Lecture Notes in Computer Science 1768

Edited by G. Goos, J. Hartmanis, and J. van Leeuwen

T0122171

Berlin
Heidelberg
New York
Barcelona
Hong Kong
London
Milan
Paris
Singapore
Tokyo

Andreas Pfitzmann (Ed.)

Information Hiding

Third International Workshop, IH'99
Dresden, Germany, September 29 - October 1, 1999
Proceedings

Series Editors

Gerhard Goos, Karlsruhe University, Germany
Juris Hartmanis, Cornell University, NY, USA
Jan van Leeuwen, Utrecht University, The Netherlands

Volume Editor

Andreas Pfitzmann
Technische Universität Dresden, Fakultät Informatik
Institut für Systemarchitektur, 01062 Dresden, Germany
E-mail: pfitza@inf.tu-dresden.de

Cataloging-in-Publication Data applied for

Die Deutsche Bibliothek - CIP-Einheitsaufnahme

Information hiding : third international workshop ; proceedings /
IH '99, Dresden, Germany, September 29 - October 1, 1999. Andreas
Pfitzmann (ed.). - Berlin ; Heidelberg ; New York ; Barcelona ; Hong
Kong ; London ; Milan ; Paris ; Singapore ; Tokyo : Springer, 2000
(Lecture notes in computer science ; Vol. 1768)
ISBN 3-540-67182-X

CR Subject Classification (1998): E.3, K.6.5, K.4.1, K.5.1, D.4.6, E.4, C.2, H.4.3,
H.5.5, H.3

ISSN 0302-9743
ISBN 3-540-67182-X Springer-Verlag Berlin Heidelberg New York

Springer is a company in the BertelsmannSpringer publishing group.
© Springer-Verlag Berlin Heidelberg 2000
Printed in Germany

Typesetting: Camera-ready by author, data conversion by DA-TeX Gerd Blumenstein
Printed on acid-free paper   SPIN: 10719724   06/3142   5 4 3 2 1 0

Preface

Now that I have compiled these proceedings, it is a great pleasure to thank all involved.

The first thanks go to the scientific community interested in hiding information or in stopping other people doing this. At the initiative of Ross Anderson in 1995, we came together for the first international meeting at IH'96 in Cambridge, and subsequently met at IH'98 in Portland. Our community now consists of about 200 people collaborating around the world – and making remarkable progress. It is our common conviction that in the long run, much more security is achieved by open discussion and public selection of mechanisms and implementations than by "security by obscurity". This is especially true for large commercial systems, and it is most probably also true within the field of information hiding. Trying to hide the design and implementation of hiding mechanisms may be particularly tempting – since hiding is an issue anyway. But as shown by the breaks of quite a few digital copy- protection systems within the last few years, "security by obscurity" may prove not to be commercially viable, at least not in civil societies.

The scientific community submitted 68 papers to this conference IH'99. This was many more papers than we had expected, and they were of much higher quality than we had dared to hope for. Many thanks to all authors.

To cope with this situation, the program committee, consisting of Ross Anderson (Cambridge University), David Aucsmith (Intel, Portland, OR), Jean-Paul Linnartz (Philips Research, Eindhoven), Steve Low (University of Melbourne), Ira Moskowitz (US Naval Research Laboratory), Jean-Jacques Quisquater (Université catholique de Louvain), Michael Waidner (IBM Research, Zurich), and me, decided to ask additional experts to help in the review of papers.

We got reviews by Christian Cachin (IBM Research, Zurich), LiWu Chang (US Naval Research Laboratory), Elke Franz (Dresden Univ. of Technology), Ton Kalker (Philips Research, Eindhoven), Herbert Klimant (Dresden Univ. of Technology), Markus Kuhn (Cambridge University), Peter Lenoir (Philips Research, Eindhoven), Thomas Mittelholzer (IBM Research, Zurich), Luke O'Connor (IBM Research, Zurich), Fabien Petitcolas (Cambridge University), Ahmad-Reza Sadeghi (Univ. des Saarlandes), Andreas Westfeld (Dresden Univ. of Technology), and Jan Zöllner (Dresden Univ. of Technology). Thanks to all program committee members and reviewers who between them contributed over 200 reviews, which I batched and delivered in anonymized form to the whole program committee. (Special thanks go to Ross Anderson for handling all reviews of papers of which I was one of the authors.)

Due to the space limitations of a three day, single stream workshop, the program committee could only accept 33 papers to allow speaker slots of 30 minutes. This meant we had – regrettably – to reject some papers which deserved acceptance. As a result, we did not provide space for an invited talk this year. To open the floor to additional ideas, we did arrange a rump session.

Within the program committee, we had quite a few discussions on the merits of borderline papers, but in the end, we achieved a consensus on the program. Many thanks to all members of the committee; it was a pleasure to work with you. It was an achievement that, in spite of a very tight schedule and many more papers than expected, we managed to finish the job and to provide feedback to all the authors three days before schedule.

IH'99 would have never become a reality without the organizational help of my secretary Martina Gersonde, who handled everything to do with accommodation, registration, printing the pre-proceedings, and organizing the various social events. During her holidays, Anja Jerichow stepped in. They and Kerstin Achtruth provided all sorts of services during the workshop. Petra Humann and Andreas Westfeld provided IT support both around and during the workshop. Hannes Federrath, being the art director of our institute in his spare time, handled all issues concerning our website and added the flavor and style to our basic functionality. As all preparation for the workshop was done completely online to avoid the costs of printing and mailing, this was especially valuable.

At this year's information hiding workshop, watermarking was the big dominating theme – at least for industry. At IH'96 and IH'98, we had a much more balanced mixture of the different fields of information hiding. I hope this will be the case again for IH'01, wherever it will take place. IH'99 could be called the "Workshop on Watermarking Resistant to Common Lossy Compression". We now know fairly well how to achieve this, but have more or less no idea how to achieve real security against well targeted attacks on watermarks. Industry's hope of copy protection by watermarking either needs a real scientific breakthrough – which I do not expect since there are so many kinds of slight changes an un-marking tool might make after the watermark has been embedded – or a more realistic perspective: systems that use copyright registration as the primary control mechanism and watermarking only as a secondary means to help keep honest people honest. If this is not commercially viable, then other means are needed to reward content providers than giving them the illusion of copy control. Perhaps as a researcher outside of industry, it falls to me to say this so frankly.

November 1999   Andreas Pfitzmann

Table of Contents

Watermarking: Embedding Techniques

Watermarking: New Designs and Applications

Watermarking: Improving Robustness

Watermarking and Software Protection

The Difficulty of Separating Private and Public Information

Stego-Engineering

An Information-Theoretic Approach to Steganography and Watermarking

Thomas Mittelholzer*

IBM Zurich Research Laboratory
Säumerstrasse 4, CH-8803 Rueschlikon, Switzerland
tmi@zurich.ibm.com

Abstract. A theoretical model for steganography and digital watermarking is presented, which includes a stego encoder, a stego channel and a stego decoder. The first part states the basic steganographic and watermarking problems in terms of mutual information of the involved quantities such as the secret message, the stego message and the modified stego message. General lower bounds on the robustness-related mutual information are derived. In the second part, perfect steganography is considered and some new schemes are presented that achieve perfect secrecy and provide robustness against some attacks. In the last part, the robustness of some simplistic schemes is evaluated by tight lower bounds on the robustness-related mutual information. From these bounds, two criteria for robust embedding are derived.

1 Introduction

With the use of the Internet for the distribution of multimedia data, steganography has become a topic of growing interest. A number of programs for embedding hidden messages in images and audio files are available and the robustness of such embeddings is a controversial issue. Steganography is still in an experimental phase and no general theory is available that states the theoretical possibilities and limits.

In this paper, we propose an information theoretic approach to steganography. The basis for this approach is a model that characterizes the embedding process and the attacker's modification of the steganogram. Other authors have proposed a different information theoretic approach to steganography [1], [2], which is based on hypothesis testing and not on mutual information. In [3], a criterion for perfect steganography is considered, which relies on mutual information as in this paper. The approach is promising, but the robustness issue of digital watermarking is not addressed.

The goal of this paper is to present a general model, which allows one to study two basic issues of a steganography scheme. The first issue is the perfect

---

* Most of this work has been done while the author was with Digital Copyright Technologies in Zurich. This work was supported by the latter and the Swiss National Science Foundation under grant No. 5003 − 045334 (KryPict).

secrecy of the embedded message. This notion of a perfect steganographic system is formulated and examples of perfect steganographic systems are presented. We show also that a certain spread-spectrum-like scheme can give perfect stego systems. This system has similar robustness properties against attacks as other stego systems based on spread-spectrum techniques (cf. [4]).

The second basic issue is the robustness of the embedding. This issue is treated by making a suitable definition of a stego channel and by using mutual information as a measure for robustness. General bounds for the robustness-related mutual information are derived and, in the case of Gaussian signals, explicit formulas and tight bounds are given.

2   A Model for Steganography and Digital Watermarking

A stego system is used to transmit secret information V from a sender, say Alice, to a receiver, Bob, in such a way that an intermediate party, Eve, is not able to notice that the stego message $\mathbf{X}$ contains hidden secret information. If Eve has control over the channel, Eve can modify a suspect message $\mathbf{X}$ and transform it into a modified version $\mathbf{Y}$. If such modification attacks might occur, the stego system should be robust against small distortions in the sense that the secret information will still reach Bob.

The proposed stego model is intended to give a framework for digital watermarking. Compared to Simmons' work [5], different criteria are used to characterize a valid stego message/image and possible attacks on stego messages. In the digital watermarking framework, unlike in the Prisoners' Problem, the intermediate party cannot check whether a watermarked image was formed according to preset rules, e.g., satisfying an authentication scheme; the only requirement is that the watermark is unnoticeable. When attacking the stego message, Eve has a different goal than Simmons' warden because she just wants to destroy the secret message (digital watermark) while maintaining an acceptable quality of the resulting modified image.

2.1   The Model

In a steganographic scheme, a secret message V is hidden with some cover data. The embedding of the secret message is done by the stego encoder which, depending on some secret key $\mathbf{K}$ merges the secret message V into the cover data $\mathbf{U}$, which is a sequence of random variables. For each key value $\mathbf{k}$, the stego encoder $f_{\mathbf{k}}(.,.)$ produces the stego message $\mathbf{X} = f_{\mathbf{k}}(\mathbf{U}, V)$, which is again a sequence of random variables (cf. Fig. 1). It is assumed that the encoder has an encoder inverse $g_{\mathbf{k}}(.,.)$, i.e., $g_{\mathbf{k}}(f_{\mathbf{k}}(\mathbf{U}, V), \mathbf{U}) = V$. The stego message should look genuine, i.e., the stego message should not be distinguishable from a typical message of the message source. A possible way to impose this condition mathematically is by choosing a suitable distortion measure $d(.,.)$ and by requiring for every key value $\mathbf{k}$ the *encoder constraint*

$$Ed(\mathbf{U}, \mathbf{X}) \leq \delta \tag{1}$$

where the expectation operator E is with respect to the joint probability distribution on $\mathbf{U}$ and $\mathbf{X}$. The bound δ is chosen suitably small to guarantee that the stego message $\mathbf{X}$ is essentially indistinguishable from the cover data $\mathbf{U}$. The secret key $\mathbf{K}$, which is used for the embedding, is usually assumed to be a vector of statistically independent and uniformly distributed random variables. A commonly used distortion measure is the squared error distortion $d(\mathbf{x}, \mathbf{y}) = 1/n \cdot \sum_{i=1\ldots n}(x_i - y_i)^2$ for vectors of length n.

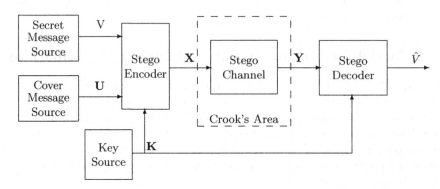

Fig. 1. Model for Stego System

In digital watermarking applications the embedding of the secret message should be robust in addition to satisfying the encoder constraint (1). This robustness requirement can be modelled by a *stego channel* in the following way. The attacker (i.e., the crook) is allowed to modify the stego message only in a limited way for otherwise the quality of the message will suffer too much, i.e., a distorted image $\mathbf{Y}$ after an attack must still have a reasonable quality. This quality requirement, which will be called the *channel constraint*, can be expressed as

$$Ed(\mathbf{X}, \mathbf{Y}) \leq \varepsilon \qquad (2)$$

where the expectation is with respect to the joint probability distribution on $\mathbf{X}$ and $\mathbf{Y}$. This implies that the distorted image $\mathbf{Y}$ must be close to the stego image $\mathbf{X}$ for small ε. The channel constraint can also be generalized to include geometric transformations by the attacker. For example, to cope with orthogonal transformations of the image, one would impose the constraint

$$\min Ed(\mathbf{X}, \tau(\mathbf{Y})) \leq \varepsilon \qquad (3)$$

where the minimum is taken over all orthogonal transformations τ.

The stego channel is different from the channel models that are commonly used in communications [6], [7], such as the discrete memoryless channel. A stego channel can be much more general, e.g., an additive noise channel or a channel that performs compression. The channel constraint (2) specifies a whole class of channels, namely, all possible channels that satisfy (2). By choosing a particular attack, the attacker selects (or creates) one fixed channel from this class of channels.

In Fig. 1 it is implicitly assumed that the attacker has no knowledge of the secret message V, the secret key $\mathbf{K}$ or the source message $\mathbf{U}$ other than that contained in her observation $\mathbf{X}$. For instance, if she knew $\mathbf{U}$, she could set $\mathbf{Y} = \mathbf{U}$ and deceive the receiver. The restricted knowledge of the attacker can be stated explicitly by saying that there is the following Markov chain of random variables

$$(V, \mathbf{K}, \mathbf{U}) \rightarrow \mathbf{X} \rightarrow \mathbf{Y}. \tag{4}$$

The goal of the decoder is to reconstruct the secret message V from the received (distorted) message $\mathbf{Y}$ using the secret key $\mathbf{K}$. In many cases, it is assumed that the decoder has no knowledge of the cover message $\mathbf{U}$, but there are applications where the decoder has access to the cover message and this knowledge can help in the decoding process.

It is important to note that in the model shown in Fig. 1 the cover message source must produce a cover message with a certain kind of uncertainty. A Gaussian source of independent random variables would be a good source, but an image source, which only produces images of typewritten text would be a bad source. For such a text-image source, one could feed the image to a text scanner and reproduce the original text with high probability. This text-image source is bad because there is enough redundancy to allow almost perfect reconstruction (on the text level). A good cover message source produces little redundancy or, equivalently, much uncertainty remains even if parts of the message are known.

2.2   Basic Issues: Secrecy and Robustness

A watermark scheme is a stego system, where the digital watermark is the secret information V and typically contains a small amount of information. To be of practical use, the embedding must be extremely robust against modifications of the stego message, e.g., image watermarking should prevent a crook, like Eve, from removing the watermark by making a modified image $\mathbf{Y}$, which is of good enough quality to be resold.

From an information theoretic viewpoint the two basic issues, secrecy and robustness, can be characterized using the notion of mutual information (cf. [8]). The stego encoder should be designed such that for given encoder and channel constraints (1) and (2)

   (i) there message V as possible, i.e., the mutual information $I(V; \mathbf{X})$ between V and $\mathbf{X}$ is minimized, and
   (ii) the stego message is robust in the sense that – given the secret key $\mathbf{K}$ – the mutual information $I(V; \mathbf{Y}|\mathbf{K})$ between the modified stego message $\mathbf{Y}$ and the embedded secret message V is maximized over the class of allowed channels.

If the cover message $\mathbf{U}$ is known, then the above conditions should be adapted as follows: (i') if Eve knows $\mathbf{U}$, then $I(V; \mathbf{X}|\mathbf{U})$ should be minimized; (ii') if Bob knows $\mathbf{U}$ then $I(V; \mathbf{Y}|\mathbf{U}, \mathbf{K})$ should be maximized. It is important to note that if Eve knows $\mathbf{U}$, she can completely remove the watermark by setting $\mathbf{Y} = \mathbf{U}$. Thus, in a watermarking application, one must ensure that Eve never gets possession of the cover message.

If $I(V; \mathbf{X}) = 0$ [or $I(V; \mathbf{X}|\mathbf{U}) = 0$ when Eve knows $\mathbf{U}$] then Eve obtains no information whatsoever about the secret message. Such a system will be called a *perfect stego system*. In the watermark context, the minimum value of $I(V; \mathbf{Y}|\mathbf{K})$ [or $I(V; \mathbf{Y}|\mathbf{U}, \mathbf{K})$ when Bob knows $\mathbf{U}$] should be about 1 bit because one needs at least about one bit to make a reliable decision about whether $\mathbf{Y}$ contains a digital watermark or not. More generally, one needs about $H(V)$ bits to read the secret message V.

It is important to note that even if $I(V; \mathbf{Y}|\mathbf{K})$ is sufficiently large, the task of the actual extraction of the secret information V from $\mathbf{Y}$ might be difficult. For a stego or watermarking scheme to be practical, this decoding process must be reasonably simple.

If one wishes to use the more general channel constraint (3) instead of (2), one should consider $\max I(V; \tau(\mathbf{Y})|\mathbf{K})$ over all orthogonal transformations and design the encoder to maximize this expression.

2.3   Basic Bounds

Using the stego model given in Section 2.1, one can obtain some useful and intuitively appealing bounds on the basic mutual information quantities considered in Section 2.2. We make no restriction on the nature (discrete or continuous) of the considered random variables but we do assume that in the continuous case the considered entropies and mutual informations are well defined.

Proposition 1. *Let V, $\mathbf{U}$, $\mathbf{K}$, $\mathbf{X}$ and $\mathbf{Y}$ be (vector) random variables denoting the secret message, the cover message, the secret key, the stego message and the modified stego message, respectively, which are related by the stego model shown in Fig. 1. Then, the following statements hold:*

(i) *The mutual information between the secret message and the modified message conditioned on knowing the secret key is upper bounded by the mutual information between the stego message and the modified message also conditioned on knowing the secret key, i.e.,*

$$I(V; \mathbf{Y}|\mathbf{K}) \leq I(\mathbf{X}; \mathbf{Y}|\mathbf{K}). \tag{5}$$

(ii) *The mutual information between the secret message and the modified message conditioned on knowing the secret key is upper bounded by the mutual information between the secret message and the stego message also conditioned on knowing the secret key, i.e.,*

$$I(V; \mathbf{Y}|\mathbf{K}) \leq I(V; \mathbf{X}|\mathbf{K}). \tag{6}$$

(iii) Knowledge of the cover message can be useful for extracting the secret message from the modified stego message when the secret key is known, i.e.,

$$I(V; \mathbf{Y}|\mathbf{K}, \mathbf{U}) \geq I(V; \mathbf{Y}|\mathbf{K}). \tag{7}$$

Proof. The following identities can be easily derived from the definition of mutual information:

$$I(V; \mathbf{Y}|\mathbf{K}) = I(V, \mathbf{K}; \mathbf{Y}) - I(\mathbf{K}; \mathbf{Y}) \tag{8}$$
$$I(\mathbf{X}; \mathbf{Y}|\mathbf{K}) = I(\mathbf{X}; \mathbf{Y}) - I(\mathbf{K}; \mathbf{Y}). \tag{9}$$

The Markov chain (4) implies $I(V, \mathbf{K}; \mathbf{Y}) \leq I(\mathbf{X}; \mathbf{Y})$ and claim (i) follows from (8) and (9).

Note that V and $\mathbf{K}$ are statistically independent, hence, claim (ii) is equivalent to $I(V; \mathbf{Y}, \mathbf{K}) \leq I(V; \mathbf{X}, \mathbf{K})$. This inequality holds because there is a Markov chain $V \to (\mathbf{X}, \mathbf{K}) \to (\mathbf{Y}, \mathbf{K})$, which is obtained from (4).

Using the fact that V, $\mathbf{U}$ and $\mathbf{K}$ are statistically independent one can rewrite the left side of claim (iii) as

$$I(V; \mathbf{Y}|\mathbf{K}, \mathbf{U}) = H(V|\mathbf{U}, \mathbf{K}) - H(V|\mathbf{U}, \mathbf{K}, \mathbf{Y}) = H(V|\mathbf{K}) - H(V|\mathbf{U}, \mathbf{K}, \mathbf{Y})$$
$$\geq H(V|\mathbf{K}) - H(V|\mathbf{K}, \mathbf{Y}) = I(V; \mathbf{Y}|\mathbf{K}),$$

where the inequality follows from the fact that additional conditioning on $\mathbf{U}$ decreases the entropy of V.

It is important to note that the upper bound (6) on $I(V; \mathbf{Y}|\mathbf{K})$ is tight and, in general, much smaller than the trivial bound $H(V)$. This means that, when extracting the watermark without knowledge of the cover image $\mathbf{U}$, one cannot obtain the full information on the message V and, therefore, the message should be coded using a suitable error correcting code.

When the cover image $\mathbf{U}$ is known at the stego decoder, the upper bound on the information about V that can be extracted from the modified stego message $\mathbf{Y}$ is $H(V)$. The following theorem gives some general lower bounds for the robustness-related mutual information quantities in the case of real-valued images.

Theorem 1. *Supposed that the cover image* $\mathbf{U} = [U_1, \ldots, U_n]$, *the stego image* $\mathbf{X} = [X_1, \ldots, X_n]$, *and the modified stego image* $\mathbf{Y} = [Y_1, \ldots, Y_n]$ *have real-valued random components. If the channel constraint is based either on the distortion measure* $d_1(\mathbf{x}, \mathbf{y}) = \frac{1}{n} \cdot \sum_{i=1,\ldots,n} (x_i - y_i)^2$ *or* $d_2(\mathbf{x}, \mathbf{y}) = \max_i (x_i - y_i)^2$, *then the following bounds hold:*

(i) $I(\mathbf{X}; \mathbf{Y}) \geq \max\{H(\mathbf{X}), H(\mathbf{Y})\} - \frac{n}{2} \log_2(2\pi e \varepsilon)$

(ii) $I(V; \mathbf{Y}|\mathbf{U}, \mathbf{K}) \geq H(\mathbf{Y}|\mathbf{U}, \mathbf{K}) - \frac{n}{2} \log_2(2\pi e \varepsilon)$

Proof. We start the proof by stating two identities, which are easy to derive ((10) follows from the Markov property (4) and the fact that $\mathbf{X}$ is uniquely determined by $V, \mathbf{U}$ and $\mathbf{K}$; (11) is analogous to (8)):

$$I(\mathbf{Y}; V, \mathbf{U}, \mathbf{K}) = I(\mathbf{Y}; \mathbf{X}) \tag{10}$$
$$I(V; \mathbf{Y}|\mathbf{U}, \mathbf{K}) = I(\mathbf{Y}; \mathbf{X}) - I(\mathbf{Y}; \mathbf{U}, \mathbf{K}) \tag{11}$$

To show (i), we consider the following chain of inequalities, where the first step follows from the fact that conditioning does not increase entropy.

$$I(\mathbf{X}; \mathbf{Y}) = H(\mathbf{Y}) - H(\mathbf{Y}|\mathbf{X}) = H(\mathbf{Y}) - H(\mathbf{Y} - \mathbf{X}|\mathbf{X}) \tag{12}$$
$$\geq H(\mathbf{Y}) - H(\mathbf{Y} - \mathbf{X}) \tag{13}$$
$$\geq H(\mathbf{Y}) - \sum_{i=1}^{n} H(Y_i - X_i) \tag{14}$$
$$\geq H(\mathbf{Y}) - \frac{1}{2} \cdot \sum_{i} \log_2(2\pi e E[(Y_i - X_i)^2]) \tag{15}$$
$$= H(\mathbf{Y}) - \frac{1}{2} \cdot \log_2((2\pi e)^n \prod_{i} E[(Y_i - X_i)^2]) \tag{16}$$
$$\geq H(\mathbf{Y}) - \frac{1}{2} \cdot \log_2((2\pi e)^n (\sum_{i} E[(Y_i - X_i)^2]/n)^n) \tag{17}$$
$$\geq H(\mathbf{Y}) - \frac{n}{2} \cdot \log_2(2\pi e \varepsilon) \tag{18}$$

Inequality (14) follows from $H(\mathbf{Y} - \mathbf{X}) \leq \sum_{i=1}^{n} H(Y_i - X_i)$ (see Chap. 9 in [8]). The entropy of the n components are maximized if they are Gaussian, in which case, $H(Y_i - X_i) \leq \frac{1}{2} \log_2(2\pi e E[(Y_i - X_i)^2])$ (cf. Chap. 9 in [8]). This implies (15). Inequality (17) follows from the fact that the geometric mean is upper bounded by the arithmetic mean. The last inequality is a consequence of the channel constraint (2) with respect to the distortion measure $d_1(.,.)$ or $d_2(.,.)$.

The same argument can also be applied to $I(\mathbf{X}; \mathbf{Y}) = H(\mathbf{X}) - H(\mathbf{X}|\mathbf{Y})$ and this implies that one can take $\max\{H(\mathbf{X}), H(\mathbf{Y})\}$ in (i).

The second statement (ii) follows from (11) and statement (i).

In the case of binary (black-and-white) images, one can derive similar bounds on the robustness-related mutual information as above. The relevant distortion measure is based on the average Hamming distance given by $\frac{1}{n} d_H(\mathbf{x}, \mathbf{y})$, if the images have n components. Since the encoder $f_{\mathbf{K}}(.,.)$ has an encoder inverse, when given $\mathbf{U}$ and $\mathbf{K}$, the secret message V uniquely determines the stego message $\mathbf{X}$ and, conversely, $\mathbf{X}$ uniquely determines V. Thus, $H(V|\mathbf{U}, \mathbf{K}) = H(\mathbf{X}|\mathbf{U}, \mathbf{K})$. This implies $I(V; \mathbf{Y}|\mathbf{U}, \mathbf{K}) = H(V) - H(\mathbf{X}|\mathbf{U}, \mathbf{K}, \mathbf{Y})$ and the last entropy term equals $H(\mathbf{Y} - \mathbf{X}|\mathbf{U}, \mathbf{K}, \mathbf{Y})$. A similar proof as above implies the following theorem.

Theorem 2. *If in a stego system the stego image $\mathbf{X} = [X_1, \ldots, X_n]$ and the modified stego image $\mathbf{Y} = [Y_1, \ldots, Y_n]$ have binary components satisfying the* *channel constraint* $E[\frac{1}{n}d_H(\mathbf{X}, \mathbf{Y})] \leq \varepsilon \leq 1/2$, *then*

$$I(V; \mathbf{Y}|\mathbf{K}, \mathbf{U}) \geq H(V) - nh(\varepsilon), \tag{19}$$

where $h(p) = -p\log_2(p) - (1-p)\log_2(1-p)$ *is the binary entropy function.*

3   Perfect Steganography

A stego system is considered perfect if it satisfies the encoder constraint (1), the role of which is to ensure imperceptibility, and Shannon's perfect secrecy condition $I(V, \mathbf{X}) = 0$ [9]. Thus, it is not astonishing that one obtains a perfect stego system if the secret message is first encrypted using the Vernam cipher (or one-time pad) and then embedded using any embedding function. A justified criticism of the simple Vernam stego system is that it does not provide robustness. For instance, an additive white Gaussian noise attack on the stego message is likely to lead to decoding errors. This is the motivation to consider a generalization of the Vernam cipher for which the robustness can be adapted and increased.

3.1   Permutation Modulation

The proposed perfect stego scheme is based on an encoding technique, which is called permutation modulation and which was introduced by Slepian [10]. The cover message is modelled as a finite sequence of real random variables $\mathbf{U} = [U_0, U_1, \ldots, U_{n-1}]$. The secret key $\mathbf{K} = [K_0, K_1, \ldots, K_{n-1}]$ is a vector of statistically independent, identically distributed (i.i.d.) real random variables. The secret message is a discrete random variable V, which selects a permutation of n letters.

The perfect stego encoder is given by the following encoding rule

$$\mathbf{X} = \mathbf{U} + \mathbf{K}^V \tag{20}$$

where $\mathbf{K}^V = [K_{v_0}, K_{v_1}, \ldots, K_{v_{n-1}}]$ denotes the vector $\mathbf{K}$ with components permuted according to the permutation V, which is given by $(v_0, v_1, \ldots, v_{n-1})$.

Proposition 2. *Suppose that the secret message* V, *the cover message* $\mathbf{U}$ *and the secret key* $\mathbf{K}$ *are jointly statistically independent. Then,*

(i) $I(V; \mathbf{X}|\mathbf{U}) = 0$
(ii) $I(V; \mathbf{X}) = 0$.

Proof. Claim (i): Since V and $\mathbf{U}$ are statistically independent, $I(V; \mathbf{X}|\mathbf{U}) = I(V; \mathbf{X}, \mathbf{U})$. Since $\mathbf{K}^V$ is determined by $\mathbf{X}$ and $\mathbf{U}$, and since by hypothesis $\mathbf{U}$ is statistically independent of the pair $(V, \mathbf{K}^V)$, one obtains

$$\begin{aligned} I(V; \mathbf{X}, \mathbf{U}) &= H(V) - H(V|\mathbf{X}, \mathbf{U}) \\ &= H(V) - H(V|\mathbf{K}^V, \mathbf{U}) \\ &= H(V) - H(V|\mathbf{K}^V). \end{aligned}$$

It remains to show that $H(V) - H(V|\mathbf{K}^V) = 0$ or, equivalently, that V and $\mathbf{K}^V$ are statistically independent.

Let $p(.|.)$ denote the conditional probability density function (pdf) of $\mathbf{K}^V$ given V (a similar argument goes through for discrete random variables, where the pdf is replaced by a conditional probability distribution). Since all components of $\mathbf{K}$ are i.i.d., the conditional pdf does not depend on the permutation $V = v$, i.e.,

$$p(k_{v_0}, k_{v_1}, \ldots, k_{v_{n-1}}|v) = p(k_0)p(k_1)\cdots p(k_{n-1}). \tag{21}$$

where $p(.)$ denotes the pdf of the components K_i. Hence, K^V and V are statistically independent.

Claim (ii): $I(V; \mathbf{X}) = 0$ follows from claim (i), using $H(V|\mathbf{X}, \mathbf{U}) \le H(V|\mathbf{X})$.

In communications, one considers additive noise channels for applying permutation modulation. This situation can also be modelled in the stego context where the intended recipient, Bob, has access to the cover message and where the crook, Eve, is only allowed to distort the stego message by additive noise. In this case, Bob can form $\mathbf{Y} - \mathbf{U} = \mathbf{K}^V + \mathbf{Z}$, where $\mathbf{Z}$ denotes the additive noise introduced by Eve.

If the i.i.d. components of the key $\mathbf{K}$ are symmetrical random variables, i.e., $p(k_i) = p(-k_i)$, then the encoder can be extended to include sign changes. The resulting scheme is again a perfect stego scheme. If one uses no permutations but only sign changes and a secret key $\mathbf{K}$ of coin-tossing ± 1 valued components, one obtains the Vernam cipher with a ± 1 embedding.

Example 1. Suppose that in a mini stego system, the secret key $\mathbf{K}$ consists of 8 components, which are ± 1 valued. Choose a sample vector $\mathbf{k}$ with 4 components having value 1 (and 4 components having value -1). One obtains a perfect stego system because (21) is satisfied. By permuting the components of $\mathbf{k}$, a total of $\binom{8}{4} = 70$ different vectors are produced, i.e., 70 different messages can be embedded. Compared to the Vernam stego system of length 8, the rate has been reduced to $(\log_2 70)/8$ bit per component. In exchange, the minimum squared Euclidean distance between distinct embedded codewords is $2^2 + 2^2$, which is twice the squared minimum distance of the Vernam scheme. This illustrates how the information rate can be traded for increased robustness.

3.2 Cyclic Shift Modulation

A low rate modulation scheme is now introduced which is based on maximum-length sequences (m-sequences). The resulting scheme has robustness properties similar to watermarking schemes that rely on spread-spectrum sequences [4]. The detection process makes use of the good correlation properties of m-sequences.

Let $\mathbf{s} = [s_0, s_1, \ldots, s_{n-1}]$ be a ± 1 valued m-sequence of length n ($n = 2^m - 1$) and let $\mathbf{k} = [k_0, k_1, \ldots, k_{n-1}]$ be the secret key with i.i.d. and symmetrically distributed components. The code set for the embedding is constructed as follows:

$$C = \{\mathrm{Sh}^j(\mathbf{s}) \odot \mathbf{k} : j = 0, 1, \ldots, n-1\} \cup \{\mathbf{k}\}, \tag{22}$$

where $\mathrm{Sh}^j(\mathbf{s}) = [s_j, s_{j+1}, \ldots, s_{j+n-1}]$ is the cyclic rightward shift by j positions of $\mathbf{s}$ (the indices are reduced modulo n) and $\odot$ denotes componentwise multiplication of two vectors. There are $M = n + 1 = 2^m$ codewords in C; hence, one can encode m bits using this code of length $n = 2^m - 1$. An additional bit b can be encoded by selecting the polarity (± 1) of each codeword. The embedding (or encoding) of a secret message $v \in \{0, 1, \ldots, 2^m - 1\}$ within a cover message $\mathbf{u}$ can be defined by

$$\mathbf{x} = \mathbf{u} + (-1)^b \cdot \mathbf{c} \tag{23}$$

where $\mathbf{c} = \mathrm{Sh}^v(\mathbf{s}) \odot \mathbf{k}$ if $v \neq 2^m - 1$ and $\mathbf{c} = \mathbf{k}$ if $v = 2^m - 1$. The stego scheme based on (23) will be called a *Cyclic Shift Modulation* (CSM) scheme. In a CSM scheme the m-sequence $\mathbf{s}$ need not be kept secret; the only secret parameter that has to be passed over a secure channel to the intended receiver is the secret key.

Noting that the conditional probability density of $\mathbf{X} - \mathbf{U}$ given V satisfies $p(\mathrm{Sh}^j(\mathbf{s}) \odot \mathbf{k}|v) = p(\mathbf{k})$, a proof similar to that of Proposition 2 gives the following

Theorem 3. *Cyclic shift modulation provides a perfect stego system, i.e.,*

$$I(V; \mathbf{X}|\mathbf{U}) = 0 = I(V; \mathbf{X}).$$

The decoding at the receiver is based on correlation. Recovering the secret message v from the received message $\mathbf{y}$ is equivalent to finding the corresponding codeword that was embedded. For each code sequence $\mathbf{c}$, the decoder forms the scalar product

$$< \mathbf{y}, \mathbf{c} >= \sum_{j=0}^{n-1} y_j c_j$$

and chooses as the decoder output $\hat{\mathbf{c}}$ (one of) the codeword(s) that maximize(s) the magnitude of this scalar product. The additional bit b, which selects the polarity of the codeword, can be recovered from the sign of $< \mathbf{y}, \mathbf{c} >$.

If the secret key $\mathbf{K}$ consists of random ± 1 valued i.i.d. components, then the resulting code C has optimal cross correlation properties, i.e., Welch's lower bound on the maximum value c_{max}^2 of $(< \mathbf{c}, \mathbf{c}' >)^2$ for $\mathbf{c} \neq \mathbf{c}'$ is achieved, which states that $c_{max}^2 \geq n(M - n)/(M - 1)$ (cf. [11]). This optimality result follows from the correlation property of the code as stated in the following theorem.

Theorem 4. *If the secret key $\mathbf{K}$ consists of random ± 1 valued i.i.d. components, then the code defined by (22) has the cross correlation values*

$$< \mathbf{c}, \mathbf{c}' >= \begin{cases} n & \text{if } \mathbf{c} = \mathbf{c}' \\ -1 & \text{otherwise} \end{cases} \tag{24}$$

where n denotes the code sequence length.

Proof. The case $\mathbf{c} = \mathbf{c}'$ is evident.

Suppose $\mathbf{c} \neq \mathbf{c}'$ and consider the case, where the code sequences are of the form $\mathrm{Sh}^j(\mathbf{s}) \odot \mathbf{k}$ and $\mathrm{Sh}^h(\mathbf{s}) \odot \mathbf{k}$, respectively. For notational convenience for the indexing, we consider $\mathrm{Sh}^j(\mathbf{s})$ to be a length-n subsequence of the infinite periodically continued m-sequence **s**. Using the fact that the key components satisfy $k_i^2 = 1$, one has

$$< \mathbf{c}, \mathbf{c}' > = \sum_{i=0}^{n-1} s_{j+i} k_i s_{h+i} k_i$$

$$= \sum_{i=0}^{n-1} s_{j+i} s_{h+i}$$

$$= -1$$

where the last equality follows from the correlation property of m-sequences. Finally, the case where one of the two code sequences equals **k** can be proved similarly.

For general secret keys, without the ± 1 restriction on the components K_i, the cross correlation values will be scaled by the variance $\sigma^2 = Var(K_i)$ and (24) no longer holds. However, one expects that the peak-to-off-peak ratio will be roughly the same as for the m-sequence because, when taking the average over all secret keys, one obtains

$$E_{\mathbf{K}}[< \mathbf{c}, \mathbf{c}' >] = \begin{cases} n \cdot \sigma^2 & \text{if } \mathbf{c} = \mathbf{c}' \\ -\sigma^2 & \text{otherwise.} \end{cases}$$

Remark 1. One might also expect that a standard synchronous CDMA scheme based on the code C given by (22) will provide a perfect stego system. However, this is not the case because standard encoding by selecting the parity of each spreading sequence $\mathbf{c}_j$ according to the bits of the secret message does not yield a resulting sum vector $\mathbf{x} = \sum(-1)^{v_j} \cdot \mathbf{c}_j$ that is statistically independent of the secret message $[v_0, v_1, \ldots, v_n]$. Thus, one does not obtain the desired result $I(V; \mathbf{X}) = 0$.

4   The Robustness of Some Simple Schemes

For the evaluation of stego and watermarking schemes on the basis of information theory and, in particular, using criteria (i) and (ii) in Section 2.2, one needs a stochastic model of the message source. In this section, we either assume that the cover image is Gaussian or that the cover image has an arbitrary real-valued probability distribution while the stego channel satisfies certain orthogonality conditions. Using this simplistic model, one can find tight bounds on $I(V; \mathbf{Y})$ for various scenarios and make some interesting conclusions. In particular, some of the experimental results presented in [12] can be given a theoretical explanation.

The main focus of this section is the robustness of the embedding of the secret message V. For simplicity, we assume that the secret message V is identical with the embedded vector $\mathbf{V}$ (that is, no encryption and no error-correcting scheme is used). Thus, we assume that $\mathbf{V}$ is a vector of i.i.d. zero-mean Gaussian random variables and that the stego encoder is a sum encoder, i.e.,

$$\mathbf{X} = \mathbf{U} + \mathbf{V}. \tag{25}$$

In the remaining part of this section, we will make the simplifying assumption that the cover message $\mathbf{U}$ has independent components and, hence, also $\mathbf{X}$ has independent components. This assumption can be approximately met by choosing a sparse sub-image, i.e., by selecting a suitable subset $U_{i_1}, U_{i_2}, \ldots, U_{i_{n'}}$ of the components of $\mathbf{U}$. The setting is further simplified by considering each component individually, i.e., by studying random variables instead of random vectors.

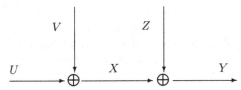

Fig. 2. Sum Encoder and Additive Noise Stego Channel

Example 2. (**Additive Noise Attack**) The attacker is only allowed to distort the stego message X with additive white Gaussian noise (AWGN) Z; thus, the distorted message is given by $Y = X + Z$. Fig. 2 shows the block diagram of the corresponding system. The robustness-related mutual information is given by the well-known formula (cf. Chap. 10.1 in [8])

$$I(Y;V) = \frac{1}{2}\log_2(1 + \frac{Var(V)}{Var(U) + Var(Z)}). \tag{26}$$

This formula implies $I(Y;V) > 0$, i.e., an AWGN attack can never completely remove the information about the secret message V. Note that for a given variance $VarZ$, the Gaussian distribution is the worst stego-message independent attack [8]. If the cover message U is known at the receiver, then one has to consider the conditional information, which is the capacity formula for a Gaussian channel (cf. Chap. 10 in [8])

$$I(Y;V|U) = \frac{1}{2}\log_2(1 + \frac{Var(V)}{Var(Z)}).$$

Since the mutual information $I(V;Y)$ remains invariant, when Y is normalized to have zero mean, we can without loss of essential generality assume that Y has zero mean, which will be done within the remaining part of this paper.

In a general attack, the distortion introduced by the attacker is

$$Z = Y - X. \tag{27}$$

By normalizing the cover image U, we can assume that U is zero-mean. Thus, we have that X, Y, and Z are zero mean and the channel constraint $E[(Y-X)^2] \leq \varepsilon$ implies $Var(Z) \leq \varepsilon$.

The attacker can choose the distortion Z to depend on X, which generalizes the AWGN attack. The distortion Z can be split into the projection Z^π onto the space spanned by the random variable X, which minimizes the expectation $E[(Z - Z^\pi)^2]$, and the orthogonal complement $Z^\perp$ (cf. Chap. 11 in [13]). Thus, one has the orthogonal decomposition

$$Z = \rho \cdot X + Z^\perp,$$

where $\rho = E[ZX]/E[X^2]$.

Since X is the sum of the independent random variables U and V, the random variable $X^\perp \triangleq (VarV)U - (VarU)V$ is orthogonal to X. The pairs of random variables (U, V) and $(X, X^\perp)$ are related by an invertible linear transformation and, thus, the Markov chain (4) can be rewritten as $(X, X^\perp) \to X \to Y - X$, yielding the Markov chain

$$X^\perp \to X \to Z. \tag{28}$$

If U and V are zero-mean Gaussian then X and $X^\perp$ are also zero-mean Gaussian. Being orthogonal, X and $X^\perp$ are statistically independent. By (28), $X^\perp$ and Z are also statistically independent. Thus, also $Z^\perp = Z - \rho \cdot X$ is independent of $X^\perp$ and, by construction, it is orthogonal to X. Therefore, $Z^\perp$ being orthogonal on X and $X^\perp$, it is orthogonal on U and V. These results are summarized in the following lemma.

Lemma 1. *If U and V are statistically independent, zero-mean Gaussian random variables, then*

$$E[Z^\perp U] = 0 \qquad and \qquad E[Z^\perp V] = 0. \tag{29}$$

Remark 2. The equations (29) are crucial to derive the lower bound given in the next theorem. Note that U need not be necessarily Gaussian for (29) to hold. For non-Gaussian U, it is enough e.g. that the attacker's distortion is restricted to be of the form $Z = \rho'X + Z^\perp$, where ρ' denotes any real number and $Z^\perp$ is independent of X. For the non-Gaussian case, (29) can be viewed as an orthogonality condition on the stego channel.

The first two steps in the derivation of the lower bound rely on the fact that conditioning reduces entropy and the Gaussian distribution maximizes entropy for a given variance, i.e., for any real number μ one has

$$I(V; Y) = H(V) - H(V|Y)$$
$$= H(V) - H(V - \mu Y|Y)$$
$$\geq H(V) - H(V - \mu Y) \tag{30}$$
$$\geq H(V) - \frac{1}{2}\log_2(2\pi e Var(V - \mu Y)). \tag{31}$$

Since all involved random variables are zero-mean, (29) implies that

$$Var(V - \mu Y) = E[(\mu(X + \rho \cdot X + Z^\perp) - V)^2]$$
$$= E[(\mu(1 + \rho)U + (\mu(1 + \rho) - 1)V + \mu Z^\perp)^2]$$
$$= \mu^2(1 + \rho)^2 VarU + (\mu(1 + \rho) - 1)^2 VarV + \mu^2 VarZ^\perp$$
$$= \mu^2[(1 + \rho)^2 VarX + VarZ^\perp] + (1 - 2\mu(1 + \rho))VarV.$$

This variance is minimized by setting $\mu = E[VY]/E[Y^2]$, which yields

$$Var(V - \frac{E[VY]}{E[Y^2]}Y) = (VarV)\left(1 - \frac{VarV}{VarX + \frac{VarZ^\perp}{(1+\rho)^2}}\right)$$

and gives the lower bound

$$I(V; Y) \geq \frac{1}{2}\log_2\left(\frac{1}{1 - \frac{VarV}{VarX + \frac{VarZ^\perp}{(1+\rho)^2}}}\right). \tag{32}$$

The attacker wants to minimize $I(V; Y)$. Without any channel constraint, the lower bound is minimized by choosing $\rho = -1$, which actually implies $I(V; Y) = 0$. Choosing $\rho = -1$ means that Y consists only of the distortion term $Z^\perp$, which in general is not allowed because of the channel constraint

$$\rho^2 VarX + VarZ^\perp = VarZ \leq \varepsilon. \tag{33}$$

The lower bound (32) is minimized by maximizing $VarZ^\perp/(1+\rho)^2$. When taking the constraint (33) into account, this is a constraint maximization problem. It is easily solved by using (33) to eliminate the term $VarZ^\perp = \varepsilon - \rho^2 VarX$ and then finding the maximum of $VarZ^\perp/(1 + \rho)^2 = (\varepsilon - \rho^2 VarX)/(1 + \rho)^2$ with respect to ρ. The maximum is achieved for $\rho = -\varepsilon/VarX$ and the lower bound on the mutual information becomes

$$I(V; Y) \geq \frac{1}{2}\log_2\left(\frac{1}{1 - \frac{VarV}{(1+\varepsilon/(VarX - \varepsilon))VarX}}\right). \tag{34}$$

When $\varepsilon = 0$, we obtain the lower bound

$$I(V; X) \geq \frac{1}{2}\log_2\left(\frac{1}{1 - \frac{VarV}{VarX}}\right)$$

which actually holds with equality since (30) and (31) hold with equality because the random variables in question are independent and Gaussian. Recalling (6), this proves the following theorem.

Theorem 5. *Suppose that the distortion $Z = Y - X$ of the stego message X satisfies the channel constraint $E(Z^2) \leq \varepsilon$ and that the secret message V is zero-mean Gaussian. If the cover image component U is Gaussian, then the mutual information between the secret message V and the stego image Y is bounded by*

$$\frac{1}{2} \log_2 \left(\frac{1}{1 - \frac{VarV}{(1+\varepsilon/(VarX-\varepsilon))VarX}} \right) \leq I(V;Y) \leq \frac{1}{2} \log_2 \left(\frac{1}{1 - \frac{VarV}{VarX}} \right).$$

Remark 3. The lower bound also holds in the case, where U is not necessarily Gaussian but the stego channel satisfies the orthogonality constraint (29). For non-Gaussian U, the upper bound no longer holds. When there is no attack, i.e., $\varepsilon = 0$, one has the the lower bound $1/2 \cdot \log_2(1/(1 - VarV/VarX)) \leq I(V;X)$.

The derivation above gives a characterization of the worst case attack, viz., produce a distortion $Z = \rho X + Z^\perp$ with $\rho = -\varepsilon/VarX$ and where $Z^\perp$ is zero-mean Gaussian with variance $\varepsilon(1-\varepsilon/VarX)$ and statistically independent of X. This attack achieves the lower bound.

Theorem 5 can be used to give the following robustness criteria of a stego scheme in the Gaussian case:

- One should choose $Var(V)$ as large as allowed by the encoder constraint, i.e., $Var(V) = \delta$.
- If $VarX$ and, hence $E[X^2] = E[U^2] + E[V^2]$, is large compared to the channel constraint ε, then $I(V;Y) \approx I(V;X)$. Thus, when having the choice to embed the watermark at particular locations within the cover image, one should choose those components for embedding that have large $E(U^2)$ (i.e., high dynamic range).

These two design criteria for a robust stego scheme are in accordance with the findings in [12], where the most robust stego schemes resulted from embedding the watermark with maximal allowed strength at locations of edges (with high dynamic range) in the image.

5 Conclusions

A model for a stego system was presented, which gives a novel characterization of the two critical components, the embedding process and the attacker's modification of a stego message. The definition of the two components is based on a requirement on the maximum distortion between the cover message, the stego message and the modified stego message. This model leads to an information-theoretic approach to steganography, which allows one to describe the two basic issues, secrecy and robustness, in terms of mutual information. In particular, Shannon's definition of perfect secrecy can be readily extended to steganography.

Based on permutation modulation and on maximum-length sequences, two classes of perfect stego schemes were proposed. The robustness of these schemes can be adapted by decreasing the rate of the hidden secret information which, in turn, increases the robustness.

For some simplistic schemes, in particular, for cover images with statistically independent Gaussian components, tight bounds have been established for the robustness-related mutual information. These bounds provide a theoretical basis for some design criteria that have been derived from experiments in [12].

References

1. C. Cachin, "An Information-Theoretic Model for Steganography," *Proceeding of the Second Intern. Information Hiding Workshop*, Portland, Oregon, USA, April 15 - 17, 1998. 1

2. J.R. Hernandez and F. Pérez-Gonzáles, "Throwing More Light on Image Watermarks," *Proceeding of the Second Intern. Information Hiding Workshop*, Portland, Oregon, USA, April 15 - 17, 1998. 1

3. J. Zöllner, H. Federrath, H. Klimant, A. Pfitzmann, R. Piotraschke, A. Westfeld, G. Wicke, G. Wolf, "Modeling the Security of Steganographic Systems," *Proceeding of the Second Intern. Information Hiding Workshop*, Portland, Oregon, USA, April 15 - 17, 1998. 1

4. I.J. Cox, J. Kilian, T. Leighton, and T. Shamoon, "Secure spread spectrum watermarking for images, audio and video," *IEEE Proc. Int. Conf. Image Processing*, 1996, vol. 3, pp. 243–246. 2, 9

5. G.J. Simmons, "The Prisoners' Problem and the Subliminal Channel," *Crypto'83 Proc.*, Ed. D. Chaum, Plenum Press, New York, 1984, pp. 51–67. 2

6. R.G. Gallager, *Information Theory and Reliable Communication*, Wiley & Sons, New York, 1968. 3

7. Shu Lin and D.J. Costello, Jr., *Error Control Coding: Fundamentals and Applications*, Prentice-Hall, New Jersey, 1983. 3

8. T.M. Cover and J.A. Thomas, *Elements of Information Theory*, Wiley 1991. 4, 7, 12

9. C. Shannon, "Communication Theory of Secrecy Systems," *Bell System Technical Journal*, vol. 28, pp. 656–715, 1949. 8

10. D. Slepian, "Permutation Modulation," *Proc. of the IEEE*, Vol. 53, No., 3, March 1965, pp. 228–236. 8

11. L.R. Welch, "Lower Bounds on the Maximum Cross Correlation of Signals," *IEEE Trans. on Information Th.*, vol. IT-20, May 1974, pp. 397–399. 10

12. C.I. Podilchuk, W. Zeng, "Image-Adaptive Watermarking Using Visual Models," *IEEE J. Selected Areas in Communications*, vol. 16, No. 4, May 1998, pp. 525–539. 11, 15, 16

13. A.N. Shiryayev, *Probability*, GTM 95, Springer, 1984. 13

One-Time Hash Steganography

Natori Shin

Department of Information Science, University of Tokyo
natori@is.s.u-tokyo.ac.jp

Abstract. In this paper we first generalize the steganography system model which Christian Cachin proposed, and specialize it to be suitable for computer oriented steganography systems. Based on this model, we introduce a new perfectly secure steganography scheme, one-time hash steganography, with which one can hide a secret bit into any cover-data that satisfies certain condition (partial recomputability). Finally we prove that there exists a perfectly secure steganography system with given cover-data source if and only if the cover-data source is partially recomputable to its sender.

1 Introduction

Steganography is the art and science of hiding data into innocent-looking cover-data so that no one can detect the very existence of the hidden data [2,4]. It is somewhat different from cryptography, since the goal of steganography is undetectability, not secrecy only. For example, a ciphertext may contain peculiar words like "QJYZQDFLKJ," but a stego-text (data-embedded text file) should be read as an ordinary text file so as not to draw suspicion of secret message.

Steganography itself has long history [10], and recent proliferation of digital communication increased the importance of computer based steganography, with which one can hide the digital communication channel itself. For example, although e-mail encryption program can secure the contents of a mail, it cannot hide the very fact of mail delivery by itself. If you send an encrypted mail to your girlfriend in hostile country, you might be arrested as a suspected spy unless you enable the policemen to read the contents. With a secure steganography system that hides the mail transfer protocol into another protocol, you can send encrypted mails without the fear of drawing such suspicion.

This type of application of steganography systems is more serious in the areas where the use of cryptography is limited by law. Some countries ban unlimited use of strong cryptography, and retain the right of court-authorized wiretapping. Some say that enabling court-authorized wiretapping cost-effectively prevents criminal activities [8]. Some say that it costs much and can make total system vulnerable [1]. The importance of steganography appears here. If the people whose communications are wiretapped could use a secure steganography system, the effect of court-authorized wiretapping would decrease. If the secure steganography system were easy to use and can provide enough bandwidth, the

A. Pfitzmann (Ed.): IH'99, LNCS 1768, pp. 17–28, 2000.

effect of wiretapping would be little. The hidden communication with steganography systems could be banned, but it would be very hard (or impossible) to detect and sue it. Most criminals would use the secure steganography system for criminal activities and only the criminal communications would be private. Therefore, when and how a steganography system can be secure is essential to the measurement of the cost-effectiveness of cryptography restriction policies such as key escrow policy.

This paper answers both of these questions. Specifically, this paper gives both a necessary and sufficient condition for the existence of a steganography system that is perfectly secure from passive adversaries and a constructive proof of the sufficiency of the condition. To do this, we first construct a new model for steganography system, which is based on the one Cachin introduced in [6]. Next, we introduce the notion of *partial recomputability*. Roughly speaking, a *partially recomputable* random variable is a random variable the realization of which can be tweaked without distorting its distribution. Then, we introduce a perfectly secure steganography system, one-time hash steganography system. This system can take arbitrary message source as cover-data, provided the message source is partially recomputable. Finally, we show that if there exists a perfectly secure steganography system, its cover-data is always partially recomputable. This leads to the conclusion that there exists a perfectly secure steganography system that takes given message source as cover-data, if and only if the message source is partially recomputable.

The paper is organized as follows. Section 2 contains basic definitions. Section 3 briefly describes related works. Section 4 describes our model of steganography system. Section 5 introduces one-time hash steganography, the main contribution of this paper. Section 6 discusses the condition for the existence of perfectly secure steganography system. Section 7 contains conclusions.

2 Terms and Definitions

2.1 Preliminary Definitions

Uppercase variables like S, C or E denote random variables and uppercase bold variables like $\mathbf{M}, \mathbf{K}$ or $\mathbf{E}$ denote finite sets of symbols except otherwise specified. $\mathbf{Z}$ denotes the set of all integers. $\mathbf{Z}_{[a,b]}$ denotes $\{x \in \mathbf{Z} \mid a \leq x \leq b\}$. $|\mathbf{M}|$ denotes number of elements in $\mathbf{M}$. $X \in \mathbf{M}$ means that any realization of X is one of $\mathbf{M}$. $X \equiv Y$ means that the distribution of X is equivalent to that of Y. $H(X)$, $H(X|Y)$ and $I(X;Y)$ denote the entropy of X, the conditional entropy of X conditioned on Y and the mutual information between X and Y, respectively.

2.2 Basic Model of a Steganography System

Fig. 1 shows the generally accepted model of a steganography system (or stegosystem for short), based upon the agreement made at the First International Workshop on Information Hiding [12]. The sender of a secret message embeds *embedded-data* into *cover-data* using a *key*, and sends the result, *stego-data*, to the recipient. The recipient then extracts the embedded-data from stego-data using a key that may or may not equal to the one used in embedding.

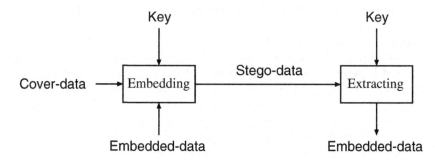

Fig. 1. Basic model of a stegosystem

There can be two kinds of attacks against a stegosystem [3]. One is *passive attack*, to detect (and possibly prove to a third person) the existence of a secret message embedded in stego-data. An attacker who does this kind of attack is called *passive adversary*. The other is *active attack*, to modify the stego-data slightly in order to destruct the embedded-data. Attacker of this kind is called *active adversary*.

In this paper, we consider only passive type attacks, and the robustness of the embedded message is out of scope.

3   Related Works

Cachin made an information-theoretic model of a stegosystem and introduced the notion of "perfectly secure" as a special case of "ϵ-secure" [6]. A stegosystem is ϵ-secure against passive adversaries if the relative entropy between probability distribution of cover-data and that of stego-data is less than or equal to ϵ. He call a 0-secure stegosystem perfectly secure, in which case both distributions are identical.

Zöllner et al. analyzed their stegosystem model with information theoretic approach and got several conditions for a stegosystem to be perfectly secure [15]. In particular, they proved that the cover-data of a perfectly secure stegosystem should not be known to passive adversaries.

In order to send a secret bit, one can generate many cover-data candidates and select one candidate that has the secret bit as its keyed hash value, and send the candidate as a real cover-data [3,5]. This "hash and choose" type of steganography is called *selection method* in [5], and described as tantamount to one-time pad in encryption. The one-time hash steganography we describe later in section 5 is a provably secure version of this *selection method*.

4 Generalizing the Basic Model

As stated in section 1, our primary goal in this paper is to answer the questions: when and how one can construct a perfectly secure stegosystem. In order to treat this topic in its most general form, we generalize the basic model for stegosystem shown in Fig.1 as follows.

- Sender may use environmental input other than cover-data and embedded-data.
    - For example, some information about the mail writer is indispensable to generate or tweak the contents of a mail algorithmically without introducing unnaturalness. Stegosystems that employ *selection method* requires multiple cover-data candidates, which can also be regarded as additional environmental input to embedding algorithm.
- The message recipient extracts need not be exactly equal to the original message. In other words, stegosystem can make error in our model.

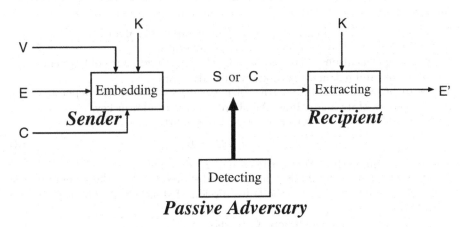

Fig. 2. Our model of a stegosystem

Fig. 2 shows our model of a stegosystem. In this model, a stegosystem consists of an embedder $\mathcal{E}$, an extractor $\mathcal{D}$ and several random variables that form inputs and outputs of $\mathcal{E}$ and $\mathcal{D}$.

We denote the embedding process as

$$S = \mathcal{E}(E, C, K, V) \tag{1}$$

where $E \in \mathbf{E}$ denotes embedded-data, $C \in \mathbf{M}$ denotes cover-data, $V \in \mathbf{V}$ denotes environmental-data, $K \in \mathbf{K}$ denotes shared secret key, and $S \in \mathbf{M}$ denotes stego-data. Similarly, we denote the extracting process as

$$E' = \mathcal{D}(S, K) \tag{2}$$

where $E' \in \mathbf{E}$ denotes an approximation of original E.

The goal of a passive adversary is to detect whether the sender is using a stegosystem or not by eavesdropping a message (S or C) [6]. The message the passive adversary eavesdrops is a realization of either S (in the former case) or C (in the latter case). The more the distribution of S gets similar to that of C, the harder for the passive adversary to detect the use of stegosystem. In the extreme case, both distributions become identical and eavesdropping becomes meaningless. We call this type of stegosystem perfectly secure. It is impossible for any passive adversary of any computational power to detect the usage of perfectly secure stegosystem.

The model we described above is fairly general. For example, under the conditions of $H(V) = 0$ and $E' = E$, the above model is equivalent to the basic model. Under the conditions of $V = R$ (here R denotes a random number source private to the sender) and $E = E'$ and some assumptions on conditional entropies, the above model is equivalent to the one introduced in [6]. It is easy to apply above model in the midst of protocol by defining V to contain the log of all the symbols so far transmitted.

Now we make some additional assumptions to make the model suitable for computer based stegosystems and to exclude some absurd situations.

- Both embedder and extractor should be computable algorithms.
- Sender can use private random number generator.
- All the specifications of stegosystem (such as the algorithms of key generator, embedder and extractor) are known to adversaries.
  - In other words, the security of a stegosystem does not depend on the secrecy of its algorithms. All shared secret resides in key.
- E' provides some information about E. In short,

$$I(E'; E) > 0 \tag{3}$$

  - This implicitly excludes the case of $H(E) = 0$.
- The secret key K should be generated and shared between the sender and the recipient securely prior to the transmission of stego-data. (The key sharing method is out of the scope of this paper.)
- The value of S depends upon K. In short,

$$H(S|CEV) > 0 \tag{4}$$

  - If the computation of S is independent from K, K has nothing to do for extracting. In such case, E' depends upon S only. Since we assume that the algorithms for extraction and key generation are publicly known, any passive adversary can compute their own E', which has the same distribution of the recipient's E'. Therefore, all information that the recipient gets in a stego-data is available to all passive adversaries. We exclude this situation from our model.

5 One-Time Hash Steganography

5.1 Partial Recomputability

Let us consider here when one can construct a perfectly secure stegosystem.

At least the cover-data C (the message to be sent in non-steganographic communication) should be indeterminable to any passive adversary, since if C is determinable to a passive adversary, S of any perfectly secure stegosystem is also determinable to him and the sender cannot alter S to contain any information about E and K. In order to hide data into the indeterminable part of the cover-data, it is desirable for the sender to know what causes the indeterminability. For example, if $C \equiv f(R, X)$ holds for certain random variables R, X and a function f and any adversary can not get any information about R and the sender knows something about R, it is likely that the sender can modify or regenerate R and recompute $f(R, X)$ again and again to use *selection method* (see section 3).

Based on above consideration, we define the following condition.

Definition 1. *A random variable C is partially recomputable to an entity P if and only if there exist random variables $X, R_1, R_2, \cdots, R_{n_r}$ $(n_r \geq 2)$ and a function f such that for all $i \in \mathbf{Z}_{[1,n_r]}$*

$$f(C, R_i, X) \equiv C \tag{5}$$

$$H(f(C, R_i, X)|CX) > 0 \tag{6}$$

hold and P can get all realizations of $X, R_1, R_2, \cdots, R_{n_r}$ and $R_1, R_2, \cdots, R_{n_r}$ are mutually independent random variables private to P.

The crucial point of partial recomputability is that if a random variable is partially recomputable to an entity P, P can replace the realization of the random variable in probabilistic way without distorting the distribution of the random variable.

Following are some examples of partially recomputable random variables. (Here we always assume that the one who tries to recompute the random variables has private random number generator).

Example 1. Any distribution-known random variable $C \in \mathbf{M}$ is partially recomputable if $H(C) > 0$ holds, since one can mimic the random variable with his private random number generator (see [7] for details) and the condition $H(C) > 0$ guarantees that the output of the random number generator affect the recomputed value of C (i.e., equation (6) holds).

Example 2. Any random variable $C \in \mathbf{M}$ is partially recomputable if there exist two symbols $a, b \in \mathbf{M}$ such that both probabilities $\Pr(C = a)$ and $\Pr(C = b)$ are known and positive. One can use following function to recompute C. (We assume here that $p = \Pr(C = a) < q = \Pr(C = b)$. $R \in \{0,1\}$ is a random variable such that $\Pr(R = 1) = p/q$ holds. v is a dummy input).

$$f(c, r, v) = \begin{cases} c & (\text{if } c \notin \{a, b\}) \\ b & (\text{if } c = a \lor (c = b \land r = 0)) \\ a & (\text{if } c = b \land r = 1) \end{cases} \tag{7}$$

Example 3. Any digital signature that requires a random number to create is partially recomputable to its signer. To recompute a signature, the signer have only to compute his signature again with new random number, which may or may not equal to the one used in the computation of the original signature.

5.2   Definition of One-Time Hash Stegosystem

Based on the above definition, here we introduce one-time hash stegosystem (or OTH stegosystem for short), which can hide an embedded-data bit $E \in \mathbf{E} = \{0, 1\}$ of any distribution into any cover-data $C \in \mathbf{M}$ that is partially recomputable to its sender. The principal idea of OTH stegosystem is fairly simple: the sender generates some candidates for the cover-data, hashes each of them by shared one-time hash, chooses one candidate according to the hash values and the secret bit to transmit, sends it to the recipient. The recipient applies shared one-time hash, and gets an approximation of the original secret bit.

The key K of OTH stegosystem should be uniformly random in $\{0, 1\}^{|\mathbf{M}|}$. Note that the key should never be reused.

Following is the embedding algorithm of OTH stegosystem written in Pascal-like pseudo language. Here we assume that cover-data C is partially recomputable as $C \equiv f(C, R_i, X)$ $(i \in \mathbf{Z}_{[1,n_r]})$. The numbering function g is an injection from $\mathbf{M}$ to $\mathbf{Z}_{[1,|M|]}$ and shared between embedder and extractor. $n \in \mathbf{Z}_{[2,n_r]}$ is the number of recomputation and can be chosen arbitrarily. (In general, increasing this value makes the embedding process take longer and the error rate lower). Both n and g are part of the algorithm and can be public.

Input

embedded-data	$e \in \{0, 1\}$
cover-data	$c \in \mathbf{M}$
key	$k = b_1 b_2 \cdots b_{|\mathbf{M}|} \in \{0, 1\}^{|\mathbf{M}|}$
environmental inputs:	
samples of recomputable part (realizations of $R_1, R_2, \cdots, R_n$)	$r_1, r_2, \cdots, r_n$
environmental input for recomputation (realization of X)	x

Output
  stego-data $s \in \mathbf{M}$

Embedding Steps

```
1: count_0 := 0; count_1 := 0
2: for i := 1 to n do
3:     a_i := f(c, r_i, x)
4:     if (b_{g(a_i)} = 0) then
5:         pool[0, count_0] := a_i;  count_0 := count_0 + 1
6:     else
```

7: $pool[1, count_1] := a_i;\ count_1 := count_1 + 1$

8:   **endif**

9: endfor

10: if $count_0 < count_1$ **then** $greater\_half := 1$ **else** $greater\_half := 0$ **endif**

11: $count_{min} := \min(count_0, count_1)$

12: Choose a random number $r \in \mathbf{Z}_{[0,n-1]}$

13: $s := \begin{cases} pool[0, \lfloor r/2 \rfloor] & \text{(if } r < 2count_{min} \ \wedge \ e = 0) \\ pool[1, \lfloor r/2 \rfloor] & \text{(if } r < 2count_{min} \ \wedge \ e = 1) \\ pool[greater\_half, r - count_{min}] & \text{(if } 2count_{min} \leq r) \end{cases}$

The extracting algorithm of OTH stegosystem is as follows.

Input

key $k = b_1 b_2 \cdots b_{|\mathbf{M}|} \in \{0,1\}^{|\mathbf{M}|}$

stego-data $s \in \mathbf{M}$

Output

extracted data $e' \in \{0,1\}$

Extracting Step

1: $e' := b_{g(s)}$

5.3   Security of One-Time Hash Stegosystem

Theorem 1. *One-time hash stegosystem is perfectly secure.*

Proof. At the entrance of step 13 in embedding steps, variables $pool[0, 0]$, $pool[0, 1]$, $\cdots$, $pool[0, count_0 - 1]$, $pool[1, 0]$, $pool[1, 1]$, $\cdots$, $pool[1, count_1 - 1]$ are permuted realizations of $f(C, R_i, X)$ $(i \in \mathbf{Z}_{[1,n]})$. Let us consider $f(C, R_i, X)$ for certain $i \in \mathbf{Z}_{[1,n]}$. The realization of $f(C, R_i, X)$ must place somewhere in $pool$ at the entrance of step 13. Let $pool[j, k]$ denote the place. The probability that the realization of $f(C, R_i, X)$ is selected as stego-data is, if $k < count_{min}$,

$$\Pr(e = j \ \wedge \ k = \lfloor \frac{r}{2} \rfloor) = \Pr(e = b_{g(f(C,R_i,X))}) \times \Pr(k = \lfloor \frac{r}{2} \rfloor) \tag{8}$$

$$= \frac{1}{2} \times \frac{2}{n} \tag{9}$$

$$= \frac{1}{n} \tag{10}$$

otherwise

$$\Pr(r = count_{min} + k) = \frac{1}{n} \tag{11}$$

In short, this probability is $1/n$ regardless of the position. Consequently,

$$\forall m \in \mathbf{M} \quad \Pr(S = m) = \sum_{i=1}^{n} \frac{1}{n} \Pr(f(C, R_i, X) = m) \tag{12}$$

$$= \sum_{i=1}^{n} \frac{1}{n} \Pr(C = m) \tag{13}$$

$$= \Pr(C = m) \tag{14}$$

holds (from the partial recomputability condition). This means $S \equiv C$, the perfect security.

Note that if the definition of a cover-data implies partial recomputability (i.e. equation (5) and (6) hold regardless of any external condition), OTH stegosystem that takes the cover-data is perfectly secure to any passive adversary regardless of the knowledge of the adversary, provided that realizations of R_i, K and the outputs from the sender's random number generator are kept secret.

5.4   Bandwidth of One-Time Hash Stegosystem

Though OTH stegosystem can make error and E' is not always equal to E, it contains some information about E.

Theorem 2. *On one-time hash stegosystem, $I(E; E') > 0$ always holds.*

Proof. The error $E' \neq E$ occurs if and only if $2 count_{\min} \leq r \wedge greater\_half \neq E$ holds at step 13 of embedding steps. Therefore, the error probability is

$$\Pr(E' \neq E) = \Pr(2 count_{\min} \leq r \wedge greater\_half \neq E) \tag{15}$$

$$= \frac{n - 2 count_{\min}}{n} \Pr(greater\_half \neq E) \tag{16}$$

$$= \frac{1}{2} - \frac{count_{\min}}{n} \tag{17}$$

(If $2 count_{\min} < n$ holds, $\Pr(greater\_half \neq E)$ is always $1/2$, since the key bits $b_1 b_2 \cdots b_{|\mathbf{M}|}$ are randomly generated and independent from E. Otherwise, $\Pr(E' \neq E)$ is 0 and the above equation holds anyway). From the conditions of partial recomputability, $H(f(C, R_i, X)|CX) > 0$ holds for all $i \in \mathbf{Z}_{[1,n]}$ and all random variables R_i ($i \in \mathbf{Z}_{[1,n]}$) are mutually independent. This means that $\Pr(pool[0, 0] = pool[0, 1] = \cdots = pool[0, count_0 - 1] = pool[1, 0] = pool[1, 1] = \cdots = pool[1, count_1 - 1]) < 1$. From this and the fact that the key bits $b_1 b_2 \cdots b_{|\mathbf{M}|}$ for hashing is randomly chosen, $\Pr(count_{\min} = 0) < 1$ holds. This means $\Pr(E' \neq E) < 1/2$ and $\Pr(E' = E) = 1 - \Pr(E' \neq E) > 1/2$. Therefore, E' is not independent from E and $I(E; E') > 0$ holds. $\square$

This means that equation (3) in our assumption always holds. It is easy to see that OTH stegosystem conforms to the other assumptions we made in section 4.

The above theorem guarantees that the channel capacity of the transmission channel OTH stegosystem provides is always positive. Therefore, the sender can encode his message with error-correcting code and send the result using the OTH stegosystem multiple times so as to lower the error probability.

Since any digital signature scheme that uses a random number is partially recomputable to its signer (see Example 3), OTH stegosystem can take any such digital signature as cover-data. This can be regarded as a subliminal channel [14]. Though the bandwidth of this channel is fairly narrow compared to the bandwidths of those cleverly exploits the redundancy of each signature scheme [13], this channel is perfectly secure even if the underlying signature scheme is vulnerable to the adversaries or if the signature function is not an injection from the random number input to the signature.

6   Necessary and Sufficient Condition for the Existence of Perfectly Secure Stegosystem

In the previous section, we showed that the partial recomputability of cover-data is a sufficient condition for the existence of perfectly secure stegosystem. In this section, we consider the necessary condition for the existence of perfectly secure stegosystem.

Suppose that there exists a perfectly secure stegosystem. Then,

$$C \equiv S \tag{18}$$
$$= \mathcal{E}(E, C, K, V) \tag{19}$$

holds. Let n_r be arbitrary integer bigger than one. Defining f as

$$f(C, K, (E, V)) = \mathcal{E}(E, C, K, V) \tag{20}$$

the first condition for the partial recomputability (equation (5)) is fulfilled, since

$$f(C, R_i, (E, V)) \equiv C \tag{21}$$

holds for all $i \in \mathbf{Z}_{[1,n_r]}$. (Here R_i $(i \in \mathbf{Z}_{[1,n_r]})$ denote the key candidates generated using the sender's private random number generator and $R_i \equiv K$ holds for all $i \in \mathbf{Z}_{[1,n_r]}$). From equation (4),

$$H(f(C, R_i, (E, V))|CEV) = H(S|CEV) > 0$$

holds. Therefore, C is partially recomputable to the sender.

From the above fact and the existence of OTH steganography, the next theorem holds.

Theorem 3. *For any message source C, there exists a perfectly secure stegosystem that takes C as its cover-data, if and only if C is partially recomputable to its sender.*

Note that partial recomputability is not the necessary condition for the existence of the perfectly secure stegosystems we excluded in the construction of our model. For example, even if a cover-data is not partially recomputable to its sender, there still can exist perfectly secure stegosystems that use external input of unknown distribution as its key. Such stegosystems are out of the scope of this paper.

7 Conclusions

In this paper, we generalized the steganography model described in [6] and made some conditions to make the model suitable for computer based steganography systems. Based on this model, we introduced a perfectly secure steganography system, one-time hash steganography system, which can take any cover-data that is partially recomputable to the sender. Finally, we proved that the partial recomputability of a cover-data to its sender is a necessary and sufficient condition for the existence of perfectly secure steganography system.

Acknowledgments

The author greatly appreciates Prof. Yasumasa Kanada, who awoke the author to the necessity of steganography.

References

1. H. Abelson, R. Anderson, S. Bellovin, J. Benaloh, M. Blaze, W. Diffie, J. Gilmore, P. Neumann, R. Rivest, J. Schiller, and B. Schneier, "The Risks of Key Recovery, Key Escrow, and Trusted Third-Party Encryption," *World Wide Web Journal*, v.2, n.3, 1997, pp.241–257
2. Ross Anderson (Ed.), "Information Hiding," First International Workshop IH'96 Proceedings, *Lecture Notes in Computer Science* 1174, Springer, 1996 17 17
3. Ross Anderson, "Stretching the Limits of Steganography," *Lecture Notes in Computer Science* 1174, Springer, 1996, pp.265–278   19
4. David Aucsmith (Ed.), "Information Hiding," Second International Workshop IH'98 Proceedings, *Lecture Notes in Computer Science* 1525, Springer, 1998   17
5. Tuomas Aura, "Practical Invisibility in Digital Communication," *Lecture Notes in Computer Science* 1174, pp.265–278   19
6. Christian Cachin, "An Information-Theoretic Model for Steganography," *Lecture Notes in Computer Science* 1525, Springer, 1998, pp.306–318   18, 19, 21, 27
7. Thomas M. Cover, Joy A. Thomas, "Elements of Information Theory," John Wiley & Sons. Inc, New York, 1991   22
8. Silvio Micali, "Fair Public-Key Cryptosystems," Advances in Cryptology— CRYPTO'92 Proceedings, *Lecture Notes in Computer Science* 740, Springer, 1993, pp.113–118
9. Neil F. Johnson and Sushil Jajodia, "Steganography: Seeing the Unseen," *IEEE Computer*, February 1998, pp 26–34   17

10. David Kahn, "The History of Steganography," *Lecture Notes in Computer Science* 1174, Springer, 1996, pp.1–7   17
11. Michiharu Niimi, Hideki Noda, and Eiji Kawaguchi, "An Image Embedding in Image by a Complexity Based Region Segmentation Method," *Proc. ICIP'97*, Vol.3, pp.74–77, (1997-10)
12. (Collected by) Birgit Pfitzmann, "Information Hiding Terminology," *Lecture Notes in Computer Science* 1174, Springer, 1996, pp.347–350   18
13. Bruce Schneier, "Applied Cryptography," John Wiley & Sons, 1996 (second edition)   26
14. Gustavus J. Simmons, "The Subliminal Channel and Digital Signatures," EURO-CRYPT'84, *Lecture Notes in Computer Science* 209, Springer, 1985   26
15. J. Zöllner, H. Federrath, H. Klimant, A. Pfitzmann, R. Piotraschke, A. Westfeld, G. Wicke, G. Wolf, "Modeling the Security of Steganographic Systems," *Lecture Notes in Computer Science* 1525, Springer, 1998, pp.344–354   19

Steganography Secure against Cover-Stego-Attacks

Elke Franz and Andreas Pfitzmann

Dresden University of Technology, Department of Computer Science,
D-01062 Dresden
{efl,pfitza}@inf.tu-dresden.de

Abstract. Steganography aims to secretly transmit messages by embedding them in cover data. The usual criterion each stegosystem must meet is to resist stego-only-attacks. An even stronger criterion is to resist cover-stego-attacks. The article introduces a stego paradigm which aims to meet this stronger requirement by simulating a „usual process" of data processing. The general realization of the paradigm is discussed. One possible realization is sketched.

1 Discussion of the Stego Paradigm

1.1 Goal of Steganography

One concern of privacy in everyday life is that one can communicate confidentially. However, modern electronic communication does not provide the same conditions as everyday communication. If one sends a message by email, for example, the message is public like on a postcard. One can prevent this by cryptography. However, there have been discussions by various governmental institutions about restricting cryptography in previous years. On the one hand, this makes life more difficult for criminals; on the other hand, it is an offence against privacy.

Steganography is a way to communicate confidentially despite of all restrictions: The secret message is imperceptibly embedded in other harmlessly looking data. Thus, the mere existence of a secret message is hidden.

The main goal of steganography is to embed data in such a way that it cannot be detected. Moreover, it should be possible to embed as much data as possible.

Steganography is also used for watermarking systems. These systems embed information about the copyright holder into digital works that are expected to be used without authorization. In contrast to classical steganography, the existence of an embedded watermark may be known but it must not be possible to remove this watermark.

1.2 Possible Attacks

The discussion of possible attacks and their success is necessary to evaluate the security of a system. In case of steganography, the goal of the attacker is to detect infor-

A. Pfitzmann (Ed.): IH´99, LNCS 1768, pp. 29–46, 2000.

mation hiding. In the worst case, he can extract the embedded text in all probability. Therefore, a stegosystem is called secure if it outputs stego data that do not even arouse suspicion about the presence of any embedded data.

We assume the use of a key for both embedding and extracting. This key is only known to the users. The attacker must find out the key and the stegosystem used. Consequently, he could find several possibilities to extract a message. However, if he extracts a plausible message it is very likely that he has succeeded. As in case of a ciphertext-only-attack in cryptography, it is not possible to gain absolute certainty about the success of the attack. But in practice, a probability close to one will be sufficient. The probability to falsely accuse anybody should be reasonably small. Additional measures like monitoring further actions of the people involved may strengthen suspicion. But this is beyond the scope of this paper and, therefore, will not be discussed further.

Power and knowledge of the attacker must be considered to describe possible attacks comprehensively. The power of the attacker can be described as follows:

- A *passive attacker* is only able to analyze the data he could intercept.
- An *active attacker* is allowed to modify the data.

Steganography mainly considers passive attacks as pointed out in [1]. [2] gives examples for active attacks. However, the discussion of active attacks is most common for watermarking systems [5].

The knowledge of the attacker describes which data and which details of the system such as algorithms and keys are known to him.

Usually, one assumes that the attacker can access only the stego data, i.e. he can analyze or even manipulate them (**stego-only-attack**). However, attacks on stegosystems should be discussed as comprehensively as in cryptography, because it cannot be excluded that the attacker is more knowledgeable or more powerful.

For example, one can imagine that the user of a stegosystem has not deleted the cover used. The cover is still stored on his computer, which is possibly not protected from access via the net. An attacker can try to spy out the cover stored (**cover-stego-attack**). This way, also the embedded data (emb) could be spied out if they were not deleted immediately (**emb-stego-attack**). Combined, this gives a **cover-emb-stego-attack**.

Moreover, the attacker could be able to **manipulate cover**. Imagine, the attacker knows that as covers, the user prefers interesting images he has found on web sites. Now the attacker publishes some very interesting images on a site and makes this site known to the user. It is at least possible that the user downloads some of these images and uses them as a cover. This way, the attacker can try to suggest the use of images which make stego analysis easier. Even if the stegosystem rejects covers that are not suitable for embedding it will surely be possible to find covers which will not be processed optimally and, therefore, are useful for the attacker's analysis.

The attacker could also try to manipulate emb in order to change its distribution. Suppose, emb will be compressed or encrypted before embedding. This step results in a special distribution of emb that may be optimal for embedding, whereas the embedding would yield suspicious stego data for covers with another distribution. The attacker could try to manipulate the distribution by suggesting the use of another compression or decryption. Therefore, the preprocessing of emb should be part of the stegosystem to prevent the manipulation. This way, such an attack is no longer possible and will not be discussed further.

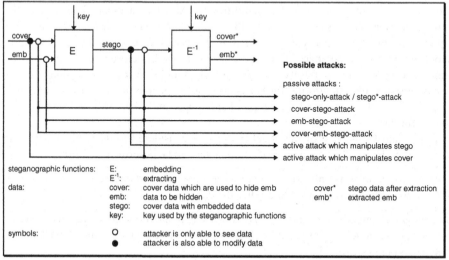

Fig. 1. Possible attacks on a stegosystem

Fig. 1 shows a common model of a stegosystem [6, 7] and possible attacks on the systems. Regarding steganography, the following attacks can be distinguished:

Passive attacks:
- stego-only-attack: Attacker analyzes the intercepted stego data.
- stego*-attack: The user has repeatedly embedded in the same cover, and the attacker has intercepted the resulting stegos. Of course, this should not happen, but it cannot surely be excluded.
- cover-stego-attack: In addition to the intercepted stego the attacker gets to know cover.
- emb-stego-attack: The attacker knows both emb and stego.
- cover-emb-stego-attack: The attacker knows cover, emb, and stego.

Active attacks:
- Manipulating stego: Stego can be manipulated to prevent the transmission of the embedded message. On the one hand, this attack foils the secret communication. On the other hand, the attacker can analyze the reaction of attacked parties: If they try to send possible stego data again it could be a sign that steganography is used.
- Manipulating cover: The attacker can try to make his attack easier as described above. In addition to the manipulated cover he uses the intercepted stego for his analysis.

As described above, there is a variety of possible attacks. For further investigations, we have chosen the cover-stego-attack and describe a paradigm that resists this attack. It will come out that the paradigm resists the stego*-attack, too, and, moreover, even the cover-emb-stego-attack.

Another classification of attacks can be found in [4].

1.3 Introduction of the Stego Paradigm

As shown in [7], deterministic steganography cannot resist cover-stego-attacks. Generally, it is necessary to add indeterminism to the embedding. [7] proposes to use a set of possible covers (called *Source*) to make the system indeterministic: The attacker cannot decide which of the possible covers was really used.

This article presents another approach: The stegosystem simulates a usual process that modifies data. There are differences between the input and the output of the process which must be used to embed the secret message. Indeterminism means in this case that the attacker cannot decide whether the differences between intercepted data are caused by the stegosystem or by the simulated process (Fig. 2). The former means that data have been embedded, the latter means that this is not the case.

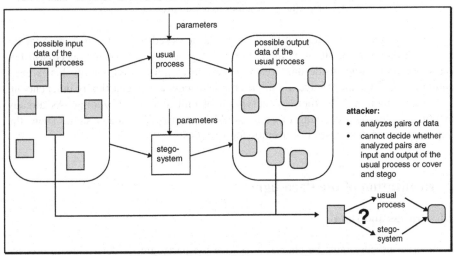

Fig. 2. Introduction of the stego paradigm

In general, there are no restrictions on the usual process. In case of a deterministic process, several output data are produced by different parameters or other influences. An indeterministic process creates different output data even if an event is repeated under nearly the same conditions (the same input data, almost the same circumstances).

The simulation of a usual process provides steganography that is even resistant to cover-stego-attacks: Given an exact simulation of a usual process. Every cover will be processed by the simulation as it would be done by the original process. The input and output of the stegosystem and of the usual process correspond to each other. Of course, the differences between the input and output of the usual process will not be suspicious to an attacker. Therefore, the differences caused by the simulation will not be suspicious, too.

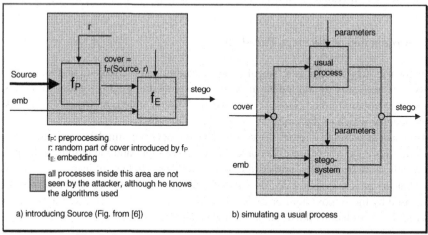

Fig. 3. Comparing possibilities to resist cover-stego-attacks

Fig. 3 compares this paradigm to the method proposed in [7]. Even if the attacker knows all data outside the gray area, a cover-stego-attack will not be successful because the processing inside this area is uncertain to him. Additionally, this is even valid regarding the knowledge of emb if emb and stego are stochastically independent. This requirement can be met by encryption of emb before embedding. As already mentioned, this preprocessing of emb should be part of the stegosystem. Then, the stegosystem can even resist cover-emb-stego-attacks.

2 Realization of the Paradigm

2.1 Process and Data

A concrete process must be chosen to realize the paradigm. A deterministic process would be easier to simulate because its behavior is determined. But the set of possible outputs is limited, because plausible parameters must be used. Therefore, the possible outputs may not supply suitable differences for embedding data. The cover must be rejected in this case. This is not critical as long as the possible covers are not limited too much. Otherwise, the stego data would be suspicious anyway.

An indeterministic process presents a larger set of possible output data. It is more likely that the differences between the input data and some of these output data are suitable for embedding. Of course, it is also possible that a special cover cannot be used. But we think that the set of possible covers will not be limited too much. Thus we focus on an indeterministic process.

As an example of an indeterministic process we discuss the scan process. There are some special features which must be considered:

- The input of the scanning is an analogue image. Repeated scanning of this image while using the same parameters yields a set of different digital images, which is caused by the indeterminism of the scanning.
- The input of the stegosystem is an already digitized image, i.e. it is a possible output of the scan process. Therefore, we have the special case that both input and output data of the stegosystem must belong to the possible output data of the scan process (Fig. 4).
- This, however, presents just another possibility to realize the stegosystem: Instead of mimicking the differences between input and output, the stegosystem can also mimic the differences between possible outputs. This has the advantage, that input and output of the stegosystem is completely digital.
- If the differences between cover and stego correspond to differences between images scanned, an attacker cannot decide whether the differences were caused by the scan process or by the embedding. This requirement should be met for any pair of data the attacker can intercept, and especially it should hold even if the attacker could intercept more than two images. Therefore, the system is not only resistant to cover-stego-attacks but also to stego*-attacks.

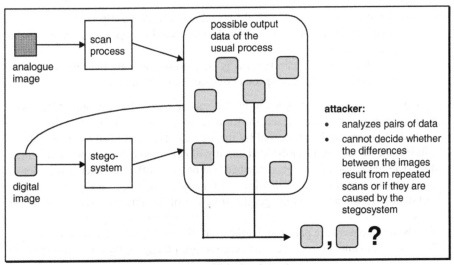

Fig. 4. A stegosystem which simulates the scan process

The problem which must be solved is to describe the scan process as exactly as possible. The stegosystem must process the permissible covers correctly by using this description: It takes the cover and generates differences which could be found between repeated scans while hiding the data to be embedded within these differences. If a cover is not suitable for embedding, the stegosystem should reject it.

The differences between repeated scans are especially important since cover and stego must be possible outputs of the scan process. These differences must be mimicked by the stegosystem. A description of the scan process, however, describes possible effects in a single image. (And thereby, possible effects in most of the images which can be found on computers, because they had to be digitized, too.) Nevertheless, such a description will reveal possible differences between images scanned: Parts of the image which are digitized more indeterministically are likely to be more different from image to image than parts which are digitized rather deterministically.

We have to assume that the attacker knows the scan process: The description used by the stegosystem to simulate the scan process must be at least as good as the description of the scan process known to the attacker. Otherwise, the attacker could be able to distinguish between the two processes.

2.2 Possible Levels of the Stegosystem

There are several levels of generality to describe the stegosystem:

1. The lowest level is a stegosystem that describes possible differences specifically for each cover to be used. Before embedding, the potential cover must be scanned several times. The stegosystem evaluates the differences between the digitized images in order to derive the stego image as digital image, which might result from another scan.
   ☺ Possible differences are described for each cover very exactly.
   ☹ It is a very expensive realization. Each cover requires repeated scanning and a special evaluation.
   ☹ The simulation of the scan process is very limited as only the differences between repeated scans of one special cover are described.

2. A more elaborate solution is given by the second level. The possible differences between repeated scans are described for a set of images. Each cover of the set described can correctly be processed by the stegosystem: The resulting stego image will include the data to be embedded and it will belong to the set of possible output data. The limitation of the sets described can be very different. Therefore, a lot of stegosystems are possible on this level. Limitations can concern e.g. the material and quality of the analogue image, the structure of the image, and the number of colors.
   ☺ The more covers are permissible, the more flexible the stegosystem is.
   ☺ It is a real simulation of the scan process, even though only for a limited set of covers.
   ☹ The more covers are permissible, the more extensive the necessary description is.
   ☹ It cannot be guaranteed that every cover of the set described will be processed correctly: Because not every single cover is evaluated, a cover may represent a special case.

3. The highest level is a stegosystem that meets the theoretical ideas of the realization of the stego paradigm. It can correctly process any cover.
   ☺ This stegosystem is the most flexible one.

⊗ This system needs a universally valid description of all properties of the scanner, which has not been found yet. It is not even clear whether such a description can be found or if an attacker can still find covers which are not covered by the description, respectively. Therefore, it is not yet clear whether a stegosystem of the third level is feasible at all.

A stegosystem of the first level is surely feasible and maybe it is the first step to define a stegosystem of the second level. We want to define a stegosystem of the second level: Based on a limited set of possible covers, the behavior of the scanner is to be described. The set contains grayscale images scanned from black and white photos. Further restrictions of the covers (e.g. regarding to the structure of the pictures) may become necessary, but they are not mentioned at this point.

3   Description of the Scan Process

3.1   Scanner Type and Principles

Several types of scanners are in use. The flatbed scanner is chosen as a model because of its widespread use.

The scan process can be generally described as follows:

1. *Scanning:*
The analogue image is scanned by a CCD-line (charge coupled device). This CCD-line and the necessary optics are fixed on a block which will vertically be moved over the image while scanning.

The analogue image is put on a thick glass pane. While scanning, the image is exposed. The image reflects the light so that it shines on the CCD elements. The CCDs convert the incoming light into analogue voltage.

2. *Processing inside the scanner:*
These analogue values are possibly edited by a preprocessor and then digitized. The scanning result can be improved by further operations, e.g. to reduce streaks (see 3.3) or to optimize the range for conversion. Such operations are performed by the firmware of the scanner.

3. *Transmission:*
Finally, the digital data are transmitted to the computer.

4. *Processing outside the scanner:*
After all, the data can be modified by the computer according to the user's wishes, e.g. changing the brightness or the contrast.

A special software is necessary for scanning. Some of their tasks are to give a preview of the scanned image and to select the image areas to be scanned. Settings may also allow to choose the image type, the resolution, or the exposure. These settings can also be chosen automatically by the firmware of the scanner.

The precision of the scan depends on the positioning of the block with the CCD elements, the precision of the CCD elements (with respect to reproducibility), and the processing of the values scanned, especially the analogue-digital conversion. Overall, mechanics and electronics, but also the processing of the data are important.

The possible horizontal resolution of the scanner is determined by the number of CCD elements, i.e. it is a function of the electronic. The possible vertical resolution is determined by the positioning of the scanning block, it is a mechanical problem.

3.2 Indeterministic Parts of the Scan Process

The repeated scanning of one image will result in digital images that look alike to the human eye. However, even if the same settings were used while scanning, the single pixels of the images are not identical. This is conditional on the indeterminism of the scan process which causes noise. The indeterminism is especially caused by the characteristic of the scanner, which consists of the following points:

- indeterminism of analogue electronics,
- irregularities of exposure,
- precision of the mechanics,
- material of the parts of the scanner (e.g. the glass pane),
- operations performed inside the scanner, which possibly contain random decisions or rounding errors.

Moreover, electronics and mechanics and with those the result of a scan can also be influenced by other parameters like temperature or soiling.

It is assumed that the transmission of the data to the computer and the processing of the digital data are deterministic.

Besides the described indeterministic parts, it is assumed that the single components of the scanner cannot be exactly the same (see Sect. 3.3). This is one reason for the differences between different copies of a scanner. Every scanner owns a typical behavior. Therefore, the exact description of the scan process, which is a requirement for the simulation, must be done separately for every scanner.

Moreover, the characteristics of the components change over time. The change of a scanner during time (concerning its electronics, mechanics and material) is assumed to be a slow process. The stegosystem reflects the behavior of the scanner at a special time. The time interval between the creation of stego images known to a stego analyst is expected to be not significant. Thus, we do not need to reflect these changes.

3.3 Effects Expected and their Influence on the Differences between Repeated Scans

The sources for indeterminism mentioned can produce two problems: noise caused by reproducing errors (*reproducing noise*) and noise caused by calibrating errors (*cali-*

brating noise). The former is produced by the inherent noise of analogue devices, the latter results from the differences between the single components.

As mentioned in Sect. 2.1, describing the effects of the scan process will lead to assumptions on possible differences between repeated scans. The more noisy the digitalization of an analogue image, the more differences are likely between the results of different scans. In the following, obvious effects expected to appear in the digitized images and possible differences between repeated scans resulting from these effects are discussed.

Influence of electronics:

The CCD elements cause a reproducing noise which is spread over the whole image. Moreover, the noise depends on the gray to be taken (signal dependent noise with a constant relative error). Because the CCD elements do not scan just a point each but possibly overlapping areas, they could yield transition zones between light and dark areas instead of sharp edges. Besides this optical problem, there are also other influences which might cause this effect, e.g. dispersion and reflection of light, the influence of neighboring CCD elements, or hysteresis between the scans per row.

It is not possible to produce and calibrate the elements so that they yield exactly the same value for the same shade of gray in the analogue image. This could produce a calibrating noise, which might be noticed as tiny streaks in vertical direction in the image scanned. Therefore, the scan direction of an image can possibly be determined: Comparing the gray scales of a digital image, there should be less variance inside the columns than inside the rows within homogenous areas.

The different behavior of the elements may also be recognizable in the difference images: Elements working more noisy will yield results more scattered than elements working more deterministically. These different amounts of reproducing noise could be noticed as vertical streaks as well.

Effects expected:	→	Possible differences:
reproducing noise which is spread over the whole image	→	(at least small) differences spread over the whole image
signal dependent noise with a constant relative error	→	stronger differences in light areas (corresponds to a high signal) than in dark ones
different degree of reproducing noise for different CCD elements	→	vertical streaks within homogenous areas

Influence of exposure:

Irregularities of exposure can produce both typical effects for a special scanner (noise depending on the position of the analogue image while scanning) and reproducing noise.

Effects expected:	➔	Possible differences:
noise depending on the position	➔	differences depending on the position
reproducing noise	➔	(at least small) differences spread over the whole image

Influence of mechanics:

It is expected that the horizontal steering of the block is very exact. Minute irregularities of the steering might map the results of a single CCD element not to the same 'column' of the analogue image but sometimes to the neighbored 'columns' instead.

Irregularities of the positioning in vertical direction (i.e. the „stops" for each row to be scanned) may slightly shift the position of the CCD line with regard to the 'rows' of the analogue image sometimes.

Besides the steering and positioning while scanning, the block must be positioned again for the next scan. It must change its direction after scanning the area selected and move back. Resulting from these movements, there might be differences between the starting positions of the block, which would cause a shift of the pixels between repeated scans.

The following illustrates the scale in which irregularities of the mechanics have an effect on the digitized image: Assumed, the scanner used has a maximum physical resolution of 600 dpi, i.e. 600 points per 2.54 cm. There are only 0.042 mm between two adjacent points. A shift of the pixels is caused even if the scanner works exactly in the range of a hundredth of a millimeter.

Effects expected:	➔	Possible differences:
irregularities of the horizontal steering	➔	differences on vertical gray edges
irregularities of the positioning in vertical direction	➔	differences on horizontal gray edges, maybe stronger than on vertical edges
shift of the block while moving back	➔	differences on gray edges depending on the shift

Influence of the surrounding:

Soiling or signs of wear of the glass pane or the optical parts can cause typical errors for a special scanner but also a calibrating noise which is spread over the whole image.

Both the results of the CCD elements and the mechanical functionality can be slightly affected by surroundings, like the temperature. The resulting reproducing noise is spread over the whole image, too.

Effects expected:	➔	Possible differences:
typical errors for a special scanner	➔	differences depending on the position
noise spread over the whole image	➔	(at least small) differences spread over the whole image

Influence of random decisions:

While converting analogue to digital data random decisions can be necessary if there is a borderline case (that effects reproducing noise).

Effects expected:	→	Possible differences:
noise spread over the whole image	→	(at least small) differences spread over the whole image

To conclude, the following differences between repeated scans are expected:
- differences spread over the whole image,
- differences depending on the gray value,
- stronger differences on gray edges,
- vertical streaks within homogenous areas, and
- differences depending on the position of the analogue image while scanning.

However, we have described obvious effects and possible differences but we do not want to exclude the possibility that there are also other differences caused by other effects.

The indeterminism of the scanning causes different kinds of noise, which will cause differences between repeated scans. Regarding to one image, the stegosystem must construct these differences while embedding. In the following we want to sketch how one could describe the differences.

4 Description of the Possible Differences

4.1 Strategies and Assumptions

This chapter describes the main work to be done. Some first results will be represented to give an impression that the paradigm is feasible.

As described above, various differences between repeated scans are possible. To find a description of the differences that can be used by the stegosystem, we want to perform two steps. First, we want to examine various scanners to answer the following questions:
- Which of the differences expected can be found?
- How strong are these differences?
- In which way do the features of a scanner influence the differences?
- Is it possible to derive the differences, which must be simulated, from the features of the scanner?

This step will yield an overall impression of the scanners' behavior, at best. However, we need exact instructions how to generate the differences for the stegosystem.

Therefore, a further step is necessary: We want to choose a special scanner in order to describe the differences caused by it as exactly as possible. This step includes the following tasks:
- The differences, which are typical for this scanner, must be found out.

- Appropriate methods to describe these differences depending on the features of the image must be chosen.
- The set of covers must be defined.
- Finally, the values of the differences must be evaluated for the permissible covers.

There are a lot of possible settings for the scan process, e.g. regarding the resolution, the gamma correction, or the brightness. During the investigation of different scanners, it is necessary to try various settings in order to find out dependencies or differences which were not considered otherwise. However, if the scan process is to be described exactly, we want to use the standard settings. The main reason for this is the fact that the stegosystem must work plausibly, i.e. it must simulate differences between scans which are done with plausible settings.

To get an impression of the differences caused only by the scanner, the image is repeatedly scanned without changing its position. For practice, it is also important to consider the case that the image was removed and later again put on the glass pane.

Difference images were computed to show the differences between repeated scans. A difference image is defined as follows: Each pixel represents the absolute difference between the pixels of the two compared images at this position.

These difference images were processed in order to visualize the differences. An inverted difference image is defined as follows: A white pixel at position (x, y) means that the pixel at (x, y) in the first image is equal to the pixel at (x, y) in the second image. A black pixel, however, means that the pixels at this position are different. In a strengthened difference image, the meaning of a white pixel is the same. The gray values of the other pixels correspond to the differences at the respective position multiplied by 10 (and, of course, subtracted from 255, which stands for white).

4.2 Comparing Different Scanners

Three flatbed scanners (single pass) were compared in order to get an impression of possible differences. Important technical data are listed in Tab. 1. In the following, a comparison of possible differences while using common settings is represented.

Table 1. Some technical data of the scanners used

Scanner	Gray Mode	Optical Resolution
1) HP ScanJet 6100C	10 bits internal (1024 shades of gray); 8 bits external (256 shades of gray)	600 dpi x 600 dpi
2) Primax Colorado Direct / D600	10 bits internal (1024 shades of gray); 8 bits external (256 shades of gray)	300 dpi x 600 dpi
3) Mustek ScanExpress 12000P	12 bits internal (4096 shades of gray); 8 bits external (256 shades of gray)	600 dpi x 1200 dpi

Fig. 5 shows the image that was scanned to visualize the possible differences between repeated scans. We can represent only some of the results here. The appropriate scans were done with settings suggested. Especially, the automatically adjusted values for *brightness* and *contrast* were not changed. It is assumed that 150 dpi are a quite common *resolution* for scanning a photograph. The *gamma correction* with gamma 2.2, especially suggested for the first scanner, was used. The image was scanned twice *without changing the position* of the analogue image. This way, the differences observed were only caused by the scanner.

Fig. 5. Image that was scanned

The difference images, which were evaluated between two scans using the HP ScanJet 6100C, are shown in Fig. 6. In contrast to the expectations, there are more differences in dark areas than in light ones. Generally, the differences are spread over the whole image. One can easily recognize the vertical streaks.

The values of the differences do not differ very much. Especially, there are no stronger differences on gray edges. Therefore, it can be assumed that the mechanics of the scanner works very exactly.

At the moment, we cannot give an explanation for the horizontal streaks which appear regularly in the difference image.

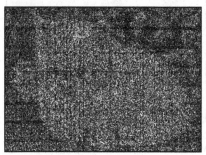

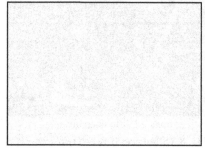

a) inverted difference image   b) strengthened difference image

Fig. 6. Differences between two scans using the HP ScanJet 6100C (150 dpi, gamma 2.2).

Possible differences between scans using the second scanner (Primax Colorado Direct) are shown in Fig. 7. The differences caused by the first and the second scanner are quite different. Now there are strong differences on gray edges, the cat's silhouette is completely recognizable. Therefore, the mechanics of the scanner seems to work less exactly. Neither horizontal nor vertical streaks appear. The streaks might go down within the overall noise.

However, the differences are not spread over the whole image, within the white areas of the image there are no differences at all. This uncovers another effect of the scan process: Within areas of saturation different gray values of the analogue image may be mapped on the same digital value.

a) inverted difference image   b) strengthened difference image

Fig. 7. Differences between two scans using the Colorado Primax (150 dpi, gamma 2.2).

The differences caused by the third scanner (Fig. 8) are quite similar to the differences caused by the second one: The gray edges are clearly recognizable, within the white areas there are no differences (of course, areas of saturation differ from scanner to scanner). But in contrast to Fig. 7, there are also some vertical streaks. We are not absolutely sure what caused the streaks in this difference image. One possible reason might be that there are stronger differences between the reproducing noise of the appropriate elements than would be overloaded by the overall noise.

a) inverted difference image   b) strengthened difference image

Fig. 8. Differences between two scans using the Mustek ScanExpress (150 dpi, gamma 2.2).

To conclude, it is useful to compare different scanners if one wants to get an overall impression of possible differences. The results have strengthened the assumption that the differences between repeated scans strongly depend on the characteristics of the scanner:

- The better the mechanics of the scanner, the less differences on gray edges can be found.
- Saturation may cause the effect that different (light) values of the image to be scanned are represented by the same digital values. Inside such areas, there will be no differences between repeated scans. The first scanner works with an intelli-

gent microprocessor chip, which performs a lot of operations to improve the scan result [8]. It can be assumed that the processing inside the other scanners is less successful with regard to handling the saturation.

- Comparing more homogenous areas, the values of the differences seem to depend on the quality of the CCD elements. Generally, the first scanner produces less noise than the others. Between the scans of the second and the third scanner, there are more and stronger differences.

Even if the scanner works very exactly there will still be enough space for embedding data. In general, there are indeterministic parts that cannot be removed despite of all elaborate technologies because they are effected by analogue processes.

As mentioned above, it is necessary to try various settings in order to find out dependencies or differences which were not considered. For example, scanning the image with the first scanner without gamma correction results in a difference image that clearly shows the signal dependent noise: The most and strongest differences could be found within the light areas. This characteristic of the difference image is changed by the gamma correction because it maps the higher values, which represent the light grays, onto less values. This way, differences can get lost.

Furthermore, scanning with higher resolution shows regularly looking horizontal streaks (using the first scanner again). Scanning an homogenous image shows that these streaks depend on the position of the image on the glass pane. We are not yet sure about the reason for this effect.

The image was also scanned after putting it on the glass pane again. It was assumed that this would yield stronger differences on gray edges, especially for the first scanner. Tests confirmed this assumption. For the second scanner, the difference images did not differ so much because there were already differences on gray edges caused by irregularities of the mechanics. The third scanner has produced strong shifts between different scans (without moving the analogue image).

4.3 Describing a Special Scanner

Because this step is not yet accomplished we want only to sketch the procedure.
According to Sect. 4.1, the differences which are typical for a scanner must be found out first. After that, an appropriate method for describing the differences depending on the image's characteristic must be chosen. That means, it must be possible to describe the image in a way that it is divided according to the differences.

Methods to describe images are known from image processing. There are both point processes and area processes. The latter seem to be more useful.

Assumedly, the second scanner is to be used as a model for the stegosystem. Typical differences caused by this scanner are strong differences on gray edges and differences spread over the whole image except the white areas. Further evaluation of the difference image has shown that there is a shift in vertical direction.

An appropriate procedure could be to filter out the edges, connect this result with the direction of the change from light to dark in vertical direction, and to add noise to the whole image except the white areas.

The last step is to define the set of permissible covers and to evaluate the chosen characteristics for these images. Of course, this requires the scanning of the images.

Generally, the result of the analysis is something like a table that contains every characteristic analyzed. For these characteristics, the likelihood for possible differences and the likelihood for possible distances between differences are given. If the stegosystem wants to process a cover, it tries to match all characteristics and modifies the cover as described. If there is any characteristic, which is not described, the cover is rejected.

If one takes into consideration the great variety of features that are possible in an image, it seems to be very hard to define a useful description which can completely cover at least a group of permissible covers. Maybe it is only possible to realize a stegosystem of the first stage (Sect. 2.2) that generates a stego after analyzing a number of scans of the chosen cover.

It is very important to verify the chosen measures, even at this time. Thus, the stegoparadigm and possible realizations are presented before practical results have been achieved.

5 Summary

The article discusses a possibility to generate stegosystems which are resistant to cover-stego-attacks. It comes out that such a system also resists cover-emb-stego-attacks and stego*-attacks. The method proposed is to simulate a usual process while embedding. To get as many suitable covers as possible, the simulation of an indeterministic process is suggested. As an example, the scan process was looked at.

Possible differences between repeated scans were pointed out. Results of some tests showed that the differences depend on the characteristics of the scanner used.

The main goal was to describe a stegosystem that is resistant to cover-stego-attacks. However, such a stegosystem may have additional features: Most of the pixels of an image must be changed, and the values of the differences are quite strong in some cases. That could be used to embed more data or to embed the data more robustly, respectively.

Further investigations will be done to accomplish the description of the differences depending on the covers permitted. The continuous validation of the descriptions is necessary.

References

1. R.J. Anderson, F.A.P. Petitcolas: On the Limits of Steganography. IEEE Journal on selected areas in communications, vol. 16 / 4, 474-481, 1998.
2. S. Craver: On Public-Key Steganography in the Presence of an Active Warden. Information Hiding, Proceedings, Workshop, Portland, Oregon, USA April 1998, LNCS 1525, Springer-Verlag, Berlin 1998, 355-368.
3. E. Franz, A. Pfitzmann: Einführung in die Steganographie und Ableitung eines neuen Stego-paradigmas. Informatik-Spektrum 21, 183-193, Springer-Verlag 1998.
4. N.F. Johnson, S. Jajodia: Steganalysis of Images Created Using Current Steganography Software. Information Hiding, Proceedings, Workshop, Portland, Oregon, USA April 1998, LNCS 1525, Springer-Verlag, Berlin 1998, 273-289.
5. F.A.P. Petitcolas, R.J. Anderson, M.G. Kuhn: Attacks on Copyright Marking Systems. Information Hiding, Proceedings, Workshop, Portland, Oregon, USA April 1998, LNCS 1525, Springer-Verlag, Berlin 1998, 218-238.
6. B. Pfitzmann: Information Hiding Terminology. Information Hiding, Proceedings, Workshop, Cambridge May/June 1996, LNCS 1174, Springer-Verlag, Berlin 1996, 347-350.
7. J. Zöllner, H. Federrath, H. Klimant, A. Pfitzmann, R. Piotraschke, A. Westfeld, G. Wicke, G. Wolf: Modeling the Security of Steganographic Systems. Information Hiding, Proceedings, Workshop, Portland, Oregon, USA April 1998, LNCS 1525, Springer-Verlag, Berlin 1998, 344-354.
8. http:www.scanjet.com/products/classics/6100C/index.htm

Secure Steganographic Methods for Palette Images

Jiri Fridrich and Rui Du

Center for Intelligent Systems, Dept. of SS&IE,
SUNY Binghamton, Binghamton, NY 13902-6000
{fridrich,bh09006}@binghamton.edu

Abstract. In this paper, we study non-adaptive and adaptive steganographic techniques for images with low number of colors in palette image formats. We have introduced the concept of optimal parity assignment for the color palette and designed an efficient algorithm that finds the optimal parity assignment. The optimal parity is independent of the image histogram and depends only on the image palette. Thus, it can be used for increasing the security of steganographic techniques that embed message bits into the parity of palette colors. We have further developed two adaptive steganographic methods designed to avoid areas of uniform color and embed message bits into texture-rich portions of the cover image. Both techniques were tested on computer generated images with large areas of uniform color and with fonts on uniform background. No obvious artifacts were introduced by either technique. The last, embedding-while-dithering, technique has been designed for palette images obtained from true color images using color quantization and dithering. In this technique, both the color quantization error and the error due to message embedding are diffused through the image to avoid introducing artifacts inconsistent with the dithering algorithm.

1   Introduction

The purpose of steganography is to hide messages in otherwise innocent looking carriers. The purpose is to achieve security and privacy by *masking the very presence of communication*. Historically, the first steganographic techniques included invisible writing using special inks or chemicals. It was also fairly common to hide messages in text. By recovering the first letters from words or sentences of some innocent looking text, a secret message was communicated. Today, it seems natural to use binary files with certain degree of irrelevancy and redundancy to hide data. Digital images, videos, and audio tracks are ideal for this purpose.

Each steganographic technique consists of an embedding algorithm and a detector function. The embedding algorithm is used to hide secret messages inside a cover (or carrier) document. The embedding process is usually protected by a keyword so that only those who posses the secret keyword can access the hidden message. The detector function is applied to the stego-document and returns the hidden secret message. For secure covert communication, it is important that by injecting a secret message into a cover document no *detectable changes* are introduced. The main goal is to not raise suspicion and avoid introducing statistically detectable modifications

A. Pfitzmann (Ed.): IH'99, LNCS 1768, pp. 47-60, 2000.

into the stego-document. The embedded information is undetectable if the image with the embedded message is consistent with the model of the source from which the cover images are drawn. We point out that the ability to detect the presence does not automatically imply the ability to read the hidden message. We further note that undetectability should not be mistaken for invisibility – a concept tied to human perception. At present, the formal theoretical framework for steganography similar to Shannon information theory is still missing. For a comprehensive treatment of this topic, see [1].

The undetectability is directly influenced by the size of the secret message and the format and content of the cover image. Obviously, the longer the message, the larger the modification of the cover image and the higher the probability that the modifications can be statistically detected. The choice of the cover image is also important. Natural photographs with 24 bits per pixel provide the best environment for message hiding. The redundancy of the data helps to conceal the presence of secret messages. Image formats that utilize color palettes provide efficient storage for images with limited number of colors, such as charts, computer art, or color quantized true color images. The palette image format GIF is recognized by all browsers and is widely used over the Internet. Posting a GIF file on one's web page will undoubtedly raise less suspicion than sending an image in the BMP format. Despite their usefulness and advantages, palette images provide a hostile environment for the steganographer. The limited number of palette colors makes the process of secure message hiding a difficult challenge. The most common steganographic technique – the least significant bit embedding (LSB) cannot be directly applied to palette images because too many new colors would be created. Most current steganographic algorithms for palette images introduce easily detectable artifacts in the palette or in the image data [8,9].

On the highest level, the typical palette image format consists of three parts: a header, a palette, and image data or pointers to the palette. The palette contains the RGB triplets of all colors that occur in the image. Secret messages can be hidden either in the palette itself or in the image data. Gifshuffle [10] is a program that uses the *palette order* to hide up to $\log_2(256!)=210$ bytes in the palette by permuting its entries. While this method does not change the appearance of the image, which is certainly an advantage, its security is weak because many image processing software products order the palette according to luminance, frequency of occurrence, or some other scalar factor. A randomly ordered palette is suspicious, which goes against the basic requirement of secure steganography. Also, displaying the image and resaving it may erase the information because the palette may be reordered. An alternative and perhaps more secure approach is to hide encrypted messages in the LSBs of the palette colors. In order to make the message readable from an image with a reordered palette, care needs to be taken during message embedding so that the message is readable at the receiving end. The common disadvantage of all techniques that embed message bits into the palette is a rather limited capacity independent of the image size.

Practical methods should have capacity proportional to the image size, or the number of pixels. Many currently available software tools [3,4,7,10–13] decrease the color depth of the GIF image to 128, 64, or 32 before the embedding starts. This way, when the LSBs of one, two or three color channels are perturbed, the total number of newly created colors will be at most 256. Thus, it will be possible to embed one, two, or three bits per pixel without introducing visible artifacts into the cover image. However, as pointed out by Johnson [8,9], the new palettes will have easily detectable groups of close colors. It is thus relatively easy to distinguish images with and without secret messages. It appears that secure schemes should not manipulate the palette but rather embed message bits in the image data.

In the next section, we discuss methods that embed message bits as parities of colors. In Sect. 3, we define the energy of distortions due to message embedding and introduce the concept of optimal parity assignment that minimizes this energy. An efficient algorithm for the optimal parity is presented and the proof of optimality is given. The technique is further extended to multiple pixel embedding. It is shown that the optimal parity assignment is also optimal for multiple-pixel embedding. In Sect. 4, we study adaptive steganographic techniques. Two methods are introduced and their performance is tested on computer generated fractal images. A new technique for palette images obtained through color quantization and dithering of true-color images is described in Sect. 5. In this new dithering-while-embedding technique, the image modifications due to message embedding are diffused through the image in the same way as the quantization error during dithering. Finally in Sect. 6, we summarize the new techniques and conclude the paper by outlining future research directions.

2   Message Hiding Using the Parity of Palette Colors

One of the most popular message hiding schemes for palette-based images (GIF files) has been proposed by Machado [11]. In her method called EZ Stego, the palette is first sorted by luminance. In the reordered palette, neighboring palette entries are typically near to each other in the color space, as well. EZ Stego embeds the message in a binary form into the LSB of randomly chosen pointers to the palette colors. One can say that this method consists of three steps: parity assignment to palette colors (ordering the palette), random, key-dependent selection of pixels, and embedding message into color parities of the selected pixels. Message recovery is simply achieved by selecting the same pixels and collecting the LSBs of all indices to the ordered palette. This algorithm is based on the premise that close colors in the luminance-ordered palette are close in the color space. However, since luminance is a linear combination of three colors, occasionally colors with similar luminance values may be relatively far from each other.

To alleviate this problem, Fridrich [6] has proposed to hide message bits into the parity bits of closest colors[1]. For the color of each pixel, into which we embed message bits, the closest colors in the palette are searched till a palette entry is found with the desired parity bit. The parity of each color could be assigned randomly or

---

[1] Using parity for message embedding has previously been proposed by Petitcolas [1] and Crandall [5].

simply by calculating $R+G+B$ mod 2. Because the parity bits are randomly distributed, we will never have to depart from the original color too much. This way, we avoid the problem of occasionally making large changes in color, which will certainly contribute to the undetectability of the message. In the absence of a rigorous security definition for steganography, the following quantities were accepted as measures of security:

1. The distance D between the original and the stego-image

$$D^2 = \sum_{i,j=1}^{M,N} d^2{}_{ij},$$

where $d_{ij}^2 = (R_{ij}-R_{ij}')^2 + (G_{ij}-G_{ij}')^2 + (B_{ij}-B_{ij}')^2$ for the (i,j)-th pixel of the original and the stego-image.
2. The maximal color change $\max_{i,j} d_{ij}$.

Both the average power per pixel and the maximal color change for the new technique [6] have decreased 4–5 times when compared to the EZ Stego, which is a significant performance improvement.

In the next section, we investigate the problem of optimal parity assignment for the palette in order to further improve the scheme described in this section.

3   Optimal Parity Assignment

The parity assignment directly influences the energy of image modifications due to message embedding. Obviously, if close colors are assigned opposite parities, the energy of the modifications will be smaller. A natural question to ask is whether it is possible to further improve the performance by using an optimized palette parity assignment. For a practical method, which does not have access to the original image, the palette parity assignment has to be reconstructable from the modified image at the receiving end.

Let the image palette contain N colors $c_1, c_2, ..., c_N$ with parities P_i, $P_i \in \{0,1\}$. The parity assignment determines an isolation s_i for the i-th color (s_i is the distance from color c_i to the closest color with different parity). The colors occur in the original image with frequencies $p_1, ..., p_N$, $p_1+ ... + p_N = 1$. Provided the message carrying pixels are selected non-adaptively, for a message of length k, approximately kp_i pixels of color c_i will contain message bits. The average square of the distance between the original and the stego-image can be expressed as:

$$\frac{1}{2}kE(P_1,...,P_N) = \frac{1}{2}k\sum_{i=1}^{N} p_i s_i^2 .$$

The quantity E does not depend on the message length and will be called the *energy of the parity assignment*. The optimization problem is to assign parities $P_1, ..., P_N$ to colors $c_1, ..., c_N$ so that E is minimal. The following algorithm always finds the optimal parity assignment that minimizes E:

3.1   Algorithm for Optimal Parity Assignment

1. Calculate the distances between all pairs of colors $d_{ij} = |c_i - c_j|$. The distance can be calculated either in the RGB or the YUV space. Set $C = \varnothing$.
2. Order the distances starting from the smallest to the largest, $\{d\} = d_{i(1)j(1)} \leq d_{i(2)j(2)} \leq ....$
3. Iteratively repeat step No. 4 until C contains all N colors.
4. Choose the next distance d_{kl} in the ordered sequence $\{d\}$ such that either $c_k \notin C$ or $c_l \notin C$. If more than one d_{kl} is the smallest, randomly choose one. If there is no such d_{kl} this means that C contains all N colors and we are done. If both $c_k \notin C$ or $c_l \notin C$, assign two opposite parities to both k and l. If $c_k \notin C$ and $c_l \in C$, set $P_k = 1 - P_l$. Update $C = C \cup \{c_k\} \cup \{c_l\}$.

It is clear that once a parity of a color is defined, it cannot be changed later by the algorithm. It is also clear that at the end all colors will have assigned parities. What needs to be proved is that the parity assignment has the minimal energy E. We point out that the minimal value of E can occur for more than one parity assignment (see Fig. 1).

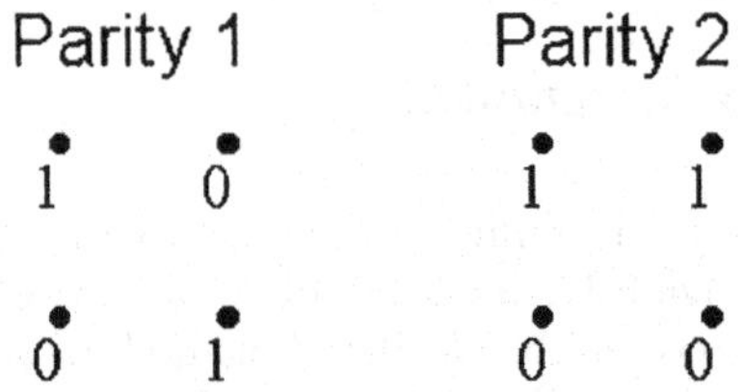

Parity 1   Parity 2

•   •   •   •
1   0   1   1

•   •   •   •
0   1   0   0

Fig. 1. Example of two different optimal parity assignments

Proof. Let d_i denotes the distance from color i to its closest color in the color space. Obviously, for any parity assignment, $P_1, ..., P_N$, we have the inequality

$$E(P_1, ..., P_N) = \sum_{i=1}^{N} p_i s_i^2 \geq \sum_{i=1}^{N} p_i d_i^2 .$$

The optimality of the parity found by the algorithm will be proven by showing that $d_i = s_i$ for each i. Let d_{ij} be the first occurrence of the index i (color i) in the non-decreasing sequence $\{d\}$. Then the color j must be the closest color to i, because if we had a different color k, $k \neq j$, with $d_{ik} < d_{ij}$, the color i would have to occur in $\{d\}$ prior to d_{ij}. It is true that there might be more than one color j that is closest to i, but in either case we have $d_i = s_i$, because according to Step 4, we always assign the parities of i and j to opposite values. This concludes the proof.

Note that the optimal parity assignment *does not* depend on the frequency of occurrence of pixels, $p_1, \ldots, p_N$. This somewhat contradictory and surprising result enables us to calculate the optimal parity assignment from the modified image without accessing the original image. We just need to order the palette before applying the algorithm (one can use the alphabetical RGB order, for example). If any random decisions are made during the algorithm run, we need to seed a PRNG with the same seed, as well. Another possibility would be to agree on a fixed order in the sequence $\{d\}$, the parity assignment for the first pair, and a rule for assigning the parity when both new nodes $c_i \notin C$ and $c_j \notin C$. Either way, the optimal parity can be utilized for decreasing the energy of modifications in images.

Numerical experiments indicate that when using the optimal parity as opposed to the parity $R+G+B$ mod 2, the energy E is decreased by 25–35% depending on the image.

3.2   Multiple-Pixel Embedding

It is possible to further decrease the energy of modifications due to message embedding by using clusters of q pixels for one message bit rather than single pixels. The image is first divided using a PRNG into disjoint clusters of random q pixels and the message bit is encoded as a parity of the sum of all q pixel parities. This has the benefit that in order to change the parity of the whole sum one can select a pixel with the smallest isolation among all q pixels. As a consequence, the energy of modifications due to message embedding must decrease. The previous method is a special case of this multiple pixel encoding with $q = 1$.

Below, we show that the optimal parity for this method is the same as for the single pixel embedding. The energy E of the parity assignment is defined in a similar manner

$$E(q) = \frac{1}{2} \sum_{i=1}^{N} p_i^{(q)} s_i ,$$

where $p_i^{(q)}$ is the probability that among randomly chosen q pixels in the image the one with the smallest isolation is the i-th color. If $p_i^{(q)}$ does not depend on s_i, the optimal parity is again only a function of the palette and not of the image. To calculate the probabilities $p_i^{(q)}$, we rearrange the colors c_i so that their isolations form a non-decreasing sequence. It can easily be shown that

$$p_i^{(q)} = \left(\sum_{j \geq i}^{N} p_j^{(q)} \right)^q - \left(\sum_{j > i}^{N} p_j^{(q)} \right)^q .$$

Because the probabilities $p_i^{(q)}$ do not depend on the isolations, s_i, the optimal parity for single pixel embedding is also optimal for multiple pixel embedding. The energy $E(q)$ as a function of q is depicted for two test images "Fox" and "Mandrill" in Figs. 2–5. Observe that even with $q = 2$, the energy of modifications could decrease by more than a third. For the test image "Fox", the energy went down to 50% of its original value for $q = 3$. This observation suggests that the multiple pixel embedding technique is a useful and significant security improvement.

Fig. 2. Test image "Fox"

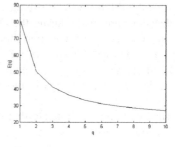

Fig. 3. Energy of modifications as a function of the number of pixels q for the test image "Fox"

Fig. 4. Test image "Mandrill"

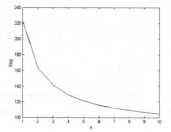

Fig. 5. Energy of modifications as a function of the number of pixels q for the test image "Mandrill"

In this section, we have shown that any method in which pixels are selected in a random (non-adaptive) manner and in which the message bits are embedded by changing the parity of pixels (the analog of LSB encoding for palette images), cannot perform better than our method. This is because our method uses the best parity assignment possible. The result is general and holds for both single pixel embedding and multiple pixel embedding. The next section is devoted to adaptive methods for message embedding to avoid areas of uniform color and avoid creating detectable artifacts in singular images with large areas of uniform color.

4   Adaptive Methods

In this section, we explore the idea of an adaptive steganographic technique that would introduce less detectable artifacts into the cover image by adapting the message embedding technique to the content of the cover image. *Non-adaptive* steganographic techniques are techniques in which the modifications due to message embedding are uncorrelated with image features. Examples are LSB encoding in randomly selected pixels, message embedding by randomly modulating pixel values or frequency bins in a fixed band, etc. In *adaptive steganography* the modifications are correlated with the image content (features). For steganography, this could mean that the pixels carrying message bits are selected adaptively and depend on the image. For example, we could avoid areas of uniform color and select only pixels with large local standard deviation. This however creates a problem with message recovery if the original unmodified image is not available. We have to be able to extract the same set of message carrying pixels at the receiving end from the modified image.

The capacity of adaptive schemes is necessarily image dependent and, in some cases, it is not even possible to calculate the capacity before the actual embedding starts. But this is a price we have to pay for increased security. There are several different ways how a non-adaptive scheme can be turned into an adaptive one. For example, the message carrying part and the part that determines the pixel selection do not interact. For example, one can calculate the local standard deviation (STD) from the 7 most significant bits and embed message bits into the LSB. This approach is plausible only for high color images and cannot be adopted for palette images.

Method 1. The image is divided into disjoint blocks (for example 3×3 blocks) completely covering the image. At most one bit will be assigned to each block (either the LSB of the middle pixel or its parity, or the parity of the whole block, etc.). A threshold for local STD is selected. A pseudo-random non-intersecting walk over the blocks is generated from a secret key. If the local STD of a block is above the threshold AND stays above the threshold after message embedding, we select the block for message embedding. If the STD falls below the threshold after message embedding, we make the change anyway but do not include the block for message embedding, and continue message embedding with the same bit in the next block. This process will guarantee that at the receiving end it is enough to regenerate the same random walk over the blocks and read the message bits only from blocks whose STD is above the threshold. Note that the local standard deviation can be replaced with a different quantity, such as the number of colors in the block. Actually, our experiments show that the number of colors works better than the standard deviation for computer generated low-color images.

The advantage of Method 1 is that any pixel(s) in the block can be modified, which will generally lead to smaller modifications especially for images with low color depth. The disadvantage is that it is not possible to say whether or not a message of a given length will fit into the image before one actually starts the embedding process. Another disadvantage is somewhat decreased capacity. At most one bit is inserted into each block, and only blocks with local STD above the threshold are considered for embedding. It is, however, only natural that more secure schemes will have smaller capacity, while "greedy" schemes emphasizing the capacity will offer less security. It will be up to the end user to decide about the priorities.

We tested Method 1 for several fractal GIF images[2] shown in Figs. 6–8. The image in Fig. 6 depicts a Julia set generated on a computer. Julia sets are fractal sets parametrized using complex numbers. The image is a bad cover image for steganography for at least three reasons:

1. There are large areas with flat color. Such areas should be avoided otherwise detectable artifacts will be created.
2. The image has been computer generated and has a known complicated inner structure common to all Julia sets. For example, the bands of close colors gradually changing from white to dark red form lines of constant potential and have to form simply connected sets. Therefore the band boundaries, too, should be avoided while embedding a message.
3. The title of the image contains fonts and any subtle change to those fonts will be easily detected.

 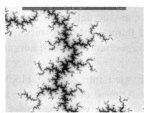 

Fig. 6. Fractal cover image 640×480, 195 colors   **Fig. 7.** Fractal cover image, 636×476, 236 colors   **Fig. 8.** Fractal cover image 636×476, 183 colors

A non-adaptive technique, no matter how good, will always create some easily detectable artifacts (see Figs. 9–10). On the one hand, we are tempted to say that the image should not be used for secure steganography. On the other hand, we intuitively feel that those areas with complex structure *can* hold some additional information without causing suspicious artifacts. A smart adaptive technique should be able to recognize which portions of the image can be used for data hiding.

A freeware software utility called MandelSteg [7] uses fractal images for generating cover images. The parameters of the Julia set form a portion of the secret key. The algorithm is naïve, non-adaptive, and provides very poor security. First, the fact that the software that generates the images is available to anybody enables an efficient search for the parameters of the Julia set by anybody skilled in the art of fractals. Second, the fractal images have complicated inner structure that follows strict rules. Any non-adaptive technique must introduce severe and easily detectable artifacts, such as those depicted in Figs. 9–10.

A version of Method 1 has been used with the local statistics corresponding to the

---

[2] Images provided courtesy of J. C. Sprott, Fractal Gallery,
http://sprott.physics.wisc.edu/fractals.htm.

number of different colors in a pixel's neighborhood. We embed a bit of information whenever there are at least three different colors in the 3×3 neighborhood. This in fact will guarantee that there will be no artifacts in the potential lines around the Julia set and no artifacts in the fonts (white characters on uniform background). A detailed inspection of the stego-image with over 1000 embedded bits did not reveal any suspicious artifacts.

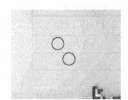

Fig. 9. Artifacts in equipotential bands

Fig. 10. Artifacts in the fonts

Fig. 11. Fonts on a complex background

Method 2. Method 1 performs satisfactorily even for difficult cover images, such as the images in Figs. 6–8. However, the price we paid was a capacity decreased by a factor of more than 9. Method 2 has been designed with the intent to put on average more bits per pixel while retaining the adaptive property. The message embedding process starts with pseudo-randomly selecting the message carrying pixels. Before we explain the selection process, we introduce some definitions. A 2×2 block is good if it has at least three different colors. In all other cases, the block is bad. A pixel is termed good if all four 2×2 squares that contain that pixel are good. The message carrying pixels are selected pseudo-randomly from the set of all good pixels in the image. Then, all palette colors are assigned the optimal parity using the algorithm from Sect. 3. Finally, we walk through the selected pixels and compare the parity of each pixel to the message bit. If there is a match, we do not modify the pixel and move to the next pixel. If there is no match, we modify the pixel color by searching through the palette for closest neighbors with the correct parity so that after the change all four blocks containing the pixel P stay good. Then, we again move to the next pixel. The embedding procedure guarantees that the set of good blocks for the original image and for the modified image are identical. This enables the detection algorithm to recover the message from color parities by going through the good pixels in the same pseudo-random manner as during the embedding.

The capacity of Method 1 and 2 is compared in Table 1. We ran a series of experiments for different seeds for the PRNG that was used to generate the pseudo-random walk and calculated the standard deviation of the capacity. All three test images shown in Figs. 6–8 were used for this experiment. As expected, Method 2 has significantly higher capacity than Method 1.

To find out the energy of modifications due to message embedding, we used the same three test images and for different seeds we calculated the average MSE distortion per pixel. The results are shown in Table 2. We have also experimented with different combinations of the block size (2×2 and 3×3) and different number of colors (2, 3 or 4) for the goodness criterion. The combination of 2×2 pixels and at least three colors gave us the best results with no perceptible artifacts.

Table 1. Comparison of capacity for Method 1 and 2

		Capacity as a percentage of the total number of pixels		
		Figure 6	Figure 7	Figure 8
Method 1		6.51~6.53%	3.16~3.18%	1.11~1.12%
Method 2	2 colors	55.64%	25.92%	10.37%
	3 colors	43.63%	16.94%	1.32%

The mean-square-error between the original and the stego-image for all three fractal test images with embedded different size of data is illustrated in Tables 2–4.

Table 2. MSE for Fig. 6 and different message length

Size of embedded data	2371 Bytes	1331 Bytes	645 Bytes	132 Bytes
Method 1	0.26±0.005	0.15±0.003	0.07±0.002	0.017±0.001
Method 2	0.54±0.01	0.30±0.007	0.15±0.015	0.039±0.011

Table 3. MSE for Fig. 7 and different message length

Size of embedded data	1019 Bytes	739 Bytes	466 Bytes	132 Bytes
Method 1	0.15±0.005	0.11±0.005	0.07±0.003	0.02±0.002
Method 2	0.35±0.009	0.25±0.01	0.16±0.006	0.05±0.004

Table 4. MSE for Fig. 8 and different message length

Size of embedded data	376 Bytes	285Bytes	192 Bytes	132 Bytes
Method 1	0.05±0.004	0.04±0.003	0.03±0.002	0.02±0.002
Method 2	0.40±0.042	0.29±0.02	0.20±0.024	0.15±0.02

Tables 2–4 show that the for images in Figs. 6 and 7 the average power per pixel due to message embedding is about 4–5 times bigger for Method 2 than for Method 1. This can be attributed to the fact that in Method 1 we can select the message carrying pixel as the one with the smallest isolation out of nine pixels. Also, in Method 2 occasionally large modifications may result due to the fact that all eight 2×2 squares must stay good after embedding. For image in Fig. 8, the difference is even more pronounced. Both methods can embed messages into computer generated fractal images without introducing any artifacts into regions of uniform color, areas with equipotential lines around the Julia sets, and aliased fonts on uniform background. Method 1 provides better security because it introduced smaller power per pixel due to message embedding. Method 2 has higher capacity but may occasionally introduce large changes in color.

5   Embedding while Dithering

As the last steganographic method of this paper, we describe a technique appropriate for message hiding in palette images obtained from true-color images using color quantization and dithering. Given a true color image, we first derive the color palette using some of the standard color quantization algorithms [2]. If the true color image is not known and only its quantized form is available, we could increase the color depth using for example the method described in [14]. We continue by calculating the optimal parity assignment for the palette. Then we pseudo-randomly select the message carrying pixels in the image (in a non-adaptive manner). Finally, we perform the quantization and dithering by scanning the image by rows. For a non-message carrying pixel, we perform the standard quantization and dithering step. When we come to a message carrying pixel, we quantize its color to the closest palette color *with the right parity*. This way, both the quantization error and the error due to message embedding will be scattered and diffused through the whole image. We conjecture that the artifacts introduced by this method will be less detectable because they should be consistent with the dithering mechanism.

We have tested the method on 24 bit scans of photographs. As expected, such images typically provide enough texture and color variations, and even when as much as 50% of all pixels in the image have been used for embedding, we could not identify any visible artifacts or suspicious patterns. The method performed satisfactorily even for "singular" images, such as the cartoon of the Tweety Bird shown in Fig. 12. The image is a true color cartoon on a background that gradually changes color. We have again embedded a message of length equal to one half of the number of all pixels. Fig. 13 is a close-up of the original Tweety's eye and beak, and Figs. 14 and 15 show the same close-up for the non-adaptive naïve method with non-optimal palette, respectively. The non-optimized, non-adaptive method performs poorly and one can identify a suspicious pattern in Tweety's eye. On the other hand, the edges and contrast of the original picture has been more or less preserved. The dithering-while-embedding method does not introduce suspicious patterns but the image edges (see the black lines are somewhat blurred due to the diffused error. The color variations in Tweety's beak have also been flattened out due to color quantization.

6   Conclusion and Future Directions

In this paper, we study non-adaptive and adaptive steganographic techniques for images in palette image formats. We have introduced the concept of optimal parity assignment and designed an efficient algorithm that finds the optimal parity assignment. The optimal parity is independent of the image histogram and depends only on the image palette. Thus, it can be used for increasing the security of steganographic techniques that embed message bits into the parity of palette colors. We have shown that the optimal palette improves the average power per pixel due to message embedding by 25–35% (for method introduced in [6]). The optimal parity is also optimal for multiple pixel embedding.

We have developed two new methods for adaptive message embedding in palette images. The techniques tend to avoid areas of uniform color and embed message bits into texture-rich portions of the cover image. Both techniques utilize the optimal parity assignment. The first technique embeds one message bit into a group of 3×3 pixels. The second technique has higher capacity, but provides less security when measured by the average distortion power per pixel. Both techniques were tested on computer generated images with large areas of uniform color and with fonts on uniform background. No obvious artifacts were introduced by either technique. An image with simple vertical bands of thickness of at least 3 with different colors would be classified by both techniques as a zero capacity image. This intuitively corresponds to our feeling that such an image should not be used as a cover image and the algorithms work as we would expect. At this point, we stress that it is almost impossible to design an algorithm that would work well on all low-color images, especially computer generated images or images with well-defined inner structure.

Fig. 12. Test image Tweety Bird   **Fig. 13.** Original   **Fig. 14.** Non-adaptive non-optimized   **Fig. 15.** Dithering-while-embedding

For example, an image with fonts of uniform color on a complex background, rather than a uniform background as in Fig. 6, will not be handled by our adaptive algorithm correctly (see Fig. 11). The border pixels of fonts may be changed. In a situation like this, it becomes increasingly difficult to automatize the process of secure adaptive selection of pixels. Image understanding and interpretation of image features comes into play. While a human can easily recognize that a pixel is actually a dot above the letter "i" and thus must not be changed, it would be very hard to design an algorithm that would recognize this automatically.

The last technique described in this paper has been designed for embedding large messages into palette images obtained from true color images using color quantization and dithering. The basic idea behind this embedding-while-dithering method is to dither both the color quantization error and the error due to message embedding to avoid introducing artifacts inconsistent with the dithering algorithm. We argue that the stego-image will correspond to an image obtained by quantizing and dithering a slightly noisier version of the original image, thus making the stego-image free of artifacts incompatible with dithering.

Our future research effort will be directed towards a more formal approach to adaptive message embedding including estimates for capacity. The dithering-while-embedding method could also be improved by making it adaptive to the image content.

Acknowledgements

The work on this paper was supported by Air Force Research Laboratory, Air Force Material Command, USAF, under a grant number F30602-98-C-0009. The U.S. Government is authorized to reproduce and distribute reprints for Governmental purposes notwithstanding any copyright notation there on. The views and conclusions contained herein are those of the authors and should not be interpreted as necessarily representing the official policies, either expressed or implied, of Air Force Research Laboratory, or the U. S. Government.

Special thanks belong to Maurice Maes and Ton Kalker of Philips Labs, who helped the author to greatly simplify the proof of optimality of the parity assignment introduced in Section 3.

References

1. Andersen, R.J., Petitcolas, F.A.P., On the limits of steganography. *IEEE Journal of Selected Areas in Communications, Special Issue on Copyright and Privacy Protection* **16** No.4 (1998) 474–481.
2. Balasubramanian, R., Bouman, C.A., Allebach, J.P.: Sequential Scalar Quantization of Color Images. Journal of Electronic Imaging **3** No.1 (1994) 45–59.
3. Black W. (anonymous): StegoDos.
   ftp://ftp.csua.berkeley.edu/pub/cypherpunks/steganography/ stegodos.zip
4. Brown, A.: S-Tools. http://idea.sec.dsi.uimi.it/pub/security/crypt/code/s-tools3.zip
5. Crandall, R.: Some notes on Steganography. Posted on Steganography Mailing List, December (1998).
6. Fridrich, J.: A New Steganographic Method for Palette-Based Images. Proc. of the IS&T PICS conference, April 1998, Savannah, Georgia (1998) 285–289.
7. Hastur, H.: Mandelsteg. http://idea.sec.dsi.uimi.it/pub/security/crypt/codev (1994)
8. Johnson, N.F., Jajodia, S.: Steganography: Seeing the Unseen." IEEE Computer, February 1998 (1998) 26–34.
9. Johnson, N.F., Jajodia, S.: Steganalysis of Images Created Using Current Steganography Software. Proc. 2nd Workshop on Info Hiding, April 1998, Portland, Oregon (1998).
10. Kwan, M.: Gifshuffle. http://www.darkside.com.au/gifshuffle/
11. Machado, R.: EZ Stego. http://www.stego.com/
12. Maroney, C.: Hide and Seek. ftp://ftp.csua.berkeley.edu/pub/cypherpunks/steganography/ hdsk1.0b.zip
13. Nelson, L.: Gif-It-Up. http://www.cs.cf.ac.uk/User/L.Nelson
14. Schmitz, B.E., Stevenson, R.L., Color Palette Restoration. Graphical Models and Image Processing **57** No.5 (1995) 409–419.

Attacks on Steganographic Systems

Breaking the Steganographic Utilities EzStego, Jsteg, Steganos, and S-Tools–and Some Lessons Learned

Andreas Westfeld and Andreas Pfitzmann

Dresden University of Technology
Department of Computer Science
D-01062 Dresden, Germany
{westfeld,pfitza}@inf.tu-dresden.de

Abstract. The majority of steganographic utilities for the camouflage of confidential communication suffers from fundamental weaknesses. On the way to more secure steganographic algorithms, the development of attacks is essential to assess security. We present both *visual attacks*, making use of the ability of humans to clearly discern between noise and visual patterns, and *statistical attacks* which are much easier to automate.

The visual attacks presented here exemplify that at least EzStego v2.0b3, Jsteg v4, Steganos v1.5, and S-Tools v4.0 suffer from the misassumption that least significant bits of image data are uncorrelated noise. Beyond that, this paper introduces more objective methods to detect steganography by statistical means.

1 Introduction

Steganography is no routine means to protect confidentiality. Normally, cryptography is used to communicate confidentially. Cryptographic algorithms—the security of which can be proven or traced back to known hard mathematical problems—are widely available. However, in contrast to steganography, cryptographic algorithms generate messages which are recognisable as encrypted messages, although their content remains confidential.

Steganography[1] embeds a confidential message into another, more extensive message which serves as a carrier. The goal is to modify the carrier in an imperceptible way only, so that it reveals nothing—neither the embedding of a message nor the embedded message itself.

The functioning of a steganographic system is shown in Fig. 1: The sender creates a steganogram using the embedding function which function has two parameters:

1. a carrier medium containing randomness (e. g., noise), and
2. the message to be embedded.

---

[1] στεγαν ʃς + γρ⟨φειν, covered writing

A. Pfitzmann (Ed.): IH'99, LNCS 1768, pp. 61–76, 2000.
© Springer-Verlag Berlin Heidelberg 2000

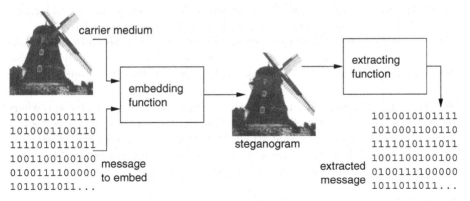

Fig. 1. Steganographic system

Multimedia data, such as audio and video, are excellent carriers. After digitisation, they contain so-called quantisation noise which provides space to embed data. Lossy compression may introduce another kind of noise. Using the extracting function, the recipient must be able to reproduce the embedded message from the steganogram.

A steganogram should have the same statistical characteristics as the carrier media so that the use of a steganographic algorithm can not be detected. Consequently, a (potential) message can be read from both the steganogram and the carrier medium. A message read from a steganogram must not be statistically different from a potential message read from a carrier medium—otherwise, the steganographic system would be insecure.

Some steganographic utilities use secret keys. We can distinguish two kinds of keys: steganographic keys and cryptographic keys [4]. A steganographic key controls the embedding and extracting process. For example, it can scatter the message to be embedded over a subset of all suitable places in the carrier medium. Without the key, this subset is unknown, and each sample used to detect embedding by a statistical attack is a mixture of used and unused places (i. e., of all potential places) which spoils the result. A cryptographic key, however, is used to encrypt the message before it is embedded. For both applications the "secret", which conceals the message, is detached from the actual algorithm in the form of a parameter—the key. If the key is confidential, the steganographic algorithm can be public (Kerckhoffs' Principle). It is possible to decide whether the bits read are in fact an encoded message of a potential steganogram only if one has the appropriate decryption key. Encryption is also advisable in addition to steganographic utilities which do not implicitly encrypt.

To decouple the security of steganographic algorithms from the appearance of the hidden message, we use pseudo random bit-strings to generate these messages in our experiments. Such bit-strings have all statistical properties of encrypted messages. In this paper, we will concentrate on images, the most widespread carrier medium.

Related to this work is the Final Year Project of Tinsley [5] on Steganography and JPEG Compression. He describes statistical attacks applied to Jsteg [14] using a different statistical model. Fravia's pages explain brute force attacks to steganography [11]. Finally, there was an introduction to "Steganalysis" given by Johnson at the previous Workshop on Information Hiding in 1998 [2].

In the following sections, we present our attacks on EzStego v2.0b3, Jsteg v4, Steganos v1.5, and S-Tools v4.0, going into details of each utility attacked where needed. To have a fundamental example, we first describe EzStego in Sect. 2. In Sect. 3, we describe our visual attacks. Thereafter, we describe our statistical attacks in Sect. 4. Finally, we present our conclusions and outlook in Sect. 5.

2   EzStego

The utility EzStego (by Romana Machado) embeds messages in GIF files. GIF files [12] contain a colour palette with up to 256 different colours out of 2^{24} possible, and the Lempel-Ziv-Welch (LZW) compressed [3,6,8] matrix of palette indices. EzStego embeds messages into the pixels without any length information. It leaves the colour palette unmodified.

The steganographic algorithm creates a sorted copy of the palette. It sorts in a way that we can hardly tell the difference between two adjacent colours in the sorted palette. Sorting by luminance is not optimal in any case because two colours with the same luminance could be radical different. We can interpret each colour as a point in a three-dimensional space, the RGB (red, green, blue) colour cube.

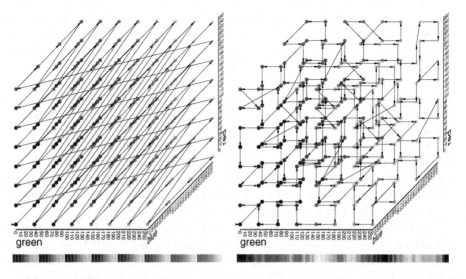

Fig. 2. Colour order in the palette (l.) and sorted as used by EzStego (r.)

Fig. 2 shows the order of colours in the RGB cube. On the left the colours look more sorted than on the right. This is the order of the colours in the palette, in most cases a numerical order. On the right the colours are sorted by EzStego to follow a shortest path through the RGB cube.

The embedding function of EzStego works line by line on the unbroken sequence of pixels from top left to bottom right. After embedding, each pixel holds one steganographic value (i. e., one bit of the embedded message). The steganographic value of a pixel is the least significant bit its index would have in the sorted palette. The embedding function matches the steganographic value with the bit to be embedded (i. e. if the bit to be embedded is not already there), and replaces the colour by its neighbour in the sorted palette if necessary.

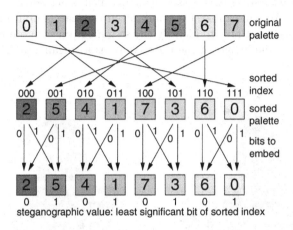

Fig. 3. Embedding function of EzStego

Fig. 3 shows the embedding function of EzStego with a reduced palette. For example, we find index 7 for a given pixel in the carrier image. If we want to embed a '1', we replace the index by 3, and if we want to embed a '0' we change nothing. Because the colour of index 7 in the original palette is at index 100 (=4) in the sorted palette, and the colour of index 3 is at index 101 (=5) in the sorted palette, both colours are neighbours in the sorted palette, i. e. hardly to distinguish. A change from index 7 to index 3 (and vice versa) is imperceptible for our eyes unless we compare it directly with the original image.

Everybody can extract the (imaginary) message bits easily. If there is one embedded bit per pixel we can draw them as an image—e. g. white for the steganographic value '1', and black for the value '0'.

3   Visual Attacks

Independently from each other, several authors assumed that least significant bits of luminance values in digital images are completely random and could therefore be replaced (references: Contraband [9], EzStego [10], Hide & Seek [13], PGMStealth [15], Piilo [16], Scytale [17], Snow [18], Steganos [19], Stego [20], Stegodos [21], S-Tools [22], White Noise Storm [23]). By the visual attacks described in this section, we will reveal that this assumption is wrong. The majority of steganographic algorithms embeds messages replacing carefully selected bits by message bits. Actually, it is difficult to distinguish randomness and image contents by machine, and it is even more difficult to distinguish least significant bits and random bits. It is extremely difficult to specify permissible image content in a formal way. A substitute is having people realise what image content is. However, the border becomes blurred and depends on our imagination—who did not already detect shapes in a cloud formation? The human sight is trained to recognise known things. This human ability is used for the visual attacks. Fig. 5 represents the least significant bits of Fig. 4, which is actually not an attack on steganography. We still can see the windmill in the least significant bits in both images, and we are not able to identify the steganogram with our eyes, although the upper half of the image on the right contains a steganographic message.

Fig. 4. Windmill as carrier medium (l.), and steganogram (r.)

Fig. 5. Least significant bits of the images in Fig. 4, black for LSB=0, white for LSB=1

3.1   The Idea of Visual Attacks

The idea of visual attacks is to remove all parts of the image covering the message. The human eye can now distinguish whether there is a potential message or still image content. The filtering process depends on the presumed steganographic utility, and it has the following structure:

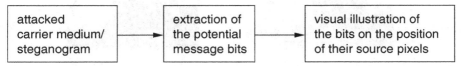

3.2   An Embedding Filter for Visual Attacks

An embedding filter for visual attacks graphically presents the values pixels yield when the extraction function is applied to them. EzStego uses the colours of pixels, defined by the palette, to determine the embedded bits. The embedding filter for visual attacks on EzStego replaces the original palette by a black and white palette. This is depicted in Fig. 6.

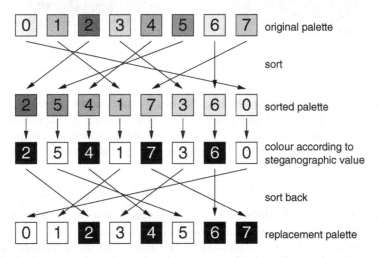

Fig. 6. Assignment function of replacement colours; colours that have an even index in the sorted palette become black, the rest becomes white.

3.3   Experiments

The following examples of visual attacks clearly show the assumption to be a myth that least significant bits are completely random and therefore might be replaced. To produce these examples, we developed small Java applications [24].

Fig. 7. EzStego; filtered images of Fig. 4: nothing embedded (l.), 50 % capacity of the carrier used for embedding (r.)

Fig. 8. GIF image of a flooring tile as carrier medium, and its filtered image

EzStego—continuous embedding. Messages, that do not use the maximum length possible, leave the rest of the carrier medium unchanged. EzStego does not encrypt the message contents. It is easy to recognise where the message is in Fig. 7, but it depends on the image content, as Fig. 8 shows. There is no embedded message in the flooring tile image.

S-Tools—spread embedding. The S-Tools spread a message over the whole carrier medium. In contrast to EzStego, there is no clear dividing line between the unchanged rest, left over with shorter messages, and the steganographically changed pixels. Both of them are mixed. In the right images of Fig. 9, Fig. 10, and Fig. 11 there are eight colors, one bit in each of the three colour components, because S-Tools embeds up to three bits per pixel (see [24] for the coloured version).

Steganos—continuous embedding with fill up. Steganos uses the carrier medium completely in every case. It will fill up shorter messages, as shown in Fig. 13. Filtered steganograms never contain content of the initial image (Fig. 12).

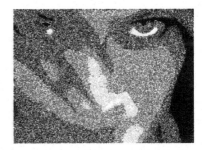

Fig. 9. True Colour BMP image as carrier medium, and its filtered image

Fig. 10. S-Tools; steganogram with maximum size of embedded text, and its filtered image

Jsteg—embedding in a transformed domain. Jsteg [14] embeds in JPEG images. In JPEG images, the image content is transformed into frequency coefficients to achieve storage as compact as possible. There is no visual attack in the sense presented here, because one steganographic bit influences up to 256 pixels.

4   Statistical Attacks

4.1   Idea of the Chi-square Attack

The embedding function of EzStego overwrites least significant bits of the sorted indices. Overwriting least significant bits transforms values into each other which only differ in the least significant bit. These *pairs of values* are called PoVs in the sequel. If the bits used for overwriting the least significant bits are equally distributed, the frequencies of both values of each PoV become equal. Fig. 14 uses the example of Fig. 3 to show how the frequencies of the colours of a picture are changed, when EzStego is used to embed an equally distributed message. The idea of the statistical attack is to compare the theoretically expected frequency distribution in steganograms with some sample distribution observed in the possibly changed carrier medium.

 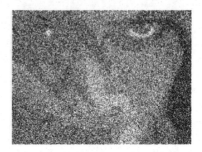

Fig. 11. S-Tools; steganogram with 50 % capacity of the carrier medium used, and its filtered image

Fig. 12. True Colour BMP image as carrier medium, and its filtered image

A critical point is how to obtain the theoretically expected frequency distribution (i. e., the frequency of occurrence we would expect after applying steganographic changes). This frequency must not be derived from our random sample, because this random sample could have been changed by steganographic operations. But in most cases we don't have the original to compare with or to derive the expected frequency from. In the original, the theoretically expected frequency is the arithmetic mean of the two frequencies in a PoV. The dashed line in Fig. 14 connects these arithmetic mean values. Because the embedding function overwrites the least significant bits, it does not change the sum of these two frequencies. The count taken from the odd value frequency is transferred to the corresponding even value frequency in each PoV, and vice versa. As the sum stays constant, the arithmetic mean is the same for a PoV in both, the original carrier medium and each corresponding steganogram. This fact allows us to obtain the theoretically expected frequency distribution from the random sample. So we don't need the original carrier medium for the attack.

The degree of similarity of the observed sample distribution and the theoretically expected frequency distribution is a measure of the probability that some embedding has taken place. The degree of similarity is determined using the Chi-square test (e.g., [1]). This test operates on a mapping of observations into categories. It performs the following steps:

Fig. 13. Steganos; steganogram with only one byte of embedded text, and its filtered image

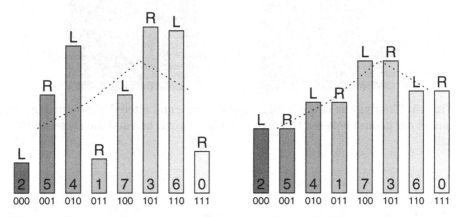

Fig. 14. Histogram of colours before and after embedding a message with EzStego

1. We shall suppose that there are k categories and that we have a random sample of observations. Each observation must fall in one and only one category. The categories are all palette indices, the colour of which is placed at an even index within the sorted palette. Without restricting generality, we concentrate on the odd values of the PoVs of the attacked carrier medium. Their minimum theoretically expected frequency must be greater than 4, we may unify categories to hold this condition.

2. The theoretically expected frequency in category i after embedding an equally distributed message is

$$n_i^* = \frac{|\{\text{colour}|\text{sortedIndexOf(colour)} \in \{2i, 2i+1\}\}|}{2}$$

3. The measured frequency of occurrence in our random sample is

$$n_i = |\{\text{colour}|\text{sortedIndexOf(colour)} = 2i\}|$$

4. The χ^2 statistic is given as $\chi^2_{k-1} = \sum_{i=1}^{k} \frac{(n_i - n_i^*)^2}{n_i^*}$ with $k-1$ degrees of freedom.

5. p is the probability of our statistic under the condition that the distributions of n_i and n_i^* are equal. It is calculated by integration of the density function:

$$p = 1 - \frac{1}{2^{\frac{k-1}{2}} \Gamma(\frac{k-1}{2})} \int_0^{x_{k-1}^2} e^{-\frac{x}{2}} x^{\frac{k-1}{2}-1} dx \tag{1}$$

Fig. 15. Flooring tile as steganogram of EzStego, and filtered; this visual attack cannot distinguish between the upper, steganographic half and the lower, original half.

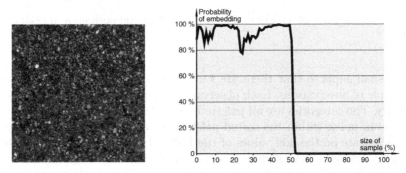

Fig. 16. Probability of embedding with EzStego in the flooring tile image (Fig. 15)

4.2   Experiments

EzStego—continuous embedding. Fig. 15 depicts a steganogram, in which a secret message of 3 600 bytes has been embedded, the same message as in Fig. 4. Fig. 15 looks pretty much like Fig. 8, due to the contents of the picture. The visual attack reaches its limit. The diagram in Fig. 16 presents the p-value of the

Chi-square test as a function of an increasing sample. This p-value is roughly the probability of embedding. Initially, the sample comprises 1 % of the pixels, starting from the upper border. For this sample, Equ. (1) yields a probability of embedding of $p = 0.8826$. The next sample comprises an additional 1 % of the pixels, i. e. 2 % of the whole picture. The p-value increases to 0.9808. As long as the sample comprises pixels of the upper half only, in which has been embedded, the p-value does not drop below 0.77. The pixels of the lower half of the picture are unchanged, because the message to be embedded was not such long. A sample of 52 % of the pixels comprises enough unchanged pixels to let the p-value drop to essentially 0. (Here, "essentially" means that the probability is smaller than the numeric precision of the 80-bit floating point arithmetic used for the implementation.)

S-Tools—spread embedding. The S-Tools spread the embedded bits over the whole carrier medium. Therefore, diagrams of the type of Fig. 16 are not useful for S-Tools. Instead, Table 1 characterises the effectiveness of our statistical test by applying it to some files with nothing embedded, 50 % embedded, or 99.5 % embedded, respectively. Actually this simple test is too weak to detect spreaded changes (see example jungle50.bmp in Table 1). More sensitive tests take appropriate combinations of the k categories or different categories. Some experiments showed useful results with only 33 % of embedded text in colour images, but tests for less embedded text causes ε (which stands for the probability of error in Table 1) to reach 0.5 rapidly.

Steganos—continuous embedding with fill up. Table 2 gives the result of the same experiment on Steganos. If we embed only one byte with Steganos (the shortest message which is possible), we get the same small probability of error as if we use 100 % capacity of the carrier medium. This is due to the fact that the stream cipher used to encrypt the secret message fills up the message with padding bytes until the capacity of the carrier medium is exhausted.

Jsteg—embedding in a transformed domain. As already noted in Sect. 3, visual attacks do not work concerning Jsteg. Since Jsteg (as EzStego) embeds bits continuously, we use the former presentation of Fig. 16 in Fig. 17, Fig. 18, and Fig. 19. They show that our statistical test is quite effective concerning Jsteg as well.

5   Conclusions and Outlook

The embedding strategy of most stego-systems which overwrite least significant bits of the carrier medium, withstands at most the casual unsophisticated observer:

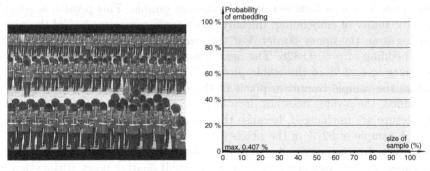

Fig. 17. JPEG image as carrier medium; nothing is embedded, and the statistical test yields a very low probability of embedding

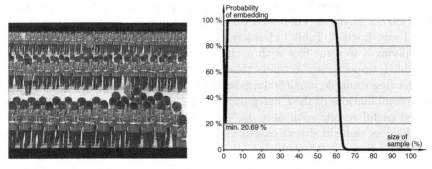

Fig. 18. Jsteg; steganogram with 50 % embedded

- The visual attacks described show that in pictures, least significant bits are not completely random, but bare a correlation with each other clearly discernible by the human sight if the pictures are presented using an embedding filter for visual attacks described above.
- Overwriting least significant bits equals frequencies of occurrence which would be unequal otherwise with very high probability. Using statistical tests, this equalisation can clearly be detected—as we have shown.

Where available, statistical tests are superior to visual attacks: They are less dependent on the cover used and they can be fully automated and thereby applied on a large scale.

By not overwriting all least significant bits, but only a fraction of them and by choosing these bits (pseudo)randomly, the error rate both of the visual and statistical attacks increases. But by that measure, the throughput of the steganographic system decreases. In the limiting case, we have a steganographic system which is nearly undetectable, but which transmits nearly nothing.

The following alternatives are promising, but need validation by a hopefully "hostile" stego-community as well:

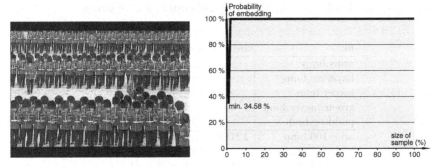

Fig. 19. Jsteg; steganogram with maximum size of embedded text

Table 1. Probability of embedding for S-Tools

file	size of embedded text	p-value
jungle.bmp	0	$0 + \varepsilon$
bavarian.bmp	0	$0 + \varepsilon$
soccer.bmp	0	$0 + \varepsilon$
groenemeyer.bmp	0	$0 + \varepsilon$
pudding.bmp	0	$0 + \varepsilon$
jungle50.bmp	18 090 bytes/50 %	$0 + \varepsilon$
jungle100.bmp	36 000 bytes/99.5 %	$1 - \varepsilon$
bavarian100.bmp	36 000 bytes/99.5 %	$1 - \varepsilon$
soccer100.bmp	36 000 bytes/99.5 %	$1 - \varepsilon$
groenemeyer100.bmp	36 000 bytes/99.5 %	$1 - \varepsilon$
		$\varepsilon < 10^{-16}$

- We should concentrate the embedding process exclusively on the randomness in the carrier medium. Of course, it is all but trivial to find out what is completely random within a carrier. [7] is an example how to design a steganographic system that way.
- We should replace the operation *overwrite* by other operations (e.g., by *increment*). Then the frequencies are not balanced, but circulate in the range of values.

Cryptography gained the security of today's state-of-the-art systems by an iterative process of designing and publishing cryptosystems, analysing and breaking them, and then re-designing hopefully more secure ones—and exposing them once more to attacks. This iterative process has to take place concerning steganography as well. Since steganography has at least one more parameter than cryptography, the choosing of cover within a carrier, validation is more complex and may take longer and proofs of security (if any) are even more limited than concerning cryptography. Within the validation circle of steganographic systems, this paper is—hopefully—a step forward.

Table 2. Probability of embedding for Steganos

file	size of embedded text	p-value
army.bmp	0	0.0095887
bavarian.bmp	0	$0 + \varepsilon$
soccer.bmp	0	$0 + \varepsilon$
groenemeyer.bmp	0	$0 + \varepsilon$
pudding.bmp	0	$0 + \varepsilon$
army100.bmp	12 000 bytes/99.5 %	$1 - \varepsilon$
bavarian1.bmp	1 byte/0.008 %	$1 - \varepsilon$
soccer1.bmp	1 byte/0.008 %	$1 - \varepsilon$
groenemeyer1.bmp	1 byte/0.008 %	$1 - \varepsilon$
pudding1.bmp	1 byte/0.008 %	$1 - \varepsilon$
		$\varepsilon < 10^{-16}$

References

1. Wilfrid J. Dixon, Frank J. Massey: Introduction to Statistical Analysis. McGraw-Hill Book Company, Inc., New York 1957. 69
2. Neil F. Johnson, Sushil Jajodia: Steganalysis of Images Created Using Current Steganography Software, in David Aucsmith (Ed.): Information Hiding, LNCS 1525, Springer-Verlag Berlin Heidelberg 1998. pp. 32–47. 63
3. M. R. Nelson: LZW Data Compression. Dr. Dobb's Journal, October 1989. 63
4. Birgit Pfitzmann, Information Hiding Terminology, in Ross Anderson (Ed.): Information Hiding. First International Workshop, LNCS 1174, Springer-Verlag Berlin Heidelberg 1996. pp. 347–350. 62
5. Robert Tinsley, Steganography and JPEG Compression, Final Year Project Report, University of Warwick, 1996. 63
6. Terry Welch: A Technique for High-Performance Data Compression. IEEE Computer, June 1984. 63
7. Andreas Westfeld, Gritta Wolf: Steganography in a Video Conferencing System, in David Aucsmith (Ed.): Information Hiding, LNCS 1525, Springer-Verlag Berlin Heidelberg 1998. pp. 32–47. 74
8. Jacob Ziv, Abraham Lempel: A Universal Algorithm for Sequential Data Compression. IEEE Transactions on Information Theory, May 1977. 63

Internet Sources
9. Contraband, http://www.galaxycorp.com/009 65
10. EzStego, http://www.fqa.com/romana/ 65
11. Fravia's Steganography, http://www.fravia.org/stego.htm 63
12. GIF, http://members.aol.com/royalef/gif89a.txt 63
13. Hide and Seek, http://www.rugeley.demon.co.uk/security/hdsk50.zip 65
14. Jsteg, ftp://ftp.funet.fi/pub/crypt/steganography/ 63, 68
15. PGMStealth, http://www.sevenlocks.com/security/SWSteganography.htm 65
16. Piilo, ftp://ftp.funet.fi/pub/crypt/steganography/ 65
17. Scytale, http://www.geocities.com/SiliconValley/Heights/5428/ 65
18. Snow, http://www.cs.mu.oz.au/ mkwan/snow/ 65
19. Steganos, http://www.demcom.com/deutsch/index.htm 65

20. Stego, http://www.best.com/ fqa/romana/romanasoft/stego.html 65
21. Stegodos, http://www.netlink.co.uk/users/hassop/pgp/stegodos.zip 65
22. S-Tools, ftp://idea.sec.dsi.unimi.it/pub/security/crypt/code/
    s-tools4.zip 65
23. White Noise Storm, ftp://ftp.funet.fi/pub/crypt/mirrors/
                idea.sec.dsi.unimi.it/cypherpunks/steganography/wns210.zip 65
24. http://wwwrn.inf.tu-dresden.de/ westfeld/attacks.html 66, 67

Developments in Steganography

Joshua R. Smith and Chris Dodge

Escher Labs
101 Main Street, Cambridge, MA 02139, USA
jrs@escher-labs.com

Abstract. This paper presents two main results. The first is a new approach to steganography in which data is encoded in correlations among the pixels in an image. Almost all previous steganographic methods encode data in correlations between the pixels and a known external reference signal. This method hints at the existence of public key watermarking techniques, which will be defined.

The other result is a method for greatly increasing the capacity of a printed steganographic channel. Because it is specific to printed images, this method is useful for steganographic problems such as stealth barcoding, but not for digital watermarking. The two results are complementary in that higher noise levels are encountered in the intra-image correlation encoding method, but the second method works by eliminating image-induced noise.

1 Introduction

The first half of this paper introduces a new approach to steganography in which data is encoded in correlations among the pixels in an image, rather than in correlations between image pixels an a known external reference signal. This method hints at the existence of *public key watermarking schemes.* We will define *weak* and *strong* public key watermarking, show that the new method is an example of a weak public key watermarking system, and conjecture that strong public key watermarking systems exist.

The second half of the paper presents *quadcluster encoding,* method of steganographically encoding data in printed form at higher densities than had been possible using the communications theory picture in which the cover image is treated as noise, introduced in [3]. The new method makes use of the fact that although the cover image is unknown to the receiver, it is known perfectly to the encoder; thus treating it as ordinary channel noise is overly pessimistic.

2 Background: Modulation Schemes and Inter-image Correlation

In a traditional binary phase shift modulation scheme, each bit b_i is represented by some basis function ϕ_i multiplied by either positive or negative one, depending

A. Pfitzmann (Ed.): IH'99, LNCS 1768, pp. 77–87, 2000.

on the value of the bit. The index i is being used to label the bits, and their associated carriers. The modulated message $S(x,y)$ is added pixel-wise to the cover image $N(x,y)$ to create the stego-image $D(x,y) = S(x,y) + N(x,y)$. The modulated signal is given by

$$S(x,y) = \sum_i b_i \phi_i(x,y)$$

A bit can be recovered by demodulation

$$\langle D, \phi_i \rangle = \langle S + N, \phi_i \rangle = \langle b_i \phi_i + N, \phi_i \rangle = b_i \langle \phi_i, \phi_i \rangle + \langle N, \phi_i \rangle \approx b_i$$

To the extent it is possible, the basis functions should be uncorrelated with (orthogonal to) the cover image N.

$$\langle \phi_i, N \rangle = \frac{1}{n} \sum_{x,y} \phi_i(x,y) N(x,y) \approx 0$$

where n is the total number of pixels summed over.

As pointed out in [2], the cover image N typically has a large non-zero DC component, since by convention luminosity values are taken to be positive, and thus the carrier ϕ should have zero DC component. If the carrier has a non-zero DC component, there will be a large noise contribution from the inner product of the cover image's DC component with the carrier's DC component.

2.1 Direct-Sequence Spread Spectrum

In the implementation of direct sequence spread spectrum in [3], the modulation function consists of a constant, integral-valued gain factor G multiplied by a pseudo-random block ϕ_i of $+1$ and -1 values. Each block ϕ_i has a distinct location in the (x,y) plane. The use of blocks is not a necessity. In some applications, it might be desirable to interleave the carriers so that each one is spread over the entire area of the image.

The embedded data is recovered by demodulating with the original modulating function. A TRUE ($+1$) bit appears as a positive correlation value; a FALSE (-1) bit is indicated by a negative correlation value. Once the carrier phase has been recovered, we project the stego-image onto each basis vector ϕ_i:

$$o_i = \langle D, \phi_i \rangle = \frac{1}{n} \sum_{x,y} D(x,y) \phi_i(x,y)$$

and then threshold the o_i values to recover the bits b_i.

In this scheme, as in many steganographic schemes, information is encoded in correlations between the pixel values and an external reference vector ϕ that must be made available to any decoder.

3   Intra-image Correlation

3.1   Motivation: Public Key Watermarking

We will define the term *public key watermarking* to mean a watermarking scheme with the property that the knowledge required to read (or verify) the hidden watermark data provides no additional help in stripping the watermark. This term should not be confused with public key steganography, which Anderson defined to mean the problem of communicating information through a steganographic channel using an asymmetric cryptosystem to keep the contents of the hidden data secret. A public key watermark is not supposed to be secret—it should be readable by anyone in possession of the public key—but only someone with the secret key should be able to remove it and recover a clean, unmarked original.

This is not to say that a public key watermark cannot be jammed: a large amount of noise can always be added blindly, for example. Nor is it to say that access to an oracle that can read watermark bits would not help: then modifications to the image can be tested until the watermark is unreadable.

Definition 1 *A strong public key watermarking scheme has the property that performing the decoding algorithm oneself, using the public key, confers no advantage (or vanishingly small advantage) in stripping the watermark above that provided by access to a watermark-reading oracle or server. With knowledge of the private key, the watermark can be stripped and the original source image recovered.*

Definition 2 *A weak public key watermarking scheme has the property that performing the decoding algorithm oneself, using the public key, does not confer the ability to exactly strip the watermark and recover a clean copy of the original. With knowledge of the private key, the watermark can be stripped and the original source image recovered.*

In either the strong or the weak form, the decoder must in some (strong or weak) sense not be able to determine "where" the data is hidden. A spread spectrum demodulation algorithm that was capable of extracting modulated bits given received data and an encrypted version of the carrier, without ever decrypting the carrier, would probably qualify as a strong public key watermarking system.

We conjecture that strong public key watermarking schemes exist, though producing them will require a novel combination of cryptography and signal processing. The first part of this paper presents a weak public key watermarking scheme.

3.2   Intra-image Methods

The technique introduced in this section encodes information in correlations *among* the pixels within an image, rather than in correlations between an image and an external reference. A consequence of this approach is that the ability to read the message does not confer the ability to exactly strip out the message. Thus, the method is a weak public key watermarking system.

The only previous investigation of intra-image correlation we are aware of is the "texture-block coding" scheme described in [1]. In this scheme, a textured region is identified by a human operator, copied, and then pasted into another area of the image, replacing whatever pixels were originally at the destination location. The shape of the region can be tailored to represent information, for example, the characters "MIT." The main drawback of this scheme is the requirement to manually identify regions of corresponding texture. For the scheme to be imperceptible, the source and destination regions have to be similar-looking regions of high texture. This means that the information is not stored in a predefined set of pixels. Thus an additional drawback is that decoding requires calculating the full 2d autocorrelation function of the image, in order to discover where the information is encoded. The information cannot be placed in a fixed location because its location depends on the human user's choice.

The method presented in this section is automatic on encode and decode, and does not require a full autocorrelation calculation to perform the extraction. The method is as follows. Break the pixels of the cover image into two disjoint subsets of equal size. Then we can treat the pixels in the first subset as a vector D_1, and the pixels from the second subset as vector D_2. Information can be encoded in correlations between these two portions of the image, rather than between the image and an external carrier. A TRUE bit will be represented by positive correlations between the sub-regions, and FALSE will be represented by negative correlations (anti-correlation). Consider two sub-regions of an image that are being used to encode a single bit b (either +1 or -1). We can write the first sub-region as $D_1 = N_1 + \chi$ and the second as $D_2 = N_2 + b\chi$, where N_1 and N_2 are portions of the original unmodified "noise" image, b is the bit being encoded (+1 or -1) and χ is a random sequence that is generated in the course of encoding, but then may be thrown away. Like classical correlation-based steganography methods, the decoder does not need to know the original image N. The novel feature of this scheme is that the decoder does not need to know χ, either. The decoder does needs to know, for each D_1 pixel, which D_2 pixel is associated with it.

The naive decoding algorithm would take the inner product of $\langle D_1, D_2 \rangle$. Because of the large DC components of N_1 and N_2, however, the signal would be swamped. To see this, we can write an expansion of N_1 into its DC component plus all other terms, $N_1 = N_1^0 + N_1'$, where N_1^0 is the DC component. The naive inner product is

$$\langle D_1, D_2 \rangle = \langle N_1^0 + N_1' + \chi, N_2^0 + N_2' + b\chi \rangle$$

Since images are by convention positive, both images will have large DC components N_1^0 and N_2^0, which will make a large contribution to this inner product. Subtracting off the DC components before taking the inner product eliminates the large contribution that would otherwise arise. Thus a much better demodulation method is

$$\langle D_1 - \langle D_1 \rangle, D_2 - \langle D_2 \rangle \rangle$$

where $\langle D_1 \rangle$ denotes the mean of D_1, taken bit-blockwise.

3.3   Geometric Interpretation

Classical schemes add a vectorial component to the image and represent information in the angle (typically 0 or 180 degrees) between this component and a
known external reference vector.[1] The method presented here represents information in the relative angle between two vectors that are parts of the image; the
absolute angle of these vectors may be completely unknown to the receiver.

Because data extraction in traditional methods is accomplished by measuring
the angle to a reference vector that must be specified to the receiver, the knowledge required to optimally read data necessarily confers the ability to exactly
strip out that data. In order to extract data using the method presented here,
the receiver need know nothing about the absolute angle (in Hamming space)
at which the data is stored.

3.4   A Weak Public-Key Watermarking Scheme

Successfully decoding a bit reveals, for the blocks or sets of correlated pixels,
whether the correlation is positive or negative. But for any pair of pixels, it
does not reveal whether the positive correlation was due to a $(+1, +1)$ change,
or a $(-1, -1)$ change. Similarly, negative correlation could be caused by either
$(+1, -1)$ or $(-1, +1)$. (An additional source of confusion arises from the image
noise.) This information (whether the contribution made by a pair of pixels to the
overall positive correlation is due to a $(+1, +1)$ change or a $(-1, -1)$ change),
which constitutes the absolute angle at which the data is encoded, is known
only by the encoder, not the decoder. A decoder who came into possession of
this information could exactly strip out the watermark, and recover the original
image.

The absolute angle at which the data is encoded can be viewed as a private
key that can be used to strip out the hidden data (that is χ is a private key).
The public key needed to read the data is the sequence of paired pixels.

3.5   Attacks

Although the receiver does not *need* knowledge of χ to read the data, this is
unfortunately not equivalent to the statement that the receiver *cannot acquire*
some knowledge of where the information is stored. Knowledge that a pair of
pixels is probably positively correlated, plus knowledge of whether each pixel is
greater or less than the mean value of its block, yields some information about
χ. An estimate of χ, even if it is not exactly correct, can be used to reduce the
power of the watermark.

There are two attacks on the intra-image encoding method that will reliably
eliminate the watermark, though at the cost of further damage to the image.

---

[1] This is because the inner product $\langle a, b \rangle = |a||b| \cos(\theta)$. If a and b are normalized so
that $|a| = |b| = 1$, then the inner product returns the cosine of the angle between a
and b.

The first attack is to bring the correlation of each of the blocks toward zero. If a pair of blocks is positively correlated, than add negative correlation until the correlation score is close to zero. Flip a coin to determine whether to stop on the positive side of zero, or the negative side. (Replacing all positive correlations by negative correlations would have the effect of inverting, but not removing, the watermark).

The second attack is simply to blindly encode some other message. This attack highlights the fact that this scheme is not as asymmetric as one would like. Though the ability to read does not confer the ability to recover the unmarked image, it does confer the ability to overwrite the original watermark.

3.6   Capacity of Intra-image Correlation Scheme

For purposes of analysis, this scheme can be mapped onto a classical inter-image correlation method. The channel capacity formula is

$$C = W \log_2(1 + \frac{S}{N})$$

The demodulation method is $\langle b\chi + N_1 - \langle N_1 \rangle, \chi + N_2 - \langle N_2 \rangle \rangle = b + \langle N_1, \chi \rangle + b \langle \chi, N_2 \rangle + \langle N_1 - \langle N_1 \rangle, N_2 - \langle N_2 \rangle \rangle$, as compared with $\langle b\phi + N_1, \phi \rangle = b + \langle \phi, N_1 \rangle$ for classical schemes. Assuming that N_1 and N_2 are uncorrelated with ϕ and χ, then $\langle N_1, \chi \rangle = \langle \chi, N_2 \rangle = \langle \phi, N_1 \rangle$. Thus the noise power for the traditional algorithm is $\langle \phi, N_1 \rangle$, and the noise power for the intra-image method is $2 \langle \phi, N_1 \rangle + \langle N_1 - \langle N_1 \rangle, N_2 - \langle N_2 \rangle \rangle$. Clearly the noise power is significantly higher for the intra-image method.

3.7   Implementation

We have used the intra-image correlation method to encode the Gatlin image used in [3] with 100 bits of information.[2] A gain of 14 percent of the total dynamic range (changes of ± 9, with the original image ranging from 0 to 64) was required to recover all 100 bits accurately. As expected, the performance is worse than [3], which hid 100 bits in the same image using lower gains. The level of gain required is clearly unacceptable from a perceptibility standpoint. However, the quadcluster noise reduction scheme in the second half of the paper could be combined with the intra-image encoding scheme to improve performance.

4   Quadcluster Encoding

A shortcoming of the intra-image encoding method is that it effectively has less signal-to-noise to work with, because (to translate into traditional terminology) the demodulating carrier has been corrupted with noise. The quadcluster encoding method allows the effect of cover image noise to be eliminated completely in

---

[2] Specifically, we are using the first 320 x 320 pixels of the Gatlin image, which is available in Matlab via the "load gatlin" command.

Fig. 1. 320 by 320 image encoded with 100 bits using intra-image correlation encoding. As expected, this method requires higher gain to achieve the same level of capacity achieved by the direct sequence scheme in [3].

a printed context. This noise reduction would render the intra-image encoding technique practical (in a printed context).

The cover image is often taken to be noise that limits the performance of the steganographic communication channel, as in the scheme and analysis presented in [3]. Although the cover image is not known in advance by the receiver, the cover image is not strictly speaking noise. For example, the "noise" due to the cover image will be the same each time the image is scanned, unlike the true noise that arises from the circuitry in the scanner, which will be different each time the image is scanned. Furthermore, the cover image is known in advance to the encoder, unlike true channel noise. Because the cover image noise is not truly noise, it turns out not to limit the communications rate. We will make use of this insight, as well as the fact that the cover image does not occupy all the spatial bandwidth that is accessible to modern printers and scanners.

The quadcluster method can be explained as follows. Up-sample the cover image by a factor of 2 in each dimension, so that each original pixel is mapped to a cluster of 4 identical pixels. The up-sampled image now contains 4 times more pixels than the original, since each original pixel has been copied 4 times. We will use the term *sub-pixels* to refer to the 4 identical pixels that were copied from a particular original pixel. Now if we encode data using any modulation-based information hiding scheme, such as the ones described in [3], but leave one sub-pixel in each quadcluster unchanged, we can achieve complete immunity to the effects of "noise" due to the cover image. Without loss of generality, suppose that the unmodified pixel is the top left member of the cluster. To demodulate, we subtract the value of the unmodified top left pixel from the other pixel values in the same cluster, and then perform the usual demodulation operation of projecting onto the basis function that was used to encode the information. We will describe better implementations of this basic idea later.

Current consumer ink jet printers have resolution specifications of 1440 dots per inch and higher, and photos meant for display on personal computer screens typically need only 72 to 100 dots per inch resolution to display them at reasonable size, so the up-sampled and encoded image can typically be printed at twice the original resolution (that is, exactly the same size as the original) by taking advantage of this unused resolution.

In practice, leaving one sub-pixel unmodified is not be the best implementation. In our implementation described below, we generated one carrier "chip" value ($+G$ or $-G$) for each pixel, not for each sub-pixel. The change made to each sub-pixel is determined by the product of the sub-carrier, the carrier, and the bit value. The sub-carrier values are chosen to sum to zero. This way, the original pixel value can be recovered by averaging the four associated sub-pixels. In our implementation, a fixed sub-carrier pattern of $+1,-1,+1,-1$ was used (with the labeling starting in the top left corner of the quadcluster and moving around clockwise). A variety of other sub-carrier sequences could be chosen, as long as the constraint that the sub-carrier values in a cluster sum to zero is obeyed. Each pixel can be upsampled by factors other than 2 in each dimension, for example 3x3 for nine sub-pixels, or 4x4 for 16 sub-pixels. In the context of printers with different horizontal and vertical resolution specifications, 8x4 might be a sensible upsampling. In general, the requirement is that it must be possible to estimate the original source pixel value from the sub-pixels.

4.1   Registration

It is a commonplace of the information hiding literature that spread spectrum techniques suffer from a need for precise registration between the encoded image and the demodulating carrier. The quad-cluster method is even more sensitive to misregistration than ordinary spread spectrum methods, and shows that ordinary spread spectrum methods actually do have some robustness to misregistration, when compared with the worst case.

Suppose that an image encoded with the spread spectrum method described in [3] has been placed on the scanner with a slight skew. Consider a 32x32 pixel block at the top left corner of the image, and suppose this block represents a single bit. Suppose further that because of the skew, the carrier being used to demodulate is registered correctly for the top left 16x16 quarter of this block, and misregistered in the rest of the block. A signal strength could be chosen such that this bit would be correctly demodulated, despite the fact that three quarters of the pixels are misregistered. Because this algorithm makes no assumptions about the cover image, treating it as noise, misregistration causes the signal power from the misregistered region to drop to zero, but has on average no effect on the noise power from this region. Since the contents of the cover image are treated as noise, there is a significant noise contribution from the cover image regardless of whether it is properly registered. Misregistered noise is no more harmful than "properly registered" noise.

In the quad-cluster method, misregistration causes a significant increase in cover image noise, as well as a decrease in signal. When the carrier is properly registered, there is zero contribution from cover image noise. When the carrier is "fully misregistered" (meaning every pixel in a carrier block misregistered), the cover image contributes potentially just as much noise as in the ordinary spread spectrum technique. Thus the quad-cluster method is much more sensitive to registration, as measured by the fall off of SNR as a function of the number of misregistered pixels.

4.2 Implementation

The obvious question given the discussion in the previous section is whether it is possible in practice to register the image and the carrier precisely enough to get the benefits of the quad-cluster method. Perhaps the increased noise due to misregistration offsets the noise savings offered by the method.

The answer to the question of whether precise enough registration is possible is a resounding yes. In the 320x320 pixel Gatlin image, shown in figure 2, in which 100 bits were hidden in [3] "on screen" (not printed and scanned) and with perfect registration, we can now hide 1024 bits and extract them with 100 percent accuracy after printing and scanning.

First the dynamic range of the original 6 bit gray scale image was expanded to fit into a standard 8 bit range of brightness values. The original was upsampled from 320 x 320 pixels to 640 x 640 pixels using nearest-neighbor interpolation - i.e. each source pixel was duplicated into a 2x2 block. This image's dynamic range was then slightly compressed and its bias was slightly raised in order to avoid non-linear clipping distortion caused by pixel saturation. 1024 data bits were encoded with the quad-cluster modulation method at a gain setting of 7.8 percent (changes of +-20 out of 255) using a carrier block size of 10 x 10.

The test image was printed on an HP895C ink jet printer and on an Epson Color Stylus 740 ink jet at maximum nominal resolution (600 dpi and 1440dpi, respectively) on plain copier paper. The final printed size of the image was 4.4" x 4.4". The scanning was performed on a Hewlett Packard ScanJet4c with a scaling setting of 500 percent, yielding a color-scanned image of approximately 1675 pixels x 1675 pixels. The scanned image was low-pass filtered with a 2D Gaussian kernel and subsequently downsampled, using nearest-neighbor interpolation, to a 640 x 640 image.

This post-processed scanned image was block-aligned and decoded by an algorithm implemented in C. Although the original test image was monochrome, we used a color scanning process to "oversample" the image, thereby smoothing out some of the noise introduced by the scanning circuitry. The red, green, and blue color planes were separately aligned in order to account for non-colinearity of the red, green, and blue detectors in the scanner.

Using this procedure, a decoding accuracy of 100 percent was achieved: all 1024 bits were decoded correctly. Presumably, even better overall performance could be achieved by going to higher data densities and employing an error correcting code. From the perspective of decreasing perceptibility, a gain of 9 (rather than 20) resulted in 98 percent bit decoding accuracy, and rendered the hidden data effectively invisible. The gain of 20 was chosen partly to exagerate the changes so that they would become visible.

Fig. 2. Unmarked Gatlin image.

Fig. 3. Gatlin image with 1024 bits encoded using quadcluster encoding at a gain level of 7.8 percent (±20/255), 10x10 block size. The linear resolution of this image is greater than the original by a factor of 2.

5   Conclusion

The intra-image encoding method is first example of a weak public key watermarking scheme. The ability to read the message does not confer the ability to produce a "clean" copy. As a steganographic method, it suffers from poor performance, due to its high susceptibility to image noise. The quad-cluster method utilizes the advance knowledge of cover image "noise" available to the encoder, plus the high spatial frequencies accessible to modern printers and scanners, to effectively cancel the effects of image noise. The quad-cluster method is certainly very useful by itself for imperceptibly encoding large amounts of data in images. It also should render the intra-image encoding technique usable as a steganographic technique (i.e. a method for transmitting large amounts of data, not as a watermarking technique), by reducing the image noise levels encountered by the intra-image encoding scheme. The application of the intra-image encoding technique for weak public key watermarking in a printed context (in which one might imagine gaining the benefit of the quad-cluster method) is less compelling, since once the image is printed, there is no longer any possibility of recovering a clean original, regardless of what encoding scheme is used.[3]

In introducing the quad-cluster modulation scheme, we have pointed out that the level of channel noise is substantially different for the transmitter and the receiver. For the transmitter, the cover image is not strictly speaking noise, because the transmitter has exact knowledge of the cover image; for the receiver, it is more accurate to call the cover image noise. Quad-cluster encoding makes use of the higher spatial frequencies accessible to modern printers, but it also makes use of the steganographic channel's "asymmetric noise levels." One interesting open question is how the asymmetric noise levels alter the usual channel capacity calculation. Another open problem that arises from the second half of this paper is finding other modulation schemes that make use of the noise level asymmetry of steganographic channels. Finally, finding examples of strong public key watermarking schemes, or proving the non-existence of such schemes, is the most significant open problem posed by this paper.

References

1. W. Bender, D. Gruhl, and N. Morimoto. Techniques for data hiding. *IBM Systems Journal*, 35(3 and 4), 1996. 80
2. J.P. Linnartz, T. Kalker, and G. Depovere. Modelling the false alarm and missed detection rate for electronic watermarks. In *Proceedings of the Second International Information Hiding Workshop*, Portland, Oregon, 1998. 78
3. J. R. Smith and B. O. Comiskey. Modulation and information hiding in images. In *Proceedings of the First International Information Hiding Workshop*, Isaac Newton Institute, Cambridge, U.K., 1996. 77, 78, 82, 83, 84, 85

---

[3] It is natural to wonder whether embedding data with a standard, symmetric watermarking scheme and then printing the encoded picture qualifies trivially as a weak public key watermarking scheme. It does not, because although the ability to read the message does not confer the ability to exactly strip the message, there is no private key that would enable recovery of the original, unwatermarked image.

An Asymmetric Public Detection Watermarking Technique

Teddy Furon[1] and Pierre Duhamel[2]

[1] THOMSON multimedia R/D France, User Interface Interactivity and Security Lab
1, av. Belle Fontaine, 35510 Cesson Sévigné, France
furont@thmulti.com
[2] Ecole Nationale Supérieure des Télécommunications de Paris, Laboratoire
Traitement Signaux et Images,
46 rue Barrault, 75013 Paris, France
duhamel@sig.enst.fr

Abstract. The new watermarking technique[1] presented in this paper is an example of an asymmetric public detection scheme. The detection process does not need the original picture nor the secret key used in the embedding process. It is the translation, in the watermarking domain, of a public key pair cryptosystem. The key idea is to filter the pseudo-noise sequence before embedding it in the cover-content. Contrary to classical techniques, the heart of the detection algorithm is not a correlation measure but a consistent statistical test hypothesis in spectral analysis. Some signal based considerations show that knowing the public key used in the detection process is no use for pirate who wants to discover the secret key. An example of a copyright protection system for digital content using this technique is briefly described.

1 Introduction

Watermarking is the art of embedding information in a cover-content in a robust and non-perceptible way. Therefore, the quality of a watermarking technique can be expressed in terms of capacity, non-perceptibility and robustness. Another distinction is whether the technique supports private watermark, where the original cover-content is needed to extract hidden information, or public watermark, where one can detect the embedded message without the original content. The terminology of public watermarking was set by B. Pfitzmann [1] during the first international Workshop on Information Hiding and is depicted in Fig. 1. It clearly appears that the embedding and detection processes have a common parameter called the key. Thus, comparing to a cryptography system, current watermarking techniques are symmetric schemes [12]. The key parameter is usually called the secret key in reference to Kerckhoffs cryptographic principle [14]: A cryptographic algorithm can not remain secret, hence the security of a cryptosystem must only rely on the key kept in a safe place. A really important constraint is intrinsic to the symmetry of these schemes. Every entity able to

---

[1] French patent application number 99-07139 filled on the first of June 1999

A. Pfitzmann (Ed.): IH'99, LNCS 1768, pp. 88–100, 2000.

detect a watermark shares the same secret key as the watermarker and thus can erase it or change the embedded message. The watermarker has to give his secret key in a secure way only to trusted entities. This constraint restricts drastically the use of watermarking technique in many domains. It is well known that no secret can be stored in consumer electronic devices or software. Smart-cards, which are considered to be the only secure equipment in consumer electronic domain, are not powerful enough or too expensive to support a complete watermark detection process. Indeed, it seems that the only way to use watermark in secure way is the case where a content owner proves its ownership detecting his watermark in the presence of a lawyer in order not to reveal his secret key in public audiences.

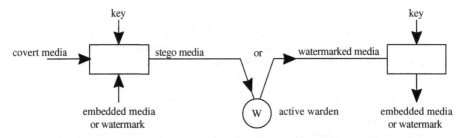

Fig. 1. Usual watermarking scheme and terminology

This major drawback has been solved in cryptography thanks to asymmetric schemes: encryption and decryption processes do not use the same key. The global system is based on a public keys pair where the private key, for example in case of certificate signature, is used in the encryption process and the public key in the decryption process. Obviously, the public key depends on the private key although it is impossible to deduce the private key from it. Transposing this idea in the watermarking domain would mean that the embedding and detection processes do not share a common secret. Moreover, knowing the detection algorithm and all its parameters is not enough to deduce the secret parameter used in the embedding process and besides it does not bring any clue in order to remove the watermark from the stego-content. F. Hartung has already presented a kind of public key watermarking technique based on classical spread spectrum watermaking scheme [19]. But it does not achieve all the desired specifications. Especially, a pirate can remove a part of the watermark. Whereas there is enough watermark signal left to allow the owner to retrieve it thanks to his private key, a detector with the public key can no more detect it.

This paper introduces a new watermark technique that is asymmetric and indeed completely different from classical spread spectrum technique. Following the reasoning of the authors, this paper firstly focuses on the cryptographic RSA scheme in order to derive some useful comparisons with the signal processing domain. To be more precise, this leads to the well known issue of blind equalization in the digital communication domain. Thanks to these comparisons, an asymmetric watermarking technique is then built up and tested with classical simulations. Finally, the use of these asymmetric watermarking technique is discussed.

2   From Cryptography to Signal Processing

Cryptography and watermarking are obviously linked, at least because watermarking, contrary to steganography, has to be robust and secure. But it is extremely hard to mix in a fruitful way these two scientific domains: Cryptography is based on number theory whereas watermarking tackles real signals. Usually, cryptography and watermarking are used separately, one after the other. The message to be hidden is encrypted before being embedded in the cover-content, or the stego-content is encrypted after the watermark embedding. But these combinations of cryptographic and watermarking techniques do not obviously improve the security or the functionalities of the global system. For example, imagine that one encrypts the message with an asymmetric cryptographic cipher like RSA, before embedding it in the cover-content with a classical spread spectrum technique, in order to build an asymmetric watermarking scheme. It is true that the only person able to embed a message is the RSA and watermark private keys holder. But, a pirate, knowing the detection process because he hacked a software or did the reverse engineering of a consumer electronic device or transformed the stego-content by an efficient attack like Stirmark [13], can erase the watermark whatever the security level of the cryptosystem used. This example is clearly not a good design of asymmetric watermarking technique. In most cases, the weakest link in a security point of view and the most constraining function is the watermark detection. That is the reason why it is necessary to invent a completely different watermarking technique truly asymmetric, getting inspired by the cryptography domain.

2.1   Example of RSA Cryptosystem

The RSA cryptosystem, invented by R. Rivest, A. Shamir and L. Adleman, is one of the most famous asymmetric schemes. This section gives a short description of the RSA encryption scheme. Key generation is done as follows: choose two large prime numbers p and q, compute $n = pq$ and $\Psi(n) = (p-1)(q-1)$ where Ψ is the Euler's function, select a random integer e prime with $\Psi(n)$ and compute the only one integer d such that $ed = 1 \mod \Psi(n)$. (n, e) is the public key whereas d is the private key. As watermarking is similar to signature in concept, the encryption with the private key is detailed: represent the message as an integer m, compute $c = m^d \mod n$, c is then the encrypted message. Decryption is easy and based on Fermat's theorem: use the public key (n, e) to compute $m = c^e \mod n$. See [2] or [14] for further details.

   The security of RSA relies on the difficulty of computing the private key d knowing the public key (n, e). The problem stems from factoring n in prime numbers: because the pirate can not find (p, q) from n (no efficient algorithm known up to now) he cannot compute $\Psi(n)$ nor d, which is the private key. Hence, it seems (it has not yet been proven that breaking RSA is equivalent to factoring) that the security of the system is based on the fact that $(p, q) \longrightarrow n = pq$ is a one way operation.

2.2 One Way Operation in Signal Processing

Compared to RSA algorithm, an asymmetric watermarking technique should add a watermark in the content using a one way operation in order to prevent pirate from removing it (operation equivalent to $(p, q) \longrightarrow n = pq$), but with the property that the detector can still retrieve the watermark (property equivalent to Fermat's theorem). It means that the detector should notice the effect of the watermark without having the knowledge of the cause. A solution was found in the digital communication field. In this domain, signals transmitted are modified by the communication channel. The channel is usually considered as a linear time-invariant (LTI) filter. The receiver has to invert the effect of the channel. This is the role of the equalizer. For this purpose, the transmitter begins to send a reference sequence known by the receiver in order to initially adjust the coefficients of the equalizer. Then, when the really informative signal is transmitted, the receiver is able to compensate the channel effect. As transmitting the referenced sequence takes time and power, communication system are desired not to need such training period. This is the problem of blind equalization based on initial adjustment of the coefficients without the benefit of a training sequence. But these methods are less efficient than classical ones especially at low signal to noise power ratio. A one way operation can be found every time blind equalization is not possible. This asymmetric technique is based on the main idea that passing through a filter, whatever white noise will produce a sequence noticeable by the shape of its power spectrum density (psd). But, with some assumptions explained in the next section, it is impossible to retrieve the original sequence. Hence, while the detection only consists of checking the psd of the watermark, a pirate can not estimate and remove the watermark. This referenced psd is the public key, whereas the private key is the set of the white noise sequence and the filter coefficients.

A Signal Processing Theorem. Second-order statistics like auto-correlation and density spectrum function of the output signal of a LTI filter provide information only on the magnitude of the filter characteristics (except for periodic signals). This statement can be done regarding the following theorem:

Consider a discrete LTI filter which impulse response $\mathbf{h} = \{h_n\}$ is real and frequency response is noted $H(f)$. Its input signal is noted $\mathbf{v} = \{v_n\}$, issued from a stationary random process, and its output $\mathbf{w} = \{w_n\}$. The following equations

(1) can be written:

$$\phi_{\mathbf{ww}}[k] = \sum_{m=-\infty}^{\infty} \phi_{\mathbf{vv}}[k-m] \sum_{u=-\infty}^{\infty} h_u h_{u+m} \quad \text{and} \quad \Phi_{\mathbf{ww}}(f) = |H(f)|^2 \cdot \Phi_{\mathbf{vv}}(f)$$

(1)

where $\phi_{\mathbf{ww}}[k]$ is the auto-correlation discrete function of $\mathbf{w}$ and $\Phi_{\mathbf{ww}}(f)$ its power spectrum density. Observing $\Phi_{\mathbf{ww}}(f)$, there is, a priori, no way to estimate $H(f)$ (or equivalently $\mathbf{h}$) due to the phase non-determination [3]. A known exception are minimum (or maximum) phase filter, because the phase of $H(f)$ is related to its magnitude.

Blind Deconvolution. Blind equalization techniques manage however to estimate filter coefficients. In the case of SISO (Single Input Single Output) system, there are mainly three classes of blind equalization algorithms based on maximum likelihood criterion, stochastic gradient iteration or high order signal statistics [3]. These techniques do not work if the broadcast signal is a gaussian white noise [18]. All the information concerning this random process are given by second-order statistics, which, according to the signal processing theorem above, bring only information on the magnitude of the filter process. But in the SIMO case (Single Input Multiple Outputs), an algorithm derived from the subspace method for example, is able to estimate the impulse responses of the different filters. These estimations feed a classical equalizer which retrieve the input of the SIMO bank of filters. In the watermarking technique described hereafter, the SISO case is mandatory to prevent the pirate from estimating the filter and retrieving the secret sequence. Thus, only one filter is used in the embedding process.

Hence, in the SISO case, if sequence $\mathbf{v}$ is issued from a gaussian stationary random process and $\mathbf{h}$ is not the impulse response of a minimum or maximum phase filter, $(\mathbf{v}, \mathbf{h}) \longrightarrow \mathbf{h} \otimes \mathbf{v}$ is a signal processing one way operation ($\otimes$ is the convolution product).

3   Asymmetric Watermarking Technique

3.1   Embedding Process

Let the sequence $\mathbf{x} = \{x_n\}$ of length N represent the content (luminance of pixels [4], DCT coefficients [6], Fourier-Mellin transform coefficients [5], wavelet transform coefficients for still picture, location of grid nodes of computer image, facial animation parameters of MPEG-4 head object, sample of sound [15]...). Assume there is an algorithm based on some Human Perception Model considerations which is able to calculate the amount of noise that each coefficient can bear without perceptible quality loss. Its output is the HPM modulation sequence noted $\mathbf{p} = \{p_n\}$ with $p_n \geq 0 \quad \forall n \in [1..N]$.

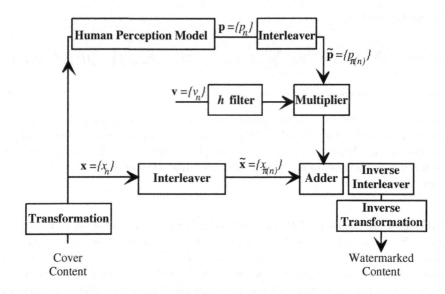

Fig. 2. Design of the embedding process

An interleaver is used in this embedding process. Its role is to mix the sequence $\mathbf{x}$ as a random permutation π. Output sequences are noted with the symbol $\tilde{}$. Hence, $\tilde{x}_n = x_{\pi(n)}$ $\quad \forall n \in [1..N]$.

According to Fig. 2, embedding process leads to the equation (2).

$$y_n = x_n + p_n.(\mathbf{h} \otimes \mathbf{v})_{\pi^{-1}(n)} \qquad \forall n \in [1..N] \tag{2}$$

with $\mathbf{v}$ white noise distributed as $\mathcal{N}(0, \sigma_{\mathbf{v}})$. Assuming that $\mathbf{x}$, $\mathbf{p}$ and $\mathbf{v}$ are statistically independent sequences, equations (3) hold:

$$\phi_{\tilde{\mathbf{y}}\tilde{\mathbf{y}}}[k] = E[\tilde{y}_n \tilde{y}_{n-k}] = E[(\tilde{x}_n + \tilde{p}_n.(\mathbf{h} \otimes \mathbf{v})_n).(\tilde{x}_{n-k} + \tilde{p}_{n-k}.(\mathbf{h} \otimes \mathbf{v})_{n-k})]$$

$$\phi_{\tilde{\mathbf{y}}\tilde{\mathbf{y}}}[k] = \phi_{\tilde{\mathbf{x}}\tilde{\mathbf{x}}}[k] + E[\tilde{p}_n \tilde{p}_{n-k}. \sum_u \sum_m h_u h_m v_{n-u} v_{n-k-m}]$$

$$\phi_{\tilde{\mathbf{y}}\tilde{\mathbf{y}}}[k] = \phi_{\tilde{\mathbf{x}}\tilde{\mathbf{x}}}[k] + \phi_{\tilde{\mathbf{p}}\tilde{\mathbf{p}}}[k].\sigma_{\mathbf{v}}^2.(\mathbf{h} \otimes \mathbf{h})_k \tag{3}$$

where E is the statistical expectation, $\sigma_{\mathbf{v}}^2$ is the variance of the sequence $\mathbf{v}$. Assuming the interleaver is perfect, that is to say its output sequences are white and stationary, then simplifications leads to:

$$\phi_{\tilde{\mathbf{y}}\tilde{\mathbf{y}}}[k] = \mu_{\mathbf{x}}^2 + (\sigma_{\mathbf{x}}^2 + \sigma_{\mathbf{p}}^2.\sigma_{\mathbf{v}}^2. \sum_u h_u^2).\delta[k] + \mu_{\mathbf{p}}^2.\sigma_{\mathbf{v}}^2.(\mathbf{h} \otimes \mathbf{h})_k \tag{4}$$

and

$$\Phi_{\widetilde{\mathbf{y}}\widetilde{\mathbf{y}}}(f) = \mu_{\mathbf{x}}^2.\delta(f) + (\sigma_{\mathbf{x}}^2 + \sigma_{\mathbf{p}}^2.\sigma_{\mathbf{v}}^2.\sum_u h_u^2) + \mu_{\mathbf{p}}^2.\sigma_{\mathbf{v}}^2.|H(f)|^2 \tag{5}$$

The secret key in the embedding process is the set of sequences $\mathbf{h}$ and $\mathbf{v}$.

3.2   Detection Process

The detection process is based on spectral analysis. Let the sequence $\mathbf{r} = \{r_n\}$ of length N represent the received content. The goal is to test two hypothesis:

- G_0: the received content is not watermarked so the power spectral density of the interleaved received sequence $\widetilde{\mathbf{r}}$ is flat. The estimated psd is expressed as $g_0(f) = \sigma_{\mathbf{r}}^2 + \mu_{\mathbf{r}}^2.\delta(f)$ $\forall f \in]-\frac{1}{2}, \frac{1}{2}]$.
- G_1: the received content is watermarked so the power spectral density of the interleaved received sequence $\widetilde{\mathbf{r}}$ is estimated as $g_1(f) = \mu_{\mathbf{x}}^2.\delta(f) + \mu_{\mathbf{p}}^2.\sigma_{\mathbf{v}}^2.|H(f)|^2 + C$ $\forall f \in]-\frac{1}{2}, \frac{1}{2}]$ such that $C = \sigma_{\mathbf{r}}^2 - \int_{-\frac{1}{2}}^{\frac{1}{2}} \mu_{\mathbf{p}}^2.\sigma_{\mathbf{v}}^2.|H(f)|^2 .df - \mu_{\mathbf{x}}^2$ according to (5).

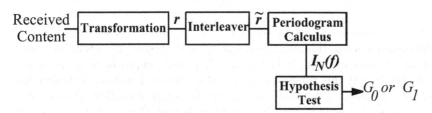

Fig. 3. Design of the detection process

In [9], a test defined by the critical region expressed in (6) is proved to be asymptotically equivalent to the likelihood ratio test.

$$\{\widetilde{\mathbf{r}} \mid 2.N.[U_{N,0}(\widetilde{\mathbf{r}}) - U_{N,1}(\widetilde{\mathbf{r}})] > d(P_{fa})\} \tag{6}$$

where $d(P_{fa})$ is a threshold depending on a desired false alarm probability and $U_{N,i}$ is the significant quantity related to the hypothesis G_i of the principal part of the log likelihood. If the estimated power spectral density is strictly positive, then $U_{N,i}$ expression is simply (7).

$$U_{N,i}(\widetilde{\mathbf{r}}) = \int_{-\frac{1}{2}}^{\frac{1}{2}} (\log g_i(f) + \frac{I_N(f)}{g_i(f)}) df \qquad i \in \{0, 1\} \tag{7}$$

where $I_N(f)=\frac{1}{N}\left|\sum_{k=1}^{N}\tilde{r}_k.\exp(2\pi jfk)\right|^2$ is the periodogram of the interleaved received sequence $\tilde{r}$, following a χ^2 distribution with two degrees of freedom [10]. The public key in the detection process is $|H(f)|$.

3.3   Security Point of View

Classical Spread Spectrum Technique. Keeping the same notation, classical spread spectrum technique can be sum up with the equation (8).

$$y_n = x_n + p_n.v_n \quad \forall n \in [1..N] \tag{8}$$

Detection is done via a correlation: a content is declared watermarked if the correlation with the referenced sequence is superior to a fixed positive threshold.

$$\langle \mathbf{y}|\mathbf{v}\rangle = \langle \mathbf{x}|\mathbf{v}\rangle + \langle \mathbf{p}.\mathbf{v}|\mathbf{v}\rangle > d'(P_{fa}) \tag{9}$$

where $\langle \mathbf{y}|\mathbf{v}\rangle = \sum_n y_n v_n$. The aim of a pirate is to create from a watermarked content a cleared content no more detectable. This can be easily done knowing the sequence $\mathbf{v}$ which is the secret key of this scheme:

$$\mathbf{y}' = \mathbf{y} - \frac{\langle \mathbf{y}|\mathbf{v}\rangle}{\langle \mathbf{v}|\mathbf{v}\rangle}.\mathbf{v} \tag{10}$$

The resulting sequence $\mathbf{y}'$ is not equal to the original one $\mathbf{x}$ due to the HPM modulation sequence $\mathbf{p}$. However, if the quality of the resulting content is correct, the pirate achieved his goal. It clearly highlights the importance of the safety of the secret key. If this scheme is designed to be used widely, such detector can not be implemented in non-secure electronic component. But, 'stealing' the secret key is not the only way to achieve pirate's aim. One can try to estimate the sequence $\mathbf{v}$ via an average process of T different watermarked contents via formula (11).

$$\hat{\mathbf{v}} = \frac{1}{T}\sum_{k=1}^{T}\mathbf{y}_k = \frac{1}{T}\sum_{k=1x}^{T}\mathbf{x}_k + (\frac{1}{T}\sum_{k=1}^{T}\mathbf{p}_k).\mathbf{v} \approx \alpha.\mathbf{v} \tag{11}$$

The only solution to avoid this attack is to desynchronise the embedded pseudo-noise sequence $\mathbf{v}$: $y_{n,k} = x_{n,k} + p_{n,k}.v_{n-t_k} \quad \forall n \in [1..N]$. But then, the detector has to get resynchronised. It means that it has to find the delay t_k for a given content r_k, calculating as many correlation as the number of possible delays. Ton Kalker and *al* [11] give a very efficient and nice implementation of this method. Nethertheless, I.J. Cox and J.P. Linnartz pointed out a more powerful attack. Assuming the pirate has a detector device he can use as many times he likes (which is the case in consumer electronic), he can finally manage to create a cleared content $\mathbf{y}'$ using the detector $O(N)$ times. This security flaw is due to the linearity of the correlation. See [12] for further details.

Asymmetric Technique. Thanks to the design of the asymmetric watermarking technique above, these threats hold no more. Obviously, the sequence **v** is stored nowhere in the detection process so nobody can steal it. This sequence is different for each content, so the average attack is useless. And finally, the detection algorithm is not linear which makes the attack of [12] non valid.

Although this watermarking technique has, for the moment, only one bit of capacity, a copy protection system for digital contents can be based on it. The idea is, as usual, to add a header to each copyrighted content. This header contains important data related to the content (identification number, rights granted to the user...) and will be bound to the content via a cryptographic signature. This is usually called a certificate. Pirate can not modify a copyrighted content or its certificate because the digital signature is then no more valid. But, he can remove the certificate, pretending the hacked content is a personal creation or whatever not copyrighted. That is the reason why copyrighted content are watermarked with an asymmetric technique. The role of this watermark is to warn the device that the content it deals with, is copyrighted. This device will read data in the certificate and will check its signature. If the signature is non valid or if no certificate is present whereas the content is watermarked, the device refuses to deal with this content. Notice that the device has no secret key but two public keys: one for the cryptosystem verifying signature, another for the watermark asymmetric detector. The content's owner has two secret keys: one for the cryptosystem making signature, another for the watermark embedding process.

A restriction may appear in the use of this watermarking technique. The comparison with asymmetric cryptosystems is not completely fulfilled. Knowing the public key $|H(f)|$, everybody can build its own private key $(\mathbf{h'}, \mathbf{v'})$ provided that $|H'(f)| = |H(f)| \quad \forall f \in] - \frac{1}{2}, \frac{1}{2}]$. As a watermark usually induces a restriction of user's rights like in the copy protection system described above, this fact is not really a dead end. Notice that the owner can still prove its ownership detecting his watermark, via a classical correlation detector, in the presence of a lawyer in order not to reveal his secret key $(\mathbf{h}, \mathbf{v})$ in public audiences.

4   Simulation

The goal of these simulations is to prove the validity of this new concept. Details of implementation are first given. A small panel of 512×512 pixels pictures is used (Lena, peppers and mandrill). Only the luminance data coded in 256 grey levels are watermarked. x_n is the luminance of the pixel located in (i, j) such that $n = i + (j - 1).512$.

4.1   Interleaver

Two interleavers are used. The direct interleaver tidies luminance pixels in a row of length 512^2 and mixes it according to a random given permutation vector. The inverse interleaver will apply the inverse permutation and will tidy the resulting row in a 512×512 pixels picture. The random permutation vector is calculated with the Moses and Oakford algorithm [17].

4.2 Human Visual System Modulation Sequence

A basic algorithm is used to calculate the modulation sequence $\mathbf{p}$. The image $\mathbf{X}$ is filtered with a laplacian high-pass filter. The absolute value of this result is tidied in a sequence $\mathbf{p}$.

$$p_{i+(j-1).512} = |\lambda \otimes \mathbf{X}|_{i,j} \qquad \lambda = \begin{pmatrix} -1 & -1 & -1 \\ -1 & +8 & -1 \\ -1 & -1 & -1 \end{pmatrix} /9 \qquad (12)$$

Textured regions or edges lead to high coefficients whereas uniform regions lead to very low values. This follows very roughly the eye's behavior, but no precise theoretical model sustains this choice. This algorithm is very fast and experimental results are satisfactory as noted in [11].

4.3 Role of the Length of Sequences

To embed the watermark, two strategies can be chosen. Add a filtered pseudo-random sequence $\mathbf{w}$ as long as the sequence $\widetilde{\mathbf{x}}$, or use a shorter pseudo-random sequence that one repeats several times before adding it to the sequence $\widetilde{\mathbf{x}}$. This last choice is usually made in classical spread spectrum technique [11]; to detect the watermark, the received sequence $\widetilde{\mathbf{r}}$ is then averaged. Hence, the watermark to cover-content power ratio is increased leading to a better false alarm probability. But, this 'tiling' process is also interesting for a pirate using the average attack. With the asymmetric watermarking scheme described before, the two strategies are illustrated. N_{seq} is the number of time the filtered pseudo-random sequence is repeated. Thus, $N_{seq} * N = 512^2$. Original and watermarked pictures are given to the detector. The result is the quantity $2.N.[U_{N,0}(\widetilde{\mathbf{r}}) - U_{N,1}(\widetilde{\mathbf{r}})]$. The sign of this quantity figures out if the content is watermarked (positive) or not (negative), whereas its absolute value shows how reliable is the decision. It means that the threshold $d(P_{fa})$ is set to zero. Figure 4 plots the average of these quantities calculated for the three different pictures and for 30 different pseudo-random sequences. On the abscissa is the parameter N_{seq}. It appears that high reliability occurs when embedding long sequences rather than short ones tiled several times, thanks to the consistence of the test hypothesis designed. The conclusion of this simulation is to set the parameter N_{seq} to one, which means that the sequence $\mathbf{w}$ is not repeated.

4.4 JPEG Test

The three pictures watermarked with the parameter N_{seq} set to 1, are then compressed with the JPEG algorithm with a quality factor Q. Figure 5 plots the average of the resulting quantities $2.N.[U_{N,0}(\widetilde{\mathbf{r}}) - U_{N,1}(\widetilde{\mathbf{r}})]$. For quality factors Q

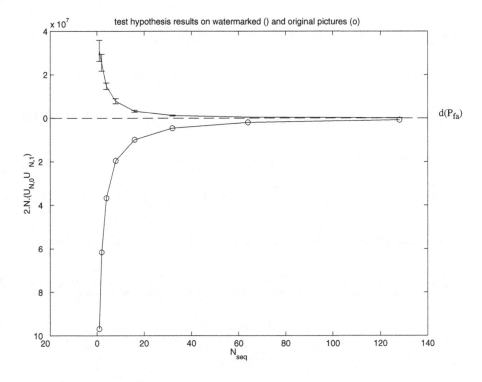

Fig. 4. Role of the length of the sequences

higher than 10, the results are far bigger than the one computed with the original image. But, as the results are indeed compared to $d(P_{fa})$, the watermark is only robust to $Q = 70$ JPEG compression. This is not a good robustness compared to actual watermarking techniques. Indeed, it can be compared to the first watermarking techniques presented a few years ago. But, authors believe a far better robustness can be reached if DCT or DWT coefficients are watermarked instead of pixels' value. In the same way, Fourrier-Mellin transformation might be useful to derive an asymmetric watermarking technique robust to rotation, scaling and translation processes. The simualtion shows that the basic concept of the watermarking technique is valuable and allows us to foresee a fair robustness using clever transformations like DCT or DWT coefficients.

5   Conclusion

This article is a description of the concept of the first truly asymmetric watermarking technique. The main advantage is that no secret is stored in the detector. Hence, the owner of copyrighted content must not rely on the security of the detection device. Thanks to the consistence of the detector, this technique

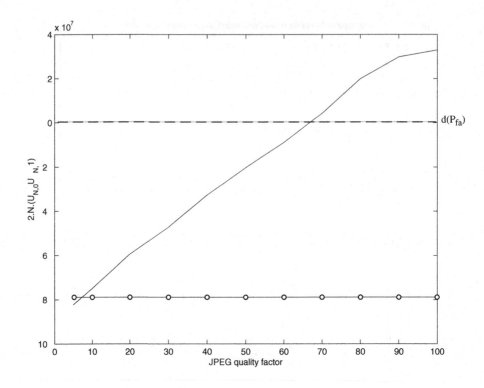

Fig. 5. Robustness to JPEG compression

is absolutely robust against average attack. The simulations show that this concept is valuable and may solve the open issue left in [16] about 'public key steganography against an active warden'. There are several technical problems left which need to be solved: some are related to the concept itself (large size of the public key, synchronization, increase of capacity, domain of application restricted...), others are related to the implementation of it (which transformation has to be used in order to achieve better robustness against scaling, rotation and compression - Can this concept be used for sound samples?).

6   Acknowledgments

The authors would like to acknowledge Eric Moulines (ENST Paris) for very fruitful discussions on test hypothesis in spectral analysis.

References

1. B. Pfitzmann, "Information Hiding Terminology", in *Proceedings of the First Int. Workshop on Information Hiding*, May 1996. 88

2. A. J. Menezes, P. C. van Oorschot, and S. A. Vanstone, *Handbook of Applied Cryptography*, Computer Sciences Applied Mathematics Engineering, CRC press, 1997. 90

3. J. G. Proakis, *Digital Communications*, Electrical Engineering Series, McGraw-Hill International Editions, third edition, 1995. 92

4. J. R. Smith and B. O. Comiskey, "Modulation and Information Hiding in Images", in *Proceedings of the First Int. Workshop on Information Hiding*, May 1996. 92

5. J. J. K. O'Ruanaidh, T. Pun "Rotation, Scale and Translation Invariant Spread Spectrum Digital Image Watermarking", in *Signal Processing, v 66 no 3*, May, 1998. 92

6. I. J. Cox, J. Kilian, T. Leighton, and T. Shamoon, "Secure Spread Spectrum Watermarking for Images, Audio and Video", in *Proceedings of IEEE-ICIP'96, v III*, Oct. 1996. 92

7. M. Barni, F. Bartolini, V. Cappellini, A. Lippi, and A. Piva, "A DWT-based Technique for Spatio-frequency Masking of Digital Signatures", in *Proceedings of SPIE Security and Watermarking of Multimedia Contents, v 3657*, Jan 1999.

9. K. Dzhaparidze, *Parameter Estimation and Hypothesis Testing in Spectral Analysis of Stationary Time Series*, Springer Series in Statistics, Springer-Verlag, 1986. 94

10. K. Fukunaga, *Introduction to Statistical Pattern Recognition*, Computer Science and Scientific Computing, Academic Press, second edition, 1990. 95

11. T. Kalker, G. Depovere, J. Haitsma, and M. Maes, "A Video Watermarking System for Broadcast Monitoring", in *Proceedings of SPIE Security and Watermarking of Multimedia Contents, v 3657*, Jan 1999. 95, 97

12. I. J. Cox and J. P. Linnartz, "Some General Methods for Tampering with Watermark", in *IEEE Journal on Selected areas in communications, v 16 no 4*, May 1998. 88, 95, 96

13. F. A. P. Petitcolas, R. Anderson, and M. Kuhn, "Attacks on copyright marking systems", in *Proceedings of the Second Int. Workshop on Information Hiding*, April 1998. 90

14. B. Schneier, *Applied Cryptography*, John Wiley & Sons, Inc., second edition, 1996. 88, 90

15. M.D. Swanson, B. Zhu, A.H. Tewfik and L. Boney, "Robust Audio watermarking using perceptual masking", in *Signal Processing, v 66 no 3*, May, 1998. 92

16. R. Anderson, "Stretching the limits of steganography", in *Proceedings of the First Int. Workshop on Information Hiding*, May 1996. 99

17. D. Knuth, *The art of computer programming*,vol II, Addison-Wesley series in Computer Science and Information Processing, second edition, 1981. 97

18. D. Donoho, *On minimum entropy deconvolution*, D. Findley Academic Press in Applied Time Series Analysis, second edition, 1981. 92

19. F. Hartung and B. Girod, "Fast Public-Key Watermarking of Compressed Video", in *Proceedings IEEE International Conference on Image Processing*, October 1997. 89

Zero Knowledge Watermark Detection

Scott Craver

Department of Electrical Engineering
Princeton University
Princeton, NJ 08544

Abstract. In order for digital watermarking technology to be truly usable, one must be able to employ it without annihilating its effect. The act of revealing a watermark within an object, in order to prove ownership or detect theft of said object, may open the door to subsequent theft, by providing attackers with the information they need to remove the watermark. The idea of *zero-knowledge* watermarking, of proving the existence of a mark without revealing what that mark is, can help address this problem and others.

1 Introduction

1.1 The Problem

Digital watermarking has been proposed as a solution to a number of media security problems. Robust digital watermarks, designed to survive within a media object unless an unreasonable amount of damage has been inflicted upon it, or unless an unreasonable amount of time is spent; have been aimed at both theft detection (i.e., Digimarc's MarcSpider service) and at resolving ownership in a court of law. Fragile watermarks, such as described in [13] and [14], designed to break (but break *intelligently*) when an image is inappropriately altered, have been proposed for authentication of recorded media and tamper-proofing documents.

Robust watermarking, which is the focus of this paper, is subdivided into application domains depending on the type of watermarking scheme employed, specifically the degree to which a watermark is concealed:

- If a watermark is hidden just enough to be imperceptible to the user, but is otherwise detectable by software, one can use it to communicate information about the image's owner and copyright status, and thus prevent accidental theft.
- If a watermark is detectable by at least one party, that party can search the Internet for all images containing the watermark, and thus detect theft.
- Finally, if a watermark is concealed to the point that removal and forgery is reliably difficult, it has potential for use as evidence of theft.

No single existing scheme admits all of these applications, due to the secrecy needed for the final application, and the lack of secrecy needed for the first application.

A. Pfitzmann (Ed.): IH'99, LNCS 1768, pp. 101–116, 2000.

1.2   Private Watermarks May Offer More Security...

A key issue in this paper is the distinction between *private* watermarks and *public* watermarks. A private watermark is one embedded using a secret key, a key which is needed for the mark's subsequent detection. The key acts as a *selection channel* (see [1]), engineering robustness through the secrecy of this information. The secret key parameterizes a watermark's "location" in an object, like a map to buried treasure, allowing insertion and removal of the mark with a small amount of degradation if the secret location is known. Those not possessing this information can at best dig up every possible location in the media object, inflicting an unreasonable amount of damage on the marked property.

Public watermarks, in contrast, are embedded in a location known to all, so that watermark detection software can scan any image for any marks which it may contain. This is far more useful, as it can be used both to detect and prevent theft. A private scheme can only detect a mark with the help of its creator, and is therefore relegated to providing evidence after theft is discovered. Employing private marks for theft detection is possible if one can trust the program or service performing the detection. Even so, public marks are more amenable than private marks to web-crawling, because everyone's public mark can be detected in the same way, with the results stored in advance of a user performing a search. A search engine for private marks would have to search each image for each possible mark, or employ an entirely different approach altogether. The downside of a public watermark is that so much information about the mark's embedding is made public, in order to allow a detector to find any watermark without help, that one can also engineer a removal tool for all watermarks. With no secret information protecting the watermark's integrity, it is not robust to direct removal, and one can only suspect that freeware watermark removal tools will appear on the internet.

1.3   ...But, All Watermarks Are Public!

It is easy for one to conclude that private watermarks are more secure than public ones. Many consider "public robust watermarking" somewhat contradictory, since the public mark's lack of secrecy allows instant removal. Unfortunately, the secret information in a private watermarking scheme is not secret either, a fact which reveals one of the darker secrets of the watermarking world: *present watermarking schemes require complete disclosure of watermark information when the watermark is actually used.* When one considers the entire watermarking life cycle, it becomes clear that existing watermarking schemes are ultimately public.

What we call private watermarks may use secret information to prevent the mark's removal, but this secrecy exists only as long as the mark is not used. Once the watermark is presented as evidence of ownership (its intended use,) enough information is divulged that the mark can then be removed. Avenues both technical and legal exist for an attacker, who likely already has a copy of the marked content, to obtain the final piece of information needed to unmark the media.

An intriguing feature of both private and public watermarks is now evident: usefulness of either kind of watermark is achieved through publicity. So-called private watermarks are only deemed such because the mark's use is factored out of the problem; researchers consider the difficulty of eliminating a private mark while the mark is not yet revealed as evidence.

1.4 A Real Private Watermark

What we need, then, is a watermarking scheme in which the watermark's presence can be verified without ever revealing enough information to remove the mark.

This paper presents floor plans for such a scheme, using zero-knowledge proofs in a novel way to separate the detection and authentication steps in the watermarking process, resulting in a watermark which is public enough to be detectable by others, yet private enough to be difficult to remove.

2 Zero-Knowledge Protocols

A discussion of zero-knowledge protocols can be found in [11], and we summarize the concepts here. A zero-knowledge proof is a method by which one can prove knowledge of a fact without revealing that knowledge to another party. The set of possible uses for such an idea is impossible to fathom, but one can instantly see its potential for solving our watermarking problem.

2.1 The Problem

Figure 1 illustrates a general problem of knowledge proof through a communications channel. Alice possesses a piece of information, such as an identifier, password or PIN number, the knowledge of which she would like to demonstrate in order to receive some kind of service (a ballot, for instance, or access to her bank account or credit card balance.) This is made possible by Bob, who possesses a database of identifying information. Alice's goal is either that of convincing Bob that she knows this information, or enlisting Bob's help to convince Carl, a third party. Carl may be a Clerk verifying Alice's credit card, for instance. His main distinction from Bob is that he is not necessarily under Bob's control, but nevertheless a direct participant in the authentication protocol. A final character is Eve, an eavesdropper, who observes all data sent between the other parties.

In a modern example, Alice possesses an account number and expiration date on a credit card, Bob is a bank with a database of clients and numbers, and Carl is a clerk who needs the card authenticated in order to allow a purchase, and who participates in the protocol by passing the card information along to Bob.

Even if the protocol prevents impersonation of Alice by anyone without her information, at least five kinds of fraud are yet possible:

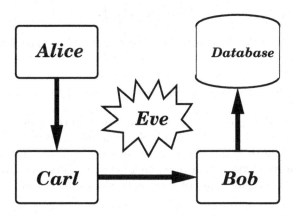

Fig. 1. A diagram of the authentication process.

- **Eve** may obtain all the information needed to impersonate Alice.
- **Databases** of identifiers can be compromised by a hacker, who may then impersonate any of Bob's customers. Unlike an eavesdropper, who exploits the insecurity of the channel, the hacker exploits the fact that Alice's identifier is stored in numerous locations beyond Alice's control.
- **Carl** may absorb enough information from participating in the protocol to impersonate Alice.
- **Bob** may himself be crooked, or have a crooked employee. This is different from Carl, who is not in Bob's control but is easier to remove from the protocol.
- **Alice** herself may take advantage of the previous four possibilities, by making a transaction and later claiming that it was the result of fraud.

The solution to this problem, then, is an identification protocol in which no useful information is sent over the channel, stored in the database, or made known to anyone other than Alice. This may at first seem impossible, since some kind of information must be transmitted and verified by Bob. However, modern cryptography has taught us an important difference between information and knowledge: knowledge is useful information, and information is not useful unless it can be extracted in a reasonable amount of time. Consider that the binary representation of a sufficiently large composite number contains within itself all the information needed to determine its factors, but that these factors are practically impossible to extract from the string. All the factor information is there, but from a computational perspective the possessor of the string has no knowledge of the factors.

In a similar vein, zero-knowledge protocols rely on a computational separation of information from useful information to prevent anyone but Alice from gaining knowledge of her identifying information. The general idea is illustrated here with two specific protocols, one relying on the hardness of the graph isomorphism problem, one relying on the hardness of discrete log.

2.2   Two Zero-Knowledge Proof Methods

Both of these protocols, and more, can be found in [11]. For a more in-depth discussion, see [10].

Protocol 1 *A zero-knowledge proof based on graph isomorphism.*

In this protocol, Alice possesses as secret information the isomorphism between two graphs. She can construct a graph H_1, scramble it to produce a graph H_2, and then publish both graphs, keeping the isomorphism to herself. To prove her identity, she must convince Bob that she knows this isomorphism. This is done by performing the following set of steps until Bob is convinced:

1. Alice produces a third graph H_3, by scrambling either H_1 or H_2, and sends it to Bob.
2. Bob now knows all three graphs, and depending on the outcome of a coin toss challenges Alice to either:
   (a) Reveal the isomorphism between H_1 and H_3
   (b) Reveal the isomorphism between H_2 and H_3
3. Alice reveals the desired isomorphism, using knowledge of the isomorphism between H_1 and H_2.
4. The graph H_3 is discarded. A new one will be constructed for every iteration of this protocol.

At this point, Alice has revealed no information about the isomorphism connecting H_1 and H_2. Had she answered both challenges, she would have given away her isomorphism. On the other hand, someone attempting to impersonate Alice without knowledge of the secret isomorphism could, at best, succeed at cheating with probability $\frac{1}{2}$: a forger can scramble one of Alice's graphs to generate an H_3, and would therefore know the isomorphism between it and the graph he scrambled. However, the isomorphism to the other of Alice's graphs can not be determined (and thus, both challenges can not be met) unless the isomorphism between H_1 and H_2 is known.

With a fair coin and sufficient security measures, Alice and Bob can perform this protocol N times to yield a probability of 2^{-N} that Alice is cheating. Once a reasonably small probability is reached, Bob agrees that Alice is indeed Alice. □

Note that proof is not absolute, but beyond a reasonable doubt, where a reasonable doubt is expressed as a threshold of probability of impersonation. No polynomial-time algorithm is known for determining the isomorphism between two graphs, although the problem is not NP-complete, and so the information of the isomorphism can be published and transmitted even though knowledge of the isomorphism is hidden from everyone but Alice.

Protocol 2 *A zero-knowledge proof based on discrete logarithm.*

The reader will note the similarities to the previous protocol. In this protocol, a large prime p and generating element a are publicly known, and Alice publishes a number with a secret discrete logarithm mod p to base a. That is, she chooses a random x and computes $M = a^x \pmod{p}$, publishing M and keeping x secret. Determining x giving M is difficult, and Alice proves knowledge of x to confirm her identity.

1. Alice generates another random number y, computes $N = a^y \pmod{p}$, and sends N to Bob.
2. Bob now knows M and N, and depending on the outcome of a coin toss challenges Alice to either:
   (a) Reveal y, the logarithm of N
   (b) Reveal $y + x \pmod{p-1}$, the logarithm of MN
3. Alice reveals the desired logarithm, using knowledge of the logarithm of M.
4. The number N is discarded. A new one will be constructed for every iteration of this protocol.

At this point, Alice has revealed no information about x. Had she provided both y and $y + x \pmod{p-1}$ she would have given x away. On the other hand, someone without knowledge of x attempting to impersonate Alice could, at best, succeed at cheating with probability $\frac{1}{2}$: Either a forger could construct a valid $N = a^y$ and pass the first challenge but not the second, or he could construct a fake $N = M^{-1}a^z \pmod{p}$ such that he knows the logarithm of MN, but can not determine the logarithm of N. Again, this algorithm is performed until the the probability of cheating falls beneath a certain threshold.   □

Several common features of these two protocols are worth mentioning. Both utilize *blinding,* a transformation of a problem into a related one which preserves important properties of the original problem whilst concealing sensitive information about it. For instance, the problem of finding the logarithm of M is transformed into the problem of finding the logarithm of MN. The goal is proof that one knows a solution to the original problem by proving the associated problem.

Another feature of these protocols is that they are *challenge-response* protocols. Usually necessary to implement blinding, a challenge-response protocol ensures honesty on the part of the prover by requiring her to disclose enough information to bound the cheating probability. In the case of blinding, Alice is challenged either to solve her transformed problem, or to show that the blinding is fair, i.e. that the transformed problem is derived from the original. Note that, should Alice do both, she will have given away all the information Bob needs to solve the original problem.

3   Zero-Knowledge Watermark Detection

We have seen how zero-knowledge protocols offer a way to prove knowledge of data without revealing it. It is natural to suspect that this can be applied to digital watermarking as well. Unfortunately, the problem domain of watermarking has a key difference from that of authentication which prevents a direct translation of zero-knowledge concepts. This difference is described below and overcome in the next section.

3.1 Applying Zero-Knowledge Methods to Watermarking

The key difference between watermarking and authentication is the need for a secure method of publishing data. In the protocols above, Alice publishes a pair of graphs or an integer M in a public directory. We did not mention the possibility of an attacker performing a denial-of-service attack by destroying the directory; the security of the directory was assumed.

In watermarking, we may assume that Alice has a web site with some data for use in authentication, but ultimately data must be embedded in the media object itself. If this information is made known then Bob can simply eliminate it from his copy, under the assumption that removing information degrades content no more severely than embedding it in the first place. However much of a mark is made public can be removed.

One possibility, described in [3], is that of a supraliminal channel. A hash based on high-level components of a media object could be used to generate secure, public data, since an attacker would have to change the image's semantic content in order to change the data. This would not, however, allow Alice to *embed* any new information. This approach might allow one to associate important parameters (such as integers p and a from protocol 2) with an image, but would not allow one to safely publish a constructed value (such as the integer M, or at least one of H_1 and H_2 in protocol 1.) Given that an image is not to be drastically altered, a supraliminal channel based on that image is read-only and completely out of Alice's control.

3.2 An Initial Attempt: Zero-Knowledge Watermarking with the Pitas Scheme

The scheme of Pitas (see [9]) is well known to the watermarking community, and has mathematical simplicity of the embedding method as an advantage. Its disadvantages also hinge on this simplicity (see [8,4]), although it should be pointed out that some attacks only take advantage of a specific implementation of the scheme.

The general idea is that an image's pixels are divided into two sets, and the statistical properties of each set is altered in such a way that two randomly chosen subsets of the image would not possess this statistical difference. A common implementation of the scheme is the increasing and decreasing of pixel intensity values in each set by an amount k, so that the means of the two sets are expected to differ by $2k$. Note that the watermark is a specification of sets of pixels, which is itself a binary image of the same dimensions as the original image.

The zero-knowledge version of this scheme is illustrated in figure 2. Alice watermarks an image I with a mark ω to create an image $\hat{I}$. She then *blinds* her image and watermark by permuting both with the same operation ρ. She can then prove the presence of $\rho(\omega)$ in $\rho(\hat{I})$ without divulging ω. Here's the protocol:

Protocol 3 *A zero-knowledge proof based on the Pitas Scheme.*

Alice publicly commits to a watermark plane Ω. To prevent invertibility attacks on her part, all legal watermarks ω must be "legal" scramblings of Ω. She wishes to prove that an image $\hat{I}$ contains a mark ω.

1. Alice generates a random legal scrambling ρ, computes $\hat{J} = \rho(\hat{I})$, and sends $\hat{J}$ to Bob.
2. Bob now knows $\hat{I}$ and $\hat{J}$, and depending on the outcome of a coin toss challenges Alice to either:
   (a) Reveal ρ, to verify that $\hat{J}$ is a legal permutation of $\hat{I}$
   (b) Reveal $\rho(\omega)$, and demonstrate its presence in $\hat{J}$.
3. Alice reveals the desired value.
4. Alice shows that $\rho(\omega)$ is a legally constructed watermark by illustrating the legal scrambling σ such that $\sigma(\Omega) = \rho(\omega)$.
5. The permutation ρ is discarded. A new one will be constructed for every iteration of this protocol.

The extra watermark Ω prevents another kind of cheating available to an impostor. One could scramble $\hat{I}$, and then by inspection find some watermark present in the scrambled image. In the standard implementation of the Pitas scheme, this can be done by simply selecting high pixel values for one subset and low pixel values for another subset so that their mean difference is as desired. (simply use the most significant bitplane of the original image as the watermark!) This *invertibility attack* is discussed in detail in [4]. With hope, it will be difficult to fake a mark which also belongs to the set of "legal scramblings" of the public mark Ω.   □

There are problems with this approach, both in the embedding method and the blinding implementation. First we notice that any scrambling random enough to safely blind the image turns even the slightest misalignment of I and $\hat{I}$ into total misalignment of $\rho(\hat{I})$ and $\rho(\omega)$. This is only as problematic as sensitivity of the Pitas scheme itself to slight spatial perturbations, however. If Alice can unperturb $\hat{I}$ until ω can be found within it, any scrambling of the mark is found perfectly well in any equivalent scrambling of $\hat{I}$, so this problem is avoided. It is likely that Alice will attempt to align and detect the original watermark in the original image before involving herself in a challenge-response protocol to prove its presence. Yet another problem is the fact that some information is revealed about the blinded image. Uncommon intensity values in the image are mapped to uncommon values in the scrambled image, giving an attacker a great deal of information by narrowing down the set of original pixels mapping to a scrambled pixel.

The space of legal scramblings must itself be engineered to be difficult for one to travel through it. If Alice can shuffle her mark Ω very slightly—for instance, if

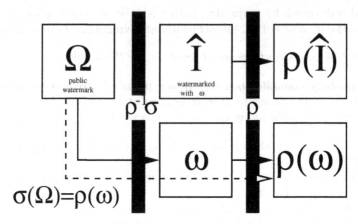

Fig. 2. A blinded Pitas scheme. A public watermark plane is scrambled into a specific watermark, and second scrambling is used to conceal the plane whilst preserving its alignment with the image.

a legal scrambling is a composition of permutations in which a pair of rows and the corresponding pair of columns is swapped—then she may be able to perform hill-climbing to find a fake watermark in the image. The astute reader may discover that this protocol is also vulnerable to a birthday attack: Alice could use two different legal scramblings ρ_1 and ρ_2, one to scramble the image and the other to scramble the watermarking plane, and this would not be discovered in the protocol. If Alice can, in a reasonable amount of time, discover such a pair of legal scramblings such that $\rho_2(\omega)$ is strongly detectable in $\rho_1(\hat{I})$, then the protocol is defeated.

3.3   A Second Method: Zero-Knowledge Watermarking Based on Hard Problems

The previous scheme can be improved in several ways. If the protocol can force the scrambling of the watermark and image data to be the same, then we can prevent birthday attacks. Further, unreasonably stiff requirements are placed on the scrambling method used: it must be secure, in that the scramblings can be verified to belong to a legal set; but "additive" in the sense that Alice can present to Bob the composition of two scramblings $\rho \cdot \sigma$ without giving away information about σ. Fortunately, a more refined blinding scheme can solve both of these problems. Based on the hard problem of finding a Hamiltonian path in a graph, but certainly adaptable to similar problems, this scheme can use any trustworthy scrambling method, relies on entirely upon the hardness of the problem for its security, and blinds data in such a way as to prevent birthday attacks.

Consider the NP-complete problem of locating a Hamiltonian path in a graph. A graph of n nodes containing a secret, difficult-to-find Hamiltonian path can be used to induce a secret permutation on a data set. The nodes of the graph, given a canonical ordering, are assigned in a 1-to-1 manner to the set of data points, also given a canonical ordering. Here we assume that the data set is at least as large as the number of nodes in the graph. Traversing the path from beginning to end induces an ordering on these assigned data points.

If the path is difficult to find, then the graph can be published, fixing the order in which the nodes can be assigned. A standard method of flattening image data, such as traversal along an approximating polygon of a space-filling curve, fixes the order of the data set to be watermarked. The secret path then describes a secret permutation used in the watermarking process, and which can be kept secret even when the watermark is revealed.

Figure 3 illustrates the setup procedure. Alice publishes a single graph Ω, isomorphic scramblings of which will be used to watermark images. This graph is the most unwieldy component of the scheme, but only one is needed; a pseudo-random scrambling algorithm is used to produce all subsequent watermarking graphs by renumbering the nodes of Ω, and only the scrambling seed values need be stored. Unlike the previous scheme, this does not require any special scrambling method; any cryptographically secure generator will do. Also, unlike in the previous scheme, the scrambling seeds used to craft individual watermarks may be published.

The watermarking step is relatively straightforward. A watermarking key consisting of a pseudo-random seed s is used to scramble Ω into a watermark graph ω. The pixels of the image to be marked are ordered in a standard way, possibly preconditioned by chopping into pieces of size $|\Omega|$. Each image data set I is then put into correspondence with the graph ω as described above, the secret path inducing a permutation of I, and this pseudo-randomly scrambled vector is subjected to an embedding scheme of our choosing.

We can use the Pitas scheme as in the previous example, but with our data set effectively whitened by the pseudo-random scrambling, we can simply add a signal, or attempt more advanced techniques. The choice of embedding method is largely orthogonal to the protocol, but may be guided by the desire to blind the pixel values during detection, below.

Finally, the watermark verification step: Alice reveals the watermark seed s, if it hasn't already been made public, and the graph ω and image data set I are prepared and put in correspondence. Alice then selects a secret session key x. This key is used as a seed to scramble both ω and I into a graph τ and image J, and the scrambled versions are sent to Bob. As mentioned above, some conditioning of the pixel values may be desired to control the information that the histogram reveals about the scrambling. Bob then Challenges Alice either to:

1. Reveal x, and possible conditioning information; or
2. Reveal the secret path in this new scrambled graph τ, inducing an ordering along J under which a watermark can be detected.

Notice that revealing x will reveal the scrambling of both the graph τ and the image J, so that Bob can verify that they were indeed scrambled in the same

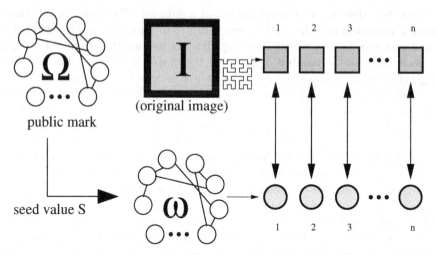

Fig. 3. The watermark setup and insertion process. A public graph is scrambled using a watermark key (pseudo-random seed) s, and the resulting graph nodes and image pixels are ordered, then put in correspondence. A path along the original graph implies a second, secret ordering of the image pixels.

way. This prevents the birthday attack possible with the previous scheme. The problem with this scheme may be the difficulty of generating public keys. One must construct a hard instance of the Hamiltonian path problem, which does contain a solution. This cannot simply be done by creating a random graph, and metrics of likelihood of hardness such as closeness to the problem's phase transition are inadequate as *guarantees* of hardness [12]. Other hard problems can likely be adapted to this protocol framework as well.

3.4   Public-Key Watermarking Using Invertibility Attacks

Invertibility attacks, described in [4], belong to a class of attacks called *interpretation attacks* in [5], and *ambiguity attacks* in [6]. In this kind of attack, one "finds" a watermark in an already watermarked object and claims it to be his own.

Some image watermarking schemes involve adding a mark to an image, and then testing a suspect image by subtracting the original from it, and correlating the difference with the mark. In this case, an invertibility attack consists of *subtracting* an arbitrarily chosen watermark from an image, and claiming the result of the subtraction to be one's original! Watermarking schemes which do not require the original are typically attacked by finding a watermark, by inspection, which correlates with the image and thus triggers a watermark detector. This watermark is then processed until it resembles a real mark statistically.

In any case, an invertibility attack can be prevented by specifying a class of "legal" marks, such that one can not easily find a counterfeit mark which is also legal. In the case of a scheme requiring an original image, the mark is required to be a one-way function of the original image. If an original is not used, the mark can be the output of a process which is difficult to invert, such as a good pseudo-random number generator with a given seed, or a one-way hash of a known identifier.

With this extra requirement preventing invertibility, it may seem that watermark inversion attacks are rendered useless. However, it turns out that they can be used constructively, as *a component in a zero-knowledge watermarking protocol*. This surprising result stems from the fact that determining the legality of a watermark may be difficult without knowledge of the seed values controlling the process, allowing a real watermark to hide in a field of fake ones.

Protocol 4 *A zero-knowledge watermarking protocol using invertibility attacks*

First, we specify the meaning of a legal mark. To utilize protocol 2, we will define a watermark as an integer in the range $0 \cdots p$ for a fixed prime p, and a legal watermark as a watermark of the form $a^x (\mathrm{mod}\ p)$, for a fixed a. The watermark value can be used to parametrize an embedding method, say as a seed for a pseudo-random number generator. Note that, if a is a generator of $\mathbf{Z}/\mathbf{pZ}$, then *all watermarks are legal*. However, one can only use a watermark if one knows its discrete logarithm, and due the hardness computing this, knowledge of a mark's logarithm is taken as proof that the mark was deliberately constructed that way.

First, the setup:

- Alice constructs a legal watermark $M = a^x (\mathrm{mod}\ p)$ from a secret x.
- Alice embeds M in an image I to obtain $\hat{I}$.
- Alice then uses invertibility attacks to find other (fake) watermarks $F_0, F_1, F_2, \cdots F_{n-1}$ in the image. None of these fake marks have a known discrete logarithm.
- Alice takes the unordered set $\{F_0, F_1, \cdots F_{n-1}, F_n = M\}$ to be her public watermark, not revealing which is the real one.

The value of n is chosen to be large enough that removing n watermarks (or enough watermarks to make the probability of damaging M high) will degrade the image severely. Each fake watermark must correlate with the image in a way that does not single out the real one. It is not necessary that the watermarks be orthogonal, but non-orthogonal watermarks need to be larger in number to prevent damage to M.

The effect of orthogonality is important because, as n increases, so too does the difficulty of finding n orthogonal fake watermarks in a scheme which does not require the original image. An original-based scheme allows one to select as many orthogonal watermarks as the watermark space has rank, since any watermark can be subtracted from an image. Unfortunately, if Alice uses a watermarking scheme relying on original images, she will have to include $n+1$ original images in the final watermark. The size of such a mark is prohibitive, and so a non-original scheme is assumed.[1]

In any case, Alice can now reveal the watermark set and show the detection value of each mark in the set. With the right choice of n, Bob is unable to effectively destroy the real mark. Alice must now prove that at least one watermark is legal. Assuming the scheme does not require original images, the protocol is like protocol 2:

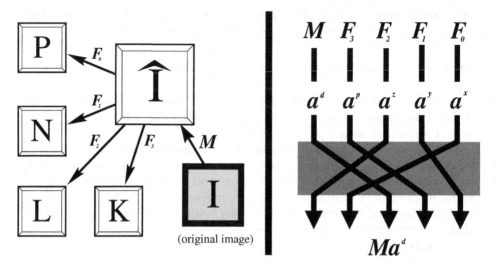

Fig. 4. Zero-knowledge watermarking using invertibility attacks. Left, the original image I is watermarked, then a sufficiently large number of fake originals is produced using other (invalid) marks. Right, the validity of at least one mark is later is proved after blinding and scrambling.

1. Bob and Alice select the watermarks which are successfully found in the image $\hat{I}$ by the detector.
2. Alice blinds each such watermark with a different discrete power: $W_i = F_i a^{y_i}$
3. Alice reorders the set $\{W_i\}$ and sends it to Bob.
4. Bob now knows $\{W_i\}$, a and p, and depending on the outcome of a coin toss challenges Alice to either:
   (a) Reveal all blinding exponents $\{y_i\}$, to verify that each blinded mark W_i is a legally blinded version of a member of the set $\{F_i\}$.
   (b) Select one of the marks W_k (the blinding of her real watermark, which is therefore of the form $a^{x+y_k (mod\ p-1)}$,) And reveal its logarithm.

---

[1] The reader will also note that if an original-based scheme is used, the legal watermark must be based on information about the original, such as $M = H(I) \cdot a^x (\mathrm{mod} p)$ for a hash function H.

5. Alice reveals the desired value(s).

6. The blinding factors y_i are discarded. New ones will be constructed for every iteration of this protocol.

Alice can not meet the second challenge without knowing the discrete logarithm of at least one of her original marks. The blinding prevents Bob from finding out which watermark is the legitimate one.   □

4   Discussion

Note that only one of these n watermarks is embedded. The scheme's security rests on the fact that the number of watermarks claimed to lie in the image is so large that they all could not have been added in the first place, and certainly can not all be directly removed by inverting the process. What makes this scheme work, then, is that data is published in an image and combined with data already there, so that the publication is secure as long as one does not reveal which data was added. This is in the spirit of the "supraliminal" channel, proposed in [3]: *the watermark collection can be considered a "semi-supraliminal" message, since most of it is actually based on content already in the image, and can not be manipulated so as to sufficiently alter the watermark without inflicting an unreasonable amount of damage upon the content.*

Another way to view the scheme is to observe that the information needed to detect the watermark—the entire watermark set—is separated from the information used to prove that the watermark set is valid—the real watermark M and the logarithm x of the real watermark. It is this information which would allow an attacker to remove the real watermark, and it is this information which is proven in a zero-knowledge protocol. We have, in effect, separated detection from verification, and so separated detection from removal.

As mentioned above, the effectiveness of the scheme depends on the choice of n, and in the case of non-original-image based schemes, the choice of n is itself constrained by the ability to find n sufficiently distinct watermarks which all trigger the detector.

Another security issue is that the revealed watermark can be fed into a detector, which, by the method of [7] can be used as an oracle to direct the watermarked image through image space into a region containing no detectable marks. It is unclear if this attack will work, because one must remove considerably more watermarks than were inserted in the first place.

Still another issue is that one can not put the same watermark in two different objects. Some watermark schemes require this anyway (such as a scheme in which each watermark is a function of the original image,) but the ability to use the same mark in multiple images would greatly improve its applicability to roles filled by public watermarks, such as searching databases or the Internet for multiple watermarked images. The fact that the part of the mark used in detection is made public may allow public use as well as use in resolving ownership.

5   Conclusion

A difficult problem in watermarking today is that of providing enough information to verify the presence of one's watermark without revealing enough information to remove that watermark. Until this problem is solved, all watermarks can be considered public in the sense that they must be made public when ultimately used. Using Zero-knowledge protocols, watermarks can be made public enough to be detected yet private enough to be unremovable. One approach uses the amenability of the Pitas scheme to blinding; an improved version does not require a specific embedding method, is not as susceptible to birthday attacks, and relies upon the hardness of an NP-complete problem for its security. Finally,invertibility attacks can be used to conceal a true watermark among fakes, and a zero-knowledge proof can be employed to demonstrate that at least one mark is not fake, without revealing which mark is the real one.

References

1. R.J. Anderson, "Stretching the Limits of Steganography." in *Information Hiding,* Springer Lecture Notes in Computer Science v 1174 (May/June 1996), pp 39–48. 102

2. I.J. Cox, J. Kilian, T. Leighton, and T. Shamoon, "Secure spread spectrum watermarking for multimedia," Technical Report 95-10, NEC Research Institute, 1995.

3. S. Craver, "On Public-Key Steganography in the Presence of an Active Warden." in *Information Hiding II,* Springer Lecture Notes in Computer Science v 1525 (April 1996), pp 355–368. 107, 114

4. S. Craver, N. Memon, B. L. Yeo, and M. M. Yeung, "Resolving Rightful Ownerships With Invisible Watermarking Techniques:, Limitations, Attacks, and Implications" *IEEE Journal on Selected Areas of Communications,* special issue on Copyright and Privacy Protection, April 1998 (IBM Research Report, RC 20755, March 1997.) 107, 108, 111

5. S. Craver, B. L. Yeo, and M. M. Yeung, "Technical Trials and Legal Tribulations." *Communications of the ACM,* July 1998, pp 44–54. 111

6. F. H. Hartung, J. K. Su, and B. Girod, "Spread spectrum watermarking: malicious attacks and counterattacks." in *Proceedings of SPIE* (San Jose, CA, February 1999,) pp. 147–158. 111

7. J. M. G. Linnartz and M. van Dijk, "Analysis of the Sensitivity Attack against Electronic Watermaks in Images," in *Information Hiding II,* Springer Lecture Notes in Computer Science v 1525 (April 1998), pp 258–272. 114

8. M. Maes, "Twin Peaks: The Histogram Attack on Fixed Depth Image Watermarks." in *Information Hiding II,* Springer Lecture Notes in Computer Science v 1525 (April 1998), pp 290–305. 107

9. I. Pitas, "A Method for Signature Casting on Digital Images." in *Proceedings of ICIP,* vol 3, IEEE press, 1996, pp 215–218. 107

10. A. Salomaa, *Public-Key Cryptography, 2nd ed.* Berlin: Springer-Verlag, 1996. 105

11. B. Schneier, *Applied Cryptograpy: Protocols, Algorithms, and Source Code in C, 2nd ed.* New York: John Wiley and Sons, 1996. 103, 105

12. Vandegriend, B. and Culberson, J. "The Gn,m Phase Transition is Not Hard for the Hamiltonian Cycle Problem." *Journal of Artificial Intelligence Research* v 9 (July-Dec 1998), pp 219–245. 111

13. P. Wong, "A Watermark for Image Integrity and Ownership Verification." In *Proceedings of IS&T PIC Conference* (Portland, OR, May.). 1998. 101

14. M. M. Yeung and F. Mintzer, "An Invisible Watermarking Technique for Image Verification." in *Proceedings of ICIP* (Santa Barbara, CA, Oct.). IEEE press, 1997. 101

Proving Ownership of Digital Content

André Adelsbach, Birgit Pfitzmann, and Ahmad-Reza Sadeghi

Universität des Saarlandes, Fachbereich Informatik,
D-66123 Saarbrücken, Germany
anadel@krypt.uni-sb.de
{pfitzmann,sadeghi}@cs.uni-sb.de

Abstract. Protection of digital property has become crucial in the widespread and rapidly growing use of digital media. Making the misuse of copyrighted works detectable, and thus deterring people from misuse, is the most promising measure currently known. To achieve this, most proposals apply watermarking techniques and focus on resolving the ownership in disputes which may arise after a misuse has been detected. Here a trusted third party (judge) compares the ownership claims of disputing parties. However, this does not necessarily imply determining the rightful owner, since she might not be participating in the dispute. Moreover, in contrast to disputes, one is in practice often confronted with only a single claim of ownership, e.g., in electronic market places where buyers intend to purchase digital items from someone claiming to be the rightful copyright holder. Proof of ownership is highly desirable in such situations because on the one hand, the buyers are ensured not to buy digital items from fake copyright holders and on the other hand, the copyright holders are protected against unauthorized reselling of their digital works.
In this paper we present the first general model and generic protocols for proving ownership of digital works. We also introduce concrete instantiations of our generic protocols, e.g., by applying watermarking schemes.

1 Introduction

It is a very difficult, if not impossible task in open environments to prevent digital content from being copied, redistributed and misused. Therefore the most promising measure for copyright protection is to deter people from *misusing* or illegally *redistributing* copyrighted content.

One way to deter the misuse is to make it *detectable*. If a person accused of misuse by the rightful copyright holder claims to be the rightful owner himself, then an ownership dispute arises. Motivated by such scenarios, previous proposals for copyright protection focus on *resolving disputes* in favor of the rightful copyright holder. In other words, these proposals aim at providing the copyright holders with means to show the precedence of their ownership claims over all others. Today watermarks [3,10,18,7] (sometimes assisted by registration [9]) are promising means for solving ownership disputes [20,15,18,7].

However, we believe that it is more desirable to have a real proof of ownership, i.e., to be able to directly verify the rightfulness of an ownership claim for a

A. Pfitzmann (Ed.): IH'99, LNCS 1768, pp. 117–133, 2000.
© Springer-Verlag Berlin Heidelberg 2000

certain work: The result of an ownership dispute is the decision made by an honest third party (e.g., a judge) after comparing several claims of ownership. This result does not determine the rightful ownership in general, since the rightful copyright holder might not be participating in the dispute. Furthermore, in contrast to disputes, one is often faced with only a single claim of ownership and has to decide on its rightfulness. An important example is purchasing digital items in electronic market places. Suppose a cheater obtains a digital work, claims to be the rightful copyright holder and starts selling (illegally redistributing) copies. Without proof of ownership honest buyers, purchasing this work, will get into trouble when the real owner later detects the (unintentional) misuse. In such a situation, a proof of ownership is desirable: On the one hand it guarantees the buyers that they obtain the rights of usage from the real copyright holder. On the other hand it makes the professional unauthorized reselling and redistributing of copyrighted works very difficult because honest buyers request an ownership proof from the seller. The ownership proofs should be transferable, i.e., the buyers should be able to show them to third parties to prove that they took good care in purchasing the work.

In this paper we present a general model for ownership proofs of digital works. The copyright holders are required to register their works at a registration center before distributing them. One might think that it is trivial to achieve proofs of ownership when involving a registration center. However, the crucial point is that ownership refers not only to the original work but also to all *similar* works which have not been registered explicitly. This has two implications: First, a rightful copyright holder should also be able to perform ownership proofs on similar works (e.g., images with reduced quality). Secondly, multiple registrations of similar works have to be avoided by the registration center; otherwise a cheater may imperceptibly modify a work and register it under his name and thus be able to perform fake ownership proofs. Our ownership proof scheme utilizes a similarity test function both in the ownership proofs and in the registration process to handle the mentioned implications.

The outline of this paper is as follows: In Section 2, we introduce a model for copyright ownership. Section 3 defines ownership proof schemes. In Section 4, we introduce a generic scheme for proof of ownership based on an arbitrary similarity test. Section 5 presents instantiations of the similarity test, e.g., by using (robust, non-blind) watermarking schemes, and thus leads to concrete ownership proof systems. Finally, Section 6 proposes measures based on authentication trees to make a cheating registration center accountable, thus reducing the necessary trust in such institutions.

2   Model of Copyright Ownership

The object to be protected is called a *work* W. We denote the set of all possible works by $\mathcal{W}$ and the set of all possible *copyright owners (holders)* by $\mathcal{H}$.

We model *ownership* as a *relation* between a copyright holder and a work. From a legal point of view one becomes the copyright holder of a new work upon

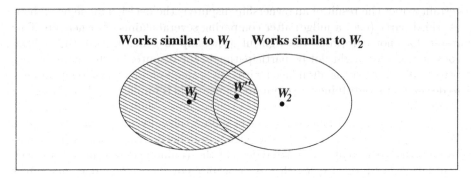

Fig. 1: Situation where the similarity relation is not an equivalence relation

its creation even without having the corresponding work registered [17]. However, in practice original works should be registered before being published to obtain a piece of evidence. Now the crucial point is that the copyright holder also holds the copyright in all works that are similar to her original work. Therefore the ownership relation

$$H \sim_{orig} W \iff H \text{ has registered the new work } W, \tag{1}$$

which models only the original work W as H's property, is not sufficient in practice.

A work W'' is considered similar to W ($W \rightarrow_{sim} W''$), e.g., if it is a *trivial or imperceptible transformation* of W. Transformations achieved by existing standard software (e.g., for images these are geometric transformations or color manipulations) fall into the class of trivial transformations.

Now assume we were given a *similarity relation* $\rightarrow_{sim}$. We improve the ownership relation in (1) by considering H's copyright in all works W'' similar to her original work W:

$$H \overset{W}{\sim}_{holder} W'' \iff H \sim_{orig} W \wedge W \rightarrow_{sim} W'' \tag{2}$$

This definition of the ownership relation would be sufficient if the underlying similarity relation $\rightarrow_{sim}$ were an equivalence relation. This is because an equivalence relation partitions $\mathcal{W}$ into equivalence classes, i.e., rightful ownership relations would not collide. However, considering $\rightarrow_{sim}$ as an equivalence relation does not always make sense, since it is not symmetric in general (e.g., a detailed and a rough map of the same geographic area). If the underlying similarity relation is not an equivalence relation, the above definition (2) may lead to ownership conflicts as shown in Figure 1.

A copyright holder H_1 has registered the work W_1, i.e., $H_1 \sim_{orig} W_1$ holds. Later a copyright holder H_2 registers a work W_2. This is possible because W_2 is not similar to W_1, i.e., $H_2 \sim_{orig} W_2$. If the similarity relation is not an equivalence relation, the set of works similar to W_1 may intersect with the set of works similar to W_2. Our ownership relation (2) considers both H_1 and H_2 to be the copyright holders of W''. However, in practice only H_1 is the rightful copyright holder of W'' because W_1 was registered before W_2. Thus we have to further enhance our ownership relation in (2) by the *registration time* of the original work to comply with the practical needs. We redefine the ownership relation as follows.

Definition 1 (Ownership Relation). *The ownership relation is*

$$H \overset{W}{\sim}_{holder} W'' \iff (H \sim_{orig} W \wedge W \to_{sim} W'') \tag{3}$$
$$\wedge (\nexists \hat{W} : \hat{W} \to_{sim} W'' \wedge (\hat{W} \text{ was registered before } W)).$$

By $\mathcal{W}_W = \{ W'' \in \mathcal{W} | H \overset{W}{\sim}_{holder} W'' \}$ we denote the set of all works which are considered the property of the owner H of W. We will refer to this set as a *work class*. Our ownership proof scheme will allow H to prove her ownership of all works in the work class $\mathcal{W}_W$. In principle, this ownership relation depends on the current time. However, we can usually omit a time parameter because once $H \overset{W}{\sim}_{holder} W''$ is established, it does not change.

So far, we assumed the existence of a similarity relation $\to_{sim}$. For concrete implementations we have to define this relation and in particular find a method to test it. In real life, official experts decide (e.g., in disputes) whether a work represents someone's own creativity or is just a trivial derivation from an already protected work. Hence they test what we call the *perfect similarity relation*. It would be much more efficient and less costly if we were able to test the perfect similarity relation between works in an automatic way. Unfortunately, no known tool can do this in a reasonable amount of time. We will therefore work with other similarity relation which can be automatically tested; we call them *restricted similarity relations*.

One can also imagine hybrid similarity tests, i.e., an automatic test assisted by a human expert, e.g., if the decision certainty of the automatic test falls under a given threshold.

3　Definition of Ownership Proof Schemes

The involved roles in a scheme for proof of ownership are (supposed) copyright holders H, one[1] registration center RC and third parties D, D'. Except later in Section 6 we always assume that RC is trusted by all parties.

The model consists of four protocols: First all necessary keys are generated and distributed authentically. Then the copyright holder registers her original work W at RC. From now on she, and no other, can prove to any (correct) D her ownership of any work in $\mathcal{W}_W$.[2] The last protocol enables D to show any other correct party D' that H has proved her ownership to him.

The protocols are summarized in the following definition:

---

[1] If there are several, they must act in a coordinated way so that ownership proofs are globally valid. Hence for our purposes they are equivalent to one.

[2] We need the correctness of D here because a dishonest party can, e.g., always refuse to accept the proof.

Definition 2 (Ownership Proof Scheme). *A scheme for proof of ownership consists of four protocols* initialize, register, prove *and* show.

- *The initialization protocol* **initialize** *sets up the system and includes the key generation for all involved parties. Every party X generates its own key pair $k_X = (sk_X, pk_X)$ and obtains the authentic public keys of the other involved parties. Depending on the used cryptographic schemes[3], keys may consist of several subkeys. The key distribution may be achieved by a public-key infrastructure and may also be executed successively, i.e., the keys may be generated and distributed on demand.*

In the following it is tacitly assumed that each honest party X inputs its own identity Id_X and the identities of the assumed other participants. Moreover, a text value reg_text could be input that could contain or point to additional registration-relevant information; we omitted this in the definition.

- *The registration protocol* **register** *is a two-party protocol between H and RC. Here H inputs her original work W, and RC inputs W and the content of a secret local memory mem_{RC}. The outputs to H are a proof string $proof_H$ and possibly an (imperceptibly) modified[4] work $W' \in \mathcal{W}_W$. The output to RC is a typically modified content of its secret local memory mem'_{RC}. Instead, both parties may obtain an output failed.*
- *The protocol* **prove** *for ownership proofs involves up to 3 parties: at least H and D, and in some cases also RC. H inputs the work $W'' \in \mathcal{W}_W$ for which she wants to prove her ownership based on a registered work W, and $proof_H$ obtained in register. D inputs the work W''. If RC takes part, it inputs W'' and the content of its secret local memory mem_{RC}. The output to D is a pair ($result, proof_D$), where the boolean value result indicates whether or not H is the rightful owner of W''. If RC participates, it obtains an output mem'_{RC}.*
- *The* **show** *protocol involves up to 3 parties, but at least D and D'. D inputs a work $W'' \in \mathcal{W}$, the identity of the copyright holder Id_H and $proof_D$ obtained in a run of prove for W''. D' also inputs the work W'' and Id_H. If RC takes part, it inputs the content of its secret local memory mem_{RC}, the work W'' and the identity Id_H. The output is a boolean value result for D' and a value mem'_{RC} for RC if it is involved in the protocol.*

We now define the requirements on ownership proof schemes. The fact that RC is honest and its in- and outputs contain the registered works and their owners implies that the relation $\sim_{orig}$ from Formula (1) is well-defined in any protocol run, and thus also the ownership relation.

---

[3] Different basic cryptographic primitives may be used such as signatures, authentication codes, commitments or even more complicated ones like asymmetric fingerprinting.

[4] RC may need to modify the original work to perform a similarity test on it, e.g., in an implementation with watermarks (see Section 5.2). In this case H should only make the version W' publicly available.

Definition 3 (Ownership Proof Requirements). *Suppose that RC is honest and initialize has been executed. In the following, prot(in, •) for a protocol prot and some input parameters in means that the honest participants execute this protocol and use these inputs. We sort the requirements by the party mainly interested in them.*

For the registration center RC:

- *(RU) Uniqueness: No party $H^\star$ can successfully register a work that RC already considers copyrighted, i.e., if register($\hat{W}$, •) ended successfully, no later execution register(W, •) with $\hat{W} \to_{sim} W$ succeeds.[5]*

For the copyright holder H:

- *(HE) Effectiveness: H can successfully execute register(W, •) for a new work W unless $\hat{W} \to_{sim} W$ for an already registered work $\hat{W}$.*

- *(HA) Authenticity: No party $H^\star \neq H$ can successfully execute register(W, Id_H, •) for any work W, nor prove(W'', Id_H, •) with a correct party D for any work W''.*

- *(HAD') Authenticity w.r.t. D': No party can successfully execute show(W'', Id_H, Id_D, •) with a correct party D', unless H has successfully registered a work W with $W'' \in \mathcal{W}_W$ and executed prove(W'', Id_D, •).*

After successful registration of a work W by H we additionally require for H and an honest D:

- *(HP) Provability: H can successfully prove its ownership to D, i.e., prove(W'', $proof_H$, •) for any $W'' \in \mathcal{W}_W$ outputs (true, •) to D.*

- *(HU) Uniqueness: No other party $H^\star$ can successfully execute prove(W'', •) with D on a work $W'' \in \mathcal{W}_W$.*

For the third party D:

- *(DC) Correctness: The protocol prove(W'', Id_H, •) outputs true to D only if H is indeed the copyright holder, i.e., $W'' \in \mathcal{W}_W$ for a work W such that RC performed register(W, Id_H, •) with an output other than failed.*

- *(DS) Showability to a correct D': If D has executed prove(W'', Id_H, •) with the output (true, $proof_D$), then it can execute show(W'', Id_H, $proof_D$, •) with any correct D' with the output true.*

For a second third party D':

- *(D'C) Correctness: The protocol show(W'', Id_H, •) outputs true to D' only if H is indeed the copyright holder, i.e., $W'' \in \mathcal{W}_W$ for a work W such that RC performed register(W, Id_H, •) with an output other than failed.*

---

[5] This could be weakened so that the owner of $\hat{W}$ is allowed to register such works W to extend the coverage of his copyright in cases where $\to_{sim}$ is not an equivalence relation. The effectiveness requirement and the scheme below could easily be adapted to this.

Some of these requirements could be omitted or weakened for certain applications. In particular, authenticity is not always needed, and weaker versions of (DC) and (D'C) are possible where other parties are allowed to make or show ownership proofs, as long as the correct identity Id_H of the owner is used. On the other hand, one could add authenticity for D with respect to D'.

4 Generic Ownership Proof Schemes

In the generic schemes we assume that an arbitrary similarity relation $\rightarrow_{sim}$ and a similarity test sim_test for it are given. Moreover, an algorithm sim_init may be given that performs set-ups for later similarity tests for a given work. We distinguish these relations with respect to two criteria:

1. *Type of similarity relation:* If similarity is an equivalence relation, it results in a partition of the set W of works. Thus the problem of overlapping work sets mentioned in Section 2 does not arise, which will simplify the scheme significantly.
2. *Type of similarity test:* There are *private* and *public* similarity tests. Private tests require secret information only known to the registration center. Public tests only need non-critical information which can be made publicly available for testing the similarity to the work W. In all cases, this information must initially be generated for a work W with sim_init, and we denote the output of this algorithm by (W', $simrec_W$, $testinf_W$). Here W' is the possibly modified (watermarked) work, $simrec_W$ a private record and $testinf_W$ the non-critical information. We denote a private test by $sim\_test(W'', simrec_W)$ and a public test by $sim\_test(W'', testinf_W)$. As $testinf_W$ can always be a part of $simrec_W$, we can generically use the private notation when RC is carrying out the test.

We omit the details of the initialization protocol and assume that it has been performed before the other protocols, in particular that all necessary keys have been distributed authentically. We also omit details of the message formats. In particular, where a signature is sent we assume that all message parts that are not known a priori are also sent and that techniques of robust protocol design like protocol- and message-type tags are used.

Registration: In the *register* protocol, H sends her original work W to RC in a signed message. Then RC performs a local test, denoted by *registered?*, to check whether W is similar to an already registered work. This is necessary to prevent *multiple registrations* of similar works. In principle RC iterates over all registered original works W_i performing the similarity test $sim\_test(W, simrec_{W_i})$. If one of these tests outputs *true*, then *registered?*(W) ends with *true* and the *register* protocol ends with *failed*. Otherwise, RC executes sim_init for W, which produces a possibly modified version W' of the original work and also $simrec_W$ and $testinf_W$. RC stores all these values in a new registration record rec_W for W in

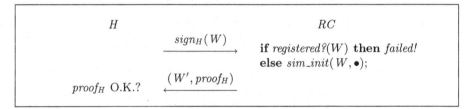

Fig. 2: Registration protocol *register*

its secret local memory mem_{RC}.[6] It sends W' to H together with the generic ownership certificate[7]

$$proof_H = sign_{RC}(Id_H, h(W), h(W'), testinf_W, reg\_time, reg\_text),$$

where $h(W)$, $h(W')$ denote hash values under a collision-free hash function h and reg_time the registration time. We also showed where a textual description reg_text of the registration could be handled in the protocol. The generic registration protocol is shown in Figure 2.

Proof of ownership: If H wants to prove the ownership of a work $W'' \in \mathcal{W}_W$ to a third party D, it starts the *prove* protocol by sending W'' and

$$init\_proof_D = sign_H(Id_H, Id_D, h(W''), prove\_time, proof_H)$$

to D. By this signature, H nonrepudiably states that she initiated *prove* with D for the work W'' at the time $prove\_time$ and used the ownership certificate $proof_H$. D verifies that $init\_proof_D$ and $proof_H$ are correct. Then D looks whether the hash value of W'' is explicitly contained in $proof_H$. If yes, D immediately outputs $result = true$ and $proof_D = init\_proof_D$. This should be the most common case because it occurs when H legally redistributes one of its own registered works. The following more complicated cases, where H proves ownership in a modified work W'', are mainly needed for the hopefully rare case that an illegal redistribution has happened.

If $h(W'')$ is not contained in $proof_H$, then D has to execute a subprotocol $test(init\_proof_D, W'')$ to verify that $W'' \in \mathcal{W}_W$ holds for the work W indicated by $h(W)$. If yes, this protocol also outputs $proof_D$.

The generic protocol for the ownership proof is shown in Figure 3. Depending on the type of the similarity relation, the subprotocol *test* for works that are not the registered original is implemented as follows:

1. $\rightarrow_{sim}$ is an equivalence relation: According to Section 2, ownership is then defined by Formula (2). Hence it suffices to test if $W \rightarrow_{sim} W''$, i.e., to carry out $sim\_test(W'', \bullet)$ without considering other registered works.

---

[6] If it is possible for a similarity relation that W' is similar to an already registered work while W was not, the above iteration should be repeated for W' and, if necessary, another W' be generated.

[7] In schemes where always $W' = W$ one can obviously omit W' and h(W), similarly $testinf_W$ if it is always empty.

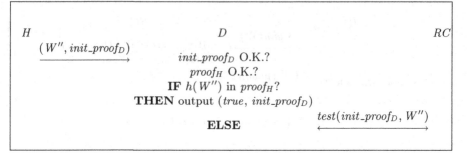

Fig. 3: Protocol for proof of ownership *prove*

(a) *sim_test* is public: In this case, D can perform *test* locally by executing $sim\_test(W'', testinf_W)$. The result of *test* is the output of the similarity test and $proof_D = init\_proof_D$.

This is the only case where *test* is computable locally and thus ownership proofs even for non-original works are possible with RC being *offline*.

(b) *sim_test* is private: In this case, D sends W'' and $init\_proof_D$ to RC, which computes $result = sim\_test(W'', simrec_W)$. RC replies with

$$proof_D = sign_{RC}(init\_proof_D, confirm\_time, result).$$

2. $\rightarrow_{sim}$ is not an equivalence relation: This complicates *test* because one has to consider the similarity to all works registered before W (see Section 2). Thus D has to contact RC by sending $(W'', init\_proof_D)$, no matter if *sim_test* is private or public. To determine the rightful copyright holder, RC, in principle, iterates in *ascending order of registration time* over all registered works W_i and performs $sim\_test(W'', simrec_{W_i})$. If the first work W_i for which the similarity test returns *true* was registered by H, then *result* is *true*, otherwise *false*. RC also sends $proof_D$ as above.

Showing a proof: Using $proof_D$, D can run the *show* protocol with any third party D' to prove that he has successfully executed *prove* together with H for a work W''. D starts by sending W'' and $proof_D$, and D' verifies all components of $init\_proof_D$, which is always a part of $proof_D$. Then there are two cases:

– If $proof_D$ consists solely of $init\_proof_D$, then D' first tests if $h(W'')$ is contained in $init\_proof_D$ and, if yes, outputs *true*. Otherwise, such a proof is only allowed if similarity is an equivalence relation and the test is public. Then D' locally carries out $sim\_test(W'', testinf_W)$.
– Otherwise $proof_D$ must also contain a signed confirmation of RC, and D' verifies that.

The protocol *show* is illustrated in Figure 4.

This finishes the description of the generic protocols. To prove their security, we first need the following lemma.

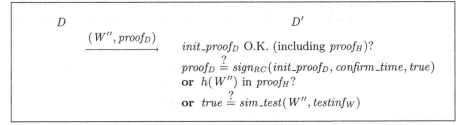

Fig. 4: The protocol *show* to show a proof

Lemma 1 (Correctness of *registered?* and *test*).

1. *registered?(W) ends with true if and only if a similar work W_i, i.e., with $W_i \rightarrow_{sim} W$, was registered before.*
2. *If $H \overset{W}{\sim}_{holder} W''$ and H generates init_proof$_D$ correctly, then the result of test(init_proof$_D$, W'') is true.*
3. *If init_proof$_D$ (including proof$_H$) is acceptable, i.e., they pass the test used in prove and show, and test(init_proof$_D$, W'') = true, then $H \overset{W}{\sim}_{holder} W''$ where Id_H and $h(W)$ are the values contained in init_proof$_D$.*

Proof (Sketch). 1. The correctness of *registered?* is obvious because it is simply an exhaustive search for a similar work over all already registered works.

2. If $H \overset{W}{\sim}_{holder} W''$, the first registered work W to which W'' is similar has been registered by H. Together with the assumption that *init_proof$_D$* is correct, the definition of *test(init_proof$_D$, W'')* immediately implies that it ends with *true*.

3. The acceptability of *init_proof$_D$* implies that a work W indicated in *proof$_H$* has been registered by H. Now *test(init_proof$_D$, W'') = true* implies $W \rightarrow_{sim} W''$. If the similarity test is not an equivalence relation, it further implies that H was the first person to register a work to which W'' is similar. Thus $H \overset{W}{\sim}_{holder} W''$ holds.

Theorem 1 (Correctness of the Generic Protocols). *The protocols for proof of ownership described above fulfil all the requirements from Definition 3.*

Proof (Sketch).

1. (***RU***): This is clear by construction.
2. (***HE***): By the precondition and Lemma 1, *registered?(W)* ends with *false* and thus the registration is successful.
3. (***HA***): This is clear by the initial signatures in both protocols.
4. (***HAD'***): If *show(W'', Id_H, Id_D, •)* ends with *true* for a correct D', then D' must have obtained a correctly signed *init_proof$_D$*. Hence H must have executed *prove(W'', Id_D, proof$_H$)*. Thus H has successfully registered a work W where $h(W)$ occurs in *proof$_H$*. Moreover, D' verifies $W \rightarrow_{sim} W''$ either

by testing that $h(W'')$ is explicitly contained in $proof_H$, or by performing the public similarity test, or by verifying the signed confirmation from RC on this similarity.

5. (**HP**): H has obtained $proof_H$ in $register(W)$ and therefore sends a correctly generated $init\_proof_D$ to D in $prove(W'', proof_H, \bullet)$. If $h(W'')$ is contained in $proof_H$, the correct D immediately accepts. Otherwise it executes $test(init\_proof_D, W'')$, which ends with $true$ by Lemma 1.

6. (**HU**): Let a work W'' with $H \overset{W}{\sim}_{holder} W''$ be given. First, the other party $H^\star \neq H$ cannot use Id_H in $prove(W'', \bullet)$ because of the initial signature. Hence we assume that D obtains $true$ in an execution of $prove(W'', Id_{H^\star}, \bullet)$. For this, it must accept some $init\_proof_D$ including $proof_{H^\star}$. Then either $h(W'')$ must be directly contained in $proof_{H^\star}$ or $test(init\_proof_D, W'')$ must have the result $true$. By Lemma 1 (Parts 1 and 3), both cases would imply $H^\star \overset{\bullet}{\sim}_{holder} W''$, which is impossible.

7. (**DC**): If D obtains the output $true$ in $prove(W'', Id_H, \bullet)$, then it accepted $init\_proof_D$. Furthermore either $h(W'')$ was directly contained in $proof_H$, then $H \overset{W}{\sim}_{holder} W''$ follows immediately, or $test(init\_proof_D, W'')$ has ended with $true$. The latter, together with Lemma 1, also implies $H \overset{W}{\sim}_{holder} W''$.

8. (**DS**): In $show(W'', proof_D)$, D' first accepts $init\_proof_D$ because it only carries out the same tests as D did. Now, if D had accepted the similarity of W'' because $h(W'')$ is contained in $proof_H$ or because it passes the public similarity test with $testinf_W$, then D' accepts by the same criterion. Otherwise D has a signed confirmation from RC, which D' also accepts.

9. (**D'C**): If D' obtains the output $true$ in $show(W'', Id_H, \bullet)$, then it accepted $init\_proof_D$, where $proof_H$ implies that such a work W was successfully registered under Id_H. Then D' either verifies for itself that $W \to_{sim} W''$, or it verifies the signed confirmation of RC. The latter implies that RC has executed $test(init\_proof_D, W'')$ for the same $init\_proof_D$ and W''. Thus Lemma 1 implies that $H \overset{W}{\sim}_{holder} W''$.

Note that RC really has to be trusted: A cheating RC can violate most requirements, e.g., by issuing wrong ownership certificates or cheating in the similarity test. In Section 6 we discuss measures to make RC accountable.

5   Instantiations

We now discuss some instantiations of the generic scheme for proof of ownership. This means that we have to present concrete similarity tests sim_test and corresponding initialization algorithms sim_init. Some possible approaches for defining and testing similarity between two works W_1 and W_2 are:

1. *Exhaustive search:* One defines explicit trivial transformations and performs an exhaustive search over all combinations for a certain depth, trying to derive W_2 from W_1. This test is very simple, but not computationally practical.

2. *Characteristics:* Similar digital works have similar main features. One could compute a kind of signature on these features, here called *characteristics.*[8] Using an appropriate metric one can compare the characteristics of works instead of the works themselves. Works are called similar if their characteristics are close with respect to the defined metric.

3. *Robust watermarks:* Under certain prerequisites, robust watermarks can be applied to test the similarity between works. Assume a work W_1 is first watermarked and later the watermarked version is transformed into a work W_2. Then the similarity between W_1 and W_2 can be tested by detecting the embedded watermark. Note that we only use watermarking as means for testing the similarity relation, not directly for ownership proofs.

4. *Methods for content-based information retrieval:* Content-based retrieval of multimedia data is an intensive research field, e.g., [14,16,13]. It typically yields rather coarse similarity relations that can be combined with others in our context.

A combination of several such automatic similarity tests is possible, and even a hybrid *sim_test* with a human expert, and may produce the best results at reasonable costs. In *registered?* the similarity of one work with all registered works has to be tested. Here a hybrid similarity test may first use information-retrieval methods to efficiently preselect possibly similar works. Afterwards more exact similarity tests should be applied to the remaining works. Finally a human expert may verify the similarity if the certainty of the automatic similarity tests is below a specified threshold.

5.1 Instantiation with Characteristics

Characteristics represent the main features of a work which have a short distance (with respect to a specific metric) for similar works.

One can obtain a similarity test which tests an *equivalence relation* and is *public* by using publicly computable robust characteristics, given by an algorithm *char*, and defining works to be similar if they have the same characteristics. Robustness in this context simply means invariance against certain transformations of the underlying work.[9] An instantiation of the generic scheme may be implemented as follows:

$$W' = W,$$
$$testinf_W = char(W),$$
$$sim\_test(W'', testinf_W) = true \iff char(W'') = testinf_W.$$

---

[8] In the literature such values are called signatures and used for authenticating digital content [11] and database retrieval of multimedia data [19]. However, here the term signature might be confused with cryptographic digital signatures.

[9] We are only aware of the use of characteristics for the purpose of copyright protection in the case of textual data [2,8]. For other types of works, one might use transformation-invariant aspects similar as in watermarking schemes, e.g., the most significant DCT coefficients of images are not much affected by compression.

This also defines *sim_init*: on input W it outputs W' and *testinf$_W$*. Note that the test is indeed public and defines an equivalence relation. Hence we are in the nice case where all ownership proofs can be performed with RC being offline.

However, in practice such characteristics will only be invariant against certain kinds of transformations. Another problem is similar to one with publicly verifiable watermarks [4]: one could continuously compute the characteristics and modify the work until the characteristics have another value. To prevent this kind of attack, *private* characteristics may be used, but this also makes offline ownership proofs of non-original works impossible.

5.2   Instantiation with Watermarks

Here we show how to use a *private*, *non-blind*, and *detectable* watermarking scheme to implement a similarity test. Such watermarking schemes need a private key when inserting a watermark in a work. For watermark detection, one needs the private key, the original work, and the watermark. We use this class of watermarking schemes because they can provide the highest robustness. Any others are easier to apply.

The quality of the resulting similarity test is mainly influenced by the robustness of the watermarking scheme against malicious and non-malicious modifications of the work.

Let the watermarking scheme be given by two algorithms $mark(W, WM_W, sk_W^{WM})$ and $detect(W'', W, sk_W^{WM}, WM_W)$. Here W is the original work, WM_W the watermark to be embedded, sk_W^{WM} a secret watermarking key and W'' the work in which the watermark should be detected.

An instantiation of the generic scheme may be implemented as follows:

$$W' = mark(W, WM_W, sk_W^{WM}),$$
$$simrec_W = (W, WM_W, sk_W^{WM}),$$
$$sim\_test(W'', simrec_W) = detect(W'', W, sk_W^{WM}, WM_W).$$

The algorithm *sim_init*, on input W, chooses WM_W and sk_W^{WM} and computes W' and *simrec$_W$* as above. To enable fast lookup of registration records, *sim_init* may also generate a unique record identifier reg_id_W, which is output as *testinf$_W$*.

Such a similarity relation defined by watermarking is somehow unnatural because "really" similar works that have been created independently and even equal works are not considered similar. A work W'' is only considered similar to a work W if it was generated by applying certain transformations to the watermarked version W'. However, this similarity test is suitable for ownership proofs on (maliciously) modified works and to prevent the registration of imitations.

An alternative that leads to a more natural similarity relation is to use an *invertible* (see [5]) watermarking scheme and let RC *remove* the watermark from W. The resulting *fake* original should be used instead of W as the reference work in the detection process, while W itself can now play the role of W'.

Note that a cheating D who wants to remove a watermark from a work W' cannot misuse the two-party tests with RC as an oracle for trying out many variants of W', since RC only executes *test* if H certifies by $init\_proof_D$ that she really initiated an ownership proof with D for a certain W''. Alternatively, this adversary might try to use RC as an oracle by attempting to register many variants of W', until such a registration is successful. However, RC may limit the number of unsuccessful registrations of a user and even accuse him of plagiarism because the presence of the watermark is most likely not by accident.

6   Accountability of the Registration Center

So far we considered ownership proof systems where the registration center is fully trusted by the other parties. Looking through the functions of RC in the generic protocols, a cheating RC could

1. refuse a registration, after obtaining the original work, claiming that a similar work has already been registered by another user $H^\star$,
2. issue an incorrect ownership certificate, which will not be accepted in ownership proofs,
3. collude with a cheater $H^\star$ and issue him an ownership certificate for an already registered work, or
4. return a wrong *test* result in the *prove* protocol.

To make RC accountable, we extend the registration protocol such that RC has to commit to the content of its local memory mem_{RC}.[10] Concretely, we use authentication trees [12] for the content of mem_{RC} and let RC bind itself to these trees by signing the corresponding roots. The extended registration protocol is shown in Figure 5 and will now be explained step by step. We omit the signatures of H on its messages.

Step 1: H initiates the protocol by sending a commitment $com = commit(W)$ to the original work W to RC.

Step 2: RC replies with an acknowledgment

$$receipt = sign_{RC}(Id_H, com, root_{T_{pub}}, root_{T_{record}}),$$

where $root_{T_{pub}}$ and $root_{T_{record}}$ are the roots of two *authentication trees* T_{pub} and T_{record}. The leaves of T_{pub} are the public test information $testinf_{W_i}$ of all the works W_i currently registered, and the leaves of T_{record} the entire registration records rec_{W_i} for these works. In order to later allow also H in person to convince himself that some W_i is similar to his new work, one should include a possibly downgraded version of W_i' in $testinf_{W_i}$.[11]

---

[10] The problem is that in general RC needs the original work W to carry out the similarity tests, i.e., before it can promise that it will accept this work as new. However, once it has W, it could construct a similar work and claim that this is older. Hence we let RC fix the older works, but without showing them. This is what a commitment achieves, see [1].

[11] One may include W_i' itself, but this is inadequate for situations where H may be an attacker who has licensed a low-quality copy W of W_i' and should not obtain the high-quality version W_i'. In this case, only reduced-quality or visibly watermarked versions should be used.

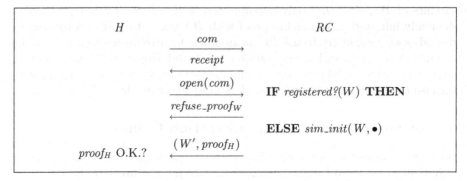

Fig. 5: The extended *register* protocol, which makes *RC* accountable

Step 3: *H* opens the commitment *com*, i.e., sends *W* and verification data.

Step 4: *RC* runs the local *registered?* algorithm.

a) If *RC* finds a similar registered work W_i, it has to prove this fact to *H*. For this it sends *H* the proof string

$$refuse\_proof_W = sign_{RC}(testinf_{W_i}, authpath(i, root_{T_{pub}}), receipt).$$

where $authpath(i, root_{T_{pub}})$ denotes the authentication path to the *i*-th leaf in the tree with this root.

b) Otherwise *RC* performs $sim\_init(W, \bullet)$ and sends the work W' and the ownership certificate

$$proof_H = sign_{RC}(Id_H, h(W), h(W'), testinf_W, root'_{T_{record}}, reg\_time, reg\_text),$$

to *H*. The new component $root'_{T_{record}}$ denotes the root of the record authentication tree augmented by the record rec_W for the newly registered work.

Disputes: Next we discuss how the additional measures in the extended registration protocol make *RC* accountable for the above-mentioned cheating possibilities.

1. By sending the signed $root_{T_{pub}}$ to *H*, *RC* commits to the public information about already registered works before *H* shows her original work *W*. To refuse the registration of *W*, *RC* has to find a similar work W_i and prove to *H* that $testinf_{W_i}$ was contained in the tree T_{pub} before *RC* obtained *W* by showing the authentication path from $testinf_{W_i}$ to $root_{T_{pub}}$.

   If *H* does not accept $refuse\_proof_W$, i.e., if she does not immediately see the similarity to the version of W'_i included in $testinf_{W_i}$ and if the automatic similarity test is private, she can initiate a trial. There, a judge *J* requests the registration record rec_{W_i} from *RC* and asks *RC* to authenticate it by showing $authpath(i, root_{T_{record}})$. This is why $root_{T_{record}}$ was included in the signature *receipt*. Then *J* can test whether *W* is really similar to W_i by performing the same sim_test algorithm as *RC* performs in the normal case; all the necessary inputs are contained in rec_{W_i}.

2. If H finds out that RC has issued a wrong ownership certificate to her, she may start a trial in which the judge verifies the certificate by requesting the authentic registration record rec_W from RC.
3. If the rightful copyright holder H finds out that there has been a fake ownership proof with a second certificate, she can initiate a trial. In the trial the judge requests RC to show the authenticated records corresponding to these two certificates and verifies whether RC has performed the algorithm *registered?* correctly.
4. RC may cheat in the 2-party *test* protocol, by returning a wrong result to D. If H suspects RC of cheating in the *test* protocol, she can initiate a trial in which RC has to show all registration records rec_{W_i} up to rec_W to J and authenticate them by $authpath(i, root'_{T_{record}})$. This enables J to execute *test* himself and verify the result given by RC.[12]

Note that even in this scheme, a cheating registration center may violate the requirements of an ownership proof system. However, our protocols then end with a trial and in the worst case with an ownership dispute, where any honest third party J will decide in favour of the rightful copyright holder.

7   Conclusion

We have presented the first general model for proof of ownership of digital works. We have discussed the advantages of proving the ownership over resolving the ownership in disputes. A significant issue is that the ownership of digital works refers not only to the original work, but also to similar works. We have defined the requirements on ownership proof schemes and proposed generic protocols for them based on arbitrary similarity tests of digital works for the case where the registration center is trusted. We have also discussed the case where the trust in the registration center is reduced and introduced measures for making a cheating registration center accountable. We have shown concrete instantiations of the generic scheme by using characteristics and watermarks.

Acknowledgments: We would like to thank Michael Steiner for fruitful discussions and comments.

References

1. Gilles Brassard, David Chaum, Claude Crépeau: Minimum Disclosure Proofs of Knowledge; Journal of Computer and System Sciences Vol. 37, 1988, pp. 156-189. 130
2. Sergey Brin, James Davis, Hector Garcia-Molina: Copy Detection Mechanisms for Digital Documents; 1995 ACM SIGMOD International Conference on Management of Data, ACM SIGMOD Record Vol. 24, No. 2, 1995, pp. 398-409. 128

---

[12] To also enable D to hold RC accountable for cheating in *test*, RC additionally has to apply public timestamping techniques (e.g., [6]) to $root_{T_{record}}$.

3. Ingemar J. Cox, Joe Kilian, Tom Leighton, Talal Shamoon: A Secure, Robust Watermark for Multimedia; Information Hiding, LNCS 1174, Springer-Verlag, Berlin, 1996, pp. 185-206. 117

4. Ingemar J. Cox, Paul M. G. Linnartz: Some General Methods for Tampering with Watermarks, IEEE Journal on Selected Areas in Communications, Vol. 16, No. 4, May 1998, pp. 587-593. 129

5. Scott Craver, Nasir Memon, Boon-Lock Yeo, Minerva M. Yeung: Resolving Rightful Ownerships with Invisible Watermarking Techniques: Limitations, Attacks, and Implications; IEEE Journal on Selected Areas in Communications, Vol. 16, No. 4, May 1998, pp. 573-586. 129

6. Stuart Haber, W. Scott Stornetta: How to time-stamp a digital document; Journal of Cryptology, Vol. 3, No. 2, 1991, pp. 99-111. 132

7. Frank Hartung, Martin Kutter: Multimedia Watermarking Techniques; Proceedings of the IEEE, Vol. 87, No. 7, July 1999, pp. 1079-1107. 117

8. Nevin Heintze: Scalable Document Fingerprinting; 2nd USENIX Workshop on Electronic Commerce, 1996, pp. 191-200. 128

9. Alexander Herrigel, Joseph Ó Ruanaidh, Holger Petersen, Shelby Pereira, Thierry Pun: Secure Copyright Protection Techniques for Digital Images; Information Hiding, LNCS 1525, Springer-Verlag, Berlin, 1998, pp. 169-190. 117

10. M. Kutter: Watermarking resisting to translation, rotation and scaling; Proc. of SPIE, Multimedia systems and applications, Boston, USA, 1998, pp. 423-431. 117

11. Ching-Yung Lin, Shih-Fu Chang: Generating Robust Digital Signature for Image/Video Authentication; Multimedia and Security Workshop at ACM Multimedia 98, Bristol, UK, Sep. 1998.
    Available at http://www.ctr.columbia.edu/ cylin/pub/acmmm98.ps. 128

12. Ralph C. Merkle: Protocols for Public Key Cryptosystems; Proc. 1980 IEEE Symposium on Security and Privacy, Oakland, CA, USA, pp. 122-134. 130

13. Ruggero Milanese, Michel Cherbuliez, Thierry Pun: Invariant Content-Based Image Retrieval Using the Fourier-Mellin Transform; International Conference on Advances in Pattern Recognition, Springer-Verlag, Berlin, 1999, pp. 73-82. 128

14. Greg Pass, Ramin Zabih, Justin Miller: Comparing Images Using Color Coherence Vectors; Proc. 4th ACM Multimedia Conference, Boston, ACM Press, New York 1996, pp. 65-73 128

15. Lintian Qiao, Klara Nahrstedt: Watermarking Methods for MPEG Encoded Video: Towards Resolving Rightful Ownership; International Conference on Multimedia Computing and Systems, Austin, Texas, USA, 1998, pp. 276-285. 117

16. S. Ravela, R. Manmatha: Image Retrieval by Appearance; Proc. 20th Annual International ACM SIGIR Conference on Research and Development in Information Retrieval, 1997, pp. 278-285. 128

17. Thomas J. Smedinghoff, Ed.: Online Law; Addison Wesley, 1996. 119

18. Mitchell D. Swanson, Mei Kobayashi, Ahmed H. Tewfik: Multimedia Data-Embedding and Watermarking Technologies; Proceedings of the IEEE, Vol. 86, No. 6, June 1998, pp. 1064-1087. 117

19. H. Wang, F. Guo, D. D. Feng, J. S. Jin: A Signature for Content-Based Image Retrieval Using a Geometrical Transform; Proc. 6th ACM International Conference on Multimedia, ACM Press, New York 1998, pp. 229-234. 128

20. W. Zeng, B. Liu: On resolving rightful ownerships of digital images by invisible watermarks; Proc. International Conference on Image Processing, Vol. I, St. Barbara, CA, USA, October 1997, pp. 552-555. 117

Error- and Collusion-Secure Fingerprinting for Digital Data

Hans-Jürgen Guth and Birgit Pfitzmann

Universität des Saarlandes,
Saarbrücken, Germany
guth@krypt.uni-sb.de
pfitzmann@cs.uni-sb.de

Abstract. Fingerprinting means making copies of the same data identifiable by hiding additional information (a fingerprint) in the data. Embedding the additional data can be done by watermarking techniques, which are mainly a branch of signal processing. Most watermarking methods, however, do not treat colluding adversaries who have obtained more than one copy, compare their copies, see differences and use this information to make a copy without a fingerprint. Therefore, there are cryptographic fingerprinting methods to obtain collusion tolerance on top of a watermarking layer. But the most important fingerprinting method by Boneh and Shaw excludes a priori any errors on the watermarking layer, i.e., it is assumed that no changes to the fingerprint occur except those based on the information from collusion attacks. This is a stronger assumption than what most underlying watermarking schemes offer.
This assumption can be justified by making each individual mark fault-tolerant on the watermarking layer, e.g., by replication, but that would imply a significant increase in the data size needed. Instead, here we implement the fault tolerance more efficiently on the cryptographic layer by generalizing Boneh and Shaw's fingerprinting methods. Our remaining assumption on the underlying watermarking is quite reasonable for watermarking methods that would be built according to the best currently known principles.

Keywords: Fingerprinting, watermarking, collusions, errors, marking assumption, probabilistic method, copyright protection, fault tolerance.

1 Introduction

Alice wants to communicate confidentially with her partners Bob, Chris, Dominique and a few others to discuss a problem on her new research project. But she cannot rely on all of them not to forward her e-mail, which includes many expensively measured data, to a competitor company. If one or more of her partners does so and she hears of that, i.e., finds her data somewhere where she has not sent it, she wants to identify at least one of the original persons who has given away a copy of her data to claim compensation.

A. Pfitzmann (Ed.): IH'99, LNCS 1768, pp. 134–145, 2000.

1.1 Fingerprinting

Now Alice does not send exactly the same data to any two persons. This presupposes that the transmitted data can be changed in some way without changing its meaning. The changes are embedded extra information and called fingerprint. We do not deal with the embedding (watermarking) process in detail in this paper. However, we concentrate on methods for digital data, and we aim at schemes that are provable under reasonable assumptions; see Section 3.2.

The main problem in fingerprinting (beyond those of watermarking) is that it requires *collusion tolerance*. If two or more recipients of the data work together, they can compare their copies, see differences and get some information about the fingerprint. Then they can try to mask the identity of a new copy of the same data much better than by changing the data at random only.[1] In the sequel, the former is called *collusion (attack)*, the latter *error (attack)*.

If the fingerprints have a code length of l bits, it must be decided from application to application whether l bits can be embedded into the data. Actually, collusion-tolerant codes are long and may not be feasible for some mass applications. However, the above example shows that there are also real applications with a small number of copies, and highly valuable data that is worth the effort of fingerprinting.

Note that Alice, as long as she uses a symmetric protocol as described here, cannot prove anything and therefore cannot claim compensation. But the existence and practicability of a symmetric protocol is a requirement for all known asymmetric protocols [13,14,2].

1.2 Previous Work

In their 1986 paper [3], Blakley, Meadows and Purdy give a construction for a fingerprint that has exponential length in the size of the collusions and is error-tolerant by replication of the marks.

Boneh and Shaw [4,5] give a construction that has about cubic length. They require a marking assumption, which excludes errors, i.e., no single mark (the encoding of one bit of the code), must be destroyed by errors. This could again be achieved by replicating the marks, i.e., essentially on the underlying watermarking layer, but our schemes will be much more efficient. More details about this class of schemes are given in Section 2.1.

Cox et al. [8] propose a fingerprinting scheme in a different model (independent components and Euclidean distance as the measure of similarity) instead of under the marking assumption. The collusion tolerance is proven in this model in [10] and lower bounds in [9]. This scheme yields shorter fingerprints where the model applies. The relation between the models has not been fully explored yet, but the usage of the Euclidean distance seems to be a stricter assumption

---

[1] Here "random changes" includes tricky transformations suitable for the data domain: Unless those destroy a fingerprint completely, they typically result in random changes on the fingerprint level, at least if the fingerprint was randomly placed in the available positions in the data.

than the marking assumption. In particular the model does not seem applicable to abstract content like text or programs.

2   Basic Concepts and the Marking Assumption

For example, let $w^{(1)} = 10101110$ and $w^{(2)} = 01000000$ be binary words which are used as fingerprints and are each embedded in a longer stream of data. Assume that Bob receives the data stream with $w^{(1)}$ in it and Dominique the one with $w^{(2)}$, and that they know that both are fingerprinted versions of the same original. So they can collude and construct a word $w^{(1,2)}$ from $w^{(1)}$ and $w^{(2)}$ by setting $w^{(1,2)}$ to an arbitrary value at every bit position that they have seen in $w^{(1)}$ or $w^{(2)}$. In the example, they can obtain every word with a zero in its fourth and eighth position. In general, if they have a set of words C, the set of words they can construct in this way is defined as $F(C)$ and called the *feasible set of the coalition* C.

Every bit position that they cannot change in this way, because they see no differences there, is called an *undetectable bit position*.

Now Boneh and Shaw's marking assumption is: Undetectable bit positions are not changed by a coalition.

The underlying embedding in digital data is usually done by a kind of spread-spectrum method: Certain coefficients of the data (usually after a transformation into a frequency domain) are chosen according to public criteria. They must be neither redundant nor imperceptible so that an adversary cannot simply delete them altogether. Then a small percentage of them is selected secretly and randomly, and those are used for the actual embedding.[2]

Fully realizing the marking assumption on this layer would require a significant amount of fault tolerance because standard transformations might change some of these coefficients. Thus, even for a very small error rate, one would have to replicate each bit a number of times. Note that if the scheme were used for pure watermarking, one could use a better error-correcting code for the embedded information; but that would not be compatible with using a separate collusion-tolerant coding on top (i.e., with the notion of undetectable bits). This is why we integrate the error tolerance on the fingerprinting layer.

---

[2] Most current products and prototypes are broken [12]; see also [11] for an overview. However, the attacks mainly exploit that these prototypes lack any preprocessing to realign the redistributed data. Hence the case is not hopeless, in particular if the unmarked original is available during extraction as in our case, see [11]. Pattern matching for substrings, low-level features etc. should go a long way. For high-value data even manually assisted methods can be used. On the other hand, watermarking is likely to always retain its status as a game of wits and resources, because any real theory of undetectability must be based on a probability space of all "possible" data items (in reality and according to the a priori knowledge of the adversary). This will usually be impossible to determine.

2.1 Existing Solutions under the Marking Assumption

Under the marking assumption several types of solutions exist, given that n copies shall be distinguished altogether:

1. *n-frameproof* codes guarantee that no copy is identified falsely [4,7,16,15].
2. *Totally secure* codes additionally guarantee that it is impossible to make a copy that cannot be identified. However, these codes do not exist if collusions of size of at least $n/2$ are considered [15,4].
3. With *n-secure* codes, it is impossible to make a copy that cannot be identified, and it is only possible with a probability of at most ϵ_I (first-order error) to make a copy that will be falsely identified [4].

All goals can also be restricted to collusions of a maximum size c among the n overall copies [3,4]. We will consider both the case with $c = n$ and the case with a smaller c.

3 An *n*-Secure Error-Tolerant Code

We now construct an n-secure code that does not need the marking assumption. Obviously, we still need *some* requirements on the underlying watermarking scheme (discussed in detail below) but these are much less stringent. Essentially one assumption is that the adversary cannot exceed a certain error rate in the fingerprint without decreasing the data quality so much that the data owner no longer cares. The other assumption is that errors are distributed approximately randomly among the bits of the fingerprint. The latter is not even an assumption if the fingerprint was originally placed randomly in the available marks.

In our scheme, there is also a small probability of at most ϵ_{II} (second-order error) that no copy can be identified. Just like ϵ_I, it can be made exponentially small in the code parameters. We show an alternative that has $\epsilon_{II} = 0$ in Section 5. However, we prefer the model in this section because of the following advantage: If the error rate does exceed the assumed maximum, the consequence is that no copy is identified. In contrast, in all current schemes with $\epsilon_{II} = 0$, the consequence is that an honest person is wrongly identified, which seems far worse.

3.1 The Code

For this construction, see also Figure 1. The number of copies to be identified and distinguished is n. Every codeword, respectively fingerprint of a copy, consists of $n + 1$ blocks, and each block contains only ones or only zeros. The first block, B_0, consists of d_0 bits, which are all zero. This block is the same in every codeword, and so it is undetectable for arbitrary coalitions. Similarly, the last block, B_n, consists of d_n bits, which are all one in every codeword. The blocks B_1 to B_{n-1} are the same as in the n-secure code by Boneh and Shaw, only their lengths d_1 to d_{n-1} have to be adjusted to the new circumstances, which requires to reconsider the security including the errors.

Copy	B_0	B_1	B_2	B_3	B_4	B_5
		Blocks of the error- and collusion-tolerant code				
			Blocks of the collusion-tolerant code			
1	0 0 0	1 1 1	1 1 1	1 1 1	1 1 1	1 1 1
2	0 0 0	0 0 0	1 1 1	1 1 1	1 1 1	1 1 1
3	0 0 0	0 0 0	0 0 0	1 1 1	1 1 1	1 1 1
4	0 0 0	0 0 0	0 0 0	0 0 0	1 1 1	1 1 1
5	0 0 0	0 0 0	0 0 0	0 0 0	0 0 0	1 1 1

Fig. 1. The error- and collusion-tolerant code for the example $n = 5$ and $d_i = 3$ for $0 \leq i \leq n$.

Thus the fingerprint of the m-th copy has only ones in every block B_k for $k \geq m$, and only zeros in the other blocks. As mentioned before, the bit positions of the codewords are assumed to be mapped into the available marking positions in random order. (Of course this order must be the same for all codewords for one data item.)

3.2   The Identification Mechanism

To identify a found copy, the data owner tests for each pair of adjacent blocks B_{s-1} and B_s whether they contain approximately the same number of ones. If this is not the case, Copy s is identified. This means that it is said that the owner of Copy s, which is the only copy in which the two blocks are distinguishable, must have taken part in the redistribution.

This is essentially as in [4], except that they have a different test for their edge blocks B_1 and B_{n-1}, while we use our new edge blocks B_0 and B_n only in the parameter estimation. The reason for our use of B_0 and B_n is that they are not affected by a collusion attack, because their bits are undetectable in every case. Only errors change their bits in the same way as the whole data stream. Therefore we have reference values for our test of adjacent blocks.

The test on adjacent blocks can be seen as a normal statistical test for the following hypothesis, which holds if information from Copy s has not been used to generate a word and the underlying watermarking scheme has certain properties:

Hypothesis: The Hamming weights w_{s-1}, w_s of Blocks B_{s-1}, B_s are distributed like the result of the following random experiment: An urn contains $d_s + d_{s-1}$ balls (the positions in the two blocks). Among them are $w_s + w_{s-1}$ "success balls" (the ones); i.e., this sum is fixed in the experiment while w_{s-1} and w_s individually are not. We draw d_s balls without putting them back (the bits for Block B_s) and call the number of drawn "success balls" w_s.

This is the standard random experiment for the hypergeometric distribution, which we denote by $\mathcal{H}(w_{s-1} + w_s, d_{s-1}, d_s)$. One of our two assumptions can now be made precise:

Assumption 1: The hypothesis is correct for the case where the adversary does not have Copy s.

This means that changes due to both detected bits and errors are distributed equally between the bits of two adjacent blocks. If the underlying watermarking scheme chooses the positions for the bits of the code randomly among the available marks, this is not even an assumption, but guaranteed. On the physical level it means that every block is a representative sample of bits of the word with regard to all "serious" transformations or changes of the data.

The following test therefore achieves a first-order error of ϵ_I:

Test: For $s = 1, \ldots, n$: Given the weights w_{s-1} and w_s of Blocks B_{s-1} and B_s of length d_{s-1} and d_s, let X be a random variable that is hypergeometrically $\mathcal{H}(w_{s-1} + w_s, d_{s-1}, d_s)$-distributed. Let b_s be a value such that

$$P(X > b_s) \leq \epsilon_I.$$

Then Copy s is identified if and only if

$$w_s > b_s.$$

The test is as tight as possible if b_s is minimal.

4   Determining the Block Length

As a simplification, we use a uniform block length d for all blocks. Then the expected weight of Block B_s in the hypothesis is $(w_s + w_{s-1})/2$. We therefore express the bounds for the test as $b_s = (w_s + w_{s-1})/2 + a_s$, and simplify this again by using the same $a = a_s$ for all blocks and all joint weights $w_s + w_{s-1}$. The requirement on b_s therefore becomes

$$P\left(w_s - \frac{w_s + w_{s-1}}{2} > a\right) \leq \epsilon_I, \tag{1}$$

and the test becomes

$$w_s > w_{s-1} + 2a. \tag{2}$$

For the second condition, i.e., that no copy at all can be identified with a probability of at most ϵ_{II}, one needs some assumption about errors. Here it is given as maximum bit-error rates p_0 with which a zero changes to a one and p_1 with which a one changes to a zero.[3] The actual number of errors in the edge blocks is then determined by $f_0 = \mathcal{B}(d, p_0)$ for Block B_0 and $f_1 = \mathcal{B}(d, p_1)$ for Block B_n, where $\mathcal{B}$ is the binomial distribution. Our second assumption is therefore:

---

[3] If a bit is not readable or has disappeared (whatever that means for a given embedding scheme), it will be set randomly to one or zero, as with other communication channels.

Assumption 2: The adversary cannot achieve error rates beyond p_0 and p_1 on the fingerprinting level without changing the real data so much that the data owner no longer cares about redistribution.

More precisely, the error rates of the adversary's transformation are defined over all potential positions for marks for the given public fingerprinting algorithm. In order to determine p_0 and p_1 in practice, one has to use information about the individual changeability of the given type of data. For example, information could come from a data-analyzing program or the used embedding software.

4.1   The Worst-Case Attack

The worst case for the second-order error is that all n recipients of copies collude. Then they can detect and distinguish the blocks $B_1, \ldots, B_{n-1}$. The worst they can do is to carry out the following steps:

1. They change the real data as much as possible, i.e., such that the error probabilities p_0 and p_1 on the fingerprinting level result.
2. They withdraw the changes on the detectable bits to make the following steps precise.
3. They choose a value $f_0^* \in \mathbb{N}$ and hope that the actual number f_0 of errors in Block B_0 is at least f_0^*.
4. They put as many ones into Block B_1 as the test (Formula 2) between Blocks B_0 and B_1 allows so that Copy 1 is not identified if indeed $f_0 \geq f_0^*$. As $w_0 = f_0$, this means $w_1 = f_0^* + \lfloor 2a \rfloor$.
5. Similarly, they put as many ones as possible into Block B_s for $s = 2, \ldots, n-1$, i.e., $w_s = w_{s-1} + \lfloor 2a \rfloor$. Hence $w_{n-1} = f_0^* + (n-1)\lfloor 2a \rfloor$.
6. Finally, they can only hope that the test between B_{n-1} and B_n does not identify Copy n, i.e., that $w_n \leq w_{n-1} + \lfloor 2a \rfloor$. Here $w_n = d - f_1$, where f_1 is the actual number of errors in Block B_n.

We now have to make d so large that the success probability of this attack is bounded by ϵ_{II} even for the adversary's optimal choice of f_0^*.

4.2   Bounds on the Parameters

First we determine the bound a for the test, i.e., one that fulfils Formula (1). For this, the hypergeometric distribution is first replaced by the binomial distribution as in [4]. Hence the calculated a, and thus d, is larger than actually needed. Then the Chernoff bound is used, which states that for a $\mathcal{B}(n, p)$-distributed random variable X and $a > 0$

$$P(X - np > a) < e^{\frac{-2a^2}{n}} \tag{3}$$

(see [1], Theorem A.4 and the preceding remark). For our case, this means

$$P\left(w_s - \frac{w_s + w_{s-1}}{2} > a\right) < e^{\frac{-2a^2}{d}} \quad \text{for } a > 0.$$

Hence the following condition is sufficient:

$$e^{\frac{-2a^2}{d}} \leq \epsilon_I \iff \frac{2a^2}{d} \geq -\ln \epsilon_I \iff a \geq \sqrt{-\frac{d}{2} \ln \epsilon_I}. \tag{4}$$

We saw that the worst-case attack succeeds if $f_0 \geq f_0^*$ and $w_n \leq w_{n-1} + \lfloor 2a \rfloor$. The second condition means

$$d - f_1 \leq f_0^* + (n-1)\lfloor 2a \rfloor + \lfloor 2a \rfloor \iff f_1 \geq d - f_0^* - n\lfloor 2a \rfloor.$$

As the expected values of f_0 and f_1 are dp_0 and dp_1, we write the adversary's choice of f_0^* as

$$f_0^* = dp_0 + a_0$$

and our choice of d as

$$d = dp_0 + n\lfloor 2a \rfloor + dp_1 + a^* \tag{5}$$

with $a^* > 0$. Then the adversary's success conditions become

$$f_0 - dp_0 \geq a_0 \quad \text{and} \quad f_1 - dp_1 \geq a^* - a_0 =: a_1.$$

The two events are independent, and thus the adversary's success probability is

$$P_{adv} = P(f_0 - dp_0 \geq a_0)P(f_1 - dp_1 \geq a_1).$$

If $a_0 > 0$, we can use the Chernoff bound from Equation 3 for any $a_0 > a_0' > 0$ and obtain

$$P(f_0 - dp_0 \geq a_0) < e^{\frac{-2a_0'^2}{d}}$$

and thus also

$$P(f_0 - dp_0 \geq a_0) \leq e^{\frac{-2a_0^2}{d}}.$$

If $a_0 \leq 0$, we bound the probability by 1. The bounds for f_1 are analogous. The adversary maximizes P_{adv} under the constraint $a_0 + a_1 = a^*$ by setting $a_0 = a_1 = a^*/2$. Thus it is sufficient if

$$e^{\frac{a^{*2}}{d}} \leq \epsilon_{II} \iff a^* \geq \sqrt{-d \ln \epsilon_{II}}.$$

Setting a to its minimum value from Formula (4) and substituting a^* according to Formula (5), the last inequality becomes

$$d(1 - p_0 - p_1) - n\lfloor \sqrt{-2d \ln \epsilon_I} \rfloor \geq \sqrt{-d \ln \epsilon_{II}}.$$

Hence it is sufficient to choose

$$d > \frac{1}{(1 - p_0 - p_1)^2} \left(n\sqrt{-2 \ln \epsilon_I} + \sqrt{-\ln \epsilon_{II}} \right)^2.$$

4.3   Comparison

As an example of what this means in practice, consider the case $\epsilon = \epsilon_I = \epsilon_{II}$ and $p = p_0 = p_1$. Then we need

$$d > \frac{1}{(1-2p)^2}\,(\sqrt{2n}+1)^2(-\ln\epsilon).$$

For $p_0 = p_1 = 0$, the d calculated here is essentially identical with the d in [4]. Hence we see that our code length grows gradually with the bit error rate, starting with the usual length for the error-free case. In contrast, any repetition code for the individual marks would lead to an expansion by at least a factor of 3 even for very low error rates.

5   Alternative without Second-Order Error

In this section, we show an alternative to the previous section where $\epsilon_{II} = 0$ as with the original Boneh-Shaw scheme. However, recall from the introduction to Section 3 that this alternative has another disadvantage.

Now we stay even closer to Boneh and Shaw's scheme: We omit our edge blocks and treat the blocks B_1 and B_{n-1} separately again. With the marking assumption, one was able to assume that any one in Block B_1 identifies Copy 1, and any zero in Block B_{n-1} identifies Copy $n-1$. We now code only the edge blocks with an error-correcting code (ECC) to allow a similar reasoning. Unfortunately, most ECCs are not collusion-tolerant. Hence only a repetition code seems appropriate. To code only one bit of information ("Copy 1 identified" or not, and similarly for Copy $n-1$), it is even optimal in order to correct as many errors as possible.

The maximum number of errors occurring is again estimated using the Chernoff bound. For that, the bit-error rates p_0 and p_1 must be known. Here the problem comes in that the merchant does not know the actual error rates used and thus, if they exceed the assumed rates, he will identify a wrong copy. (In the other scheme, this case was noticed and no identification was made.) If one wanted to add measures to estimate the actual error rates, it seems one would have to send a codeword through this "communication channel" without admitting collusion attacks. But this seems to lead to our undetectable edge blocks again, i.e., to the code proposed in Section 3.

The algorithm for identifying at least one copy is the following:

1. **Test of the edge blocks B_1 [respectively B_{n-1}]:**
   If B_1 [B_{n-1}] contains at least $dp_0 + \sqrt{-\frac{d}{2}\ln\epsilon_{II}}$ ones [$dp_1 + \sqrt{-\frac{d}{2}\ln\epsilon_{II}}$ zeros], Copy 1 [Copy n] is identified.
2. **For all blocks B_s with $2 \le s \le n-1$:**
   Let X be a hypergeometric $\mathcal{H}(w_{s-1}+w_s, d_{s-1}, d_s)$-distributed random variable. If
   $$P(X \ge w_s) \le \epsilon_I,$$
   then Copy s is identified.

Corollary 1. *For*

$$d > \frac{1}{(1 - p_0 + p_1)^2} (\sqrt{2n} + 1 - 2\sqrt{2})^2 (- \ln \epsilon_I)$$

the code is n-secure with a first-order error of ϵ_I, under the same assumptions as in Sections 3 and 4.

The proof is almost identical to that in Section 4.2.

6   An Error-Tolerant c-Secure Code for $c < n$

We now want to construct a code Γ_2 that is shorter if the maximum number c of copies used for making an untraceable copy is much smaller than the overall number of copies, which is now called N. Again we can follow the approach from [4] quite closely; we only have to deal with the additional error probabilities. Some words of an n-secure code Γ (here called inner code) with $n > c$ are concatenated. An outer (L, N)-code K specifies which ones they are.

The N words of K are n-ary, of length L, and are chosen secretly, independently and with uniform distribution. Each digit specifies which word of the inner code has to be concatenated according to the following construction:

Construction. *Let $\Gamma = \{w^{(1)}, w^{(2)}, \ldots, w^{(n)}\}$ be an n-secure code of length l and $n > c$.*
For all $v = v_1 v_2 \ldots v_L \in K$ let $W_v = w^{(v_1)} \| w^{(v_2)} \| \ldots \| w^{(v_L)}$, where $\|$ means concatenation. Then the code Γ_2 is

$$\Gamma_2 = \{W_v \mid v \in K\}.$$

Now we describe the algorithm for identification.

Input: Parameters n, L, N, and a found word $w = w_1, \ldots, w_L$ where $w_L \in \{0, 1\}^l$ for $1 \leq i \leq L$.
Output: A number of an identified copy or a message that nothing has been identified.

1. Use the identification mechanism of the inner code Γ to identify digits $x_1, \ldots, x_L \in \{1, \ldots, n\}$. The resulting word is called x in the sequel, and each of its digits a *component*. If this identification is not possible (due to the second-order error of the test or due to too many errors), output a message like "We apologize for not identifying a copy" and stop.
2. Find the word $v \in K$ that agrees with x in the largest number of digits.
3. Output the number of the copy that belongs to v.

Theorem 1. *To build a c-secure code Γ_2 with a first-order error of ϵ_I and a second-order error of ϵ_{II} according to the description above, it suffices that*

$$L \geq \frac{c \ln \frac{2}{\epsilon_I}}{\frac{c}{n} - 1 + \ln \frac{n}{c}},$$

where the first- and second-order error $\epsilon_{I,n}$ and $\epsilon_{II,n}$ of the underlying n-secure code must be chosen such that

$$\epsilon_{I,n} \leq \frac{\epsilon_I}{2L(n-1)}$$

and

$$\epsilon_{II,n} \leq \frac{\epsilon_{II}}{L}.$$

Proof (Sketch): One component can be identified, perhaps falsely, with probability $1 - \epsilon_{II}/L$. Thus, all L components can be identified with probability at least $1 - \epsilon_{II}$. Therefore, the second-order error is ϵ_{II} at most.

The rest is similar to the proof in [4]: Let C be the coalition, or equivalently its set of codewords from K. We say that a component is falsely identified if it is given a value that no codeword in C had. Each component is falsely identified as any specific value with probability at most $\frac{\epsilon_I}{2L(n-1)}$, the first-order error of the n-secure code. There are $(n-1)$ possible wrong values. Therefore all L components are correct with probability at least $1 - \frac{\epsilon_I}{2}$.

The coalition C consists of at most c elements and therefore a word $v \in C$ must exist that agrees with x in at least $\frac{L}{c}$ positions. On the other hand, as each v' is chosen randomly, a word v' from $K \setminus C$ agrees with x only in $\frac{L}{n}$ positions on average. One can use the Chernoff bound (as in [6]) to determine a value of L so that the probability that x agrees with v' in at least $\frac{L}{c}$ positions is smaller than $\frac{\epsilon_I}{2}$. The value for L is the one from the theorem.

Altogether, the first-order error of the c-secure code is $1 - (1 - \frac{\epsilon_I}{2})^2 \leq \epsilon_I$.

7   Conclusion

We have constructed fingerprinting methods that are secure against both errors and collusions and more efficient than simple realizations of the marking assumption (see the end of Section 4). Nevertheless, there is still a tradeoff between implementing robustness on the watermarking layer and error tolerance in the code. The most important open questions therefore concern the actual combination of the codes presented here with embedding methods, in particular estimating the actual bit error rates that result from tolerable data modifications in different watermarking methods.

Acknowledgments

We thank Ahmad-Reza Sadeghi and Michael Waidner for helpful discussions.

References

1. N. Alon and J. Spencer. *The probabilistic method*. J. Wiley and Sons, New York, 1992. 140

2. I. Biehl and B. Meyer. Protocols for collusion-secure asymmetric fingerprinting. In *STACS 97, Lecture Notes in Computer Science, vol. 1200*, pages 399–412, Berlin, 1997. Springer-Verlag. 135

3. G. R. Blakley, C. Meadows, and G. B. Purdy. Fingerprinting long forgiving messages. In *CRYPTO '85, Lecture Notes in Computer Science, vol. 218*, pages 180–189, Berlin, 1986. Springer-Verlag. 135, 137

4. D. Boneh and J. Shaw. Collusion-secure fingerprinting for digital data. In *CRYPTO '95, Lecture Notes in Computer Science, vol. 963*, pages 452–465, Berlin, 1995. Springer-Verlag. 135, 137, 138, 140, 142, 143, 144

5. D. Boneh and J. Shaw. Collusion-secure fingerprinting for digital data. *IEEE Transactions on Information Theory*, pages 1897–1905, 1998. 135

6. B. Chor, A. Fiat, and M. Naor. Tracing traitors. In *CRYPTO '94, Lecture Notes in Computer Science, vol. 839*, pages 257–270, Berlin, 1994. Springer-Verlag. 144

7. Y. M. Chee. Turan-type problems in group testing, coding theory and cryptography. Ph. d. thesis, University of Waterloo, Waterloo, Canada, 1996. 137

8. I. Cox, J. Kilian, F. T. Leighton, and T. Shamoon. A secure, robust watermark for multimedia. In *Information hiding: first international workshop, Lecture Notes in Computer Science, vol. 1174*, pages 185–208, Berlin, 1996. Springer-Verlag. 135

9. F. Ergun, J. Kilian, and R. Kumar. A Note on the Limits of Collusion-Resistant Watermarks. In *EUROCRYPT '99, Lecture Notes in Computer Science, vol. 1592*, pages 140–149, Berlin, 1999. Springer-Verlag. 135

10. J. Kilian, T. Leighton, L. R. Matheson, T. G. Shamoon, R. E. Tarjan, and F. Zane. Resistance of digital watermarks to collusive attacks. *Technical report TR-585-98*, Department of Computer Science, Princeton University, 1998. 135

11. L. R. Matheson, S. G. Mitchell, T. G. Shamoon, R. E. Tarjan, and F. Zane. Robustness and security of digital watermarks. In *2nd International Conference on Financial Cryptography, Lecture Notes in Computer Science, vol. 1465*, pages 227–240, Berlin, 1998. Springer-Verlag. 136

12. F. A. P. Petitcolas, R. J. Anderson, and M. G. Kuhn. Attacks on copyright marking systems. In *Information Hiding: 2nd international workshop, Lecture Notes in Computer Science, vol.1525*, pages 218–238, Berlin, 1998. Springer-Verlag. 136

13. B. Pfitzmann and M. Schunter. Asymmetric fingerprinting. In *EUROCRYPT '96, Lecture Notes in Computer Science, vol. 1070*, pages 84–95, Berlin, 1996. Springer-Verlag. 135

14. B. Pfitzmann and M. Waidner. Asymmetric fingerprinting for larger collusions. In *4th ACM Conference on Computer and Communications Security*, pages 151–160, New York, 1997. acm press. 135

15. D. R. Stinson, T. van Trung, and R. Wei. Secure frameproof codes, key distribution patterns, group testing algorithms and related structures. Submitted to Journal of Statistical Planning and Inference, version from http://cacr.math.uwaterloo.ca/~dstinson/index.html#pubs, November 1997. 137

16. D. R. Stinson and R. Wei. Combinatorial properties and constructions of traceability schemes and frameproof codes. *SIAM J. on Discrete Mathematics*, pages 41–53, 1998. 137

Computing the Probability of False Watermark Detection*

Matt L. Miller and Jeffrey A Bloom

Signafy, Inc.,
4 Independence Way, Princeton, NJ 08540

Abstract. Several methods of watermark detection involve computing
a vector from some input media, computing the normalized correlation
between that vector and a predefined watermark vector, and comparing
the result against a threshold. We show that, if the probability density
function of vectors that arise from random, unwatermarked media is a
zero-mean, spherical Gaussian, then the probability that such a detector
will give a false detection is given exactly by a simple ratio of two definite
integrals. This expression depends only on the detection threshold and
the dimensionality of the watermark vector.

1 Introduction

Digital data hiding, also referred to as digital watermarking, is the practice of
making imperceptible changes in digitized media to hide messages. A basic watermarking system consists of a watermark embedder and a watermark detector
(see figure 1). In general, the inputs to the embedder are a message to be hidden
and some media in which to hide it, such as an audio stream, an image, or a
video stream. The output of the embedder is media that is perceptually very
similar to the input media, but contains the input message as a hidden watermark. The input to the detector is some media that may or may not contain
the watermark. The detector's output is a judgment about whether or not a
watermark is present in its input, along with the message that the watermark
contains.

Several applications of such invisible watermarking systems have been suggested. These include identifying the content creator, identifying the content
recipient in a transaction, monitoring broadcast and publication channels for
tracking purposes, assuring that the media item is an authentic, unmodified
copy of the original, and restricting the use of media to avoid illegal duplication.
These applications of watermarking are discussed in more detail in [1].

Recently, watermarking systems have begun to be considered for widespread
deployment as parts of copy-protection systems. Primarily for protection of video
or audio media, watermarks would be used in addition to encryption techniques.
Standardization movements that will likely involve watermarking include efforts

---

* The authors are now with NEC Research Institute, 4 Independence Way, Princeton,
NJ, 08540.

A. Pfitzmann (Ed.): IH'99, LNCS 1768, pp. 146–158, 2000.

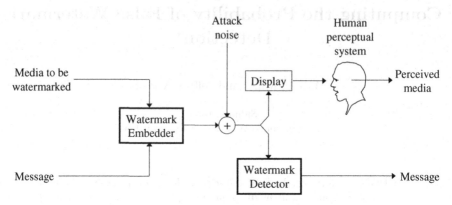

Fig. 1. Typical Watermarking System

by the Copy Protection Technical Working Group to protect DVD video [2], efforts by a group of 4 companies (IBM, Intel, Matsushita, and Toshiba) working through the DVD forum to protect DVD audio, and an effort by the Recording Industry Association of America (RIAA) through its Secure Digital Music Initiative (SDMI) to protect music distributed on the internet [3].

A critical issue for many applications is the probability that the watermark detector incorrectly identifies some unwatermarked media as containing a watermark. Such an error can lead to the mistaken prevention of a legitimate operation. For example, in the case of DVD copy protection, the presence of a watermark on a RAM disk will prevent that disk from being played on a DVD player. If the watermark is really there, this is the correct behavior, since copy protected video that appears on a home-recordable disk must have been copied illegally. But if the detection is false and the video does not really contain a watermark, then it is a legal copy and should have been playable. A false watermark detection could thus prevent people from watching their legitimate home recordings and would be viewed as an equipment malfunction. For this reason, the probability of false detection should be as low as the probability of malfunction in consumer electronics equipment.

The required probability of false detections can be extremely low in some applications. The Consumer Electronics Manufacturer's Association (CEMA) has set the requirement for DVD at roughly one false detection in 10^{10} seconds - roughly 300 years - of unwatermarked video. Such probabilities are too low to be verified by experimentation, so it is necessary to estimate the false detection behavior of a given detector analytically.

The problem of analyzing false detection behavior has received little attention in the literature. Linnartz and Kalker have made an in-depth analysis of the probability of false detection in an image watermarking method [4]. Hernández and Pérez-González include false detection probability in their framework for discussing watermarking systems [5]. Stone analyzed the behavior of watermark detectors that use the correlation coefficient as a detection metric [6] and his analysis was applied to a specific video watermarking system by McKellips [7].

In the present paper, we analyze the behavior of watermark detectors that use correlation coefficient as their detection metric. In section 2 we give a basic framework for watermark detectors and discuss possible detection metrics that they can use. Section 3 reviews two earlier methods for estimating the probabilities of false detection when the detection metric is correlation coefficient. Section 4 gives our method, which is exact under a single, reasonable assumption. Finally, section 5 shows the results of experimental simulations, and section 6 offers conclusions and discusses future work.

2   Watermark Detection

The probability of false watermark detection is determined by the design of the watermark detector and the distribution of media processed by it. The embedding algorithm is not relevant to computing this probability, because we assume that no watermark has been embedded (otherwise a detection would not be false). We therefore begin by describing a generic framework for watermark detection and will not discuss embedding.

Figure 2 shows a basic design for a watermark detector. The input media is first processed by a watermark extractor which generates an n-dimensional extracted vector, V. Examples of watermark extraction include various combinations of spatial registration [8], frequency transforms [9,10,11], block averaging [12,13], spectral shaping [14,15], whitening [16], and subtraction of the unwatermarked original media [9,17]. Reasons for applying these processes include the following: increasing robustness to certain common types of attack, increasing signal-to-noise ratio, reducing the size of data to make detection cheaper, and generating vectors that are well distributed for standard detection measures.

The extracted vector is then compared against an n-dimensional watermark vector W, to obtain a detection measure C. In our analysis we assume that the detector uses a single watermark vector, which is a predefined constant. When used in a typical application, a watermark detector may check the extracted vector against multiple watermark vectors and decode the resulting detection measures into one of several possible messages. The effect of this decoding process on the probability of a false detection is usually a straightforward function of the probability of obtaining a false detection with only one watermark vector. Thus, when we limit our analysis to a single watermark vector, we obtain a result that is widely useful for computing false detection rates of real detectors with multiple watermark vectors.

Finally, the detection measure is compared against a threshold T, and the result of this comparison determines whether the detector reports that the watermark is present or not. Generally, larger C indicates greater probability that the watermark is present, so the detector reports a detection if $C > T$.

The exact formula used for computing the detection measure is critical to determining the probability of false detection. Three types of measure are corre-

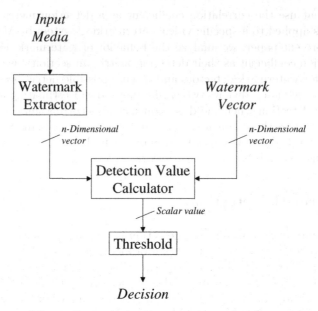

Fig. 2. Basic design for a watermark detector

lation, correlation coefficient, and a slight variant of correlation coefficient that we refer to as simply normalized correlation.

Correlation: The correlation measure is computed as

$$C_c = W \cdot V = \sum_i w_i v_i. \tag{1}$$

This type of detection measure is known to be optimal for certain types of communications channels, which suggests its use for watermark detection. However, it is argued in [5] and [18] that a watermark in digital media behaves very differently from those communications channels for which correlation is optimal. Furthermore, if we are to calculate the probability of false detection resulting from the use of correlation, we need to know the variance of the elements of vectors extracted from random media. This variance is difficult to obtain with enough precision to guarantee the kinds of extremely low probabilities required in many applications.

The probability of false detections resulting from an image watermark detector using correlation is analyzed in detail in [4]. This detection measure will not be considered further in the present paper.

Correlation Coefficient: To remove dependence on the variance of extracted vector elements, we can use the correlation coefficient, which is defined as

$$C_{cc} = \frac{\tilde{W} \cdot \tilde{V}}{\sqrt{\left(\tilde{W} \cdot \tilde{W}\right)\left(\tilde{V} \cdot \tilde{V}\right)}} \qquad (2)$$

where

$$\tilde{W} = W - \bar{W}, \qquad (3)$$
$$\tilde{V} = V - \bar{V}. \qquad (4)$$

This differs from correlation by subtracting out the means of V and W, and dividing by the product of their standard deviations. The latter difference makes a qualitative change in the behavior of detection values which, as will be shown in section 4, causes the false detection probability to be independent of the variances of the extracted watermark elements.

Normalized Correlation: A detection measure that is simpler than correlation coefficient is obtained by not subtracting out the means of V and W. This yields

$$C_{nc} = \frac{W \cdot V}{\sqrt{(W \cdot W)(V \cdot V)}} \qquad (5)$$

We refer to this measure as *normalized correlation*.

If we restrict W to have variance of exactly 1, then this detection metric is equivalent to the one used in [9], namely

$$C'_{nc} = \frac{W \cdot V}{\sqrt{V \cdot V}}. \qquad (6)$$

Since $W \cdot W$ is a constant n, these two metrics differ only by a constant factor of $\sqrt{n}$ and their behaviors are the same.

For the sake of simplicity, the analysis presented in section 4 concentrates only on normalized correlation. However, we can apply the same analysis to correlation coefficient by observing that subtracting the means from V and W amounts to projecting them into an $(n\text{-}1)$-dimensional subspace. The correlation coefficient is then just the normalized correlation, computed in this subspace. Thus, the analysis of section 4 will apply equally well to both normalized correlation and correlation coefficient, with the proviso that the dimensionality, n, be replaced with $n-1$ when computing the probability of false detections using correlation coefficient.

3   Approximate Methods of Computing Probability of False Detections

Two approximate methods have been used in the past to estimate the probability of false detections when using normalized correlation or correlation coefficient as a detection measure. Both of these rely on the assumption that the elements of watermarks extracted from unwatermarked media are drawn from identical, independent distributions.

3.1   Approximate Gaussian Method

The simplest method, which we will refer to as the approximate Gaussian method, is to treat the distribution of normalized correlations as a Gaussian with standard deviation $1/\sqrt{n}$. If n is large, then the body of the distribution is very similar to a Gaussian. Thus, we can approximate the false detection probability as

$$P_{fd} \approx \operatorname{erfc}\left(T\sqrt{n}\right) = \int_{T\sqrt{n}}^{\infty} \frac{1}{\sqrt{2\pi}} e^{-\frac{x^2}{2}} \, dx. \tag{7}$$

For relatively low thresholds, and relatively high false detection probabilities, this approximation can be quite accurate. However, as the threshold increases out into the tails of the distribution, we begin to dramatically overestimate the probability of false detections. This is clear from the fact that the normalized correlation is bounded between plus and minus 1. Thus, if T is higher than 1, the true probability of a false detection (or, indeed, any detection at all) is zero. But the approximation based on assuming a Gaussian distribution yields a non-zero probability.

3.2   Fisher Z-statistic Method

A more accurate approximation is described in [6], and employed in [7]. This relies on the Fisher Z-statistic [19], computed from the correlation coefficient as

$$Z = \frac{1}{2} \log \frac{1+C}{1-C}. \tag{8}$$

When elements of V are drawn from identical, independent, Gaussian distributions, the values of Z form an approximately Gaussian distribution with standard deviation[1] $1/\sqrt{n-2}$. If we assume the distribution of Z is truly Gaussian, then we can estimate the probability of false detection by

$$P_{fd} \approx \operatorname{erfc}\left(T_Z\sqrt{n-2}\right), \tag{9}$$

where

$$T_Z = \frac{1}{2} \log \frac{1+T}{1-T}. \tag{10}$$

This approximation is much more accurate than the approximate Gaussian method. However, as will be shown in section 5, it begins to underestimate the probability of false detections as the threshold approaches one.

---

[1]   In [6], the standard deviation was given as $1/\sqrt{n-3}$. The difference is because Stone was analyzing correlation coefficient, which has one fewer dimension than normalized correlation.

4 Exact Method of Computing Probability of False Detections

In this section, we develop a new method for computing the probability of false detections when using normalized correlation or correlation coefficient. We begin with a single assumption about the distribution of vectors extracted from random, unwatermarked media:

> *Assumption: the probability density function (PDF) of vectors extracted from unwatermarked media is radially symmetric.*

In other words, we assume that the relative likelihood of a given vector being extracted from unwatermarked media is dependent only on the vector's length, and independent of the vector's direction.

While the above assumption is true for many distributions, the most plausible such distribution in a watermark detector is the one that arises when the elements of extracted vectors are drawn from identical, zero-mean, independent, Gaussian distributions. This yields an n-spherical Gaussian. Thus, the above assumption can be seen as essentially the same as the assumption that underlies the Z-statistic method of approximating probability of false detections.

Next, we simplify the PDF by scaling the extracted vectors to unit length before computing the detection measure. The scaled, extracted vector will be denoted V' and is defined as

$$V' = \frac{V}{\sqrt{V \cdot V}}. \tag{11}$$

Observe that V' yields a detection if, and only if, V yields a detection, since

$$C_{nc} = \frac{W \cdot V'}{\sqrt{(W \cdot W)(V' \cdot V')}} = \frac{W \cdot V'}{\sqrt{W \cdot W}} = \frac{W \cdot V}{\sqrt{(W \cdot W)(V \cdot V)}}. \tag{12}$$

So the probability of false detections is unaffected by the introduction of this scaling step. Every V' lies on the unit n-sphere and has the same likelihood of occurring as any other V' because of the radial symmetry of the PDF for V.

Now, we turn our attention to a geometric interpretation of the detection region defined by a given watermark vector W, and a given threshold T. Since

$$\frac{W \cdot V'}{\sqrt{(W \cdot W)(V' \cdot V')}} = \cos\alpha, \tag{13}$$

where α is the angle between W and V', we can replace the threshold on normalized correlation between W and V' with a threshold on the angle between them:

$$C > T \Longleftrightarrow \alpha < T_\alpha, \tag{14}$$

where

$$T_\alpha = \cos^{-1} T. \tag{15}$$

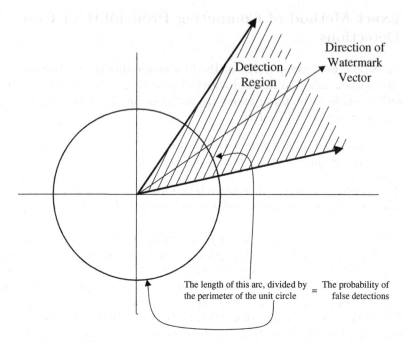

Fig. 3. Two dimensional detection region

This means that the detection region is an n-cone that subtends an angle of $2T_\alpha$. Figure 3 illustrates the 2-dimensional case. It shows the unit 2-sphere (circle), upon which V' is uniformly distributed, together with the detection region for a given watermark vector and T. Figure 4 is the same diagram for the 3-dimensional case.

The probability of false detections is given by dividing the $(n$-1)-content of the unit n-sphere's surface into the $(n$-1)-content of the intersection of the surface with the detection region. The following derivation of the resulting equation is obtained from [20].

The $(n$-1)-content of the intersection between an n-cone and the surface of an n-sphere is given by

$$\mathrm{Cap}(n, \theta) = S_{n-1} I_{n-2}(\theta) \tag{16}$$

where θ is half the angle subtended by the n-cone, and where

$$S_d = \frac{d\pi^{\lfloor d/2 \rfloor}}{\lfloor d/2 \rfloor!} \tag{17}$$

and

$$I_d(\theta) = \int_0^\theta \sin^d(u) du \tag{18}$$

for any d.

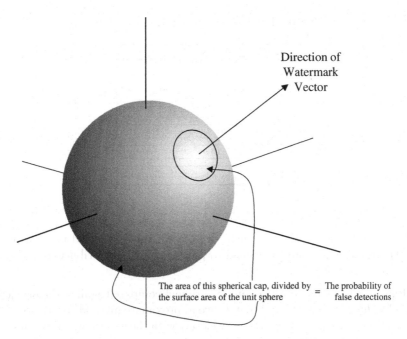

Direction of
Watermark
Vector

The area of this spherical cap, divided by $=$ The probability of
the surface area of the unit sphere   false detections

Fig. 4. Three dimensional detection region

Note that $\mathrm{Cap}(n, \frac{\pi}{2})$ is half the $(n\text{-}1)$-content of the surface of the unit n-sphere. Thus, the ratio of the portion of the surface that is within the detection region to the whole surface and hence, the probability of a false detection, is given by

$$P_{fd} = \frac{\mathrm{Cap}(n, T_\alpha)}{2\mathrm{Cap}(n, \frac{\pi}{2})} = \frac{I_{n-2}(T_\alpha)}{2I_{n-2}(\frac{\pi}{2})} \tag{19}$$

where T_α is as defined in equation 15.

To compute this probability, we need to evaluate the function $I_d(\theta)$. Table 1 shows the closed-form solutions for $d = 1$ through $d = 5$. Values of $I_d(\theta)$ for $d > 5$ can be computed by means of the recursive formula at the bottom of this table.

5   Results

To verify that the formula derived in section 4 is correct, we compared its predictions against results obtained from over a billion synthetic vectors drawn from a radially symmetric, pseudorandom distribution. Each vector had 10 elements $(n = 10)$. This dimensionality gives high enough false detection rates that we can obtain reasonable statistics from a billion trials. It also shows the differences between predictions made using the new method and using the two approximate

Table 1. Closed-form solutions for $I_d(\theta)$

d	$\mathbf{I_d}(\theta)$
0	θ
1	$1 - \cos(\theta)$
2	$\dfrac{\theta - \sin(\theta)\cos(\theta)}{2}$
3	$\dfrac{\cos^3(\theta) - 3\cos(\theta) + 2}{3}$
4	$\dfrac{3\theta - \left(3\sin(\theta) + 2\sin^3(\theta)\right)\cos(\theta)}{8}$
5	$\dfrac{4\cos^3(\theta) - \left(3\sin^4(\theta) + 12\right)\cos(\theta) + 8}{15}$
≥ 6	$\dfrac{d-1}{d}I_{d-2}(\theta) - \dfrac{\cos(\theta)\sin^{d-1}(\theta)}{d}$

methods of section 3. Each element of a vector was generated using a pseudo-random number generator designed to produce normal distributions [21] with 0 mean and unit variance.

Figure 5 shows the results of our experiment compared against the predictions made by the new method and by the two approximate methods of section 3. The new method's predictions match very closely with the experimental results, while the approximate methods quickly deviate from them.

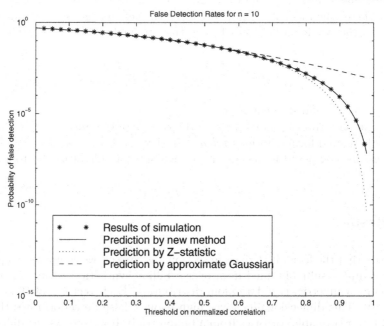

Fig. 5. False detection rates for various thresholds, watermark vector length 10

In figures 6 and 7, we explore the relationship between the new method and the two approximate methods for vectors with more elements. It is clear that, at higher thresholds, the approximate Gaussian method tends to overestimate the false detection probabilities, while the Z-statistic method tends to underestimate false detection probabilities, though providing closer approximations to the exact result obtained with the new method. However, when the threshold is low, all three methods give very similar results, regardless of the dimensionality of the vectors. Thus, the approximate methods may be acceptable when a low threshold is predicted to yield the desired false detection rate, either because the desired rate is relatively high, or because the vectors are long. The new method is to be preferred when the detection threshold must be set at a higher level.

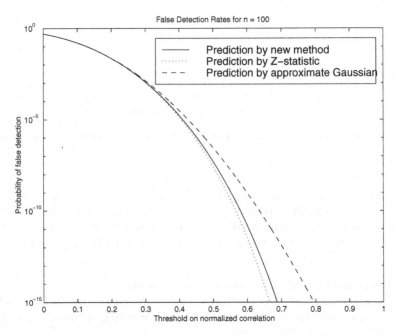

Fig. 6. False detection rates for various thresholds, watermark vector length 100

6   Conclusion and Future Work

In this paper, we have presented a formula (equation 19) for the probability that a watermark detector will report false detections, if the watermark detector uses normalized correlation as its detection measure. This formula holds exactly if the distribution of vectors extracted from unwatermarked data is radially symmetric, which is the case when the elements of the vectors are drawn from independent, identical, zero-mean Gaussian distributions.

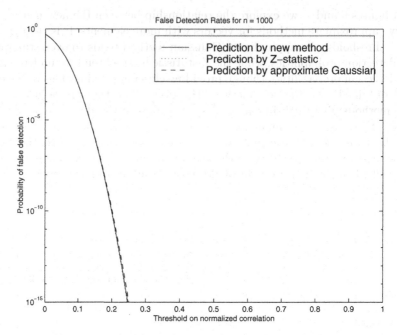

Fig. 7. False detection rates for various thresholds, watermark vector length 1000

Of course, in an actual application, the distribution of extracted vectors is unlikely to be prefectly symmetric. Thus, the next problems to be studied are the effects of other types of distributions on the probability of false detections. In particular, we expect that real distributions can differ from symmetric distributions in the following ways:

- The elements of extracted vectors can be correlated.
- In a watermark detector that uses integer arithmetic, the elements of the vectors are quantized. This results in a joint probability distribution that is quantized to a rectilinear grid.
- In most systems, the possible values in extracted watermarks are bounded. This means that the probability distribution is bounded by an n-cube.

We plan to address these questions in the future.

Acknowledgements

The authors are grateful to Dr. Warren Smith and Dr. Harold Stone for their helpful discussions and insights.

References

1. I.J. Cox, M. Miller, J-P. Linnartz, and T. Kalker. A review of watermarking principles and practices. In K.K. Parhi and T. Nishitani, editors, *Digital Signal Processing for Multimedia Systems*, chapter 17. Marcel Dekker, Inc., 1999.
2. J. A. Bloom, I. J. Cox, T. Kalker, J-P. Linnartz, M. L. Miller, and B. Traw. Copy protection for DVD video. *Proceedings of the IEEE Special Issue on Identification and Protection of Multimedia Information*, 87:1267–1276, 1999.
3. Secure digital music initiative. *http://www.riaa.com/tech/sdmiinfo.htm*.
4. J-P. Linnartz, T. Kalker, and G. Depovere. Modelling the false alarm and missed detection rate for electronic watermarks. *Proc. Second International Workshop on Information Hiding*, pages 329–343, 1998.
5. Juan Ramón Hernández and Fernando Pérez-González. Shedding more light on image watermarks. In David Aucsmith, editor, *Information Hiding 1998*, pages 191–207. Springer-Verlag, 1998.
6. Harold S. Stone. Analysis of attacks on image watermarks with randomized coefficients. *Tech. Rep. 96-045, NEC Research Institute, Princeton, NJ*, 1996.
7. Andrew McKellips. Watermark detection false positive analysis. *Signafy Technical Report, TR-118*, 1997.
8. Geoffrey B. Rhoads. Image steganography system featuring perceptually adaptive and globally scalable signal embedding. *U S Patent 5,748,763*, 1998.
9. I.J. Cox, J. Kilian, T. Leighton, and T. Shamoon. Secure spread spectrum watermarking for multimedia. *IEEE Trans. Image Proc.*, 6(12):1673–1687, 1997.
10. C. I. Podilchuk and W. Zeng. Image-adaptive watermarking using visual models. *IEEE Trans. on Selected Areas of Communications*, 16(4):525–539, 1998.
11. J. J. K. O'Ruanaidh, W. J. Dowling, and F. Boland. Phase watermarking of digital images. *Proc. ICIP 96*, pages 239–242, 1996.
12. Ton Kalker, Geert Depovere, Jaap Haitsma, and Maurice Maes. A video watermarking system for broadcast monitoring. *Proc. SPIE*, 3657 Security and Watermarking of Multimedia Contents:103–112, 1999.
13. I. J. Cox and K. Tanaka. *NEC data hiding proposal*. Technical report, NEC Copy Protection Technical Working Group. Response to call for proposal issued by the Data Hiding SubGroup. Available at http://www.dvcc.com/dhsg, July, 1997.
14. Ingemar J. Cox, Matt L. Miller, Kazuyoshi Tanaka, and Wakasu. Digital watermarking. *U S Patent filed November 5, 1996*, 1996.
15. R. D. Preuss, S. E. Roukos, A. W. F. Huggins, H. Gish, M. A. Bergamo, P. M. Peterson, and D. A. G. Embedded signalling. *U S Patent 5,319,735*, 1994.
16. Geert Depovere, Ton Kalker, and J-P Linnartz. Improved watermark detection reliability using filtering before correlation. *Proc. ICIP 98*, pages 430–434, 1998.
17. M. D. Swanson, B. Zhu, and A. H. Tewfik. Transparent robust image watermarking. *Proc. ICIP 96*, pages 211–214, 1996.
18. Ingemar J. Cox, Matt L. Miller, and Andrew L. McKellips. Watermarking as communications with side information. *Proceedings of the IEEE Special Issue on Identification and Protection of Multimedia Information*, 87:1127–1141, 1999.
19. H. D. Brunk. *An introduction to mathematical statistics*. Ginn and Company, 1960.
20. Warren D. Smith. *Studies in computational geometry motivated by mesh generation*. Ph.D. Thesis, Applied Mathematics, Princeton University, 1988.
21. J.H. Ahrens and U. Dieter. Extensions of Forsythe's method for random sampling from the normal distribution. *Math. Comput.*, 27:927–937, 1973.

Optimum Decoding of Non-additive Full Frame DFT Watermarks

Alessia De Rosa[1], Mauro Barni[2], Franco Bartolini[1],
Vito Cappellini[1], and Alessandro Piva[1]

[1] Department of Electronic Engineering, University of Florence
Via di Santa Marta 3, 50139 - Florence, Italy
Tel:+39 055 4796380, Fax:+39 055 494569
derosa@lci.die.unifi.it
[2] Department of Information Engineering, University of Siena
Via Roma 56, 53100 - Siena, Italy

Abstract. The problem of optimum watermark recovery in a non additive, non Gaussian framework is addressed. Watermark casting is carried out on the frequency domain according to an additive-multiplicative rule. The structure of the optimum decoder is derived based on statistical decision theory. The Neyman-Pearson criterion is used to minimize the probability of missing the watermark for a given false detection rate. Experimental results highlights the superiority of the novel detector scheme with respect to conventional correlation-based decoding.

1 Introduction

Digital watermarking has recently received great attention as a tool for copyright protection. The watermarking process can be seen as a communication task consisting of two main steps: *watermark casting*, in which the watermark is transmitted over the channel the host data acts the part of (the watermark-channel), and *watermark detection*, in which the signal is received and extracted from data; from this point of view the image itself is considered as channel-noise. In many image watermarking techniques watermark casting is based on additive algorithms operating either in the spatial or in the frequency domain and the watermark-channel is often modeled as an AWGN channel. Under these hypotheses optimum detection, in the sense of minimizing the error probability, is achieved through correlation-based decoding, as described in [1,2].

As a matter of fact, the embedding rule is not always additive, and the Gaussian approximation is not verified in most practical cases, so that correlation-based detector is not optimum. In this paper, a new optimum technique to retrieve the watermark inserted in a digital image is presented. Watermark casting, described in the next section, operates in the DFT domain following an additive-multiplicative embedding rule. Watermark extraction, presented in section 3, is performed without resorting to the original image; note that the watermark channel is assumed to be neither additive nor Gaussian. Statistical channel modeling is obtained in section 4, and the model used in section 5 to actually implement the optimum decoder. In section 6 experimental results are presented and discussed, which support the validity of the method.

A. Pfitzmann (Ed.): IH'99, LNCS 1768, pp. 159–171, 2000.

2   Watermark Casting

According to the approaches proposed by Cox et al. [3] and Barni et al. [4], watermark embedding is achieved by modifying a set of full-frame transformed coefficients of the image. In particular, aiming at making our system translation-invariant, we propose to modify the magnitude of DFT coefficients instead of those of the DCT [5][6]. The amount of modification each coefficient undergoes is proportional to the magnitude of the coefficients itself as expressed by the following rule:

$$y_i = x_i + \gamma m_i |x_i|, \tag{1}$$

where x_i indicates the original coefficient, y_i the marked coefficient, m_i the i-th component of the watermark, i accounts for the position of the marked coefficient within the frequency spectrum, and γ is a parameter controlling the watermark strength. In the case of DFT watermarking, equation (1) is rewritten as:

$$y_i = x_i + \gamma m_i x_i, \tag{2}$$

where x_i denotes the magnitude of the i-th DFT coefficient, and y_i the corresponding marked magnitude. The watermark consists of a pseudo-random sequence of N real numbers $\{m_1, m_2, \ldots m_N\}$; each value m_i being a uniformly-distributed, zero mean random number. Since the magnitude of the marked coefficients y_i has to be non-negative, it must be guaranteed that:

$$|\gamma m_i| < 1. \tag{3}$$

Hence, we will assume that m_i's take values in the finite interval $[-1, 1]$, and $\gamma \leq 1$: the last condition is also necessary to ensure the perceptual invisibility of the watermark.

Since watermark detection is performed without resorting to the non-marked image (blind detection), the mark is always inserted in the same set of coefficients. In Fig. 1 the region of the DFT spectrum the watermark is embedded in is depicted. In particular, to account for the symmetry properties of the DFT magnitude spectrum, the coefficients to be modified are those between the k-th and the $(k + n)$-th diagonal in the first quadrant and the corresponding symmetricals in the second quadrant: these regions are then duplicated in the third and fourth quadrants.

To enhance the robustness of the watermark, the characteristics of the Human Visual System are often exploited to adapt the watermark to the image being signed through perceptual masking [7]. In the following section the structure of the optimum decoder is derived without taking into account neither visual masking nor the presence of attacks aiming at removing the watermark from the image. Instead, the effect of visual masking and attacks on the optimum decoder performance will be investigated experimentally in section 6, where watermark casting is performed by exploiting the masking characteristics of the HVS. Even in this case the optimum decoder results in a superior robustness.

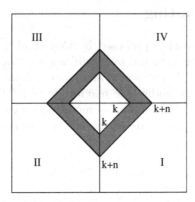

Fig. 1. The marked area of the frequency spectrum: the regions are duplicated to account for the simmetry properties of the magnitude of the DFT spectrum

3   Watermark Detection

During watermark detection we want to verify if a given code is present in an image. Basing on hypothesis testing or decision theory, the problem is one of taking measurements and then estimating in which of a finite number of states the underlying system resides. In particular the analyzed system is the possibly marked image and the system observation variable is the vector $\mathbf{y} = \{y_1, y_2, \ldots y_N\}$ of possibly marked DFT coefficients selected to be marked. We define two possible hypotheses: the system contains a certain parameter, i.e. the watermark $\mathbf{m}^* = \{m_1^*, m_2^*, \ldots m_N^*\}$ (H_1) or the system does not contain this parameter (H_0); consequently the parameter space can be defined as $M = M_0 \cup M_1$, where $M_1 = \{\mathbf{m}^*\}$ and $M_0 = \{\mathbf{m}_j \neq \mathbf{m}^*\}$, including $\mathbf{m} = \mathbf{0}$. We look for a test of the simple hypothesis H_1 versus the composite alternative H_0 that is optimum with respect to a criterion.

3.1   The Likelihood Ratio

In Bayes theory of hypothesis testing, the criterion is minimum Bayes risk, where Bayes risk is defined as the average of a loss function with respect to the joint distribution of the measurement $\mathbf{y}$ and the parameter $\mathbf{m}$ [8]. The decision rule Φ maps each $\mathbf{y}$ into 0 or 1, corresponding to H_0 or alternative H_1:

$$\Phi(\mathbf{y}) = \begin{cases} 1 & , \quad \mathbf{y} \in S_1 \quad (H_1 \text{ is in force}) \\ 0 & , \quad \mathbf{y} \in S_0 \quad (H_0 \text{ is in force}) \end{cases}, \tag{4}$$

where S_0 e S_1 are acceptance and rejection regions for H_0.

The set S_1 or, equivalently, the test $\Phi(\mathbf{y})$ are selected so that the Bayes risk is minimized:

$$S_1 = \{\mathbf{y} : \ f_{\mathbf{Y}}(\mathbf{y}|M_1)/f_{\mathbf{Y}}(\mathbf{y}|M_0) > p_0 L_{01}/p_1 L_{10}\}, \tag{5}$$

and

$$\Phi(\mathbf{y}) = \begin{cases} 1, & f_{\mathbf{Y}}(\mathbf{y}|M_1)/f_{\mathbf{Y}}(\mathbf{y}|M_0) > p_0 L_{01}/p_1 L_{10} \\ 0, & \text{otherwise} \end{cases}, \qquad (6)$$

where $f_{\mathbf{Y}}(\mathbf{y}|M)$ is the pdf of the random variable $\mathbf{Y}$; $p_0 = P(\mathbf{m} \subset M_0)$ and $p_1 = P(\mathbf{m} \subset M_1)$ are the a priori probabilities of H_0 and H_1; $L_{01} = L[M_0, \Phi(\mathbf{y}) = 1]$ and $L_{10} = L[M_1, \Phi(\mathbf{y}) = 0]$ are the losses substained when a hypothesis is in force and we decide for the other.

The term $f_{\mathbf{Y}}(\mathbf{y}|M_1)/f_{\mathbf{Y}}(\mathbf{y}|M_0)$ is called likelihood ratio

$$\ell(\mathbf{y}) = \frac{f_{\mathbf{Y}}(\mathbf{y}|M_1)}{f_{\mathbf{Y}}(\mathbf{y}|M_0)} = \frac{f_{\mathbf{Y}}(\mathbf{y}|\mathbf{m}^*)}{f_{\mathbf{Y}}(\mathbf{y}|M_0)}, \qquad (7)$$

whereas the term $p_0 L_{01}/p_1 L_{10}$ is the threshold λ: if the likelihood ratio exceeds the threshold, then H_1 is accepted, otherwise H_0 is accepted.

The pdf $f_{\mathbf{Y}}(\mathbf{y}|M_0)$ is:

$$f_{\mathbf{Y}}(\mathbf{y}|M_0) = f_{\mathbf{Y}}(\mathbf{y}|\mathbf{m}_1)f(\mathbf{m}_1) + \ldots + f_{\mathbf{Y}}(\mathbf{y}|\mathbf{m}_P)f(\mathbf{m}_P) \qquad (8)$$

$$= \sum_{j=1}^{P} f_{\mathbf{Y}}(\mathbf{y}|\mathbf{m}_j)f(\mathbf{m}_j),$$

where $f(\mathbf{m}_j) = \prod_{i=1}^{N} f(m_{j,i})$, because watermark components are statistically independent, and $f(m_{j,i})$ is the pdf of the i-th component of the j-th watermark and P is the number of watermarks in M_0. According to the assumptions that watermark components are uniformly distributed in $[-1; 1]$, M_0 consists of an infinite number of watermarks, and $f_{\mathbf{Y}}(\mathbf{y}|M_0)$ can be written as:

$$f_{\mathbf{Y}}(\mathbf{y}|M_0) = \int_{[-1,1]^N} f_{\mathbf{Y}}(\mathbf{y}|\mathbf{m})f(\mathbf{m})d\mathbf{m}. \qquad (9)$$

By assuming that a given DFT coefficient y_i depends only on the corresponding watermark component m_i, and that DFT coefficients are independent each other, for the integral (9) the following expression can be used:

$$\int_{[-1,1]^N} f_{\mathbf{Y}}(\mathbf{y}|\mathbf{m})f(\mathbf{m})d\mathbf{m} = \qquad (10)$$

$$= \int_{-1}^{1} \ldots \int_{-1}^{1} f_{Y_1}(y_1|m_1) \ldots f_{Y_N}(y_N|m_N)f(m_1) \ldots f(m_N)dm_1 \ldots dm_N$$

$$= \int_{-1}^{1} f_{Y_1}(y_1|m_1)f(m_1)dm_1 \ldots \int_{-1}^{1} f_{Y_N}(y_N|m_N)f(m_N)dm_N$$

$$= \prod_{i=1}^{N} \int_{-1}^{1} f_{Y_i}(y_i|m_i)f(m_i)dm_i = \prod_{i=1}^{N} \frac{1}{2} \int_{-1}^{1} f_{Y_i}(y_i|m_i)dm_i.$$

Hence, the likelihood function can be expressed as:

$$\ell(\mathbf{y}) = \frac{f_{\mathbf{Y}}(\mathbf{y}|\mathbf{m}^*)}{\int_{[-1,1]^N} f_{\mathbf{Y}}(\mathbf{y}|\mathbf{m})f(\mathbf{m})dm} = \frac{f_{\mathbf{Y}}(\mathbf{y}|\mathbf{m}^*)}{\frac{1}{2^N}\prod_{i=1}^{N}\int_{-1}^{1} f_{Y_i}(y_i|m_i)dm_i}. \tag{11}$$

Unfortunately, each i-th integral in the above expression can not be solved analitically, thus calling for a numerical solution. To simplify the decoder, we have developed an approximate decoding algorithm which couple effectiveness and simplicity. The simplified decoder relies on the assumption that the watermark strength γ is much lower than 1. Note that this assumption is verified in virtually all practical applications, since the watermark energy has to be kept low due to the invisibility requirement.

It can be demonstrated that if $\gamma \ll 1$, the i-th integral $\frac{1}{2}\int_{-1}^{1} f_{Y_i}(y_i|m_i)dm_i$ can be approximated by $f_{Y_i}(y_i) = f_{Y_i}(y_i|0)$, that is the pdf conditioned by the null watermark. By repeating the above analysis for all the integrals at the denominator of $\ell(\mathbf{y})$, we can easily prove that

$$f_{\mathbf{y}}(\mathbf{y}|M_0) \simeq f_{\mathbf{y}}(\mathbf{y}|\mathbf{0}). \tag{12}$$

Under this hypothesis, the watermark decoder assumes the form sketched in Fig. 2, where decoding is looked at from the point of view of classical detection theory and considering as the test function the following equation:

$$\ell(\mathbf{y}) = \frac{f_{\mathbf{Y}}(\mathbf{y}|\mathbf{m}^*)}{f_{\mathbf{Y}}(\mathbf{y}|\mathbf{0})}. \tag{13}$$

The signal space is composed by two subspaces containing the given code $\mathbf{m}^*$ and the null code $\mathbf{m} = \mathbf{0}$ respectively. The noise space is constituted by the vector $\mathbf{x}$ with the non-marked coefficients; the observations space contains marked coefficients vector $\mathbf{y}$. The decision rule permits to pass from the observations space to the decision space, which in our case contains two possible alternatives only: the presence and the absence of watermark $\mathbf{m}^*$.

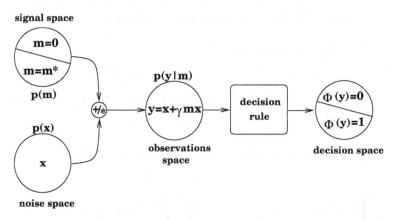

Fig. 2. Watermark detection system

3.2   Threshold Selection

It is important now, for a correct behaviour of the watermark detection system, to properly choose the decision threshold λ. A possible choice considers the minimization of the error probability, that is:

$$P_e = p_0 P_{FA} + p_1 [1 - P_D], \tag{14}$$

where P_{FA} is the probability of revealing the presence of $\mathbf{m}^*$ when $\mathbf{m}^*$ is not actually present (false positive), and $[1 - P_D]$ the probability of missing the presence of the mark (false negative):

$$
\begin{aligned}
P_{FA} &= P[\Phi(\mathbf{y}) = 1 | M_0] = P[\ell(\mathbf{y}) > \lambda | M_0] \tag{15} \\
P_D &= P[\Phi(\mathbf{y}) = 1 | M_1] = P[\ell(\mathbf{y}) > \lambda | M_1].
\end{aligned}
$$

From decision theory [9], it is known that P_e is minimized if $\lambda = 1$, that is $p_0 = p_1 = 1/2$ and $L_{01} = L_{10} = 1$: in such a way $P_{FA} = 1 - P_D$ and the probability of false positive and false negative are the same.

Experimental results show that when the watermark image is attacked the proposed threshold leads to a higher watermark missing rate than was expected [10]. In particular, the probability of missing an embedded watermark results to be considerably higher than the probability of false positive detection. To solve this problem, a different approach to threshold selection is proposed here. Instead of minimizing the error probability P_e, we chose to fix a constraint on the maximum false positive probability (e.g. 10^{-6}). By relying on equation (15) and assuming that ℓ is normally distributed, the situation reported in Fig. 3 is obtained: to minimize P_e the threshold is in the intersection of the two functions; otherwise, given a value for the false positive probability ($P_{FA} = \overline{P_{FA}}$), the corresponding threshold $\overline{\lambda}$ is obtained.

To design the optimum decoder we refer to the Neyman-Pearson criterion, which can be summarize by saying that the optimum test, amongst all the criterions that verify the relation:

$$P_{FA} \leq \overline{P_{FA}},$$

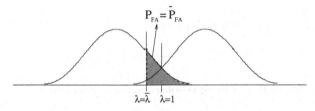

Fig. 3. The pdf's of ℓ under hypotheses H_0 (on the left) and H_1 (on the right): the false positive probability is the area under the tail of pdf of ℓ conditioned to H_0

is the one that minimizes the false negative probability $(1 - P_D)$, or equivalently the one maximizing the correct detection probability P_D [9]. The threshold is computed by solving the following equation:

$$P_{FA} = P[\Phi(\mathbf{y}) = 1|M_0] = P[\ell(\mathbf{y}) > \lambda|M_0] = \int\limits_{\lambda}^{+\infty} f(\ell|M_0)d\ell, \qquad (16)$$

where $f(\ell|M_0)$ is pdf of ℓ under hypotheses H_0 [8]. By fixing $P_{FA} = \overline{P_{FA}}$ and by evaluating the integral (16), the value for λ can be estimated.

The estimation of the pdf of DFT coefficients, that is needed to implement the optimum decoder, is addressed in the following section.

4   Statistical Modeling of DFT Coefficients

For describing the magnitude of the DFT spectrum, what is needed is a parametric pdf which is defined on the positive real axis only, and which is both flexible and easy to handle from mathematical point of view. Parametrization should permit the description of random variables characterized by pdf's with different variance and shape. A possible solution is to describe the DFT coefficients through the Weibull distribution, defined as:

$$f_W(x) = \frac{\beta}{\alpha}\left(\frac{x}{\alpha}\right)^{\beta-1}\exp\left[-\left(\frac{x}{\alpha}\right)^{\beta}\right], \qquad (17)$$

where $\alpha > 0$ and $\beta > 0$ are real-valued positive constants controlling the pdf mean, variance and shape. In particular, the mean and the variance of the Weibull pdf can be expressed as follows:

$$\mu_X = \alpha\Gamma\left(1 + \frac{1}{\beta}\right), \qquad (18)$$

and variance:

$$\sigma_X^2 = \alpha^2\left\{\Gamma\left(1 + \frac{2}{\beta}\right) - \left[\Gamma\left(1 + \frac{1}{\beta}\right)\right]^2\right\} = \alpha^2\Gamma\left(1 + \frac{2}{\beta}\right) - \mu_X^2 . \qquad (19)$$

Limit cases are obtained by letting $\beta = 1$ and $\beta = 2$, when exponential and Rayleigh distribution are obtained respectively.

By relying on watermark rule, the pdf $f_y(y)$ of marked coefficient y subject to a watermark value m can be written as

$$f_Y(y|m) = \frac{1}{1 + \gamma m}f_X\left(\frac{y}{1 + \gamma m}\right). \qquad (20)$$

By inserting equation (17) in equation (20), the pdf of marked DFT coefficients is achieved:

$$f_Y(y|m) = \frac{\beta}{\alpha(1 + \gamma m)}\left(\frac{y}{\alpha(1 + \gamma m)}\right)^{\beta-1}\exp\left[-\left(\frac{y}{\alpha(1 + \gamma m)}\right)^{\beta}\right]. \qquad (21)$$

5   Implementation of the Optimum Decoder

By assuming DFT coefficients $\{y_i\}$ are independent each other and by relying on equation (21), $f_{\mathbf{Y}}(\mathbf{y}|\mathbf{m})$ can be expressed:

$$f_{\mathbf{Y}}(\mathbf{y}|\mathbf{m}) = \prod_{i=1}^{N} f_{Y_i}(y_i|m_i) \tag{22}$$

$$= \prod_{i=1}^{N} \frac{\beta_i}{\alpha_i(1+\gamma m_i)} \left(\frac{y_i}{\alpha_i(1+\gamma m_i)}\right)^{\beta_i-1} \exp\left[-\left(\frac{y_i}{\alpha_i(1+\gamma m_i)}\right)^{\beta_i}\right].$$

Hence, the likelihood ratio is:

$$\ell(\mathbf{y}) = \left\{ \frac{\prod_{i=1}^{N} \frac{\beta_i}{\alpha_i(1+\gamma m_i^*)} \left(\frac{y_i}{\alpha_i(1+\gamma m_i^*)}\right)^{\beta_i-1} \exp\left[-\left(\frac{y_i}{\alpha_i(1+\gamma m_i^*)}\right)^{\beta_i}\right]}{\prod_{i=1}^{N} \frac{\beta_i}{\alpha_i} \left(\frac{y_i}{\alpha_i}\right)^{\beta_i-1} \exp\left[-\left(\frac{y_i}{\alpha_i}\right)^{\beta_i}\right]} \right\} \tag{23}$$

$$= \prod_{i=1}^{N} \left(\frac{1}{(1+\gamma m_i^*)}\right)^{\beta_i} \exp\left[-\left(\frac{y_i}{\alpha_i(1+\gamma m_i^*)}\right)^{\beta_i} + \left(\frac{y_i}{\alpha_i}\right)^{\beta_i}\right].$$

The natural logarithm is a monotone function: hence $\ln \ell(\mathbf{y})$ can be used instead of $\ell(\mathbf{y})$ producing the log likelihood ratio:

$$\mathcal{L}(\mathbf{y}) = \ln \ell(\mathbf{y}) \tag{24}$$

$$= \sum_{i=1}^{N} [-\beta_i \ln(1+\gamma m_i^*)] + \sum_{i=1}^{N} \left[-\left(\frac{y_i}{\alpha_i(1+\gamma m_i^*)}\right)^{\beta_i} + \left(\frac{y_i}{\alpha_i}\right)^{\beta_i}\right],$$

and the decision rule can be given the form:

$$\mathcal{L}(\mathbf{y}) > \ln \lambda. \tag{25}$$

By relaying on the expression (16), the value for the threshold $\ln \lambda$ is achieved:

$$\ln \lambda = 3.3 \sqrt{2 \sum_{i=1}^{N} \left[\frac{[(1+\gamma m_i^*)^{\beta_i} - 1]}{(1+\gamma m_i^*)^{\beta_i}}\right]^2 + \sum_{i=1}^{N} \left(\frac{[(1+\gamma m_i^*)^{\beta_i} - 1]}{(1+\gamma m_i^*)^{\beta_i}}\right)} + \tag{26}$$

$$- \sum_{i=1}^{N} [\beta_i \ln(1+\gamma m_i^*)].$$

6   Experimental Results

In order to asses the performance of the optimum detection scheme proposed so far a set of gray scale 512×512 standard images ("Boat", "Bridge", "Lena", etc.)

were labeled, and several common signal processing techniques and geometric distortions applied to them. Based on such experiments, the algorithm robustness against various kind of attacks has been measured.

Let us note that the log likelihood ratio $\mathcal{L}$ and the threshold $\ln \lambda$, needed for the implementation of the optimum decoder, depend on some parameters:

- the vector $\mathbf{y} = \{y_1, y_2, \ldots y_N\}$ of DFT coefficients selected to be marked;
- the parameters α_i and β_i characterizing the pdf's of DFT coefficients y_i;
- the watermark power γ;
- the watermark $\mathbf{m}^*$ that has to be detected.

DFT coefficients to be modified are between the 79-th and the 150-th diagonal in the first quadrant and the corresponding symmetricals in second quadrant. The region of the DFT spectrum the watermark is embedded in was split into 16 smaller sub-regions, as shown in Fig. 4. According to the approach we followed throughout the experiments, the coefficients of each sub-region are assumed to have the same pdf. The parameters α and β characterizing the coefficients of each sub-region were evaluated by applying the Maximum Likelihood criterion to the DFT samples contained in it. The equations (24) and (26) can then be written as:

$$\mathcal{L}(\mathbf{y}) = \sum_{l=1}^{16} \left\{ \sum_{i=1}^{N_l} [-\beta_l \ln(1 + \gamma m_i^*)] + \sum_{i=1}^{N_l} \left[-\left(\frac{y_i}{\alpha_l(1 + \gamma m_i^*)} \right)^{\beta_l} + \left(\frac{y_i}{\alpha_l} \right)^{\beta_l} \right] \right\},$$
$$(27)$$

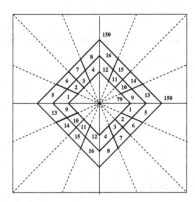

Fig. 4. The marked area of the magnitude of DFT spectrum has been divided into 16 zones for the statistical estimation of the coefficients pdf.

$$\ln \lambda = 3.3 \sqrt{2 \sum_{l=1}^{16} \sum_{i=1}^{N_l} \left[\frac{[(1 + \gamma m_i^*)^{\beta_l} - 1]}{(1 + \gamma m_i^*)^{\beta_l}} \right]^2 + \sum_{l=1}^{16} \sum_{i=1}^{N_l} \left(\frac{[(1 + \gamma m_i^*)^{\beta_l} - 1]}{(1 + \gamma m_i^*)^{\beta_l}} \right)} + \tag{28}$$

$$- \sum_{l=1}^{16} \sum_{i=1}^{N_l} [\beta_l \ln(1 + \gamma m_i^*)],$$

where l denotes the l-th sub-region in which the watermarked area of DFT spectrum has been split into.

The watermark power γ is chosen so that watermark invisibility is ensured. In order to enhance the robustness of the watermark, the characteristics of the Human Visual System can be exploited to mask the watermark, following the approach used in [7]. Through perceptual masking, it is possible to embed within the images, watermarks of higher energy than it is possible without masking, while preserving watermark invisibility. By masking the watermark, the amount of energy that is inserted in the image depends on the masking image: in particular, since the watermark is inserted non-uniformly in the image, the mean value $\bar{\gamma}$ has to be considered in the implementation of the optimum decoder.

In the following, we present some experiments to evidence the performance of the optimum decoder with respect to the performance of the correlation decoder by Barni et al. [4,11]; more specifically, the results presented refer to the standard image "Lena". The image was signed with $\bar{\gamma}$ equal to 0.22, value that guarantees the invisibility of the watermark; then, the watermarked image was attacked. For each attack the response of the detector for 1000 randomly generated watermarks, including the one actually embedded within the image, has been measured. The response relative to the true watermark and the highest response among those corresponding to the other watermarks are plotted along with the detection threshold. In this way both false positive and false negative detection errors are taken into account. As it can be seen the new algorithm permits to obtain a significant improvement with respect to conventional correlation decoding.

First, JPEG coding with decreasing quality was applied: the detector responses for both the Optimum Decoder (OD) and for the Correlator Decoder (CD) are plotted in Fig. (5). As it can be observed, OD response is above the threshold until quality is larger than 3%, while OC response is above the threshold until quality is larger than 6%. The above analysis is further confirmed by the results depicted in figure 6, where robustness against joint compression and filtering is accounted for. More specifically, the results refer to the case in which JPEG compression is preceded by 3x3 median filtering. As in figure 5, the detector output is plotted versus the JPEG quality factor used to code the image.

As a further test, the watermarked image was corrupted by adding a zero mean Gaussian noise with increasing variance. In Fig. (7) the responses of the two detectors are plotted; we can note that the OD response is above the threshold until variance is less than 2000, while the other detector reveals the watermark if variance is less than 1000.

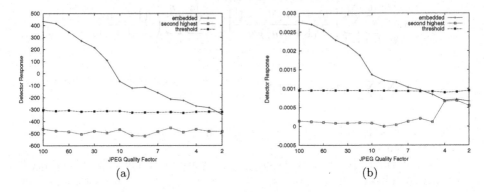

Fig. 5. Optimum detector responses (a) and correlator detector responses (b) on watermarked and JPEG compressed Lena image with decreasing qualities and 0% smoothing.

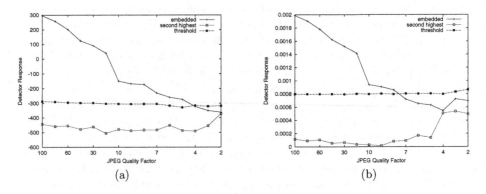

Fig. 6. Optimum detector responses (a) and correlator detector responses (b) on watermarked, joint median filtered (3 × 3 window) and JPEG compressed Lena image with decreasing qualities.

The signed image was resized from 512×512 to smaller size (until 160×160): the relative responses of the two detectors are plotted in Fig. (8). OD detects the watermark in the 224×224 cropped image; OC detects the watermark in 272×272 cropped Lena.

As a final test we have printed, photocopied and scanned the watermarked image: while OD response is over the threshold, CD fails the detection of the watermark in the elaborated image. To summarize, in all cases the use of the optimum decoder results in a superior robustness.

Eventually, *StirMark* [12,13,14] has been used to globally verify the robustness of the proposed decoder. We have not considered geometric attacks, since for such attacks a syncronization process in watermark detection is necessary,

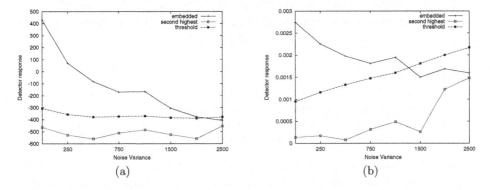

Fig. 7. Optimum detector responses (a) and correlator detector responses (b) on watermarked image corrupted by addition of zero mean Gaussian noise with increasing variance.

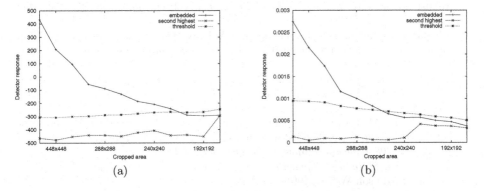

Fig. 8. Optimum detector responses (a) and correlator detector responses (b) on watermarked and cropped image with decreasing size of cropped area.

even if for some of them the watermark has been detected by OD (e.g. small rotations). For the other attacks proposed in *StirMark*, OD response is always above the threshold; in particular, OD detects the watermark in the image attacked by median filtering, Gaussian filtering, sharpening, colour quantization, JPEG compression and frequency mode Laplacian removal.

7   Conclusions

In this paper, an optimum watermark detector has been proposed. The new method, based on Bayes decision theory, results optimum without AWGN channel assumption. Experimental results have demonstrated the validity of the method; in particular, the use of the optimum decoder results in a superior robustness respect on the previous correlation decoder by Barni et al. [4,11]. Future research will focus on the extension of the analysis carried out in this work to video sequence and colour images watermarking.

References

1. G. F. Elmasry and Y. Q. Shi, "Maximum likelihood sequence decoding of digital image watermarking", in *Proc. SPIE's Int. Symposium on Optical Science, Engineering and Instrumentation*, San Josè, CA, USA, January 25-27 1999, pp. 425-436. 159

2. F. P. Gonzalez J. R. Hernandez, "Throwing more light on image watermarks", in *2nd International Workshop on Information Hiding, Lecture Notes in Computer Science*, Portland, Oregon, USA, April 1998, vol. 1525, pp. 191-207. 159

3. I. Cox, J. Kilian, F. T. Leighton, and T. Shamoon, "Secure spread spectrum watermarking for multimedia", *IEEE Trans. Image Processing*, vol. 6, no. 12, pp. 1673-1687, December 1997. 160

4. M. Barni, F. Bartolini, V. Cappellini, and A. Piva, "A DCT-domain system for robust image watermarking", *Signal Processing*, vol. 66, no. 3, pp. 357-372, May 1998. 160, 168, 171

5. M. Barni, F. Bartolini, V. Cappellini, and A. Piva, "Copyright protection of digital images by embedded umperceivable marks", *Image and Vision Computing*, 1998. 160

6. J. J. K. Ó Ruanaidh and T. Pun, "Rotation, scale and translation invariant spread spectrum digital image watermarking", *Signal Processing*, vol. 66, no. 3, pp. 303-317, May 1998. 160

7. F. Bartolini, M. Barni, V. Cappellini, and A. Piva, "Mask building for perceptually hiding frequency embedded watermarks", in *Proc. IEEE Internat. Conf. Image Processing '98*, Chicago, Illinois, USA, October 4-7 1998. 160, 168

8. L. L. Scharf, *Statistical Signal Processing: Detection, Estimation, and Time Series Analysis*, Addison-Wesley, 1991. 161, 165

9. J. V. Di Franco and W. L. Rubin, *Radar Detection*, Artech House, Inc., Dedham, Ma., 1980. 164, 165

10. A. Piva, M. Barni, F. Bartolini, and V. Cappellini, "Threshold selection for correlation-based watermark detection," in *Proc. COST 254 Workshop on Intelligent Communications*, L'Aquila, Italy, June 4-6 1998, pp. 67-72. 164

11. A. Piva, M. Barni, F. Bartolini, and V. Cappellini, "Dct-based watermark recovering without resorting to the uncorrupted original image", in *Proc. IEEE Internat. Conf. Image processing '97*, Santa Barbara, CA, October 26-29 1997, pp. 520-523. 168, 171

12. F. A. P. Petitcolas, "Weakness of existing watermarking schemes", [Online], 1999, WWW:http://www.cl.cam.ac.uk/fapp2/watermarking/stirmark/index.html. 169

13. M. G. Kuhn F. A. P. Petitcolas, R. J. Anderson, "Attacks on copyright marking systems", in *Proc. Information Hiding, Second International Workshop, David Aucsmith (Ed)*, Portland, Oregon, USA, April 15-17 1998, pp. 219-239. 169

14. F. A. P. Petitcolas and R. J. Anderson, "Evaluation of copyright marking systems", in *IEEE Multimedia Systems (ICMCS'99)*, Florence, Italy, June 7-11 1999, pp. 574-579. 169

Watermark Detection after Quantization Attacks

Joachim J. Eggers and Bernd Girod

Telecommunications Laboratory, University of Erlangen-Nuremberg
Cauerstr. 7/NT, 91058 Erlangen, Germany
{eggers,girod}@LNT.de

Abstract. The embedding of additive noise sequences is often used to hide information in digital audio, image or video documents. However, the embedded information might be impaired by involuntary or malicious "attacks." This paper shows that quantization attacks cannot be described appropriately by an additive white Gaussian noise (AWGN) channel. The robustness of additive watermarks against quantization depends strongly on the distribution of the host signal. Common compression schemes decompose a signal into sub-signals (e.g., frequency coefficients) and then adapt the quantization to the characteristics of the sub-signals. This has to be considered during watermark detection. A maximum likelihood (ML) detector that can be adapted to watermark sub-signals with different robustness is developed. The performance of this detector is investigated for the case of image watermark detection after JPEG compression.

1 Introduction

In the last decade, the digital representation of continuous signals (e.g., audio, images, video) has become very popular due to the possibility of efficient transmission and copying without quality degradation. On the other hand, unauthorized copying is also simplified. One approach to solve this problem is to mark a valuable digital document such that a copyright can be proven or the distribution path be reconstructed. The watermarking process produces a perceptually equivalent digital document rather than a bit-exact copy.

A general watermark embedding scheme can be described by

$$\underline{s}_k = \underline{x} + \underline{w}_k, \tag{1}$$

where $\underline{w}_k$ denotes the signal modification introduced by the watermarking process, $\underline{x}$ the original document, and $\underline{s}_k$ the published document (watermarked document). $\underline{x}$ is also called "host signal" or "private document". In many schemes $\underline{w}_k$ is explicitly given, but there are also schemes where the signal modification depends on the private document $\underline{x}$. In the remainder of this article, signals are denoted by vectors (e.g. $\underline{x}$), th nth signal sample by $x[n]$, and random variables by boldface. Here, the index k allows for the possibility of embedding different watermarks. Later, the index will be also used to denote sub-signals.

The watermark detector receives a signal

$$\underline{r}_k = \underline{s}_k + \underline{e} = \underline{x} + \underline{w}_k + \underline{e}, \tag{2}$$

A. Pfitzmann (Ed.): IH'99, LNCS 1768, pp. 172–186, 2000.

where $\underline{e}$ denotes the distortion that might be introduced by the watermark channel. Here, only independent watermarks are considered. That is, $\underline{w}_i$ and $\underline{w}_j$, $j \neq i$, are independent of each other. In this case, a different watermark than the one to be detected appears as additive noise. This noise can be included in $\underline{e}$ and thus, the index k can be neglected.

A complete characterization of the watermark channel is still an open problem. In contrast to many other communications problems, the channel distortion might be introduced intentionally to remove or obscure the transmitted information (the watermark). Besides attacks that exploit possible weaknesses of protocols for watermarking schemes, desynchronization and compression attacks usually are most successful. The latter will be discussed in this article. Therefore, we assume perfect synchronization of the watermark detector. This assumption is not too restrictive, since many desynchronization attacks can be counter-attacked by improved detectors [5,13].

In Section 2, watermark detection is discussed. We derive a decision rule that can be adapted to the different robustness of different parts of an embedded watermark. A detailed analysis of watermark detection after scalar quantization is presented in [1]. This analysis is based on the theory of dithered quantizers, as described e.g. in [3,6,10]. Due to space constraints, here only the main aspects of this analysis are summarized in Section 3. To demonstrate the importance of the detection problem after quantization attacks, we discuss an example image watermarking scheme. This scheme is described in Section 4, and, in Section 5, the corresponding detection results are discussed. Section 6 concludes the paper.

2 Watermark Detection

Signal detection has been intensively analyzed by communication engineers. However, the quantization attack is a very special transmission channel, thus we derive a special watermark detection scheme.

2.1 Bayes' Hypothesis Test

The watermark detection problem can be stated as a simple hypothesis test.

> hypothesis H_0 : the watermark $\underline{w}$ is not present,
> hypothesis H_1 : the watermark $\underline{w}$ is present.

The problem of hypothesis testing is to decide which of the hypotheses is true, when a document $\underline{r}$ ist given. Usually it is not possible to separate all watermarked and un-watermarked documents perfectly; a received signal $\underline{r}$ might be watermarked with probability $p(H_1|\underline{r})$ or not watermarked with probability $p(H_0|\underline{r})$. We can trade off the probability p_{FP} of accepting H_1 when H_0 is true (*false positive*) and the probability p_{FN} of accepting H_0 when it is false (*false negative*). Bayes' solution is the decision rule

$$\frac{p_{\mathbf{r}}(\underline{r}|H_1)}{p_{\mathbf{r}}(\underline{r}|H_0)} \begin{cases} > K \Rightarrow \text{accept } H_1 \\ \leq K \Rightarrow \text{accept } H_0, \end{cases} \tag{3}$$

where $K = \text{cost}_{p_{FP}} p_{H_0} / (\text{cost}_{p_{FN}} p_{H_1})$ is a constant depending on the a priori probabilities for H_1 and H_0 and the cost connected with the different decision errors [2]. For

$K = 1$, the decision rule (3) forms a **maximum-likelihood (ML) detector**. For equal a priori probabilities, the overall detection error probability is $p_e = \frac{1}{2}(p_{FP} + p_{FN})$. Receiver operating characteristic (ROC) graphs, as proposed in [8], can be computed using different thresholds K.

2.2   Correlation Detection

The watermark information is spread by an independent, mean-free, pseudo-noise sequence over the complete original signal. For an AWGN channel and $K = 1$ the hypothesis test (3) can be implemented as a correlation detector [4]:

$$H_1 : \quad \frac{r^T w}{M \sigma_{\mathbf{w}}^2} > \frac{1}{2}, \tag{4}$$

where $\sigma_{\mathbf{w}}^2$ denotes the watermark power and M is the signal length. The AWGN channel model implies that $\mathbf{x}$ and $\mathbf{e}$ are jointly Gaussian random processes and statistically independent from a possibly included watermark $\mathbf{w}$. In Section 3, it is shown that this assumption is not valid for a quantization attack.

2.3   Generalized Watermark Detection

The description of the watermark detection problem is generalized in this subsection, such that the characteristics of the quantization attack described in Section 3 can be exploited. We do not restrict the channel distortion to be AWGN. However, we assume to know a signal decomposition

$$x[n] = \sum_{i=1}^{i_{\max}} \sum_{m=0}^{\tilde{M}_i - 1} \tilde{x}_i[m] \psi_i \left[n - m \frac{M}{\tilde{M}_i} \right] \tag{5}$$

so that all $i_{\max}$ signals $c_i[m] = \tilde{r}_i[m]\tilde{w}_i[m]$ of length $\tilde{M}_i$ are white and stationary. The function $\psi_i[\cdot]$ denotes the ith function of the set of basis functions used for the decomposition. For instance, the decomposition could be a block-wise frequency transform, where m denotes the block index and i the frequency component. $\tilde{r}_i$ and $\tilde{w}_i$ are the sub-signals of r and w that are defined just like $\tilde{x}_i$ in (5). The received sub-signals $\tilde{r}_i$ are different for both hypotheses:

$$H_1 : \quad \tilde{r}_i = \tilde{x}_i + \tilde{w}_i + \tilde{e}_{1i} \tag{6}$$
$$H_0 : \quad \tilde{r}_i = \tilde{x}_i + \tilde{e}_{0i}. \tag{7}$$

The channel distortion depends on the considered hypotheses and can even depend on the watermark in case of hypothesis H_1. The proper choice of a signal decomposition is not discussed further in this article. *The goal of the decomposition is to separate signal components that can hide watermarks with different robustness.* For the experiments described in Section 4, the 8×8 block-DCT is used. In this case, the basis functions are two-dimensional.

With help of a signal decomposition, watermark detection can be separated into two steps:

1. Estimate the expectations $\mathrm{E}\{\mathbf{c_i}\}$ with $i = 1, \ldots, i_{\max}$ by

$$\mathrm{E}\{\mathbf{c_i}\} \approx C_i = \frac{1}{\tilde{M}_i} \sum_{m=1}^{\tilde{M}_i} c_i[m], \tag{8}$$

and combine these values to form the vector $\underline{C} = (C_1, C_2, \ldots, C_{i_{\max}})^T$. C_i is equal to the correlation of the sub-signals $\underline{\tilde{r}}_i$ and $\underline{\tilde{w}}_i$. For sufficiently large $\tilde{M}_i$, we can assume that the C_i are normally distributed with variance [9]

$$\mathrm{Var}\{\mathbf{C_i}\} = \frac{1}{\tilde{M}_i} \mathrm{Var}\{\mathbf{c_i}\}. \tag{9}$$

Thus, the collection of all sub-channels $\underline{C}$ can be described by a multivariate Gaussian random variable $\underline{\mathbf{C}}$ with mean vector $\underline{C}_\mu$ and covariance matrix $\underline{\underline{\Phi}}_{CC}^{H_1}$ in the case of hypothesis H_1 or with mean vector[1] $\underline{0}$ and covariance matrix $\underline{\underline{\Phi}}_{CC}^{H_0}$ for H_0, respectively.

2. Apply the Bayesian hypothesis test (3) with the sample vector $\underline{C}$. Using the multivariate Gaussian PDF, the decision rule is given by

$$H_1: \quad K < \frac{(2\pi)^{-\frac{i_{\max}}{2}} \left|\underline{\underline{\Phi}}_{CC}^{H_1}\right|^{-\frac{1}{2}} \exp\left(-\frac{1}{2}(\underline{C} - \underline{C}_\mu)^T \underline{\underline{\Phi}}_{CC}^{H_1}{}^{-1}(\underline{C} - \underline{C}_\mu)\right)}{(2\pi)^{-\frac{i_{\max}}{2}} \left|\underline{\underline{\Phi}}_{CC}^{H_0}\right|^{-\frac{1}{2}} \exp\left(-\frac{1}{2}(\underline{C} - \underline{0})^T \underline{\underline{\Phi}}_{CC}^{H_0}{}^{-1}(\underline{C} - \underline{0})\right)}$$

or equivalently

$$\begin{aligned}
H_1: \quad \log(K) < &\frac{1}{2}\left(\log\left(\left|\underline{\underline{\Phi}}_{CC}^{H_0}\right|\right) - \log\left(\left|\underline{\underline{\Phi}}_{CC}^{H_1}\right|\right) - \underline{C}_\mu^T \underline{\underline{\Phi}}_{CC}^{H_1}{}^{-1} \underline{C}_\mu\right) \\
&+ \frac{1}{2}\underline{C}^T \left(\underline{\underline{\Phi}}_{CC}^{H_0}{}^{-1} - \underline{\underline{\Phi}}_{CC}^{H_1}{}^{-1}\right)\underline{C} + \underline{C}^T \underline{\underline{\Phi}}_{CC}^{H_1}{}^{-1} \underline{C}_\mu.
\end{aligned} \tag{10}$$

The decision rule (10) has quadratic terms in $\underline{C}$ and thus defines a parabolic hypersurface in the $i_{\max}$-dimensional space. The analytic computation of the decision error probability is hard due to the quadratic terms. In addition, decision boundaries obtained from (10) are not very robust to an inaccurate estimation of the channel parameters. This will be demonstrated in Section 5. A simplification of rule (10) results by assuming equal covariance matrices $\underline{\underline{\Phi}}_{CC}^{H_1}$ and $\underline{\underline{\Phi}}_{CC}^{H_0}$, in which case the decision hyper-surface becomes a hyper-plane.

Fig. 1 shows a two-dimensional example. Here, the channel distortion is caused by the quantization of watermarks in two different DCT coefficients. More details are explained in Section 4. The measured correlations $\underline{C} = (C_{24}, C_{40})^T$ are plotted for both hypotheses and denoted by "×" and "+" for H_1 and H_0, respectively. The samples leading to detection errors when using (10) are circled. The figure also depicts the parabolic and planar decision boundaries. Both rules are almost identical in the range where both hypotheses might be confused. Therefore, in practice both rules perform similarly, since they differ mainly in the regions of low probabilities.

---

[1] The conditional expectation $\mathrm{E}\{\underline{C}|H_0\}$ is zero, since the watermark $\mathbf{w}$ is mean-free and independent from the unmarked document.

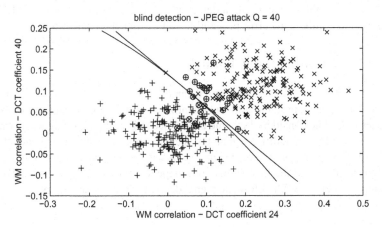

Fig. 1. Combined detection of two watermark components after a quantization attack

In Section 4 we will treat the 8×8 block-DCT as a decomposition that yields almost uncorrelated sub-channels. For uncorrelated sub-channels the covariance matrices $\underline{\underline{\Phi}}_{CC}^{H_1}$ and $\underline{\underline{\Phi}}_{CC}^{H_0}$ are diagonal and thus given by the conditional variances $\text{Var}\{\mathbf{C}_i|H_1\}$ and $\text{Var}\{\mathbf{C}_i|H_0\}$ for each channel. We assume $\sigma_{\mathbf{C}_i}^2 = \text{Var}\{\mathbf{c}_i\}/\tilde{M}_i = \text{Var}\{\mathbf{c}_i|H_1\}/\tilde{M}_i = \text{Var}\{\mathbf{c}_i|H_0\}/\tilde{M}_i$ to obtain a decision hyper-plane. Defining $\mu_{\mathbf{C}_i} = \text{E}\{\mathbf{C}_i|H_1\}$ and setting $K = 1$ yields the detection rule

$$H_1: \quad \sum_{i=1}^{i_{\max}} \left(\frac{C_i}{\mu_{\mathbf{C}_i}} - \frac{1}{2}\right) \frac{\mu_{\mathbf{C}_i}^2}{\sigma_{\mathbf{C}_i}^2} > 0. \tag{11}$$

The ratio $\alpha_i = \mu_{\mathbf{C}_i}^2/\sigma_{\mathbf{C}_i}^2$ can be interpreted as a weight for the correlation result computed for sub-channel i. This weight is largest for the sub-channels that provide the most robust watermark detection. The error probabilities for this detector are given by

$$p_{FP} = \frac{1}{2}\text{erfc}\left(\frac{\frac{1}{2}\sum_{i=1}^{i_{\max}}\alpha_i}{\sqrt{2\sum_{i=1}^{i_{\max}}\frac{\alpha_i^2}{\mu_{\mathbf{C}_i}^2}\text{Var}\{\mathbf{C}_i|H_0\}}}\right) \tag{12}$$

$$p_{FN} = \frac{1}{2}\text{erfc}\left(\frac{\sum_{i=1}^{i_{\max}}\alpha_i\left(\frac{1}{\mu_{\mathbf{C}_i}}\text{E}\{\mathbf{C}_i|H_1\} - \frac{1}{2}\right)}{\sqrt{2\sum_{i=1}^{i_{\max}}\frac{\alpha_i^2}{\mu_{\mathbf{C}_i}^2}\text{Var}\{\mathbf{C}_i|H_1\}}}\right) \tag{13}$$

where $\text{erfc}(x) = \frac{2}{\sqrt{\pi}}\int_x^\infty \exp(-\xi^2)\,\mathrm{d}\xi$.

The detector (11) is completely determined by the α_i and $\mu_{\mathbf{C}_i}$. These values can be defined independently from $\text{E}\{\mathbf{C}_i|H_1\}$, $\text{Var}\{\mathbf{C}_i|H_1\}$, and $\text{Var}\{\mathbf{C}_i|H_0\}$, which, of course, does not give an optimal detector. However, in this case (13) and (12) can also be used to compute the error probabilities of mismatched detection[2].

3   The Quantization Channel

Quantization of a watermarked signal can decrease the robustness of watermark detection. We investigate scalar uniform quantization following the additive embedding of a watermark. The considered scheme is depicted in Fig. 2. Although every watermark can be described by an additive signal, the special property of the investigated watermark is its independence from the host signal $\underline{x}$. In this section, we assume that the samples of the watermark and the host signal are independent identically distributed and Δ is the quantizer step size. Therefore, no signal decomposition is necessary.

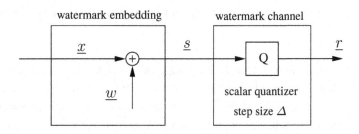

Fig. 2. Additive watermark embedding and subsequent quantization

It is known that the quantization channel can be modeled by an AWGN channel in the case of *fine quantization* [1]. However, for *coarse quantization*, as common for compression, better models are necessary. Here, only the most important results are summarized. A detailed description is given in [1].

The channel distortion $\underline{e}$ equals the quantization error $\underline{e} = \underline{r} - \underline{s}$. The watermark is detected via correlation according to (4). We introduce a slight extension to improve the detection with help of the original signal $\underline{x}$. This is expressed by the subtraction of $\underline{x}$, weighted by a factor γ_x. Thus we define

$$c[n] = (r[n] - \gamma_x[n]x[n])w[n]. \tag{14}$$

The normalized conditional expectation $E\{c|H_1\}$ is given by

$$\frac{E\{c|H_1\}}{\sigma_w^2} = \frac{E\{(r - \gamma_x x)w\}}{\sigma_w^2} = \frac{E\{ew\}}{\sigma_w^2} + 1. \tag{15}$$

We would like to obtain the value 1, meaning the correlation $E\{ew\}$ between the quantization error e and the watermark w should be zero. This is assumed when the quantization attack is modeled by an AWGN channel.

---

[2] Here, mismatched detection means to use a detector that was designed for the case of a different attack.

The value of $\mathrm{E}\{\mathbf{ew}\}/\sigma_{\mathbf{w}}^2$ can be determined for a given quantizer if the PDFs of the original signal $\mathbf{x}$ and the watermark $\mathbf{w}$ are known. Here, we investigate a Gaussian and Laplacian host signal $\mathbf{x}$ with zero mean and unit variance. We consider watermarks with Gaussian, uniform or bipolar ($w[n] = \pm\sigma_{\mathbf{w}}$) distributions. All three signal characteristics are frequently used in watermarking schemes. For convenience, the standard deviations of the input signal and the watermark are normalized by the quantizer step size Δ. This defines the normalized parameters $\chi = \sigma_{\mathbf{x}}/\Delta$ and $\zeta = \sigma_{\mathbf{w}}/\Delta$.

We are mainly interested in the robustness of an additive watermark against quantization of different coarseness. Fig. 3 shows the cross-correlation $\mathrm{E}\{\mathbf{ew}\}$ for a constant watermark-to-host-signal ratio ζ/χ and increasing quantizer step size Δ. In this case ζ/χ represents the embedding strength and an increasing step size Δ equals a decreasing value of χ.

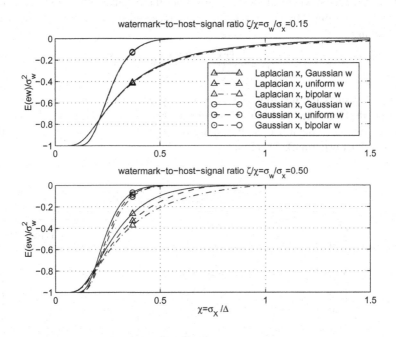

Fig. 3. Predicted cross-correlation $\mathrm{E}\{\mathbf{ew}\}/\sigma_{\mathbf{w}}^2$ for $\zeta/\chi = 0.15$ and $\zeta/\chi = 0.5$.

For a fixed ratio ζ/χ and varying χ, the correlation $\mathrm{E}\{\mathbf{ew}\}$ becomes zero for sufficiently large χ (fine quantization) and converges towards -1 for the limit $\chi \to 0$. The behavior of $\mathrm{E}\{\mathbf{ew}\}$ for large χ is intuitively clear, since in this case the host signal has an approximately constant PDF over the range of a step size Δ. At the limit $\chi \to 0$, the quantizer step size Δ becomes arbitrarily large, which leads to a zero quantizer output, assuming zero is a reconstruction value, and thus to the quantization error $e[n] = -x[n] - w[n]$. As a result, the normalized expectation $\mathrm{E}\{\mathbf{ew}\}/\sigma_{\mathbf{w}}^2$ converges to -1 and the conditional expectation $\mathrm{E}\{\mathbf{c}|H_1\}$ becomes zero.

The characteristic of the watermark PDF does not have a significant influence for small ratios ζ/χ. More important is the influence of the host signal's distribution, especially, since this cannot be modified in watermarking schemes. The plots in Fig. 3 show that the watermark embedded in a signal with a Gaussian distribution resists quantization better than an equivalent watermark embedded in a signal with Laplacian distribution. In general we observe that with more peaky host signal PDFs – everything else being equal – the watermark is somewhat less robust against quantization attacks.

The expressions for the variances $\mathrm{Var}\{\mathbf{c}|H_1\}$ and $\mathrm{Var}\{\mathbf{c}|H_0\}$ are slightly more complicated and thus not derived here. The formulas given in [1] reveal that $\mathrm{Var}\{\mathbf{c}|H_1\}$ and $\mathrm{Var}\{\mathbf{c}|H_0\}$ are indeed different. However, they are approximately equal for common signal settings. The variances depend on the interference from the original document and, therefore, on the choice of γ_x. The weight $\gamma_x = 0$ has to be used when no knowledge about the original is available at the watermark decoder ("blind" detection). In applications, where full knowledge about the original can be exploited, the weight can be determined by the correlation of the received signal $\underline{r}$ with the original signal $\underline{x}$, yielding

$$\gamma_x = \frac{\mathrm{E}\{\mathbf{rx}\}}{\sigma_{\mathbf{x}}^2} = \frac{\mathrm{E}\{\mathbf{ex}\}}{\sigma_{\mathbf{x}}^2} + \frac{\mathrm{E}\{\mathbf{x}\}^2}{\sigma_{\mathbf{x}}^2} + 1. \tag{16}$$

Fig. 4 depicts the resulting detection error probalities after quantization of different strength. Here, the quality of the received signal $\underline{r}$, is measured by the host-signal-to-noise ratio after quantization. Again, we observe that the Laplacian host signal provides less robust watermark detection.

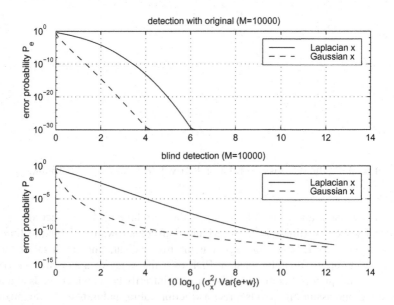

Fig. 4. Predicted error probabilities for $\zeta/\chi = 0.15$ and Gaussian watermark **w**.

4 An Example Image Watermarking Scheme

The investigation of image watermark detection after quantization reveals the importance of the problems discussed in Section 2 and Section 3. The presented scheme is not fully optimized, but sufficiently good to give realistic results.

4.1 Host Data

The theoretical analysis of watermark detection after quantization has been made without specifying the data to be watermarked. Therefore, the results can be applied easily to many different signals. The following examples are for natural images. The watermark is embedded into the coefficients of an 8×8 block-DCT of the luminance component. Many different domains for the watermark embedding process have been proposed in recent publications, where, besides the DCT domain, wavelet domains are very popular [7,8,15]. We choose the block-wise DCT since this is also used by JPEG compression. We do not claim that the block-wise DCT is the optimal image decomposition for watermarking purposes. Two advantages of the proposed watermarking domain are:

– During JPEG compression, the coefficients of the 8×8 block-DCT are quantized with a uniform scalar quantizer, where the step size Δ_i can be different for each of the 64 frequencies. Therefore, defining the watermark in the DCT domain simplifies the optimization of detection after the compression attack.
– Quantizer step sizes for JPEG-baseline compression are optimized for subjectively quality and can be parameterized via a quality factor QF ($QF = 100$: highest quality with step size $\Delta = \Delta_{\min}$ for all coefficients; $QF = 1$: lowest quality with step size $\Delta = 256\Delta_{\min}$). Therefore, an invisible watermark can be achieved by adapting its strength to the quantization noise produced via JPEG compression with a sufficiently high quality factor.

4.2 Embedding Scheme

Fig. 5 depicts the scheme for the signal dependent additive watermark embedding. The signal decomposition is performed as in JPEG compression [14]. Image samples are denoted by $I(u, v, m)$, where (u, v) are the row and column indices of the m-th block (where the blocks are numbered in row-scan). All blocks are DCT transformed and the coefficients for the same frequency from all blocks are grouped into a sample sequence – a *sub-signal*. This sub-signal can be described relatively accurately by a white, stationary random variable $\tilde{x}_i$. Since each sub-signal can be quantized differently, each sub-signal has its own *sub-channel*. Due to the 8×8 blocks, this scheme gives 64 vectors $\underline{\tilde{x}}_i$, where the index i denotes the sub-channel number. The sub-channels are numbered according to the common zigzag-scan of the DCT coefficients. The length of the vectors $\underline{\tilde{x}}_i$ equals the number of 8×8 blocks in the given image.

The main idea for the adaptation of the watermark strength is that the embedding should introduce roughly the same distortion as JPEG compression with a certain quality factor QF_e. Therefore, uniform scalar quantization with step size Δ_i (which is used

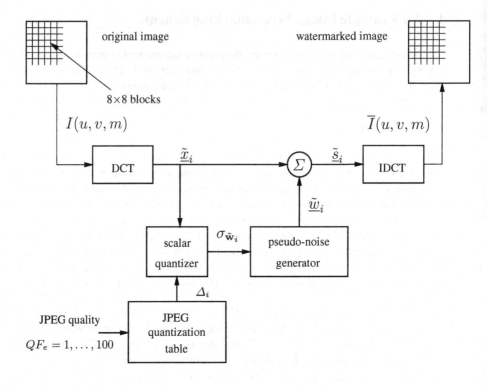

original image   watermarked image

8×8 blocks

$I(u, v, m)$ $\overline{I}(u, v, m)$

DCT $\tilde{\underline{x}}_i$ Σ $\tilde{\underline{s}}_i$ IDCT

$\tilde{\underline{w}}_i$

scalar quantizer $\sigma_{\tilde{\mathbf{w}}_i}$ pseudo-noise generator

Δ_i

JPEG quality   JPEG quantization table

$QF_e = 1, \ldots, 100$

Fig. 5. JPEG-adapted additive watermarking

in JPEG compression with a certain quality QF_e) is applied to the elements of the vector $\tilde{\underline{x}}_i$. Now, the watermark variance $\sigma_{\mathbf{w}_i}^2$ for every sub-channel is chosen equal to the variance of the corresponding quantization errors. A Gaussian pseudo-noise vector $\tilde{\underline{w}}_i$ with the correspondent standard deviation is computed for each sub-channel and added to $\tilde{\underline{x}}_i$. Finally, the elements of the resulting 64 watermarked vectors $\tilde{\underline{s}}_i$ are inverse DCT transformed.

In [11,12], it is suggested that the watermark frequency spectrum should be directly proportional to the host signal's. However, that work uses mean square error, and for subjective quality we should not satisfy this condition exactly.

4.3 Simulation Settings

In order to reduce the number of free parameters, we will discuss only the results for an embedding quality of $QF_e = 70$, which gives a watermarked image with sufficiently high quality. As a test image, we use the 256×256 gray-scale "Lenna" picture. The given image size leads to 1024 8×8 blocks, and thus to 1024 samples for each sub-channel $\tilde{\underline{x}}_i$.

200 differently watermarked images $\overline{I}(u, v, m)$ were produced, using the scheme depicted in Fig. 5, where the watermarks were obtained by different seeds for

the pseudo-random number generator. Note that, in contrast to an AWGN-channel, the quantization channel can only be investigated by varying input sequences. The watermarked images were JPEG compressed and decompressed, each with 20 different quality factors which are equally increased from $QF_a = 5$ to $QF_a = 100$.

For watermark detection, the attacked public document is transformed again by the 8×8 block-DCT. Then the signals $\tilde{r}_i$ for the different sub-channels i are correlated with the corresponding watermarks $\tilde{\underline{w}}_i$. For a fair test, the detection process is carried out for both hypotheses H_1 and H_0, i.e., for documents that are or are not watermarked by $\tilde{\underline{w}}_i$. For simplicity we chose as reference an un-watermarked image, which was compressed in the same way the watermarked image was compressed.

5   Experimental Results

5.1   Detection Optimized for the Applied Attack

The detection rule (11) derived in Section 2 is determined by the weights $\alpha_i = \mu_{C_i}^2/\sigma_{C_i}^2$ and the expected correlations μ_{C_i}. These parameters are computed for each sub-channel and each of the 20 JPEG attacks, so that the detector defined by (11) can be optimized for a given attack. We found that the values derived experimentally by 200 different watermark realizations match to the values computed via the theoretic model presented in [1]. Therefore, it is possible to substitute the simulations by theoretic modeling.

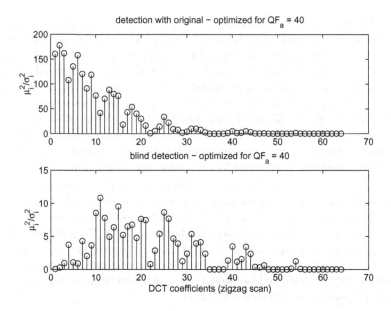

Fig. 6. Detection weights $\alpha_i = \mu_{C_i}^2/\sigma_{C_i}^2$ for all 64 DCT coefficients.

Channel weights. Fig. 6 depicts the weights determined after JPEG compression with $QF_a = 40$. The robustness of watermark detection is very different for the sub-channels (the DCT coefficients). This is due to the different quantization of each sub-channel, the adapted watermark strength and the differently distributed host signals. Further, it can be observed that the weights differ for detection with original and blind detection. The small weights for the low frequency coefficients in the case of blind detection are reasonable, since here the interference from the original is large. Enlarging the watermark power for these coefficients can increase the detection weights, but also degrades the subjective quality of the watermarked image. Detection with original is not affected by interference from the original document. Therefore, the low frequency coefficients provide the most robust detection after JPEG compression.

The results are similar for compression with other quality factors. However, especially in the case of blind detection the higher frequency coefficients get larger weights for high quality compression.

Detection error probabilities. With help of the measured or computed values α_i and μ_{C_i}, the detection error probabilities can be investigated. When the strength of the conducted JPEG compression is known, the watermark detection can be optimized by plugging the appropriate weights into (11). The error probabilities for blind detection are shown in Fig. 7 and Fig. 8. Plots with linear and logarithmic axes are provided. The values found by actually counting detection errors are only depicted in the plots with linear axis due to the relatively small number of simulations. The results in Fig. 7 are achieved by considering only the watermark components embedded in the 12-th and 13-th DCT coefficient.

The plots show the results derived by estimating the necessary means and variances from the experimentally found correlation values. In addition these values are computed by modeling the host data by a Gaussian or generalized Gaussian random variable. The plots reveal that the Gaussian model – in contrast to the generalized Gaussian model – does not agree with the experimental results. This emphasizes the importance of the host signal's PDF. A Gaussian host signal would provide much better robustness, but the actual image data is *not* Gaussian distributed. In the upper plots of Fig. 7 and Fig. 8, the circles indicate the error rates found by actually counting the detection errors of the proposed detector. When using only a subset of all sub-channels, more errors occur and the error probabilities predicted by (12) and (13) can be verified with less simulations.

The plots also depict the error probabilities that can be expected for a detector that is designed after modeling the quantization attack by an AWGN channel. The AWGN model does not consider that coarse quantization removes parts of the embedded watermark, so the normalized expected correlation is always 1. The presented results demonstrate that this assumption leads to severe degradations of the detection performance. This is especially true when all sub-channels are considered since in this case un-robust sub-channels are weighted too strongly. Here, it would be better to detect the watermark only in a small subset of all sub-channels.

With help of the proposed detector – optimized for the given attack – even blind detection of a watermark embedded with quality $QF_e = 70$ is still possible after com-

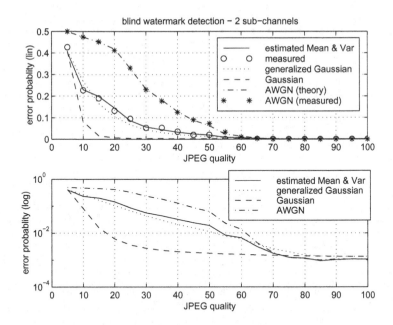

Fig. 7. Error probabilities for blind watermark detection after JPEG compression considering sub-channel 12 and 13. The detector is always optimized for the special attack.

pression attacks down to qualities about $QF_a = 20$. Naturally, detection with original is much more robust, so we do not present these results here.

5.2 Detection Optimized for a Worst Case Attack

The detection error probabilities presented in the previous subsection are very promising. However, full knowledge about the compression attack might not always be available. If this is the case, we have to find a detector that works for a large set of possible attacks. The error probabilities using a detector optimized for an attack with $QF_a = 40$ are shown in Fig. 9. These plots allow also the comparison of the performance of the parabolic and planar detection boundaries as discussed in Section 2.3. Due to the optimization of the detector for attacks with $QF_a = 40$, the parabolic detector fails completely for weak attacks ($QF_a \geq 80$). The planar detector is much more robust. We cannot expect to get error probabilities as low as with a fully optimized detector. However, the error rate is still lower than 10^{-10} for all attacks with $QF_a \geq 40$. Again, the AWGN model is in general not appropriate. It fits only in the case of very weak attacks.

6 Conclusion

Quantization attacks against embedded watermarks have different severity, depending on the PDF of the host signal. The AWGN model is not appropriate for quantization

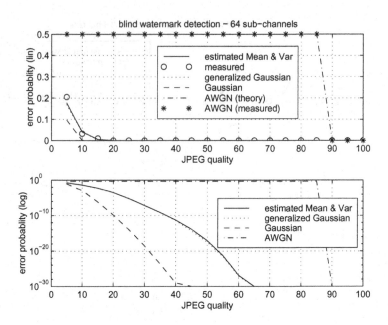

Fig. 8. Error probabilities for blind watermark detection after JPEG compression considering all sub-channels. The detector is always optimized for the special attack.

channels. This has to be considered when the watermark detector is optimized to resist certain compression attacks. An example image watermarking scheme is presented, and the proposed detection principle experimentally verified. With this scheme, it is possible to detect watermarks without using the original document with low error probabilities even after JPEG-compression with $QF_a = 20$. In practical schemes it is sufficient to use a detector that is optimized for a worst case attack, e.g., a strong attack that still provides an attacked document with good subjective quality.

References

1. J. J. Eggers and B. Girod. Quantization Effects on Digital Watermarks. *Signal Processing*, 1999. Submitted.
2. I. A. Glover and P. M. Grant. *Digital Communications*. Prentice Hall, London, New York, Toronto, Sydney, 1998.
3. R. M. Gray and T. G. Stockham. Dithered quantizers. *IEEE Transactions on Information Theory*, 39(3):805–812, May 1993.
4. J. C. Hancock and P. A. Wintz. *Signal Detection Theory*. McGraw-Hill, Inc, New York, St. Louis, San Francisco, Toronto, London, Sydney, 1966.
5. F. Hartung, J. K. Su, and B. Girod. Spread spectrum watermarking: Malicious attacks and counter-attacks. In *Proceedings of SPIE Vol. 3657: Security and Watermarking of Multimedia Contents*, San Jose, Ca, USA, January 1999.
6. N. S. Jayant and P. Noll. *Digital Coding of Waveforms*. Prentice Hall, 1984.

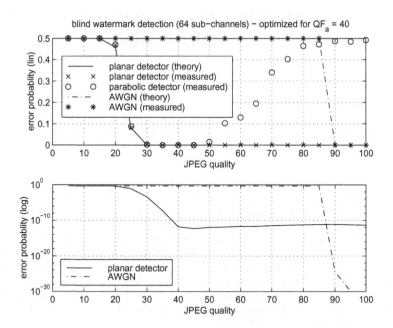

Fig. 9. Error probability of blind watermark detection after JPEG compression considering all sub-channels. The detector is optimized for an attack with $QF_a = 40$.

7. D. Kundur and D. Hatzinakos. Digital watermarking using multiresolution wavelet decomposition. In *Proceedings IEEE International Conference on Acoustics, Speech, and Signal Processing 1998 (ICASSP 98), Seattle, WA, USA*, volume 5, pages 2969–2972, May 1998.
8. M. Kutter and F. A. P. Petitcolas. A fair benchmark for image watermarking systems. In *Proceedings of SPIE Vol. 3657: Security and Watermarking of Multimedia Contents*, San Jose, Ca, USA, January 1999.
9. A. Papoulis. *Probability, Random Variables, and Stochastic Processes*. McGraw-Hill, New York, 3rd edition, 1991.
10. L. Schuchman. Dither signals and their effect on quantization noise. *IEEE Transaction on Communication Technology (COM)*, 12:162–165, December 1964.
11. J. K. Su and B. Girod. On the imperceptibiliy and robustness of digital fingerprints. In *Proceedings IEEE International Conference on Multimedia Computing and Systems (ICMCS 99)*, Florence, Italy, June 1999.
12. J. K. Su and B. Girod. Power-spectrum condition for L_2-efficient watermarking. In *Proceedings of the IEEE International Conference on Image Processing 1999 (ICIP 99)*, Kobe, Japan, October 1999. Accepted.
13. J. K. Su, F. Hartung, and B. Girod. A channel model for a watermark attack. In *Proceedings of SPIE Vol. 3657: Security and Watermarking of Multimedia Contents*, San Jose, Ca, USA, January 1999.
14. G. K. Wallace. The JPEG still picture compression standard. *Communications of the ACM*, 34(4):31–44, April 1991.
15. L. Xie and G. R. Arce. A Blind Wavelet Based Digital Signature for Image Authentication. In *Proceedings European Signal Processing Conference (EUSIPCO 98)*, Greece, September 1998.

Content-Based Watermarking for Image Authentication

Pedro Lamy, Jose' Martinho, Tiago Rosa, and Maria Paula Queluz

Instituto de Telecomunicações – Instituto Superior Técnico
Av. Rovisco Pais, 1049-001 Lisboa, Portugal
Paula.Queluz@lx.it.pt

Abstract. This paper is focused on digital image authentication, considered as the process of evaluating the integrity of image contents relatively to the original picture and of being able to detect, in an automatic way, malevolent content modifications. A computationally efficient watermarking technique for image authentication, robust to small distortions caused by compression is proposed and described. In essence, a content-dependent authentication data is embedded into the picture by exploiting the rank order relationship of image projections throughout the entire image. The viability of the proposed method as a means of protecting the content is assessed under JPEG compression and semantic content modifications.

1 Introduction

The recent development of digital multimedia communications together with the intrinsic capability of digital information to be copied and manipulated requires new copyright protection and authentication schemes to be developed. This paper is devoted to the second issue, the one of image or video content authentication. Authentication in this context should be understood as the procedure to guarantee that the content has not been altered, or at least the visual (or semantic) characteristics of the image are kept[1].

Since digital images can be altered or manipulated with ease, the ability to detect changes in digital images can be crucial for many applications such as news reporting, medical archiving, photographic databases of historical, political and sports events, mainly when acceded over a network. Another need for image authentication arises in commercial image transaction. It is also important when acceding through the Internet to images stored on Internet-attached servers, given the opportunities for malicious parts to intercept and replace images that have been transmitted to others.

Digital authentication and integrity verification is nowadays a current procedure in electronic exchange of messages. It uses the concept of *digital signature*, derived from a recent encryption technique called Public Key Encryption [1]. Public Key Encryption employs two different keys: a private key, which is held by the message

---

[1] It could also be necessary to authenticate the identity of the owner, but this question will be not considered here.

A. Pfitzmann (Ed.): IH´99, LNCS 1768, pp. 187-198, 2000.

generator and a corresponding public key, produced based upon the private key, which needs not to be kept secret. A digital signature is produced by first creating a hash[2] of the original message, and then encrypting the hash using the sender's private key. Message integrity can be confirmed by comparing the decrypted digital signature (using the public key) and a hash of the message in question – if they match, message integrity can be assured. Integrity verification based on digital signatures is a very powerful tool, as changing a single bit in the original message produces a very different hash (and signature) output. Also, reverse engineering a message so that it will have a given hash value is virtually impossible. It has however a clear drawback for some applications: strict information integrity is required and no modification on the information bitstream is allowed.

The digital signature technique described above is very general and it could be applied to any kind of digital information, including digital images and video, as already proposed for the so-called Trustworthy Digital Camera [2]. However, reliable image/video authentication technology should be able to protect images from malicious manipulation in every stage of transmission and storage, from the time they were first produced. This means that the most important place to implement it is at the moment of image creation (within a scanner, still camera, or video system) and that the digital signature produced at that time should survive to authorized content modifications (such as compression for audio-visual information) that can occur afterwards. This clearly invalidates the use of digital signatures as defined above for applications where such modifications are allowed. This limitation has recently motivated the research on image authentication techniques that are robust to authorized content modification but sensitive to malevolent manipulations.

The existing proposals for image authentication can be divided into two broad categories, depending on the way chosen to convey the authentication data: *labeling* based approaches, when the data is written in a separate file [2][5][6][7][8]; *watermarking* based approaches, when it is embedded in the picture [3][4][9][10]. Watermarking techniques for content authentication are usually designed to be *fragile watermarks,* since they should not tolerate malicious tampering that modifies the content of the image. In this case the goal is to embed a mark in the host signal (image or video) such that any changes applied to the signal will cause a change in the values of the extracted mark. Once more, it is desirable to have robustness to some form of modifications, such as compression. To achieve this, most of the proposed fragile watermarking approaches perform embedding simultaneously with compression [4][9][10].

In this paper, we propose a computationally efficient watermarking technique for authentication of visual information, robust to small distortions caused by compression. In section 2, a detailed description of the new technique is presented. The viability of the new method as a means for protecting the content is assessed under JPEG compression and non-authorized image modifications in section 3. Finally, in section 4, conclusions are drawn and future research directions are suggested.

---

[2] A hash is a mathematical function that maps values from a large domain into a smaller range. A simple kind of hash is, for example, a checksum.

2 Authentication Scheme

The approach for content authentication proposed here exploits the rank order relationship of image projections throughout the entire image. Related work has been presented in [9][10], where a digital signature is embedded in the wavelet bands by changing the median of a local area to a value that depends on its neighbors. In [9][10], and to allow the watermarked image to be stored or transmitted in lossy compressed forms, the embedding must be done jointly with compression. The method we propose here can be applied before compression (e.g., to the original image at the acquisition time), in a way that, up to a certain degree, is robust to JPEG compression and without compromising the image quality.

2.1 Image Projections

Let $\mathbf{x}$ represents a vector of dimension N, whose elements are pixel values taken at a pre-defined walk along an image. The projection of $\mathbf{x}$ in a direction defined by a N-dimensional vector $\mathbf{y}$, is given by:

$$P = <\mathbf{x}, \mathbf{y}> = \frac{\mathbf{x}.\mathbf{y}}{\|\mathbf{y}\|} = \frac{1}{\|\mathbf{y}\|} \sum_{i=1}^{N} x(i).y(i), \tag{1}$$

where $\|\mathbf{y}\|$ is the norm of vector $\mathbf{y}$.

Suppose that the original image is perturbed by some form of additive noise, such that vector $\mathbf{x}$ is modified to $\mathbf{x'}$, according to:

$$\mathbf{x'} = \mathbf{x} + \mathbf{n}. \tag{2}$$

The resulting projection on direction $\mathbf{y}$ is now:

$$P' = <\mathbf{x}, \mathbf{y}> + \frac{1}{\|\mathbf{y}\|} \sum_{i=1}^{N} n(i) y(i) \tag{3}$$

$$= P + \delta P.$$

Robustness of image projections to noise requires that $\delta P \approx 0$, which can be guaranteed if $\mathbf{n}$ has zero or nearly zero mean and N is sufficiently large. In fact, let n and y be random variables, independently distributed, with means μ_n and μ_y respectively. It is known that the expected value of their product is given by:

$$\mathrm{E}[n.y] = \mu_n \mu_y. \tag{4}$$

If the noise has zero mean, this expected value is equal to zero. As, apart from the normalizing constants N and $\|\mathbf{y}\|$, the second term of equation (3) represents an estimate of $\mathrm{E}[n.y]$, which will be the more accurate with increasing N, $\delta P \approx 0$ if $\mu_n \approx 0$ and N is large enough. This suggests the use of image projections in authentication schemes that have to be resistant to compression, as long as compression noise can be considered as having zero or nearly zero mean.

2.2 Embedding Method

The embedding procedure starts by decomposing the image into M sets of N pixels each. The optimum size of the sets result from a trade-off between robustness to compression and the capacity of protecting small portions of the image. Each set is stored in a vector of dimension N, with x_k being the vector resulting from set k.

The vectors are associated three by three, resulting in triads (x_k, x_l, x_m) of image vectors, with $k<l<m$. For each triad, its constitutive vectors are projected in secret directions – y_1, y_2, y_3 – as defined by eq. (5)

$$P_k =< x_k \cdot y_1 >$$

$$P_l =< x_1 \cdot y_2 >$$

$$P_m =< x_m \cdot y_3 > . \tag{5}$$

These projections are sorted in ascending order, resulting in P_1, P_2 and P_3, with $P_1 \le P_2 \le P_3$. The range between P_1 and P_3 is then split into intervals of length

$$\Delta = \max(\Delta_{min}, \alpha(P_3 - P_1)) \tag{6}$$

with Δ_{min} being the minimum interval length that guarantees robustness to authorized manipulations (such as compression). $\alpha<1$ is a tuning parameter that, as with Δ_{min}, must be estimated from statistical tests. The boundaries between intervals are numbered from bottom to top by $b_0, b_1, ..., b_n$, with $b_0 = P_1$, $b_1 = P_1 + \Delta$, $b_2 = P_1 + 2\Delta$, ..., $b_n = P_3 = P_1 + n\Delta$.

To embed a binary digit, the pixels involved in the computation of the projections are altered such that P_2, the median value of the projections, is modified to its nearest interval boundary of *even* parity, if the binary digit to insert is a '0', or of *odd* parity, if the binary digit to insert is a '1'. A similar embedding procedure was proposed in [9][10] but applied in the wavelet coefficient domain.

Supposing that P_2 is in the *k-th* interval

$$(k-1)\Delta + P_1 < P_2 < k\Delta + P_1 \tag{7}$$

the rule for inserting a '0' is then:

$$P_2 \rightarrow P_2 + dP_2 = \begin{cases} k\Delta + P_1 & \text{if } k \text{ is even} \\ (k-1)\Delta + P_1 & \text{if } k \text{ is odd} \end{cases} \tag{8}$$

and for inserting a '1' is:

$$P_2 \rightarrow P_2 + dP_2 = \begin{cases} k\Delta + P_1 & \text{if } k \text{ is odd} \\ (k-1)\Delta + P_1 & \text{if } k \text{ is even} . \end{cases} \tag{9}$$

If P_2 alone is modified, the mean value of the image will change. Instead, it is possible to modify the three projections P_1, P_2 and P_3, in order that the mean value of the image remains constant. Also, condition (8) and (9) can be verified with smaller variations on P_1, P_2 and P_3 than that required for P_2 alone, minimizing the appearance of image artifacts. Supposing once more that P_2 falls into the k-th interval, the modifications on P_1, P_2 and P_3 will be:

$$dP_1 = dP_3 = -\frac{1}{3} dP; \; dP_2 = \frac{2}{3} dP \tag{10}$$

where

$$dP = \begin{cases} k\Delta + P_1 - P_2, & \text{if } k \text{ even and } bit = '0' \text{ or } k \text{ odd and } bit = '1' \\ (k\text{-}1)\Delta + P_1 - P_2, & \text{if } k \text{ even and } bit = '0' \text{ or } k \text{ odd and } bit = '1' \end{cases} \tag{11}$$

and '*bit*' is the watermark value to be inserted. As $\sum\limits_{i=1}^{3} dP_i = 0$, the mean value of the image will remain constant.

From eq. (1), a variation of dP_i in P_i can be obtained by changing, in average, the value of the image pixels involved in the computation of P_i by: $\dfrac{\|\mathbf{y}\|}{\sum\limits_{i=1}^{N} y(i)} dP_i$

The decision for inserting a logical '0' or '1' is done accordingly to the image characteristics, which favors the algorithm capacity for detecting non-authorized manipulations:

If $P_1 = \; <\mathbf{x_i}, \mathbf{y_1}>$ and $P_3 = \; <\mathbf{x_j}, \mathbf{y_3}>$,   with $i, j = k, l$ or m and $i \neq j$ $\qquad$ (12)

then $\begin{cases} \text{if } i < j, & \text{bit } = '0'; \\ \text{otherwise, bit } = '1'. \end{cases}$

To check the authenticity of an image, the process has to be reversed on the receiving end. First, from the image under evaluation the different triads of pixel vectors are obtained and the respective projections are computed. For each triad, the embedded bit is extracted by computing for each median projection the nearest boundary: if the parity of this boundary is even, a '0' is extracted; otherwise a '1' is extracted. Image integrity is decided by comparing the extracted bits with those obtained from the rule expressed in eq. (12).

2.3 Constraints on Δ and Δ_{min}

Being δP_{max} the absolute value of the maximum expected variation in the image projections due to compression (to be obtained from statistical tests), it follows immediately that

$$\Delta_{min} \geq 2 \, \delta P_{max} . \tag{13}$$

In fact, and supposing P_1 and P_3 are not modified by compression, the margin for modification in P_2 that assures a correct recover of the boundary parity and inserted bit is $\pm \Delta/2$.

Note that equation (13) does not *a priori* guarantee robustness to compression, as P_1 and P_3 may also change after compression resulting in different interval size and interval boundaries. Suppose that P_2 was modified at the insertion to the *k-th* boundary, i.e., $P_2+dP_2= P_1+k\Delta$. To recover the right boundary at the verification, it must be assured that:

$$P_1' + k\Delta' - \frac{\Delta'}{2} \le P_2' \le P_1' + k\Delta' + \frac{\Delta'}{2} \tag{14}$$

where

$$\Delta' = \alpha \, (P_3' - P_1') = \Delta + \alpha \, (\delta P_3 - \delta P_1) \tag{15}$$
$$P_i' = P_i + \delta P_i, \quad i = 1,2,3$$

are, respectively, the interval width and projections values after compression and δP_i, $i=1,2,3$ are the projections variation due to compression. Introducing (15) in (14), after some manipulations results in:

$$\frac{\Delta}{2} \ge \delta P_2 - (1 - \frac{\alpha}{2} - \alpha \, k)\delta P_1 - (\frac{\alpha}{2} + \alpha \, k)\delta P_3 . \tag{16}$$

Supposing that $(1-\alpha/2-\alpha k) > 0$, the maximum value for the right-hand side of eq. (16) is attained when:

$$\delta P_1 = -\delta P_2 = \delta P_3 = -\delta P_{max} \tag{17}$$

resulting in

$$\Delta_{min} \ge 4 \, \delta P_{max} . \tag{18}$$

Equation (18) expresses the worst case Δ value for which the system is resistant to maximum variations of δP_{max} in the original image projections.

2.4 Generation of Projection Directions

Most watermarking algorithms assume that it is desirable to have secure data-embedding and extraction procedures. Typically, a secret key determines how the data is embedded in the host signal. A user needs to know that key to extract the data.

In the proposed method, security resides in the directions onto which image vectors are projected. In the results presented in this paper, these directions - y_1, y_2 and y_3 - were obtained from a random-number generator uniformly distributed in [0,1]. The seeds to generate each direction result from a linear combination of a secret key and: the horizontal image size for y_1, the vertical image size for y_2, the total image size for y_3. In this way, if the image size is modified through scaling or cropping, so will the directions and the resulting image projections be, and the change will be detected by the watermarking extraction procedure.

2.5 Summary of Insertion and Verification Algorithms

The algorithms for inserting and extracting the authentication data can be summarised as follows:

Insertion algorithm
- i)   From the image to mark, obtain M vectors, each one containing N image pixels; Associate the vectors three by three (form vector triads);
- ii) From a secret key, image size and a random numbers generator (uniformly distributed in $[0,1]$), obtain three N-dimensional random vectors: y_1, y_2 and y_3;
- iii) Project each vector triad onto the directions obtained in *ii)* (eq. (1) and (5));
- iv) For each vector triad, sort in ascending order the respective projections, obtaining P_1, P_2 and P_3. Compute Δ (eq. (6)) and the bit to insert (eq. (12));
- v)   For each vector triad, insert the bit obtained in *iv)* (eq. (10) and (11)).

Extraction algorithm
- i)   For the image whose integrity has to be verified, apply steps *i)* to *iv)* of the insertion algorithm (in step *iv)*, eq. (11) gives now the bit to be extracted);
- ii) For each vector triad, obtain the embedded bit by computing the nearest interval boundary of P_2. If the parity of this boundary is even, the extracted bit is ´0´; otherwise it is ´1´;
- iii) Compare the bits obtained in *i)* and *ii)*. If they match, a correct bit has been extracted.

3 Results

In the implemented authentication system, image vectors were obtained by splitting the image into non-overlapping lines and columns. With reference to fig.1, where an image and its pixel positions are represented, a line vector - **l** - is obtained by reading the image pixels along a line, in the positions marked with a cross; a triad of line vectors is obtained by reading three spatial consecutive image lines. A column vector - **c** - is obtained by reading the image pixels along a column, in the positions marked with a circle; a triad of column vectors is obtained by reading three spatial consecutive image columns.

The manipulation of the pixels values inside the grey box of fig. 1, if strong enough, will modify the relationship between image projections for the first line vector triad and for the two first column vector triads. The intersection of those triads allows the integrity evaluator to localize the modification inside the image.

Image projections were computed replacing in eq. (1) the normalizing constant $\|y\|$ by N.

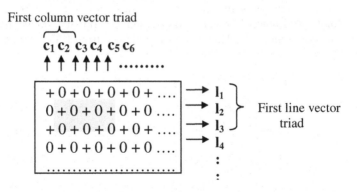

Fig. 1. Interlaced structure used for scanning line and column image vectors. Symbols '+' and '0' represent, respectively, pixel sites used to produce line and column vectors.

3.1 Estimation of Δ_{min}

As mentioned previously, the robustness of the embedding method to compression and its sensitiveness to content tampering depends on the insertion parameters Δ and Δ_{min}. The larger Δ is, the more robust the algorithm will be to compression errors. However, larger values of Δ will also imply stronger modifications on the pixel values and the appearance of horizontal and vertical stripes on the image. Also, it reduces the capability for detecting content manipulations. In what concerns the parameter Δ_{min} it should be set to a value that guarantees a maximum value for the probability of false positives (i.e., the probability of erroneously decide that the image has been tampered). Suppose that:

   i)   the minimum relevant area from the point of view of content manipulation has dimension of $n{\times}n$ pixels (which comprises $n/3$ projection triads in each direction);

   ii)   an image is considered authentic if, for any sequence of $n/3$ spatial adjacent projection triads (in horizontal and vertical directions), no more than m have resulted in a wrong extracted bit.

If p is the probability of extracting a wrong bit due to compression then, the probability of a false positive - P_{fp} - due to compression errors is:

$$P_{fp} = 1 - \sum_{0}^{m}\binom{n/3}{i} p^{i} (1-p)^{n/3-i} . \tag{19}$$

This equation can be used to obtain an estimate for Δ_{min}. Defining m, n and an objective value for P_{fp}, eq. (19) can be solved for p. Then, through eq. (13) we obtain $\Delta_{min}=2\delta P$ where δP is the modification on the image projections due to compression, whose probability of being exceeded is p.

Figure 2 presents the cumulative distribution function of δP, defined as the absolute difference between original and compressed image projections, for the luminance component. This figure was obtained from JPEG compression tests, with

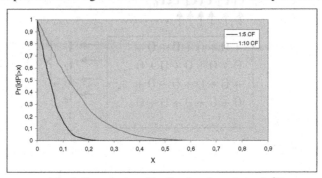

Fig.2 Cumulative distribution function of δP

compression factors of 1:5 and 1:10, and over a database of still images. Using this figure, and with m, n and P_{fp} already settled, it is possible to infer an estimate for δP and Δ_{min}.

3.2 Probability of False Negatives

Another important quantity to assess is the probability of false negatives, i.e., the probability of missing the detection of an unauthorized content modification. The probability of having projection P_2 in a odd (or even) parity boundary is 0.5. Also, the probability of having the correct relationship between P_1 and P_3 (expressed by eq. (12)) is 0.5. Accordingly, the probability of extracting a "good" bit is, for each vector triad, 0.25. Imposing once more that an image is considered authentic if, for any sequence of $n/3$ spatial adjacent projection triads no more than m have result in a wrong extracted bit, the probability of a false negative – P_{fn} – will be:

$$P_{fn} = \sum_{i=0}^{m} \binom{n/3}{i} 0.25^{n/3-i} 0.75^{i}. \tag{20}$$

For $n/3=8$ and $m=1$ we get $P_{fn}=9.84\text{E-}04$. This value can be reduced by increasing n or by embedding more than one bit in each triad. Of course, in both cases, the value of Δ_{min} should be increased to maintain the same probability of false positives.

3.3 Robustness to Compression

Several tests were performed in order to find the best practical values for parameters α, Δ_{min}, m and n, beginning with first estimates for these parameters, obtained as described in sections 3.1 and 3.2. The parameter α has been set to 0.25. With Δ given by eq. (6), this result in a constant number of 4 intervals between P_1 and P_3 for every

a)   b)   c)

Fig. 3. "Cameraman": a) Original Image; b) Watermarked and modified Image (Image modification is highlighted by a circle); c)Result of the verification algorithm

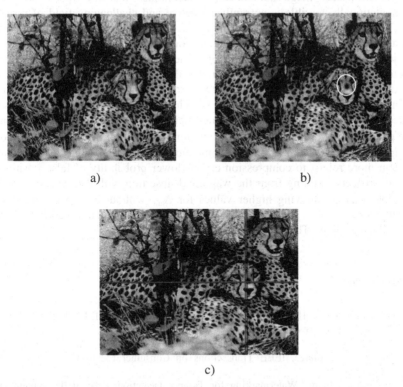

a)   b)

c)

Fig. 4. "Jaguar": a) Original Image; b) Watermarked and modified Image (Image modification is highlighted by a circle); c) Result of the verification algorithm

projection triad. We have also concluded that a value for Δ_{min} of 0.6 guarantees robustness to JPEG compression up to compression factors of 1:10, without compromising the image quality after the insertion. In what concerns parameters m and $n/3$ they have been set to 1 and 8, respectively.

3.4 Sensitivity to Semantic Content Modifications

In order to evaluate the sensitivity of the proposed method to semantic content modifications, the same database of still images used for the compression tests was employed. Figures 3 and 4 show some examples of semantic content modification that in all cases were detected and localized by the algorithm. In figures 3-b) and 4-b), a circle highlights image manipulations. Image vectors for which a wrong bit was detected are also signaled in figures 3-c) and 4-c).

4 Conclusions and Further Work

Content-based image authentication techniques that are robust, reliable and computationally feasible is currently an active and challenging field of research. In this paper a new contribution on this subject is given. A new fragile watermarking technique was described, that exploits the rank orders relationship of image projections throughout the entire image. The viability of the method as a means of protecting the content was assessed under JPEG compression and semantic content modifications. With the present system, robustness to JPEG compression up to compression factors of about 1:10 can be achieved. At the same time, it is possible to detect and localize quite small image modifications. A key element of the algorithm is the parameter Δ_{min} related with the minimum modification that has to be imposed on image projections to embed the authentication data. Larger values of Δ_{min} result in a system more robust to compression errors (lower probability of false positives), but image artifacts resulting from the watermark insertion will also be more evident. A possible way of allowing higher values for Δ_{min} without compromising the image quality is to use perceptual models of the human visual system together with the data insertion algorithm. This is the subject of current work.

References

1. W. Diffie and M. Hellman, New Directions in Cryptography, IEEE Trans. on Information Theory 22 (6) (November 1976) 644-654
2. G. L. Friedman, The Trustworthy Digital Camera: Restoring Credibility to the Photographic Image, IEEE Transactions on Consumer Electronics 39 (4) (November 1993) 905-910
3. J. Fridrich, Image Watermarking for Tamper Detection, Proc. ICIP, September 1998, pp. 404-408

4. D. Kundur and D. Hatzinakos, Towards a Telltale Watermarking Technique for Tamper-Proofing, Proc. ICIP, September 1998, pp. 409-413
5. C.-Y. Lin and S.-F. Chang, A Robust Image Authentication Method Surviving JPEG Lossy Compression, Proc. of IS&T/SPIE Symposium on Electronics Imaging, San Jose, USA, January 1998
6. M. P. Queluz, Towards Robust, Content Based Techniques for Image Authentication, Proc. IEEE 2nd Worshop on Multimedia Signal Processing, Los Angeles, CA, December 1998, pp. 297-302
7. M. P. Queluz, Content-based Integrity Protection of Digital Images, Proc. SPIE - Security and Watermarking of Multimedia Contents, San Jose, CA, January 1999, pp. 85-93
8. M. Schneider and S.-F. Chang, A Robust Content Based Digital Signature for Image Authentication, Proc. ICIP, September 1996, pp. 227-230
9. L. Xie and G. Arce, Joint Wavelet Compression and Authentication Watermarking, Proc. ICIP, October 1998, pp. 427-431
10. L. Xie and G. Arce, A Blind Wavelet Based Digital Signature for Image Authentication, Proc. EUSIPCO, September 1998.

Fast Robust Template Matching for Affine Resistant Image Watermarks

Shelby Pereira and Thierry Pun

University of Geneva - CUI,
24 rue General Dufour, CH 1211 Geneva 4, Switzerland,
{Shelby.Pereira,Thierry.Pun}@cui.unige.ch
http://cuiwww.unige.ch/~vision

Abstract. Digital watermarks have been proposed as a method for discouraging illicit copying and distribution of copyrighted material. This paper describes a method for the secure and robust copyright protection of digital images. We present an approach for embedding a digital watermark into an image using the Fourier transform. To this watermark is added a template in the Fourier transform domain to render the method robust against general linear transformations. We detail a new algorithm for the accurate and efficient recovery of the template in an image which has undergone a general affine transformation. Furthermore we demonstrate how the template can be used as a tool for asserting the presence of a watermark. We also systematically evaluate the algorithm and present results which demonstrate the robustness of the method against some common image processing operations such as compression, rotation, scaling and aspect ratio changes.

1   Introduction

The World Wide Web, digital networks and multimedia afford virtually unprecedented opportunities to pirate copyrighted material. Digital storage and transmission make it trivial to quickly and inexpensively construct exact copies. Consequently, the idea of using a robust digital watermark to detect and trace copyright violations has therefore stimulated significant interest among artists and publishers.

In order for a watermark to be useful it must be robust against a variety of possible attacks by pirates. These include robustness against compression such as JPEG, scaling and aspect ratio changes, rotation, cropping, row and column removal, addition of noise, filtering, cryptographic and statistical attacks, as well as insertion of other watermarks. A discussion of possible attacks is given by Petitcolas and Craver [15,3]. Watermarking methods have become increasingly more robust against the above mentioned attacks.

Many of the current techniques for embedding marks in digital images have been inspired by methods of image coding and compression. Information has been embedded using the Discrete Cosine Transform (DCT) [8,2], Wavelets [1],

A. Pfitzmann (Ed.): IH'99, LNCS 1768, pp. 199–210, 2000.
© Springer-Verlag Berlin Heidelberg 2000

Linear Predictive Coding [10], and Fractals [17] as well as in the spatial domain [16,21]. While these methods perform well against compression, they lack robustness to geometric transformations. Consequently methods have emerged which exploit the properties of the Discrete Fourier Transform (DFT) to achieve robustness against rotation and scaling. The DFT methods can be divided into two classes, those based on invariance [12,7] and those which embed a template into the image which is searched for during the detection of the watermark and yields information about the transformation undergone by the image [13,18]. However both these methods exploit the properties of log-polar-maps (LPM) and can only be used to detect changes of rotation and scale. Similarly the log-log-map (LLM) [4] has also been proposed as a means of detecting changes in aspect ratio. However, once again general transformations cannot be recovered.

The method we propose in the text that follows consists of embedding a watermark in the DFT domain. The watermark is composed of two parts, a template and a spread spectrum message containing the information or payload. The template contains no information in itself, but is used to detect transformations undergone by the image. Once detected, these transformations are inverted and then the spread spectrum signal is decoded. The payload contains information such as the owner of the image, a serial number and perhaps flags which indicate the type of content e.g. religion, pornography, or politics. This can be useful for indexing images or even for tracking pornography on the web.

System security is based on proprietary knowledge of the keys (or the seeds for pseudo-random generators) which are required to embed, extract or remove an image watermark. In the case of a public watermarking scheme the key is generally available and may even be contained in publicly available software. In a private watermarking scheme the key is proprietary. From the point of view of embedding watermarks in documents given the keys or seeds the sequences themselves can be generated with ease. A mark may be embedded or extracted by the key owner which, in our model, is the Copyright Holder. Our system is a private watermarking scheme in which the cryptography aspects are detailed by Herrigel [7] and will not be addressed here. In what follows, we limit ourselves to the image processing aspects of the problem.

The main contribution of this article lies in the development of a method for recovering a watermark from an image which has undergone a general affine transformation. Unlike algorithms which use log-polar or log-log-maps, we propose searching the space of possible affine transformations. Since an exhaustive search leads to an intractable problem, we demonstrate how a careful pruning of the search space leads to robust detection of transformations reasonable quickly. The proposed method is evaluated relative to the benchmark series of tests proposed by Kutter and Petitcolas [9] and implemented in the software package Stirmark3 [14]. The algorithm performs very well relative to the extensive series of tests implemented in the benchmark.

The rest of this paper is structured as follows. In section 2 we describe the embedding approach. Section 3 describes the extraction algorithm. In Section 4, we present our results. Finally, section 5 contains our conclusions.

2 Embedding

In this section we describe the embedding approach. First we show how the message is encoded. Secondly we review some key properties of the DFT before demonstrating how the encoded message is inserted in this domain. We conclude this section by showing how the template is also embedded in the DFT domain.

2.1 Encoding the Message

In image watermarking, we are given a message to be embedded which can be represented in binary form as $m = (m_1, m_2...m_M)$ where m_i in$\{0, 1\}$ and M is the number of bits in the message. In realistic applications M is roughly 60 bits which contain the necessary copyright information as well as flags which can be used to indicate the type of content in the image. In our scheme, the binary message is first coded using the well known BCH codes [19] to produce the message m_c of length $M_c = 72$. We then apply the mapping $0 \rightarrow -1$ and $1 \rightarrow 1$ to produce the bipolar signal $\tilde{m}_c = (\tilde{m}_{c1}...\tilde{m}_{cM_c})$ which can then be embedded as described in section 2.3.

2.2 The DFT and Its Properties

Definition Let the image be a real valued function $f(x_1, x_2)$ defined on an integer-valued Cartesian grid $0 \leq x_1 < N_1, 0 \leq x_2 < N_2$.

The Discrete Fourier Transform (DFT) is defined as follows:

$$F(k_1, k_2) = \sum_{x_1=0}^{N_1-1} \sum_{x_2=0}^{N_2-1} f(x_1, x_2)e^{-j2\pi x_1 k_1/N_1 - j2\pi x_2 k_2/N_2} \tag{1}$$

The inverse transform is

$$f(x_1, x_2) = \frac{1}{N_1 N_2} \sum_{k_1=0}^{N_1-1} \sum_{k_2=0}^{N_2-1} F(k_1, k_2)e^{j2\pi k_1 x_1/N_1 + j2\pi k_2 x_2/N_2} \tag{2}$$

The DFT of a real image is generally complex valued. This leads to magnitude and phase representation for the image:

$$A(k_1, k_2) = |F(k_1, k_2)| \tag{3}$$

$$\Phi(k_1, k_2) = \angle F(k_1, k_2) \tag{4}$$

General Properties of the Fourier Transform It is instructive to study the effect of an arbitrary linear transform on the spectrum of an image.

Once $N_1 = N_2$ (i.e. square blocks) the kernel of the DFT contains a term of the form:

$$x_1 k_1 + x_2 k_2 = \begin{bmatrix} x_1 & x_2 \end{bmatrix} \begin{bmatrix} k_1 \\ k_2 \end{bmatrix} \tag{5}$$

If we compute a linear transform on the spatial coordinates:

$$\begin{bmatrix} x_1 \\ x_2 \end{bmatrix} \rightarrow T \begin{bmatrix} x_1 \\ x_2 \end{bmatrix} \tag{6}$$

then one can see that the value of the DFT will not change[1] if:

$$\begin{bmatrix} k_1 \\ k_2 \end{bmatrix} \rightarrow (T^{-1})^T \begin{bmatrix} k_1 \\ k_2 \end{bmatrix} \tag{7}$$

Since our watermarks are embedded in the DFT domain, if we can determine the transformation T undergone by the image in the spatial domain, it will be possible to compensate for this transformation in the DFT domain and thereby recover the watermark. The matrix T is an arbitrary matrix which can be a composition of scale changes, rotations, and/or skews. In section 3.1 we will discuss how to recover watermarks when an arbitrary matrix T is applied to the image.

DFT: Translation Another important property of the DFT is its translation invariance. In fact, shifts in the spatial domain cause a linear shift in the phase component.

$$F(k_1, k_2) \exp\left[-j(ak_1 + bk_2)\right] \leftrightarrow f(x_1 + a, x_2 + b) \tag{8}$$

From equation 8 of the Fourier transform it is clear that spatial shifts affect only the phase representation of an image. This leads to the well known result that the magnitude of the Fourier transform is invariant to translations in the spatial domain. This property leads directly to the fact that the watermark is robust against cropping.

2.3   Embedding the Watermark

When working with color images, we first extract the luminance component and then rescale the RGB components accordingly. In order to embed the watermark for an image of size (m, n), we first pad the image with zeros so that the resulting size is 1024×1024. If the image is larger than 1024×1024 then the image is divided into 1024×1024 blocks and the watermark is calculated for each block. The watermark is embedded into the DFT domain between radii f_{w1} and f_{w2} where f_{w1} and f_{w2} are chosen to occupy a mid-frequency range. We note that the strongest components of the DFT are in the center which contains the low frequencies as illustrated in figure 1. Since during the recovery phase the image represents noise, these low frequencies must be avoided. We also avoid the high frequencies since these are the ones most significantly modified during lossy compression such as JPEG.

---

[1] The DFT will be invariant except for a scaling factor which depends on the Jacobian of Transformation, namely the determinant of the transformation matrix T.

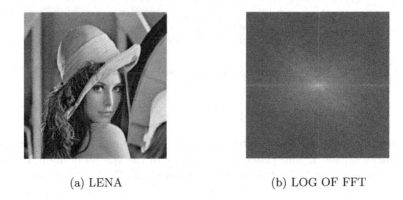

(a) LENA   (b) LOG OF FFT

Fig. 1. Original lena image and log of magnitude of FFT

To embed the mark between the chosen radii, we first generate a sequence of points $(x_1, y_1)...(x_{M_c}, y_{M_c})$ pseudo-randomly as determined by a secret key. Here, x_i, y_i are integers such that $f_{w1} < \sqrt{x_i^2 + y_i^2} < f_{w2}$. We note that only half the available points in the annulus $\{f_{w1}, f_{w2}\}$ can be marked since the DFT must be symmetric in order to yield a real image upon inversion. In what follows we work in the upper half plane and assume that the corresponding modifications are made in the lower half plane $(\pm x_i, y_i)$ to fulfill the symmetry constraints.

Since the magnitude of the DFT is positive valued, in order to encode the bipolar message $\tilde{M}_c$, we adopt the following differential encoding scheme. For each message bit $\tilde{m}_{c_i}$ we modify the points (x_i, y_i) and $(y_i, -x_i)$ such that $k_w \tilde{m}_{c_i} = (x_i, y_i) - (y_i, -x_i)$. In other words 2 points 90° apart are modified such that the difference is equal to the desired message value. The parameter k_w is the strength of the watermark. The watermark strength can be set interactively or can be set adaptively as function of the average value and standard deviation of the DFT components of the image lying between f_{w1} and f_{w2}. If the strength is set interactively, the user can examine the artifacts introduced in the image as the strength is increased and finally settle on a strength which is as high as possible while at the same time leaving the watermark relatively invisible.

2.4   Embedding the Template

The template contains no information but is merely a tool used to recover possible transformations in the image. In previous work the template consisted of a random arrangement of peaks in the FFT domain [13]. We have found experimentally that using templates of approximately 8 points works best. In section 3.1 we provide a theoretical justification using probabilistic arguments to justify this choice. The points of the template are distributed uniformly in the DFT with radii varying between f_{t1} and f_{t2}. The angles (θ_i) and radii (r_{ij}) are chosen pseudo-randomly as determined by a secret key. The strength of the template is determined adaptively as well. We find that inserting points at a strength equal to the local average value of DFT points plus three standard deviations yields a good compromise between visibility and robustness during decoding. We note in particular that points in the high frequencies are inserted less strongly since in these regions the average value of the high frequencies is usually lower than the average value of the low frequencies. We also note that it is critical that the points be inserted strongly enough so that they remain peaks after interpolation errors from possible transformations. The reason for this will be clear in the next section.

3   Decoding

The watermark extraction process is divided into two phases. First we have the template detection phase and then we decode the watermark if the template has been detected. The main idea is to search possible transformations while taking care not to examine the large amount of cases that cannot lead to a successful template match.

3.1   Template Detection

The template detection process involves several steps which are enumerated below. We first present the basic algorithm and then indicate how to effectively prune the search space by applying a few heuristics.

1. Calculate the FFT of the image zero padded to 1024×1024.
2. Extract the positions of all the local peaks (p_{xi}, p_{yi}) in the image. We denote this set of peaks as P.
3. Choose two points in the template (x'_1, y'_1) and (x'_2, y'_2).
4. For all pairs of points $(p_{xi}, p_{yi}); (p_{xj}, p_{yj})$ perform the following steps
   (a) Compute the transformation matrix A which maps the two template points to the point pair $(p_{xi}, p_{yi}); (p_{xj}, p_{yj})$
   (b) Apply the transformation to the other template points
   (c) Count the number of transformed template points lie within a small radius r_{min} of any peak in the set P. These are the matched template points
   (d) If we have at least N_m matches we conclude that the template is found and terminate the search, otherwise we proceed to the next point pair.
5. If all point pairs have been tested and we never obtain N_m matches, we conclude that no watermark has been found.
6. If we have at least N_m matches, recalculate the linear transformation A using all the matched points such that the mean square estimation error in equation 9 is minimized.

$$mse = \frac{1}{nummatches} \left\| A \begin{bmatrix} x'_1 & y'_1 \\ \vdots & \vdots \\ x'_l & y'_l \end{bmatrix}^T - \begin{bmatrix} p_{x1} & p_{y1} \\ \vdots & \vdots \\ p_{xl} & p_{yl} \end{bmatrix}^T \right\|^2 \qquad (9)$$

We note that A is a 2×2 linear transformation matrix so that we understand the notation $\|.\|$ to mean the sum of the magnitude of the two rows of the error matrix. The rows contain the errors in estimating the x and y from the known template positions x' and y' after applying the transformation A. If we have less than N_m matches we conclude that no watermark is found.

Some observations are necessary. In step 1 we pad to 1024×1024 in order to obtain a good resolution in the FFT domain. This is important in order to obtain accurate estimates of the transformation matrix. We also note that the re-estimation in step 6 is important since it increases the accuracy of the matrix A. Finally we note that step 4d contains a criterion for asserting the presence of a watermark. Consequently the template serves the dual purpose of recovering geometrical transformations and asserting the presence of a watermark even if the watermark itself may be falsely decoded. Some alternate schemes consist of using cross-correlation as in [20,22,5] or Bayesian models as in [11]. The advantage of using the template is that it is much more robust than the watermark itself since we concentrate a significant amount of energy into a few points in the FFT.

Step 4 contains the most costly part of the algorithm. As it stands the cost of the algorithm is $O(N^2 M)$ where N is the number of points in P and M is the number of points in the template. N can be as large as 500 points so that we find that the algorithm may take up to 5 minutes in some cases on a pentium 400MHz machine to find a search.

However the search space can be drastically pruned by exploiting two heuristics. Firstly we observe that if we choose in step 5 the points (x'_1, y'_1) and (x'_2, y'_2) which are (r'_1, θ'_1) and (r'_2, θ'_2) in polar coordinates then if $r'_1 > r'_2$ we need only consider points in the P where $r_1 > r_2$. Similarly if $r'_1 < r'_2$ we need only consider points in the P where $r_1 < r_2$. Here we are in fact exploiting the fact that for realistic transformations small and large frequencies will never be inverted. This immediately reduces the search space by a factor of 2.

The second important observation is that for transformations which are likely to occur in practice the difference in θ between two template points will change only slightly. In practice we can limit the change in θ to roughly $\pm 20°$. Exploiting this observation further reduces the search space to $\frac{40°}{360°}$ of the original size. When we apply these heuristics we obtain an algorithm which finds the affine transformation in roughly 15 seconds on a pentium 400MHz.

Since we are using the template to assert the presence of a watermark, it is important to evaluate the probability of a false detection in order to justify the approach. The evaluation of this probability is relatively straightforward. We first note that on a 1024×1024 grid with 500 points (which for simplicity we assume are uniformly distributed) the probability of finding a point in a given location is $500/1024^2 \approx \frac{1}{2000}$. Since we work on a discrete grid, when we look for a match we also look in the 8 surrounding neighbors (i.e. r_{min} equals one pixel in step 5c), we multiply by 9 to obtain $\frac{9}{2000}$. We must now count the number of transformations which will be calculated. If we ignore the heuristics used to prune the search space, an exhaustive search involves $2N^2 = 2 \times 500^2$ transformations. The factor of 2 comes from the fact that the ordering is essential. By pruning the search space, we reduce the number of calculated transformations by a factor of 2×9 so that roughly 3000 transformations are evaluated. Now if we embed a template with 8 points and insist that all 8 points be matched at detection, we obtain that the probability of a false match given by equation 10. This probability is extremely small and in practice no false detections have been encountered.

$$P_{false} = \frac{9}{2000}^{8} \times 3000 \approx 5.0 \times 10^{-16} \tag{10}$$

3.2   Decoding the Watermark

Once the transformation matrix A has been detected the decoding of the watermark is straightforward and proceeds as follows.

1. Calculate the FFT of the windowed image I_w of size (I_m, I_n).
2. Generate the sequence of points $(x_1, y_1)...(x_{M_c}, y_{M_c})$ pseudo-randomly as determined by the secret key used during embedding.
3. Calculate the normalized coordinates in Fourier domain of the points as follows
   $(x_{ni}, y_{ni}) = (x_i/1024, y_i/1024)$.
4. Apply the transformation matrix A to the normalized coordinates to yield
   $(\tilde{x}_1, \tilde{y}_1)...(\tilde{x}_{M_c}, \tilde{y}_{M_c})$
5. Extract the watermark from the transformed coordinates, taking into account the 90° coding scheme used during embedding and using bilinear interpolation to obtain values for samples which do not correspond directly to samples directly on the calculated FFT. This yields the bipolar signal $\tilde{m}'$.
6. We then take the sign of $\tilde{m}'$ and apply the transformation $-1 \rightarrow 0$ and $1 \rightarrow 1$ to yield the recovered binary bit sequence b.
7. The bit sequence b represents the recovered message encoded by the BCH error correcting codes. This sequence is now decoded to yield the recovered message m_r. For a message of length 72, if there are fewer than 5 errors, the 60 bit recovered message m_r will be identical to the embedded message m since these errors will be corrected by the BCH codes.

We note that in the first step we do not pad the image with zeros since this leads to artifacts in the DFT domain. Rather, we perform directly the FFT on the windowed image and then work in normalized frequencies. We note that when performing the FFT, it is not necessary for the image size to be a power of 2 in order to transform from the spatial domain to DFT and vice-versa since we adopt the FFTW package [6] to calculate FFTs of arbitrary size efficiently.

4   Results

In this section we evaluate the proposed approach relative to a standard series of tests detailed by Petitcolas and Kutter [15,9] and then compare the results to the performance of two commercially available algorithms.

4.1 Test Results

We use the stirmark [14] program to evaluate the algorithm. The tests are divided into the following 8 sections: signal enhancement, compression, scaling, cropping, shearing, rotation, row/column removal, and random geometric distortions. We use the images of Lena, Mandrill and Fishingboat. The original and watermarked images appear in figures 2 and 3 respectively. We note that for a PSNR of 38dB, the watermark is invisible. For each attack we consider the attack by itself and where applicable after JPEG compression at a quality factor of 90. For each image we assign a score of 1 if for that case, the watermark is correctly decoded. If the watermark is incorrectly decoded, we assign a value of 0. We then compute an average for each section and summarize the results.

(a) LENA   (b) MANDRILL   (c) FISHINGBOAT

Fig. 2. Original images

In the signal enhancement section which includes Gaussian, median, and sharpening filters as well as the Frequency Mode Laplacian Removal attack, the watermark was correctly decoded in all cases. The algorithm is successful against JPEG down to a level of 75 quality factor. In all cases the combinations of rotations, scales and cropping were correctly recovered. Against scaling the watermark is successfully recovered in the range 0.75 to 2, but fails when the image is scaled to 0.5. This can be expected since 75% of the information is lost in this case. The watermarked is recovered when up to 50% of the image has been cropped. Furthermore, the watermark is also successfully recovered against shearings of 0.01% and 0.1% and combinations of row and column removal. Unfortunately the watermark is never recovered when the random geometric distortions implemented by the stirmark program are applied. We summarize the results in table 1 where we compute the average for each section. We note that for the compression section we first calculate the average for JPEG compression and then compute the average of the results with the results of GIF compression as

(a) LENA   (b) MANDRILL   (c) FISHINGBOAT

Fig. 3. Watermarked images with PSNR> 38dB

Table 1. Results: summary and comparison

	Proposed approach	Digimarc	Suresign
Enhancement	1	1	1
Compression	0.74	0.81	0.95
Scaling	0.78	0.72	0.95
Cropping	0.89	1	1
Shearing	1	0.5	0.5
Rotation	1	0.94	0.5
Row/column removal+flip	1	1	1
Random Geometrical Distortions	0	0.33	0

done in Petitcolas' benchmark tests for the commercially available watermarking packages Digimarc[2] and Suresign[3].

Relative to the benchmark series of tests, the watermark performs well and comparably to commercially available algorithms. The algorithm fails for random geometric distortions since the FFT is severely distorted. However, to our knowledge, at this time no algorithm systematically decodes watermarks successfully after being attacked by the random geometric distortions implemented in the Stirmark3 [14] package.

The major improvement lies in the fact that the algorithm recovers general affine transforms. We note in particular that the algorithm is successful 100% of the time in cases of shearing whereas the other algorithms only recover the watermark in cases where the shearing is small. Since the general affine transformation is not included in version 3.0 of the Stirmark benchmark tests used for our results, we tested the algorithm on images which have undergone a relatively

---

[2] Digimarc Batch Embedding Tool c01.00.13 and Readmarc v1.5.8 used for the tests
[3] SureSign Server version 1.94 used for the tests

large general linear transformation given by the matrix $A = \begin{bmatrix} 1.3 & 0.1 \\ -0.05 & 0.8 \end{bmatrix}$. In all cases our algorithm successfully decodes the watermark.

5 Conclusion

In this article we have described a new algorithm for recovering watermarks which have undergone an arbitrary linear transformation. The main idea consists of pruning a relatively large search space to obtain a fast decoding algorithm which recovers the general affine transformation. The method is robust against a wide variety of tests as indicated by the results obtained when evaluated relative to the extensive series of benchmark tests proposed in [9] and is comparable to currently available commercial algorithms with the major improvement lies in its ability to detect general affine transformations whereas other algorithms are generally limited to rotations and scales.

Acknowledgments

We thank Gabriela Csurka, Frederic Deguillaume, and Svyatoslav Voloshynovski for there valuable insights. We also thank Fabien Petitcolas for making test results available for comparison and for providing the Stirmark3 software package. We are also grateful to Dr. Alexander Herrigel and Digital Copyright Technologies for their work on the security architecture for the digital watermark and for the ongoing collaboration. This work is financed by the Swiss Priority Program on Information and Communication Structures (project Krypict) and by the European Esprit Open Microprocessor Initiative (Project JEDI-FIRE). This work is part of the European Patent application EU 978107084.

References

1. Marco Corvi and Gianluca Nicchiotti. Wavelet based image watermarking for copyright protection. In Michael Frydrych, Jussi Parkkinen, and Ari Visa, editors, *The 10th Scandinavian Conference on Image Analysis*, pages 157–163, Lappeenranta, Finland, June 1997. Pattern Recognition Society of Finland. 199

2. I. Cox, J. Killian, T. Leighton, and T. Shamoon. Secure spread spectrum watermarking for images, audio and video. In *Proceedings of the IEEE Int. Conf. on Image Processing ICIP-96*, pages 243–246, Lausanne, Switzerland, September 16-19 1996. 199

3. S Craver, N Memon, BL Yeo, and MM Yeung. Can invisible watermark resolve rightful ownerships? In *Fifth Conference on Storage and Retrieval for Image and Video Database*, volume 3022, pages 310–321, San Jose, CA, USA, February 1997. 199

4. F. Deguillaume, G. Csurka, J. J. K. Ó Ruanaidh, and T. Pun. Robust 3d dft video watermarking. In *IS&T/SPIE Electronic Imaging'99, Session: Security and Watermarking of Multimedia Contents*, San Jose, CA, USA, January 1999. 200

5. J. F. Delaigle, C. De Vleeschouwer, and B. Macq. Watermarking algorithm based on a human visual model. *Signal Processing*, 66:319–335, 1998. 205
6. Matteo Frigo and Steven Johnson. fftw-1.3. MIT, Boston, Massachusetts, 1997-98. 206
7. Alexander Herrigel, Joe J. K. Ó Ruanaidh, H. Petersen, Shelby Pereira, and Thierry Pun. Secure copyright protection techniques for digital images. In *International Workshop on Information Hiding*, Portland, OR, USA, April 1998. 200
8. C.-T. Hsu and J.-L. Wu. Hidden digital watermarks in images. *IEEE Transactions on Image Processing*, 8(1):58–68, January 1999. 199
9. M. Kutter and F. A. P. Petitcolas. A fair benchmark for image watermarking systems. In *Electronic Imaging '99, Security and Watermarking of Multimedia Contents*, volume 3657, pages 219–239, San Jose, CA, USA, January 1999. 200, 206, 209
10. K. Matsui and K. Tanaka. Video-Steganography: How to secretly embed a signature in a picture. In *IMA Intellectual Property Project Proceedings*, pages 187–206, January 1994. 200
11. J. J. K. Ó Ruanaidh and G. Csurka. A bayesian approach to spread spectrum watermark detection and secure copyright protection for digital image libraries. In *IEEE Conf. on Computer Vision and Pattern Recognition*, Fort Collins, Colorado, USA, June 1999. 205
12. Joe J. K. Ó Ruanaidh and Thierry Pun. Rotation, scale and translation invariant spread spectrum digital image watermarking. *Signal Processing*, 66(3):303–317, May 1998. (Special Issue on Copyright Protection and Control, B. Macq and I. Pitas, eds.). 200
13. S. Pereira, J. J. K. Ó Ruanaidh, F. Deguillaume, G. Csurka, and T. Pun. Template based recovery of Fourier-based watermarks using Log-polar and Log-log maps. In *Int. Conference on Multimedia Computing and Systems, Special Session on Multimedia Data Security and Watermarking*, Juin 1999. 200, 203
14. F. A. P. Petitcolas. http://www.cl.cam.ac.uk/ fapp2/watermarking/stirmark/. In *Stirmark3.0(60)*, 1999. 200, 207, 208
15. F. A. P. Petitcolas and R. J. Anderson. Attacks on copyright marking systems. In *2nd International Information Hiding Workshop*, pages 219–239, Portland, Oregon, USA, April 1998. 199, 206
16. I Pitas. A method for signature casting on digital images. In *Proceedings of the IEEE Int. Conf. on Image Processing ICIP-96*, pages 215–218, Lausanne, Switzerland, September 16-19 1996. 200
17. J. Puate and F. Jordan. Using fractal compression scheme to embed a digital signature into an image. In *Proceedings of SPIE Photonics East'96 Symposium*, November 1996. 200
18. G. B. Rhoads. Steganography systems. In *International Patent WO 96/36163 PCT/US96/06618*, November 1996. 200
19. C. Britton Rorabaugh. *Error Coding Cookbook : Practical C/C++ Routines and Recipes for Error Detection and Correction*. McGraw Hill Text, 1996. 201
20. M. D. Swanson, B. Zhu, and A. H. Tewfik. Multiresolution scene-based video watermarking using perceptual models. *IEEE Journal on Selected Areas in Communications*, 16(4):540–550, May 1998. 205
21. A. Z. Tirkel, C.F. Osborne, and T.E. Hall. Image and watermark registration. *Signal processing*, 66:373–383, 1998. 200
22. George Voyatzis and Ioannis Pitas. Protecting digital image copyrights: A framework. *IEEE Computer Graphics and Applications*, 19(1):18–23, January 1999. 205

A Stochastic Approach to Content Adaptive Digital Image Watermarking

Sviatoslav Voloshynovskiy[1], Alexander Herrigel[2],
Nazanin Baumgaertner[2], and Thierry Pun[1]

[1] CUI - University of Geneva, Department of Computer Science
24 rue General Dufor, CH-1211 Geneva 4, Switzerland
[2] DCT - Digital Copyright Technologies, Research & Development
Stauffacher-Strasse 149, CH-8004 Zurich, Switzerland

Abstract. This paper presents a new stochastic approach which can be applied with different watermark techniques. The approach is based on the computation of a Noise Visibility Function (NVF) that characterizes the local image properties, identifying textured and edge regions where the mark should be more strongly embedded. We present precise formulas for the NVF which enable a fast computation during the watermark encoding and decoding process. In order to determine the optimal NVF, we first consider the watermark as noise. Using a classical MAP image denoising approach, we show how to estimate the "noise". This leads to a general formulation for a texture masking function, that allows us to determine the optimal watermark locations and strength for the watermark embedding stage. We examine two such NVFs, based on either a non-stationary Gaussian model of the image, or a stationary Generalized Gaussian model. We show that the problem of the watermark estimation is equivalent to image denoising and derive content adaptive criteria. Results show that watermark visibility is noticeably decreased, while at the same time enhancing the energy of the watermark.

1 Introduction

Digital image watermarking is applied today as a popular technique for authentication and copyright protection of image data. Based on global information about the image characteristics, many approaches and commercial solutions embed the watermarking signal as random noise in the whole cover image with the same strength regardless of the local properties of the image. This embedding may lead in practice to visible artifacts specially in the flat regions which are characterized by small variability. In order to decrease these distortions the given watermark strength has to be decreased. This, however, reduces drastically the robustness of the watermark against different sorts of attacks, since the image regions which generate the most visible artifacts determine the final maximum strength of the watermark signal to be embedded.

We present for this problem an effective solution[1] which embeds the watermark

---

[1] This work has been supported by the Swiss National Science Foundation (Grant 5003-45334) and the EC Jedi-Fire project (Grant 25530)

A. Pfitzmann (Ed.): IH'99, LNCS 1768, pp. 211–236, 2000.

into the cover image according to the local properties of the image, i.e. applying this technique every watermarking algorithm will be *content adaptive*. In contrast to recently published results we present a new stochastic approach to identify the regions of interest for the embedding. This approach has the advantage that it is applicable for very different types of images and is not constrained with the identification of an adequate set of parameters to be determined before the identification of the local charactersitics as it is the case in [8]. In addition, the approach presented may be applied to different domains, such as coordinate, Fourier and wavelet. We show the interrelationship to the image denoising problem and prove that some of the applied techniques are special cases of our approach. Comparing the derived stochastic models with results recently published we have noticed that some heuristically derived formula are close to our problem solution. The stationary Generalized Gaussian model is superior concerning the strength of the watermark to be embedded as well as the image quality.

2   State-of-the-Art Approaches

Some authors tried to develop content adaptive schemes on the basis of the utilization of luminance sensitivity function of the human visual sytem (HVS) [1]. Since the derived masking function is based on the estimation of the image luminance a soley luminance based embedding is not efficient against wavelet compression or denoising attacks. Another group of watermarking algorithms exploites transfer modulation features of HVS in the transform domain to solve the compromise between the robustness of the watermark and its visibility [3]. This approach embeds the watermark in a predetermined middle band of frequencies in the Fourier domain with the same strength assuming that the image spectra have isotropic character. This assumption leads to some visible artifacts in images specially in the flat regions, because of anisotropic properties of image spectra. A similar method using blocks in DCT (discrete cosine transform) domain was proposed in [4]. In the context of image compression using perceptually based quantizers, this concept was further developed in [5] to a content adaptive scheme, where the watermark is adjusted for each DCT block. However, as the original image is required to extract the watermark, the practical applications of this approach are very limited since it can be shown that the usage of the cover image will results in watermark schemes which can be easily broken. Another DCT based algorithm which uses luminance and texture masking was developed by [6]. The next group of methods is also based on the image compression background [7] and practically exploits 3 basic conclusions of the above paper: (1) all regions of high activity are highly insensitive to distortion; (2) the edges are more sensitive to distortion than highly textured areas; (3) darker and brighter regions of the image are less sensitive to noise. The typical examples of this approach are ([8], [9]). The developed methods consist of a set of empirical procedures aimed to satisfy the above requirements. The computational complexity and the absence of closed form expressions for the perceptual mask complicate the analysis of the received results. However, experiments performed in these papers show high robustness of these approaches. A very similar method was proposed in [10], where edge detectors are used to overcome the problem of visibility of the watermark around the edges.

The goal of this paper is to develop a coordinate domain content adaptive criterion which may easily be applied to any watermarking technique in coordinate, Fourier, DCT or wavelet domains as perceptual modulation function. The basic idea of our approach consists in the adequate stochastic modelling of the cover image. This allows the estimation of the image as well as the watermark and makes the application of the information theory to the watermarking problem possible. Knowing stochastic models of the watermark and the cover image, one can formulate the problem of watermark estimation/detection according to the classical Bayessian paradigm and estimate the capacity issue of the image watermarking scheme. Developing this concept we show that the problem of watermark estimation is equivalent to image denoising, and derive content adaptive criteria. Finally, we will show the relevance of the developed criterion to the known empirical results.

3   Problem Formulation

Consider the classical problem of non-adaptive watermark embedding, i.e. embedding the watermark regardless of the image content. In the most general case it can be defined according to the next model:

$$y = x + n, \tag{1}$$

where y is the stego image ($y \in \mathcal{R}^N$ and $N = M \times M$), x is the cover (original) image and n is associated with the noise-like watermark image encoded according to the spread spectrum technique [11]. Our goal is to find an estimate $\hat{n}$ of the watermark n either directly, or equivalently, an estimate $\hat{x}$ of the cover image x and then compute an estimation of the watermark as:

$$\hat{n} = y - \hat{x}, \tag{2}$$

where $\hat{n}$ and $\hat{x}$ denote the estimates of the watermark and the cover image respectively. The decision about the presence/absence of the watermark in a given image is then made by a robust detector. This detector must consider the prior statistics of the watermark and the possible errors of its estimation due to the decomposition residual coefficients of the cover image and the possibly applied attack. The generalized scheme of such an approach could be schematically represented according to figure (1). This generalized idea has found practical applications in the watermarking algorithm [1] and steganography method [12]. The key moments of the above approach are the design of the corresponding estimator and the robust detector. The problem of estimation of the cover image from its noisy version is known as image denoising or image smoothing. We will concentrate our consideration on its analysis and its solution in this paper, and show a way of deriving some stochastic criteria for content adaptive watermarking. To solve this problem we use the *Maximum a Posteriori Probability (MAP)* approach.

Our stochastic approach is based on two models of the image where the image is assumed to be a random process. We consider a stationary and non-stationary process to model the cover image. The stationary process is characterized by the constant parameters for the whole image and the non-statinary has spatially varying parameters. To estimate the parameters a maximum likelihood estimate is used in the specified neighbourhood set. We assume that image is either a non-statinary Gaussian process or a stationary Generalized Gaussian. In contrast to many information theory approaches for watermarking, we don't consider the distribution of an image as purely stationary Gaussian, since the image regions of interest for watermarking have different local features. In addition, the channel capacity is not uniform since the image contents of every window constitute a channel capacity which is closely linked to the local image characteristics which are not uniform over the whole image and dependent from visible artifacts.

4   Watermark Estimation Based on MAP

To integrate the watermarking problem into a statistical framework, a probabilistic model of the watermark and the cover image must be developed. If the watermark has the distribution $p_n(n)$ and the cover image the distribution $p_x(x)$, then according to the MAP criterion, the watermark estimate could be found as:

$$\hat{n} = argmax_{\tilde{n} \in \mathcal{R}^N} L(\tilde{n}|y), \tag{3}$$

where $L(\tilde{n}|y)$ is the log function of the *a posteriori* distribution:

$$L(\tilde{n}|y) = \ln p_x(y|\tilde{n}) + \ln p_n(\tilde{n}). \tag{4}$$

The estimate $\hat{n}$, found according to equation (2), leads to the next formulation:

$$\hat{x} = argmax_{\tilde{x} \in \mathcal{R}^N} \{\ln p_n(y|\tilde{x}) + \ln p_x(\tilde{x})\}. \tag{5}$$

The problems (3), (4) and (5) are according to the formulation (2) equivalent to each other. The formulation (5) is the typical image denoising problem, and will be considered further in the present paper.

To solve this problem it is necessary to develop the accurate stochastic models for the watermark $p_n(n)$ and the cover image $p_x(x)$.

Under the assumption that the watermark is received using spread spectrum technique, it is possible to model it as Gaussian random variable. Let samples $n_{i,j}$ ($1 \leq i, j \leq M$) be defined on vertices of an $M \times M$ grid, and let each sample $n_{i,j}$ take a value in $\mathcal{R}$. Let further all the samples be *independent indentically distributed (i.i.d)* . Then:

$$p_n(y|x) = \frac{1}{\sqrt{(2\pi\sigma_n^2)^N}} \cdot \exp\{-\frac{1}{2\sigma_n^2}(y-x)^T(y-x)\}, \tag{6}$$

where σ_n^2 is the variance of the watermark. This assumption is reasonable, because of the fact that the Gaussian distribution has the highest entropy among all other distributions and hence, from the security point of view, any spread spectrum encoding algorithm should approach this distribution in the limit. Thus, the watermark could be modelled as $n \sim N(0, \sigma_n^2)$. The next important question is the development of an adequate *prior* model of the cover image.

5   Stochastic Models of the Cover Image

One of the most popular stochastic image model, which has found wide application in image processing, is the *Markov Radom Field (MRF)* model [13]. The distribution of MRF's is written using a Gibbs distribution:

$$p(x) = \frac{1}{Z} e^{-\sum_{c \in A} V_c(x)}, \tag{7}$$

where Z is a normalization constant called the *partition function*, $V_c(\cdot)$ is a function of a local neighboring group c of points and A denotes the set of all possible such groups or cliques.

In this paper we will consider two particular cases of this model, i.e. the Gaussian and the Generalized Gaussian (GG) models. Assume that the cover image is a random process with non-stationary mean. Then using autoregressive (AR) model notations, one can write the cover image as:

$$x = A \cdot x + \varepsilon = \bar{x} + \varepsilon, \tag{8}$$

where $\bar{x}$ is the non-stationary local mean and ε denotes the residual term due to the error of estimation. The particularities of the above model depend on the assumed stochastic properties of the residual term:

$$\varepsilon = x - \bar{x} = x - A \cdot x = (I - A) \cdot x = C \cdot x, \tag{9}$$

where $C = I - A$ and I is the unitary matrix. If A is a low-pass filter, then C represents a high-pass filter (decomposition operator).

We use here two different models for the residual term ε. The first model is the non-stationary (inhomogeneous) Gaussian model and the second one is the stationary (homogeneous) Generalized Gaussian (GG) model.

The choice of these two models is motivated by the fact that they have found wide application in image restoration and denoising ([14], [15]), and that the best wavelet compression algorithms are based on these models ([16], [17]).
Their main advantage is that they take local features of the image into account. In the first case, this is done by introducing the non-stationary variance using a quadratic energy function, and in the second case, by using an energy function, which preserves the image discontinuities under stationary variance. In other words, in the non-stationary Gaussian model, the data is assumed to be *locally i.i.d.* random field with a Gaussian probability density function (pdf), while in the stationary GG model the data is assumed to be *globally i.i.d.*.

The autocovariance function in the non-stationary case can be written as:

$$R_x = \begin{pmatrix} \sigma_{x_1}^2 & 0 & \cdots & 0 \\ 0 & \sigma_{x_2}^2 & 0 & \vdots \\ \vdots & 0 & \ddots & 0 \\ 0 & 0 & 0 & \sigma_{x_N}^2 \end{pmatrix}, \tag{10}$$

where $\{\sigma_{x_i}^2 | 1 \leq i \leq N\}$ are the local variances.
The autocovariance function for the stationary model is equal to:

$$R_x = \begin{pmatrix} \sigma_x^2 & 0 & \cdots & 0 \\ 0 & \sigma_x^2 & 0 & \vdots \\ \vdots & 0 & \ddots & 0 \\ 0 & 0 & 0 & \sigma_x^2 \end{pmatrix}, \tag{11}$$

where σ_x^2 is the global image variance.

According to equation (9) the non-stationary Gaussian model is characterized by a distribution with autocovariance function (10):

$$p_x(x) = \frac{1}{(2\pi)^{\frac{N}{2}}} \cdot \frac{1}{|\det R_x|^{\frac{1}{2}}} \cdot \exp\{-\frac{1}{2}(Cx)^T R_x^{-1} Cx\}, \tag{12}$$

where $|\det R_x|$ denotes the matrix determinant, and ^{T} denotes transposition. The stationary GG model can be written as:

$$p_x(x) = (\frac{\gamma\eta(\gamma)}{2\Gamma(\frac{1}{\gamma})})^{\frac{N}{2}} \cdot \frac{1}{|\det R_x|^{\frac{1}{2}}} \cdot \exp\{-\eta(\gamma)(|Cx|^{\frac{\gamma}{2}})^T R_x^{-\frac{\gamma}{2}} |Cx|^{\frac{\gamma}{2}}\}, \tag{13}$$

where $\eta(\gamma) = \sqrt{\frac{\Gamma(\frac{3}{\gamma})}{\Gamma(\frac{1}{\gamma})}}$ and $\Gamma(t) = \int_0^\infty e^{-u} u^{t-1} du$ is the gamma function, R_x is determined according to (11), and the parameter γ is called the *shape parameter*. Equation (13) includes the Gaussian ($\gamma = 2$) and the Laplacian ($\gamma = 1$) models as special cases. For the real images the shape parameter is in the range $0.3 \leq \gamma \leq 1$.

Having defined the above models of the watermark and the cover image, we can now formulate the problem of image estimation according to the MAP approach.

6   Image Denoising Based on the MAP Approach

MAP estimate of the cover image results in the following general optimization problem:

$$\hat{x} = argmin_{\tilde{x} \in \mathcal{R}^N} \{\frac{1}{2\sigma_n^2} \|y - \tilde{x}\|^2 + \rho(r)\}, \tag{14}$$

where $\rho(r) = [\eta(\gamma) \cdot |r|]^\gamma$, $r = \frac{x - \bar{x}}{\sigma_x} = \frac{Cx}{\sigma_x}$ and $\| \cdot \|$ denotes the matrix norm. $\rho(r)$ is the energy function for the GG model.

In the case of the non-stationary Gaussian model (12) $\gamma = 2$ (i.e. convex function) and σ_x^2 is spatially varying. The advantage of this model is the existence of a closed form solution of (14) in form of adaptive Wiener or Lee filters [18]. In the case of stationary GG model the general closed form solution does not exist, since the penalty function could be non-convex for $\gamma < 1$. In practice, iterative algorithms are often used to solve this problem. Examples of such algorithms are the stochastic [13] and deterministic annealing (mean-field annealing) ([20]), graduated nonconvexity [19], ARTUR algorithm [21] or its generalization [22]. However, it should be noted that for the particular case of $\gamma = 1$, a closed form solution in wavelet domain exists: it is known as soft-shrinkage ([23], [14]). Of course, it is preferable to obtain the closed form solution for the analysis of the obtained estimate. To generalize the iterative approaches to the minimization of the non-convex function (14) we propose to reformulate it as a *reweighted least squares (RLS)* problem. Then equation (14) is reduced to the following minimization problem:

$$\hat{x}^{k+1} = argmin_{\tilde{x} \in \mathcal{R}^N} \{ \frac{1}{2\sigma_n^2} \|y - \tilde{x}^k\|^2 + w^{k+1} \|r^k\|^2 \}, \tag{15}$$

where

$$w^{k+1} = \frac{1}{r^k} \rho'(r^k), \tag{16}$$

$$r^k = \frac{x^k - \bar{x}^k}{\sigma_x^k}, \tag{17}$$

$$\rho'(r) = \gamma [\eta(\gamma)]^\gamma \frac{r}{\|r\|^{2-\gamma}}, \tag{18}$$

and k is the number of iterations. In this case, the penalty function is quadratic for a fixed weighting fuction w.

Assuming w is constant for a particular iteration step, one can write the general RLS solution in the next form:

$$\hat{x} = \frac{w\sigma_n^2}{w\sigma_n^2 + \sigma_x^2} \bar{x} + \frac{\sigma_x^2}{w\sigma_n^2 + \sigma_x^2} y. \tag{19}$$

This solution is similar to the closed form Wiener filter solution [18]. The same RLS solution could also be rewritten in the form of Lee filter [18]:

$$\hat{x} = \bar{x} + \frac{\sigma_x^2}{w\sigma_n^2 + \sigma_x^2} (y - \bar{x}). \tag{20}$$

The principal difference with classical Wiener or Lee filters is the presence of the weighting function w. This weighting function depends on the underlying assumptions about the statistics of the cover image. In the rest of this paper, we will only consider the Lee version of the solution which coincides with the classical case of Gaussian prior of the cover image ($w = 1$). It is important to note that the shrinkage solution of image denoising problem previously used only in the wavelet domain can easily be obtained from (15) in the next closed form:

$$\hat{x} = \bar{x} + \max(0, |y - \bar{x}| - T)sign(y - \bar{x}),$$

where $T = \frac{\sigma_n^2}{\sigma_x}\sqrt{2}$ is the threshold for practically important case of Laplacian image prior. This coincides with the soft-thresholding solution of the image denoising problem [14].

The properties of the image denoising algorithm are defined by the multiplicative term:

$$b := \frac{\sigma_x^2}{w\sigma_n^2 + \sigma_x^2} \tag{21}$$

in equations (19) and (20). It is commonly known, that the local variance is a good indicator of the local image activity, i.e. when it is small, the image is flat, and a large enough variance indicates the presence of edges or highly textured areas. Therefore, the function b determines the level of image smoothing. For example, for flat regions $\sigma_x^2 \to 0$, and the estimated image equals local mean, while for edges or textured regions $\sigma_x^2 >> \sigma_n^2$, $b \to 1$ and the image is practically left without any changes. Such a philosophy of the adaptive image filtering is very well matched with the texture masking property of the human visual system: the noise is more visible in flat areas and less visible in regions with edges and textures. Following this idea we propose to consider the texture masking property according to the function b based on the stochastic models (12) and (13).

7   Texture Masking Function

In order to be in the framework of the existing terminology, we propose to relate the texture masking function to the *noise visibility function (NVF)* as:

$$NVF = 1 - b = \frac{w\sigma_n^2}{w\sigma_n^2 + \sigma_x^2}, \tag{22}$$

which is just the inverted version of the function b.

In the main application of the proposed NVF in context of watermarking, we assume that the noise (watermark) is an i.i.d. Gaussian process with unit variance, i.e. $N(0,1)$. This noise excite the perceptual model (22), in analogy with the AR image model. The NVF is the output of the perceptual model (22) to a noise $N(0,1)$. This model is schematically shown in figure (2). The particularities of the developed perceptual model are determined by the weighting w, which are defined according to eqs. (17) and (18).

7.1   NVF Based on Non-stationary Gaussian Model

In the case of non-stationary Gaussian model the shape parameter γ is equal to 2 and the autocovariance function is defined according to (10). The weighting function w is then equal to 1 according to equation (17) and NVF can simply be written in the form:

$$NVF(i,j) = \frac{1}{1 + \sigma_x^2(i,j)}, \tag{23}$$

where $\sigma_x^2(i,j)$ denotes the local variance of the image in a window centered on the pixel with coordinates (i,j), $1 \le i,j \le M$. Therefore, the NVF is inversely proportional to the local image energy defined by the local variance. In order to estimate the local image variance the *maximum likelihood (ML)* estimate can be used. Assuming that the image is a locally i.i.d. Gaussian distributed random variable, the ML estimate is given by:

$$\sigma_x^2(i,j) = \frac{1}{(2L+1)^2} \sum_{k=-L}^{L} \sum_{l=-L}^{L} (x(i+k,j+l) - \bar{x}(i,j))^2 \tag{24}$$

with

$$\bar{x}(i,j) = \frac{1}{(2L+1)^2} \sum_{k=-L}^{L} \sum_{l=-L}^{L} x(i+k,j+l), \tag{25}$$

where a window of size $(2L+1)\times(2L+1)$ is used for the estimation. This estimate is often used in practice in many applications. However, the above estimate is assymptotically unbiased. To decrease the bias, it is necessary to enlarge the sampling space. From the other side, enlarging the window size violates the requirement of data being locally Gaussian, since the pixels from different regions occur in the same local window. In order to have a more accurate model, it is reasonable to assume that flat regions have a Gaussian distribution while textured areas and regions containing edges have some other highly-peaked, near-zero distribution (for example Laplacian). This assumption requires the analysis of a mixture model with the Huber energy function (so called Huber-Markov Random Fields) and is the subject of our ongoing research. In this paper, we concentrate on the analysis of the eq. (22) and its relation to the stationary GG version of NVF.

7.2 NVF Based on Stationary GG Model

For the stationary GG model we rewrite eq. (22) in the following form, taking eqs. (17) and (18) into account:

$$NVF(i,j) = \frac{w(i,j)}{w(i,j) + \sigma_x^2}, \tag{26}$$

where $w(i,j) = \gamma[\eta(\gamma)]^\gamma \frac{1}{\|r(i,j)\|^{2-\gamma}}$ and $r(i,j) = \frac{x(i,j) - \bar{x}(i,j)}{\sigma_x}$.

The particularities of this model are determined by the choice of two parameters of the model, e.g. the shape parameter γ and the global image variance σ_x^2. To estimate the shape parameter, we use a *moment matching* method as the one used in [17]. The analysis consists of the next stages. First, the image is decomposed according to the equation (9), using equation (25) as an estimate of the local mean. In the second stage, the moment matching method is applied to the residual image and the shape parameter and the variance are estimated. Some typical examples of these estimations are shown in figure (3). The shape parameter for most of real images is in the range $0.3 \leq \gamma \leq 1$. As a comparison with frequently used pdfs such as Gaussian and Laplacian (also known as double-exponential), we have given the plots of these distributions and their corresponding penalty (energy) function in figures 4(a) and 4(b), respectively. The derivatives of these energy functions and their corresponding weighting functions are shown in figures 4(c) and 4(d). Comparing these pdfs, it is clear that smaller shape parameters lead to a distribution, which is more highly-peaked near zero. Another important conclusion regards the convexity of the energy function, which is concave (non-convex) for $\gamma < 1$, convex for $\gamma = 1$ and strictly convex for $\gamma > 1$. This causes the known properties of this non-convex function in the interpolation applications and the corresponding discontinuity preservation feature, when it is used in restoration or denoising applications. Despite of the nice edge preserving properties, the use of the non-convex functions causes the known problems in the minimization problem (15). However, in the scope of this paper we are mostly interested in the analysis of the properties of the term (26), under condition that the cover image is available for designing the content adaptive watermarking scheme.

8   Stochastical NVFs and Empirical Models

In the derivation of the content adaptive function we explicitly used stochastic modelling of images. However, it is also very important to investigate the relevance of these analytical results with the empirically obtained results, which reflect the particularities of the human visual system.

Obviously, the development of a complete model of the HVS that reflects all its particularities is quite a difficult task. Therefore, most of the developed empirical models utilize only the main features which are important for certain applications, and give reasonable approximations for the practical use. Such sort of models have been used in deterministic image denoising and restoration algorithms ([24], [25]). They have also been used in the field of image compression to reduce the visual artifacts of the lossy compression algorithms and to design special quantization schemes (see for applications in DCT domain [26], and in wavelet domain [27] and [28]). This fact explains the appearance of a great amount of watermarking algorithms based on the transform domain embedding ([5]). Another reason that motivates the use of the transform domain is the decrease of the inter-pixel redundancy by performing image decomposition in the transform domain. In our case image decomposition is obtained in a natural way directly in the coordinate domain by decomposing the image into low-frequency and high-frequency fractions. This is similar to the Gaussian and Laplacian pyramids and to the wavelet decomposition, where scale and orientation (3 directions) are additionally exploited.

To take the texture masking properties into account, it was proposed in [24] to use the NVF for image quantization in the coordinate domain in prediction schemes and also to extend it to the problem of image denoising. The most known form of the empirical NVF is widely used in image restoration applications [25]:

$$NVF(i,j) = \frac{1}{1 + \theta \sigma_x^2(i,j)}, \tag{27}$$

where θ is a tuning parameter which must be chosen for every particular image. This version of NVF was the basic prototype for a lot of adaptive regularization algorithms.

Comparing the above function with the stochastically derived NVF based on the non-stationary Gaussian model, it is very easy to establish the similarity between them. The only difference is the tuning parameter θ which plays the role of the contrast adjustment in NVF. To make θ image-dependent, it was proposed to use:

$$\theta = \frac{D}{\sigma_{x_{max}}^2}, \tag{28}$$

where $\sigma_{x_{max}}^2$ is the maximum local variance for a given image and $D \in [50, 100]$ is an experimentally determined parameter.

9   Content Adaptive Watermark Embedding

Using the proposed content adaptive strategy, we can now formulate the final embedding equation:

$$y = x + (1 - NVF) \cdot n \cdot S, \tag{29}$$

where S denotes the watermark strength. The above rule embeds the watermark in highly textured areas and areas containing edges stronger than in the the flat regions.

In very flat regions, where NVF approaches 1, the strength of the embedded watermark approaches zero. As a consequence of this embedding rule, the watermark information is (nearly) lost in these areas. Therefore, to avoid this problem, we propose to modify the above rule, and to increase the watermark strength in these areas to a level below the visibility threshold:

$$y = x + (1 - NVF) \cdot n \cdot S + NVF \cdot n \cdot S_1, \tag{30}$$

with S_1 being about 3 for most of real world and computer generated images. We are now investigating more complex cases, to replace this fixed value by an image-dependent variable, which takes the luminance sensitivity of HVS into account.

Finally, the watermark detection and the message demodulation will be accomplished in accordance with the general scheme presented in (1), where the estimation $\hat{x}$ of the cover image is done using the image denoising algorithm (15).

The performance of the resulting watermarking algorithm depends strongly on the particular scheme designed to resist geometrical distortions or the basic image processing operations such as filtering, compression and so on. Examples of such distortions are integrated in StirMark watermarking benchmark [2]. For instance, the coordinate domain method given in[1] uses properties of the autocorrelation function of a spatially spreaded watermark, while the Fourier domain approach developed by [3] utilizes a pre-defined template to detect and compensate the undergone geometrical distortions. The adaptive approach proposed here can be integrated into these methods to achieve the best trade-off between the two contradicting goals of increasing the robustness by increasing the watermark strength and at the same time, decreasing the visual artifacts introduced by the watermarking process. This is the subject of our current research.

Here, we address mainly the problem of content adaptive watermark embedding, and investigate its visibility aspects in the next section.

10 Results of Computer Simulation

To illustrate the main features of the proposed content adaptive embedding method, we tested our algorithm on a number of real world and computer generated images. In this paper we will restrict our consideration to several images with most typical properties. The first stage of modeling consists of the calculation of the NVFs according to the developed stochastic models of the cover image. The NVFs based on non-stationary Gaussian (a) and stationary GG (b) models for Barbara and Fish images are shown in Figures (5) and (6), respectively. The NVF calculated according to the non-stationary Gaussian model is smoother and the intensity for the edges is about the same order as that of textured regions. The NVF calculated from stationary GG model looks more *noisy* due to the discontinuity preserving properties of the non-convex energy function of GG prior. From the point of view of noise visibility, both functions reflect the regions of reduced visibility. This corresponds to the desirable features of a content adaptive watermarking approach. To demonstrate the possibility of integrating this adaptive approach into transform domain based techniques, another set of experiments was performed, which demonstrate the relationship between coordinate domain and Fourier domain properties of the cover image and the corresponding NVFs. The magnitude spectrum of Camaraman image (7a) and the corresponding spectra of the NVFs based on the non-stationary Gaussian (7b) and on the stationary GG (7c) model were calculated. It is important to note that the spectra of real images are characterized by a high level of spatial anisotropy, where the principal component directions are determined by the properties of the image. These directions in the spatial spectrum of the original image are determined by the spatial orientation of the edges and textures in the coordinate domain and play a very important role for the high quality image aqcuisition systems under resolution constraints of imaging aperture [30] . The prospective watermarking techniques have to take these properties into account, to survive denoising or lossy compression attacks. Such a strategy implies that the watermark should be most strongly embedded in these directions. The comparison of the spectrum of the cover image with the spectra of corresponding NVFs, shows that the directions of the principal components coincide. This can be the solution to finding a compromise between making the watermark as robust as possible and avoiding the visible distortions that are introduced by the watermarking process. The next stage of modeling is the comparison of the visual quality of the stego images generated using the different developed NVFs. The test consists in the direct embedding of a Gaussian distributed watermark according to the equation (1) and to the content adaptive schemes described in equation (30), using both NVFs. The strength of the watermark (i.e. its standard deviation) is equal to 5, 10 and 15 for the non-adaptive scheme (1). The corresponding results are shown in Figure (8) in parts (a),(d) and (g). The *peak-signal-to noise ratio (PSNR)* was chosen as the criterion for the comparison of the introduced distortions in the stego image or equivalentlly to estimate the general energy of the watermark

$$PSNR = 10 \log_{10} \frac{\|255\|^2}{\|x - y\|^2}$$

The resulted PSNRs for Barbara image are gathered in table (1).

Table 1. Comparison of the watermark strength for different watermark embedding methods

Embedding method	Barbara: Watermark strength		
Non-adaptive	5.0	10.0	15.0
Adaptive non-stationary Gaussian NVF	6.5	15.0	23.0
Adaptive stationary GG NVF	8.0	20.0	31.0
Adaptive Kankanhalli	9.8	19.6	30.38
PSNR (dB)	34.1	28.3	24.7

To receive similar PSNR values in case of adaptive embedding, the watermark strength was increased in these cases to the values given in table (1). The resulting images are depicted in figure (8), parts (b), (e), (h) and figure (8), parts (e), (f), (i) for the non-stationary Gaussian and the stationary GG based NVFs, respectively. The corresponding images in the appendix show that even the PSNR is very similar, the image qualities are quite different. Comparing both visual quality and objective parameters given by the watermark strength, the adaptive scheme based on NVF calculated from stationary GG model seems to be superior to other schemes. This can be explained regarding the above

Table 2. Comparison of the watermark strength for different watermark embedding methods

Embedding method	Fish: Watermark strength		
Non-adaptive	5.0	10.0	15.0
Adaptive non-stationary Gaussian NVF	6.5	14.5	23.0
Adaptive stationary GG NVF	9.0	21.0	35.0
Adaptive Kankanhalli	10.5	21.7	32.2
PSNR (dB)	34.64	28.67	25.26

mentioned properties of the local variance estimation in equation (23), given by the ML-estimate (24). In particular, the watermark is very visible on the edges, because here the requirement of data being local stationary is violated. This decreases the performance of the ML-estimate. In the stationary GG model, only the global variance estimation is needed (equation (26)), where the data is considered to be globally i.i.d.. Therefore, distortions due to edges are considerably smaller than in the non-stationary Gaussian model embedding scheme. The same experiments were performed for Fish image and the results are shown in table (2). In some watermarking algorithms [1], the watermark is embedded in the coordinate domain as a pseudo-random spatially spreaded binary sequence -1;1. To investigate the visibility aspects of this watermark in the scope of the proposed approach, a similar test was performed. The results are shown in figure (9). The PSNR values and the watermark strengths practically coincide with the data given in table (1).

Based on the empirical evaluation of different test people, we think that the image quality of our approach is better than the results of the Kankanhalli approach (see the corresponding stego images in the appendix(figures 11, 12).

The stationary GG model shows a superior performance in this case too. The third stage of the modeling consists in the investigation of the watermark robustness against adaptive Wiener denoising. The resulting PSNR of the watermark after the above attack was determined as

$$PSNR_n = 10 \log_{10} \frac{\|255\|^2}{\|n - n_a\|^2}$$

where n_a is the watermark after attack. The results of this experiment are presented in table (2). The watermarks before and after this attack are shown in figure (10) for a PSNR equal to 28.3 dB. Inspection of the results of figure (10) show that the watermark survives mostly in the highly textured regions and areas with edges, where its strength was increased according to the developed content adaptive scheme. Therefore, the obtained results clearly indicate the advantages of the proposed approach for digital image watermarking.

Table 3. The watermark PSNR after adaptive Wiener denoising attack for different watermark embedding methods

embedding method	watermark PSNR (dB) (after adaptive Wiener denoising)
non-adaptive	25.99
adaptive non-stationary Gaussian NVF	26.86
adaptive stationary GG NVF	26.97

11 Conclusions and Future Work

In this paper we have presented a new approach for content adaptive watermarking which can be applied to different watermarking algorithms based on the coordinate domain, the Fourier or wavelet domains. In contrast to state-of-the-art heuristic techniques our approach is based on a stochastic modelling framework which allows us to derive the corresponding analytic formula in a closed form solution. It is, therefore, not necessary to investigate in practice the different parameter sets for different image classes but to apply mathematical expressions which can be easily computed. In addition, we have shown the close relationship of the derived optimization problems and the corresponding solutions to image denoising techniques. We have shown that some of the heuristically derived solutions are special cases of our model. Running different tests we have sucessfully compared our approach against other techniques. The test results have also shown that some assumptions in many information theoretic papers for watermarking are not satisfied, namely, the distribution of the image is not stationary Gaussian and the channel capacity is not uniform meaning that depending on the sample, the image contents constitute a channel capacity which is closely linked to the local image characteristics which are not uniform. It is, therefore, necessary to consider the enhanced information theory based approaches which satisfy these constraints. Based on the identified relationship to image denoising problems, we are going to develop the corresponding attacks on commercial watermark schemes to test our models as the basis of a new piracy tool and for further enhancement of the existing watermarking techniques. In the future, we will apply the presented model also for the construction of more robust encoder and decoder schemes.

12 Acknowledgements

We appreciate usefull comments of S. Pereira, G. Csurka and F. Deguillaume during the work on the paper. S. Voloshynovskiy is grateful to I. Kozintsev, K. Mihcak, A. Lanterman and Profs. P. Moulin and Y. Bresler for fruitfull and helpfull discussions during his staying at University of Illinois at Urbana-Champaign.

References

1. M.Kutter: *Watermarking Resisting to Translation, Rotation and Scaling*, Proc. of SPIE, Boston, USA, November 1998. 212, 213, 222, 224
2. M.Kutter, F.Petitcolas: *A fair benchmark for image watermarking systems*, SPIE, Vol.3657, San Jose, January 1999, pp.226-239. 222
3. J.Ruanaidh, T.Pun: *Rotation, Scale and Translation Invariant Spread Spectrum Digital Image Watermarking*, Signal Processing, May 1998, Vol.66, No.3, pp.303-317. 212, 222
4. M.Swanson, B.Zhu, A.Twefik: *Transparent Robust Image Watermarking*, Proc. of 3rd IEEE International Conference on Image Processing ICIP96, 1996, Vol.3, pp.211-214. 212
5. C.Podilchuk, W.Zeng: *Image Adaptive Watermarking Using Visual Models*, IEEE Journal on Selected Areas in Communication, May 1998, Vol.16, No.4, pp.525-539. 212, 220
6. J.Huang, Y.Shi: *Adaptive Image Watermarking Scheme Based on Visual Masking*, Electronic Letters, April 1998, Vol.34, No.8, pp.748-750. 212
7. N.Jayant, J.Johnston, R.Safranek: *Signal Compression Based on Models of Human Perception*, Proc. of the IEEE, 1993, Vol.81, No.10, pp.1385-1422. 212
8. M.Kankanhalli, R.Ramakrishnan: *Content Based Watermarking of Images*, ACM Mulimedia98, Bristol, UK, 1998, pp. 61-70. 212
9. F.Bartolini, M.Barni, V.Cappelini, A.Piva: *Mask Bilding for Perceptually Hiding Frequency Embedded Watermarks*, Proc. of 5th IEEE International Conference on Image Processing ICIP98, Chicago, Illinois, USA, October 4-7, 1998, Vol.1, pp. 450-454. 212
10. J.F.Delaigle, C.De Vleeschouwer, B.Macq: *Watermarking Algorithm Based on a Human Visual Model*, Signal Processing, 1998, Vol.66, pp. 319-335. 213
11. I.Cox, J.Kilian, T.Leighton, T.Shamoon: *Secure Spread Spectrum Watermarking for Multimedia*, NEC Research Institute Tech Rep. 95-10, 1995. 213
12. L.Marvel, C.Retter, C.Boncelet: *Hiding Information in Images*, Proc. of 5th IEEE International Conference on Image Processing ICIP98, Chicago, Illinois, USA, October 4-7, 1998, Vol.1. 213
13. S.Geman and D.Geman: *Stochastic Relaxation, Gibbs Distributions and the Bayesian Restorations of Images*, IEEE Trans. on Pattern Analysis and Machine Intelligence, 1984, Vol.14, No.6, pp.367-383. 215, 217
14. P.Moulin, J. Liu: *Analysis of Multiresolution Image Denoising Schemes Using Generalized-Gaussian Priors*, Proc. IEEE Sig. Proc. Symp. on Time-Frequency and Time-Scale Analysis, , Pittsburgh, PA, October 1998. 215, 217, 218
15. S.Chang, B.Yu, M.Vetterli: *Spatially Adaptive Wavelet Thresholding with Content Modeling for Image Denoising*, Proc. of 5th IEEE International Conference on Image Processing ICIP98, Chicago, Illinois, USA, October 4-7, 1998. 215
16. S.LoPresto, K.Ramchandran, M.Orhard: *Image Coding Based on Mixture Modeling of Wavelet Coefficients and a Fast Estimation-Quantization Framework*, Data Compression Conference 97, Snowbird, Utah, 1997, pp.221-230. 215
17. S.Mallat: *A Theory for Multiresolution Signal Decomposition: The Wavelet Representation*, IEEE Trans. on Pattern Analysis and Machine Intelligence, 1989, Vol.11, No.7, pp.674-693. 215, 220
18. J.S.Lim: *Two-Dimensional Signal and Image Processing*, Englewood Cliffs, NJ: Prentice-Hall, 1990. 217
19. A.Blake, A.Zisserman: *Visual Reconstruction*, MA: The MIT Press, 1987. 217

20. D.Deiger, F.Girosi: *Parallel and Deterministic Algorithms from MRFs Surface Reconstruction*, IEEE Trans. on Pattern Analysis and Machine Intelligence, 1991, Vol.13, No.6, pp.401-412. 217

21. P.Charbonnier, L.Blanc-Feraud, G.Aubert, M.Barlaud: *Deterministic Edge-Preserving Regularization in Computed Images*, IEEE Trans. on Image Processing, 1997, Vol.6, No.2, pp.298-311. 217

22. A.Dalaney, Y.Bresler: *Globally Convergent Edge-Preserving Regularization: An Application to Limited-Angle Tomography*, IEEE Trans. on Image Processing, 1998, Vol.7, No.2, pp.204-221. 217

23. M.Nikolova: *Estimees Locales Forment Homogenes*, Comptes Rendus Ac. Sci. Paris, Serie I, 1997, Vol.325, pp.665-670. 217

24. G.L.Adelson, A.N.Natravali: *Image Restoration Based on Subjective Criterion*, IEEE Trans. Syst., Man, Cyber. SMC-6, 1976, pp.845-853. 220, 221

25. S.Efstratiadis, A.Katsaggelos: *Adaptive Iterative Image Restoration with Reduced Computational Load*, Optical Engineering, Dec. 1990, Vol.29, No.12, pp.1458-1468. 220, 221

26. A.Watson: *DCT Quantization Matrices Visually Optimized for Individual Images*, in Proc. SPIE Conf. Human Vision, Visual Processing and Digital Display IV, 1993, Vol.1913, pp.202-216. 220

27. A.Watson, G.Yang, J.Solomon, J.Villasenor: *Visual Thresholds for Wavelet Quantization Error*, in Proc. SPIE Human Vision and Electronic Imaging, 1996, Vol.2657, pp.381-392. 220

28. A.S.Lewis, G.Knowles: *Image Compression Using 2-D Wavelet Transform*, IEEE Trans. Image Processing, No.4, 1992, pp.244-250. 220

29. S.Pereira, J.Ruanaidh, F.Deguillaume, G.Cscurka, and T.Pun: *Template Based Recovery of Fourier-Based Watermarks Using Log-Polar and Log-Log Maps*, Proc. Int. Conference on Multimedia Computing and Systems, June 1999.

30. I.Prudyus, S.Voloshynovskiy, T.Holotyak: *Adaptive Aperture Formation in Radar Imaging Systems with Nonlinear Robust Image Restoration*, In IX European Signal Processing Conference Eusipco-98, Island of Rhodes, Greece, September 8-11 1998, vol. 3, pp.1365-1368. 223

13   Appendix

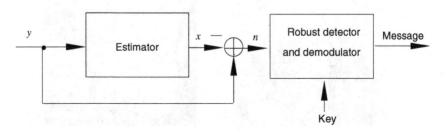

Fig. 1. Block diagram of the watermark detection algorithm according to equation (2).

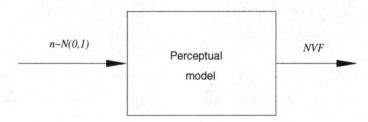

Fig. 2. Generation of the NVF from perceptual model.

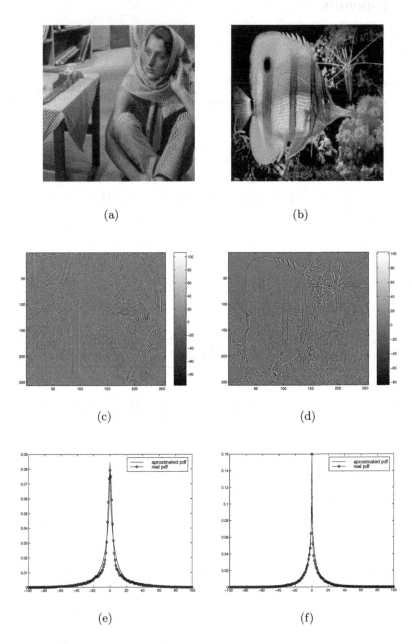

Fig. 3. Results of the GG model parameter estimation: cover images Barbara and Fish (a) and (b); residual decomposed images (c) and (d); histogram plots and their approximation by GG pdfs (e) and (f). The estimated parameters are $\sigma_x = 17.53$ and $\gamma = 0.64$ for Barbara image and $\sigma_x = 13.40$ and $\gamma = 0.68$ for Fish image.

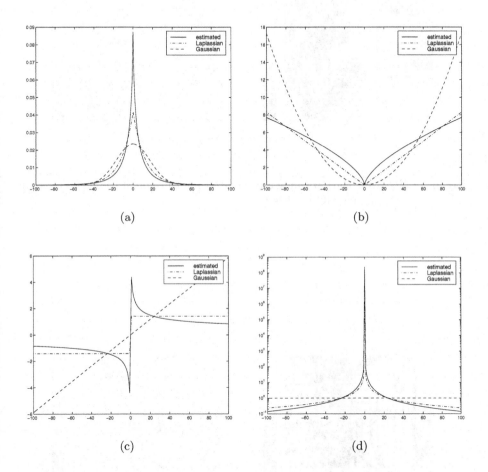

Fig. 4. Comparative analysis of the estimated distribution $\gamma = 0.64$ with Gaussian and Laplacian (a); corresponding energy (penalty) functions ρ (b); the derivatives from the energy functions ρ' (c) and weighting functions w (d). For all distributions $\sigma_x = 17.53$.

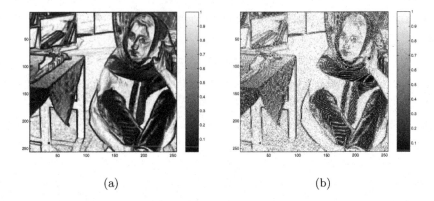

Fig. 5. NVFs from Barbara image calculated for the non-stationary Gaussian (a) and the stationary GG models (b).

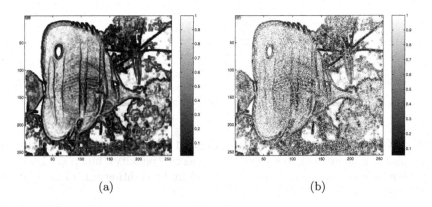

Fig. 6. NVFs from Fish image calculated for the non-stationary Gaussian (a) and the stationary GG models (b).

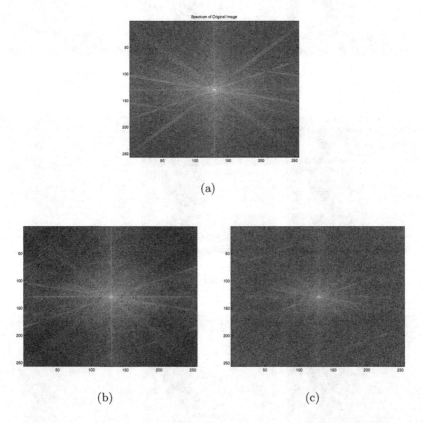

(a)

(b)   (c)

Fig. 7. Magnitude spectrum of the original image Cameraman (a), and spectra of NVFs calculated according to non-stationary Gaussian (b) and stationary GG (c) models.

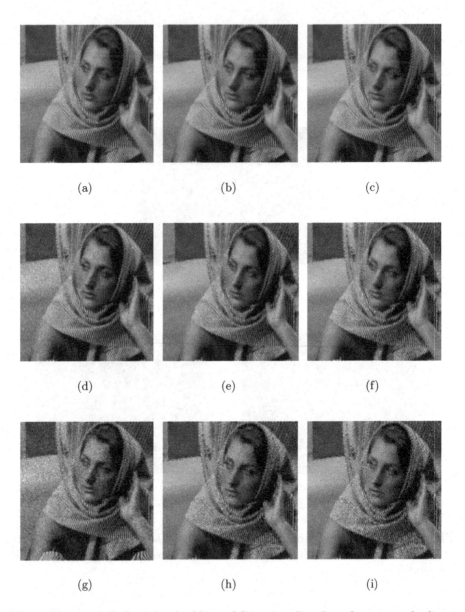

Fig. 8. Test on visibility of embedding of Gaussian distributed watermark: direct embedding according to scheme (1) with the watermark strength 5 (a), 10 (d) and 15 (g); and adaptove shemes with NVF (23) (b, e, h) and NVF (26) (c, f, i) with the corresponding watermark strengthes given in Table (1).

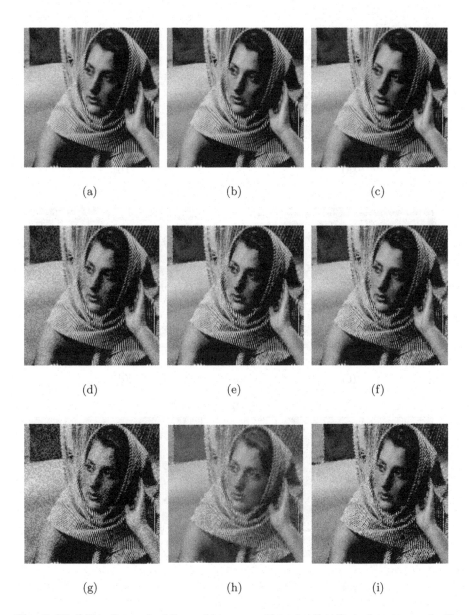

(a)   (b)   (c)

(d)   (e)   (f)

(g)   (h)   (i)

Fig. 9. Visibility for embedding of binary uniformly distributed watermark. For reference see Figure (8).

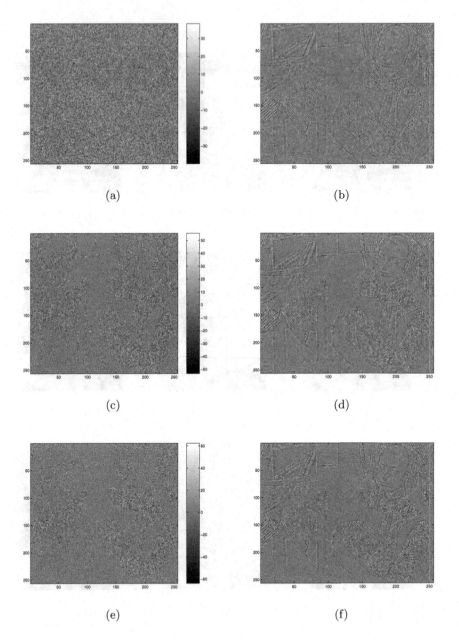

Fig. 10. Results of adaptive Wiener denoising attack: left column represents watermark embedded according to the direct scheme (1) (a), adaptive ones with NVF (23) (c) and NVF (26) (e), and right column shows the remained watermark after denosing attack for the corresponding images from right column.

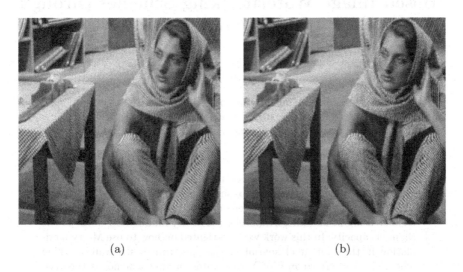

(a)   (b)

Fig. 11. The Barbara stego images calculated for the Kankanhalli (a) and the stationary GG model (b).

(a)   (b)

Fig. 12. The Fish stego images calculated for the Kankanhalli (a) and the stationary GG model (b).

Performance Improvement of Spread Spectrum Based Image Watermarking Schemes through M-ary Modulation

Martin Kutter

Swiss Federal Institute of Technology (EPFL)
Ecublens, 1014 Lausanne, Switzerland
martin.kutter@kutter.ch

Abstract. In spread spectrum communication the use of M-ary modulation is a popular extension to binary signaling usually resulting in a significant performance improvement. Furthermore it was shown that for increasing M and for certain schemes M-ary modulation works at the channel capacity. In this work we investigated on how to use M-ary modulation in the context of spatial spread spectrum based watermarking schemes. The performance of M-ary watermarking schemes is theoretically analyzed and the results verified through empirical test. We show that in general M-ary modulation based on the biorthogonal extension of the Hadamard matrix results in a significant performance improvement for values of $M > 4$. Furthermore we show that the performance improvement does not decrease under noise like distortion such as lossy JPEG compression.

1   Introduction

Digital watermarking, the art of hiding information in multimedia data, has become a very popular research area for the past 7 years. The reason for its fast growing interest is mainly due to potential applications addressing issues such as copyright protection, data monitoring, and data authentication. For a in-depth introduction to the topic and an overview of current state of the art techniques for a variety of multimedia data, the reader is referred to [1].

Most digital image watermarking methods employ some kind of spread spectrum modulation [8,10]. This approaches have proven to be efficient, robust and cryptographically secure. From communication theory, we know that the performance and reliability of modulation schemes may be increased through channel coding. However, this concept is not very efficient if applied to watermarking techniques because in watermarking the message is usually of limited size (such as 64 or 128 bits) and not continuous. Furthermore the channel distortion is very variable because it depends on the image size, the image content, as well as processing applied to the watermarked image. It is therefore very difficult to identify appropriate code lengths [7].

Another approach to increase the performance of communication schemes is based on M-ary modulation [10]. Often in communication, a binary information

A. Pfitzmann (Ed.): IH'99, LNCS 1768, pp. 237–252, 2000.

is transmitted on a bit by bit basis, usually referred to as *binary signaling*. In such schemes, the smallest information entity is a bit which can take on two values. In communication the states of the smallest piece of information transmitted are called *symbols*. For binary signaling, we have two symbols. The idea of M-ary modulation is to increase the size of the transmitted information, resulting in an increase of the number of different symbols. The M in M-ary refers to the number of symbols used in the communication scheme. Therefor, binary signaling is a special case of M-ary modulation with $M = 2$. In general for large values of M this schemes result in a significant performance improvement. For small values of M, the performance does not necessarily increase, and even decreases in some cases.

In this paper we investigate the performance of M-ary modulation in the context of digital image watermarking. We start by reviewing the common spatial spread spectrum watermarking scheme in Sec. 2. In Sec. 3 we look at the extension of this scheme for M-ary modulation based on biorthogonal modulation functions generated using the Hadamard matrix. Results will be shown in Sec. 4 and conclusions are drawn in Sec. 5.

2   Spatial Spread Spectrum Watermarking

We start the technical description of the proposed method, by first introducing the underlying digital watermarking scheme for binary signaling, that is $M = 2$. This scheme is based on a previous work [6,5] and can be viewed as some sort of spread spectrum watermarking with the difference that, in the watermark recovery process, an additional step which predicts the embedded watermark is introduced to increase detector performance.

2.1   Watermark Embedding

The generic watermark embedding system is depicted in Fig. 1. Our goal is to embed an N bit long information $B = \{b_1, b_2, \ldots, b_N\}$ in an image I. The image I defines a set of pixels used to represent the visual information. Each pixel is a sets of three tristimulus values:

$$I(x, y) = \{R(x, y), G(x, y), B(x, y)\} \tag{1}$$

where $(x, y) \in \mathbb{Z}^2$ is the spatial location in the Cartesian coordinate system, and $R(x, y)$, $G(x, y)$, $B(x, y)$, are the three tristimulus values in a color coordinate system such as the *red-green-blue* color coordinate system [3].

The watermark embedding process takes place in the watermarking space $\mathcal{E}$. To project an image into the watermarking space the transformation χ is applied to the image, i.e. $\chi : (I) \rightarrow (C)$, where C is the projected image. Once the watermark is embedded in the watermarking space, the inverse projection is applied to compute the watermarked image, that is $\chi^{-1} : (\hat{C}) \rightarrow (\hat{I})$. For the moment the only constraint on the projection is that it has to maintain the

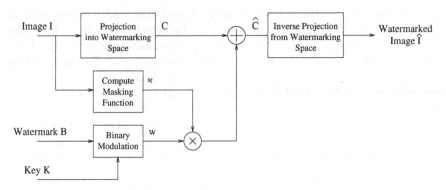

Fig. 1. Watermark embedding system for binary signaling.

spatial dimensionality of the input data. That is, the image representation in the watermarking space has to be two dimensional.

In binary signaling we have two symbols Y^0 and Y^1, corresponding to the bit values of 0 and 1, respectively. It is well known, that for binary signaling, the optimal modulation functions are antipodal signal pairs [10,4], that is $s^0 = -s^1$, where s^0, and s^1 are the signals corresponding to the symbols Y^0 and Y^1, respectively. For the embedding of the N bit watermark we use a set S^k of N two dimensional orthogonal functions $s_i, i = \{1, \ldots, N\}$, where k defines the secret key used as initializing seed to generate the set. Each function s_i in the set is used to represent one bit value of the watermark. In our case the functions can be considered as uniformly distributed random sets of random variables. The random variables are all independent and have a zero mean bilevel distribution with unit variance. In order not to introduce initial *inter symbol interference (ISI)*, the orthogonal functions are designed such that they are non overlapping. That is, if $S_i = \{(x,y), \forall s_i(x,y) \neq 0\}$ is the set of all locations for which the function s_i has non-zero values, then the intersection of all sets of non zero locations is the empty set, $S_i \cap S_j = \emptyset, \forall i \neq j$.

The watermark w is defined as the superposition of all modulated and weighted functions s_i:

$$w(x,y) = \sum_{i=1}^{N} b_i' \alpha(x,y) s_i(x,y) \qquad (2)$$

where $\alpha(x,y)$ is a local weighting factor with the purpose to adapt the watermark to the human visual system, and b_i' represents the bit value mapped from $\{0,1\}$ to $\{-1,1\}$. The watermarked image is now given by adding the watermark w to the image representation in the embedding space $\mathcal{E}$ and applying the inverse transformation:

$$\hat{I} = \chi^{-1}(C + w). \qquad (3)$$

The weighting function α depends on the visual characteristics of the original image I and the watermark embedding space. Finding the optimal weighting function is a very difficult and delicate issue because it depends on both, the image and the metric used to measure the distortion. Because in this work we focus on the performance improvements through M-ary modulation and not optimal weighting of the watermark, we use a simple function for α in order to facilitate tractability of the problem. This approach is a valid basis because using more sophisticated functions increases the watermark energy by maintaining the visual distortion and hence results in an increase of the overall system performance.

In order to remain as general as possible, we do not watermark all locations in the watermarking domain. To describe the occupancy in the watermarking domain we define the density D as:

$$D = \frac{|\{\bigcup_{i=1}^{N} S_i\}|}{|\{S\}|} \tag{4}$$

where $|\{.\}|$ refers to the set cardinality and S represents the universal set. The probability for a location to be assigned to any set is equiprobable and hence given by D/N. It is obvious that the density has a direct impact on the watermark robustness and should therefore be set to 1 all the time. Nevertheless, the density gives us additional control over the watermark visibility and there is a trade-off between the watermark visibility and robustness.

2.2   Watermark Detection

The introduced watermarking scheme can be seen as a modulation system in which the image acts as additive noise. If the statistics of the image were Gaussian, common models could be used to design efficient detectors. However, it is well known that the statistics of images are in general very difficult to model. Nevertheless, it is a common method in digital watermarking to use a linear correlator as detection statistics. In our case we slightly modify this scheme by introducing a pre-processing step to compute a prediction of the embedded watermark and hence improve detector performance.

The linear detector is shown in Fig. 2. Let $\hat{F}$ be the preprocessed watermarked image given by:

$$\hat{F} = \hat{I} * H \tag{5}$$

where the operator $*$ expresses convolution, and H is a space variant linear filter defined by its impulse response $h_{m,n}(x,y)$. The coordinates (x,y) define the spatial position and (m,n) the relative shift to the local position. We assume that the projection into the watermarking space is a linear operation with the property that we can inverse the operators:

$$\hat{C}_F = \chi(\hat{I} * H) = \chi(\hat{I}) * H \tag{6}$$

where $\hat{C}_F$ is the projection of the watermarked and filtered image $\hat{F}$ into the watermarking space. This property means that, convolving the projection of the

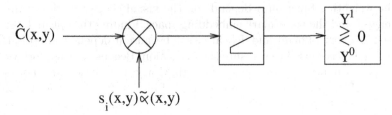

Fig. 2. Linear correlator detector with pre-processing step to predict the embedded watermark.

image in the watermarking space is the same as projecting the filtered image into the watermarking space. Now we continue our analysis by expanding the watermarked and preprocessed image into its components:

$$\hat{C}_F = (C + w) * H$$
$$= C * H + w * H \tag{7}$$

We use this expression to derive the detector statistic r_i for bit i conditioned on the modulation function s_i, that is $r_i|s_i$:

$$r_i|s_i = < \hat{F}, s_i\tilde{\alpha} >$$
$$= < C * H + w * H, s_i\tilde{\alpha} > \tag{8}$$

$$= \sum_{(x,y)} \left[\left(\sum_{(m,n)} w(x-m, y-n)h_{m,n}(x,y) \right) s_i(x,y)\tilde{\alpha}(x,y) \right]$$
$$+ \sum_{(x,y)} \left[\left(\sum_{(m,n)} C(x-m, y-n)h_{m,n}(x,y) \right) s_i(x,y)\tilde{\alpha}(x,y) \right] \tag{9}$$

where $< . >$ denotes the inner product operator. Because we do not have the original weighting function in the detection process, an estimate $\tilde{\alpha}$ of it is used.

Using this expression as a starting point we may now proceed to compute the expectation and variance of the detector statistic. After some algebra we find the expectation as:

$$E[r_i] = b_i' \frac{D}{N} \sum_{(x,y)} E[\alpha(x,y)\tilde{\alpha}(x,y)] h_{0,0}(x,y) \tag{10}$$

and the variance:

$$Var[r_i] = \frac{D}{N} \sum_{(x,y)} E[C_F^2(x,y)\tilde{\alpha}^2(x,y)] \tag{11}$$

$$+ \frac{ND - D^2}{N^2} \sum_{(x,y)} E\left[\alpha^2(x,y)\tilde{\alpha}^2(x,y)\right] h_{0,0}^2(x,y)$$

$$+ \frac{D^2}{N} \sum_{(x,y)} \sum_{(m,n)\neq 0} E\left[\tilde{\alpha}^2(x,y)\alpha^2(x-m,y-n)\right] h_{m,n}^2(x,y)$$

$$+ \frac{D^2}{N^2} \sum_{(x,y)} \sum_{(m,n)\neq(x,y)} E\left[\alpha(x,y)\tilde{\alpha}(x,y)\alpha(m,n)\tilde{\alpha}(m,n)\right] \qquad (12)$$

$$h_{x-m,y-n}(m,n)h_{m-x,n-y}(x,y)$$

Looking at these results we can make several observations. The detector performance increases with increasing pulse size, that is the size of the image, and the expectation is inversely proportional to the watermark length and proportional to the embedding density. The variance has a major contribution from the filtered image. The variance terms due to the correlation of the watermark can be decreases by decreasing the embedding density.

Next we have to look at the error performance of the proposed scheme. We consider a symbol-by-symbol hard decoder and assume that there is no inter symbol interference. This approach is justified by the fact that ISI is by an order of magnitude smaller than the interference from the image data. Fig. 3 illustrates the error region for the binary detection process by showing the conditional probability density function $f(r|Y^k)$ of the detector statistic r. As illustrated, in our case the two conditional probabilities are symmetric about the origin $r = 0$. The symbol error probability P_S, which is equivalent to the bit error for binary signaling, is given by integrating the overlapping Gaussian tails:

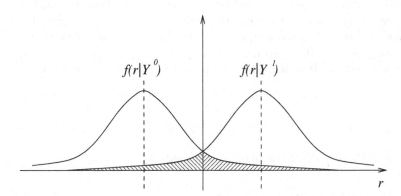

Fig. 3. Conditional probability functions for binary detection and error regions.

$$P_S = \frac{1}{2}P(\epsilon|Y^0) + \frac{1}{2}P(\epsilon|Y^1) \qquad (13)$$

where ϵ stands for the error. As we have seen, the probability function of the detector statistic, conditioned on a symbol, is the sum of non-Gaussian random variables. If the number of terms is large enough we can make use of the *central limit theorem* [2] and approximate the sum by a Gaussian distribution with mean and variance as derived in Eq. (10) and Eq. (11), respectively. Hence in our case, the conditional distribution of the detector statistic $f(r_i|s_i)$ is given by:

$$f(r_i|s_i) \simeq \frac{1}{\sqrt{2\pi\sigma_i^2}} e^{\frac{-(r_i-\mu_i)^2}{2\sigma_i^2}} \qquad (14)$$

where μ_i is the expectation as defined in Eq. (10) and σ_i^2 the variance as defined in Eq. (11);

The resulting symbol error probability P_S is given by:

$$P_S = \frac{1}{\sqrt{2\pi\sigma^2}} \int_\mu^\infty e^{\frac{-x^2}{2\sigma^2}} dx$$
$$= Q\left(\frac{\mu}{\sigma}\right) \qquad (15)$$

where $Q(.)$ is the so-called *Q-function*[1] defined as the tail integral of a Gaussian function with zero mean and unit variance:

$$Q(x) = \int_x^\infty \frac{1}{\sqrt{2\pi}} e^{\frac{-z^2}{2}} dz \qquad (16)$$

The symbol error probability is a very useful measure in digital communication because it represents the probability of detecting a symbol wrong. In digital watermarking this information is not that interesting because we do not have continuous data transmission and hence limited possibilities for efficient coding and error correction. We are mainly interested in the probability of detecting the embedded watermark without error, or the error probability of at least not detecting one bit. We denote the error probability of not detecting the right watermark by P_w. It is defined by 1 minus the probability of correctly detecting all bits:

$$P_w = 1 - (1 - P_S)^N \qquad (17)$$

where P_S is again the symbol error probability.

3   M-ary Modulation

Until now we have worked with antipodal modulation signals because they provide best performance for binary signal modulation in a noisy environment. From

---

[1] The Q-function is the complementary of the *error function* defined as: $erfc(x) = \frac{2}{\sqrt{\pi}} \int_x^\infty e^{-z^2} dz$.

modulation theory we know that increasing the number of symbols may for certain modulation schemes result in a decrease of the symbol error probability. Furthermore, in the limit, that is for $M \to \infty$, we can design schemes working at the channel capacity. We will now investigate the concept of M-ary signaling in the context of digital watermarking. The idea for an improvement of the performance is given by the fact that the fewer symbols we have to hide in an image, the more locations we can use per symbol. In the previous sections we have seen, that the expected value of the detector statistic increases with the number of locations, often referred to as *pulse size* in spread spectrum modulation. Therefore, the larger the pulse size, the higher the probability of detecting the right symbol. Modulation and demodulation systems for M-ary signaling are shown in Fig. 4 and Fig. 5, respectively. The N bit long message, which can be considered as a two symbol signal, that is $M = 2$, is first mapped to M symbols required for the M-ary modulation. This is usually done by grouping $\log_2(M)$ bits of the original message and then taking the resulting decimal value as an index to select the appropriate function from a set of basis functions. In the decoding process the received signal is correlated with all modulation functions representing the different symbols. The index of the largest correlation determines the transmitted symbol.

Fig. 4. M-ary modulation. The input message is fist mapped to M symbols by grouping $\log_2 M$ bits of the original message.

As mentioned, in M-ary signaling, every symbol conveys m bits, that is $M = 2^m$. Each symbol is represented by a bilevel spread spectrum modulation function from a basis set containing M functions. In general, the functions in a set are either *orthogonal, biorthogonal,* or *transorthogonal* [10]. The orthogonal case is the most obvious selection because it inherently results in orthogonal symbols, and therefore watermarks orthogonal to each other. One way to generate orthogonal function sets is based on the *Hadamard-Walsh functions*[9]. Given any spread spectrum function of length M, we may generate a set of M orthogonal functions by multiplying the initial spread spectrum function with the Hadamard matrix of order M. The smallest possible Hadamard matrix is of order 2 and is defined as:

$$\mathbf{H}_2 = \begin{bmatrix} 1 & 1 \\ 1 & -1 \end{bmatrix} \tag{18}$$

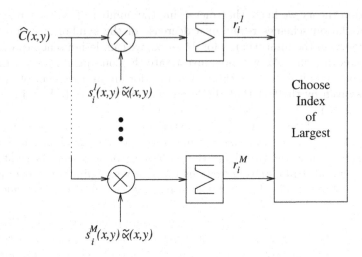

Fig. 5. M-ary demodulation scheme for orthogonal signals. The received signal is projected onto all symbol functions and the index of the largest is used to decode the message.

Any other Hadamard matrix with an order of a power of 2 may then be iteratively constructed from the $\mathbf{H}_2$ matrix. The construction is based on the *Kronecker* product recursion and given by:

$$\mathbf{H}_N = H_2 \otimes H_{N/2} = \begin{bmatrix} \mathbf{H}_{N/2} & \mathbf{H}_{N/2} \\ \mathbf{H}_{N/2} & -\mathbf{H}_{N/2} \end{bmatrix} \tag{19}$$

As an example, this construction leads us to the following Hadamard matrix of order 4:

$$\mathbf{H}_4 = \begin{bmatrix} 1 & 1 & 1 & 1 \\ 1 & -1 & 1 & -1 \\ 1 & 1 & -1 & -1 \\ 1 & -1 & -1 & 1 \end{bmatrix} \tag{20}$$

Inspecting this matrix, we can first verify that all rows are orthogonal. Furthermore, it is interesting to note that the first value in each row is 1. This means that for the purpose of modulation this information is redundant and may therefore be dropped without any loss in performance. The detector statistics for a correlator, assuming the right symbol is given, follows the expression derived in the previous sections, with the difference that it does not depend on the bit value anymore. We have seen in Sec. 2 that for antipodal sequences the distance between the two conditional expectations for bit values of 0 and 1 is twice the expected value of one conditional expectation. This is due to the fact that the antipodal signal design provides largest distance for fixed energy. For an orthogonal signal design this is not the case because the expectation for a wrong symbol is 0, which means that the distance between the symbols is only once the mean of the conditional expectation. This fact has been realized long ago and it was proposed to use biorthogonal basis sets for M-ary modulation.

Sets of biorthogonal basis functions can be generated from orthogonal sets by adding the sign reversed versions of the functions. This approach is very similar to the design of the antipodal functions. In our case, if we want do design an M-ary modulation scheme, where M is a power of 2. We start by computing an $M/2$ order Hadamard matrix $\mathbf{H}_{M/2}$. This matrix is then completed by appending its sign-reversed version to generate the M biorthogonal matrix entries:

$$\mathbf{B}_M = \begin{bmatrix} \mathbf{H}_{M/2} \\ -\mathbf{H}_{M/2} \end{bmatrix} \tag{21}$$

where $\mathbf{B}_M$ is the final matrix used to generate the set of M biorthogonal functions from one initial function. Besides the superior performance of biorthogonal function sets, there are also other advantages over orthogonal function sets. For example the number of correlators in the detection process is only half the number required for orthogonal functions. This issue is especially important for large values of M. The detector for biorthogonal M-ary signaling is shown in Fig. 6

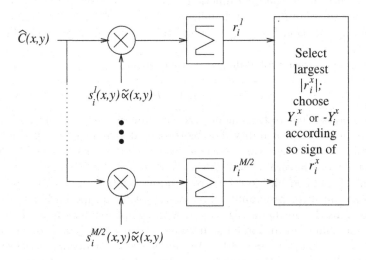

Fig. 6. M-ary demodulation scheme for biorthogonal signals. The received signal is projected onto the non sign reversed modulation functions. The symbol is found by locating the correlation with the largest absolute value and then choosing the symbol corresponding to the sign of the correlation.

To analyze the performance of M-ary biorthogonal signaling, we start by computing the probability of detecting a symbol right. Let us assume we transmitted symbol Y^0. The probability of correct detection P_C is defined as the probability that the absolute value of the detector correlation for Y^0 is larger than zero, and all other correlations are smaller than the correlation for Y^0;

$$P_C = p(abs(r_i^1) < r_i^0, \ldots, abs(r_i^{M/2-1}) < r_i^0 | r_i^0 > 0) \qquad (22)$$

where r_i^n is the detector statistic for the n_{th} of the ith M-tuple of bits from the encoded message. Under the assumption of large pulse sizes we may again use the central limit theorem and conclude that the distribution of r_i^0 approaches a Gaussian distribution with mean and variance as derived in the previous sections. The distribution of the random variable $r_i^n, n = 1, \ldots, M/2 - 1$, is as well Gaussian with the same variance as for r_i^0, but with zero mean. Assuming that there is no inter symbol interference the random variables r_i^n are independent, which means that their joint distribution is the product of the individual probability density functions and because they all have the same distribution we can raise is to the power of $M/2 - 1$. The resulting probability of correct detection is then given by:

$$P_C = \int_0^\infty \frac{e^{-\frac{(x-\mu_0)^2}{2\sigma_0^2}}}{\sqrt{2\pi\sigma_0^2}} \left[1 - 2Q\left(\frac{x}{\sigma_0}\right) \right]^{\frac{M}{2}-1} dx \qquad (23)$$

The 2 in front of the $Q(.)$ function is due to the absolute value of r_i^0 which means that to compute the probability $p(abs(r_i^1) < r_i^0)$ we have to integrate the Gaussian distribution from $-x$ to x and this is equivalent to twice the integral from 0 to x.

The symbol error probability P_s is then given by:

$$P_s = 1 - P_C \qquad (24)$$

It should be clear to the reader that the symbol error probability is different from the bit error probability. For biorthogonal signaling two distinct symbol errors can occur. Either $-s_i$ is selected instead of s_i or one of the $M - 2$ signals orthogonal to s_i. Several procedures are possible for bit-labeling, that is the assignment of grouped bits to the corresponding symbol. In general, and in order to decrease bit error probability the assignment for antipodal biorthogonal signaling assigns the antipodal signal pair with complementary label. For example in 8-ary signaling an antipodal signal pair would be assigned to the bit triple "010" and its complement "101". Assuming the error occurs of selecting $-s_i$ instead of s_i, the complementary bit-labeling results in decoding all bits wrong. However, this case is relatively rare because the distance between the antipodal signals is twice the distance to the orthogonal signals. For the second and more probable error, there are $M - 2$ equally probable decision errors and $\frac{M-2}{2}$ have bit discrepancies with Y_i^0 in any given position. The bit-error rate P_b is therefore bound by:

$$\frac{P_s}{2} < P_b \leq P_s \qquad (25)$$

where P_s is the symbol error probability.

As we have argued earlier, in digital watermarking applications we are more interested in the probability P_w of not correctly detecting the entire embedded watermark. Taking into account that the number of symbols decreases with increasing M and following the same strategy used to derive Eq. (17) we can derive the following expression for P_w:

$$P_w = 1 - P_C^{N/\log_2(M)}$$

$$= 1 - \left\{ \int_0^\infty \frac{e^{-\frac{(x-\mu_0)^2}{2\sigma_0^2}}}{\sqrt{2\pi\sigma_0^2}} \left[1 - 2Q\left(\frac{x}{\sigma_0}\right) \right]^{\frac{M}{2}-1} dx \right\}^{N/\log_2(M)} \quad (26)$$

To evaluate this expression we have to resort again to numerical methods.

4   Results

In order to illustrate the behavior of the detection error probability, we show the detection error as a function of the embedding density for different values of M. Usually in modulation the symbol error is shown as a function of the signal to noise ratio for different values of M. However, this approach is not suitable for watermarking systems because both, the signal and noise depend on the embedding density. The watermarking space is defined as the gray scale representation of the image. The weighting function $\alpha(x, y)$ is defined as a fraction of the luminance and a minimum offset, that is $\alpha(x, y) = C(x, y)/128 * \beta + \delta$, where β defines the embedding strength and δ the offset. The term 128 was only introduced to normalize the luminance and has no functional impact. The tests were performed using the following parameter settings: $\beta = 4$, $\delta = 1$, $N = 240$. Each test was repeated 100 times and using a different key for each test. In the detection process we use a cross-shaped prediction filter [6,5] as motivated below with its coefficients defined as:

$$H_+^W : h_+(x, y) = \begin{cases} 1 & x = 0, y = 0 \\ -\frac{1}{2W-2} & x = 0, 0 < |y| \le \frac{W-1}{2} \\ -\frac{1}{2W-2} & y = 0, 0 < |x| \le \frac{W-1}{2} \\ 0 & \text{otherwise} \end{cases} \quad (27)$$

where W defines the filter size. For the tests the size was set to $W = 7$. Other filters are also possible, For example filters based on the adaptive Wiener filter result in an impressive performance increase. However, the goal of this work is to investigate the impact of M-ary modulation and for this purpose the cross-shaped prediction filter provides a good trade-off between computational complexity and performance.

Fig. 7(a) shows the theoretical detection error probability as a function of the density D. Changing the density may actually be considered as some sort of changing the signal to noise ratio. The curves clearly show the significant performance improvement for large values of M. For small values of $M \leq 4$ the performance is approximately equivalent. This results agree with the theoretical performance results known from standard M-ary modulation [10] in that small values of M do not necessarily result in a performance increase.

Empirical detector results are shown if Fig. 7. The curves show an interpolation of the data points. We can clearly see the relative correspondence of the theoretical results shown in Fig. 7(a) and the empirical results in Fig. 7(b). Again, for small values of M, the performance does not increase, or decreases even for some densities. However, as soon as M is larger than 4, the detector performance increase significantly.

As a last test set Fig. 8 shows the watermark detection error for the *lena* and *baboon* images using M-ary modulation and lossy JPEG compression. The watermark embedding was performed using the same parameters as in the previous example. The density was fixed to $D = 0.5$. The graphs clearly illustrate the significant improvement with increasing values of M even under large JPEG compression. As an example, for a detection error probability of 0.1, the compression quality goes down to 25% for $M = 256$, and only 55% for $M = 2$.

5   Conclusions

The concept of M-ary modulation has been applied to spatial spread spectrum watermarking. The theoretical analysis using a linear correlator statistic with a preprocessing step prior to the detection have been derived. The theory was then verified with empirical results. We may conclude that in general M-ary modulation may significantly improve the robustness of digital watermarking schemes for values of M larger than 4. As we have seen, increasing values of M also increases the overall performance. However, it should be noted that large values of M result in an increased demodulation time. For real applications values of M between 8 and 64, in some cases 256 seem appropriate. Values larger than 256 would in general require to much processing time and are hence not suitable for digital watermarking applications. Comparing M-ary modulation to channel coding we may conclude that in any case M-ary modulation seems more appropriate for watermarking application because it results in any case in a performance improvement for values of $M > 4$. As opposed to M-ary modulation, in channel coding [7] the issue is much more delicate and the performance improvement is not guaranteed because it depends on the pulse size, as well as the watermark length and code length.

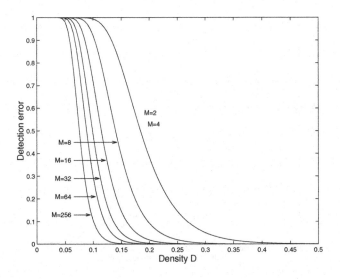

(a) Theoretical results.

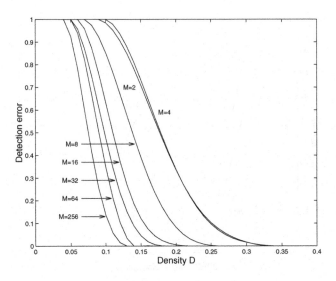

(b) Empirical results.

Fig. 7. Theoretical end empirical watermark detection error as function of the embedding density D for the *lena* image. For small values of M the detector performance is approximately the same. However, with values of M large than 4, the detector performance increases significantly with increasing M.

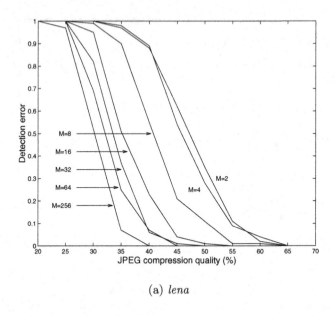

(a) *lena*

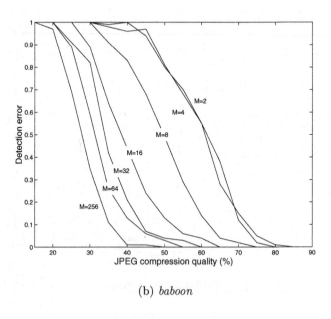

(b) *baboon*

Fig. 8. Empirical watermark detection error probability for the *lena* and *baboon* image using M-ary modulation. The curves show the detector improvement for large values of M. The detection error largely improves with increasing M, with exception for very small values of M.

References

1. Frank Hartung and Martin Kutter. Multimedia watermarking techniques. *Proceedings IEEE:Special Issue on Identification and Protection of Multimedia Information*, July 1999. 237
2. Carl W. Helstrom. *Probability and Stochastic Processes for Engineers*. Macmillan, 1991. 243
3. Anil K. Jain. *Fundamentals of Digital Image Processing*. Prentice-Hall, 1989. 238
4. Saleem A. Kassam. *Signal Detection in Non-Gaussian Noise*. Springer-Verlag, 1998. Chapter 2. 239
5. Martin Kutter. Watermarking resisting to translation, rotation, and scaling. In Andrew G. Tescher, Bhasjaran Vasudev, V. Michel Bove, and Barbara Derryberry, editors, *Multimedia Systems and Applications*, volume 3528, pages 523–431, San Jose, CA, USA, November 1998. IS&T, The Society for Imaging Science and Technology and SPIE, The International Society for Optical Engineering, SPIE. 238, 248
6. Martin Kutter, F. Jordan, and Frank Bossen. Digital watermarking of color images using amplitude modulation. *Journal of Electronic Imaging*, 7(2):326–332, April 1998. 238, 248
7. J.R. Hernández F. Pérez-González and J.M. Rodríguez. The impact of channel coding on the performance of spatial watermarking for copyright protection. In *International Conference on Acoustic, Speech and Signal Processing (ICASP)*, volume 5, pages 2973–2976, May 1998. 237, 249
8. Raymond L. Pickholz, Donald L. Schilling, and Laurence B. Milstein. Theory of spread-spectrum communications–a tutorial. *IEEE Transactions on Communications*, 30(5):855–884, May 1982. 237
9. Andrew J. Viterbi. *CDMA: Principles of Spread Spectrum Communication*. Addison-Wesley Publishing Company, 1995. 244
10. Stephen G. Wilson. *Digital Modulation and Coding*. Prentice Hall, 1996. 237, 239, 244, 249

On the Design of a Watermarking System: Considerations and Rationales

Jean-Paul Linnartz, Geert Depovere, and Ton Kalker

Philips Research Laboratories
Prof. Holstlaan 4, WY8, 5656, AA Eindhoven, The Netherlands
{linnartz,kalker,depovere}@natlab.research.philips.com

Abstract. This paper summarizes considerations and rationales for the design of a watermark detector. In particular, we relate watermark detection to the problem of signal detection in the presence of (structured) noise. The paper builds on the mathematical results from several previously published papers (by our own research group or by others) to verify and support our discussion. In an attempt to unify the theoretical analysis of watermarking schemes, we propose several extensions which clarify the interrelations between the various schemes.
New results include the matched filter with whitening, where we consider the effect of the image and watermark spectra and imperfect setting of filter coefficients. The paper reflects our practical experience in developing watermarking systems for DVD copy protection and broadcast monitoring. The aim of this paper is to further develop the insight in the performance of watermark detectors, to discuss appropriate models for their analysis and to provide an intuitive rationale for making design choices for a watermark detector.

1 Introduction

The understanding of reliable methods to detect embedded data or watermarks has progressed substantially over the past years. Many of the first proposals for watermarking emerged from the image processing community. It was also recognized that detection theory and spread-spectrum communication have several aspects in common with watermark detection, and results from these fields are now also exploited to improve the detection performance. This paper reviews the relation with detection theory and develops an intuitive understanding of the behavior of various approaches to watermark detection. It is not intended as a *how to* recipe, but rather as an attempt towards the development of a better understanding and a unified and more rigid theoretical modeling of watermark detection. Hitherto, several detection principles have been proposed and verified experimentally, but theoretical support often was meagre. Our discussion mostly refers to theoretical models, rather than to experiments. Nonetheless most of the models have been verified by experiments reported in previous publications. New results are obtained to further verify and illustrate detection performance. Our experiments have been conducted during the development of watermarking systems, both for a consumer electronics application, viz., the JAWS system [1] [2]

A. Pfitzmann (Ed.): IH'99, LNCS 1768, pp. 253–269, 2000.
© Springer-Verlag Berlin Heidelberg 2000

proposed by the Millennium Group as a solution to DVD copy protection[3], and for a professional application, viz., the VIVA system for automated monitoring of advertisements and news clips in television broadcasts [1]. In this paper, we address a large and important class of watermarks in which a pseudo-noise pattern is added to the luminance of the image pixels. This watermarking technique may involve adaptive embedding, based on perceptual masking models [4].

We are most concerned with the application of *embedded signaling*, i.e., of carrying additional data along with images or video. The three prime optimization criteria are low perceptibility, cost (intemately related to complexity), and robustness against common processing operations [5]. Robustness against intentional attempts to remove the watermark, and confidentiality in covert communication (hiding the fact that additional data is embedded) are of secondary importance. We do not specifically address the temporal aspect of motion pictures, so our results apply to images as well as to video. It has been shown that a watermark embedder can exploit its knowledge about the image. This leads to the modeling of a communication channel with side information at the transmitter [6]. Our paper (which primarily focusses on detection) ignores this aspect.

The outline of the paper is as follows. Section 2 formulates a watermarking model and defines parameters that we will use in our discussions in Section 3. The subsections of Section 3 address specific watermark detectors or refinements of these. Our discussion progresses from very basic schemes, such as the correlator in Section 3.1, and develops further sophistications step by step. Section 3.2 discusses some important ingredients of the correlator concept, in particular the size of the watermark alphabet. Section 3.3 addresses non-stationarity in the image. It justifies Wiener filtering on theoretical grounds, but finds that under slightly different assumptions for the embedding process, another adaptive filtering is preferable. The model in Section 3.4 addresses spectral prefiltering, but finds shortcomings in some implementations, which can be resolved by the whitening filter of Section 3.5. Section 3.6 provides a frequency-domain interpretation of the whitened matched filter. It extends the classic discussion of whether one should mark the perceptually relevant or irrelevant areas of the image. This section also relates the effect of MPEG compression to the theory of quantization and dithering. Section 3.7 discusses phase-only matched filtering and relates this to the theoretical model of Section 3.3. Section 3.8 discusses the problem of threshold setting. Section 4 supports the discussion of Section 3 by a mathematical analysis. It provides a derivation of new results for watermark detecting with imperfect prefiltering. Section 5 concludes the paper.

2   Preliminaries

We consider two stochastic processes: $\mathcal{W}$ generates watermarks W and $\mathcal{P}$ generates images P. Processed images, derived from $\mathcal{P}$ will be denoted as $\mathcal{Q}$ and $\mathcal{R}$. The watermark is seen as a random process because it is created from a pseudo-random sequence generator, which is fed by a random *seed*. We want our system performance to be sufficiently independent of the choice of this seed. Earlier analysis has shown that this can be ensured if certain restrictions are imposed on the sequence generation process. DC-freeness is one such requirement [7].

The image and its watermark have a size of N_1 by N_2 pixels with a total of $N = N_1 N_2$ pixels. The intensity level (called *luminance*) of the pixel with coordinates $n = (n_1, n_2)$, $(0 \leq n_1 \leq N_1 - 1, 0 \leq n_2 \leq N_2 - 1)$ for image P (upper case!) is denoted as $p(n)$ (lower case!). The set of all pixel coordinates is denoted as A. We restrict our discussion to gray scale images in which $p(n)$ takes on real or integer values in a certain interval. Whenever convenient we will represent $p(n)$ as a z-expression $p(z)$ defined by

$$p(z) = \sum_{n \in A} p(n) z^{-n} = \sum_{n \in A} p(n) z_1^{-n_1} z_2^{-n_2}. \tag{1}$$

2.1 Image Model

In some (but not all) analyses, we will make the simplification that the stochastic processes W and P are wide-sense stationary (WSS) and ergodic [8]. By ergodicity we are allowed to approximate the statistical k-th moment $\mu_k(p)$ by the spatial k-th moment $m_k(p)$, viz.,

$$\mu_k(p) = \mathrm{E}[p^k(n)] = m_k(p) = \frac{1}{N} \sum_{n \in A} p^k(n). \tag{2}$$

WSS means that the statistical autocorrelation function $\Gamma_{p,p}(n, m)$ only depends on the difference vector $\Delta = (\Delta_1, \Delta_2) = (n - m)$. That is,

$$\Gamma_{p,p}(n, m) = \mathrm{E}[p(n)p(m)] = C_{p,p}(\Delta) = \frac{1}{N} \sum_{n} p(n) p(n + \Delta). \tag{3}$$

A simple model for images is the first-order separable autocorrelation function [9]

$$C_{p,p}(\Delta) = m_1^2(p) + \sigma_p^2 \alpha^{|\Delta|}, \tag{4}$$

where $|\Delta| = |\Delta_1| + |\Delta_2|$. The standard deviation s_p is defined as $\sigma_p^2 = m_2(p) - m_1^2(p)$. The quantities $m_1(p)$ and $m_2(p)$ are referred to as the *DC-component* and the *power* of the image p, respectively. The value α reflects the correlation between adjacent pixels in the image. In other parts of the discussion we refine the WSS, ergodicity and autocorrelation models by assuming that these properties only apply locally.

We denote $\tilde{p}(n)$ as the DC-free component of the image, that is $\tilde{p}(n) = p(n) - m_1(p)$, so

$$C_{\tilde{p}\tilde{p}}(\boldsymbol{\Delta}) = \sigma_{\tilde{p}}^2 \alpha^{|\boldsymbol{\Delta}|}. \tag{5}$$

To avoid problems discussed elsewhere [7], we will assume that in the watermark detector all signals have been processed by subtracting the DC-component such that $\tilde{p} = p$, or, equivalently $m_1(p) = 0$.

2.2   Watermark Model

A watermark $w(\boldsymbol{n})$ is modeled as a sample drawn from the stochastic process W. The *energy* in a watermark w equals $NC_{w,w}(0) = Nm_2(w)$ and is denoted as E_w. Similarly as in the case of images we assume that w is DC-free, i.e. $\tilde{w} = w$. *White watermarks* have a spatial autocorrelation function which approaches the discrete Dirac distribution when the image size is large enough: $C_{w,w}(\boldsymbol{\Delta}) = N^{-1}E_w\delta(\boldsymbol{\Delta})$.

Our method of creating a *low-pass watermark* is by spatially filtering a white watermark source W with a first-order two dimensional spatial smoothing IIR filter $S_\beta(\boldsymbol{n})$,

$$S_\beta(\boldsymbol{z}) = \frac{1 - \beta^2}{(1 - \beta z_1^{-1})(1 - \beta z_2^{-1})}. \tag{6}$$

In this case the autocorrelation becomes:

$$C_{ww}(\boldsymbol{\Delta}) = \frac{E_w}{N}\beta^{|\boldsymbol{\Delta}|}. \tag{7}$$

The watermark is embedded according to

$$r(\boldsymbol{n}) = p(\boldsymbol{n}) + \phi(\boldsymbol{n})w(\boldsymbol{n}), \tag{8}$$

where $\phi(\boldsymbol{n}), (\phi(\boldsymbol{n}) > 0)$ denotes a local embedding depth, which adaptively depends on a local neighborhood of $\boldsymbol{n}$. Mostly, a global embedding depth condition guarantees that $m_2(\phi w) \approx m_2(\phi)m_2(w)$ equals E_w/N, thus $m_2(\phi) = 1$.

3   Discussion

Several early papers [10] [11] [12] propose a watermarking system which is equivalent to increasing the luminance of one set of pixels in the image by one quantization step, and decreasing it by one quantization step in a second set of pixels. The number of elements in both sets was taken equal. Thus, $w \in \{-1, 0, +1\}$. We denote $A_- = \{\boldsymbol{n} : w(\boldsymbol{n}) = -1\}$ and $A_+ = \{\boldsymbol{n} : w(\boldsymbol{n}) = +1\}$. Here, $A_+ \cap A_- = \emptyset$ and $A_+ \cup A_- \subseteq A$. Watermarks are detected by computing the sum of all pixel luminance values at locations where the watermark is negative, i.e., $s_- = \sum_{n \in A_-} r(n)$ and the sum of all luminance values where the watermark is positive, i.e., $s_+ = \sum_{n \in A_+} r(n)$. Then, an expression such as $d = (s_+ - s_-)/N$ is used as a decision variable. This scheme was later improved and the underlying model generalized to include

- adaptive embedding, to exploit masking properties of the image,
- real-valued watermarks w,
- embedding in different domain such as the DCT transform domain
- methods to exploit correlation in image pixels to improve the detector performance

3.1   Generalization to Correlation

The detector of the previous subsection is a special case of a *correlator detector* or *matched filter* [14]. In a correlator detector, a decision variable d is extracted from the suspect image $R = \{r(n)\} = P + W$ according to correlation with a locally stored copy of a (not necessarily equal) watermark $\hat{w}(n)$, so

$$d = C_{\hat{w},r}(0) = \frac{1}{N} \sum_n \hat{w}(n) r(n) = d_p + d_w. \tag{9}$$

Here the watermark contribution d_w equals $d_w = C_{\hat{w},w}(0)$ if the watermark is present and $d_w = 0$ otherwise. The image contribution $d_p = C_{\hat{w},p}(0)$ is a zero-mean *projection* of the image p on the watermark $\hat{w}$. Its variance determines the amount of noise or interference to the watermark.

Ignoring some subtleties, the matched filter theorem [14] can be summarized as the statement that $\hat{w}(n) = w(n)$ is the optimum choice for the local copy $\hat{w}$. Important assumptions are that the watermark signal (and its location or phase) are known and that the noise is additive, white and Gaussian. Under these conditions the decision variable d has the best achievable signal to noise ratio SNR, which is defined as $g = m_2(d_w)/m_2(d_p)$. Also, once d is known, no other properties can be extracted from R that would further improve the detector reliability.

The white noise assumption is equivalent to assuming that pixels in an image have random luminance values, independent from pixel to pixel. This may not model real-world images very well, but the matched filter theory also provides a foundation for further improvement, in casu the *whitened matched filter* which we will address later.

The Gaussian assumption may also lack realism, but up to now we have not found any paper in open literature which describes how to exploit the precise probability distribution of image luminance values to enhance detector reliability. Experiments, e.g. [11][7], confirmed that after accumulation of many pixels, $d_p(w)$ has a Gaussian distribution if N is sufficiently large and if the contributions to the summing are sufficiently independent. In [15] the model for the tails of the distribution is refined, leading to the conclusion that the Gaussian assumption for correlation values leads to pessimistic predictions for false positives.

3.2 Corollary

The concept of the matched filter directly suggests how to handle watermarks which draw w-values from a larger alphabet than $\{-1, 0, +1\}$. The matched filter detector multiplies every pixel of the suspect image with the luminance value of the reference watermark, $\hat{w} = w$. Thus, the detector should weigh most heavily the pixels (or frequencies) in which most watermark energy has been put, in fact, the best weighing is proportionally to the strength of the watermark. The use of a multi-valued watermark has several advantages.

– It is stronger against specific attacks, such as collusion attacks [16] or the histogram attack [17].
– Moreover, it is useful to have real-valued watermarks (or a discrete alphabet of sufficient size) when adaptive embedding is used. If the pixel modification ϕw is quantized and if w only has binary values (+1, -1), undesired discontinuities may occur. In such case, the effect of a carefully calculated ϕ is reduced to a crude switching of the watermark level. Boundaries may be particularly disturbing to the human eye.
– Real-valued watermarks occur naturally if the watermark is defined in one domain (e.g. spatial domain) but detected in another domain (e.g. JPEG or MPEG DCT coefficients).

Another observation is that detection based on correlation is equivalent to extracting a decision variable which is a linear combination of pixel luminance values. Hence correlation can be performed in any transform domain for which energy preservation is guaranteed. It can be calculated for instance in pixel domain, in an image-wide DCT, block-based DCT or FFT. While several embedding methods have been based on modifying MPEG or JPEG DCT coefficients, such watermarks can also be detected by correlation in the spatial domain, or vice versa. Domain transforms can further be used to speed up the correlation calculation or as a computationally efficient manner to search for watermarks in altered (e.g. shifted) images [1].

An aspect relevant to the complexity of the detector, is the ability to use *tiling* [1]. This is a method of spatially repeating a watermark pattern of size M_1 by M_2 with $M_1 < N_1, M_2 < N_2$ in the image, according to

$$r(\boldsymbol{n}) = p(\boldsymbol{n}) + \phi(\boldsymbol{n})w(n_1 \mathrm{mod} M_1, n_2 \mathrm{mod} M_2). \tag{10}$$

Since correlation is linear, i.e., $C_{p+q,w} = C_{p,w} + C_{q,w}$, the computational speed detection can be improved by a factor $N_1 N_2/(M_1 M_2)$ by cyclically wrapping the suspect image to one of size $M_1 M_2$, on which correlation is then performed [1].

3.3   Exploiting Non-stationarity

Most watermarks are embedded with an adaptive depth ϕ which depends on the masking properties of the image. Ideally the detector should take this into account. This section presents an optimum method for this. Let's assume that the image can be partitioned into I sub-images A_0, A_1, .., A_i, .. A_{I-1}, with N_0, N_1, .. ,N_i, .., N_{I-1} pixels, respectively, with $\sum_I N_i = N$. Each sub-image A_i has its own variance $\sigma_{p,i}^2$, autocorrelation α_i, and masking properties ϕ_i, which are constant within A_i. In practice, feature extraction algorithms may be used to partition A [1]. The problem of optimal detection relates to *diversity* [18] radio reception, a system which combines signals received by multiple antennas. Borrowing from this theory, one can extract I decision variables $d_0, d_1, ..d_{I-1}$, defined as

$$d_i = \frac{1}{N_i} \sum_{n \in A_i} r(n)\hat{w}(n) = d_{i,w} + d_{i,p}. \tag{11}$$

Here $d_{i,w} = N_i^{-1} \sum_{n \in A_i} \phi(n)w(n)\hat{w}(n) = \phi_i N_i^{-1} \sum_{n \in A_i} w(n)\hat{w}(n)$ and $d_{i,p} = N_i^{-1} \sum_{n \in A_i} p(n)\hat{w}(n)$. We define $E_{i,w} = \sum w^2(n)$, so if $\hat{w} = w$, $d_{i,w} = \phi_i N_i^{-1} E_{i,w}$. Section 3.8 describes how to estimate the variance $\sigma_{i,p}^2 = m_2(d_{i,p})$ in a practical detector. In the case that the local copy $\hat{w}$ is white Gaussian noise, it not hard to show that $sigma_{i,p}^2$ is proportional to the variance of the pixel data $m_2(p)$.

A single decision variable can be combined from

$$d = \sum_{i=0}^{I-1} d_i f_i. \tag{12}$$

Using Cauchy's inequality, the selection of the weigh factor f_i can be optimized for optimal SNR as follows,

$$g = \frac{\{\sum_{i=0}^{I-1} d_{i,w} f_i\}^2}{\sum_{i=0}^{I-1} \sigma_{i,p}^2 f_i^2} \leq \frac{\sum_{i=0}^{I-1} d_{i,w}^2 \sigma_{i,p}^{-2} \sum_{i=0}^{I-1} \sigma_{i,p}^2 f_i^2}{\sum_{i=0}^{I-1} \sigma_{i,p}^2 f_i^2} \tag{13}$$

$$= \sum_{i=0}^{I-1} \frac{d_{i,w}^2}{\sigma_{i,p}^2} = \sum_{i=0}^{I-1} \frac{\phi_i^2 E_{i,w}^2}{N_i^2 \sigma_{i,p}^2} = \sum_{i=0}^{I-1} \frac{\phi_i^2}{\sigma_{i,p}^2},$$

where we assume (without loss of generality) that $E_{i,w}/N_i = 1$. Equality holds if

$$f_i = \frac{d_{i,w}}{\sigma_{i,p}^2} = \frac{\phi_i E_{i,w}}{N_i \sigma_{i,p}^2} = \frac{\phi}{\sigma_{i,p}^2}. \tag{14}$$

---

[1] We will use later that this partitioning is not particular to the spatial domain, but may also occur in frequency domain.

Next we will consider two special cases of this result. These special cases can be shown to be approximately equivalent to a previously proposed detection methods.

The first case is that of an embedder using white Gaussian noise as a watermark pattern, with $\phi_i \approx \sigma_{i,p}$. This approximates a typical embedder which assumes that the perceptivity of a watermark is related to the standard deviation $\sigma_{i,p}$ in the pixel luminance. Inserting this into the formula for optimum weighing of the subimage decision variables f_i, we find $f_i = E_{i,w}\sigma_{i,p}^{-1}$ as the optimal choice. We will use this in our discussion of phase-only matched filtering in Section 3.7.

The second case is fixed-depth embedding, i.e., $\phi_i = $ constant. Our generic formula Equation 14 proposes that a detector should weigh $f_i = \sigma_{i,p}^{-2}$. Intuitively we explain this as follows: one division by $\sigma_{i,p}$ makes the noise power identical for all pixels, the second division weighs pixels proportionally to their strength. Radio engineers call the latter weighing *maximum ratio combining* [18]. This special case relates to extracting a Wiener filtered copy from the suspect image $R = Q - Wiener(Q)$, proposed in [19], which corresponds to

$$f_i = 1 - \frac{N_i\sigma_{i,p}^2}{N_i\sigma_{i,p}^2 + E_{i,w}} \tag{15}$$

Since one can approximate this as

$$f_i \approx \frac{E_{i,w}}{N_i\sigma_{i,p}^2}, \tag{16}$$

we can now provide a justification for the use of wiener filtering on theoretical grounds. We refer to [19] for a quantification of the improvement gains. Also, [20] develops a model for the impact of adaptive filtering, though it was used as an attack to minimize $C_{w,r}$ by $R = Wiener(Q)$.

3.4   Prefiltering

In this section we consider watermark detection when correlation is preceded by filtering of the image. In the following sections we will also consider prefiltering of the watermark. When an image is linearly filtered, a new image R is created in which each pixel luminance is a combination of pixel luminance values in the original image Q. Most filters operate locally, thus combining pixels in the neighborhood (small Δ) of the pixel that is created in the new image, according to the convolution

$$R = \sum_{\Delta} h(\Delta)Q(n + \Delta), \tag{17}$$

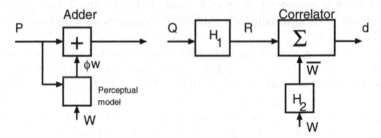

Fig. 1. Embedder and Correlator detector with prefiltering

Here $h(\Delta)$ are the filter coefficients of a *filter* H. Referring to Figure 1, this role is conducted by filter H_1, $R = H_1(Q)$, for the image and by filter H_2 for the watermark, $\hat{W} = H_2(W)$.

When a correlation detector is preceded by filtering, the SNR in the decision variable differs from the result for an unfiltered image [19] [20] [21] [22]. For linear prefiltering it is not difficult to show that the situation of Figure 1 is equivalent to correlation with W on the image $(H_2^* H_1)(R)$, where H_2^* denotes the time-inverse of the filter H_2.

An edge-enhancement filter [21] or median filter [23] filter can be used to predict the image in pixel n from the neighbouring pixels. This prediction is extracted from the actual luminance, according to $R = H_2(Q) = Q - Pre(Q)$, where $Pre()$ denotes pre-filtering. This exploits the redundancy in the pixels of the video. These filters reduce $m_2(d_p)$, the variance of the noise, and were shown to give a performance improvement. However these do not necessarily also maximize $E[d_w]$ or the signal to noise ratio. Optimization of the SNR g leads to the *whitened matched filter*.

3.5 Whitening Prefilter

For non-white noise, one can first prefilter the suspect image Q into R, such that its frequency spectrum is sufficiently white (see Figure 2. Subsequently, a matched filter Σ_1 is used for $R = H_1(Q)$. Readers who are familiar with information theory (e.g. [14]) may wish to skip the next paragraph, which sketches the proof by contradiction to see that this detector is optimum.

If the prefilter H_1 is invertible, $R = H_1(Q)$ and Q intrinsically carry the same information, so optimum detectors for R and Q must have the same reliability. Let $\Sigma_2(Q)$ be a fictitious detector which detects watermarks in Q more reliably than $H_1(\Sigma_1(Q))$, i.e., the concatenation of Σ_1 and H_1 executed on Q. Then, for images R (with white noise), the detector $\Sigma_2(H_1^{-1}(R))$ would outperform $\Sigma_1(R)$. This is at odds with the the matched filter theorem that $\Sigma_1(R)$ is optimum for R. So, $H_1^{-1}(\Sigma_2))$ cannot outperform Σ_1. This implies that $\Sigma_2(Q) = \Sigma_2(H_1^{-1}(H_1((Q)))$ cannot perform better than $\Sigma_1(H_1(Q))$. Thus, $\Sigma_1(H_1(Q))$ must be optimum

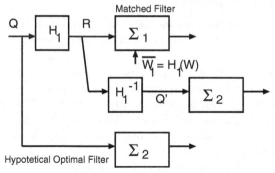

Fig. 2. Whitening Matched Filter H_1 and Σ_1, and fictitious better detector Σ_2

Whitening can be interpreted as a form of (high-pass) prefiltering before correlation. The whitened matched filter differs from the prefilter concept of he previous section in the sense that not only the suspect image but also the locally stored reference watermark is filtered ($\hat{W} = H_1(W)$). In fact in Figure 2, Σ_1 is a matched filter for R, where the watermark component in R is $H_1(W)$.

Implementation-wise we observe that the correlator, the correlator with prefiltering, and the whitened matched filter all create a decision variable which is a *linear* combination of the pixel luminance values. Thus, any of these can be implemented just as correlator, without any prefiltering. In other words, using the implementation of Figure 1, the detector does not have to execute filtering operartions H_1 and H_2 in real-time. Both H_1 and H_2 can be incorporated in a precomputed $\hat{W}$. We refer to Section 4 for an analysis of the performamance and the sensitivity to the accuracy of the filter setting. Experiments with whitening are reported in [22].

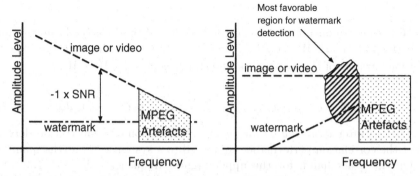

Fig. 3. Frequency components in image and watermark, without and with whitening

3.6   Frequency Components

The whitening concept throws new light on the discussion whether the watermark should be located in perceptually relevant or irrelevant areas (or frequency components) of the image. Whitening enhances high frequency components, which are relatively weak in a typical image. Whitening weakens the low frequency components, which are strong in a typical image. Thus these prefiltering methods tend to weigh high frequency components more heavily in the decision variable than low frequency components. The intuition behind it is that at low frequencies, the image itself causes stronger interference to the watermark than at higher frequencies.

A limitation of these models is that they not model typical distortion by MPEG or JPEG very well. In a first order approximation, these techniques can be interpreted to crudely quantize the medium to high-frequency components, and remove (i.e., quantize to zero) the upper higher frequencies. For the medium to upper frequencies, the watermark may not be affected so dramatically, because typically the image *dithers* [24] the watermark. Dithering is illustrated in Figure 4.

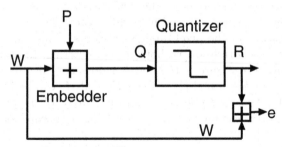

Fig. 4. Watermark embedding and lossy compression interpreted as a dithering system on watermarks.

Dithering can ensure that the error $E = R - W$ is statistically uncorrelated with the watermark W, i.e., $C_{w,e} = 0$ [24]. It follows the that the expected decision variable of the watermark detector becomes, for $\hat{W} = W$,

$$\mathrm{E}[d] = C_{w,R} = C_{w,w+e} = C_{w,w} + C_{w,e} = C_{w,w} = \mathrm{E}[d_w] \qquad (18)$$

That is, after *dithering by the image*, compression or quantization does not affect the correlation performance compared to a system without the quantizer.

On the other hand, for the upper highest frequencies the dithering effect is lost[2] and the watermark components in these frequencies do not contribute

---

[2] Formally speaking, the probability density of the amplitude of the image components do not satisfy the particular relation to the quantization step size as it was derived in [24]

to d_w. As these frequencies may nonetheless contain noise, the detector must avoid to excessively weigh upper high frequencies in the correlation. This requires a modification to $\hat{W}$ or H_2 in Figure 1.

3.7   Phase Only Matched Filtering

A refinement of the whitened matched filter is to adaptively whiten the spectrum of the incoming video. Instead of using a fixed H_1, the detector calculates an FFT of Q, and sets amplitudes to unity at all frequencies, thereby preserving only phase information [25].

This idea agrees with the result in Section 3.3. The rationale is that the watermark is only a small perturbation of the luminance. We partition the image into I spectral components. Even if it has been watermarked the suspect image gives a good estimate of the spectral components σ_i of P. It turns out that it is reasonable to assume that the embedding depth is likely to be more or less proportional to σ: even if this is not the case for freshly watermarked content, this is almost always true after common processing (JPEG, MPEG). Using the results of Section 3.3, the weigh factor is found as $f_i = \phi_i E_{i,w}/\sigma_{i,p}^2$, i.e. $f_i = E_{i,w}/\sigma_{i,p}$ which corresponds to phase-only filtering. We refer to [25] for an analysis of the performance of the phase only matched filter.

3.8   Adaptive Threshold Setting

Up to this point we have primarily described the extraction of a real-valued decision variable. Next we will discuss the extraction of a hard *watermark present - not present* decision. Detection theory suggests that a threshold can be used, and almost all practical systems use this method. A suspect signal (or an extracted set of features) is correlated with some pattern to obtain a correlation value. If this value is larger than a signal-dependent threshold then the watermark is said to be present. Otherwise the watermark is said to be absent. The setting of the threshold determines the trade-off between the false negative and the robustness to image processing. [3].

Only if non-adaptive embedding is used and the image is not modified the detector can exploit that $d_w = E_w$. In practice, the value d_w is not known exactly to the detector, because the algorithm for adaptive embedding may not be known or can not be repeated in the detector. Also, minor shifts and scaling of the image severely affects the value of d_w [26]. Moreover MPEG compression, or other processing may affect the high frequency components of the watermark in the image.

This makes the determination of the false negative rate problematic, unless extensive statistical assumptions are made about the processing that is likely to

---

[3] Traditionally, the false alarm probability versus missed detection probability are compared. However, the watermark embedder has full knowledge about the original image, thus is it can ensure detection. The threshold setting determines what modifications can be tolerated.

affect the image. An appropriate design approach is to determine a required false positive rate and to set the threshold accordingly. The problem of guaranteeing a certain false negative rate, i.e., how to make ϕ, or more precisely the correlation $C_{\hat{w},\text{MPEG}(\phi w)}$ large enough, then becomes mostly an embedding issue.

Various authors observed that d_p is in good approximation a Gaussian random variable [8] [7] [20] [15]. The ratio of the threshold setting over $m_2(d_p)$ determines the false positive rate, according to

$$P_{fp} = \text{erfc}\sqrt{\frac{d_{thr}^2}{m_2(d_p)}}$$

Since $m_2(d_p)$ significantly differs from image to image, it appeares useful to estimate $m_2(d_p)$ from the image. A practical solution is to use decision variables gathered during a search for shifts of the image [25]. For all attempts in the search that failed, $d_w \approx 0$ so $d \approx d_p$. One can set the threshold level according to

$$d_{thr}^2 = m_2(d_p)\{\text{erfc}^{-1}(P_{fp})\}^2$$

where erfc^{-1} is the inverted error function. This operation is mathematically equivalent to the concept of normalized correlation [27].

4   Error Performance for Whitening

This section presents a theoretical study of the whitened matched filter. We consider a low-pass watermark W, which is generated by spatially filtering a white watermark V with a first-order two dimensional spatial smoothing IIR filter $S_\beta(z)$, We further consider a low-pass image P, which is generated by spatially filtering a white image S with a first-order two dimensional spatial smoothing IIR filter $S_\alpha(z)$. After watermark embedding, the image is denoted $Q = P + W$. We apply a first order *whitening filter* at the input of the correlation receiver. This filter aims at transforming the non-white input signal of the receiver Q to a signal with a constant power spectrum. As shown in Section III, also the watermark has to be filtered in the same way. In order to keep the model as general as possible, we use the filter $G_\alpha(z) = S_\gamma^{-1}(z)$ as whitening filter.

In the correlator detector, a decision variable d is extracted by correlating the filtered received image Q with a filtered locally stored copy of the watermark W, i.e. $d = d_p + d_w$, where

$$d_p = \frac{1}{N}[S_\alpha(z^{-1})S_\gamma^{-1}(z^{-1})S(z^{-1})S_\beta(z)S_\gamma^{-1}(z)V(z)]_0,$$

and

$$d_w = \frac{1}{N}[S_\beta(z^{-1})S_\gamma^{-1}(z^{-1})V(z^{-1})S_\beta(z)S_\gamma^{-1}(z)V(z)]_0.$$

We introduce:

$$T_\alpha(z) = S_\alpha(z)S_\alpha(z^{-1}).$$

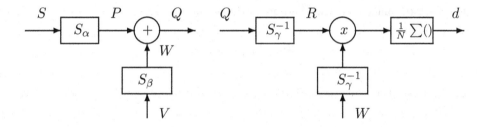

Fig. 5. Watermark Embedding and Correlation Detection.

Using results from the previous sections, the error probability is given by

$$P = \frac{1}{2} \operatorname{erfc} \left(\frac{\mathrm{E}[d_w]}{2\sqrt{2}\sigma_{d_p}} \right),$$

with

$$\mathrm{E}[d_w] = \frac{1}{N} [\frac{T_\beta(z)}{T_\gamma(z)}]_0 E_w$$
$$= \frac{E_w}{N} [\frac{1+\gamma^2 - 2\alpha\beta}{1-\gamma^2}]^2.$$

For the variance we find

$$\sigma_{d_p}^2 = \frac{1}{N^2} \mathrm{E}[[S_\alpha(z^{-1})S_\beta(z)T_\gamma^{-1}(z)S(z^-1)V(z)]_0]^2,$$
$$= \frac{\sigma_p^2 E_w}{N^2} [\frac{T_\alpha(z)T_\beta(z)}{T_\gamma(z)^2}]_0$$
$$= \frac{\sigma_p^2 E_w}{N^2}$$
$$[\frac{(1+\alpha\beta)(\gamma^4 + 2\gamma^2(2-\alpha\beta) + 1) - 2(\alpha+\beta)(2\gamma^3 - (\alpha+\beta)\gamma^2 + 2\gamma)}{(1-\gamma^2)^2(1-\alpha\beta)}]^2$$

Inserting these results in the formula for the error rate gives

$$P = \frac{1}{2} \operatorname{erfc} \left(\sqrt{\frac{E_w}{8\sigma_p^2}} \right.$$
$$\left. \frac{(1+\gamma^2 - 2\beta\gamma)^2(1-\alpha\beta)}{(1+\alpha\beta)(\gamma^4 + 2\gamma^2(2-\alpha\beta) + 1) - 2(\alpha+\beta)(2\gamma^2 - (\alpha+\beta)\gamma + 2)} \right),$$

It should be noted that in the case the whitening filter exactly matches the the received image, i.e. $\alpha = \gamma$ the above expression reduces to

$$P = \frac{1}{2} \operatorname{erfc} \left(\sqrt{\frac{E_w}{8\sigma_p^2} \frac{(1+\alpha^2 - 2\alpha\beta)}{1-\alpha^2}} \right).$$

For a white image $\alpha = 0$ we find again the result

$$P = \frac{1}{2} \operatorname{erfc} \sqrt{\frac{E_w}{8\sigma_p^2}}.$$

In the case of a white watermark, i.e. $\beta = 0$, the expression for the error rate becomes

$$P = \frac{1}{2} \operatorname{erfc} \left(\sqrt{\frac{E_w}{8\sigma_p^2}} \frac{(1+\gamma^2)^2}{(\gamma^4 + 4\gamma^2 + 1 - 2\alpha\gamma(2\gamma^2 - \alpha\gamma + 2))} \right).$$

This reduces further to

$$P = \frac{1}{2} \operatorname{erfc} \left(\sqrt{\frac{E_w}{8\sigma_p^2}} \frac{1+\alpha^2}{1-\alpha^2} \right).$$

in the case of perfect whitening: $\alpha = \gamma$.

5   Conclusions

We have reviewed various recently proposed watermark detection methods from a detection theory point of view. It appeared that many improvements which have been found from experiments can be explained by extending methods and theories known from communications. These considerations have been a reference for our design of two watermarking systems, which have been demonstrated and evaluated in practical applications [1].

Earlier publications confirmed that the use of crude statistical models for images can be useful to create some basic understanding of typical detectors. Here we summarized such results and compiled a consistent intuition for the effect of various sophistications of watermark detectors.

As the models used here have a relatively large scope, we not only justified detector refinements proposed in previous papers, but also found limitations and possibilities for further improvements.

New mathematical results of the effect of imperfect whitening showed that the accuracy with which prefiltering is performed only has a minor effect on the reliability of the detector.

We must leave several aspects for further investigation, such as a comparison of the performance of fixed prefilters (or fixed whiteners) with phase-only matched filtering.

References

1. T. Kalker, G. Depovere, J. Haitsma, M.J. Maes, "A video watermarking system for broadcast monitoring", Proceedings of SPIE, Security and Watermarking of Multimedia Content, Volume 3657, pp. 103–112, 1999. 253, 254, 258, 267

2. J.P.M.G. Linnartz, "The ticket concept for copy control based on embedded signalling", ESORICS '98, 5th. European Symposium on research in Computer Security, Louvain-La-Neuve, September 1998, Lecture Notes in Computer Science, 1485, Springer, pp. 257-274. 253

3. J. Bloom, I.J. Cox, A.A.C. Kalker, J.P.M.G. Linnartz, Math Miller and B. Traw, "Copy Protection for DVD", IEEE Proceedings, Special issue on Information and Protection of Multimedia Information, July 1999, Vol. 87, No. 7, pp. 1267-1266. 254

4. I. J. Cox, M. L. Miller, "A review of watermarking and the importance of perceptual modeling", Proc. of Electronic Imaging 97, Feb. 1997. 254

5. I.J. Cox and J.P.M.G. Linnartz, "Some general methods for tampering with watermarks", IEEE Journ. of Sel. Areas in Comm., Vol. 16. No. 4, May 1998, pp. 587-593. 254

6. I.J. Cox, M.L. Miller, and A.L. McKellips. "Watermarking as communications with side information", IEEE Proc., Vol. 87, No. 7, pp. 1127-1141. 254

7. J.P.M.G. Linnartz, A.C.C. Kalker, and G.F. Depovere, "Modelling the false-alarm and missed detection rate for electronic watermarks". Workshop on Information Hiding, Portland, OR, 15-17 April, 1998. Springer Lecture Notes on Computer Science, No. 1525, pp. 258-272, pp. 329-343. 255, 256, 257, 265

8. J.P.M.G. Linnartz, A.C.C. Kalker, G.F. Depovere and R. Beuker, "A reliability model for detection of electronic watermarks in digital images", Benelux Symposium on Communication Theory, Enschede, October 1997, pp. 202-209. 255, 265

9. N.S. Jayant and P. Noll., "Digital Coding of waveforms", Prentice Hall, 1984. 255

10. I. Pitas, T. Kaskalis, "Signature Casting on Digital Images", Proceedings IEEE Workshop on Nonlinear Signal and Image Processing, Neos Marmaras, June 1995. 256

11. W. Bender, D. Gruhl, N. Morimoto and A. Lu, "Techniques for data hiding", IBM Systems Journal, Vol. 35. No. 3/4 1996. 256, 257

12. W. Bender, D. Gruhl, N. Morimoto, "Techniques for Data Hiding", Proceedings of the SPIE, 2420:40, San Jose CA, USA, February 1995. 256

13. I. Cox, J. Kilian, T. Leighton and T. Shamoon, "A secure, robust watermark for multimedia", in Proc. Workshop on Information Hiding, Univ. of Cambridge, U.K., May 30 - June 1, 1996, pp. 175-190

14. J. Wozencraft and I. Jacobs, "Principles of Communication Engineering", Wiley, 1965. 257, 261

15. M. L. Miller and J. A. Bloom, "Computing the probability of false watermark detection", in Proc. Workshop on Information Hiding 99, Dresden. 257, 265

16. I. Cox, J. Kilian, T. Leighton and T. Shamoon, "A secure, robust watermark for multimedia", in Proc. Workshop on Information Hiding, Univ. of Cambridge, U.K., May 30 - June 1, 1996, pp. 175-190. 258

17. M. Maes, "Twin peaks: the histogram attack on fixed depth watermarks", Workshop on Information Hiding, Portland, OR, 15-17 April, 1998. Springer Lecture Notes on Computer Science, No. 1525, pp. 290-305. 258

18. "Wireless Communication, The Interactive MultiMedia CD ROM", Baltzer Science Publishers, Amsterdam, 3rd Edition, 1999, http://www.baltzer.nl/wirelesscd. 259, 260

19. L.M. Marvel, C.G. Boncelet, C.T. Retter, "Reliable blind information hiding for images", Workshop on Information Hiding, Portland, OR, 15-17 April, 1998. Springer Lecture Notes on Computer Science, No. 1525, pp. 48-61. 260, 261

20. J.R. Hernandez, F. Perez-Gonzalez, J.M. Rodriguez and G. Nieto, "Performance analysius of a 2D Multipulse Amplitude Modulation Scheme for data hiding and watermarking of still images", IEEE JSAC, Vol. 16, No. 4, May 1998, pp. 510-524. 260, 261, 265

21. G.C. Langelaar, J.C.A. van der Lubbe, J. Biemond, "Copy protection for multimedia data based on labeling techniques", 17th Symposium on Information Theory in the Benelux, Enschede, The Netherlands, May 1996. 261

22. G.F.G. Depovere, A.C.C Kalker, and J.P.M.G. Linnartz, "Improved watermark detection reliability using filtering before correlation", Int. Conf. on Image Processing, ICIP, October 1998, Chicago IL. 261, 262

23. G. Langelaar, R. Lagendijk and J. Biemond, "Removing Spread Spectrum Watermarks", Proceedings of Eusipco-98, Volume IV, pp. 2281–2284, Rhodes, 1998. 261

24. S.P. Lipshitz, R.A. Wannamaker and J. Vanderkooy, "Quantization and Dither: A theoretical survey", J. Audio Eng. Soc., Vol. 40, No. 5, May 1992, pp. 355-375. 263

25. T. Kalker and A.J.E.M Janssen, "Analysis of SPOMF Detection", Accepted at ICIP-99, Kobe, Japan, 1999. 264, 265

26. J.P.M.G. Linnartz, A.A.C. Kalker, J. Haitsma, "Detecting electronic watermarks in digital video", Paper 3010, Invited paper for special session at ICCASP-99, Phoenix, AR, March 1999. 264

27. M. Wu, M. Miller, J. Bloom, I. Cox, "Watermark detection and normalized correlation", presented at ICCASP 99, Phoenix, AR, March 1999, also at DSP Conference in Florance. 265

A Bayesian Approach to Affine Transformation Resistant Image and Video Watermarking

Gabriella Csurka[1], Frédéric Deguillaume[1], Joseph J. K. Ó Ruanaidh[1,2], and Thierry Pun[1]

[1] CUI, University of Geneva,
24 rue Général Dufour, CH 1211 Geneva, Switzerland
{Gabriela.Csurka,Frederic.Deguillaume,Thierry.Pun}@cui.unige.ch
http://cuiwww.unige.ch/~vision
[2] Siemens Corporate Research,
755 College Road East, Princeton, NJ 08540, US
oruanaidh@scr.siemens.com

Abstract. This paper proposes a new approach for assessing the presence of a digital watermark in images and videos. This approach relies on a Bayesian formulation that allows to compute the probability that a watermark was generated using a given key. The watermarking itself relies on the discrete Fourier transform (DFT) of the image, of video frames or of three dimensional chunks of video scene.

Two kinds of information are hidden in the digital data: a watermark and a template. Both are encoded using an owner key to ensure the system security and are embedded in the 2D or 3D DFT magnitude of the image or video. The watermark is encoded in the form of a spread spectrum signal. The template is a key based grid and is used to detect and invert the effect of an affine geometric transformation (rotations, scaling and/or aspect ratio change) or in the case of the video framerate changes, aspect-ratio modification and rescaling of frames.

It is shown that, for the spread spectrum signal described in the paper, it is possible to positively detect the presence of a watermark without necessarily decoding it, given only the key used to generate it. To do that, the Bayesian approach allows the deduction of the relative log-probability of the presence of a watermark in an image given only the key. All that is required for positive watermark verification is the key. This approach also allows to infer the number of bits contained in the watermark.

The performance of the presented techniques and the usefulness of the relative log-probability are shown through various applications and experimental results.

1 Introduction

The popularity of the World Wide Web has clearly demonstrated the commercial potential of the digital multimedia market and consumers are investing heavily in digital audio, image and video recorders and players. Unfortunately, digital

A. Pfitzmann (Ed.): IH'99, LNCS 1768, pp. 270–285, 2000.

networks and multimedia also afford virtually unprecedented opportunities to pirate copyrighted material. Digital storage and transmission make it trivial to quickly and inexpensively construct exact copies. Therefore, digital image and video watermarking and copyright protection has recently become a very active area of research.

The main idea of the method presented here is to use a *Bayesian approach* to image and video watermark detection, in order to compute the probability that a watermark was generated using a given key (section 5). All that is required for positive watermark verification is the key. This technique works even when the binary message cannot be decoded; this is interesting, because it suggests that the watermark algorithm can be used either to extract binary messages, or for binding a watermark to the key, i.e. it is not necessary to decode the watermark to verify the ownership.

The watermark used in this paper is a Gold Code based spread spectrum sequence (see section 3) which encodes the message, containing information such as owner identification, a serial number, type of content, etc., or alternatively a hash number to a table that contains these elements. The major advantage of a spread spectrum system is that it transforms the narrow band data sequence into a noise-like wide-band signal, using pseudo-random sequences that are difficult to detect and extract.

The watermark, in the form of a spread spectrum sequence, is embedded in a mid-frequency range of the discrete Fourier transform (DFT) domain of the image or video as a compromise between the visibility of the watermark and robustness to lossy compression and other attacks (section 3). Due to the properties of the Fourier transform and spread spectrum techniques this method resists to spatial and/or temporal shifts, to simple filtering, noise adding, JPEG respectively MPEG compression. However, if the modification suffered by the image or video are geometric transformations such as rotation, scaling, cropping, aspect ratio change respectively changes of frame-rate the positions where the mark was embedded also change. In order to be able to synchronize and to decode the message in these cases, a template is used to detect and invert the effect of a *general affine geometric transformation* undergone by the image, or a shift in the log-log-log map[1] in the 3d DFT of the video prior to extracting the mark (section 4).

Several applications are presented in the second part of the paper, which show the usefulness of the proposed Bayesian approach (section 6).

2   Background

Most of the current watermarking techniques for digital images, inspired by methods of image and video coding and compression, work in the transformed

---

[1] The reason not to search for affine transform in the case of videos is that, from one hand the 3D linear transform depends on more parameters and the template search has a high computational cost and on the other hand it unlikely that video frames be rotated or transformed by a random linear transform.

frequency domain. The reason is that data loss usually occurs among the high frequency components. Hence the watermark has to be placed in the significant frequency components of the Discrete Cosine Transform (DCT) [1] or Discrete Fourier Transform (DFT) [8,9] of the image. Some other approaches have been proposed that rather embed the mark in the image in the spatial domain [7,5]. Geometric distortions are determined manually [1], using an empirical search [5,7], using template-grid and automatic template matching [9] or working in a geometric distortion invariant space [8].

In the case of video watermarking the challenge is to mark a group of images which are strongly intercorrelated and often manipulated in a compressed form, e.g. MPEG. A first group of video watermarking methods therefore directly operate on MPEG data to avoid full decompression [4]. Other approaches, less dependent on the type of video compression and more resistant to rescaling, change of frame-rate and re-compression in a different format, mark the uncompressed video sequence. Each video frame is then marked individually as a still image or the video is considered as a three-dimensional signal and the mark is embedded into the 3D DFT domain [2]. In another approach, Swanson et al. [12] make use of a temporal wavelet transform of the video; 2D wavelet frames are then marked instead of the original video frames.

One of the key element to make a watermark robust is to embed it in the perceptually significant components of the image taking account of the behavior of the human visual system (HVS) [1]. Another key element is the use of spread spectrum techniques to encode the information before embedding it in the images [13,1]. A good spread spectrum sequence is one which combines desirable statistical properties such as uniformly low cross correlation with cryptographic security. It was shown in [10] that m-sequences and Gold Code based spread spectrum sequences perfectly fulfil these requirements.

3   The Watermark

The approach presented here uses spread spectrum to encode the message, that can contain information such as the owner of the image, a serial number and perhaps flags which indicate the type of content e.g. religion, pornography, or politics, or alternatively a hash number to a table that contains these informations. System security is based on proprietary knowledge of the keys (or the seeds for pseudo-random generators) which are required to embed, extract or remove an image watermark.

Let the message be represented in binary form as $\widehat{\boldsymbol{b}} = (\hat{b}_1, \hat{b}_2, ...\hat{b}_M)^\top$ where $\hat{b}_i \in \{0,1\}$ and M is the number of bits in the message to be encoded. The binary form of the message $\widehat{\boldsymbol{b}}$ is then transformed to obtain the vector $\boldsymbol{b} = (b_1, b_2, ...b_M)^\top$, with $b_i \in \{1, -1\}$ by exploiting the basic isomorphism between the group[2] $(\oplus, \{0,1\})$ and the group $(*, \{1,-1\})$. The mapping $1 \to -1$ and $0 \to 1$ is an extremely important step because it essentially enables us to replace the exclusive-OR operator used in finite field algebra with multiplication.

---

[2] The bit addition modulo 2, $\oplus$ is equivalent to exclusive-OR.

Defining a set of random sequences v_i each corresponding to a bit b_i, the encoded message can be obtained by:

$$w = \sum_{i=1}^{M} b_i v_i = \mathbf{G}b \qquad (1)$$

where b is a $M \times 1$ vector of bits (in ± 1 form), w is a $N \times 1$ vector and $\mathbf{G}$ in $N \times M$ matrix such that the ith column is a pseudo-random vector v_i.

Clearly, the effectiveness of this scheme depends on the specific choice for the random vectors v_i. It is shown in [10], how pseudo-random sequences can be used to spread the signal spectrum. In order to despread the signal these pseudo-random sequences need to have good randomness properties, long periods and different sequences must be well separated in term of correlation. In other words, the specific choice of method for generating the pseudo-random sequence has direct implications on the reliability and security of the embedded mark.

Maximum length sequences or simply m-sequences perfectly fulfil these requirements. They are the largest codes that can be generated by a shift register of a given length. They exist for all integer values n with period $N = 2^n - 1$ and can be easily generated by proper connections of feedback paths in an n-stage shift register circuit [10]. The autocorrelation function and spectral distribution resemble that of white Gaussian noise. Cross-correlation between shifted versions of m-sequences are equal to -1, whereas autocorrelations are equal to N. Therefore, one alternative to choose v_i to encode the message b is to consider an m-sequence v_1 and for each i, v_{i+1} results from v_i by a circular shift of length 1 (each element of v_i is shifted to right and the last element becomes the first).

Another alternative for v_i is to use Gold Codes [10,3]. A family of Gold Codes is obtained using an m-sequence v_1 and a q-decimation of it. The decimation v_1' is obtained by sampling every q^{th} element of v_1. Note that v_1' has period N if and only if $\gcd(N,q)=1$, where "gcd" denotes the greatest common divisor. Each element v_{i+1} of the family can then be obtained as follows: take v_1' (of length N), circular shift it by i and multiply element by element with the vector v_1.

Gold sequences have the advantage that for a given register length n there are more choices for the "key" than with shifted m-sequences. Indeed, for a register length n, there are $2^n - 1$ possible m-sequences ($2^n - 1$ possible seed as initial element in the register) but for Gold Codes there is in addition the possibility to choose a different decimation q. In addition, it is known that Gold sequences have better cross correlation properties if only part of the sequence is used. This could have implications if the watermark is partially destroyed by image cropping or filtering.

The watermark, in the form of a spread spectrum sequence, is embedded in a mid-frequency range of the discrete Fourier transform (DFT) domain of the image or video. The upper and the lower frequency bound are fixed in advance as a compromise between the visibility of the watermark (low frequencies contain the most of the image information) and robustness to lossy compression (which remove high frequencies). Note that for videos the mark can be embedded in the 2D DFT of each frame as for still images or into the magnitude of the 3D DFT of video chunks [2]. In the case of the 3D DFT the third dimension corresponding to the temporal frequencies also has to be taken into account. These frequencies have the following properties. Null or low temporal frequencies are linked to static components in the input scene, while higher frequencies are related to moving objects and varying areas. Therefore again, due this time to a compromise between the static and moving components, a mid range is considered.

The spread spectrum message w is added only to the magnitudes of the DFT and the phase is left unaltered. The strength of the watermark, corresponding to a modulation factor ($s_w w \rightarrow w$) can be set either interactively or adaptively as a function of the average and standard deviation of the DFT components of the chosen frequency range. Note, that w contains positive and negative values (it is easy to see from (1) that $w_i \in \{-M, M\}$). To have a better security, for each w_i a pair of location $\{(u_i^1, v_i^1), (u_i^2, v_i^2)\}$ in the specified frequency band of the magnitude domain is chosen pseudo-randomly in function of the owner key. Then, if $w_i > 0$, it is added to the magnitude at the position (u_i^1, v_i^1), otherwise to the magnitude at the position (u_i^2, v_i^2). To be more robust, instead of simply adding the values of the spread spectrum, one can modify the magnitude values at (u_i^1, v_i^1) and (u_i^2, v_i^2) in such a way that their difference becomes equal to w_i. Finally, from the marked spectrum and the unchanged phase the DFT is inverted (inverse Fourier transform) yielding the watermarked image.

In order to extract the watermark, the DFT of the marked image or video is considered. As the pair of positions of the magnitude components modified is known (it depends on the owner key), there is no need of the original image to extract the watermark. The difference between the pair-wise coefficients allows to obtain a spread spectrum signal $w' = w + e$, where w is the embedded watermark and e is an additive error. In order to decode the message from w', for each i the dot product ("cross-correlation") between v_i and $w' = \sum_{i=1}^{M} b_i v_i + e$ is performed:

$$B'_j = <w', v_j> = \sum_{i=1}^{M} b_i <v_i, v_j> + <e, v_j> \qquad (2)$$

It can be shown that for m-sequences and Gold Codes $<v_i, v_j> = -1$ for $i \neq j$ and $<v_i, v_i> = N$. Replacing them in (2), gives $B'_j = b_j N - (M-1) + <e, v_j>$. Generally $M \ll N$. Moreover the distribution of e can be approximated by a normal distribution with zero mean, so $<e, v_j>$ is negligible comparing to N. Therefore, each embedded information bit b_j can be retrieved as follows:

$$b'_j = sign(B'_j) = sign(b_j) = b_j$$

4 Affine Transformation Resistant Watermarking

The watermarking method described in the previous section presents an inherent invariance to spatial shifts for images and videos and/or temporal shift for videos due to the basic properties of the Fourier transform. It also resists to simple filtering, noise adding, JPEG respectively MPEG compression because the spread-spectrum sequences are very robust to noise or partial cancelation. However, if the modification suffered by the image or video are geometric transformations such as affine geometric transformation (rotations, scaling and/or aspect ratio change), cropping[3] respectively changes of frame-rate the positions where the mark was embedded also change. In order to be able to synchronize and to decode the message in these cases, a *template* is used to detect and invert the geometric transformation undergone by the image or video prior to extracting the mark.

The template is defined as a sparse set of positions in the 2D or 3D DFT. These positions are owner key dependent and therefore it is possible to create a reference template during the extraction. The magnitude values at these positions are modified to become local maxima (peaks) in the DFT magnitude domain in order to facilitate the template search process.

4.1 Template search in 2D DFT. First, all local maxima (peaks) in the magnitude of the 2D DFT are extracted. The geometric transformation is then estimated by a point matching algorithm between the extracted peaks and the reference template points as follows. It is assumed that the more general global transformation applied to an image is an affine transformation (which is a linear transform defined by a 2×2 matrix $\mathbf{T}$ plus a translation). Due to the properties of the Fourier transform, the magnitude is invariant to the translation, and therefore the corresponding transformation in the DFT magnitude depends only on four parameters (the coefficients of $\mathbf{T}^{-\top}$). Consequently, it is sufficient to have two pairs of matches between the local peaks and the template points to be able to estimate the geometric transformation. An exhaustive search is performed considering each pair of peaks with each pair of template points. The corresponding linear transformation is applied to all the other template points and the transformation for which there is a maximum number of match between the peaks and the transformed template points is retained. In order to optimize the exhaustive search, only those pairs of matches are considered that satisfy some predefined constraints. These constraints concern the distance between the pairs of points, the angle defined by the pair of point and the origin of the DFT (0 frequency) and the order of the points as a function of the distance from the origin, before (reference template points) and after the transformation (the considered pair of peaks). These constraints are based on the assumption that the geometric distortion of the image cannot be very important. Finally, to have a more accurate estimation of the linear transformation, it is reestimated using a least median square technique on the set of found matches.

4.2 Template search in 3D DFT. One alternative is to generalize the above technique for the 3D DFT. However, the 3D linear transform depends on 9 pa-

---

[3] Note that cropping in direct domain corresponds to a horizontal and/or vertical scaling in the frequency domain, and therefore it is a particular case of a linear transform in the DFT.

rameters (three matches) and therefore the template search would have a high computational cost. Furthermore, it is unlikely that video frames be rotated or transformed by a random linear transform. Generally, the changes suffered by a video are frame cropping, frame scaling and/or changes of aspect ratio, or changes of frame-rate. Therefore, instead of a generalization of the above technique, a log-log-log map of the 3D DFT is used which allows to find independent scalings along the three axes corresponding to a aspect-ratio change and a frame-rate change. The log-log-log is a bijective function (if the origin $(0, 0, 0)$ was extracted) and it converts the DFT (k_x, k_y, k_z) space to a (μ_x, μ_y, μ_z) logarithmic space as follows:

$$\mu_t = sign(k_t) \cdot ln(|k_t|), \quad \text{where} \quad t \in \{x, y, z\} \tag{3}$$

From the signed shifts $\triangle \mu_x$, $\triangle \mu_y$ and $\triangle \mu_z$ in the log-log-log space obtained by the template matching the rescaling factors s_x, s_y, s_z of the 3D DFT are $s_x = e^{\triangle \mu_x}$, $s_y = e^{\triangle \mu_y}$ and $s_z = e^{\triangle \mu_z}$.

Consequently, in the log-log-log map the scalings along the three axes are transformed to a simple 3D shift. This means that in order to retrieve the transformation a cross-correlation step needs to be applied between the reference template and the mapped DFT. However the cross-correlation can be computationally costly, and can be replaced by a point matching techniques between the local peaks and template points. As the 3D shift is defined by 3 parameters, it is sufficient to have a match between a local peaks and a template points to be able to estimate it. An exhaustive search is therefore performed considering each peak with each template point, and the corresponding shift is applied to all the other template points. The shift for which there is a maximum number of matches between the peaks and the transformed template points is retained.

5   The Bayesian Approach for Assessing the Watermark Presence

Consider a binary string b' extracted from an image, for which almost all bits agree with a known binary sequence message b which may have been embedded in the image. Generally, one can expect that about 50% of the bits of a random sequence will agree with the watermark. The question that can be asked is: What is the probability that the almost perfect agreement occurred at random? In order to answer this question, consider the probability that a random sequence will have a certain number of bits in common with a given sequence. It is easy to show that this probability is given by the Bernoulli distribution: $p(i) = C_N^i / 2^N$, where N is the number of bits in both messages and i is the number of bits found to be in common.

The implications of this result are quite far reaching. If one decodes a 100 bit watermark and finds that 80% of the bits are "correct" then one can be fairly sure that the watermark was indeed found. This is because the probability of getting 80% or more bits correct is at random is 2.17×10^{-9}. This is the probability of a false alarm – where one would say that a watermark is present when in fact there is none.

However, the original message is generally not known, and a bit by bit comparison between the extracted message (which can be corrupted) and the original one is not possible. Being able to detect a watermark without necessarily being able to decode it, can be therefore highly useful since it can help to prove ownership (the owner of the given key) in the case when due to noise the message can only partially be decoded. One expects that watermark detection will always be more robust than watermark decoding because in detection one is essentially transmitting a single bit of information which is to say whether a watermark is present or not.

In which follows, a new approach is proposed that computes the probability that the watermark was generated using a given key. The basic idea is as follows. A watermark w is embedded in the DFT domain of the image or video. The watermark is a m-sequence or Gold Code based spread spectrum signal $w = Gb$ (see (1)) and the extracted watermark can generally be estimated by $w' = Gb + e$, where e is an additive noise vector corrupting the watermark.

Assuming that the noise is approximately Gaussian distributed and applying the Bayesian approach described in [11], the *probability* that a spread spectrum signal w' extracted from the image I' contains a message of length M encoded with the key K can be computed as follows:

$$p(K, M \mid w', I') \propto \frac{\pi^{-N/2}\, \Gamma\left(\frac{M}{2}\right) \Gamma\left(\frac{N-M}{2}\right) \left|G^\top G\right|^{-1/2}}{4\, R_\delta\, R_\sigma \left(b'^\top b'\right)^{M/2} \left(w'^\top w' - f^\top f\right)^{(N-M)/2}} \tag{4}$$

where $b' = (G^\top G)^{-1} G^\top w'$ and $f = G^\top b$, are the least squares estimate for the bit sequence and the fit of the estimated watermark respectively. R_σ and R_δ are irrelevant constants introduced as normalization factors.

For m-sequences and Gold sequences, the $M \times M$ matrix $A = G^\top G$ has the following form: $A(i, j) = -1$ for $i \neq j$ and $A(i, i) = N$. The two terms in expression (4) which require the most computation are $B = (G^\top G)^{-1}$ and $|G^\top G|$. However, both the determinant and the inverse can be computed in closed form:

$$|G^\top G| = (N + M - 1)(N + 1)^{M-1} \quad \text{and} \quad B(i, j) = \begin{cases} \frac{2^N - M + 1}{2^N\,(2^N - M)} & \text{if } i = j \\ \frac{1}{2^N\,(2^N - M)} & \text{if } i \neq j \end{cases}$$

In a similar way, the *probability that no message* (a message of length 0) was embedded in the image with a given key K is:

$$p(K, 0 \mid w', I') \propto \frac{\pi^{-N/2} \Gamma\left(\frac{N}{2}\right)}{2 R_\sigma (w'^\top w')^{N/2}} \tag{5}$$

Finally, to decide if a given key was used or not to generate a watermark, the *relative log-probability*:

$$P_r = log\left(\frac{p(K, M \mid w', I')}{p(K, 0 \mid w', I')}\right) \tag{6}$$

Fig. 1. Six marked images used to test. Up: Lena (color, 512×512, PSNR=37.2), Fishingboat (gray-scale, 512×512, PSNR=39.5) and Barbara (gray-scale, 256×256, PSNR=32.5), Down: Benz (color, 640×480, PSNR=42.2), Bear (color, 394×600, PSNR=39.6) and Watch (color, 1024×768, PSNR=44.1).

is compared to 0. If $P_r > 0$ a message was embedded with the key K, otherwise no message was embedded with K. To exclude false alarms, a threshold $t > 0$ can be chosen by accepting occasional false rejections (noisy cases).

6   Applications of the Bayesian Approach

In the following, we show some experimental results and some concrete applications of this Bayesian approach. In our experiments, we used several real images and videos. In each cases we encoded the message "CUI_Tests" (72 bit) with the key (seed) 180599. Figure 1 shows the marked images[4].

6.1 Searching for the message length. We are interested here in determining the message length M using the Bayesian approach. Therefore, we consider a marked image (Lena) and we compute the relative log-probability P_r for different values of M. It can be noticed in Figure 2(Left) that the curve obtained for the correct key has reached its maximum at 72 (the correct number of bits), and that it is almost constant (the values vary between -4 and 0) for a wrong key. We have the same behavior as for the second curve if we try to detect the mark in an unmarked image (Figure 2(Right)).

---

[4] PSNR is the Peak Signal to Noise Ratio [6].

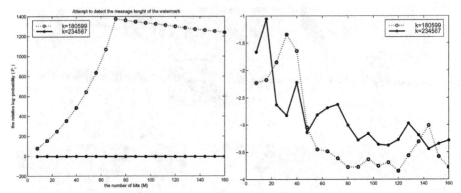

Fig. 2. An attempt to determine the correct number of bits in the watermark given only the key. Left: marked image. Right: unmarked image.

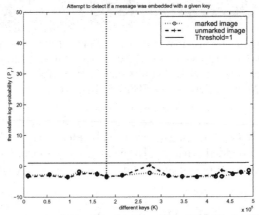

Fig. 3. An attempt to detect if a message was embedded with a given key.

6.2 Detecting the presence of the mark. The presented Bayesian approach can act concurrently to the message decoding, by estimating the probability that a watermark was generated given only the key. It can therefore be used either to extract the binary messages or to bind the watermark to the key.

Figure 3 shows several attempts on the marked and unmarked images to detect and decode the message using different keys. We can see that the relative log-probabilities were below the threshold (generally between 0 and -4), excepting, when we used the correct key and the marked image.

6.3 Stirmark attacks. To test the robustness to different attacks of our algorithm, we applied the program Stirmark 3.1[5] of Fabien Petitcolas [6] on the marked images. The results are shown in Table 1. Figures 4 and 5 show the behavior of the relative log-probability (P_r) in the case of some of the tests.

[5] http://www.cl.cam.ac.uk/ fapp2/watermarking/stirmark/.

Tests	$ber = 0$	$ber \leq 5\%$	$ber > 5\%$	$P_r \geq 1$	$P_r < 1$
JPEG	28/72	15/72	29/72	63/72	9/72
Enhancement $\pm$ JPEG	60/66	3/66	3/66	63/66	3/66
Scaling $\pm$ JPEG	57/72	5/72	10/72	67/72	5/72
ARC $\pm$ JPEG	96/96	0/96	0/96	96/96	0/96
RAC $\pm$ JPEG	80/192	40/192	72/192	176/192	16/192
RACS $\pm$ JPEG	85/192	33/192	74/192	178/192	14/192
Cropping $\pm$ JPEG	57/108	21/108	30/108	92/108	16/108
LT $\pm$ JPEG	6/36	16/36	14/36	36/36	0/36
Shearing $\pm$ JPEG	18/72	20/72	34/72	71/72	1/72
RCR $\pm$ JPEG	33/60	12/60	15/60	60/60	0/60
Flip	6/6	0/6	0/6	6/6	0/6
RGD	0/6	0/6	6/6	0/6	6/6
CR	1/4	3/4	0/4	4/4	0/4

Table 1. The results of the tests with Stirmark 3.1. We used the following notations: *ber* is the *bit error ratio*; *ber* $\leq 5\%$ means in our case 1, 2 or 3 bit errors; $\pm$ JPEG means that the results on the corresponding row contains the tests with the modified image without compression and with compression JPEG of a quality factor 90. The enhancement techniques contains Gaussian and median filtering, frequency mode Laplacian removal and sharpening. LT are general linear transforms, RGD is a random geometric distortion. CR is a GIF format based color reduction (no color reduction for the two gray scale images). The variation of the parameters of different attacks is as follows: quality factor for JPEG between 10 and 90, scaling between 0.5 and 2; aspect ratio changes (ARC) between 0.8 and 1.2; angles for the rotation with auto-crop to remove zero padded regions (RAC) between -2 and 90; angles for the rotation with auto-crop to remove zero padded regions and rescale to the original size (RACS) between -2 and 90; the percentage of the cropped region between 1% et 75%; the percentage of the shearing along the x and y axes between 1% à 5% the number of the row and/or column regularly removed (RCR) between 1 and 17.

The results show that the algorithm resist generally to the different attacks (excepting the random geometric distortion). Moreover, they show clearly that the Bayesian approach is more robust (the mark is detected for $P_r > 1$) than the message decoding (*ber* $= 0$) even if we accept[6] 1/72-3/72 bit error ratio (*ber* $\leq 5\%$).

6.4 Different size of images. In our method we consider the DFT of the whole image and embed the mark inside a fixed frequency band. These frequencies were chosen as a compromise between visibility and robustness of the mark. As we work with absolute frequencies, the choice of the correct mid-frequency band depends on the image size. A frequency band adequate for a given size can be too low for large images, too high for small images. Therefore, for different sizes of images we have to consider different frequency bands. One possibility is to use

---

[6] These few bits can be recovered if we use error correcting codes.

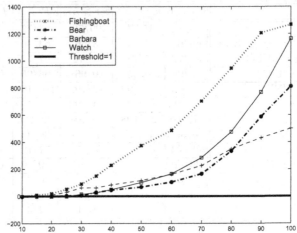

Fig. 4. The relative log-probabilities for JPEG tests with Stirmark 3.1.

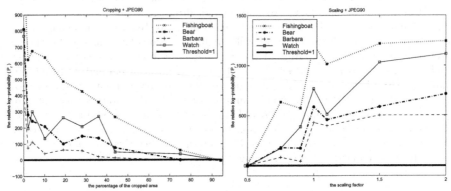

Fig. 5. The relative log-probabilities for cropping + JPEG90 (Left) and scaling + JPEG90 (Right) tests with Stirmark 3.1.

normalized frequencies instead of absolute frequencies. As we do not know the original image size during the extraction, working with normalized frequencies requires fixed sized block at the embedding, which means that we have to divide the image into blocks or if the block is bigger than the image to pad it with zeros. Another possibility is to choose several (3-5 as a function of the image sizes we want to mark) fixed absolute frequency bands, and in function of the image size embed the mark in the more appropiate corresponding frequency band. During the extraction, as the image can be cropped or scaled, therefore we do not know the original size. We thus check each frequency band and estimate the relative log-probability P_r for each of them. The correct band will be the one for which $P_r > t$.

Image	Lena	Bear	Benz
Inverting the found transformation	$P_r = -3.26$ $ber = 52.78\%$	$P_r = -3.07$ $ber = 45.83\%$	$P_r = -3.26$ $ber = 40.28\%$
Without inverting the found transformation	$P_r = 312.7$ $ber = 0\%$	$P_r = 68.6$ $ber = 1.39\%$	$P_r = 55.8$ $ber = 0\%$

Table 2. Some examples where the template does not resist to the JPEG compression (quality factor 50) and the found transform is not the correct one, however the mark was detected when we try to extract directly the mark.

Transformation	RC (-0.25)	Shearing	RCR (17,5)
Inverting the found transformation	$P_r = 524$ $ber = 0\%$	$P_r = 94.7$ $ber = 0\%$	$P_r = 158$ $ber = 0\%$
Without inverting the found transformation	$P_r = 1.58$ $ber = 16.67\%$	$P_r = 0.6$ $ber = 9.72\%$	$P_r = 69.09$ $ber = 1.39\%$

Table 3. Some examples where the mark was detected without the template, however the with template we have more accurate results.

6.5 Using or not the recovered transformation. The template points require a stronger modification of the DFT magnitudes than the watermark since we want to insure that there will be local peaks. In order not to introduce visible artifacts, we choose higher frequencies for the template peaks than for the watermark. Several attacks such as JPEG compression with a high compression rate (low quality factor) affect first the high frequencies. Moreover, due to the properties of the spread spectrum, the watermark presents good robustness even if it is corrupted or partially considered. Therefore, it can happen that the template search algorithm is less robust than the watermark detection. In this case, if we invert the transformation (which is not necessarily correct or accurate) before detecting and decoding we may obtain a wrong message (see Table 2). However, if the attack contains no geometric transformation, the position of the watermark has not changed. Therefore, it is interesting to extract the mark first without looking for the geometric transformation and compute the relative log-probability. We then search for a geometric transform, invert it, extract again the mark and compare the new relative log-probability with the first one. We keep the message for which the relative log-probability was larger.

On the other hand, it is also important to estimate the geometric transformation even if the mark was detected without it. Indeed, if the transformation is not very large (small rotation for example), the mark can be detected without inverting the transformation, but with less accuracy (see Table 3).

6.6 Resistance of the video watermarking. In order to test the robustness of the 3D DFT watermarking we use the video sequences compressed

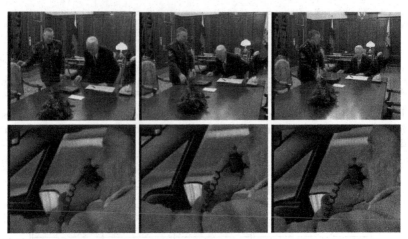

Fig. 6. Three marked frames of both considered video sequences.

Tests	$ber = 0$	$ber \leq 5\%$	$ber > 5\%$	$P_r \geq 1$	$P_r < 1$
MPEG-2	170/201	15/201	16/201	201/201	0/201
ARC+ MPEG-2	87/201	33/201	81/201	167/201	34/201
FRC+ MPEG-2	66/251	51/251	134/251	187/251	64/251
ARC+ FRC + MPEG-2	43/251	24/251	184/251	138/251	113/251

Table 4. The results for the 3D video watermarking approach. The aspect ratio changes (ARC) is 4/3 vs. 16/9; the frame-rate changes (FRC) is 25 vs. 30 fps. In the case of aspect ratio change of the frames, each frame is cropped and rescaled to the original size of the frame.

with MPEG-2. Figure 6 shows three marked frames for each of them. Both sequence have been encoded from PAL television images with a frame-rate of 25 frames/sec. The frames are of size 352×288 pixels, which is close to the 4/3 TV standard format ($352/288 = 3.667/3$). The first sequence, was 1450 frames long (58 s), and the second one, was 1749 frames long (1 min 10 s). Both video sequences were decompressed before performing any watermarking operation. The tests have been made using blocks of 16 frames long embedding the same watermark and the same template into each block. The results of the tests are shown in Table 4. Note that here each block was considered independently to test the presented algorithm on a maximum number of blocks. However, in the case of a video, generally the aspect ratio change and/or frame-rate change is the same along the whole video sequence. Therefore, it is sufficient to search for the template at the beginning of the video and once the template is detected, that is once the relative log-probability is positive, the obtained parameters can be used to invert the transformation for the next blocks.

ARC+ FRC + MPEG-2	first video	second video
Averaging the results of all blocks	$ber = 2.88\%$	$ber = 0\%$
Averaging after outliers rejection	$ber = 0\%$	$ber = 0\%$

Table 5. Example (first video) where due to the outliers rejection the mark was more accurately detected than with simple averaging.

6.7 Outliers rejection. As the video is divided into consecutive chunks of fixed length and the same watermark is embedded into the 3D Discrete Fourier Transform magnitude of each block, for a given video one can compute an averaged w' or an "averaged" sequence of bits b in order to extract the message. However, some blocks, frames or video blocks can be more affected than others and therefore can be considered as "outliers". Using the Bayesian approach these "outliers" can be rejected easily before "averaging" and in this way the watermark extraction and message decoding becomes more robust (see Table 5).

7 Conclusion

We have presented here a new approach for assessing the presence of a digital watermark in images and videos, by means of a Bayesian formulation that allows to compute the probability that a watermark was generated using a given key. The watermarking method itself relies on the discrete Fourier transform (DFT) of the image or of three dimensional chunks of video scene. The message is encoded in the spread spectrum signal using an owner key to ensure the security. The properties of m-sequences or Gold Codes were studied and exploited in order to generate this spread spectrum sequence.

In order to detect and invert the effect of an affine geometric transformation (rotations, scaling and/or aspect ratio change) or in the case of the video frame-rate changes, aspect-ratio modification and rescaling of frames, a point matching based template search algorithm was proposed.

Experimental results show on one hand the efficiency and the robustness of our watermark detection algorithm and, on the other hand, the behavior and the usefulness of the added Bayesian measure.

Acknowledgments

We are grateful to Shelby Pereira and Svyatoslav Voloshynovskyy for a number of interesting discussions on the subject, and to Dr A. Herrigel and Digital Copyright Technologies Switzerland for the ongoing collaboration. This work is financed by the European Esprit Open Microprocessor Initiative (project JEDI-FIRE) and by the Swiss Priority Program on Information and Communication Structures (project Krypict) and is part of the European Patent application EU978107084.

References

1. I. Cox, J. Killian, T. Leighton, and T. Shamoon. Secure spread spectrum watermarking for images, audio and video. In *Proceedings of the IEEE Int. Conf. on Image Processing ICIP-96*, pages 243–246, Lausanne, Switzerland, 1996.
2. F. Deguillaume, G. Csurka, J. J. K. Ó Ruanaidh, and T. Pun. Robust 3d dft video watermarking. In *IS&T/SPIE Electronic Imaging'99, Session: Security and Watermarking of Multimedia Contents*, San Jose, CA, USA, January 1999.
3. E. H. Dinan and B. Jabbari. Spreading codes for direct sequence CDMA and wideband CDMA cellular network. *IEEE Communications Magazine*, pages 48–54, june 1998.
4. F. Hartung and B. Girod. Watermarking of uncompressed and compressed video. *Signal Processing*, 66:283–301, 1998.
5. J. R. Hernández, F. Pérez-González, J. M. Rodrígez, and G. Nieto. Performance analysis of a 2-D-multipulse amplitude modulation scheme for data hiding and watermarking of still images. *IEEE Journal on Selected Areas in Communications*, 16(4):510–523, May 1998.
6. M. Kutter and F. A. P. Petitcolas. A fair benchmark for image watermarking systems. In *Electronic Imaging '99, Security and Watermarking of Multimedia Contents*, volume 3657, pages 219–239, San Jose, CA, USA, January 1999.
7. N. Nikolaidis and I. Pitas. Robust image watermarking in the spatial domain. *Signal Processing*, 66:385–403, 1998.
8. Joe J. K. Ó Ruanaidh and Thierry Pun. Rotation, scale and translation invariant spread spectrum digital image watermarking. *Signal Processing*, 66(3):303–317, May 1998. (Special Issue on Copyright Protection and Control, B. Macq and I. Pitas, eds.).
9. S. Pereira, J. J. K. Ó Ruanaidh, F. Deguillaume, G. Csurka, and T. Pun. Template based recovery of Fourier-based watermarks using Log-polar and Log-log maps. In *Int. Conference on Multimedia Computing and Systems, Special Session on Multimedia Data Security and Watermarking*, Juin 1999.
10. R. L. Pickholtz, D. L. Schilling, and L. B. Milstein. Theory of spread spectrum communications – A tutorial. *IEEE Transactions on Communications*, COM-30(5):855–884, May 1982.
11. J. J. K. Ó Ruanaidh and W. J. Fitzgerald. *Numerical Bayesian Methods Applied to Signal Processing*. Series on Statistics and Computing. Springer-Verlag, 1996.
12. M. D. Swanson, B. Zhu, and A. H. Tewfik. Multiresolution scene-based video watermarking using perceptual models. *IEEE Journal on Selected Areas in Communications*, 16(4):540–550, May 1998.
13. A. Z. Tirkel, G. A. Rankin, R. G. van Schyndel, W. J. Ho, N. R. A. Mee, and C. F. Osborne. Electronic watermark. In *Dicta-93*, pages 666–672, Macquarie University, Sydney, December 1993.

Enhanced Intellectual Property Protection for Digital Circuits on Programmable Hardware

John Lach[1], William H. Mangione-Smith[1], Miodrag Potkonjak[2]
University of California, Los Angeles

[1]Department of Electrical Engineering
56-125B Engineering IV
Los Angeles, CA 90095
{jlach, billms}@icsl.ucla.edu

[2]Department of Computer Science
4532K Boelter Hall
Los Angeles, CA 90095
{miodrag}@cs.ucla.edu

Abstract. The use of digital marks to provide ownership (watermarking) and recipient (fingerprinting) identification for intellectual property (IP) has become widespread. However, many of these techniques require a high complexity of copy detection, are vulnerable to mark removal after revelation for ownership verification, and are susceptible to reduced mark integrity due to partial mark removal. This paper presents a method for both watermarking and fingerprinting intellectual property, in the form of designs implemented on field programmable gate arrays (FPGAs), that achieves robustness by responding to these three weaknesses. The key techniques involve using secure hash functions to generate and embed multiple small marks that are more detectable, verifiable, and secure than existing FPGA IP protection techniques.

1   Introduction

1.1   Motivation

Design reuse has grown due to the continual increase in digital IC system complexity. While twenty years ago a 32-bit processor would require several ICs, a 32-bit RISC core currently requires approximately 25% of the StrongARM 110 device developed by Digital Semiconductor in collaboration with ARM Limited [1,2,3]. Design partitioning allows complex systems to be assembled from smaller modules. Although this type of design reuse has been employed for years, the boundaries of these modules have recently moved inside IC packages. Reused modules include parameterized memory systems, I/O channels, ALUs, and complete processor cores.

Design reuse has led to the rise of Intellectual Property Protection (IPP) concerns. IP modules are often designed by one company and sold in a non-physical form (e.g. HDL, netlist, layout) to others, and therefore do not have a natural physical manifestation. The IP blocks are modular and are designed to be integrated within other systems, usually on the same chip. As a result of the flexible, intangible nature of these modules, IP theft has become a problem. A thief need only resell or reuse an IP module without even reverse engineering the design, as proof of IP ownership is difficult to assert due to its inherently abstract nature.

A. Pfitzmann (Ed.): IH´99, LNCS 1768, pp. 286–301, 2000.

Existing FPGA design watermarking [4] and fingerprinting [5] techniques attempt to deter such direct theft and misappropriation of FPGA IP. Digital marks are embedded in a design layout which identify the design origin (watermarking and fingerprinting) and specific design instance recipient (fingerprinting only). These marks allow the IP owner to verify the physical layout as their property and establish the source of misappropriation, in a way that is more compelling than the existing option of verifying the design against a registered database or design history documentation. However, these existing FPGA IP protection techniques focused more on embedding the mark and keeping it secure. Little emphasis was placed on the mark itself and the quality and complexity of its detection and verification.

Our new techniques enable efficient copy detection for identifying stolen or misappropriated IP, even if it is embedded in a complex system. The techniques also provide simple mark extraction and convincing design source and instance recipient verification, without threatening the security of other designs. Finally, the embedded marks are more secure against removal attacks and more robust against partial mark removal. The new techniques provide this greater efficiency, verifiability, security, and robustness for protecting FPGA IP without increasing the user design effort, CAD tool effort, or area and timing overhead required by the existing FPGA watermarking and fingerprinting techniques.

1.2   Existing FPGA IPP Techniques

FPGA design watermarking embeds a digital mark in unused lookup tables (LUTs) throughout the design [4]. These LUTs are incorporated into the design with unused interconnect and neighboring logic block "don't care" inputs, further hiding the signature. Watermarks have been shown to be secure against removal unless the design can be reverse engineered to the netlist level, thus protecting against direct IP theft. Fingerprinting combines watermarking and a physical design partitioning technique [5]. Using solely the watermarking technique to embed recipient information would facilitate simple comparison collusion[1]. Therefore, fingerprinting efficiently generates a different design configuration for each recipient using the physical design partitioning technique[2]. Each recipient receives a different, yet functionally equivalent, set of partitioned blocks. Any attempt to eliminate differences in non-identical blocks via comparison collusion would render the design non-functional.

---

[1] Two recipients could simply XOR their bitstreams, as the only difference between the designs would be their unique fingerprints within.

[2] This partitioning technique greatly reduces the design effort for instance generation [5]. Each recipient receives a different instance of the design without having to re-place-and-route the entire design for each recipient as seed-as-fingerprint approaches require.

1.3   Copy Detection

Scanning a large set of diverse FPGA designs for potentially stolen or misappropriated copies can be a laborious process if comparisons are based on functional similarities or widely dispersed watermarks. Fortunately, existing FPGA IPP techniques restrict mark placement to logic block LUTs, and it can be quickly established where LUTs are located in an FPGA bitstream. Therefore, LUTs can be scanned for ownership marks, making copy detection reasonably efficient.

The new FPGA IPP techniques allow for even more efficient copy detection than existing techniques provide by allowing each design and every copy of each design to have the same set of watermarks. Therefore, when a set of designs is being searched, a constant, constrained set of marks is being compared to the LUT configurations, greatly reducing the search complexity. Mark security is maintained by the use of multiple watermarks (existing FPGA IPP techniques use a single large watermark) as discussed in Sections 1.4 and 1.5.

In addition, searching for multiple marks does not increase design search complexity by a significant measure even if a single mark were used in every design. This efficiency is achieved by using small marks, specifically marks that fit in the target architecture's LUTs. Therefore, for each LUT examination, the set of marks is iteratively compared to the LUT contents instead of successive LUT-sized portions of the large single mark. For example, given 16-bit LUTs, comparing 20 successive 16-bit portions of a single 320-bit mark to LUT contents requires the same complexity as comparing 20 16-bit marks.

The use of many small marks makes copy detection significantly more efficient.

1.4   Mark Verification

Publicly verifying design ownership has previously presented a risk to the design owners. Once a mark was publicly revealed for verification, it increased the possibility that other design recipients could find and remove the mark. This vulnerability is especially crucial if the same mark is used for all of the owners' IP including unrelated modules, which is necessary for efficient copy detection.

The new techniques eliminate this concern with the use of multiple watermarks. A subset of the marks is revealed for public verification, providing enough information for proof of ownership yet not enough for other recipients to remove a significant amount of marks in their copies (as well as the customers for all the other designs created by the company that possess the same set of marks). The subset may be removed, but the others will remain.

In addition, an important characteristic of any watermarking approach involves the owner being able to precisely locate the marks for ownership verification based on a predefined extraction technique. If the owner tells an independent verification team that a watermark is in locations F(seed), for some known algorithm F() and an integer seed value, they will have more credibility than if they tell the team to search the entire design until they find a watermark. The specific approach to such an implementation for watermarking verification is detailed in Section 4.4. Also, small watermarks require no cross-LUT reassembly, reducing verification complexity.

Mark location is not precisely known for fingerprinting, for which there is variability among designs released to multiple partners for comparison collusion prevention. Assuming the design recipient is not known before verification, it is necessary to make an exhaustive comparison between the ownership watermarks and all possible mark locations (i.e. all LUTs), much in the same way that copy detection searches are performed. Ownership can still be established in this method, albeit less efficiently and convincingly. However, searching possible locations for fingerprints would not be efficient, as the set of recipients could be large. Without knowing which customer distributed the design, we would have to consider each of them against the contents of each LUT. We address this point by co-locating ownership watermarks with recipient fingerprints. The most direct method is (given multiple LUTs per logic block) to use one LUT in a logic block to store the ownership watermark and the other to store the fingerprint. Therefore, once the ownership mark location is established via the exhaustive LUT search, recipient marks can be extracted and verified with the same efficiency and level of validity as the F(seed) watermark verification technique.

1.5   Mark Security and Robustness

Smaller marks reduce the possibility that a mark may be partially removed, thus increasing mark robustness for verification. For example, if ten of twenty LUTs containing the mark were erased by reverse engineering, one 320-bit mark with 50% of its bits removed may be less compelling for ownership verification than ten intact 16-bit marks due to the problems of partial mark reassembly.

Fingerprinting robustness is also enhanced by the use of smaller marks. If the physical partition boundaries are established by a collusion group, partition blocks may be exchanged. This may break up large fingerprints, rendering them unreadable and impossible to reassemble. Similarly, fingerprints in otherwise identical partition blocks may be removed by comparison collusion (see Section 0 for security against comparison collusion information), thus destroying parts of large signatures. Shorter signatures contained entirely in a LUT maintain their integrity, as each exchanged tile passes all of the design owner and recipient information, and the short signatures in non-identical partition blocks remain intact after the others are removed by comparison collusion.

Multiple distinct marks also increase mark security by reducing the possibility of repetition-based statistical attacks from the repetition of a single small watermark. For example, a single 16-bit mark repeated twenty times is susceptible to such an attack, while ten to twenty distinct marks would be less apparent.

1.6   Contributions

We present new FPGA design watermarking and fingerprinting techniques for IPP that provide for more efficient copy detection, more convincing ownership and recipient verification, and more secure and robust marks without increasing user design effort, CAD tool effort, or area and timing overhead.

2   Technological Issues

2.1   Vulnerability to Reverse Engineering

Marks can be applied to any level in the design flow, including behavioral hardware description language (HDL), synthesis to register transfer language (RTL), technology mapping, and finally physical layout involving place-and-route. A mark applied at one level transfers down to lower levels, but because a mark is nonfunctional, it may be removed by reverse engineering a design to a higher level in the design flow than that where the mark was applied. However, FPGA vendors generally believe that it is difficult to reverse engineer their devices, and they promise their customers that they will keep the bitstream specification confidential in order to raise the bar for reverse engineering [6]. Ken Hodor, product-marketing manager at Actel, claims that "antifuse-based FPGAs are by far the hardest device to reverse engineer" [7]. The SRAM-based Xilinx XC4000 devices follow a form of Pareto's rule: the first 80% of the configuration information can be determined relatively easily by inspection, the next 16% is much more difficult, etc. The irregular row and column pattern due to the hierarchical interconnect network increases the complexity.

2.2   Vulnerability to Statistical Analysis

Although the new IPP approaches help protect against mark removal through repetition-based statistical analysis, other statistic investigations could be launched. A naive approach to encoding a watermark would involve making direct use of symbols from a known alphabet or strings from a known language (e.g. ASCII encoding of words). This approach would result in a frequency distribution of symbols that is likely to be quite different from that typically found in LUTs that are used to implement digital logic. An engineer could detect a watermark through statistical analysis given a large enough sample of typical digital designs.

This problem could be attacked by creating a mapping function that translates the symbols in the watermark alphabet into appropriate symbols from typical design distributions – thus giving the watermark a statistical signature closer to a typical design. However, we do not currently have a large enough set of complete designs to be able to characterize the typical distribution, and thus producing such a mapping function is problematic. Instead, we choose to whiten the spectrum of the watermark making it not look like any particular spectrum. Thus, while it will still be possible to find a mark by asking "does this look like a typical design?" (given enough information regarding typical design characteristics) it is not possible to find the mark by asking "is there a mark in English?" This spectral whitening primarily is achieved through the application of secure hash functions.

2.3   Verifying Altered Designs

As discussed in Section 1.4, watermarking places ownership marks in specific LUTs based on the design seed and desired marks. Therefore, knowing the design seed and embedded marks, the location of each mark is known to the owner. Verification then only requires comparisons to be made between the presumed mark and the LUT bits. However, if the design has been altered (e.g. the bitstream reverse engineered to the physical design layout level and rearranged using a design or floorplan editor), the mark may have been moved to a different LUT location. If such a case arises, mark extraction for ownership or source verification involves blindly searching LUTs for the multiple ownership watermarks, much in the same manner as the ownership portion of fingerprints is extracted (see Section 1.4).

3 Related Work

Many current IP protection techniques are based on encrypted source files. For example, encrypted HDL modules disguise the form and structure from IP users. This allows the IP users the ability to incorporate soft modules and high performance simulation models into their design using a CAD tool provided with the decryption key, without exposing the IP to theft. However, this approach has been successfully attacked, often by directly attacking the CAD tool. Therefore, there is no foreseeable IP protection technique based on encrypted source files, despite stronger forms of encryption and more thorough systems engineering.

Signature hiding techniques for image, video, and audio signals have recently received a great deal of attention. Digital image steganography has been especially well explored [8,9,10], including many mark security and verification issues [11]. Digital audio protection has proven to be even more difficult, but many different techniques have nevertheless been proposed [12,13,9]. Video stream protection techniques have also been developed [14,15].

Recently, a set of techniques has been proposed for the protection of digital circuit IP through watermarking at various levels in the design hierarchy using the superimposition of additional constraints in conjunction to those specified by the user [16,17,18,19,20,21,22]. In this paper, we propose the first fingerprinting technique for FPGA designs. The majority of intellectual property is already programmable components, and all economic and historical trends indicate that the importance of these components will continue to rise.

Cryptography is used for selecting a subset of FPGA physical design constraints for mark embedding, as it provides probabilistic randomization and therefore protection from added constraints. For this task, we use the standard cryptography tools from the PGP-cryptography suite, the secure hash function MD5, and the RSA/MIT stream cipher RC4 [23].

4 Approach

4.1 General Approach

While the basic design flows for watermarking and fingerprinting are no different than described in [4] and [5] respectively, the techniques introduced here create new approaches for three sub-functions: mark preparation, mark embedding, and mark verification. The pseudo-code and explanations below represent the global flow of each technique.

Watermarking

```
1.  create initial non-watermarked design;
2.  extract timing and area information;
3.  prepare marks;
4.  establish mark locations;
5.  modify netlist and constraints for mark locations;
6.  execute place-and-route tools on modified netlist;
7.  embed marks;
8.  incorporate unused logic blocks into design;
9.  if !(meet timing criteria) {
10.    try with fewer marks, else terminate with success;}
```

Steps 1 and 2 are a part of any digital design flow. The original netlist is mapped, processes by place-and-route tools, and subjected to timing and area analysis. This timing and area information is later used for calculating the overhead incurred due to watermarking. Ownership mark preparation is then performed in Step 3, and mark locations are defined by the mark and a design seed in Step 4. The physical constraints based on the established mark locations are input to the netlist and CAD tool constraints file in Step 5, allowing the modified design to be re-processed by the place-and-route tool in Step 6. Steps 7 and 8 embed the marks in the appropriate LUTs which are incorporated into the rest of the design by receiving dummy inputs and outputting to neighboring "don't care" inputs, further hiding the marks. Timing analysis is done in Step 9, establishing the timing overhead incurred due to watermarking. If the overhead is deemed unacceptable, the process is repeated with fewer marks, which also changes the mark locations determined in Step 4.

Fingerprinting

```
1.  create initial non-fingerprinted design;
2.  extract timing and area information;
3.  while (!complete) {
4.     partition design into tiles;
5.     if (!(mark size && collusion protection)) break;
6.     for (i=1;i<=# of tiles;i++) {
7.        for (j=1;j<=# of tile instances;j++) {
8.           create tile instance(i,j);
9.           if (instance meets timing criteria) {
10.             incorporate unused logic blocks;
11.             store instance;
12. } } } }
13. prepare ownership marks;
14. for (i=1;i<=# of recipients;i++) {
15.    prepare recipient marks(i);
16.    select tile instances from database;
17.    embed marks;
18. }
```

As in watermarking, Steps 1 and 2 create the physical layout for the non-fingerprinted design, establishing the basis for all area and timing overhead. Steps 3-12 perform the design partitioning (tiling), creating a database of tile instances. Step 13 prepares the ownership marks, and Steps 14-18 are executed for each distributed instance of the design. Fingerprinting Steps 10, 13, and 17 are analogous to watermarking Steps 8, 3, and 7. However, the locations of fingerprint marks are also a function of tile instances, not the marks or design seed.

4.2   Mark Preparation

The improved method of mark preparation is the first major diversion from the original watermarking and fingerprinting techniques. Mark preparation now has the specific focus of creating small and multiple marks.

The marks to be embedded originate as 7-bit ASCII strings that can be printed using traditional I/O mechanisms[3]. Their sizes are limited by the subsequent hash function specifications. The mark strings are given to the watermarking system for embedding in the circuit and are later produced by the verification program. The marks are transformed via a hash function, creating marks each capable of fitting in a single LUT[4], while still incorporating the user-defined number of error-correction coding (ECC) bits as discussed below. This step is crucial to the enhancements enabled by small and multiple marks, as the original watermarking and fingerprinting techniques prepared one large signature. As a consequence of the hash function, the marks are whitened so as not to look like any particular statistical spectrum, as described in Section 2.2. This whitening of the signal does not mask its content but rather its existence. By making the mark have a flat distribution, the marks will be more difficult to detect.

An optional part of mark preparation may involve adding ECC, which helps combat attempts to modify or remove the marks by changing LUT bits. If the modification is small enough, ECC codes help increase the possibility of retrieving the original marks and provide proof of design tampering. A tradeoff exists between the number of bits allocated to each mark and to ECC, as the sum must not exceed the size of the target architecture's LUTs while still providing enough tampering protection through ECC.

4.3   Mark Embedding

As mentioned in above, the process of selecting the mark locations is different for watermarking and fingerprinting. Watermarking locations are determined by a secure function and a seed, which leaves a different design with the same set of marks still secure. This additional security is relevant to mark verification efficiency discussed in Sections 1.4 and 4.4.

Fingerprinting locations are independent of such functions, as they are determined by tile instances. Each tile instance is generated by placing the unused LUTs in a unique location. The CAD tool then places-and-routes the rest of the tile around the constraints. Therefore, the mark locations in each design instance are unique, which has a negative affect on mark verification efficiency. The one constant that exists is

---

[3] A set of marks indicating design instance recipient information must be included for fingerprinting.

[4] If the target architecture possesses logic blocks with multiple LUTs, a mark can transcend a single LUT to fit within a logic block's available LUTs.

that the design recipient marks are always kept in the same location relative to the ownership marks (the same logic block if the target architecture's logic blocks contain multiple LUTs), thus simplifying the process of fingerprint retrieval.

After the mark locations are determined, the process of mark embedding begins. As in the previous watermarking and fingerprinting techniques, the LUTs to be implanted with the marks are given arbitrary inputs and outputs in order to further disguise the marks. The inputs are simply taps off of passing signals, and the outputs are routes to neighboring logic block "don't care" inputs. This incorporation helps to hide the marked LUTs without severely impacting design performance, as the dummy outputs are not a functional design component.

Finally, the marks themselves are embedded in the predefined LUTs by reprogramming the respective bits in the bitstream. Therefore, the final step of mark embedding is an entirely post-processing step.

4.4   Mark Verification

When the suspicion of theft or misappropriation arises, an unbiased verification team is presented the configuration in question. For watermarking, the IP vendor must produce the design seed that they claim was used to produce the block and upon which the mark locations are based. The verification team uses the seed and reverses the signature preparation and embedding process by first identifying the LUTs used for hiding the marks. Once the marks are extracted and, if necessary, the ECC is applied, the marks are decrypted using a known key and hash function. Finally, the original ASCII signature is revealed, and if the signature identifies the IP vendor, ownership has been established. As discussed in Section 1.4, ownership can also be publicly proved by revealing a subset of the multiple watermarks found in the design without creating the possibility that other design (the same design or other designs containing the same mark set) recipients remove the ownership information.

The process is slightly different for fingerprinting, as the mark locations are unknown. The IP vendor must produce a subset of the ownership marks that they claim to be embedded in the design, but the verification process is reversed. The signatures are encrypted using a known key and are applied to the secure hash function and ECC creating the bits used to code the LUTs. The verification team then searches the LUTs for the subset of bits. If all or a large percentage of the subset is found, ownership has been established. Once the locations of the ownership marks are known, the watermarking extraction process can be implemented on instance recipient mark retrieval, as recipient marks are always in a constant location relative to the ownership marks. The relevant LUT bits are decrypted using the known key and printed out. The result is then used to establish the source of misappropriation.

5   Experimental Results

5.1   Objectives

Experiments have been used to evaluate the overhead (area and timing) of the proposed watermarking and fingerprinting approaches as well as the fingerprint security against recipient collusion.

When calculating area overhead for the proposed techniques, it must be noted that place-and-route tools rarely pack utilized logic blocks, and therefore LUTs, into a minimal area. Unused logic introduces flexibility into the place-and-route step that may be essential for completion or good performance. However, these unused LUTs can be used for embedding marks, but should not be considered area overhead. For example, an initial design may possess a region that contains 100 utilized logic blocks but also 15 unutilized logic blocks. Area overhead should not include those 15 blocks. Rather, area overhead must be calculated as the area used by the watermarked design minus the total area of the original design, including unused logic blocks and LUTs. In addition, the constraints imposed on placement for mark embedding may also contribute to timing overhead, as a marked LUT may require that a critical path be lengthened.

The fingerprinting approach incurs design effort overhead and additional area and timing overhead due to tiling. Mark security is also an issue in fingerprinting, as recipient collusion could remove parts of the instance recipient marks.

The smaller and multiple marks technique does not have an impact on the area, timing, or design effort overhead required for the existing FPGA IPP techniques. A given number of LUT bits and unused LUT locations are available, and all of the bits may be used to encode several smaller marks where one large watermark had been. For example, one 320-bit mark distributed over twenty LUTs could be transformed to twenty 16-bit marks without affecting the design.

5.2   Designs

To evaluate the area and timing overhead of the watermarking approach, we conducted an experiment on three large real-world designs: a MIPS R2000 processor core designed for FPGAs [24], a reconfigurable Automatic Target Recognition (ATR) system [25], and a digital encryption standard (DES) design [26]. The MIPS core and the DES design were both implemented on the Xilinx [27] XC4028EX-3-PG299, and the ATR system was implemented on the XC4062XL-3-PG475. For fingerprinting overhead evaluation, experiments were performed on nine MCNC designs, each of which was implemented on the XC4028EX-3-PG299. In Step 2 of both the watermarking and fingerprinting pseudo-code in Section 4.1, the number of unused LUTs was calculated and the circuit timing was noted. The original area and timing statistics for both sets of designs are displayed in Table 1.

5.3   Watermarking Results

Experimental results reveal that the new watermarking approach does not require more area or timing overhead that the existing FPGA watermarking technique. Due to the place-and-route tool not packing the logic to maximum density, there is essentially no area overhead required by the new approach. As expected, the unused logic was used to embed the marks and therefore increased the density of utilized logic blocks and LUTs. If place-and-route tools packed logic to a higher density, a certain degree of area overhead may become apparent.

Table 1. Original physical layout statistics

Design	# used LBs	# spare LBs	min period (ns)
MIPS R2000	756	268	185.0
ATR	1876	214	424.5
DES	875	149	166.3
9sym	46	49	71.6
c499	94	96	104.9
c880	110	115	110.8
duke2	93	100	87.9
rd84	27	28	50.2
planet1	95	100	145.0
s9234	195	206	135.0
sand	82	90	97.6
styr	78	81	150.6

Following the pseudo-code approach detailed in Section 4.1, location constraints were placed on each design before place-and-route. An iteratively larger number of marks (until all unused LUTs were filled) were embedded, and the circuit timing was noted and compared to the original design. The results are shown in Tables 2-4.

Table 2. MIPS R2000– Impact of number of 16-bit marks on resources and speed

# 16-bit marks	50	98	162	200	288	392	512
% resources	3.31	6.48	10.71	13.23	19.05	25.93	33.86
% timing	-1.04	-0.47	3.17	-7.15	1.65	2.47	-5.23

Table 3. ATR- Impact of number of 16-bit marks on resources and speed

# 16-bit marks	2	50	98	184	288	374	428
% resources	0.05	1.33	2.61	4.90	7.68	9.97	11.41
% timing	-10.74	3.46	-25.93	-7.99	-13.50	10.25	-1.57

Table 4. DES- Impact of number of 16-bit marks on resources and speed

# 16-bit marks	2	50	98	158	200	242	298
% resources	0.11	2.86	5.60	9.03	11.43	13.83	17.03
% timing	-22.98	-14.83	-5.07	-1.90	11.05	-11.93	-3.28

For each table, the top two rows show the number of the 16-bit (Xilinx 4000 LUT size) marks. The next two rows show the area increase and timing degradation. As mentioned above, the area overhead is nearly 0%, but the additional percentages of utilized logic blocks are noted in the tables. For timing degradation, positive percentages indicate a decrease in performance. Therefore, some marked designs recorded a timing improvement. This can be explained by the dramatically different placement and corresponding timing that often results from relatively small design changes. The timing impact of watermarking is below the characteristic variance associated with such small changes. Therefore, timing degradation is non-monotonic with the number of marks.

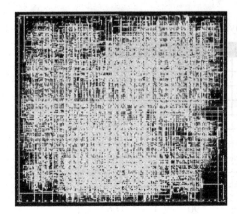

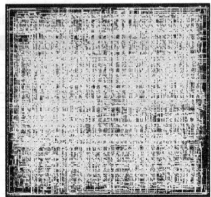

Fig. 1. DES original layout   **Fig. 2.** DES with 298 16-bit marks

Figs. 1 and 2 represent two iterations of the watermark experiment process. Fig. 1 is the original layout of the DES design with no watermarking constraints. The area and timing statistics for the design are noted in Table 1. Note that optimal logic density for the original placement does not exist, as many unused logic blocks are dispersed throughout the design. The experimental process continued until all unused LUTs contained a mark. Fig. 2 shows the final layout with 298 16-bit marks and, therefore, the maximum amount of location constraints. The location of each LUT containing a mark is hidden by the incorporation of each LUT into the design. Inputs are taken from passing signals, and the outputs are routed to neighboring logic block "don't care" inputs. Comparisons between Figs. 1 and 2 reveal that area overhead is negligible (only logic density is increased), and Table 4 indicates that the timing overhead is actually negative for this iteration of mark embedding.

5.4   Fingerprinting Results

Fingerprinting area overhead due to tiling is shown in Table 5. If more marks are needed, additional resources could be added to the design.

Table 5. Area overhead for number of 16-bit marks

Design	# 16-bit marks	% resources
9sym	16	.065
c499	26	.021
c880	36	.045
duke2	26	.075
rd84	8	.037
planet1	28	.053
s9234	46	.056
sand	26	.098
styr	20	.038

Fingerprinting timing overhead, which is variable and user specified, is show in Fig. 3. Variability is achieved by simply discarding tile instances that do not meet defined timing specifications. Therefore, Fig. 3 displays timing overhead in terms of instance yield (i.e. number of tile instances that meet the timing specifications / total number of tile instances) for certain timing specifications (measured as percent increase over the original, non-fingerprinted design timing). Results indicate that if specifications consider a 20% timing degradation acceptable, then approximately 90% of total tile instances will be acceptable.

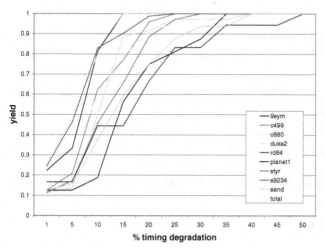

Fig. 3. Instance yield vs. timing specifications

Fingerprint design effort and mark security against comparison collusion (including relevant equations and calculations) is detailed in [5]. Security increases with the size of the tile, but back-end CAD tool effort required for tile instance generation also increases with the size of the tile. Fig. 4 displays the chance that a certain percentage (graphs in 10% increments) of design instance recipient information could be removed by a growing number of colluders (tile size of 40 logic blocks). The results show that even for small tile sizes, the likelihood that a colluding group could remove even a small number of marks is quite remote. For example, 15 colluders would have one chance in approximately 4 million to remove 30% of the marks by comparison collusion. The chance would be even more remote if larger tile sizes were used, but design effort would increase[5].

The tradeoff between design effort and fingerprint security is important to consider, as design effort may often be the limiting factor for tile size selection. Fig. 5 is a direct multiplication comparison between fingerprint security and design effort. Alternate comparisons between security and effort (e.g. security * effort^2) may be more accurate for certain applications. High security against large colluding groups is not necessarily required for many of today's applications, as a large number of design

---

[5] For fingerprint design effort and security, the following constants were assumed: device size = 400 logic blocks, number of unused logic blocks/number of total logic blocks = 0.1, and instance yield (due to timing specifications) = 0.9.

instances are not easily available. Also, modern FPGA CAD layout technology is time consuming, so current developments place a strong emphasis on design effort.

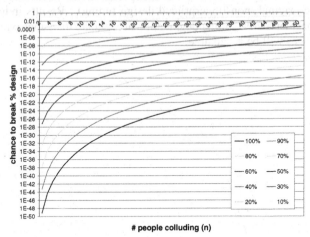

Fig. 4. Chance to remove % of recipient marks (tile size = 40)

6   Conclusion

We have introduced new FPGA design watermarking and fingerprinting techniques for IPP that are more efficient for copy detection, more convincing for ownership and recipient verification, and more secure and robust against mark removal than existing techniques. These improvements are achieved without increasing user design effort, CAD tool effort, or area and timing overhead.

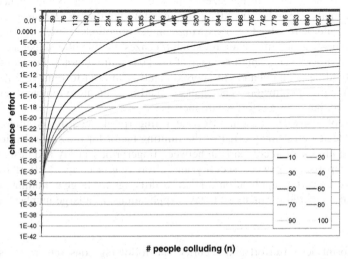

Fig. 5. Chance to remove all recipient marks * design effort

Acknowledgements

This work was supported by the Air Force Research Laboratory of the United States of America, under contract F30602-96-C-0350 and subcontract QS5200 from Sanders, a Lockheed Martin company.

References

1. Furber, S., ARM System Architecture, Menlo Park: Addison-Wesley, p. 329. 1996.
2. Montanaro, J. et al., "A 160MHz 32b 0.5W CMOS RISC Microprocessor," International Solid-State Circuits Conference, pp. 49-62, 1996.
3. Turley, J., "ARM Grabs Embedded Speed Lead," Microprocessor Report, vol. 10, 1996.
4. Lach, J., W. H. Mangione-Smith, and M. Potkonjak, "Signature Hiding Techniques for FPGA Intellectual Property Protection," International Conference on Computer-Aided Design, pp. 186-189, 1998.
5. Lach, J., W. H. Mangione-Smith, and M. Potkonjak, "Fingerprinting Digital Circuits on Programmable Hardware," International Workshop on Information Hiding, pp. 16-31, 1998.
6. Trimberger, S., Personal Communication, Xilinx Corporation, 1997.
7. Goering, R., "IP98 Forum Exposes Struggling Industry – Undefined Business Models, Unstable Core Prices Cited," EE Times, Issue 1000, March 30, 1998.
8. Brassil, J. and L. O'Gorman, "Watermarking Document Images with Bounding Box Expansion," International Workshop on Information Hiding, pp. 227-235, 1996.
9. Cox, I.J. et al., "Secure Spread Spectrum Watermarking for Images, Audio, and Video," International Conference on Image Processing, pp. 243-246, 1996.
10. Smith, J. and B. Comiskey, "Modulation and Information Hiding in Images," International Workshop on Information Hiding, pp. 207-226, 1996.
11. Craver, S. et al., "Can Invisible Watermarks Resolve Rightful Ownership?" International Society for Optical Engineering, vol. 3022, pp. 310-321, 1997.
12. Bender, W. et al., "Techniques for Data Hiding," IBM Systems Journal, vol. 35, no 3-4, pp. 313-336, 1996.
13. Boney, L. et al., "Digital Watermarks for Audio Signals," International Conference on Multimedia Computing and Systems, pp. 473-480, 1996.
14. Hartung, F. and B. Girod, "Copyright Protection in Video Delivery Networks by Watermarking of Pre-Compressed Video," European Conference on Multimedia Applications, Services and Techniques, pp. 423-436, 1997.
15. Spanos, G.A. and T.B. Maples, "Performance Study of a Selective Encryption Scheme for the Security of Networked, Real-Time Video," International Conference on Computer Communications and Networks, pp. 2-10, 1995.
16. Caldwell, A.E. et al., "Effective Iterative Techniques for Fingerprinting Design IP," Design Automation Conference, pp. 843-848, 1999.
17. Charbon, E., "Hierarchical Watermarking in IC Design," Custom Integrated Circuits Conference, pp. 295-298, 1998.
18. Hong, I. and M. Potkonjak, "Behavioral Synthesis Techniques for Intellectual Property Protection," Design Automation Conference, pp. 849-854, 1997.
19. Kahng, A.B. et al., "Robust IP Watermarking Methodologies for Physical Design," Design Automation Conference, pp. 782-787, 1998.
20. Kahng, A.B. et al., "Watermarking Techniques for Intellectual Property Protection," Design Automation Conference, pp. 776-781, 1998.
21. A. Oliveira, "Robust Techniques for Watermarking Sequential Circuit Designs," *Design Automation Conference*, pp. 837-842, 1999.

22. I. Torunoglu and E. Charbon, "Watermarking-Based Copyright Protection of Sequential Functions," *Custom Integrated Circuits Conference,* 1999.
23. Schneier, B., 1963- Applied Cryptography: Protocols, Algorithms, and Source Code in C, New York: John Wiley & Sons, 1996.
24. Hutchings, B. et al., BYUcore: A MIPS R2000 Processor for FPGAs, 1997.
25. Villasenor, J. et al., "Configurable Computing Solutions for Automatic Target Recognition," IEEE Workshop on FPGAs for Custom Computing Machines, pp. 70-79, 1996.
26. Leonard, J. and W. H. Mangione-Smith, "A Case Study of Partially Evaluated Hardware Circuits: Key-Specific DES," Field Programmable Logic, pp. 151-160, 1997.
27. Xilinx, The Programmable Logic Data Book, San Jose, CA, 1996.

Robust Watermarking for Images Based on Color Manipulation

Sebastiano Battiato[1], Dario Catalano[1*], Giovanni Gallo[1], and Rosario
Gennaro[2]

[1] Dipartimento di Matematica, Universita' di Catania.
Viale A.Doria 6, 95125 Catania.
{battiato,catalano,gallo}@dipmat.unict.it
[2] IBM T.J. Watson Research Center
PO Box 704, Yorktown Heights, New York 10598, USA
rosario@watson.ibm.com

Abstract. In this paper we present a new efficient watermarking scheme
for images. The basic idea of our method is to alter the colors of the
given image in a suitable but imperceptible way. This is accomplished
by moving the coordinates of each color in the color opponency space.
The scheme is shown to be robust against a large class of image manipulations. The robustness of the scheme is also theoretically analyzed
and it is shown to depend on the number of colors in the image being
marked.

1   Introduction

The proliferation of the Internet as a new media, opens many new possibilities
and opportunities for information and communication. If the new opportunities
are many, so are the challenges. It's clear that, in the digital world, making a
copy of a document means producing an exact copy of it: there is no degradation
in the copying process. Digital watermarking is the embedding of a mark into
digital content that can later be, unambiguously, detected to allow assertions
about the ownership or provenience of the data. This makes watermarking an
emerging technique to prevent digital piracy. There are several parameters and
criteria over which categorize watermarking schemes due to their widespread
application in several areas. Excellent overviews on various aspects of digital
watermarking can be found in [1,2,9,17,20,28]. In section 2 of this paper basic
notions about watermarks with particular reference to the case of digital images
are briefly surveyed. The contribution proposed in this paper is a novel technique
to insert an imperceptible mark in digital images. The new method is, in a
sense, similar to the technique introduced by Cox et al. [8] (see next Section).
These authors propose to edit in an imperceptible way some frequencies in the
spectrum of the signal to be marked. Differently than [8] we propose to insert

---

* Work done while the author was visiting the Computer Science Dept. of Columbia
University.

A. Pfitzmann (Ed.): IH'99, LNCS 1768, pp. 302–317, 2000.

the watermark in a suitable color space of the image (i.e. the *color opponency space* [22]): editing in an imperceptible way the palette of an image allows the insertion of a unambiguous mark. In the paper we show how this can be done efficiently and robustly. The main advantage of the proposed technique is to avoid costly computation of DCT or FT. On the other hand it could be argued that LUT (Look up Table) operations can easily destroy the proposed watermark: our claim is that for these attacks to be effective they must introduce perceptible degradation of the original picture. In the paper we support this claim through a statistical analysis and experimental evidences.

2   Watermarking Basics

Here we summarize some general parameters for categorizing watermarking schemes.

First a watermark can be *perceptible* or *imperceptible*. A perceptible watermark is typically used to encode information that should be known to the final user (i.e. ownership information or usage instruction etc.) An imperceptible watermark is more useful in those context in which the content owner doesn't want the user to know about the watermark (or at least not to know where the watermark is). Roughly speaking, by applying an imperceptible watermark to a digital image, we get a marked copy that is "almost" identical to the original unmarked one, where the meaning of "almost" depends on several parameters, one of which could be how much degradation is allowed in the marked data (with respect to the original).

Also a watermarking technique can be *fragile* or *robust*. Fragile watermarks can be easily corrupted by almost any kind of manipulation on the data (i.e. in the case of images, any image processing operation could damage the mark). Fragile watermarks are useful to preserve the integrity of the marked document, and more generally for authentication purposes (since small changes in the data will cause the corruption of the watermark). On the other hand robust watermarks have to resist the most common trasformations on the data (again in the case of images, typical procedures of image manipulation are filtering, JPEG compression, resizing, etc.) A desirable property would be also to be able to resist malicious attacks aimed at the removal of the watermark. Clearly, robust watermarks are useful in contexts where ownership has to be proved or preserved.

PREVIOUS WORK Several techniques have been proposed in the last few years. One of the first watermarking scheme has been proposed by [20]. Here the basic idea is to insert the watermarking signal (a sequence of pseudo-random bits) into the LSB position of the original image, pixel by pixel. Clearly this scheme is not robust: being embedded in the least significant bit of the pixel it can be easily removed.

Other somehow non-robust techniques are proposed in [3,5,7,15,19,18,27].

Cox et al. [8] pointed out that a watermarking scheme to be robust has to be placed in the perceptually most significant components of the digital data (their method can also be used in audio, video and multimedia in general). This approach can seem contradicting the requirement of imperceptibility of the watermark. However a reasonable tradeoff between imperceptibility and robustness can be obtained using some properties of spread-spectrum communication. This scheme is secure against almost all common signal processing and geometric distortion operations and even against some more malicious attacks.

3   Color Spaces

The watermarking technique introduced in this paper operates an editing over a color space of an image. The proposed algorithm requires, for this color space the following properties:

i) a simple and compact way to describe geometrically in the color space a small, perceptively constant region;
ii) the transformation from a standard RGB space to the color space should be fast and easily and robustly inverted.

The algorithm performs small imperceptible perturbations of the palette according to some simple geometrical rules described in the next Section. In particular a colour is *moved* inside a sphere of almost equal colors. The common RGB space, unfortunately, is not well suited to these operations: even small sphere in such a space could be perceptively not very homogeneous. Computer Graphics has, since long, recognized the need for perceptively uniform color spaces (see [12], [13]) and several color models addressing this issue are known: L*u*v*, L*a*b*, etc. The transformation from RGB to such spaces are generally nonlinear, hard to invert, and what is worse for our application introduce a requantization of the color. In short they violate the requirement ii) above. For this reason, although these spaces are ideally the best alternative to RGB, we choose to operate in the CO, *Color Opponency* space [22]. This choice grants a linear, easy to invert mapping from RGB to CO. The mapping is realized through the the equations:
RGB → Co:

$$A = R + G + B; B/Y = 2B - R - G; R/G = R - 2G + B. \tag{1}$$

CO → RGB:

$$R = \frac{A + R/G - B/Y}{3}; G = \frac{A - R/G}{3}; B = \frac{B/Y + A}{3}. \tag{2}$$

Perceptual studies strongly suggest, moreover, that this space is probably the best choice to hide small perturbations in colors, at least to an human observer. *Color Opponency* model is, indeed, very close to the chromatic channels of human visual system. Another, indirect, proof, of the suitability of *Color Opponency* in dealing with human perception is that many computer vision algorithms aimed to recognize specific texture/colors (like for example human skin [11]) adopt this model. In the following Sections it is assumed that the color are already represented in the CO space. Conversion from RGB is a pre-processing step that is taken for granted.

4   The Algorithms

A watermarking mechanism is composed by two algorithms. The watermark *insertion* algorithm which takes as input the original image and outputs the marked image and a mark that is stored in a database with the identity of the acquiring user. The watermark *detection* algorithm takes as input the original image, a watermarked image and the database of marks and outputs the mark which is associated with the input marked image.

The crucial tool used by the algorithm is to associate to each color in the image (thought of as a point in the CO space) a sphere in the CO space centered around it. The points of the sphere represent colors that are indistinguishable to the human eye from the original color.

At the moment we do not claim that our scheme is resistant against collusion attacks. Indeed, notice that if all rays (on each color sphere) have the same length in all marked images, an obviuos collusion attack can be mounted. As soon as an adversary gets at least four different marked images the mark can be removed with overwhelming probability (since four different points not belonging to the same plane, uniquely determine a sphere in the space and this would allow the adversary to reconstruct the ray and remove the mark). An easy countermeasure to this particular attack would be to choose the length of the ray randomly (in a suitable range) for each color sphere and each marked image. However it should be kept in mind that adopting this solution does not necessarily protect against more clever collusive attacks.

4.1   The Insertion Algorithm

The insertion algorithm starts by classifying the pixels of the image according to their color. Then we modify each color in the image in a random, yet imperceptible, fashion. That is, for each color in the image, we move the color space point associated with it to the border of its color sphere. The direction in which the color space point is moved is chosen at random for each color.

More in detail, we are given an image I represented as three matrices in the color opponency space, $A[i,j], R/G[i,j], B/Y[i,j]$ (the coordinates of the color of pixel (i,j)). If the image has N colors, we call COL_k, with $1 \leq k \leq N$, the set of pixels (i,j) of I that have the same color (i.e. the same coordinates $A[i,j] = x_k, R/G[i,j] = y_k, B/Y[i,j] = z_k$ in the color space.) For each k we randomly choose a ray of the color sphere centered in (x_k, y_k, z_k) and consider the plane $\pi[k]$ perpendicular to the ray and passing through its middle point. We "move" all the pixel in COL_k to the end of the ray on the opposite side of the plane $\pi[k]$ (that is, we change the representation of the colors of pixels $(i,j) \in COL_k$ to $A'[i,j] = x'_k, R/G'[i,j] = y'_k, B/Y'[i,j] = z'_k$ where (x'_k, y'_k, z'_k) is the other endpoint of the ray).

The result of this process is the watermarked image. The stored mark[1] is the vector of planes $\pi[k]$.

A pseudocode description of the insertion algorithm appears in Figure 1.

Mark-Insert

Input: An Image I, given as three matrices in the color opponency space $A[i,j], R/G[i,j], B/Y[i,j]$ where (i,j) is a single pixel.

Output:
A marked image I' given as $A'[i,j], R/G'[i,j], B/Y'[i,j]$.
A *mark* given as a vector $\pi[k]$, $k = 1, \ldots, N$ where N is the number of colors in the image. Each $\pi[k]$ is a plane in the color space.

1. For each $k = 1, \ldots, N$ where N is the number of colors
   (a) *Classify pixels by color*
      Set COL_k the set of pixels (i,j) that have color k
      Let x_k, y_k, z_k be the point in the color space associated with color k.
   (b) *Select a random direction of motion*
      Select a random ray in the color sphere centered in (x_k, y_k, z_k). Let (x'_k, y'_k, z'_k) be the other endpoint of the ray.
   (c) *Move all pixels in COL_k to the same point in the color opponency space*
      For each pixel $(i,j) \in COL_k$
         Set $A'[i,j] = x'_k, R/G'[i,j] = y'_k, B/Y'[i,j] = z'_k$
      End For.
   (d) *Save the plane normal to the direction of motion*
      Set $\pi[k]$ to be the normal plane to this ray and passing through its middle point.
   End For.
2. Return $I' = [A'[i,j], R/G'[i,j], B/Y'[i,j]]$ as the marked image.
   Save $MARK = [\pi[1], \ldots, \pi[N]]$ as the mark.

Fig. 1. Watermark Insertion Algorithm

4.2   The Detection Algorithm

Recall that a detection algorithm takes as input a received marked image, the original image and the list of stored marks.

---

[1] It is possible to reduce the size of a mark to a short random string by using strong *pseudo-random number generators* (see [21]). We use a PRNG seeded with a short random string s to generate plane coefficients in the color space. Clearly the stored mark can just be s. When the detection algorithm is run the vector $[\pi[1], \ldots, \pi[N]]$ can be reconstructed using the same process.

Let us assume for the moment that the received image has the same number of colors as the original image. The detection algorithm compares the image to each stored mark. When comparing against $MARK = [\pi[1], \ldots, \pi[N]]$, the basic idea is to look at each class COL'_k of the received marked image and check if the color point x'_k, y'_k, z'_k associated with it is located on the opposite side of the plane $\pi[k]$ (where opposite is defined with respect to the original center for COL_k, i.e. (x_k, y_k, z_k)). If this is the case we increase a counter.

At the end, after comparing the image with all the stored marks, we output the mark that scored the highest counter.

A pseudocode description of the detection algorithm appears in Figure 2. In Section 5 we present a statistical analysis that proves that with very high probability this algorithm identifies the correct mark.

Remark 1. Note that the detection algorithm could receive an image manipulated by a malicious adversary. Such an adversary is not required to keep the same number of colors in the image. In particular the adversary could "move" each pixel in COL_k to a different location in the color space. However notice that in order not to deteriorate the image the adversary must keep each pixel in COL_k inside the color sphere associated with it. Then it is easy to reduce this case to the case that the received image still has the same colors. One possibility is to "recompact" the pixels moved by the adversary to their "baricenter". Another possibility is to increment the counter whenever a large enough quorum of pixels belonging to the same class is on the correct side of the plane. So in the following we can safely assume that the received image will have N colors and the classes COL_k are the same as in the original image. The only difference is that the representative coordinate point for the class COL_k will be different in the marked image.

5   Statistical Analysis

In this section we show that the proposed algorithms work. We first show that a marked imaged that has undergone no transformation at all will be recognized uniquely with very high probability (that is we show that our algorithms do not create false positive or false negative errors).

We then consider an adversarial model in which the marked image is processed by an adversary who is trying to erase the watermark. We first argue that such an adversary does not have enough information to mount an effective attack and the only thing that it can do is to move the pixels of the marked image in a random fashion inside their color spheres. Then we show that with very high probability our algorithms will resist such adversarial strategy and the marked image will still be uniquely identified.

Remark 2. For simplicity's sake we first carry on the analysis in a two-dimensional color space rather than the three-dimensional one. That is we assume that each color is a point in the plane and that it will be moved to the edge of a circle centered on it. The "planes" $\pi[k]$ will become straight lines normal to the ray along which the point has been moved and passing through its

---

Mark-Detect

Input:
The original image $I = [A[i,j], R/G[i,j], B/Y[i,j]]$.
A received marked image $I' = [A'[i,j], R/G'[i,j], B/Y'[i,j]]$.
The list of stored marks $MARK_\ell = [\pi_\ell[1], \ldots, \pi_\ell[N]]$ for $\ell = 1, \ldots, M$
where M is the total number of images originally marked.
N the number of colors in the image.

Output: A mark $MARK_{id}$.

1. Set $max = 0$ and $id = 0$
2. For each $\ell = 1, \ldots, M$
    (a) Set counter $C_\ell = 0$.
    (b) For each color $k = 1, \ldots, N$
        Let (x'_k, y'_k, z'_k) be the coordinates of the color of the pixels
        of the marked image belonging to COL_k.
        Let (x_k, y_k, z_k) be the coordinates of the color of the pixels
        of the original image belonging to COL_k.
        If (x_k, y_k, z_k) and (x'_k, y'_k, z'_k) are on opposite sides of the plane
        $\pi_\ell[k]$ then increase C_ℓ by 1.
    End For
    (c) If $C_\ell > max$ then set $max = C_\ell$ and $id = \ell$
    End For.
3. Output $MARK_{id}$.

Fig. 2. Watermark Detection Algorithm

middle point. Although this gives us slightly weaker bounds on the error probability of our algorithm, it is much easier to understand the geometric intuition behind the analysis. In section 5.3 we show how to improve the error bounds by using the full three-dimensional model.

5.1   Identifying Non-manipulated Images

Let's assume that the marked image I' given to detection algorithm is the exact result of the application of the insertion algorithm to the original image I. That is, we assume that no other manipulation has been applied to the image.

Let $MARK_i$ be the correct mark that generated I' from I and let $MARK_j$ be any of the other incorrect marks.

Since the image was not manipulated in any way, the counter C_i resulting from comparing I' with $MARK_i$ will reach the value $C_i = N$. The detection algorithm will output $id = j$ only if also $C_j = N$.

When comparing I' with $MARK_j$, for each k the counter C_j will be increased iff the color (x'_k, y'_k, z'_k) in I' ended up on the opposite side of $\pi_j[k]$. This happens with probability $1/3$ since the lines intersect the circles in a way that $1/3$ of the edge is on the opposite side (see Figure A case 1). For each $k = 1, \ldots, N$ these are independent events, thus we conclude that $Prob[C_j = N] = 3^{-N}$.

The algorithm fails if there exists a $j \neq i$ such that the above will happen. Thus since there are $M - 1$ incorrect marks to be examined we have that the total probability of failure is bounded by

$$Prob[\textbf{Mark-Detect } \textit{fails }] \leq (M - 1)\, 3^{-N}$$

5.2 Identifying Manipulated Images

In this section we assume that an adversary has manipulated a marked image I' in an effort to remove the watermark embedded in it.

First of all let's try to understand what kind of attack can the adversary mount. When given a marked image, the adversary does not know in which direction colors have been moved. Indeed this information is part of the secret key used to generate the mark.

Thus the only thing that the adversary can do is to move each color in a random fashion trying to "undo" the effect of the watermark. As a first approximation let us assume that the adversary moves pixels with the same color in the same way. That is, it makes the same changes for each pixel in COL_k inside its associated color sphere (indeed the adversary is limited to move things inside the sphere, otherwise the image is deteriorated). The interesting thing is that now for each color the adversary "sees" a different color sphere associated with it, namely the one centered in (x'_k, y'_k, z'_k). For each color the probability of "undoing" the mark is $1/3$. This is because the biggest part of the "new" color circle (actually $2/3$ of it) lies on the other side of the line w.r.t. to the original color location, thus the probability that a random motion brings the point to the correct side of the plane is $1/3$ (see Figure A case 1).

Another thing that we have to make sure is that by "moving" these colors the adversary does not cause an increase of the counter for an incorrect mark. As we will see, this event will also happen with sufficiently small probability for each color.

Remark 3. It is sufficient to consider the above adversarial strategy for our purposes. Indeed (as we already mentioned in Remark 1, Section 4.2), the adversary could also "move" each pixel in COL_k in a different direction of the color space. However all these locations should be inside the color sphere. Thus it would be sufficient for the detection algorithm to look at the "baricenter" of all the pixels inside this sphere associated with COL_k and increase the counter if this point is on the opposite side of the plane. An equivalent approach would be to increase the counter only if a large quorum of the pixels fall on the opposite side of the plane. Roughly speaking such an attack will be effective if it concentrates as many pixels as possible on the correct side of the plane $\pi[k]$. Which is basically as hard as guessing where the plane is and moving *all* the pixels on the other side of it.

SOME PROBABILITY TOOLS. Our analysis uses heavily the following inequality due to Hoefding (see [14]).

Let $Z_1, \ldots, Z_N$ be independent, identically distributed (i.i.d.) random variables, each ranging over the interval $[a, b]$, and let μ denote their expected value. Then,

$$Prob\left[\left|\frac{\sum_{i=1}^{N} Z_i}{N} - \mu\right| \geq \delta\right] < 2e^{-\frac{2\delta^2 N}{b-a}} \tag{3}$$

Again let $MARK_i$ be the correct mark and $MARK_j$ be any of the other incorrect marks. The statistical analysis will work by considering the counters C_i and C_j kept by the detection algorithm as random variables. The algorithm fails when $C_j \geq C_i$, i.e. when $S = C_j - C_i \geq 0$. We show that S can be written as the sum of N i.i.d. random variables whose expected value is a negative number μ. Then we can just apply Equation (3) with $\delta = -\mu$ to get a bound on the probability that $S \geq 0$.

Consider the random variable X_k defined as follows: $X_k = 1$ if when analyzing color k in the detection algorithm we add 1 to the counter C_i, otherwise $X_k = 0$. Clearly $C_i = \sum_{k=1}^{N} X_k$. Similarly define random variable Y_k as follows: $Y_k = 1$ if when analyzing color k in the detection algorithm we add 1 to the counter C_j, otherwise $Y_k = 0$. Clearly $C_j = \sum_{k=1}^{N} Y_k$. Thus $S = \sum_{k=1}^{N} Z_k$ where $Z_k = Y_k - X_k$. All we are left to do is to estimate the distributions of X_k and Y_k.

ESTIMATE FOR X_k. When analyzing the correct mark $MARK_i$ we claim that for each color the counter C_i is increased with probability 2/3, that is $Prob[X_k = 1] = \frac{2}{3}$. Indeed in order for $X_k = 1$ we need that the adversary moved the marked color on a location that is still on the opposite side of the line $\pi_i[k]$. But since the color circle associated with this color lies for 2/3 on that side of $\pi_i[k]$ (see Figure A case 1) and the adversary chooses the direction of motion at random we have the above probability.

ESTIMATE FOR Y_k. In this case the analysis is slightly more complicated. In order for $Y_k = 1$ we need that the adversary moved the marked color on a location that is still on the opposite side of the line $\pi_j[k]$ (where $MARK_j$ is the incorrect mark being analyzed). We analyze the probability that this happens based on the location of the line $\pi_j[k]$.

Referring to Figure A, we partition the original color circle in four areas:

1. Assume that the line $\pi_j[k]$ is ortogonal to a ray contained inside the angle a. This happens with probability 1/3 since $a = \frac{2\pi}{3}$. In this case at most 2/3 of the color circle of the "marked" point lies on the opposite side of $\pi_j[k]$. Thus the probability that the adversary moves the point to the opposite side of $\pi_j[k]$ in this case is at most 2/9.
2. Assume that the line $\pi_j[k]$ is ortogonal to a ray contained inside the angle b. This happens with probability 1/6 since $b = \frac{\pi}{3}$. In this case at most 1/2 of the color circle of the "marked" point lies on the opposite side of $\pi_j[k]$. Thus the probability that the adversary moves the point to the opposite side of $\pi_j[k]$ in this case is at most 1/12.
3. Symmetrically the same probability 1/12 is obtained when the line $\pi_j[k]$ is ortogonal to a ray contained inside the angle d.

4. Assume that the line $\pi_j[k]$ is ortogonal to a ray contained inside the angle c. This happens with probability $1/3$ since $c = \frac{2\pi}{3}$. But in this case the line $\pi_j[k]$ does *not* intersect the color circle so the adversary will never manage to move the point on the opposite side of it. Thus the probability in this case is 0.

The above cases are mutually exclusive and cover all possibilities, thus we can say that $Prob[Y_k = 1] \leq \frac{2}{9} + 2\frac{1}{12} = \frac{7}{18}$. In the following we assume that the adversary is actually stronger and gets $Y_k = 1$ exactly with probability $7/18$ (this means that in practice the failure probability is smaller than the obtained bounds)

PUTTING IT ALL TOGETHER. Now we can estimate the distribution of Z_k. Given that X_k and Y_k are indendent random variables we have that

$$Z_k = \begin{cases} -1 & \text{with prob. } 11/27 \\ 0 & \text{with prob. } 25/54 \\ 1 & \text{with prob. } 7/54 \end{cases}$$

Thus $\mu = E[Z_k] = -5/18$. We can now apply Equation (3) with $b = 1$, $a = -1$, and $\delta = -\mu$:

$$Prob[S \geq 0] \leq e^{-\mu^2 N}$$

As in the previous case the probability of failure is that there exists at least one incorrect mark that causes $S \geq 0$. Thus

$$Prob[\textbf{ Mark-Detect } \textit{fails }] \leq (M-1)\, e^{-\mu^2 N}$$

5.3   Improving the Analysis

The statistical analysis in the previous section was simplified to a two-dimensional model in order to make it more intuitive. However the full three-dimensional model allows us to obtain stronger bounds on the probability of error.

In this section we simply sketch how to generalize the two-dimensional arguments to the case in three dimension and provide the stronger bounds. The final version of this paper will contain all the missing details.

First of all let's recall some fact of basic geometry. A sphere of ray R has area $4\pi R^2$. If we take a plane perpendicular to a ray and distant h from the center, the area of the spherical cap on the opposite side of the plane from the center is $2\pi R(R - h)$. Since in our case we choose a plane passing through the middle point of the ray, we obtain that the area of the spherical cap on the opposite side of the plane is πR^2, i.e. $1/4$ of the total.

This immediately generalizes the bound on the probability of error in the case of images non-manipulated. In that case we can strenghten the upper bound on the probability of failure to $(M - 1)4^{-N}$.

FIGURE A

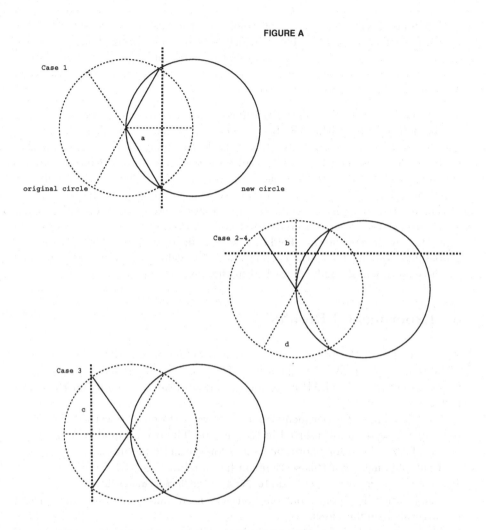

For the case of images manipulated by an adversary we use again the same notation as before. In this case $Prob[X_k = 1] = 3/4$ since to a random motion of the marked point "undoes" the mark only if it brings the point on the above spherical cap. When analyzing incorrect marks we can argue that $Prob[Y_k = 1] < 7/16$, by generalizing the case-by-case analysis done in the two-dimensional case. Thus $\mu = E[Z_k] < -5/16$ in this case (and the probability of failure still bounded by $(M-1)e^{-\mu^2 N}$.)

THE PRACTICAL MEANING OF THIS ANALYSIS. The first thing to notice is that the error probability goes down exponentially with the number of colors in the image. For non-manipulated images the theoretical bounds are already very strong. For manipulated images the theoretical bounds start becoming meaningful for images ranging around one thousand colors.

For images with, say, $N = 256$ colors the theoretical bound says that the probability of failure is $(M-1)e^{-25}$ which is clearly not strong enough. However one must remember that in the analysis we were quite "generous" with upper bounding. In practice the probability of failure is much smaller than that and our experimental results seem to confirm this.

THRESHOLD DETECTION. The algorithms assume that the image being analyzed by the detection algorithm has been generated by one of the marks in the list MARK. If this is not the case (for example the image arrives from another vendor) then the algorithm, as is, will still identifies a mark from the list as the correct one. In order to avoid this problem it is sufficient to modify the algorithm so that it accepts an identification as correct only if the counter C_{id} of the selected mark is higher than a given threshold T. A statistical analysis similar to the one described above (and not reported here for space limitations) show that by setting the threshold to $T \approx N/2$ one obtains bounds on the failure probability comparable to the current ones. The value $T \approx N/2$ is also justified by the experimental results described in the next section.

6   Experimental Results

A first version of the proposed marking and detection algorithm has been implemented in MATLAB 5.0. This has been done for sake of fast prototyping. On the other side MATLAB image processing libraries works only on 256 colors pictures.

The first kind of experiments that we have performed concerned the invisibility of the watermark inserted in the picture. The overall quality of a picture is not affected, both for photographs and for synthetic pictures.

Example images for this section can be found at this URL
http://www.dipmat.unict.it/~anile/FuzzyArith/home/papers.htm
Small differences comes out only on very high quality monitors and just at the highest magnifications.

The second kind of experiments that we have performed have been aimed to tune the detection algorithm. We call a color that has been recognized as marked a *positive color*. For a given mark M, we are interested in determining a threshold value T such that if more than T positive colors have been found then, with a high probability, the image comes, perhaps after some manipulation, from an image containing mark M. To this aim we have taken an ensemble of about 200 unmarked pictures and submitted them to the detection algorithm in search of a mark M. The algorithm gave an average of about 38% of positive colors, with a variance of $\sigma^2 = 7.5\%$. As a safe rule of thumb, hence, we suggest to classify as definitively suspect an image such that more than $T = (38 + 2\sigma^2)\%$ colors have been recognized as marked. With this safely set threshold we have observed no false positive (unmarked images detected as marked) in our set.

The third kind of experiments that we have done uses a small "library" of 15 marks. We have submitted to the detection algorithm an ensemble of 100 pictures. Of these, 33% were marked with marks from the library, 33% were unmarked, 33% were marked with a mark outside of the library. All the unmarked images have been recognized as such using the threshold discussed above relatively to every marks in the library. Of the 33% of images that have been stained with a mark outside of the library all have been classified as unmarked. Of the remaining group all the pictures have been recognized as marked because the number of colors in agreement with a watermark exceeded the threshold T. Moreover, in total agreement with the theoretical analysis reported in the previous Section, the threshold has been trespassed only relatively to the original inserted watermark. Results are also summarized in the following table, where the number n indicates the number of positive colors detected both on images marked with marks outside the library (denoted with M1) and marked with marks of the correct library (denoted with M2).

	$0 < n \leq T/2$	$T/2 < n < T$	$n \geq T$
Unmarked	25	8	0
Marked M1	20	13	0
Marked M2	0	0	33

We have repeated the previous experiment using the same marks library, with another ensemble of 200 pictures where, this time, 50% of them were unmarked, and 50% of them were marked with a random mark from the library and successively manipulated with a random combination of 4 of the following operators: trimming/cropping, geometrical distortion, scaling and rotation, equalization, contrast stretching, median and gaussian filtering (with a small kernel). All this operation has been realized using the standard *Stirmark 3.0* package (see [16], [24] for more details). The detection algorithm has correctly classified all the unmarked images as such. Of the marked images almost all have been correctly recognized as marked with the correct mark, although the value observed for the counters were much closer (from above) to the threshold than in the previous experiment. Only in one case a marked image produced a counter value slightly below the threshold, without attaining, in such a case, the maximum value of the counter for the correct mark. Results are summarized in the next table.

	$n < T$	$T < n < 3/2T$	$n > 3/2T$	Correct Mark identified
Marked	8	70	22	99
Unmarked	100	0	0	—

Finally we have simulated some malicious attacks oriented to remove the mark from an image. In order to do so we are presented with the following alternatives:

i) To randomly change all colors in the picture palette by a large amount;

ii) To randomly change all colors in the picture palette by a small amount;

iii) To randomly change a portion of all colors in the picture palette by a large amount;

iv) To randomly change a portion of all colors in the picture palette by a small amount;

The mark becomes difficult to detect in case i), but in this case the picture is visibly degraded from the original: although almost mark free the picture is now close to useless if fidelity to the original is an important issue.

The strategy in case ii) seems to produce the best results for a malicious attack. In this case, indeed, we observed an attenuation of the watermark with an almost imperceptible degradation of the picture. In all of our experiments, however,the correct watermark has always been recognized. In case iii) the mark has been still recognized in all our experiments and at the same time frequently the image could be visibly degraded. In case iv) the mark is recognized by our detection algorithm with a slight decrease of the maximum number of positive colors detected.

Lately, we have implemented the two algorithms in C++ to better test the method with images having more than 256 colors.
Early experimental results showed its robustness against requantization attacks [2]. In particular we noticed that the number of recognized colors is "proportional" to the number of colors of the final, requantized image (the less is the number of colors of the requantized image, the less is, clearly, the number of recognized colors).
However, we point out, that the number of positive colors remains more than T even for "strong" requantizations (from 16 million to 256 colors).

7   Conclusions and Future Works

In this paper we have presented a new watermarking scheme that works moving the colors of a picture inside the CO color space according to a predefined scheme. The mark inserted in this way can be easily detected. Its statistical properties have been analyzed and the dependence of its robustness to malicious attack is shown to be dependent on the number of colors in a picture. Early experimental results show that the proposed method is resistant to several attacks, under different strategies, moreover the mark is resistant to geometrical transformation, equalization and smoothing. Future works includes to explore the importance of the color space in granting a transparent and robust mark also under collusive-attacks.

Acknowledgments

The authors wish to thank the anonymous referees for their helpful suggestions and comments.

---

[2] Requantization attacks have been simulated using Stirmark software

References

1. J.M.ACKEN How Watermarking Adds Value to Digital Content *Communications of the ACM* July 1998/Vol.41, No.7 pp.75-77   302
2. A.E.BELL, G.W.BRAUDAWAY, F.MINTZER Opportunities for Watermarking Standards *Communications of the ACM* July 1998/Vol.41, No.7 pp.57-64   302
3. W.BENDER, D.GRUHL, N.MORIMOTO Techniques for data hiding. *Proc. of SPIE* Vol. 2420, pag.40 1995   303
4. D.BONEH, J.SHAW Collusion-secure fingerprinting for digital data. *Proc. Advances in Cryptology - Crypto'95*, Springer Verlag LNCS no.963 pp.452-465, 1995
5. J.BRASSIL, S.LOW, N.MAXEMCHUK, L.O'GORMAN Electronic marking and identification techniques to discourage document copying. *Proc. of Infocom '94* pp.1278-1287, 1994   303
6. D.H.BALLARD, C.M.BROWN *Computer Vision*, Prenctice Hall, Inc. 1982
7. G.CARONNI   Assuring ownership rights for digital images. *Proc. of reliable IT Systems, VIS'95* Vieweg Publishing Company, 1995   303
8. I.COX, J.KILIAN, T.LEIGHTON, T.SHAMOON A secure, robust watermark for multimedia. *IEEE Transaction on Image Processing*, Vol.6(12) pp.1673-1687, 1997   302, 303
9. S.CRAVER, BOON-LOCK YEO, M.YEUNG Technical Trials and Legal Tribulations *Communications of the ACM* July 1998/Vol.41, No.7 pp.45-56   302
10. F.ERGUN, J.KILIAN, S.R.KUMAR A note on the limits of collusion-resistant watermarks *Proc. Advances in Cryptology - Eurocrypt '99*, Springer Verlag LNCS no.1592 pp.140-149, 1999
11. M.M. FLECK, D.A. FORSYTH, C. BREGLER *Finding Naked People*, Lectures in Computer Science, 1996   304
12. J.D.FOLEY, A.V. DAM, S.K. FEINER, J.F. HUGHES *Computer Graphics, Principles and Practice*, Addison Wesley, 1990   304
13. A.S. GLASSNER *Principle of Digital Images*, Morgan Kaufmann Publishers Inc., 1995   304
14. O.GOLDREICH Foundations of Cryptography (Fragments of a Book). Available online from http://theory.lcs.mit.edu/~ oded/frag.html.   309
15. E.KOCH, J.RINDFREY, J.ZHAO Copyright protection for multimedia data *Proc. of the Int. Conf. on Digital Media and Electronic Publishing* 1994   303
16. M.KUTTER, F.A.P. PETITCOLAS *A fair benchmark for image watermarking systems*, To in E. Delp et al. (Eds), in Vol.3657, proceedings of *Electronic Imaging'99, Security and Watermarking of Multimedia Contents*, San Josè, CA USA, 1999   314
17. C.LUO, E.KOCH, J.ZHAO In Business Today and Tomorrow *Communications of the ACM* July 1998/Vol.41, No.7 pp.67-72   302
18. B.M.MACQ, J.J.QUISQUATER Cryptology for digital TV broadcasting. *Proc. of IEEE*, 83(6) pp.944-957, 1995   303
19. K.MATSUI, K.TANAKA Video-steganography *IMA Intellectual Property Project Proceedings*, Vol.1, pp.187-206, 1994   303
20. N.MEMON P.WAH, WONG Protecting Digital Media Content *Communications of the ACM* July 1998/Vol.41, No.7 pp.35-43   302
21. A.MENEZES, P.VAN OORSCHOT, S.VANSTONE Handbook of Applied Cryptography.   306
22. A.N.NETRAVALI, B.G. HASKELL *Digital Pictures:Representation and compression*, Application of Communication Theory, Plenum Press, NY, 1988   303, 304

23. C.I.PODILCHUK, W.ZENG *Image Adaptive Watermarking Algorithm Based on a Human Visual model, Signal Processing*, Vol.66, No.3, 1998, pp.337-355

24. F.A.P. PETITCOLAS, R.J. ANDERSON, M.G. KUHN *Attacks on copyright marking systems*, in David Aucsmith (Ed): Proceedings of *Information Hiding, Second International Workshop, IH'98*, LNCS 1525, Springer-Verlag, pp.219-239   314

25. I.PITAS, G.VOYATZIS *Protecting Digital-Image Copyrights: A Framework*, IEEE Computer Graphics and Applications, Jan. 1999,Vol.19, No.1, pp.18-24

26. R.VAN SCHYNDEL, A.TIRKEL, C.OSBORNE A Digital watermark *Proceedings of ICIP* IEEE Press, 1994 pp.86-90   303

27. K.TANAKA, Y.NAKAMURA, K.MATSUI Embedding secret information into a dithered multi-level image. *Proc. 1990 IEEE Military Communications Conference*, pp.216-220, 1990   303

28. M.YEUNG Digital Watermarking *Comm. of the ACM* July 1998/Vol.41, No.7 pp.31-33   302

Recovery of Watermarks from Distorted Images

Neil F. Johnson*, Zoran Duric**, and Sushil Jajodia***

Center for Secure Information Systems, George Mason University
Fairfax, VA 22030-4444
{njohnson,zduric,jajodia}@gmu.edu
http://ise.gmu.edu/~csis

Abstract. Many techniques for watermarking of digital images have appeared in numerous publications. Most of these techniques are sensitive to cropping and/or affine distortions (e.g., rotation and scaling). In this paper we describe a method for the recovery of original size and appearance of images based on the concept of *identification marks* ("fingerprints"); the method does not require the use of the "original" image, but only a small number of *salient* image points. We show that, using our method, it is possible to recover original appearances of distorted images. The restored image can be used to recover embedded watermarks.

1 Introduction

Interest in digital watermarking techniques is growing, motivated by the need to provide copyright protection to digital works, such as images, audio, and video, has increased over the last few years. Much of the interest has been driven by the growth of the Internet and the development of compression techniques and compression standards that make possible fast transmission of large volumes of information. These advances have made it easy to copy almost any song, image, video, or multimedia object that is available in digital form.

Watermarking can be used to identify owners, license information, or other information related to the digital object carrying the watermark. Watermarks may also provide mechanisms for determining if a work has been tampered with or copied illegally. In the domain of video and satellite broadcasts, watermarks are used to interfere with recording devices so copies of a broadcast are somewhat corrupt. Much of the focus has been on digital watermarking of images; this paper deals with images, although some of the discussion can be equally applied to other digital works.

Many proposed watermarking techniques are sensitive to image compression and transformations such as smoothing, rotation, scaling, cropping, and so on, or even printing and scanning. This interferes with the readability of the watermark.

---

* Also with Information and Software Engineering Department, George Mason University.
** Also with Computer Science Department, George Mason University.
*** Also with Information and Software Engineering Department, George Mason University.

A. Pfitzmann (Ed.): IH'99, LNCS 1768, pp. 318–332, 2000.

Publicly available tools can be used to distort images and effectively disable their watermarks. Given the volume of data on the internet, a watermark is effectively hidden if it cannot be found using a computationally simple and fast procedure.

Attacks on watermarks may be accidental or intentional. Accidental attacks may be the result of standard image processing or compression procedures. Illicit attacks may include cryptanalysis, steganalysis, image processing techniques, or other attempts to overwrite or remove existing watermarks or confuse the reader as to the authenticity of the watermark [7,8].

Many owners of watermarked works do not want the watermark to interfere with the use of the work by others; they therefore require that the watermark be imperceptible to the human visual system. This requirement works against the robustness of a watermark. Nevertheless, watermark users usually advertise the fact that a watermark exists.

In images, various image processing techniques and transformations are commonly employed to develop and apply digital watermarks. These methods can also be used to attack and disable watermarks. Even with advances in watermarking technology, watermarks may be forged or overwritten; for example, multiple watermarks may be placed in an image and one cannot determine which of them is valid [1]. Current watermark registration services are "first come, first serve", and someone other than the owner of a digital work may attempt to register a copyright first.

Attacks on watermarks may not necessarily remove the watermark, but only disable its perceptibility. If watermarks are used to locate images, how can an image be located or the watermark verified after it is disabled? To begin to understand this issue, we can ask: what features of an image are unaffected by (or invariant to) the processing that disables the watermark? Finding such features is key to reliably locating an image when an embedded watermark has been disabled.

We propose alternative methods for image recognition based on the concept of *identification marks* (id-marks or "fingerprints"), which can be used to locate corrupted copies of images [3,6]. Such a fingerprint can be used as a code to recognize an image and once an image is found, then the amount of change that occurred in the process of disabling the watermark can be determined. This same fingerprint can be used in calculating the inverse transform based on these changes over the image to recover the original appearance (scale and rotation) of the image. In doing so, we are also able to recover aspects of the embedded watermark, as we will see later.

The remainder of this paper is organized as follows: Section 2 provides formal descriptions of image processing techniques that we use in the recognition and recovery processes. Section 3 provides a brief description of our image fingerprinting and recognition methods based on invariant image properties. It shows how images can be prepared before their release to allow their easier recognition. Section 4 describes our method of recovering image parameters and appearance, and presents experimental results on images. Conclusions and suggestions about future research are presented in Section 5.

2   Affine Transforms and Displacement Fields

In this section we provide a mathematical background for our work. In Section 2.1 we formally define affine transforms and give an expression for displacement fields under affine transforms. In Section 2.2 we give the expression for normalized cross-correlation and explain its geometric meaning; we use it later in this paper to establish point correspondences in images. Finally, in Section 2.3 we introduce normal displacement fields, which we used for fine tuning of image registration parameters [3].

2.1   Affine Transforms

Let (x, y) be the image coordinates of a pixel in an image $I(x, y)$ and let the image center be at $(0, 0)$. An affine transform of $I(x, y)$ is given by

$$\begin{pmatrix} x' \\ y' \end{pmatrix} = \begin{pmatrix} a & b \\ c & d \end{pmatrix} \begin{pmatrix} x \\ y \end{pmatrix} + \begin{pmatrix} e \\ f \end{pmatrix} \tag{1}$$

where (x', y') are image coordinates in the transformed image $I'(x', y')$ and $a, \ldots, f$ are the transform parameters.

If we subtract the vector $(x\ y)^T$ from both sides of equation (1) we obtain an expression for the displacement $(\delta x, \delta y)$ of the point (x, y) due to the transform:

$$\begin{pmatrix} \delta x \\ \delta y \end{pmatrix} \equiv \begin{pmatrix} x' - x \\ y' - y \end{pmatrix} = \begin{pmatrix} a - 1 & b \\ c & d - 1 \end{pmatrix} \begin{pmatrix} x \\ y \end{pmatrix} + \begin{pmatrix} e \\ f \end{pmatrix}. \tag{2}$$

2.2   Normalized Cross-Correlation

Let $w_1 = I_1(x_1 + i, y_1 + j)$ and $w_2 = I_2(x_2 + i, y_2 + j)$, $i = -W, \ldots, W$, $j = -W, \ldots, W$ be two square image windows centered at locations (x_1, y_1) and (x_2, y_2) of images I_1 and I_2, respectively. The normalized cross-correlation of w_1 and w_2 is given by

$$NCC(w_1, w_2) = \frac{(w_1 - \overline{w}_1) \cdot (w_2 - \overline{w}_2)}{\|w_1 - \overline{w}_1\| \, \|w_2 - \overline{w}_2\|} \tag{3}$$

where w_1 and w_2 are treated as vectors. ($a \cdot b$ stands for the inner product of vectors a and b, $\overline{a}$ for the mean value of the vector elements and $\|a\|$ for the 2-norm of vector a.) For two windows whose pixel values differ by a scale factor only NCC will be equal to 1; if the windows are different NCC has value lower than 1. For two non-zero binary patterns which differ in all pixels NCC is -1. Normalized cross-correlation corresponds to the cosine of the angle between w_1 and w_2; as this angle varies between $0°$ and $180°$, the corresponding cosines vary between 1 and -1.

2.3   Normal Displacement Fields

Let $\imath$ and $\jmath$ be the unit vectors in the x and y directions, respectively; $\delta r = \imath \delta x + \jmath \delta y$ is the projected displacement field at the point $r = x\imath + y\jmath$. If we choose a unit direction vector $n_r = n_x \imath + n_y \jmath$ at the image point r and call it the normal direction, then the *normal displacement field* at r is $\delta r_n = (\delta r \cdot n_r)n_r = (n_x \delta x + n_y \delta y)n_r$. n_r can be chosen in various ways; the usual choice (and the one that we use) is the direction of the image intensity gradient $n_r = \nabla I / \|\nabla I\|$.

Note that the normal displacement field along an edge is orthogonal to the edge direction. Thus, if at the time t we observe an edge element at position r, the apparent position of that edge element at time $t + \Delta t$ will be $r + \Delta t \delta r_n$. This is a consequence of the well known *aperture problem*. We base our method of estimating normal displacement field on this observation.

For an image frame (say collected at time t) we find edges using an implementation of the Canny edge detector. For each edge element, say at r, we resample the image locally to obtain a small window with its rows parallel to the image gradient direction $n_r = \nabla I / \|\nabla I\|$. For the next image frame (collected at time $t_0 + \Delta t$) we create a larger window, typically twice as large as the maximum expected value of the magnitude of the normal displacement field. We then slide the first (smaller) window along the second (larger) window and compute the difference between the image intensities. The zero of the resulting function is at distance u_n from the origin of the second window; note that the image gradient in the second window at the positions close to u_n must be positive. Our estimate of the normal displacement field is then $-u_n'$, and we call it the *normal flow*.

3   Fingerprinting Images

The task of recognizing images can be defined as matching invariant features. These features may be salient parts of images or they may be artificial additions to them. In digital watermarking the information is typically embedded into images to facilitate identification of images. The embedded information is susceptible to attack through filtering and transformations [7,8]. To make this information robust enough it is usually necessary to distort the images to the point of making the embedded information visible.

Another approach to recognizing images is to use salient features of images as registration patterns or identification marks. In this way perceptually important image features are used for image identification. Removing these features is not possible without destroying the image. An alternative is to transform the image so that it cannot be easily recognized. Such transforms include rotating, cropping, resampling, etc. Most of these operations can be classified as affine transforms (see Section 2). They are included in widely available image processing software and are easy to perform.

In this section we introduce our methods for using salient image features in recognizing images that have been distorted by unknown affine transforms. The image features used for recognition are groups of points. [lines (edges) are also considered, but these can be considered as collections of points]. Isolated points are not sufficient for image recognition since they are not necessarily invariant, as differing images may contain similar points. However, groups of points tend to exhibit uniqueness, For example, ratios of areas enclosed by triples of points are invariant to affine transforms [3,6].

We have two basic approaches to our recognition process. One is based on finding strong, relatively unique points along image edges of high gradient magnitude. The other is based on finding corners with strong gradient magnitude within the image.

Regardless of which apporach is taken, our image recognition method consists of two parts. First, for each image we select a set of representative feature points at multiple resolutions. Second, we use these points for recognizing images. These methods are described in [3] and [6].

3.1   Selecting Feature Points

In general, our approach is based on choosing unique points in each image at multiple resolutions. The points are represented by small rectangular neighborhoods. We use neighborhood sizes ranging from 3×3 to 11×11 pixels. For each resolution we identify the feature points separately. The selected points usually differ when resolution changes. In this section, we will summarize our two techniques for identifying image feature points used to construct an "image fingerprint." The first approach we will discuss is based on finding relatively unique points along edges within an image. The second method is a further refinement of the first approach by considering corners of edges and less emphasis on uniqueness of the individual points.

Edge-Based Feature Points. This method of choosing unique feature points consists of several steps. First, we compute the image gradient ∇I over the image. We identify the image points that have large values of the gradient magnitude $\|\nabla I\|$. Note that these points typically correspond to edges (see Figure 1). We consider all the points that have gradient magnitude larger than one third of the highest gradient magnitude in the entire image. In doing so we insure that the second selection step operates on a smaller number of image points.

Second, for each of the selected points (x_i, y_i) we compute the similarity of its neighborhood, centered at (p, q), to the neighborhoods of other points in the image. This reduces the number of points to process in image recognition and identifies relatively unique points. In the remainder of this paper we will use the term *image point* to represent the point and its neighborhood. We use the normalized cross-correlation (see Section 2.2) as the similarity measure. For an image point (p, q) we obtain the similarity function $s_{p,q}(x-p, y-q)$. This function has a local maximum at $s_{p,q}(0, 0) = 1$ since the value at $(0, 0)$ corresponds to the similarity of the point with itself. If the point is *unique*, i.e. there are no other points in the image that are similar to it, $s_{p,q}(0, 0)$ is the global maximum of $s_{p,q}$ as well. If the point is unique we consider the sharpness of the peak at $(0, 0)$ and the next highest value of $s_{p,q}$ to decide if the point is a feature point.

Fig. 1. Identifying likely feature points: (a) an original image and (b) the image points with large values of gradient magnitude.

Figure 2 shows three examples of feature point selection. The points on the left and right are good feature points; their similarity functions computed over a 60×60 pixel window (lower row) have sharp peaks at the center (cross-correlation with itself), while all other similarity values are below 0.5. The center point is not a good feature point; it can be seen that its similarity function (the middle of the lower row of Figure 2) does not have a sharp peak at the center, and there are multiple other points with similarity values around 0.8 in the 60×60 pixels window centered at the point.

Corner-Based Feature Points. We rely on the cornerness measure for salient point selection. In other words, in areas of strong gradient magnitude, we look for converging edges in selecting the feature points. Consider the spatial image gradient $[E_x, E_y]^T$, computed for all points (x, y) of an image area (neighborhood) A. The matrix M is defined as

$$M = \begin{pmatrix} \sum E_x^2 & \sum E_x E_y \\ \sum E_x E_y & \sum E_y^2 \end{pmatrix} \tag{4}$$

where the sums are taken over the image neighborhood captures the geometric structure of the gray level pattern of A. M is a symmetric matrix and can therefore be diagonalized by rotation of the coordinate axes, with no loss of generality, we can think of M as a diagonal matrix [4]:

$$M = \begin{pmatrix} \lambda_1 & 0 \\ 0 & \lambda_2 \end{pmatrix} \tag{5}$$

where λ_1 and λ_2 are eigenvalues of M. We can choose λ_1 as the larger eigenvalue so that $\lambda_1 \geq \lambda_2 \geq 0$. If A contains a corner, then we expect $\lambda_1 \geq \lambda_2 > 0$, and the larger the eigenvalues, the stronger (higher contrast) their corresponding edges. A corner is identified as two strong edges; therefore as $\lambda_1 \geq \lambda_2$, a corner is a location where λ_2 is sufficiently large [10].

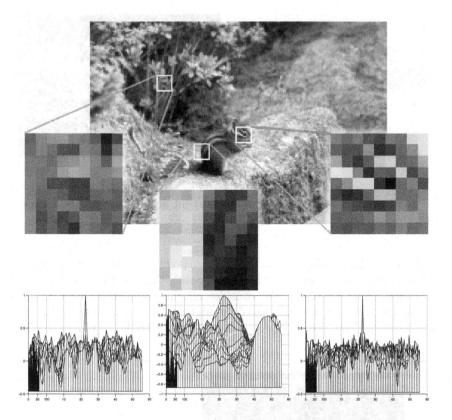

Fig. 2. Selecting feature points. Upper row: 9×9 neighborhoods of three image points. Lower row: corresponding similarity functions shown from an 80° viewing angle. The two outside points are good feature point candidates, while the center point is not.

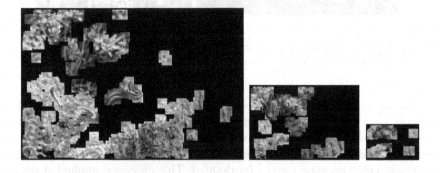

Fig. 3. Selected feature points (based on *edges*) for 1/2, 1/4, and 1/8 resolutions; each point is shown with its 9×9 neighborhood.

(a)   (b)

Fig. 4. Identifying likely feature points: (a) an original image. (b) Candidate feature points (small boxes).

Given this The method of choosing feature points based on corners consists of several steps. First, we identify the corner points that have cornerness measure larger than some threshold. We consider all the points that have cornerness measure larger than one-twentieth of the highest value of λ_2 in the entire image (see Figure 4). Also, values for λ_2 must be significantly large and $\lambda_1 < 2.5\lambda_2$.

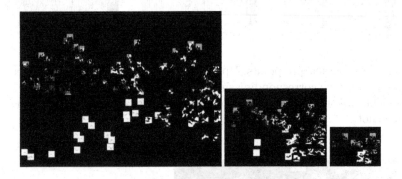

Fig. 5. Selected feature *corner* points for full, 1/2, and 1/4 resolutions; each point is shown with its neighborhood.

Second, for each of the selected corner points we compute the similarity of its neighborhood to the neighborhoods of other corner points in the image. In the remainder of this paper we will use the term image point and feature point to represent the point and its neighborhood. We use the normalized cross-correlation as the similarity measure (see [3] for details). This process is applied at multiple resolutions. Figure 5 shows selected feature points at three different resolutions. Notice that the number of feature points goes down as the resolution decreases. Also, image points that are not unique at higher resolutions may become prominent at lower resolutions. This is to counter scaling and blurring so the image can still be recognized. These sets of feature points provide a compressed representation of the original image and can be use to identify variations of the same image.

The processes described above for feature point selection are applied at multiple resolutions. Typically, as resolution changes selected feature points also change. Figure 3 shows selected feature points for the edge-based method at three different resolutions. Figure 5 shows selected feature points for the corner-based method at three different resolutions. Both of these figures illustrate that the number of feature points goes down rapidly as the resolution decreases. Also, image points that are not unique at higher resolutions may become prominent at lower resolutions.

4   Recovering Watermarks

In this section we describe our method of recovering the original size and aspect of a distorted image given the feature points identified in Section 3.1. Following the recovery process watermarks that may have been embedded in the image can be retrieved.

4.1   Estimating Transform Parameters

In this section we describe how the image size and aspect can be recovered by using the correspondences between image points in the original (I) and transformed (I') images.

Let (x_i, y_i), $i = 1, \ldots, N$ be image points in the image I and let (x_i', y_i'), $i = 1, \ldots, N$ be the corresponding points in the image I', respectively. From (1) we have

$$\begin{pmatrix} x_i' \\ y_i' \end{pmatrix} = \begin{pmatrix} a & b \\ c & d \end{pmatrix} \begin{pmatrix} x_i \\ y_i \end{pmatrix} + \begin{pmatrix} e \\ f \end{pmatrix}, \quad i = 1, \ldots, N. \tag{6}$$

We can rewrite equations (6) as

$$\begin{pmatrix} x_1 & y_1 & 1 & 0 & 0 & 0 \\ x_2 & y_2 & 1 & 0 & 0 & 0 \\ & \vdots & & & & \\ x_N & y_N & 1 & 0 & 0 & 0 \\ 0 & 0 & 0 & x_1 & y_1 & 1 \\ 0 & 0 & 0 & x_2 & y_2 & 1 \\ & & & \vdots & & \\ 0 & 0 & 0 & x_N & y_N & 1 \end{pmatrix} \begin{pmatrix} a \\ b \\ e \\ c \\ d \\ f \end{pmatrix} = \begin{pmatrix} x_1' \\ x_2' \\ \vdots \\ x_N' \\ y_1' \\ y_2' \\ \vdots \\ y_N' \end{pmatrix}. \tag{7}$$

Equation (7) can be written as

$$\mathbf{Au} = \mathbf{b} \tag{8}$$

where $\mathbf{A}$, $\mathbf{u}$, and $\mathbf{b}$ are defined by comparing equations (7) and (8).

(a)   (b)

Fig. 6. Recognizing images: (a) A distorted version of the image from Figure 1a. (b) A cropped version of image (a).

We seek $\mathbf{u}$ that minimizes $\|E\| = \|\mathbf{b} - \mathbf{Au}\|$; the solution satisfies the system [9]

$$\mathbf{A}^T \mathbf{Au} = \mathbf{A}^T \mathbf{b} = \mathbf{d}. \tag{9}$$

We observe that the problem can be further simplified if we rewrite (8) as

$$\begin{pmatrix} \mathbf{A}_1 & \mathbf{0} \\ \mathbf{0} & \mathbf{A}_1 \end{pmatrix} \begin{pmatrix} \mathbf{u}_1 \\ \mathbf{u}_2 \end{pmatrix} = \begin{pmatrix} \mathbf{b}_1 \\ \mathbf{b}_2 \end{pmatrix} \tag{10}$$

where $\mathbf{A}_1$, $\mathbf{u}_1$, $\mathbf{u}_2$, $\mathbf{b}_1$, and $\mathbf{b}_2$ are defined by comparing equations (7) and (10). Equation (9) thus separates into two equations:

$$\mathbf{A}_1^T \mathbf{A}_1 \mathbf{u}_1 = \mathbf{A}_1^T \mathbf{b}_1, \qquad \mathbf{A}_1^T \mathbf{A}_1 \mathbf{u}_2 = \mathbf{A}_1^T \mathbf{b}_2 \tag{11}$$

We solve these systems using the Cholesky decomposition [9]. Since the matrix $\mathbf{A}_1^T \mathbf{A}_1$ is a positive definite 3×3 matrix there exists a lower triangular matrix L such that $\mathbf{LL}^T = \mathbf{A}_1^T \mathbf{A}_1$. We solve two triangular systems $\mathbf{Le}_1 = \mathbf{d}_1 = \mathbf{A}_1^T \mathbf{b}_1$ and $\mathbf{L}^T \mathbf{u}_1 = \mathbf{e}_1$ for $\mathbf{u}_1$ and similarly for $\mathbf{u}_2$. Note that we need only one decomposition for both systems.

The computed $\mathbf{u}$ may be inaccurate due to various geometrical and numerical factors, to be discussed below. Given the estimate $\mathbf{u}$, based on point correspondences between images I and I', we use equation (6) to obtain the inverse affine transform of I'; we call this corrected image $I^{(1)}$. [The inversion of (6) is obtained implicitly. For each pixel position (x, y) of $I^{(1)}$ we compute the pixel position (x', y') in I' (note that x' and y' may be non-integers). We obtain the gray level for (x, y) by interpolating the gray levels of transformed image I'.]

Figure 6 shows images derived from the "original" images in Figure 1a and Figure 4. Figure 6a was created by applying an affine transform (cropping, scaling, and rotating) to the original. Figure 6b was created by cropping the image in Figure 6a.

(a)   (b)

Fig. 7. Recovering image size and aspect: (a) The recovered image from Figure 6a. (b) The recovered image from Figure 6b.

Figure 7 shows results of recovering the size and aspect of a distorted image using our method for the images in Figure 6. The estimated affine transform parameters $a, \ldots, f$ for the image in Figure 6a were $(1.082\ 0.004\ -0.015\ 1.015\ -8.51\ 2.32)^T$; the corresponding inverse transform applied to the image resulted in the image shown in Figure 7a. Similarly, the estimated affine transform parameters for the image in Figure 6b were $(1.084\ 0.004\ -0.014\ 1.015\ -20.85\ -34.81)^T$; the corresponding inverse transform applied to the image resulted in the image shown in Figure 7b. Note that the recovered parameters are very similar for both the uncropped and cropped images. Note also that the embedded watermark [2] has been successfully detected in the recovered images.

In this section we discussed various factors that may contribute to inaccuracies in estimating $\mathbf{u} = (a\ b\ e\ c\ d\ f)^T$. However, it is possible to iteratively improve on the computed solution of the system (11) using the normal flow. The technique for the refinement of image recovery based on normal displacement is explained in [3]. We show experimental results in Section 4.2.

4.2   Additional Experiments

We have experimented with the images shown in previous sections and with the images shown in Figure 8 using both a commercially available watermarking tool [2] and the watermarking technique described in [5]. A demo of the commercial watermark is available with Adobe Photoshop. The technique described in [5] embeds a watermark that corresponds to a logo or a text image into the original/cover image. We have successfully recovered the watermark in all cases. In some instances we had to go through the refinement phase to recover the watermark. An example of watermark recovery is shown in Figure 9.

Figure 9 shows an example of a watermarked image and recovery after attack. The image is watermarked using commercial software to produce the watermarked image (see Figures 9a,b). An attack on the watermark is conducted by applying Stirmark against the watermarked image (see Figures 9c,d). The

Fig. 8. Additional images used in our experiments.

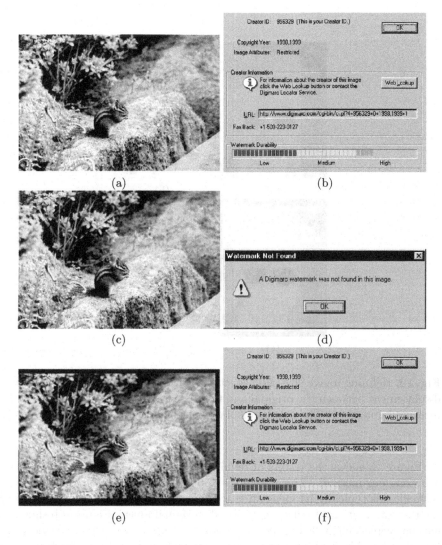

Fig. 9. Recovery of a commercial watermark [2] for an image in Figure 8. (a) The watermarked image. (b) Detection of the commercial watermark embedded in (a). (c) The distorted image. (d) Error message when attempting to read the watermark from (c). (e) The recovered image. (f) The watermark is once again available and can be read from (e).

affine transformation parameters were estimated as $(1.0255 \ 0.0012 \ -0.0049 \ 1.0045 \ 0.9685 \ 1.0939)^T$. The recovered image is shown in Figure 9e, and the watermark recovery results are shown in Figure 9f.

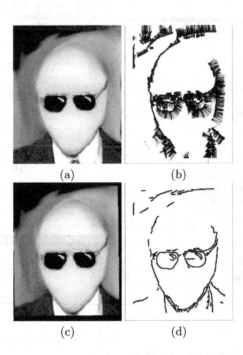

(a)   (b)

(c)   (d)

Fig. 10. Refining image size and aspect: (a) The original image. (b) The normal displacement between the original and the distorted image (not shown). (c) The recovered image. (d) The normal displacement field between images (a) and (c).

Figure 10 shows the results of refining the size and aspect of a distorted image using our method. [This method is applied when the distortion of an image is small; this typically happens after applying the recovery method described in the previous section.] Figure 10a shows the original image. Figure 10b shows the normal displacement field between the original image and the distorted image (not shown). The affine transform parameters estimated from the normal displacement field using the method described in this section are $(0.9993 \ -0.0002 \ -0.0029 \ 1.0002 \ -0.7565 \ -0.842)^T$. Figure 10c shows the recovered image that was obtained by applying the inverse affine transform to the distorted image. Finally, Figure 10d shows the normal displacement field between the images in Figure 10a and Figure 10c. The affine transform parameters estimated from this normal displacement field are $(1 \ -0.0002 \ 0.0001 \ 1.0001 \ 0.0356 \ -0.0206)^T$. Since the transform is small (the induced normal displacement field is < 0.5 everywhere) no further refinement is needed.

5   Conclusion and Future Directions

Digital works are subject to illicit copying and distribution. May owners wish for some means of of identifying ownership and copyright. Digital watermarks can fulfill this role and provide a means to identify and track digital works. However, embedded watermarks may fail to be recognized due to accidental corruption or attack by cropping and/or affine distortions (e.g., rotation, scaling, and blurring) [7,8]. This hampers the ability to locate and identify watermarked images over distributed networks such as the Internet.

In this paper, we introduced alternative methods for image recovery, based on inherent features within images that can be used to "fingerprint" images. These identification marks can be applied to locate images and recover image size and aspect from distorted images. Our methods do not rely on embedded information and can be used to recover images distorted by various geometric transformations [3,6].

We provided examples showing that it is possible to recover the original appearances of distorted images. In many cases doing so results in the recovery of embedded watermarks. We continue to investigate ways to make these methods more efficient for image recognition and recovery.

References

1. Craver, S., Memon, N., Yeo, B., Yeung, N.M., "Resolving Rightful Ownerships with Invisible Watermarking Techniques: Limitations, Attacks, and Implications," *IEEE Journal on Selected Areas in Communications*, 16(4):573–586, 1998.   319
2. Digimarc Corporation, PictureMarc^{TM}, MarcSpider^{TM}, http://www.digimarc.com   328, 330
3. Duric, Z., Johnson, N.F., and Jajodia, S., "Recovering Watermarks from Images," submitted to *IEEE Transactions on Image Processing*, 1999.   319, 320, 322, 325, 328, 332
4. Jahne, B.: Digital Image Processing, 4th ed. Springer-Verlag, 1997.   323
5. Johnson, N.F., Duric, Z., and Jajodia, S., "A Role for Digital Watermarking in Electronic Commerce," *ACM Computing Surveys*, 1999.   328
6. Johnson, N.F., Duric, Z., and Jajodia, S., "On "Fingerprinting" Images for Recognition," to appear in Fifth International Workshop on Multimedia Information Systems (MIS'99), Indian Wells, California, 1999.   319, 322, 332
7. Johnson, N.F., Jajodia, S., "Steganalysis of Images Created using Current Steganography Software," in Aucsmith, D., (ed.), Second Information Hiding Workshop, Portland, Oregon, Lecture Notes in Computer Science, Vol. 1525. Springer-Verlag, 1998.   319, 321, 332
8. Petitcolas, F., Anderson, R., Kuhn, M., "Attacks on Copyright Marking Systems," in Aucsmith, D., (ed.), Second Information Hiding Workshop, Portland, Oregon, Lecture Notes in Computer Science, Vol. 1525. Springer-Verlag, 1998.   319, 321, 332
9. Stewart, G.W. *Introduction to Matrix Computations*. Academic Press, New York, 1973.   327
10. Trucco, E. and Verri, A.: *Introductory Techniques for 3-D Computer Vision*. Prentice Hall, 1998.   323

Cocktail Watermarking on Images

Chun-Shien Lu, Hong-Yuan Mark Liao, Shih-Kun Huang, and
Chwen-Jye Sze

Institute of Information Science,
Academia Sinica, Taipei, Taiwan
{lcs,liao}@iis.sinica.edu.tw

Abstract. A novel image protection scheme called "cocktail watermarking" is proposed in this paper. We analyze and point out the inadequacy of the modulation techniques commonly used in ordinary spread spectrum watermarking methods and the visual model-based ones. To resolve this inadequacy, two watermarks which play complementary roles are simultaneously embedded into a host image. The new watermarking scheme has the characterictic that, no matter what an attack is, at least one watermark typically survives well. We also conduct a statistical analysis to derive the lower bound of the worst percentage for the likelihood that the better watermark (of the two) can be extracted. With this "high" lower bound, it is ensured that a "better" extracted watermark is always obtained. Results of extensive experiments indicate that our cocktail watermarking scheme is remarkably effective in resisting various attacks.

1 Introduction

A watermark is an identification code, which is used for ownership protection, content authentication, and side information conveyance [12]. Some requirements are needed for an effective watermarking scheme. These requirements include transparency, robustness, oblivious detection, resolution of ownership deadlock, and so on.

A major problem associated with watermarking is the fact that the current watermarking approaches are not strongly robust to attacks, so their use is limited [7]. In this paper, the above mentioned problem will be seriously addressed. We shall begin by introducing two commonly referred works. The first one is the spread spectrum watermarking technique proposed by Cox *et al.* [3]. Their method has been very popular and has been followed by many researchers [2,5,6,16]. The other one, proposed by Podilchuk and Zeng [15], is a human visual model-based watermarking scheme. Several similar methods have also been presented [4,5,18,19]. However, the reason why the two aforementioned methods succeed or fail is still not clear. We will investigate the modulation techniques used in [3,15] and clearly point out their drawbacks. We assert that in order to obtain high detector responses, most of the transformed coefficients of the host image and the watermarked image have to be modulated along the same direction. This is the key to improve the previous approaches because a watermark

A. Pfitzmann (Ed.): IH'99, LNCS 1768, pp. 333–347, 2000.
© Springer-Verlag Berlin Heidelberg 2000

detector can produce a high correlation value only when the above mentioned condition is satisfied. Unfortunately, we find that both Cox *et al.*'s method [3] and Podilchuk and Zeng's method [15] do not take this important factor into account. We have observed that an arbitrary attack usually decreases or increases the majority ($\geq 50\%$) of the transformed coefficients. In other words, the chance that an attack will make the number of increased and of decreased coefficients equal is very small. In this paper, we propose an efficient modulation strategy, which is composed of positive modulation (increasing the magnitude of the transformed coefficients) and negative modulation (decreasing the magnitude of the transformed coefficients). The two modulation rules simultaneously hide two complementary watermarks in a host image so that at least one watermark will survive under different attacks. Therefore, we call the proposed watermarking scheme "cocktail watermarking." The proposed cocktail watermarking scheme can embed watermarks firmly and make them hard to simultaneously obliterate. We also conduct a statistical analysis to derive a lower bound, which provides the worst percentage of the likelihood that the better watermark (of the two) will be extracted. With this "high" lower bound, it is ensured that a "better" extracted watermark will always be obtained. Experimental results confirm that our watermarking scheme is extremely robust to different kinds of attacks. To the best of our knowledge, there exists no single watermarking technique that can resist so many attacks.

2   Random Modulation

Two very popular watermarking techniques, which take the perceptual concept into account, were presented in [3,15]. Cox *et al.* [3] used the spread spectrum concept to hide a watermark based on the following modulation rule:

$$I_i^* = I_i(1 + \alpha \cdot n_i), \tag{1}$$

where I_i and I_i^* are DCT coefficients before and after modulation, respectively, and n_i is a value of a watermark sequence. α is a weight that controls the trade-off between transparency and robustness. In [15], Podilchuk and Zeng presented two watermarking schemes based on human visual model, i.e., the image adaptive-DCT (IA-DCT) and the image adaptive wavelet (IA-W) schemes. The watermark encoder for both IA-DCT and IA-W can be generally described as follows:

$$I_{u,v}^* = \begin{cases} I_{u,v} + J_{u,v} \cdot n_{u,v}, & I_{u,v} > J_{u,v}; \\ I_{u,v}, & otherwise, \end{cases} \tag{2}$$

where $I_{u,v}$ and $I_{u,v}^*$ are DCT or wavelet coefficients before and after modulation, respectively. $J_{u,v}$ is the masking value of a DCT or a wavelet based visual model, and $n_{u,v}$ is the sequence of watermark values. It is found from both embedding schemes that modulations take place in the perceptually significant coefficients with the modification quantity specified by a weight. The weight is either heuristic [3] or depends on a visual model [15]. Cox *et al.* [3] and Podilchuk and Zeng [15] adopted a similar detector response measurement described by

$$Sim(n, n^*) = \frac{n \cdot n^*}{\sqrt{n^* \cdot n^*}}, \tag{3}$$

where n and n^* are the original and the extracted watermark sequences, respectively. If the signs of a corresponding pair of elements in n and n^* are the same, then they contribute to the detector response. A higher value of $Sim(n, n^*)$ is stronger evidence that n^* is a genuine watermark. In Eq. (3), high correlation values can only be achieved if most of the transformed coefficients of the original source and the watermarked image are updated along the same direction during the embedding and the attacking processes, respectively. This is the key point if a watermark detector is to get a higher correlation value. However, we find that both [3] and [15] did not take this important factor into account. In fact, the modulation strategy adopted by them is intrinsically random. Usually, a positive coefficient can be updated with a positive or negative quantity, and a negative coefficient can be altered with a positive or a negative quantity as well. In other words, [3,15] did not consider the relationship between the signs of a *modulation pair*, which is composed of a selected transformed coefficient and its corresponding watermark value. This explains why many attacks can successfully defeat the above mentioned watermarking schemes.

In the following analysis, we assume that the watermark sequence n is embedded into a host image H. For the random modulation techniques proposed in [3] and [15], there are four possible types of modulations: $Modu(+, +)$, $Modu(+, -)$, $Modu(-, +)$, and $Modu(-, -)$, where $Modu(+/-, -/+)$ represents a positive/negative transformed coefficient modulated with a negative/positive watermark quantity. For a noise-style watermark with a Gaussian distribution of zero mean and unit variance, the probability of drawing a positive or a negative value is roughly equal to 0.5. In the wavelet domain, the wavelet coefficients of a high-frequency band can be modeled as a generalized Gaussian distribution [1] with the mean close to 0; i.e., the probability of getting a positive or a negative coefficient is roughly equal to 0.5. The lowest frequency component is, however, only suitably modeled by a usual Gaussian distribution with the mean far away from 0. That is, the probability of obtaining a positive coefficient is extremely different from the probability of obtaining a negative coefficient. When wavelet decomposition is executed with many scales, the lowest frequency component is tiny. Therefore, the probability of getting a positive or a negative wavelet coefficient is still close to 0.5. For the transformed coefficients in the DCT domain, the number of positive global DCT coefficients and the number of negative ones are statistically very close to each other. Hence, no matter whether the DCT or wavelet domain is employed, the probability of occurrence of each of the four types of modulations is very close to 0.25 due to their random nature. We have also analyzed the influence of a number of attacks to see how they update the magnitudes of transformed coefficients. From our observations, we find that using the random modulation proposed in [3,15], about 50% of the transformed coefficients are modulated more and the other half are modulated less. Therefore, it can be concluded that the random modulation strategy does not help to increase the detector response value at all.

For an attack like compression, the magnitudes of most of the transformed coefficients of a watermarked image are reduced after it is applied. Under these circumstances, it is hoped that every transformed coefficient will be modulated with a quantity that has a different sign with it. The reason why the above modulation strategy is adopted is that it can adapt to compression-style attacks so that more than 50% of the modulated targets can contribute a bigger positive value to the detector response. In sum, we can conclude that of the four types of modulations, only $Modu(+, -)$ and $Modu(-, +)$ will increase the detector response. On the other hand, if an attack (ex., sharpening) causes most of the transformed coefficients to increase in magnitude, then every constituent transformed coefficient should be modulated with a quantity that has the same sign with it. Under these circumstances, only $Modu(+, +)$ and $Modu(-, -)$ of the four types of modulations will increase the detector response.

3   Cocktail Watermarking

Our cocktail watermarking algorithm is based on the assumption that the original image (host image) is gray-scale. The watermark to be embedded is a Gaussian noise with zero mean and unit variance. The wavelet-based human visual system (HVS) [20] is adopted to sufficiently make use of the capacity allowed to hide watermarks. The advantage of using HVS in resisting attacks is analyzed in [11].

3.1   Wavelet Coefficients Selection

Before the wavelet coefficients of the host images are modulated, we must select the places for embedding. The wavelet coefficients are selected for modulation if their magnitudes are larger than their corresponding just noticeable difference thresholds [20]. Because two complementary watermarks need to be hidden, the length of each watermark to be hidden is one half the length of the selected coefficients. Basically, a watermark designed using our approach is image-adaptive [15]. Next, the places in the wavelet domain should be selected for watermarks hiding in an interleaving manner. We use a secret key to generate a Gaussian sequence, G, with zero mean and its length equal to the number of selected wavelet coefficients. The selected wavelet coefficients and this Gaussian form a one-to-one mapping. This mapping function is defined as

$$m(x, y) = \begin{cases} 1, & G(i) \geq 0 \\ -1, & G(i) < 0, \end{cases} \quad (4)$$

where (x, y) is the coordinate in the wavelet domain and i is the index of this Gaussian sequence, G. The locations in the wavelet domain correspond to positive/negative values will be assigned to employ positive/negative modulation rules. The value of $m(x, y)$ will be changed after modulation, as described in Sec. 3.3.

3.2   Design and Analysis of Complementary Modulation Strategy

After wavelet coefficients selection, the next step is to hide two complementary watermarks simultaneously. Recall the discussion in Sec. 2, it is known that a highly robust watermark encoding strategy should take the behavior of an attack into account. We have observed that any single attack will cause the majority of transformed coefficients ($\geq 50\%$) to either decrease or increase in magnitudes. The probability that an attack will cause the number of transformed coefficients to decrease or increase is almost equal zero. Therefore, if we embed two watermarks: one will use the $Modu(+, -)$ and $Modu(-, +)$ rule, and the other one will use the $Modu(+, +)$ and $Modu(-, -)$ rule; then, we can expect at least one of the two watermarking rules to capture a high detector response. Basically, the two embedded watermarks play complementary roles. Based on the above embedding strategy, if one watermark is severely damaged by an attack, the other will definitely survive. In this paper, we call the embedding strategy that uses $Modu(+, -)$ and $Modu(-, +)$ "negative modulation." On the other hand, the embedding strategy that uses $Modu(+, +)$ and $Modu(-, -)$ is called "positive modulation." The robustness requirement, which is a very important constraint for a good watermarking scheme, will always be satisfied in our approach since at least one of the two watermarks will survive under various kinds of attacks.

We assume that the watermark sequence, n, is a Gaussian distribution with probabilities $P(n_+)$ and $P(n_-)$ for positive and negative watermark values, respectively, where $P(n_+) = P(n_i | n_i \geq 0)$ and $P(n_-) = P(n_i | n_i < 0)$ are, respectively, equal to 0.5. In the proposed approach, all the wavelet transformed coefficients are modeled as a generalized Gaussian distribution [1]. The probabilities for both the positive and the negative coefficients, $P(w_+)$ and $P(w_-)$, are approximately equal, but $P(w_+)$ is a little bit larger than $P(w_-)$. Let $H_{s,o}(x_h, y_h)$ and $H_{s,o}^m(x_h, y_h)$ represent the original wavelet coefficients and the modulated wavelet coefficients, respectively, we define the probability, P_{nm}^M, of negative modulation as

$$
\begin{aligned}
P_{nm}^M &= P(Modu(+, -)) + P(Modu(-, +)) \\
&= P(n(m(x_h, y_h)) \cdot H_{s,o}(x_h, y_h) < 0),
\end{aligned} \tag{5}
$$

where $n(m(x_h, y_h))$ is a hidden watermark value and $m(x_h, y_h)$ is the mapping function as defined in Eq. (4). The term $n(m(x_h, y_h)) \cdot H_{s,o}(x_h, y_h) < 0$ specified in Eq. (5) is called the "**negative modulation (NM)**" event for watermark encoding. Let P_{nm}^D be a conditional probability which represents the probability that wavelet coefficients will be modulated less (in magnitude) by an attack provided that the embedding rule "**negative modulation**" has occurred. Therefore, P_{nm}^D can be defined as follows:

$$
\begin{aligned}
P_{nm}^D &= P(\text{coefficients that are decreasingly modulated by an attack} | \text{NM}) \\
&= \frac{P(n^*(m(x_h, y_h)) \cdot H_{s,o}^m(x_h, y_h) < 0 \ \& \ n(m(x_h, y_h)) \cdot n^*(m(x_h, y_h)) > 0)}{P(n(m(x_h, y_h)) \cdot H_{s,o}(x_h, y_h) < 0)}, \tag{6}
\end{aligned}
$$

where $n^*(m(x_h, y_h))$ is an extracted watermark value and $H^*_{s,o}(x_h, y_h)$ denotes a modified wavelet coefficient after attacking. This event can be interpreted as follows: at (x_h, y_h) and under the constraint of negative modulation, the modulated values (or updates) caused by the embedding process and the attacking process have the same tendency. As long as the above event is true, $n(m(x_h, y_h)) \cdot n^*(m(x_h, y_h)) > 0$ holds, and it will contribute a positive amount to the detector response. On the other hand, a "**positive modulation (PM)**" event for watermark encoding can be defined as $n(m(x_h, y_h)) \cdot H_{s,o}(x_h, y_h) > 0$. Therefore, the probability of positive modulation, P^M_{pm}, can be defined as

$$P^M_{pm} = P(Modu(+,+)) + P(Modu(-,-))$$
$$= P(n(m(x_h, y_h)) \cdot H_{s,o}(x_h, y_h) > 0). \tag{7}$$

The conditional probability, P^D_{pm}, which represents the probability that wavelet coefficients will be modulated more by an attack given that the embedding rule is positive modulation, can be represented as

$$P^D_{pm} = P(\textbf{coefficients that are increasingly modulated by an attack}|\textbf{PM})$$
$$= \frac{P(n^*(m(x_h, y_h)) \cdot H^m_{s,o}(x_h, y_h) > 0 \ \& \ n(m(x_h, y_h)) \times n^*(m(x_h, y_h)) > 0)}{P(n(m(x_h, y_h)) \cdot H_{s,o}(x_h, y_h) > 0)}. \tag{8}$$

Next, we will decide the ranges of P^D_{nm} and P^D_{pm}. In an ideal attack whose behavior completely matches negative modulation, all the coefficients of the watermarked image and the original image are decreasingly altered in magnitudes. Under these circumstances, $P^D_{nm} = P^M_{nm} = 1$. However, the above situation is only an ideal case. In fact, if an attack favors negative modulation, most ($\geq 50\%$) of the transformed coefficients will be decreased. Thus, we can get

$$P^D_{nm} \leq P^M_{nm} \tag{9}$$

and

$$P^D_{nm} \in [0.5 \ 1]. \tag{10}$$

Eq. (10) can be derived as follows. From Eq. (6), let the given "**negative modulation**" event be denoted as B, and let "$n^*(m(x_h, y_h)) \times H^m_{s,o}(x_h, y_h) < 0 \ \& \ n(m(x_h, y_h)) \times n^*(m(x_h, y_h)) > 0$" be denoted as event A. Since it is difficult for an attack to match the behavior of negative modulation completely, we know that the relation between A and B should be $A \subseteq B$. Therefore, the probability, P^D_{nm}, can be derived from Eq. (6) as

$$P^D_{nm} = P(A|B) = \frac{P(A \cap B)}{P(B)} = \frac{P(A)}{P(B)} \leq 1. \tag{11}$$

Furthermore, owing to the fact that the attack favors negative modulation, $|A|$ is greater than or equal to $\frac{1}{2}|B|$ ($|S|$ indicates the number of elements in the set S). This leads to

$$0.5 \leq \frac{P(A)}{P(B)} = P^D_{nm}. \tag{12}$$

From Eq. (10), we know that more than 50% pairs of $(n(\cdot,\cdot), n^*(\cdot,\cdot))$ will contribute to the detector response. These pairs result from the fact that more than 50% of the transformed coefficients decrease. A similar method can be used to deduce P_{pm}^{D} given positive modulation. One may ask what will happen if we do not know the tendency of an attack in advance. Fortunately, since our approach hides two complementary watermarks into a host image, there will be at least one modulation which matches the behavior of an arbitrary attack where the probability, P^{D}, is guaranteed to be larger than or equal to 0.5; i.e.,

$$P^{D} = MAX\{P_{nm}^{D}, P_{pm}^{D}\} \geq 0.5. \tag{13}$$

3.3   Complementary Watermark Hiding

The area for hiding watermarks is divided into two parts, i.e., a lowest frequency part and a part that covers the remaining frequencies. In this approach, different weights may be assigned to achieve a compromise between transparency and robustness. Here, only the frequency masking effect of the wavelet-based visual model [15,20] is considered. Owing to the lack of wavelet-based image-dependent masking effects, the heuristic weights assignment needs to be used.

The watermark embedding process proceeds as follows. First, the wavelet coefficients (H) of a host image are sorted in increasing order based on their magnitude, and the watermark sequence $(\mathcal{N})$ is sorted in increasing order, too. Each time, a pair of wavelet coefficients, $H_{s,o}(x_p, y_p)$ and $H_{s,o}(x_n, y_n)$, is selected from the top of the sorted coefficient sequence. They are then modulated and become $H_{s,o}^{m}(x_p, y_p)$ and $H_{s,o}^{m}(x_n, y_n)$, respectively, according to the following modulation rules:

Positive modulation:

$$H_{s,o}^{m}(x_p, y_p) = \begin{cases} H_{s,o}(x_p, y_p) + J_{s,o}(x_p, y_p) \times n_{bottom} \times w, & H_{s,o}(x_p, y_p) \geq 0 \\ H_{s,o}(x_p, y_p) + J_{s,o}(x_p, y_p) \times n_{top} \times w, & H_{s,o}(x_p, y_p) < 0, \end{cases} \tag{14}$$

where $J_{s,o}(.,.)$ represents the JND values of a wavelet-based visual model [20] and n_{top}/n_{bottom} represents the value retrieved from the top/bottom of the sorted watermark sequence $\mathcal{N}$. w is a weight used to control the maximum possible modification that will lead to the least image quality degradation. It is defined as

$$w = \begin{cases} w_L, & H_{s,o}(\cdot,\cdot) \in lowest - frequency\ channel \\ w_H, & H_{s,o}(\cdot,\cdot) \in high - frequency\ channel. \end{cases} \tag{15}$$

w_L and w_H refer to the weights imposed on the lowest and high frequency coefficients, respectively. If both of them are set to be one, they are diminished as in [15].

Negative modulation:

$$H_{s,o}^{m}(x_n, y_n) = \begin{cases} H_{s,o}(x_n, y_n) + J_{s,o}(x_n, y_n) \times n_{top} \times w, & H_{s,o}(x_n, y_n) \geq 0 \\ H_{s,o}(x_n, y_n) + J_{s,o}(x_n, y_n) \times n_{bottom} \times w, & H_{s,o}(x_n, y_n) < 0. \end{cases} \tag{16}$$

Based on the above mentioned positive and negative modulations, the mapping relationship between the position of a selected wavelet coefficient and the index of its corresponding watermark value is established as

$$m(x, y) = \begin{cases} i, & G(i) \geq 0 \\ -i, & G(i) < 0. \end{cases} \tag{17}$$

These mapping results will be stored for watermark detection and kept secret such that the pirates cannot easily remove the hidden watermarks. So, in the watermark detection process, we search for the positive/negative *signs* of $m(x, y)$ to detect watermarks embedded by positive/negative modulation rules. Besides, the positive/negative *values* of $m(x, y)$ determine the index of hidden watermarks.

4   Watermark Detection

In the literature, a number of authors [2,5,6,8,9] have proposed use of the public mode to extract watermarks without access to the original image, but the correlation values detected using their methods are not high enough, especially in the case of a strong attack. It is obvious that the performance of these public modes is not good enough due to lack of a precise way to predict the original image. Currently, we still need the original image to extract watermarks due to the lack of a reliable oblivious watermarking technique. Basically, the need for a host image is acceptable in destination-based watermarking [15].

4.1   Dealing with Attacks Containing Asynchronous Phenomena

In this section, we shall present a relocation strategy which can be used to tackle attacks that generate asynchronous phenomena. In what follows, we shall introduce some attacks of this sort. StirMark [13] is a very strong attacker that defeats many watermarking techniques. From analysis of StirMark [13], it is known that it introduces unnoticeable quality loss into an image with some simple geometrical distortions. Jitter attack [14], is another type, leads to spatial errors in images that are perceptually invisible. Basically, these attackers cause asynchronous problems. Experience tells us that an embedded watermark, when encountering these attacks, is often severely degraded [10]. Therefore, it is important to deal with the encountered attack in a clever way so that the damage caused by the attack can be minimized. It is noted that the order of the wavelet coefficients is different before and after an attack and might be changed significantly by attacks with the inherent asynchronous property. Consequently, in order to recover a "correct" watermark, the wavelet coefficients of an attacked watermarked image should be relocated to proper positions before watermark detection is conducted. The relocation operation is described in the following. First, the wavelet coefficients of the attacked watermarked image are re-arranged into the same order as those of the watermarked image. Generally speaking, by preserving the order, damage to the extracted watermark can always be reduced. From the experiments, we shall see that the detector response obtained by the relocation step is significantly improved. The improved results are especially remarkable for some attacks.

4.2 Detector Response

Through the watermark modulation procedures described in Eqs. (14) and (16), the distorted watermark, $\mathcal{N}^*$, is detected in the host image H and the attacked watermarked image H^* by means of

$$n^*(m(x,y)) = \begin{cases} \frac{H_{s,o}^*(x,y) - H_{s,o}(x,y)}{J_{s,o}(x,y) \times w_L}, & H_{s,o}^*(x,y) \in lowest - frequency\ channel \\ \frac{H_{s,o}^*(x,y) - H_{s,o}(x,y)}{J_{s,o}(x,y) \times w_H}, & H_{s,o}^*(x,y) \in high - frequency\ channel, \end{cases}$$

where $n^*(\cdot,\cdot)$ is the extracted watermark sequence value, $m(\cdot,\cdot)$ is a mapping function, and $H_{s,o}^*(x,y)$ is the distorted wavelet coefficient. The detector response is then calculated using the similarity measurement in Eq. (3).

According to the mapping function, the detector responses resulting from positive modulation and negative modulation are represented as $Sim^{pos}(\cdot,\cdot)$ and $Sim^{neg}(\cdot,\cdot)$, respectively. The final detector response, $Sim^{CW}(\cdot,\cdot)$, is thus defined as

$$Sim^{CW}(\cdot,\cdot) = MAX(Sim^{pos}(\cdot,\cdot), Sim^{neg}(\cdot,\cdot)), \tag{18}$$

where CW is an abbreviation for Cocktail Watermarking. Furthermore, if the relocation step is applied, then the detector response is denoted as $Sim_{Re}^{CW}(\cdot,\cdot)$; otherwise, it is denoted as $Sim_{NRe}^{CW}(\cdot,\cdot)$. A better detector response can be obtained by calculating the maximum value of $Sim_{Re}^{CW}(\cdot,\cdot)$ and $Sim_{NRe}^{CW}(\cdot,\cdot)$. That is,

$$Sim^{CW}(\cdot,\cdot) = MAX(Sim_{Re}^{CW}(\cdot,\cdot), Sim_{NRe}^{CW}(\cdot,\cdot)). \tag{19}$$

5 Experimental Results

A series of experiments was conducted to corroborate the effectiveness of the proposed method. The experimental results are reported in the following.

5.1 Complementary Effects of Cocktail Watermarking

First, a tiger image 128×128 in size was used to hide watermarks. The length of a hidden watermark depends on the host image and the wavelet-based visual model. Here, its length was 1357. Using our modulation strategy, a total of 2714 wavelet coefficients needed to be modulated. The PSNR of the watermarked image was 34.5 dB. We used 32 different attacks to test our cocktail watermarking scheme. The 32 attacked watermarked images are shown in Fig. 1. Among them, the attacked images (labeled (13) to (31)) were generated using Photo-Shop, while the others were obtained by applying common image processing techniques. The detector responses, $Sim_{NRe}^{CW}(\cdot,\cdot)$, (without employing the relocation step) with respect to the 32 attacks are plotted in Fig. 2(a). The two curves clearly demonstrated the complementary effects. It is apparent that one watermark could be destroyed while the other one survived well. From the set of attacked watermarked images, it is not difficult to find that while some attacks severely damaged the watermarked image, the embedded watermarks could still be extracted with high detector response. In addition, the probabilities, P_{pm}^D and P_{nm}^D, are corresponding to positive and negative modulations (without employing the relocation step) are plotted in Fig. 2(b). It is obvious that the cocktail watermarking strategy enables at least one watermark to achieve a high probability of survival under different kinds of attacks.

Moreover, the detector responses yielded by $Sim_{NRe}^{CW}(\cdot, \cdot)$ and $Sim_{Re}^{CW}(\cdot, \cdot)$ were also compared to identify the significance of relocation. Fig. 2(c) shows two sets of detector responses, one from detection with relocation and the other from detection without relocation. From Fig. 2(c), it can be seen that asynchronous phenomena caused by attacks could be compensated by means of the relocation strategy.

The cocktail watermarking scheme was also compared with the methods proposed by Cox et al. [3] and Podilchuk and Zeng (IA-W) [15] under the same set of attacks. In order to make a fair comparison, the parameters used by Cox et al. [3] were adopted. The PSNR of their watermarked image was 29.26 dB. Podilchuk and Zeng's method is image-adaptive and requires no extra parameter. The PSNR of their watermarked image was 30.21 dB. In our cocktail watermarking scheme and Podilchuk and Zeng's approach, 3-level wavelet transform was adopted in decomposing the tiger image. Among the three watermarked images generated, respectively, by Cox et al.'s method, Podilchuk and Zeng's method, and our method, our cocktail watermarking mode made the highest PSNR. In order to make the comparison fair, the relocation step, which would make our approach even better, was not used. Comparisons of the detector responses with respect to the 32 attacks for the three methods are shown in Fig. 2(d). From the comparisons shown in Fig. 2(d), it is obvious that our scheme is superior to the other two.

5.2   Cocktail Watermarking under Single Attack with Various Strength

We demonstrate that the detector responses of our cocktail watermarking will not drop dramatically with respect to the same attack having gentle to severe strength. In this experiment, the relocation strategy is not applied. In Fig. 3(a), a gentle decrease in detector response is illustrated for Gaussian blurring with various mask sizes. In Fig. 3(b), a gentle decrease in detector response is also obtained when the compression ratio increases. These promising results are expected because our complementary modulation strategy could capture the behaviors of attacks no matter what their strength are.

5.3   Cocktail Watermarking under Combined Attacks with Various Strength

In this section, a series of experiments were conducted to show how a combined attack would influence a cocktail watermarked image. It is shown that blurring (B) and histogram equalization (H) are two types of attacks which have opposite functions. That is, the blurring operation tends to decrease the magnitudes of most of the wavelet coefficients. Histogram equalization, on the other hand, tends to increase the magnitudes of most of the wavelet coefficients. The purpose of this experiment is to check whether this kind of combination is able to remove the watermark of a cocktail watermarked image. 20 combined attacks including B(1st attack), BH(2nd attack), BHB(3rd attack), BHBH, ..., BHBHBHBHBHBHBHBHBHBH(20-th attack), were used. The noise-style (Gaussian sequence here) watermark detection results are shown in Fig. 4. It is observed that the detector response becomes trustless once the number of attacks increases. This is because that the variance of the watermarked image after combined attacks becomes large. Under the circumstances, the difference between an extracted watermark pixel and its corresponding original watermark pixel also becomes large. However, if the sign instead of the quantity of a watermark value is used, the result will be stable as shown in our another work [11]. This is the reason why we suggest that noise-style watermark detection (considered here) is not so robust as bipolar watermark detection [11]. Even though most of the signs of noise-style watermark values are preserved, those watermark values who are changed dramatically will dominate the calculation of detector response.

6   Conclusion

A cocktail watermarking scheme which can securely protect images has been presented in this paper. The proposed scheme has two characteristics: (1) embedding two complementary watermarks makes it more difficult for attackers to succeed; (2) a relocation step is included to deal with attacks that generate asynchronous distortions. Experimental results have demonstrated that our watermarking scheme is extremely robust while satisfying typical watermarking requirements. To the best of our knowledge, no other technique so far reported in the literature can resist so many attacks.

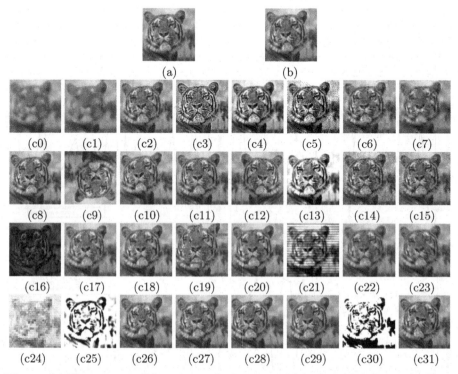

Fig. 1. (a) Host image; (b) watermarked image of (a); (c0)∼(c31) attacked watermarked images: (c0) blurred (mask size 15 × 15); (c1) median filtered (mask size 11 × 11); (c2) rescaled; (c3) sharpened (with an *XV* factor of 85); (c4) histogram equalized; (c5) dithered; (c6) JPEG compressed (with a quality factor of 5%); (c7) SPIHT (at a compression ratio of 64 : 1) [17]; (c8) StirMark attack (1 time with all default parameters); (c9) StirMark+Rotating 180°; (c10) StirMark attack (5 times with all default parameters); (c11) jitter attack (5 pairs of columns were deleted/duplicated); (c12) flip; (c13) brightness/contrast adjusted; (c14) Gaussian noise added; (c15) texturized; (c16) difference of clouds; (c17) diffused; (c18) dusted; (c19) extruded; (c20) faceted; (c21) halftoned; (c22) mosaic applied; (c23) motion blurred; (c24) patchworked; (c25) photocopied; (c26) pinched; (c27) rippled; (c28) sheared; (c29) smart blurred; (c30) thresholded; (c31) twirled.

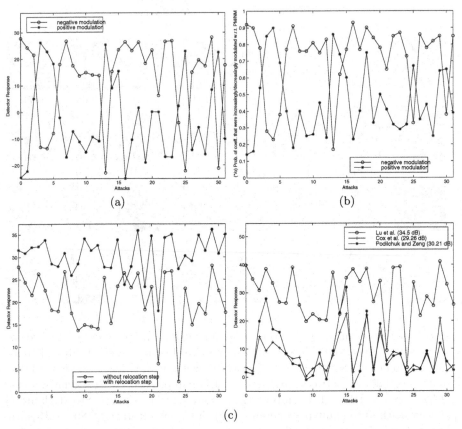

Fig. 2. Results of Cocktail watermarking in terms of detector responses (where the maximum detector response was 37.37): (a) the obtained detector responses (without the relocation step) with respect to 32 attacks; (b) probability that coefficients would be modulated more/less with respect to positive/negative modulation; (c) comparison of detector responses with/without the relocation step; (d) comparisons among our method, Podilchuk and Zeng's method [15], and Cox *et al.*'s method [3].

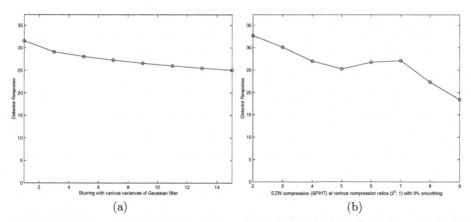

Fig. 3. Single attack with various strength (without using relocation): (a) Gaussian smoothing with various mask sizes (3×3, 7×7, ..., 31×31); (b) SPIHT compression with various compression ratios (4, 8, ..., 512).

References

1. M. Antonini, M. Barlaud, P. Mathieu, and I. Daubechies, "Image Coding Using Wavelet Transform", *IEEE Trans. Image Processing*, Vol. 1, pp. 205-220, 1992. 335, 337

2. M. Barni, F. Bartolini, V. Cappellini, and A. Piva, "Copyright Protection of Digital Images by Embedded Unperceivable Marks", *Image and Vision Computing*, Vol. 16, pp. 897-906, 1998. 333, 340

3. I. J. Cox, J. Kilian, F. T. Leighton, and T. Shamoon, "Secure Spread Spectrum WaterMarking for Multimedia", *IEEE Trans. Image Processing*, Vol. 6, pp. 1673-1687, 1997. 333, 334, 335, 342, 345

4. J. F. Delaigle, C. De Vleeschouwer, and B. Macq, "Watermarking Algorithms based on a Human Visual Model", *Signal Processing*, Vol. 66, pp. 319-336, 1998. 333

5. J. Fridrich, "Combining Low-frequency and Spread Spectrum Watermarking", *Proc. SPIE Int. Symposium on Optical Science, Engineering, and Instrumentation*, 1998. 333, 340

6. F. Hartung and B. Girod, "Watermarking of uncompressed and compressed Video", *Signal Processing*, Vol. 66, pp. 283-302, 1998. 333, 340

7. F. Hartung, J. K. Su, and B. Girod, "Spread Spectrum Watermarking: Malicious Attacks and Counterattacks", *Proc. SPIE: Security and Watermarking of Multimedia Contents*, Vol. 3657, 1999. 333

8. D. Kundur and D. Hatzinakos, "Digital Watermarking Using Multiresolution Wavelet Decomposition", *Proc. IEEE Int. Conf. Acoustics, Speech and Signal Processing*, Vol. 5, pp. 2969-2972, 1998. 340

9. M. Kutter, F. Jordan, and F. Bossen, "Digital Signature of Color Images using Amplitude Modulation", *Journal of Electronic Imaging*, Vol. 7, pp. 326-332, 1998. 340

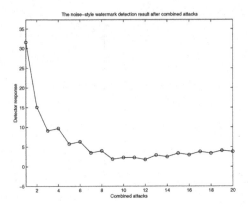

Fig. 4. Noise-style watermark detection result (without using relocation) under combined attacks (B, BH, BHB, etc.) using blurring (B) and histogram equalization (H).

10. C. S. Lu, S. K. Huang, C. J. Sze, and H. Y. Mark Liao, "A New Watermarking Technique for Multimedia Protection", to appear in *Multimedia Image and Video Processing*, eds. L. Guan, S. Y. Kung, and J. Larsen, CRC Press Inc. 340

11. C. S. Lu, H. Y. Mark Liao, S. K. Huang, and C. J. Sze, "Highly Robust Image Watermarking Using Complementary Modulations", to appear in *2nd International Information Security Workshop*, Malaysia; Lecture Notes in Computer Science, Springer-Verlag, 1999. 336, 343

12. F. Mintzer and G. W. Braudaway, "If one watermark is good, are more better?", *Inter. Conf. on Acoustic, Speech, and Signal Processing*, pp. 2067-2070, 1999. 333

13. F. Petitcolas and M. G. Kuhn, "StirMark 2.3 Watermark Robustness Testing Software", *http://www.cl.cam.ac.uk/~fapp2/watermarking/stirmark/*, 1998. 340

14. F. Petitcolas, R. J. Anderson, and M. G. Kuhn, "Attacks on Copyright Marking Systems", *Second Workshop on Information Hiding*, USA, pp. 218-238, 1998. 340

15. C. I. Podilchuk and W. Zeng, "Image-Adaptive Watermarking Using Visual Models", *IEEE Journal on Selected Areas in Communications*, Vol. 16, pp. 525-539, 1998. 333, 334, 335, 336, 339, 340, 342, 345

16. J. J. K. Ruanaidh and T. Pun, "Rotation, Scale, and Translation Invariant Spread Spectrum Digital Image Watermarking", *Signal Processing*, Vol. 66, pp. 303-318, 1998. 333

17. A. Said and W. A. Pearlman, "A New, Fast, and Efficient Image Codec based on Set Partitioning in Hierarchical Trees", *IEEE Trans. Circuit and Systems for Video Technology*, Vol. 6, pp. 243-250, 1996. 344

18. M. D. Swanson, B. Zhu, and A. H. Tewfik, "Multiresolution Scene-Based Video Watermarking Using Perceptual Models", *IEEE Journal on Selected Areas in Communications*, Vol. 16, pp. 540-550, 1998. 333

19. M. D. Swanson, M. Kobayashi and A. H. Tewfik, "Multimedia Data-Embedding and Watermarking Technologies", *Proc. of the IEEE*, Vol. 86, pp. 1064-1087, 1998. 333

20. A. B. Watson, G. Y. Yang, J. A. Solomon, and J. Villasenor, "Visibility of Wavelet Quantization Noise", *IEEE Trans. Image Processing*, Vol. 6, pp. 1164-1175, 1997. 336, 339

Hiding Signatures in Graph Coloring Solutions

Gang Qu and Miodrag Potkonjak

Computer Science Department, University of California
Los Angeles, CA 90095, USA
{gangqu,miodrag}@cs.ucla.edu

Abstract. One way to protect a digital product is to embed an author's signature into the object in the form of minute errors. However, this technique cannot be directly applied to protect intellectual properties such as solutions to hard problems which must maintain the correct functionality. This paper proposes a *constraint-based watermarking technique* and lays out a theoretical framework to evaluate this type of technique. Based on this framework, we analyze three watermarking techniques for the graph coloring problem because of its theoretical importance in complexity theory and numerous applications in real life. The first adds extra edges between some pairs of vertices and therefore forces them to be colored by different colors. The second pre-colors a set of well-selected vertices according to the watermark. And the last introduces new vertices and edges to the graph. Since credibility and overhead are the most important criteria for any efficient watermarking technique, we derive formulae which explicitly illustrate the trade-off between high credibility and low overhead. Asymptotically we prove that for almost all random graphs $G_{n,p}$, an arbitrarily high credibility can be achieved by all proposed watermarking techniques with at most 1-color-overhead. Numerical simulation on random graphs shows that a large amount of information can be embedded with very low overhead. We also watermark several sets of graphs generated from real-life benchmarks. Almost all the watermarked graphs, with a huge watermark embedded, can be colored with the known minimal number of colors for the original instances with no run-time overhead.

1 Introduction

Suppose that you have developed a very efficient heuristic to solve a well-known hard problem, for example the graph (vertex) coloring (GC) problem. You test your program on real-life benchmarks and your solutions outperform the best known solutions, then you decide to put your solutions online on a pay-per-use base to recoup the cost of developing your software. Since the solutions you post are heavily used in real-life and soon you will find yourself a target of pirates, who purchase your solutions and then resale them at a lower price. Even if you catch the dishonest buyer, he/she can claim that he/she solves the problem by himself/herself. To protect your intellectual property (IP), you need to prove to a third-party that your are the creator and owner of this solution.

A. Pfitzmann (Ed.): IH'99, LNCS 1768, pp. 348–367, 2000.

In this paper, we propose a constraint-based watermarking technique for intellectual property protection (IPP). Instead of solving the real problem and posting the answer directly, we build a watermarking engineer which takes the real problem and the owner's signature as input and gives a solution to the initial problem. Inside the watermarking engineer, we translate the signature into a set of additional constraints and add them into the original problem. Therefore, the solution will satisfy both the original and additional constraints. I.e., in this solution, there exist special structures that cannot be easily discovered without the owner's signature. Now the owner can claim his/her authorship by showing the small probability that such structures exist in a random solution without the signature. Since the signature is embedded as extra constraints, there might be some degradation in the quality of the IP. The trade-off between *credibility* (measures for the strength of proof for authorship) and *overhead* (measures for the degradation of quality of the IP) has to be balanced, based on which we build a framework to evaluate watermarking techniques. As an attempt to theoretically analyze watermarking techniques, the primary objective of this paper is to lay out analytical foundations for all watermarking techniques, not only those which we discuss here.

We take the GC problem as an example to illustrate our approach because of its theoretical importance in complexity theory and numerous applications in real life. The GC problem is to color the vertices of a graph with the fewest number of colors such that no vertices connected by an edge receive the same color. A watermarked solution is a coloring scheme from which the embedded information can be retrieved. We propose three watermarking techniques to embed signatures into solutions of the GC problem. For each technique, we explain how signatures can be put into the graph as extra constraints, then we do the asymptotic analysis to answer the questions about credibility and overhead (number of extra colors required in the GC problem). Surprisingly, the result shows that an arbitrarily high credibility can be achieved with at most one color overhead by all proposed watermarking techniques. This is tested by numerical simulation on random graphs. Finally we color several sets of random graphs, graphs from real-life benchmarks and the DIMACS challenge graph. For most instances, the watermarked graphs can be colored with no overhead with the same amount of run-time.

The rest of the paper is organized as follows. In section 2, we survey the related work on watermarking, random graphs and outline the constraint-based watermarking IPP techniques. The framework for evaluating watermarking techniques is then illustrated by analyzing the three watermarking techniques for the graph coloring problem. We report the numerical simulation and experimental results in section 6 and summarize our work in section 7. The proof and pseudo-code are listed in the Appendices.

2   Preliminary

Data watermarking, also known as data hiding, embeds data into digital media for the purpose of identification, annotation, and copyright. Recently, the proliferation of digitized media and the Internet revolution are creating a pressing need for copyright enforcement schemes to protect copyright ownership. Several techniques for data hiding in digital images, audios, videos, texts and multimedia data have been developed [1,3,4,5,9,10,11]. All these techniques take advantage of the limitation of human visual and auditory systems, and simply embed the signature to the digital data by introducing minute errors. The transparency of the signature relies on human's insensitiveness to these subtle changes.

Watermarking for the purpose of IPP, on the other hand, is more difficult because it has to maintain the correct functionality of the initial IP. A conceptually new method [6], *constraint-based watermarking*, translates the to-be-embedded signature into a set of additional constraints during the design and implementation of IP in order to uniquely encode the signature into the IP. The proof of authorship is shown by arguing the small probability for a random solution to satisfy all these extra constraints. The effectiveness of this generic scheme has been demonstrated at all stages of the design process [6].

A generic watermarking procedure consists of the following components:

- An *optimization problem* with known difficult complexity. By difficult, we mean that either achieving an acceptable solution, of enumerating enough acceptable solutions, is prohibitively costly. The solution space of the optimization problem should be large enough to accommodate a digital watermark.
- A well-defined *interpretation* of the solutions of the optimization problem as intellectual property.
- Existing *algorithms and/or off-the-shelf software* that solve the optimization problem. Typically, the "black box" software model is appropriate, and is moreover compatible with defining the watermarking procedure by composition with pre- and postprocessing stages.
- *Protection requirements* that are largely similar to well-understood protection requirements for currency watermarking.

A non-intrusive watermarking procedure then applies to any given instance of the optimization problem, and can be attached to any specific algorithms solving it. Such a procedure can be described as:

- *A use model or protocols* for the watermarking procedure. In general, each watermarking scheme must be aware of attacks based on design symmetries, renaming, reordering, small perturbations (which may set requirements for the structure of the solution space), etc.
- Algorithmic descriptions of the *pre- and post-processing* steps of the watermarking procedure. Pre- and post processing preserve the algorithms and/or software as a "black box".
- *Strength and feasibility analyses* showing that the procedure satisfies given protection requirements on a given instance. Strength analysis requires metrics, and structural understanding of the solution space (e.g., "barriers" (with

respect to local search) between acceptable solutions). Feasibility analysis requires measures of solution quality, whether a watermarked solution remains well-formed, etc.

- *General robustness analyses*, including discussion of susceptibility to typical attacks, discussion of possible new attacks, performance guarantees (including complexity analysis) and implementation feasibility.

In addition to maintaining the correct functionality of the IP, an effective watermark must satisfy the following properties:

- *high credibility:* The watermark should be readily detectable for the proof of the authorship. The probability of coincidence should be low.
- *low overhead:* The degradation of the software or design by embedding the watermark should be minimized.
- *resilience:* The watermark should be difficult or impossible to remove without the complete knowledge of the software or design.
- *transparency:* The addition of the watermark to software and designs should be transparent so that it can be used for existing design tools.
- *perceptual invisibility:* The watermark must be very difficult to detect. This is related to but not the same as the resilience problem.
- *part protection:* Ideally, a good watermark should be distributed all over the software or design in order to protect all parts of it.

The theory of random graphs was founded by Erdös and Rényi after Erdös had discovered, in the middle of this century, that probabilistic methods were often useful in tackling extremal problems in graph theory. The traditional way of estimating the proportion of graphs having a certain property is to obtain exact but complicated formulae. The new probabilistic approach is to approximate a variety of exact values by appropriate probability distributions and using probabilistic ideas.

Random graphs play a very important role in many fields of computer science. The two most frequently occurring models of random graphs are $\mathcal{G}(n, M)$ and $\mathcal{G}(n, p)$. The first consists of all graphs with n vertices and M edges, the second consists of all graphs with n vertices and the edges are chosen independently with probability $p(0 < p < 1)$. We will focus on the second model and use these conventional notations: $G_{n,p}$ for an element of $\mathcal{G}(n, p)$, $q = 1 - p, b = \frac{1}{q}$, $\alpha(G_{n,p})$ is the independent number of graph $G_{n,p}$ (i.e., the maximal cardinality of independent sets.), and $\chi(G_{n,p})$ denotes the chromatic number of $G_{n,p}$ (i.e., the minimum number of colors required to color the graph.). For almost all graphs $G_{n,p}$, we have [2]:

(1) $$\alpha(G_{n,p}) = (2 + o(1)) \log_b n$$
(2) $$\chi(G_{n,p}) = (\tfrac{1}{2} + o(1)) \frac{n}{\log_b n}$$

The graph (vertex) coloring problem is to label the vertices of a graph with minimal number of colors such that vertices connected by an edge do not receive the same color. This problem is NP-complete and has a lot of applications in various fields[1]. Many heuristics have been developed dedicated to it[12]. In the

---

[1] For example, Toft stated 75 interesting and easily-formulated graph coloring problems[8].

next three sections, we propose techniques for watermarking the solutions to
the GC problem, and lay out the theoretical framework for technique evaluation
through the analyses of these techniques.

3   Watermarking Technique #1 — Adding Edges

3.1   Generic Watermarking Procedure for the Graph Coloring Problem

The essence of constraint-based watermarking techniques is to add extra design
constraints in order to get a rather unique solution. This is shown explicitly in
Figure 1 for the GC problem.

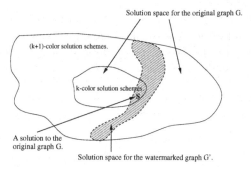

Fig. 1. Additional constraints cut the solution space.

Suppose we have a graph G which is *k-colorable*, the inner and outer regions
in Figure 1 represent the solution spaces of k-color and (k+1)-color solutions to G
respectively. We assume that when a k-color solution is required, every solution
in the inner region has equal probability being picked. The shaded area is the
solution space for the watermarked graph G', where we impose our signature as
additional constraints. Since graph G' in-herits all the constraints of graph G,
a solution to G' is also valid for G. However, the solutions to G may violate
the new constraints in G'. By coloring graph G' instead of G, we can obtain
solutions to G and more important, we force the solutions fall into the shaded
area. Denote n_k and n'_k the numbers of k-color solutions for graphs G and G'.
The chance to get a particular solution S from the constraints in G is $\frac{1}{n_k}$, which
increases to $\frac{1}{n'_k}$ if from the more-constrained graph G'. When n_k is large and
$n'_k << n_k$, the difference between $\frac{1}{n_k}$ and $\frac{1}{n'_k}$ is significant and becomes a credible
evidence for the authorship.

High credibility depends not only on the amount of constraints, but also the
"quality" of the constraints. For example, one constraint that cuts the solution
space by half is definitely better than 20 constraints each cutting the solution
space by less than 1%. Constraints for the GC problem are the edges: vertices

connected by an edge have to receive different colors. One type of straightforward watermarks is extra edges. By translating signature as extra edges, we make the original graph more constrained, and some solutions to the original graph will become invalid for the watermarked graph. The solution space eventually shrinks. There are other interpretations of signatures as constraints. However, to have a transparent watermark, we require that the watermarked graph preserve the characteristics (e.g. connectivity, randomness, acyclicity.) of the original graph. In the following sections, we propose three watermarking techniques for the GC problems of random graphs, and investigate the impact of the corresponding watermarks to the solution space.

3.2   Technique Statement

Signature embedding:

   Given a graph $G(V, E)$ and a message M to be embedded in G. Let $V = (v_0, v_1, \cdots, v_{n-1})$ and we encrypt the message into a binary string $M = m_0 m_1 \cdots$ (by stream ciphers, block ciphers, or cryptographic hash functions). Figure 2 shows how M is embedded into the graph G as additional constraints.

Input: a graph $G(V, E)$,   a message $M = m_0 m_1 \ldots$ **Output:** new graph with message M embedded

Algorithm:
 copy $G(V, E)$ to $G'(V, E')$;
 foreach bit m_i
      { find the nearest two vertices v_{i_1}, v_{i_2} that
         are not connected to vertex v_i;
         if $m_i = 0$ add edge (v_i, v_{i_1}) to E'
         else add edge (v_i, v_{i_2}) to E'
      }
 report graph $G'(V, E')$;

Fig. 2. Pseudo code for technique # 1.

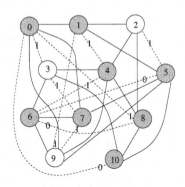

Fig. 3. An example.

   By the nearest two vertices v_{i_1} and v_{i_2} which are not connected to vertex v_i, we mean that $i_2 > i_1 > i$ (mod n), the edges $(v_i, v_{i_1}), (v_i, v_{i_2}) \notin E$ and $(v_i, v_j) \in E$ for all $i < j < i_1, i_1 < j < i_2$ (mod n). For example, in Figure 3, vertices 2 and 3 are the nearest two vertices that are not connected to vertex 0. The essence of this technique is to add an extra edge between two vertices, these two vertices have to be colored by different colors which may not be necessary in the original graph G. Figure 3 shows a graph of 11 nodes with solid lines for original edges. The message $1998_{10} = 11111001110_2$ has been embedded by 11 dotted edges, each represents one bit marked on the edge. A 4-color scheme, $\{\{v_0, v_2, v_6\}, \{v_1, v_7, v_{10}\}, \{v_3, v_8, v_9\}, \{v_4, v_5\}\}$, is shown as well.

Signature recovering:

How can we read the watermark from the solution? Given the original graph, we claim that some pairs of vertices will have different colors. For example, in Figure 3, these pairs are $\{v_0, v_3\}, \{v_1, v_4\}, \{v_2, v_5\}, \cdots, \{v_{10}, v_0\}$. In the original graph, every such pair of vertices are not directly connected by an edge, so it is not necessary to assign them different colors. However we observe that this happens in the coloring scheme shown in Figure 3. For each such pair $\{v_i, v_j\}$, we can retrieve one bit of information by counting how many nodes in between (i.e., nodes with indices bewteen i and j) are not connected to v_i. If there is none, the hidden bit is 0; if there is only 1, the hidden bit is 1; and if there are more than 1, reverse the order of v_i and v_j. This binary string is the (encrypted) message. In the same manner, it is not difficult to construct many other binary strings, even if the vertices have a standard order and the watermark is embedded in the well-accepted manner. For example, node 0 in Figure 3 has different color from both nodes 2 and 3, which are the nearest two vertices that are not connected to node 0. So both bits 0 and 1 can be claimed as the hidden bit in this case and one may have a different binary string. However, it will be hard to build one with a piece of meaningful information. In particular, if the original message is encrypted by one-way functions, forging a watermark with the same level of credibility needs to break the one-way functions.

3.3   Technique Analysis

The signature or message can be anything that is capable of identifying authorship. We can transfer it into binary (e.g., in ASCII), encrypt it by stream ciphers or cryptographic hash functions and assume the final bit stream is random. To have a quantitative analysis, we assume that exactly χ colors are required to color the graph $G_{n,p}$, where χ is given by[2]:

$$(3) \qquad \chi(G_{n,p}) = \lceil \frac{n}{2\log_b n} \rceil$$

It follows immediately that after adding k extra edges into the graph $G_{n,p}$ according to the signature , the resulting graph remains random[3] with the same number of vertices and a new edge probability:

$$(4) \qquad p' = p + \frac{2k}{n(n-1)}$$

So formula (3) for the chromatic number still holds, we denote this number by χ'. The **overhead** is defined to be $\chi' - \chi$, i.e., the number of extra colors required to color the watermarked graph. Intuitively, the more edges we add, the

---

[2] We choose expression (3) instead of (2) to simplify the asymptotic analysis, all the results hold if we replace (3) by (2).

[3] In general, the graph is not random unless k is a multiple of n. The randomness can be maintained by modifying this technique in the following way: in Figure 2, select the first vertex of each pair according to the message M instead of the given order for the vertices. E.g., the first node will be v_l where the binary expression of l: $l_2 = m_0 m_1 \cdots m_{\lfloor \log_2 n \rfloor}$. In practice, we restrict k to be multiples of n to keep the randomness.

more colors we need to mark the graph. Since the number of colors is one of the most important criteria for the quality of coloring scheme, we want to keep this overhead as low as possible. One question is: how many edges can we add into the graph without introducing a large amount of overhead? Formally speaking: finding $k(n)$, the number of edges can be embedded into an n-vertex random graph, such that $\overline{\lim_{n \to \infty}} \chi' - \chi < \infty$.

Theorem 3.1
Adding $k(n)$ edges to a random graph $G_{n,p}$, for almost all $G_{n,p}$, $\overline{\lim_{n \to \infty}} \chi' - \chi = \infty$ iff $k(n) \in \omega(n \log n)$.

Corollary 3.2 (1-color overhead)
Adding $k(n)$ edges to graph $G_{n,p}$, if $\lim_{n \to \infty} \frac{k(n)}{n \ln n} = l$, then $\overline{\lim_{n \to \infty}} \chi' - \chi \leq 1 + \frac{l}{1-p}$.
In particular, if $k(n) \in o(n \log n)$, for almost all $G_{n,p}$, the overhead is at most 1.

A good watermark should be able to provide any desired level of confidence. I.e., the authorship can be proved with a probability almost 1 when the graph goes large. Obviously one extra edge cannot bring high credibility. The following theorem answers the question: finding $k(n)$, the number of edges to be embedded into a n-vertex random graph, such that $\mathbf{Prob}[\mathcal{E}] \to 0$ as $n \to \infty$, where $\mathcal{E}$ is the event that in a random solution all these $k(n)$ constraints are satisfied.

Theorem 3.3 (arbitrarily high credibility)
Adding $k(n)$ edges to a random graph $G_{n,p}$, let $\mathcal{E}$ be the event that a random solution to the original graph also satisfies all these $k(n)$ extra constraints. Then for almost all $G_{n,p}$, $\lim_{n \to \infty} \mathbf{Prob}[\mathcal{E}] = 0$ if $k(n) \in \omega(\frac{n}{\log n})$.

To summarize the "*adding edges*" technique, we conclude: adding $k(n) \in \omega(\frac{n}{\log n}) \cap o(n \log n)$ extra edges into graph $G_{n,p}$, as n goes large, arbitrarily high credibility can be achieved with at most 1-color-overhead. More precisely, we define the *watermark potential* (by adding edges) for graph $G_{n,p}$:

$$(5) \qquad WP(G_{n,p}) = \chi(G_{n,p}) - \frac{n}{2 \log_b n}$$

This function describes the power of the "*adding edges*" technique on random graphs. We list several properties of this function with respect to n (for p, similar results hold):

(a) $0 \leq WP(G_{n,p}) < 1$ for all graph $G_{n,p}$.
(b) **periodic:** χ is a non-decreasing step function and $\frac{n}{2 \log_b n}$ is continuous and increasing. So $WP(G_{n,p})$ behaves periodically for different values of χ,
(c) **starting points:** χ increases by 1 at the start of each period $WP(G_{n,p})$ achieves its local maximum.
(d) **locally decreasing:** In each period, since χ is constant, as n increases, $WP(G_{n,p})$ decreases.
(e) **increasing period:** When n grows by 1, $\frac{n}{2 \log_b n}$ will increase roughly by $\frac{1}{2 \log_b n}$. Thus, the period is about $2 \log_b n$. (a little larger than $2 \log_b n$ to be more precise, since $b = \frac{1}{1-p}$ also increases.)

4   Watermarking Technique #2 — Selecting MIS

4.1   Technique Statement

A maximal independent set (**MIS**) of a graph is a subset of vertices S such that vertices in S are not connected and vertices not in S are connected to at least one vertex of S. This second technique takes advantage of the fact that vertices in one MIS can all be labeled by a single color.

Signature embedding:

Given a graph $G(V, E)$ and a message M to be embedded in G. We order the vertices set $V = (v_0, v_1, \cdots, v_{n-1})$ and encrypt the message into a binary string $M = m_0 m_1 \cdots$. The message M is embedded into the graph G as shown in Figure 9 (see the Appendices). The idea is to select one or more MISes according to M, assign each MIS with one color and then color the rest of the graph. The MIS containing M is constructed in the following way: choose v_i as the first vertex of the MIS, where the binary expression of i coincides the first $\lfloor \log_2 n \rfloor$ bits of M; then we cut v_i and its neighbors from the graph since they cannot be in the same MIS as v_i; we reorder the vertices and select the next vertex of the MIS based on M. When we get a MIS, we color it with one color, remove it from the original graph and start constructing the second MIS if M has not been completely embedded.

A small example of an 11-node graph with the embedded message $1998_{10} = 11111001110_2$ is shown in Figure 4, where we use three colors to color the graph $\{v_1, v_4, v_7, v_{10}\}$, $\{v_0, v_2, V_5, v_6\}$, and $\{v_3, v_8, v_9\}$. From 11 nodes, we choose node 7 to embed the first three bits of M, 111. Then all node 7's neighbors are crossed and the rest nodes are reordered; the node with the new index 3 is picked based on the next two bits 11; after cutting this node's neighbors, we obtain a MIS of the original nodes $\{1,4,7,10\}$ which we mark by one color; reorder the rest 6 nodes and continue the procedure till M is completely embedded.

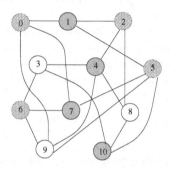

Fig. 4. An example.

Signature recovering:

The selected MIS with a particular order of its vertices is the watermark. We can retrieve a binary string from this watermark by reconstructing the MIS in the specific order. For example, in Figure 4, 11111 is the information hidden behind the MIS $\{v_7, v_4, v_1, v_{10}\}$ in that order. The first vertex v_7 is node No. 7 in the original 11-vertex graph, so we have the first three bits $111_2(= 7_{10})$. After deleting v_7 and its neighbors, there are 7 vertices left. We reorder the vertices and claim the next two bits from the second vertex of the MIS v_4, which is now node No. 3 in the new graph. From the number 3 we get bits 11. Removing v_4 and its neighbors from the new graph gives us two isolated vertices v_1 and v_{10}, no further information can be hidden and this completes the given MIS. Similarly, the rest of the (encrypted) message 001110 is hidden in the second MIS $\{v_0, v_6, v_5, v_2\}$ in that order.

The uniqueness of the selected MIS determines the credibility. In Figure 4, vertex v_1 may be involved in any of the following MISes: $\{v_1, v_3, v_7, v_8, v_9\}$, $\{v_1, v_4, v_6, v_{10}\}, \{v_1, v_4, v_7, v_{10}\}, \{v_1, v_6, v_8\}$. The order of the vertices in the MIS also plays a very important role[4]. If we order the MIS $\{v_1, v_4, v_7, v_{10}\}$ by the indices, following the same watermarking scheme, the hidden binary string becomes to 0010101 instead of 11111.

4.2   Technique Analysis

Our goal is to analyze this technique follow the framework we built in the previous section. In particular, we are interested in finding formulae for overhead and credibility.

First, we claim that after removing one randomly selected MIS, the remaining graph is still random with the same edge probability. One way to generate a random graph $G_{n+1,p}$ is to add one new vertex into a random graph $G_{n,p}$ and add an edge between the new vertex and each of the old vertex in $G_{n,p}$ with probability p. Reversing this procedure says that deleting one vertex from $G_{n,p}$ results in a random graph $G_{n-1,p}$. Since the neighbors of one vertex are also random, it follows that the graph will maintain its randomness after erasing one vertex and all its neighbors.

The first vertex of the MIS can be selected randomly, while the choices for the second vertex are restricted to $(1-p)n = qn$, because all the pn neighbors of the first vertex have been eliminated. In general, only $q^k n$ vertices are left as candidate for the (k+1)th vertex of the MIS. Therefore, we have:

Lemma 4.1

Given random graph $G_{n,p}$, almost all randomly selected MIS is of size $\log_b n$, where $b = \frac{1}{1-p}$.

The strength of the watermark relies on the uniqueness of the MISes we constructed as well as a specific order of the vertices in each MIS. To create a

---

[4]   For a given MIS of size k, selecting these k vertices in different orders delivers different messages. However, it is unlikely to get the same MIS from different messages (after encryption).

convincible watermark in a large graph, we have to add $\omega(\frac{n}{\log n})$ edges by the first technique. The same goal can be achieved by selecting only one MIS:

Theorem 4.2 (arbitrarily high credibility with 1-color overhead)
Given a random graph $G_{n,p}$, we select one MIS as in Figure 9. Let $\mathcal{E}$ be the event that in a random solution, all vertices in this MIS have the same color and they are in the order as specified by Figure 4. Then $\lim_{n \to \infty} \mathbf{Prob}\,[\mathcal{E}] = 0$. Furthermore, this introduces at most 1-color overhead.

By selecting one vertex from an n-vertex graph, we can embed $\lfloor \log_2 n \rfloor$ bits. From Lemma 4.1, at most $\log_2 \cdot n \log_b n$ bits of information could be embedded into the MIS. To embed long messages, we have to construct more MISes,[5] which may result in huge overhead.

Theorem 4.3
Given a random graph $G_{n,p}$, if we select $k(n)$ MISes as in Figure 9, assign each MIS one color and color the rest of the graph, then the overhead is at most $k(n)$ and on average at least $\frac{k(n)}{2}$.

5   Watermarking Technique # 3 – Adding Nodes and Edges

5.1   Technique Statement

Signature embedding:
    Given a random graph $G_{n,p}$ and a message M to be embedded. We order the vertices set $V = (v_0, v_1, \cdots, v_{n-1})$ and encrypt the message into a binary string $M = m_0 m_1 \cdots$ which is then embedded into $G_{n,p}$ as follows: introduce a new node v, take the first $\lfloor \log n \rfloor$ bits from M, find the corresponding vertex v' and connect it to v; take the next $\lfloor \log n - 1 \rfloor$ bits and locate the next vertex to which v is connected ($n - 1$ since v' has to be excluded); continue till we add np edges starting from v and get a new graph $G_{n+1,p}$; introduce another new node if M has not been completely embedded. We color the new graph, restrict the coloring scheme to the original graph $G_{n,p}$ and we have a solution with message M embedded.

Signature recovering:
    This watermark is hard to detect because of the invisibility of the new added nodes and their associated edges. To exhibit the hidden signature in a colored graph, we have to go through the signature embedding procedure again and show that the encrypted signature can be added into the colored graph as edges to the newly inserted vertices without any conflicts. This has to be coupled with a statement of the unlikelihood that this happens for any random message. As we discussed earlier, many different binary strings can be generated in the same way

---

[5] Alternatively, we can map long messages to a fixed length message by hash functions. Since hash function is many-to-one, this brings ambiguity which depends on the hash function itself. Such analysis is out of the scope of this paper.

from the same colored graph, but to fake one corresponds to a one-way function with a specific information is not easy.

5.2   Technique Analysis

Suppose k new nodes have been added into the initial graph $G_{n,p}$ to accommodate the message, similar to the previous two techniques, it is clear that the embedded graph is an instance of $G_{n+k,p}$[6]. This guarantees that randomness of the watermarked graph and hence the validity of the formula (3) which implies an overhead in the amount of $\chi' - \chi = \lceil \frac{n+k}{2\log_b(n+k)} \rceil - \lceil \frac{n}{2\log_b n} \rceil$, where $b = \frac{1}{1-p}$.

We have defined the watermark potential for graph $G_{n,p}$ as $WP(G_{n,p}) = \chi(G_{n,p}) - \frac{n}{2\log_b n}$. A large $WP(G_{n,p})$ means there is still room for adding new nodes and/or edges into $G_{n,p}$ without introducing a new color, especially at the starting point of each period (property (c) of function $WP(G_{n,p})$ in section 3.3). From the step function nature of χ, we have

Theorem 5.1 (1-color overhead)
Given a random graph $G_{n,p}$, we introduce $k(n)$ new vertices and associate edges based on the signature, then for almost all $G_{n,p}$, the overhead is at most 1 if $k(n) \in o(\log n)$.

A graph of χ colors is essentially a partition of the vertices to χ independent sets. The neighbors of any new vertex can be selected randomly from these χ set. However, to add one new vertex v without bringing a new color, v's neighbors have to be chosen from at most $\chi - 1$ independent sets. It is not hard to see that when many edges have to be added, it is unlikely that none of these edges ending into a specific independent set.

Theorem 5.2 (arbitrarily high credibility)
We build graph $G_{n+1,p}$ from a given random graph $G_{n,p}$ by introducing one new vertex and np edges. A coloring scheme to the initial $G_{n,p}$ is obtained by coloring $G_{n+1,p}$. Let $\mathcal{E}$ be the event: add a vertex v to the colored graph $G_{n,p}$, connect v to np random vertices, and v does not require a new color. Then $\lim_{n\to\infty} \mathbf{Prob}[\mathcal{E}] = 0$ for almost all $G_{n,p}$.

6   Simulation and Experimental Results

6.1   Numerical Simulation for Techniques # 1 and # 2

We conduct simulation in the ideal case assuming we know how to color the graph optimally. In the "adding edges" technique, we add extra edges into the original graph corresponding to the signature. Figure 5 shows for graph $G_{n,0.5}$ ($500 \leq n \leq 1000$), the number of edges can be added (y-axis) with 0-overhead ($k_0(n)$, shown as black dots) and 1-color overhead ($k_1(n)$, shown as grey triangles), the

---

[6] For the last node, we can add edges randomly or repeat the message to make sure it has $(n + k - 1)p$ neighbors.

curve in between is the difference of $k_0(n)$ and $k_1(n)$. Revisiting the properties of the watermark potential function, we see that $WP(G_{n,p})$ describes correctly the amount of information can be embedded into graph $G_{n,p}$.

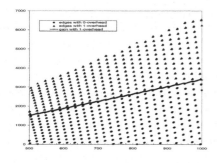

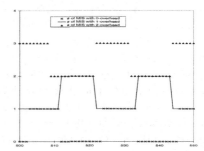

Fig. 5. Numerical data for # 1.   **Fig. 6.** Numerical data for # 2.

In Figure 6, for graph $G_{n,0.5}$ ($500 \leq n \leq 550$),the numbers of MISes (y-axis) that can be constructed within 2-color overhead are given. One observation is that the number of MISes as a function of n for the same number of overhead is piecewise constant. This has been predicted from the proof of Theorem 4.3. Another fact is that when we select one MIS, with 50% probability there will be a 1-color overhead. The reason is that the increment on $\frac{n}{2\log_b n}$ by selecting one MIS is around $\frac{1}{2}$ and $\mathbf{Prob}[\lceil x - \frac{1}{2}\rceil = \lceil x \rceil] = 0.5$.

6.2   Experimental Results

The main goal of the experiment is to compare the difficulty of coloring the original graphs vs. the watermarked graphs, as well as the quality of the solution. For this purpose, we choose three types of graphs: random graphs $G_{n,p}$, graphs generated from real-life benchmarks, and the DIMACS challenge graph. For each type of graphs, we do the simulation in three steps: (1) color the original graph, (2) apply the watermarking techniques to embed a random message, (3) color the watermarked graph. Each graph is colored 10 times and the average result is reported. All experiments are conducted on 200MHz UltraSparcII and 40 MHz SPARC 4 processors using the algorithm in [7]. The same parameters are used for the original and watermarked graph.

Table 1 shows the results on random graphs $G_{n,0.5}$, and the corresponding watermarked graphs by adding n and $2n$ random edges or by selecting one MIS. The columns labeled *color* are the average numbers of colors on 10 trials for each instance, while the *best* columns are the best solutions from the 10 trials, and the columns *mesg* measure the amount of information (in bits) being embedded in the graph.

Table 1. Coloring the watermarked $G_{n,0.5}$.

Original $G_{n,0.5}$		Adding n Edges			Adding $2n$ Edges			Selecting 1 MIS		
n	color	best	color	best	mesg	color	best	mesg	color	best	mesg
125	19	19	19	19	125	19	19	250	19	19	42
250	30	30	30.2	30	250	30.2	30	500	30	30	80
500	50.1	50	50.4	50	500	50.6	50	1000	50.2	50	81
1000	85.8	85	86	85	1000	86.8	86	2000	86	85	110

Table 2 is the result on dense/sparse random graphs. For dense graphs $G_{n,0.9}$, there is not much space left to add extra edges, so it is expensive to watermark dense graphs by adding edges. On the other hand, the size of MIS for dense graph is relatively small, therefore very limited information can be embedded by selecting MISes. For sparse graphs $G_{n,0.1}$, both techniques perform well.

Table 2. Coloring other watermarked $G_{n,p}$.

Original $G_{n,p}$			Add n Edges	Add $2n$ Edges	Select 1 MIS	Select 2 MISes
n	p	color				
125	0.9	46	49.1	52	47	47.3
250	0.9	77.9	79	82	77.2	77
250	0.1	9	9.1	9.8	9	9.8
500	0.1	13.9	14	14.2	14	14.2

When applying to the on-line challenge graph at the DIMACS site [12], for the graph with 1000 vertices and 249826 edges which implies an edge probability slightly larger than 0.5, we restrict the run-time to 1 hour and get the results from 10 trials shown in Table 3. In the 10 trials for the original graph, we find two 85-color solutions and the average number of colors is 86.1. The second column is the amount of information (in bits) being added into the graph. The last column shows the probability of coincidence, where low coincidence means high credibility. One can see both methods provide high credibility with little degradation of the solution's quality.

For the technique of "adding vertices and edges", we start from a random graph $G_{125,0.5}$ and introduce new vertex (and certain number of edges to keep the edge probability) one by one till we reach an instance of $G_{549,0.5}$. Then we color each of these 425 graphs 10 times and plot the average number of required colors in Figure 7. The results for the last 50 instances are enlarged as shown in Figure 8

The graph coloring problem has a lot of applications in real life, for example, the register allocation problem, the cache-line coloring problem, wavelength assignment in optical networks, and channel assignment in cellular systems. The instances of GC problems based on register allocation of variables in real codes and the optimal solutions are available at [13]. We watermark these graphs and

Table 3. Coloring the watermarked DIMACS benchmark.

Edges Added	Information	Colors	Overhead	Coincidence
0	0	86.1	-	-
500	500	85.8	-0.3	2.89e-03
1000	1000	87	0.9	9.55e-06
3000	3000	87	0.9	8.71e-16

MIS Selected	Information	Colors	Overhead	Coincidence
1	110	86.2	0.1	3.52e-17
2	210	86.4	0.3	1.24e-33
3	300	87	0.9	8.51e-50
4	390	87.4	1.3	5.85e-66
5	480	87.4	1.3	2.06e-82
6	590	87.9	1.8	7.24e-99

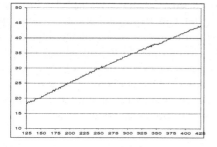

Fig. 7. Numerical data for # 1.

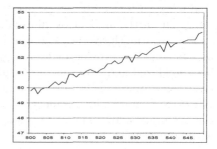

Fig. 8. Numerical data for # 2.

then color them. The *fpsol2* and *inithx* instances are colored in $1 \sim 3$ minutes, while the others are all colored in less than 0.5 minute. Table 4 reports the details. The first four columns shows the characteristic of the original graph and the known optimal solution; the next two are for technique #1, showing the number of edges (information in bits) being embedded and the overhead; followed by two columns for technique #2, where the *Size* columns are the number of vertices in the selected MISes. The last two columns are for technique #3, where we compute the average edge probability of the original graph and add edges to keep this probability unchanged. Again, in almost all examples, there is no overhead.

7   Conclusion

Most watermarking techniques lack formal analysis and their effectiveness solely relies on the experiments. In this paper, we build the first theoretical framework for analyzing watermarking techniques. In particular, we select two of the most

Table 4. Coloring watermarked real-life graphs.

Original Instance			Optimal	Add n Edge		Select 1 MIS		Add 1 Vertex	
Instance	Vertices	Edges	Coloring	Edges	Colors	Size	Colors	Edge	Colors
fpsol2.i.1.col	496	11654	65	496	65	229	65	47	65
fpsol2.i.2.col	451	8691	30	451	30	90	30	38	30
fpsol2.i.3.col	425	8688	30	425	30	64	30	40	30
inithx.i.1.col	864	18707	54	864	54	347	54	43	54
inithx.i.2.col	645	13979	31	645	31	89	31	43	31
inithx.i.3.col	621	13969	31	621	31	64	31	45	31
mulsol.i.1.col	197	3925	49	197	49	61	49	40	49
mulsol.i.2.col	188	3885	31	188	32	17	32	41	31
mulsol.i.3.col	184	3916	31	184	32	12	32	42	31
mulsol.i.4.col	185	3946	31	185	31	12	31	42	31
mulsol.i.5.col	186	3973	31	186	31	12	31	42	31
zeroin.i.1.col	211	4100	49	211	49	87	49	39	49
zeroin.i.2.col	211	3541	30	211	30	56	30	33	30
zeroin.i.3.col	206	3540	30	206	30	51	30	34	30

important criteria for any effective watermark, namely high credibility and low overhead, as the basis of our analysis. We propose three watermarking techniques for the graph coloring problem, which are provably capable to provide high credibility with at most 1-color overhead for large graphs. Asymptotic formulae are given on the amount of information that can be embedded into the graph without too much overhead as well as the amount of information that should be embedded to provide high credibility. Numerical data from simulation has been analyzed and confirms our results. Also, we watermark and then color a large range of graphs from random graphs, DIMACS challenge graph to graphs generated from real life problems. With the same amount of run-time as for the original graphs, for almost all instances, we obtain solutions of the same quality with no overhead.

References

1. H.Berghel and L.O'Gorman. *Protecting ownership rights through digital water-marking*. IEEE computer, 29(7): 101-103, 1996.   350
2. B.Bollobás. *Random Graphs*. Academic Press, London, 1985.   351
3. L.Boney, A.H.Tewfik, and K.N.Hamdy. *Digital watermark for audio signals*. International Conference on Multimedia Computing and Systems, pp. 473-480, 1996. 350
4. I.J.Cox, J.Kilian, T.Leighton, and T.Shamoon. *A secure, imperceptible yet perceptually salient, spread spectrum watermark for multimedia*. Southcon, pp. 192-197, 1996. 350
5. F. Hartung, and B. Girod, *Digital watermarking of rae and compressed video*. In Proceedings of the SPIE-The Internation Society for Optical Engineering, volume 2952, pages 205-213, 1996.   350
6. A.B. Kahng, J. Lach, W.H. Magione-Smith, S. Mantik, I.L. Markov, M. Potkonjak, P. Tucker, H. Wang and G. Wolfe. *Watermarking Techniques for Intellectual Property Protection*. 35th Design Automation Conference Proceedings, pp. 776-781, 1998. 350
7. D.Kirovski and M.Potkonjak. *Efficient Coloring of a Large Spectrum of Graphs*. 35th Design Automation Conference Proceedings, pp. 427-432, 1998.   360
8. R. Nelson, and R.J. Wilson (Editors) *Graph Colourings*. Longman Scientific & Technical, Harlow,Essex, UK 1990.   351

9. C. Podilchuk, W. Zeng, *Perceptual watermarking of still images*. IEEE Workshop on Multimedia Signal Processing, pp. 363-368, 1997. 350

10. M.D.Swanson, B.Zhu, B.Chau, and A.H.Tewfik. *Object-based transparent video watermarking*. IEEE Workshop in Multimedia Signal Processing, pp. 369-374, 1997. 350

11. M.M.Yeung, F.C.Mintzer, G.W.Braudaway, and A.R.Rao. *Digital watermarking for high-quality imaging*. IEEE Workshop on Multimedia Signal Processing, pp. 357-362, 1997. 350

12. http://dimacs.rutgers.edu/ 351, 361

13. http://mat.gsia.cmu.edu/COLOR/instances.html 361

8 Appendices

8.1 Proof of Theorem 3.1

Theorem 3.1
Adding $k(n)$ edges to a random graph $G_{n,p}$, for almost all $G_{n,p}$, $\overline{\lim_{n\to\infty}} \chi' - \chi = \infty$ iff $k(n) \in \omega(n \log n)$.

Proof:

In the original graph $G_{n,p}$, let $b = \frac{1}{1-p}$ and $\chi = \lceil \frac{n}{2\log_b n} \rceil$ as given by (3). After adding $k(n)$ extra edges, the edge probability increases to $p' = p + \frac{2k}{n(n-1)}$, and $b' = \frac{1}{1-p'}$, $\chi' = \lceil \frac{n}{2\log_{b'} n} \rceil$.

$$\chi' - \chi = \lceil \frac{n}{2\log_{b'} n} \rceil - \lceil \frac{n}{2\log_b n} \rceil \geq \frac{n}{2\log_{b'} n} - \frac{n}{2\log_b n} - 1 = \log_n (\frac{b'}{b})^{n/2} - 1$$

where $\frac{b'}{b} = \frac{1-p}{1-p'} = 1 + \frac{2k/n(n-1)}{(1-p)-2k/n(n-1)}$.

It is clear that $k(n) \in O(n^2)$, and further if $k(n) \in \Theta(n^2)$ then $\chi' - \chi \to \infty$ as $n \to \infty$. Therefore,

and
$$\lim_{n\to\infty} (\frac{b'}{b})^{\frac{n}{2}} = \lim_{n\to\infty} (1 + \frac{2}{1-p} \frac{k}{n(n-1)})^{\frac{n}{2}} = \lim_{n\to\infty} e^{\frac{k}{(1-p)(n-1)}}$$

$$\overline{\lim_{n\to\infty}} \chi' - \chi \geq \lim_{n\to\infty} \log_n (\frac{b'}{b})^{n/2} - 1 = \lim_{n\to\infty} \frac{k}{(1-p)(n-1)\ln n} - 1$$

So, if $k(n) \in \omega(n \log n)$, $\overline{\lim_{n\to\infty}} \chi' - \chi = \infty$.

On the other hand, since

$$\chi' - \chi = \lceil \frac{n}{2\log_{b'} n} \rceil - \lceil \frac{n}{2\log_b n} \rceil \leq \frac{n}{2\log_{b'} n} + 1 - \frac{n}{2\log_b n} = \log_n (\frac{b'}{b})^{n/2} + 1$$

similarly, we can see if $k(n) \in O(n \log n)$, $\chi' - \chi$ will be bounded.   □

8.2 Proof of Theorem 3.3

Theorem 3.3 (arbitrarily high credibility)
Adding $k(n)$ edges to a random graph $G_{n,p}$, let $\mathcal{E}$ be the event that a random solution to the original graph also satisfies all these $k(n)$ extra constraints. Then for almost all $G_{n,p}$, $\lim_{n\to\infty} \mathbf{Prob}[\mathcal{E}] = 0$ if $k(n) \in \omega(\frac{n}{\log n})$.

Proof:

The event $\mathcal{E}$ is probabilistic equivalent to fixing a GC solution, then selecting $k(n)$ pairs of disconnected vertices and each pair do not have the same color. For random graph $G_{n,p}$, each vertex has $p(n-1)$ neighbors, and if the graph is color by $\chi = \lceil \frac{n}{2\log_b n} \rceil$ colors as given by (3), in average there will be $\lfloor 2\log_b n \rfloor$ vertices for each color. Hence, when we select two disconnected vertices, the probability that they have different colors is $1 - \frac{\lfloor 2\log_b n \rfloor - 1}{q(n-1)}$. Assuming that $k(n)$ pairs of vertices are picked independently, then the probability that the vertices in each pair are of different colors is $(1 - \frac{\lfloor 2\log_b n \rfloor - 1}{q(n-1)})^{k(n)}$.

$$\lim_{n\to\infty} \mathbf{Prob}[\mathcal{E}] = \lim_{n\to\infty} (1 - \frac{\lfloor 2\log_b n \rfloor - 1}{q(n-1)})^{k(n)} \leq \lim_{n\to\infty} (1 - \frac{\log_b n}{qn})^{k(n)}$$

$$= \lim_{n\to\infty} (1 - \frac{\log_b n}{qn})^{\frac{qn}{\log_b n} \frac{k(n)\log_b n}{qn}} = \lim_{n\to\infty} e^{-\frac{k(n)\log_b n}{qn}}$$

$$= 0 \qquad\qquad (\text{ if } k(n) \in \omega(\frac{n}{\log n}) = \omega(\chi).)$$

$\square$

8.3   Proof of Theorem 4.2

Theorem 4.2 (arbitrarily high credibility with 1-color overhead)
Given a random graph $G_{n,p}$, we select one MIS as in Figure 9. Let $\mathcal{E}$ be the event that in a random solution, all vertices in this MIS have the same color and they are in the order as specified by Figure 4. Then $\lim_{n\to\infty} \mathbf{Prob}\,[\mathcal{E}] = 0$. Furthermore, this introduces at most 1-color overhead.

Proof:

For a random graph $G_{n,p}$, the technique in Figure 4 gives us a MIS of size $\log_b n$ by Lemma 4.1. Given a fixed solution to $G_{n,p}$, event $\mathcal{E}$ has the same probability as: constructing all MISes of size $\log_b n$ with a specific order and one randomly picked MIS has all its $\log_b n$ vertices the same color.

From the Stirling formula:

$$k! = (\frac{k}{e})^k \sqrt{2\pi k} e^{\alpha_k}$$

where $\frac{1}{12k+1} < \alpha_k < \frac{1}{12k}$, we have:

$$\mathbf{Prob}[\mathcal{E}] = \frac{1}{\frac{(nq)\cdot(nq^2)\cdots(nq^{\log_b n - 1})}{(\log_b n)!}} = (\frac{1}{q})^{\frac{\log_b n(\log_b n - 1)}{2}} (\frac{1}{n})^{\log_b n - 1} (\log_b n)!$$

$$= (b^{\log_b n})^{\frac{\log_b n - 1}{2}} (\frac{1}{n})^{\log_b n - 1} (\log_b n)! = n^{\frac{1-\log_b n}{2}} (\log_b n)!$$

$$= n^{\frac{1-\log_b n}{2}} (\frac{\log_b n}{e})^{\log_b n} \sqrt{2\pi\log_b n} e^{\alpha_{\log_b n}}$$

$$= \sqrt{2\pi n\log_b n} e^{\alpha_{\log_b n}} (\frac{\log_b n}{e\sqrt{n}})^{\log_b n}$$

$$\to 0 \qquad (n \to \infty)_1$$

where $\frac{1}{12\log_b n+1} < \alpha_{\log_b n} < \frac{1}{12\log_b n}$.

It costs exactly one color for the selected MIS, and coloring the remaining graph requires no more than the number of colors for the original graph. Therefore, this introduces at most one extra color overhead. $\square$

8.4 Proof of Theorem 4.3

Theorem 4.3
Given a random graph $G_{n,p}$, if we select $k(n)$ MISes as in Figure 9, assign each MIS one color and color the rest of the graph, then the overhead is at most $k(n)$ and on average at least $\frac{k(n)}{2}$.

Proof:
The first part is trivial from the fact that χ is non-decreasing in terms of n.

By Lemma 4.1, the MIS is of size $\log_b n$. Assuming the message is random, after we cut this MIS from the original graph $G_{n,p}$, the remaining graph will still be random with $n' = n - \log_b n$ vertices and the same edge probability p. Therefore, from formula (4) in section 3.2, we need $\chi' = \lceil \frac{n'}{2 \log_b n'} \rceil$ colors to color this remaining graph, taking into account one more color for the selected MIS, we use a total of $\chi' + 1$ colors to color the original graph $G_{n,p}$.

$$\chi' + 1 - \chi = \lceil \frac{n'}{2 \log_b n'} \rceil + 1 - \lceil \frac{n}{2 \log_b n} \rceil = \lceil \frac{n - \log_b n}{2 \log_b (n - \log_b n)} \rceil + 1 - \lceil \frac{n}{2 \log_b n} \rceil$$

$$= \lceil (\frac{n}{2 \log_b n} - \frac{1}{2}) \log_{(n - \log_b n)} n \rceil + 1 - \lceil \frac{n}{2 \log_b n} \rceil$$

$$\geq \lceil \frac{n}{2 \log_b n} - \frac{1}{2} \rceil + 1 - \lceil \frac{n}{2 \log_b n} \rceil$$

since $\quad \log_{(n - \log_b n)} n > 1$

For a uniformly distributed real number x, $\mathbf{Prob}(\lceil x - \frac{1}{2} \rceil = \lceil x \rceil) = 0.5$. Therefore, when we construct one MIS by Figure 9, we will introduce one extra color overhead with probability at least 50%. And when we construct two MISes, for sure we will introduce at least one-color-overhead since $\lceil \chi - 1 \rceil = \lceil \chi \rceil - 1$. In general, when $k(n)$ MISes are selected, the size of the remaining graph $n' \geq n - k \log_b n$ because the size of MIS decreases with the size of the graph. So

$$\chi' + k(n) - \chi \geq \lceil \frac{n}{2 \log_b n} - \frac{k(n)}{2} \rceil + 1 - \lceil \frac{n}{2 \log_b n} \rceil \sim \frac{k(n)}{2}$$

$\square$

8.5   Pseudo-code for Technique #2

Input: a graph $G(V, E)$, a message $M = m_0 m_1 \ldots$ **Output:** new graph with message M embedded

Algorithm:
 current_graph = original_graph $G(V, E)$;
 previous_graph = current_graph;
 MIS = ϕ;
 do { **if** (current_graph is empty)
     { current_graph = previous_graph - MIS;
       previous_graph = current_graph;
       report MIS and reset MIS = ϕ; }
     if (current_graph has more than 2 vertices or is connected)
     { find the vertex v corresponding to the next $\lfloor \log_2 n \rfloor$
       bits of M, where n is the size of the current graph;
       cut v and all its neighbors from the current graph;
       current_graph = current_graph - $\{v$ and its neighbors$\}$;
       MIS = MIS + v;
       reorder the vertices in current_graph;
       advance message M.
     } **else** MIS = MIS + current_graph;
   }**while**(M is not empty)
 report the current_graph;

Fig. 9. Pseudo code for watermarking technique # 2.

Robust Object Watermarking: Application to Code

Julien P. Stern[1,2], Gaël Hachez[1], François Koeune[1], and
Jean-Jacques Quisquater[1]

[1] UCL Crypto Group,
Batiment Maxwell, Place du Levant, 3, B-1348 Louvain-la-Neuve, Belgique
{stern,hachez,fkoeune,jjq}@dice.ucl.ac.be
[2] Laboratoire de Recherche en Informatique, Université de Paris-Sud,
Batiment 490, F-91405 Orsay Cedex, France
stern@lri.fr

Abstract. In this paper, we focus on a step of the watermarking process whose importance has been disregarded so far. In this perspective, we introduce the *vector extraction paradigm* which is the transformation between digital data and an abstract vector representation of these data. As an application, we propose a new, robust technique in order to insert watermarks in executable code.

1 Introduction

The tremendous growth of the Internet probably marks the beginning of a new era in communications. Any digital document can be duplicated and distributed in a matter of minutes by means of a simple mouse click. Because of the very low cost of this kind of distribution and the availability of high quality printing and audio devices, digital distribution seems to be an attractive direction for the near future. However, no valuable document is currently being sold that way, as the cost of duplication and the quality of an illegally redistributed document is just the same as the original.

As it is impossible to prevent the copy of a digital document, a new direction is being explored, which consists in dissuading an user to redistribute his legitimate copy, by permanently embedding some piece of information in the data so as to enable tracing. This leads to a very large amount of research in the domain of watermarking and techniques to robustly embed information in many different types of media have been pursued.

While many solutions exist when the data to be marked is an image, a video or an audio record, several types of data still seem to resist unobtrusive and robust information embedding. In particular, text documents, source code and machine code create difficulties, notably because their structure allows a very low level of modifications.

In this paper, we show that, as far as machine code is concerned, we can take advantage of the difficulty to modify data to create a very robust way of

A. Pfitzmann (Ed.): IH'99, LNCS 1768, pp. 368–378, 2000.

embedding information. We also argue that, paradoxically, a lower level of tolerance versus modifications yields more robust watermarking schemes. In other words, we believe that the possibility of performing unobtrusive modifications are helping an attacker to defeat a marking scheme much more than it helps a legitimate user to mark a data.

We also introduce a new paradigm, the vector extraction paradigm (VEP), which is an important step between the raw digital data and the object that will actually be marked. The VEP allows to apply generic schemes to any type of data and to define classes of attacks against which a scheme will resist against.

Our technique differs from previous approaches by the representation we take of machine code. We do not consider it as a linear succession of instructions, nor do we use its execution flow, but rather we view the code as a whole statistical object. More precisely, the entity that we are actually going to mark is the function representing the frequencies of groups of consecutive assembly instructions in the code. With this approach, we strongly limit the range of modifications that can be applied to the marked object.

Outline: In section 2, we discuss related work. Section 3 introduces the *vector extraction paradigm* and section 4 presents our solution. Finally, implementation issues are discussed in section 5.

2   Related Work

There has been a very large amount of work in the domain of watermarking. We can however distinguish two main models.

The first one represents the data to be marked as a vector and the mark as a word on an alphabet. Each "letter" of this word is embedded in each component of the data vector. In the simplest case, the data and the mark are binary strings, and each bit of the data is flipped depending on the value of the corresponding bit in the mark. This model allows a nice modeling of the watermarking process and leads to the most sophisticated watermarking protocols [1,15,13,12,14]. Its main drawback, however, is that it is mostly a theoretical model. In order to be secure in practice, the size of the marks often would have to be larger than the data itself!

The second model takes its roots in the spread spectrum technique, and was first introduced in [4]. This model, which is harder to manipulate as a building block for complicated protocols, allows for practical and robust insertion of marks. The security of such an insertion techniques has been proven in [9] under an assumption restricting the range of alterations performed on the marked data. Interestingly, [7] recently showed an attack which matches the security bound obtained in [9], namely, for a data represented as a vector of size n, $O(\sqrt{n/\log n})$ different marked copies are sufficient to delete the mark, but $\Omega(\sqrt{n/\log n})$ are not.

On the side of these generic techniques, a lot of work has been performed in order to embed marks in *specific* data. We refer the reader to [5] for a summary of such techniques when the data is an image. A more recent and less data specific survey can be found in [11].

There have been very few published results for software marking. [8] simply writes a specific mark in a specific place in the file, [6] reorders blocks of instructions to form a signature. In [2] a good summary of existing techniques is given, and a method to mark code using the topology of dynamic heap data structure is presented.

While these techniques take advantage of the structure of source or executable code, they are, in spirit, following the first model above. Hence, except possibly in the case of tremendously large data, we believe that a sufficient level of security will not be obtained.

The main difference of our approach is that we will extract a representation of machine code which allows the use of spread spectrum techniques, thus yielding more robust schemes.

3   The Vector Extraction Paradigm

A typical application of spread spectrum watermarking techniques (such as [4]) represents the data to be marked as a vector and modifies each of the vector components by a very small random (but known) amount, the *mark*. The presence of this mark is then tested by correlation. The security of such a technique relies on the assumption that in the space of the vectors which represent the data, a large degradation of the usability of the data implies a large distance between the corresponding vectors in the vector space, and conversely.

However, we believe there is one step missing: a piece of data is *not* a vector. A piece of data can be represented by many different vectors, in many different spaces. So, before actually applying marking techniques, there is a need to extract a vector from the data. This extraction step, which is implicit in most currently published works, is very important, as it will define which types of attacks the scheme will resist. We now present a robustness framework for data marking:

1. Start with a piece of data and provide a (possibly non-invertible) transformation which gives a vector from the data. Define a distance d on the vector space (We call this first step the *extraction step*);
2. List possible attacks that can modify the data without altering its usability;
3. Show that, after these attacks, the distance of the modified vector to the original one is small.

If the above can be shown, then we can apply techniques such as [4] or any other spread-spectrum techniques and apply the security framework of [9,7]. Of course, all published schemes are already using (sometimes implicitly) a vector extraction step. What we want to underline here is that this step is *fundamental*: choosing one VEP or another will result in a scheme being robust against different classes of attacks.

If we list the classical requirements on watermarks, we can separate those that will depend on the VEP from those that will only depend on the spread-spectrum technique in use. This distinction between VEP and vector marking allows us to benefit from the large attention the second problem has already received. The imperceptibility and the robustness of the watermark will depend on the VEP (as stated in the previous paragraph). But other properties such as watermark recovery with or without the original data, watermark extraction or verification of presence for a given watermark will depend on the chosen spread-spectrum technique. For example, we know from spread spectrum theory that insertion – by a malicious adversary or not – of a second watermark will not induce a sufficient modification of the first one, which will with very high probability remain visible; as this property is inherent to spread spectrum technique and does not depend on our VEP, we can rely on this theory.

Note that step 2 is very subjective because "usability" of data usually cannot be properly defined. However, consider the following setting: the data to be marked is an image, the extraction step yields a vector whose coefficients are the DCT coefficients of the image, the distance chosen is the Euclidean one. If we perform on the image a flip around its vertical central axis, we will obtain a new image, whose quality is comparable to the original one. Furthermore, this operation obviously does not remove the mark. However, the detection algorithm will fail to find the mark, because the distance between the new and the old vector will be very large.[1]

This means that marking the DCT coefficients of an image using spread spectrum techniques will not resist against this specific attack. On the other hand, it will resist against JPEG compression very well, because even a high compression will result in a small variation of the distance in the vector space.

We refer the reader to [10] for many attacks on different types of data which all work by finding a transformation which heavily modifies the structure of the extracted vector.

Now, consider the case of executable code. The margin to modify such data is low, because the *correctness* of the output of the code has to be preserved. Hence, an (hopefully) exhaustive list of attacks can be given. If we can exhibit a vector extraction step, a distance on the corresponding vector space and show that all the attacks in the list result in a small variation in distance, we will have a robust method of marking.

It is interesting to note that images were the first target of choice for watermarking, certainly because of the ease to unobtrusively modify an image. We argue that this ease turns out to be a disadvantage. As a matter of fact, it will be extremely difficult to find a vector representation and a distance that will resist against the very broad range of modifications available. Hence, we conjecture that robust image marking will be almost infeasible, at least using spread spectrum techniques.

---

[1] Of course, if we flip the image again before testing, the watermark will be detected, but this requires this specific operation to be done.

4 Our Solution

4.1 Specificity of Codemarking

Imperceptibility of the watermark is one important requirement, but its meaning will vary with the data to be watermarked. It will for example be very different for an image (invisibility) than for an audio record (inaudibleness).

As far as code is concerned, imperceptibility means the correctness of the program must be preserved. By correctness, we mean that the observable behaviour of the code is not modified. More formally, we must have this property (based on the definition of code obfuscation in [3]).

Let C be a code and and C' the watermarked C code. C and C' must have the same observable behaviour. That is, with a given input:

1. If C fails to terminate or terminate with an error, then C' must fails to terminate or terminate with an error.
2. Otherwise, C' must terminate and produce exactly the same output as C.

Note that [2] also proposed a definition for the correctness preservation of the code. This definition is based on semantic preservation but this is more restrictive than our definition.

4.2 Vector Extraction Step

The main difference of our scheme compared to previous work is in the vector extraction step that we apply to the code prior to marking. Our choice was motivated by the fact that the modifications which can be applied to a code are mainly local ones and functions reordering. Hence, we looked for a vector extraction step that would not be structurally changed by blocks reordering and that would be only slightly modified by local modifications.

Vector Extraction Let n be a security parameter. We define a set S of n ordered groups of machine language instructions. For each group of instructions i in S, we compute the frequency c_i of this group in the code (e.g. the number of occurrences of this group divided by the size of the code), and we form the vector $c = (c_1, \ldots, c_n)$. This vector, that we call the *extracted vector*, is the entity we are going to mark. The distance we define on the vector space is the Euclidean norm.

4.3 The Scheme

For clarity of discussion, we briefly detail the rest of the algorithm, which is a simple application of [4].

Initialisation We set a detection threshold δ ($0 < \delta < 1$).

Watermark Insertion

1. We apply the vector extraction step to obtain a vector c (of length n).
2. We choose a n coordinates vector $w = (w_1, \ldots, w_n)$ whose coefficients are randomly distributed following a normal law with standard deviation α.
3. We modify the code in such a way that the new extracted vector $\tilde{c}$ is $c + w$. (This step will be detailed in section 4.4).

Watermark Testing

1. We apply the extraction step to obtain a vector d.
2. We compute a similarity measure Q between $d - \tilde{c}$ and w, e.g.:

$$Q = \sum_{i=1}^{n} \frac{(d_i - \tilde{c}_i)w_i}{\sqrt{(d_i - \tilde{c}_i)^2}} \quad .$$

3. If Q is higher than δ then the algorithm outputs "marked" else it outputs "unmarked".

4.4   Details

We now consider precisely the problem of modifying the frequencies of groups of instructions in the code to obtain a given frequency.

Recall that we are starting with an extracted vector $c = (c_1, \ldots, c_n)$, with the c_i representing the number of occurrences of the group of instruction i in the code. What we want is to modify the code in such a way that the new extracted vector is $\tilde{c} = c + w$ for some vector w.

In order to do so, we will randomly perform a small modification to the code, (while preserving its correctness) and compute the new frequency vector. If the new frequency vector is closer to $\tilde{c}$ than the previous one, we accept the modification and start again, else we simply refuse the modification. Our technique is actually a very simple case of probabilistic stabilising algorithms.

The modifications that we will apply, depend on the specificity of the assembly language we are working with. A study of these modifications in the case of the x86 language is given in section 5.

4.5   Analysis of Attacks

We now informally analyze the attacks which can be applied to a program. Because of the inflexibility of machine code, we can summarise most (if not all) the attacks that can be applied, and thus argue that our solution is really robust.

We believe that there are five different attacks that can be mounted which could modify the frequencies we are working with:

Local modifications This attack modifies the code in a similar way as we did in order to insert the mark.

Code reordering This attack modifies the code by reordering large independent pieces of codes. This attack defeats many schemes which uses the structure of the code. In our case however, it will only slightly modify the frequencies (of groups larger than one instruction), and will be considered as a local modification.

Code addition The attacker can add a (possibly) large piece of code to the initial program. This piece of code should either not be executed or do nothing (to preserve the functionality of the initial program).

Code decompiling The code can be decompiled and recompiled again.

Code compression The attacker can also modify the code by using code compression tools (e.g. ASPack), which decrease code size by compressing code and adding a decompression routine at the beginning.

The "code decompiling" attack is the most serious threat. If a code can effectively be totally decompiled and recompiled, it is likely that the new frequency vector can be very far from the original one (and thus that the mark can be removed). However, code decompiling is a very difficult, time consuming operation, especially for large programs, and it should be stressed that if only minor parts of the code are decompiled and recompiled, the frequencies will not vary a lot. Hence, we consider that the effort which would have to be invested in such an attack is too important and that it is certainly a better choice for an attacker to rewrite the code from scratch.

The "code addition" attack is also an attack which could result in a large variation of the extracted vector. But once again, in practice, the size of the additional code will have to be very large in order to influence the frequencies of the instructions, and even larger (that is, *much* larger than the program itself) in order to make sure this frequency change actually obfuscates the watermark. This is due to the fact that the attacker does not know *which* deviation α was added as watermark: random frequency modifications will therefore most probably reduce the signal at some places, but also amplify it at others, leaving the mark present. To make watermark disappear, the attacker has therefore to add a very big amount of code, so that frequencies of the marked part become negligible. Thus, we consider that this attack degrades the quality of a program in a noticeable way. Additionally, this attack will be relatively easy to detect as we will very likely have a large part of the code with very unnatural frequencies.

Code compression will certainly remove the watermark. We however insist on the fact that the modified object will no more be valid code, and that the only way to use this code is to uncompress and execute it. It is therefore possible to detect compression and undo it (as the compression algorithm must be coded somehow in the beginning of the file). Once uncompressed, the watermark will reappear unmodified. These two properties together make this situation somewhat different from "classical" watermark removal attacks, in which such a detection-recovery property does not exist. Note that this resistance is more general than the "image flip" example described in section 2: in this case, the watermark could be restored if detected, but the removal was not visible (it is generally not possible to detect an image was flipped) and the modified object could perfectly be used as is. We therefore conclude our model resists this attack.

Finally, the "local modifications" attack are not a threat to our scheme. Intuitively, the spread spectrum techniques have this very nice property that if an attacker cannot perform "stronger" modifications than the original one, the mark will be recovered with very high probability (and we will of course try to insert marks with the largest possible norm). We refer the reader to the analysis of [9] for further details.

5   Implementation

Our first step was to find a set of groups of instructions which occur very frequently in an assembly program. The x86 assembly language was our target for this first implementation. However, many other languages are interesting targets, for example the JAVA bytecode.

We started sampling on about one hundred various programs. It turned out that there were about 1000 different usable groups of instructions of size lower or equal than four.

Figure 1 gives a good intuition of what we are willing to mark. They represent the number of occurrences of all the possible combinations of up to 4 instructions, with those occurring less than 50 times removed. While it is discrete, this representation shows very well how a spread spectrum approach will work.

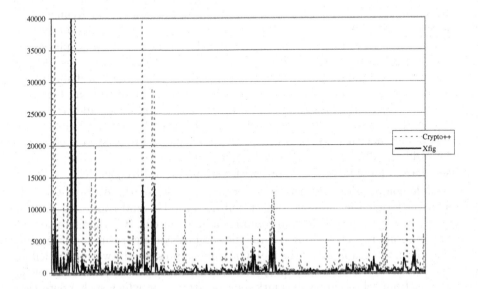

Fig. 1. Experimental distribution of the frequencies of different groups of instructions.

The second step consisted in building a "codebook" of equivalent groups of instructions. We now discuss the way to build this codebook, and give some examples.

The first remark is that every operation which can modify the frequency of our patterns and that does not modify the behaviour of the program is valid. Hence, most of the techniques used in previous low-level watermarking schemes can be used in our setting. However, we need to keep a minimal amount of control of the modifications, they must either be predictable or modify a small number of frequencies (so that we can test the result of the modification and accept it if it goes in the right direction). The simplest example would be to reorder blocks of instructions, which has already been studied in other marking schemes.

We can distinguish two kinds of code modifications:

local: This includes modifications restricted to a specific instruction block. (An instruction block is a block of instruction beginning after a jump and ending by a jump (of any kind) or the target of a jump).

widespread: This includes modifications performed on several blocks at the same time and implies the need to modify jumps and target of jumps.

Local Modifications The simplest local modification consists in modifying the order of two consecutive instructions which do not influence one another. We can, for example, swap the following pairs: (mov/push), (mov,pop), (mov/xor), (mov/and), (mov,sub), (not,xor), etc. Of course, we have to be careful. Because these modifications are data dependent, we have to verify that the registers modified in one instruction are not used in the other one. Also, flag modification must be taken in account. So, we decided, in our first attempt, to only use pairs with one instruction which does not modify any flag (mov, push, pop, lea, not, in, out, rep, set, xchg, ...).

A slightly more sophisticated modification consists in swapping small *groups* of instructions instead of single instructions. An example is:

```
mov eax,ebx
sub eax,edx
push eax
mov eax,ebx
add eax,ecx
push eax
xor eax,eax
```

which becomes

```
mov eax,ebx
add eax,ecx
push eax
mov eax,ebx
sub eax,edx
push eax
xor eax,eax
```

A even more sophisticated modification consists in replacing a group of instructions by an equivalent one. For example, we could replace:

```
mov eax,ebx
mov ebx,ecx
```

by

```
xch eax,ebx
mov ebx,ecx
```

Similarly,

```
ror eax,19
```

can be replaced by

```
rol eax,13
```

provided we make sure the overflow and carry flags will not be tested further in the code.

Widespread Modifications As already pointed out, the probably most natural widespread modification is the reordering of different blocks [6].

Another possibility is to modify the jump sequences: a typical sequence when a test is performed is:

```
cmp eax,ebx
jne _Label_A
jmp _Label_B
```

This can be replaced by:

```
cmp eax,ebx
je  _Label_B
jmp _Label_A
```

It should be remembered that any modification to the code, which preserves its correctness, and which modifies a small number of frequencies can be applied to enhance the efficiency of our scheme. Future research will include: increasing the number of modifications we allow ourself to perform on the code, as well as studying the possible modifications for other languages.

6   Conclusion

We introduced the vector extraction paradigm and proposed a concrete application of this paradigm to machine code. We argued that our new method is robust for marking machine code and showed, contrary to common beliefs, that is it easier to robustly mark data which stand minor modifications (such as code, where *correctness* has to be preserved) than data which stand large modifications (such as images, or source code).

References

1. D. Boneh and J. Shaw. Collusion-secure fingerprinting for digital data. In D. Coppersmith, editor, *Proc. CRYPTO 95*, number 963 in Lecture Notes in Computer Science, pages 452–465. Springer-Verlag, 1995. 369

2. C. Collberg and C. Thomborson. Software watermarking: Models and dynamic embeddings. In *ACM SIGPLAN-SIGACT Symposium on Principles of Programming Languages (POPL99)*, 1999. 370, 372

3. C. Collberg, C.Thomborson, and D. Low. Breaking abstraction and unstructuring data structures. In *IEEE International Conference on Computer Languages (ICCL '98)*, 1998. 372

4. Ingemar J. Cox, Joe Kilian, Tom Leighton, and Talal Shamoon. A secure, robust watermark for multimedia. In Ross Anderson, editor, *Workshop on Information Hiding*, volume 1174 of *Lecture Notes in Computer Science*. Springer-Verlag, 1996. 369, 370, 372

5. Ingemar J. Cox and Matt L. Miller. A review of watermarking anf the importance of perceptual modeling. In *Proc. of Electronic Imagining '97*, 1997. 369

6. R. Davidson and N. Myhrvold. Method and system for generating and auditing a signature for a computer program. U.S. Patent No. 5,559,884, 1996. 370, 377

7. Funda Ergun, Joe Kilian, and Ravi Kumar. A note on the limits of collusion resistant watermarks. In Jacques Stern, editor, *Advances in Cryptology - EUROCRYPT '99*, volume 1592 of *Lecture Notes in Computer Science*, pages 140–149. Springer-Verlag, 1999. 369, 370

8. K. Holmes. Computer software protection. U.S. Patent No. 5,531,021, 1994. 370

9. J. Kilian, T. Leighton, L. R. Matheson, T. G. Shamoon, R. E. Tarjan, and F. Zane. Resistance of digital watermarks to collusive attacks. Technical Report TR-58598, Departement of computer science, Princeton University, 1998. 369, 370, 375

10. Fabien A. P. Petitcolas, Ross J. Anderson, and Markus G. Kuhn. Attacks on copyright marking systems. In David Aucsmith, editor, *Second Workshop on Information Hiding*, number 1525 in Lecture Notes in Computer Science, pages 218–238. Springer-Verlag, 1998. 371

11. Fabien A. P. Petitcolas, Ross J. Anderson, and Markus G. Kuhn. Information hiding. a survey. In *Proceedings of the IEEE, special issue on protection of multimedia content*, 1999. To appear. 370

12. B. Pfitzmann and M. Waidner. Annonymous fingerprinting. In Walter Fumy, editor, *Advances in Cryptology—EUROCRYPT 97*, number 1233 in Lecture Notes in Computer Science, pages 88–102. Springer-Verlag, 1997. 369

13. B. Pfitzmann and M. Waidner. Asymmetric fingerprinting for larger collusions. In *4th ACM Conference on Computer and Communications Security*, pages 151–160, 1997. 369

14. Birgit Pfitzmann and Ahmad-Reza Sadeghi. Coin-based anonymous fingerprinting. In Jacques Stern, editor, *Advances in Cryptology - EUROCRYPT '99*, volume 1592 of *Lecture Notes in Computer Science*, pages 150–164. Springer-Verlag, 1999. 369

15. Birgit Pfitzmann and Matthias Schunter. Asymmetric fingerprinting (extended abstract). In Ueli Maurer, editor, *Advances in Cryptology—EUROCRYPT 96*, number 1070 in Lecture Notes in Computer Science, pages 84–95. Springer-Verlag, 1996. 369

Software DisEngineering: Program Hiding Architecture and Experiments

Enriquillo Valdez[1]* and Moti Yung[2]

[1] Polytechnic University, Computer and Information Science Department
Brooklyn, NY, USA
rvaldez@photon.poly.edu
[2] CertCo Inc.
New York, NY, USA
moti@cs.columbia.edu

Abstract. Protecting software is becoming important in the context of modern Internet technologies; often such protection efforts are kept as trade secrets. In this paper, we take a step toward understanding such protection mechanisms and their impact on performance and security. We present a program hiding architecture that utilizes an automatic hiding tool. The hiding tool generates programs that are resistant to reverse engineering by applying software transformations. Our approach protects against the learning of inner workings (and subsequently tampering) of executables in environments that lack appropriate hardware support and where programs may contain certain private knowledge components (proprietary algorithms). We designed and implemented a prototype of a hiding tool for Tcl. We studied the effect of transformations on the execution time of Tcl scripts and suggest a security checking experimentation as well.

1 Introduction

In the software distribution area, a crucial objective is ensuring payment for the use of software executables. Accordingly, software distributors seek to prevent activities that affect adversely their compensation for the use or sale of their software executables. Through reverse engineering efforts, an adversary can learn embedded information in programs, such as trade secrets, proprietary algorithms, cryptographic keys, etc. Such acquired information from programs can facilitate the construction of competing products or be used maliciously (e.g., in computer viruses) to learn how to tamper with programs. Thus, to prevent such activities, software distributors want programs that are hard to comprehend. Programs with such a property not only will enable software distributors to prevent disclosure of inner workings, i.e., make them resistant to observation, but also will inhibit illegal activities, such as illegal modification and unauthorized use.

* This work was supported by the National Science Foundation under Grant No. 9256688 and the NY State Center for Advanced Technology in Telecommunications.

A. Pfitzmann (Ed.): IH'99, LNCS 1768, pp. 379–394, 2000.

In this paper, we present an approach for preventing the disclosure of inner workings of programs. This approach is based on applying software transformations to conceal programs. We distinguish between two types of transformations: obfuscating and scrambling. Obfuscating transformations convert syntactically correct programs (*SCP*)s to SCPs; scrambling transformations convert SCPs to SCPs plus data (i.e., arbitrary strings).

The security of applying software transformations is based on making it difficult to observe and extract valuable information from transformed programs. This is applicable, for example, in preventing direct copying of an embedded session key in a program; the current session key in the program is stored in a location or accessed in a manner different from previous session keys. We expect our method to be an effective deterrence against the average user (and not against experts with substantial resources) from reverse engineering transformed programs. Thus, we rely on the economy (cost of software as an alternative to cost of reverse engineering) to assure that our methods are sufficient.

In our work, we incorporate both obfuscating and scrambling transformations into an automatic hiding tool that generates transformed programs. The transformed programs are input-output equivalent to their originals (i.e., the nature of their computations is transformed). We also describe a Program Hiding Architecture (*PHA*) that employs the hiding tool within a software distribution scheme. A version of the hiding tool is implemented for the Tcl environment. The choice of Tcl is due to its being an interpretive language that is easily susceptible to transformations. We perform experiments to measure the impact of transformations on the execution time and the concealment of Tcl scripts.

The organization of paper is as follows: Section 2 reviews related work in software protection. Section 3 informally discusses two types of transformations for concealing programs, measures for gauging obscurity, and security. Section 4 describes the system model and threats. Section 5 details the stages of the PHA and the hiding tool. Section 6 discusses the Tcl hiding tool and experiments for evaluating our prototype. Finally, Section 7 presents the conclusions and explores directions for future work.

2   Related Work

Software-only approaches relevant to our work (i.e., hiding of inner workings) include works from a practical perspective. Aucsmith [1] initiated the notion of tamper-proof software. He suggests verifying the integrity of programs by embedding installation-unique, self-decrypting, and self-modifying code segments that calculate digital signatures. The code segments communicate with other code segments (possibly in other programs) to verify their integrity. Aucsmith's approach is appropriate for hiding cryptographic keys. In contrast, our approach is applicable to concealing programs in general.

Developed independently from our work, Collberg et al. [2,3] describe obfuscation techniques based on compiler optimization techniques; in Section 6.1, we compare their implementation in [10] with ours. Although many of their transformations (i.e., obfuscation) may be reversed by an optimizing compiler, they introduce the useful notion of opaque constructs. The values (or properties) of opaque constructs are known at obfuscation time but are difficult for deobfuscators to determine. The opaque constructs are used to prevent the removal of extraneous code that they add to programs. Their most resilient (i.e., resistant to reverse engineering) opaque constructs are those that use pointer-based structures (and exploit the difficulty of pointer analysis). The obfuscation techniques of [2,3] can serve as a subcomponent to the work presented here; besides altering the control flow and data structure of programs, another aspect we consider and they do not, is the manipulation of programs as **data**. We view our work to be a continuation of [1,2,3]. From a theoretical perspective, work regarding program hiding appears in [6,13,14].

3   Transformations

In this section, we informally present our understanding of transformations. First, we describe two types of transformations that we consider for concealing the inner workings of programs. Next, we introduce measures for gauging the obscurity of transformed programs. Finally, we discuss the security of transformed programs.

For our work, we are interested in transformations that maintain the *input-output equivalent* property of programs (or on their parts), i.e., a particular input value will yield the same output value on the original program and on its transformed version. However, we do not necessarily seek transformations that maintain the behavior of programs, i.e., internal or external characteristics (e.g., data structures, performance, etc.).

We consider two types of transformations: *obfuscating transformations* and *scrambling transformations*. Obfuscating transformations (OB_T)s convert syntactically correct programs (SCP)s to other input-output equivalent SCPs without altering the semantics. Thus, OB_Ts do not need to be undone (e.g., the removal of symbol table information from programs). Scrambling transformations (SC_T)s convert a program (or parts of it) to data. This data requires interpretation (i.e., descrambling) before it can be executed. Thus, we consider SC_Ts, such as the RSA encryption algorithm [12], that have inverses. Applying a SC_T requires the code that does the interpretation to be available to the transformed program; e.g., the descrambling code can be inserted into the transformed program. We observed that an unlimited number of transformations can be applied on programs. This is so, since we can always add dead code, for example, at the end of a code segment thus performing OB_T and given the code segment we can always apply another scrambling of it.

From OB_Ts and SC_Ts, we derive *obfuscating fingerprints (OB_FP)s* and *scrambling fingerprints (SC_FP)s*. OB_FPs and SC_FPs serve to individualize programs (add watermarkings) and thus are useful for showing copyright infringement (i.e., illegal redistribution). They utilize users provided information to generate customized information for applying OB_Ts and SC_Ts. An example is the ciphertext generated by encrypting a user's name using a software developer's private key: the first byte of ciphertext determines a permutation order, the second byte specifies an index to the noise instruction repository, etc.

The results of applying transformations on programs are *hidden programs*. The security of hidden programs is based on the extent to which transformations make programs incomprehensible to humans or to automatic tools (i.e., deobfuscators). Similar to [2,3], we can use software complexity metrics [15] which considers syntactical features of programs (e.g., code size, nesting complexity, etc.) for gauging the difficult of understanding a program. Unfortunately, software complexity metrics are not generally applicable to SC_Ts. Potential measures for SC_Ts include those that gauge the structural features of programs, such as similarity or randomness. However, measures that allow us to examine executions are more relevant. One such measure is the number of dynamic snapshots of the state of an executing program. This can show, for example, that the nesting of transformations is useful, since it requires more dynamic snapshots to "really" start understanding the program.

Unlike the cryptography field, where certain algorithms can be shown (via a reduction method) to be secure with respect to any adversary with bounded computational power, quantifying what feasible amount of work will be needed to break (i.e., make understandable) a hidden program is difficult. We equate security as being proportional to the cost of reverse engineering (the higher the cost the more likely we can deter this activity). Conceptually, *reverse engineering cost* is the effort associated with converting a hidden program to an input-output equivalent SCP plus the cost of understanding this latter program (which is most likely obfuscated); in Section 6.2, we discuss practical aspects.

4   System Model and Threats

Next we present the system model and threats.

System Model We consider protecting executables in Low End Computer Systems (LECS)s. In LECSs, instructions/data in memory and on the system bus are observable and modifiable. An example of a LECS is the PC platform. The PC is an inherently insecure system: memory content can be probed, data on the system bus read, and system components can be replaced, e.g., CPU.

Threats In LECSs, threats to software executables include:

- Erasing Fingerprint, denoted as ERASE, is when information that encodes the identity of the user (or the buyer) (i.e., a person's name, a company name, etc.) in a program is removed.
- Information Disclosure, denoted as LEARN, is when information on inner workings, such as structure, algorithms, or cryptographic keys, is learned. This information can be acquired by studying the source of the program,

tracing execution, and monitoring memory access. Tools to accomplish LEARN include decompilers, disassemblers, and debuggers.

- Tampering, denoted as ALTER, is when unauthorized modification, such as adding, deleting, or changing instructions, of programs occurs. This can make a program inoperable or add a new behavior, such as a Trojan horse.
- Unauthorized Use, denoted as USE, is when a program is used without permission from creators or vendors. An example is breaking a clause of the licensing agreement: a user transfers the ownership of a program, but he or she keeps a copy of the program.
- Illegal Duplication, denoted as COPY, is when unauthorized copies of programs are made.

Adversarial attacks on programs involve carrying out one of the above threats. If the program is delivered over insecure channels, such as the Internet, CD-ROMs, or floppy disks, then COPY and ALTER can be perpetrated. When a program is in storage (e.g., on the hard drive), ERASE, LEARN, COPY, and ALTER can be perpetrated. It is conceivable that owners/users of LECSs will try to invoke ERASE, LEARN, and COPY, but they are less likely to invoke ALTER. Purchasers of programs can invoke ERASE by themselves, but it is very likely that they will try to collude with others to detect the fingerprint information (by comparing their different versions of the program). While executing a program, LEARN and ALTER can be committed. These strong attacks can be invoked by those who have complete control over their LECSs. An example is an adversary who replaces the CPU with in-circuit-emulator (or replaces the operating system with an emulation environment) that collects every executed instruction.

In this paper, we only address LEARN. Addressing ALTER, COPY, and USE requires different techniques than those presented here, e.g., linking programs to machines, embedding accounting mechanisms and integrity checks into programs, etc. Although we utilize software transformations with strong operators, such as encryption and compression, to protect against optimizing compilers our approach is not immune to successful attacks by a very persistent or rich adversary. An obvious attack includes the tracing of a program's execution. Our approach makes such an attack quite costly for an adversary to implement. Hidden programs (those generated by our approach) will also be vulnerable in situations where they are not often changed, because continued trace attacks will enable adversaries to construct profiles of execution patterns which can lead to their eventual breaking.

5   Program Hiding Architecture

To address LEARN, we designed a Program Hiding Architecture (PHA) to facilitate the creation and distribution of hidden programs. This architecture is based on a simple processing model: first, a program's sections are identified for obscuring and a concealment parameter is specified; next, the selected sections are processed and customized using the buyer's system information; then the hidden program is delivered to the buyer. The PHA involves interaction among parties who create, sell, buy, and use software executables: the *software developer*, the party responsible for the creation of the software executable; the *software distributor*, the party who processes and sells software executables on behalf of software developers; and the *buyer*, the party who buys and executes the software executable.

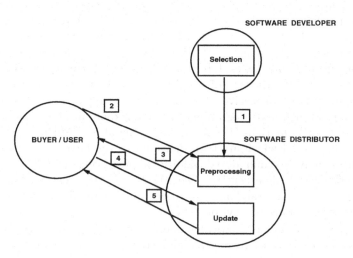

Fig. 1. Program Hiding Architecture

In the design of the PHA, we assume that software distributors will not conspire against software developers or buyers. Software developers expect software distributors to provide accurate sales reports, and buyers trust software distributors to provide safe programs, i.e., programs that do not have malicious behavior, such a Trojan horse, etc., unknown to buyers. This is important because detecting viruses in hidden programs may be difficult. We also assume that the communication between buyers and software distributors is done securely and that there exists a mechanism for handling the purchase and the delivery of hidden programs.

The PHA consists of three stages: selection, preprocessing, and update. In the first stage, selection, a software developer identifies sections to obscure in a program and selects the transformations to apply. The candidate sections selected for concealment are those that have an associated value. This value can be measured in terms of the secrets contained in sections, such as proprietary algorithms or cryptographic keys. Other candidate sections include those instrumented with software checks that detect or enforce behaviors, such as tampering and software license agreement. Of course, other less important sections (decoys) are selected as well, to conceal location of interesting program aspects. After identifying these sections, the software developer selects the transformations. The criteria for selecting transformations depend on their concealment quality and affect on performance. The activities of this stage can be performed by anyone who has knowledge of the program's structure and functionality. The output of this stage is a profile that details the sections to process and the transformations to apply. The program along with a profile is provided to trusted software distributors (see Figure 1, $\boxed{1}$) who then process requests for the program.

In the second stage, preprocessing, programs are customized, transformed, and distributed to buyers. This stage begins when a buyer locates a software distributor that has, i.e., sells, the desired executable. The buyer then engages in a delivery protocol with the software distributor in which the buyer submits system characteristic information $\boxed{2}$. This information specifies the environment, e.g., CPU ids, machine names, Internet addresses, etc., where the requested program will execute and the type of temporal access desired for the program. After the software distributor receives this information, it inputs system characteristic information, profile, and program to the hiding tool, an automatic tool which applies the transformations. The hiding tool generates a hidden program and an execution credential which are then delivered to the buyer $\boxed{3}$. In some situations, buyers may be required to do additional processing on hidden programs on their systems to enable execution. The buyers, now the users, for example, may be required to generate random keys. In Section 5.2, we discuss the execution of hidden programs in users' environments.

The last stage, update, provides maintainability of hidden programs after they have been delivered to buyers. This stage is responsible for extending or changing the functionality of hidden programs to accommodate users' needs. It provides three basic functions re-configuration, upgrade, and renewal. The re-configuration function adapts a hidden program to changes in the execution environment. This function is invoked when a user wants to enable execution on more machines, transfer use to other machines, or transfer ownership of a program to another user $\boxed{4}$. The upgrade function serves to update a hidden program by installing a new version, adding new components, or enabling features previously disabled $\boxed{5}$. The final function, renewal, extends the valid period of usability of hidden programs. Renewal is invoked when a user wants to renew the execution privileges of an exhausted hidden program.

5.1 The Hiding Tool

The core of the PHA is the preprocessing stage's hiding tool. This tool obfuscates and scrambles the content and runtime features of programs. Our basic hiding tool utilizes generic transformations that are generally applicable to all types of software executables (see Figure 2).

The inputs to the basic hiding tool[1] are the original program and a profile. The profile specifies the sections of the program to conceal and the concealment

---

[1] Currently, the basic hiding tool does not utilize system characteristic information from buyers.

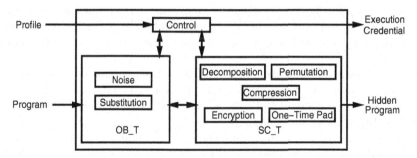

Fig. 2. The Hiding Tool

parameter. The concealment parameter specifies the type and degree of transformations to apply. For creating hidden programs, the basic hiding tool employs a straightforward procedure: a program is passed through a multistage process where on each stage a distinct transformation primitive is applied. The transformation primitives applied are noise, substitution, decomposition, permutation, compression, and encryption.

In a typical situation, when all the transformation primitives are selected, the hiding tool works as follows. First, obfuscating transformations then scrambling transformations are applied. Noise instructions are inserted either at random or at specified locations in the preselected sections. These noise instructions are randomly generated or retrieved from a repository that contains code fragments. Then the substitution primitive is applied. Original instructions are replaced with equivalent instructions in the preselected program sections. The substitute instructions are retrieved from a dictionary that contains mapping of equivalent patterns. After applying the noise and substitution primitives, the processed sections are decomposed into blocks of some finite size, and a random permutation order is applied on these blocks. Then from these blocks, blocks are randomly selected for encryption and/or compression. The last applied transformation is the one-time pad which adds, i.e., xors, all the blocks with randomly generated keys. Note that these transformation primitives can be interleaved and applied at different levels of granularity.

The hiding tool compiles the recovery information (for reversing the hidden program) as it applies transformations to the program. At termination time, the hiding tool outputs the hidden program and an execution credential, a processed version of the recovery information.

5.2   Execution Credential and Descrambling

To execute a hidden program requires both the execution credential and the descrambling routine. Because the execution credential is vulnerable to observation, we describe three concealing techniques for protecting it. The first technique is the simple wrapper: the execution credential is encrypted. The execution credential is decrypted only during the execution of the hidden program. The decryption key for the credential can be embedded in the hidden program, or provided as additional information. The second technique is the hidden credential: the execution credential is processed by the hiding tool. The third technique is the diffused credential: part of the execution credential is diffused into the hidden program. In the latter technique, a reduced version of the credential is supplied for accessing the recovery information embedded in the hidden program. This reduced credential can be provided as is, or either one of the two previous techniques can be applied.

Two important issues concerning the descrambling routine include its availability and concealment. There are three methods for making the descrambling routine available. The first method is to build in the descrambling routine into the operating system. A hidden program would invoke system calls to reveal itself. This would hide the relationship between the recovery information and the hidden program because the execution will take place in the system space not accessible to the user. The second method is to provide the descrambling routine as an external resource, such as a shared library. Descrambling routines can be placed in a standard location across all systems so that at runtime hidden programs would know where to search for them. When a hidden program executes, for example, its first task would be to load the descrambling routine from the shared library. The third method is to append the descrambling routine to the hidden program. This can be done by the hiding tool. Clearly, these methods are susceptible to observation. We can rely on the same techniques for concealing programs to conceal the descrambling routine. We can pass the descrambling routine through the hiding process. This will create a double indirection for execution where the descrambling routine must be revealed first via a simple descrambling before the hidden program.

6   Implementation and Experimentation

As a first step, we consider a version of the hiding tool (*HT*) for an interpreted environment that is easily susceptible to transformations. Such an environment allows us to manipulate a program's instructions as data. Other environments (e.g., UNIX and C) separate a program's data and instructions, and restrict modification on the program's instructions during execution. The HT will require different types of techniques (than those described here, e.g., dynamic linking) for these restrictive environments.

We implement a prototype of HT for Tcl 7.6 [16], HT-Tcl. Tcl (Tool command language) is a string-based language that has a simple syntax. Tcl programs are scripts which are parsed and interpreted by a Tcl interpreter. Tcl allowed us to treat a script, i.e., a program, as a modifiable data structure; however, certain features of the language made the process of transforming scripts cumbersome. These features include the requirement of the entire command (that may extend to several lines of the source) before evaluation by the Tcl interpreter, the lack of goto command, and Tcl's inability to manipulate binary data directly. In this prototype, we apply transformations on the script level and not on the Tcl interpreter though we extended the Tcl interpreter to support transformations.

6.1   Tcl Transformations

Available Tcl tools (e.g., tcl_cruncher [4] and frink [11]) obfuscate scripts by removing comments and deleting unnecessary white space (i.e., space, tab, newline character, etc.). Our HT-Tcl employs more sophisticated hiding techniques than these tools. In implementing HT-Tcl, we borrow from existing works: we modified tclparser [17] to provide a substitution primitive, employed pgp's [19] hex64 encoding and decoding routines, and utilized CryptoLib's [9] random byte generator, zlib library (a variation of Lempel-Ziv1977 compression algorithm) [5] and Tcl Data Transformation (Tcl-Trf) extension package [8] which provides DES. Additionally, we added an exclusive OR (xor) command to the interpreter. This command performs a bitwise exclusive OR of two binary strings.

The HT-Tcl prototype operates on the entire script and transforms only syntactically correct Tcl programs. It may break scripts that dynamically construct commands. The use of HT-Tcl requires a simpler style for writing Tcl programs. Table 1 shows the transformation primitives available to the Tcl hiding tool. In our current prototype, primitives are enabled and set in a profile file that is read at processing time (by HT-Tcl). In the profile, we also specify the type of execution credential (to generate) and the availability of the descrambling routine. For the execution credential, we can select a diffused credential or simple wrapper configuration. For the descrambling routine, we can specify whether to attach the descrambling routine to the hidden script or not.

The obfuscating transformations in Table 1 are comparable to those implemented for [2,3] in [10] for the Java environment. They insert extraneous branch and dead code. We provide similar code insertion functionality with the noise primitive; however, we cannot create predicates that reference dynamic structures as they do because Tcl does not support pointers. They convert code to subroutine call; we do not because such a simple code conversion can be easily undone. They change the access of methods and variables (e.g., make accessible to every class), but this is only applicable to languages that supports access restriction (and not to Tcl). They also remove debugging information and scramble identifiers. We provide the same functionality with the substitute primitive.

6.2   HT-Tcl Evaluation

Evaluating an implementation of a HT requires examining two factors: efficiency and security. **Efficiency** measures the overhead in code size and execution time of hidden programs. **Security** measures how well the HT conceals programs. We observed that efficiency and security are in conflict; efficiency in execution does not coincide with security. When a program, for example, has many transformations applied, it takes longer to execute than if it had fewer transformations applied. We believe that the more transformations applied to a program the

Table 1. Transformation Primitives Available for HT-Tcl

Type	Primitive	Operation
Obfuscating	Delete	inserts codes that delete variable names in the global space after last use
Obfuscating	Noise	inserts random computations and dead code
Obfuscating	Substitute	removes comments and white space, and replaces user defined variable and procedure names with other strings (having an average length of 6.5 characters)
Scrambling	Decompose	partitions a script into blocks
Obfuscating	Crunch	replaces the newline character with ";"
Obfuscating	Pad	appends ";" character to block
Scrambling	Permute	transposes the position of blocks
Scrambling	Compress	randomly picks blocks to compress
Scrambling	Encrypt	randomly picks blocks to encrypt (DES in ecb mode)
Scrambling	Encode	converts strings into hex64 format
Scrambling	Xor	xors two binary strings encoded in hex64 and returns a hex64 encoded string

Table 2. Simple Transformations (seconds)

Scripts	Original	Substitute and Crunch
10	0.387	0.377
100	0.393	0.393
1000	0.467	0.473
for	0.93	0.937
if	0.91	0.9
mflop	40.0	39.0
prime	1.19	1.17
random	0.39	0.383
read	0.743	0.753

more work it will take to extract any useful information[2]. Users of any HT will need to tradeoff between their desired concealment level, and the efficiency of hidden programs. Next, we describe experimental evaluation of efficiency and security for hidden Tcl scripts.

Efficiency Experiments We measured the execution times of Tcl scripts in order to evaluate the effects of applying the transformation primitives in Table 1. Memory performance (i.e., page faults or cache misses) and code size were not measured, because these were small Tcl scripts, and thus the execution time is the actual performance measure. The hidden scripts were run with the configuration of diffused credential and no attached descrambling routine. We measured

---

[2] Of course, this also depends on the concealment property of the transformations.

Table 3. Decompose (seconds)

	Decompose				Decompose and Xor		
	Block size % of original				Block size % of original		
Scripts	1%	25%	50%	100%	25%	50%	100%
10	0.683	0.61	0.547	0.547	1.44	0.743	0.65
100	3.07	0.623	0.583	0.563	2.35	1.02	0.777
1000	8.77	1.09	0.917	0.86	16.3	4.37	2.14
for	31.5	12.8	9.9	5.87	26.4	12.5	6.67
if	27.8	10.5	7.83	5.1	34.0	15.9	5.63
mflop	45.3	39.7	40.0	40.0	44.0	40.3	39.3
prime	2.36	1.62	1.43	1.38	2.84	1.95	1.52
random	0.953	0.707	0.62	0.59	2.08	0.86	0.727
read	1.7	1.15	1.08	0.967	2.67	1.27	1.11

Table 4. Decompose and Compress (seconds)

	Block size % of original									
	1%				25%			50%		100%
	compression				compression			compression		compression
Scripts	10%	25%	50%	100%	25%	50%	100%	50%	100%	100%
10	0.843	0.857	0.893	0.933	0.757	0.743	0.767	0.697	0.697	0.663
100	5.37	5.67	6.17	7.13	0.79	0.78	0.77	0.723	0.713	0.7
1000	12.9	12.4	10.7	7.47	1.25	1.13	0.93	1.01	0.89	0.88
for	36.7	36.3	36.0	36.0	13.2	12.8	12.5	9.53	9.57	6.2
if	33.7	33.3	33.3	34.3	10.7	10.6	10.3	8.03	7.73	5.0
mflop	48.0	48.3	49.7	51.0	39.3	39.3	39.3	39.7	39.3	39.0
prime	2.64	2.67	2.68	2.79	1.75	1.74	1.75	1.57	1.6	1.5
random	1.16	1.15	1.21	1.24	0.857	0.86	0.897	0.74	0.777	0.703
read	2.02	2.03	2.13	2.25	1.31	1.28	1.33	1.19	1.19	1.08

the execution time of a Tcl interpreter invoked with the command line arguments of a descrambling routine and hidden script. The experiments were performed on a SPARCstation 2 running Solaris 2.5.1 with a Weitek CPU and 64MB of memory.

Because our work focused on a subset of Tcl, finding suitable Tcl scripts to run experiments on was difficult. Most of the publicly available Tcl scripts combine the use of Tcl and Tk, i.e., an extension that provides a graphical user interface. We ran our experiments on scripts retrieved mostly from other work. These scripts are representative of the types of programs written by users of Tcl. The nine selected scripts are called *10, 100, 1000, for, if, mflop, prime, random,* and *read. 10, 100,* and *1000* are simple scripts in which a variable is set, repeatedly increased by 1 (the number of times the variable is increased is given by the filename minus two), and then displayed. *for* and *if* are modified

Table 5. Decompose and Encrypt (seconds)

	Block size % of original									
	1%				25%			50%		100%
	encryption				encryption			encryption		encryption
Scripts	1%	25%	50%	100%	25%	50%	100%	50%	100%	100%
10	0.867	0.87	0.92	1.0	0.74	0.753	0.8	0.7	0.717	0.683
100	5.6	6.03	6.93	8.77	0.817	0.81	0.843	0.713	0.787	0.72
1000	14.7	15.9	17.6	21.8	1.44	1.6	1.84	1.34	1.52	1.38
for	36.7	37.7	38.3	40.3	13.2	13.1	13.2	9.87	9.8	6.2
if	34.0	35.0	35.7	38.3	10.9	10.9	11.0	8.2	8.47	5.27
mflop	48.3	49.0	50.7	53.3	39.0	39.7	40.3	39.3	40.0	40.3
prime	2.64	2.73	2.81	3.12	1.77	1.79	1.89	1.64	1.64	1.52
random	1.17	1.2	1.27	1.33	0.853	0.887	0.907	0.763	0.757	0.707
read	2.02	2.07	2.21	2.38	1.28	1.28	1.31	1.18	1.2	1.1

test scripts from the Tcl distribution [16]. *mflop* calculates a benchmark (i.e., a version of flops.c) and *prime* finds the number of prime numbers from the range 1 to 100. *random* generates and displays three random numbers (from Exploring Expect by Libes, O'Reilly & Associates, Inc., 1995). *read* displays the timing result of reading a file from [18]'s distribution. In Tables 2 - 5, a data value that represents a running time is computed from the average of three runs for that particular data point.

From the performance experiments (results in Tables 2 - 5), we conclude the following: first, the substitute and crunch primitives can always be applied. The results in Table 2 show that applying substitute and crunch does not significantly affect the running times of scripts. In some cases, these primitives improve the running times by eliminating unnecessary processing of comments and white spaces by the Tcl interpreter. Second, the decompose primitive needs to be reworked to eliminate the excessive breaking of Tcl commands. The Decompose section of Table 3 contains the results of applying decompose and permute over different block sizes (on the scripts). The decompose primitive showed poor results for the *for* and *if* scripts (compared with their running times in Table 2). These poor results are due to the decompose primitive's strategy of partitioning a script at arbitrary locations which then causes the descrambling routine to check[3] excessively whether a block has complete Tcl commands before executing the block. Third, the xor primitive should be applied at a large granularity. The Decompose and Xor section of Table 3 shows that xor is useful for large block sizes. When the block size is increased from 25% to 50%, the execution times of the hidden scripts are reduced by almost a half. Fourth, the compress primitive serves to optimize large scripts. The compress primitive optimized the reading and manipulation of hidden scripts by the descrambling routine. Finally, decompose is less costly than decompose and compress which is in turn less costly

---

[3] The check consists of counting the number of matching pair of curly braces.

than decompose and encrypt (in the programs in our range these differ mostly in the fractions of a second and not in seconds). The running time values for the encrypt primitive were in the most cases slightly larger than the compress primitive.

Security Experiment We suggest that our hiding tool, when used in production, be tested via an extensive adversarial testing. An adversarial testing stage, employing users of various degrees of expertise, should be part of the implementation of the PHA since it can help in calibrating the appropriate level of security for hidden programs. Any experimental results will naturally depend on a user's craftiness, technical expertise, available time, and motivation.

As one type of experiments, we suggest the following triangle experiment. A user is given a set of three hidden programs where two have the same underlying program. The user is then asked to identify the hidden program that has a different underlying program from the set. Such an experiment maps naturally into a binomial experiment where n sets of hidden programs correspond to n repetitions of the experiment. The probability, p, that a user correctly identifies the hidden program with the different underlying program from the set by chance is $1/3$. Thus, the probability that a user gets k correct answers is $P(X = k) = \binom{n}{k} (1/3)^k (2/3)^{n-k}$. For our initial experiment, we let $n = 6$. We expect a user to get in the neighborhood of two correct answers due to chance, because the expected value is $np = 2$. Hence, we consider the obscurity property of our PHA to be good if the computed average value of users' correct answers equals two or less, fair if the average value equals three or four, and poor if it equals five or more.

For the experiment, we selected Tcl scripts with the same input/output relationships for each set. Three average users were given six sets of hidden scripts ($n = 6$) and were allowed to use any available tool at their disposal in the experiment. They spent three to four hours on their tasks. One user identified the hidden script correctly once and the two others identified correctly only twice. The results of our initial experiment are encouraging; however, they are not conclusive. To assess accurately the obscurity property of HT-Tcl, we need to run this experiment on more users.

Finally, we note that in our prototype, we concentrated on applying transformations on Tcl scripts and did not address the observable nature of the environment. To make HT-Tcl, however, a viable tool requires us (in the future) to restrict the environment (e.g., remove commands that reveal state) and disguise the use of commands (e.g., reference commands indirectly).

7 Conclusion and Future Work

In this paper we presented a program hiding architecture for making programs resistant to reverse engineering via relatively efficient transformations. We implemented a key component of the architecture, the hiding tool (HT-Tcl), for the Tcl environment. We measured the running time of scripts when transformations were applied one at a time. The results showed that the transformations did not significantly increase the running time of the Tcl scripts (when applied on large block sizes).

There are many possible directions to extend the work presented here. We can devise other types of obscuring schemes that: affect functionality without resulting in substantial performance degradation; actively make adversaries' attempts to observe programs more difficult (e.g., disable interrupts used by debugger applications); and leverage the uniqueness of environment (e.g., multithreading, remote processors, smartcards, etc.) for concealment. Another aspect to consider is further evaluation of the concealment property of the HT. We can also continue with extending HT-Tcl (e.g., provide support for the entire set of Tcl core commands, incorporate other concealment strategies, etc.), but Tcl is not a language for writing industrial strength applications. Thus, we consider implementing a variant of the PHA for the Java environment [7] which enables the development of robust applications in a distributed environment.

References

1. D. Aucsmith. Tamper Resistant Software: An Implementation. *Information Hiding - Proceedings of the First International Workshop*, pages 317-333, Springer-Verlag, 1996. 380, 381
2. C. Collberg, C. Thomborson, and D. Low. A Taxonomy of Obfuscating Transformations. Technical Report 148, University of Auckland, NZ, July 1997. http://www.cs.auckland.ac.nz/~collberg/Research/Publications/Collberg Thomborson97a/index.html. 380, 381, 382, 388
3. C. Collberg, C. Thomborson, and D. Low. Manufacturing Cheap, Resilient, and Stealthy Opaque Constructs. In *Proceedings of POPL 1998*, pages 184-196, Jan. 1998. 380, 381, 382, 388
4. L. Demailly. tcl_cruncher 1.11. http://www.sco.com/Technology/tcl/ Tcl.html. 388
5. J. Gailly and M. Adler. zlib 1.0.4. http://quest.jpl.nasa.gov/zlib/. 388
6. O. Goldreich and R. Ostrovsky. Software Protection and Simulation on Oblivious RAMs. In *Journal of the ACM*, 43(3):431-473, May 1996. 381
7. J. Gosling and H. McGilton. *The Java Language Environment*. Sun Microsystems Computer Company, Oct. 1995. ftp://java.sun.com/doc/whitepaper.ps.tar.Z. 393
8. A. Kupries. Tcl Data Transformations (Tcl-Trf v1.0b2). http://www.sco.com/Technology/tcl/Tcl.html. 388
9. J. Lacy, D. Mitchell, and M. Blaze. CryptoLib 1.2. AT&T Laboratories, 1995. 388
10. D. Low. Java Control Flow Obfuscation. Master Thesis, University of Auckland, NZ, June 1998. http://www.cs.auckland.ac.nz/~douglas/thesis.ps. 380, 388
11. L. Marshall. Frink 1.2. http://www.sco.com/Technology/tcl/Tcl.html. 388
12. R. L. Rivest, A. Shamir, and L. Adleman. A Method for Obtaining Digital Signatures and Public-Key Cryptosystems. In *CACM*, 21(2):120-126, Feb. 1978. 381
13. T. Sander and C. Tschudin. Towards Mobile Cryptography. In *Proceedings of the 1998 IEEE Symposium on Security and Privacy*, pages 215-224, 1998. 381

14. T. Sander, A. Young, and M. Yung. Non-Interactive CryptoComputing for NC^1. *IEEE FOCS*, 1999. 381

15. I. Sommerville. *Software Engineering* 5th ed. Addison-Wesley, 1996. 382

16. Tcl7.6/Tk4.2. http://www.scriptics.com/. 387, 391

17. S. Weiss. TclParser v3.00. http://www.informatik.uni-stuttgart.de/ipvr /swlab/sopra/tclsyntax/tclparseHome.h. 388

18. B. B. Welch. *Practical Programming in Tcl and Tk*. Prentice Hall PTR, 1995. 391

19. P. Zimmermann. Pretty Good Privacy package. http://web.mit.edu/network /pgp.html. 388

Chaffing at the Bit:

Thoughts on a Note by Ronald Rivest

John McHugh

CERT CC, Software Engineering Institute
Carnegie Mellon University

Abstract. Rivest developed the concept of chaffing, a technique based on blending authenticated plaintext information with non authenticated noise (chaff) to obscure the true message as a method of subverting controls on strong cryptography in an arena in which strong authentication is unregulated. Assuming a secret authentication key shared between the sender and the receiver, only the intended recipient can easily separate the message content from the noise (winnowing).
We look at ways in which the winnowing and chaffing processes might be made more efficient. We begin by considering the winnowing process as error correction (another unregulated technology) and consider the effectiveness of shorter authentication codes. In the limit, we show that we can transmit only a single bit of authentication material in place of a single bit of data, but in this limit, our process is equivalent to XORing the message with a similar sized random bit stream.

1   Introduction

A recent note by Rivest [3] develops the concept of chaffing, a technique based on blending authenticated plaintext information with non authenticated noise to obscure the true message. Assuming a secret authentication key shared between the sender and the receiver, only the intended recipient can easily separate the message content from the noise and the process of recovering the message without the key can be made arbitrarily difficult.

Rivest's work is part of a growing body of work that seeks to demonstrate the futility of attempting to guarantee government access to information through controls on cryptographic techniques. The purpose of this paper is to investigate ways in which the chaffing and winnowing processes might be made more efficient, especially for streams of data such as voice or video where communications latency and freedom from jitter are the most important factors. While we understand that the notions put forward by Rivest are more political than a serious suggestion for a new information hiding technology, they have served to motivate this work and we find the results interesting, and to some extent surprising.

2   Chaffing Overhead and Its Reduction

Rivest's underlying assumption for his exposition of chaffing is that the information is packaged into packets containing sequence numbers, data (or noise),

A. Pfitzmann (Ed.): IH'99, LNCS 1768, pp. 395–404, 2000.

and a MAC over the sequence number and data (or a random number that is not a MAC over the sequence number and noise). It is assumed that the data and noise come from the same distributions so that, short of passing the MAC test, there is no way to choose effectively between the data fields of two packets having the same sequence number. In the extreme case, the data field contains a single bit and the distribution assumption is easily shown to be satisfied. In this case, the space overhead for the scheme is $2(1 + size(seq\#) + size(MAC))$

With 1 bit of data, a 32 bit sequence number, and a 64 bit MAC, the overhead is about 200 to 1. If we transmit each packet independently, much of this overhead is necessary as we need the sequence numbers to put the packets in the proper order as they arrive having been (possibly) reordered by accidents of transmission.

If we are transmitting the data over a connection that has circuit properties such as the preservation of data order, certain efficiencies may be possible.

Consider the following example (taken from the Rivest note)

```
(1,0,351216)
(1,1,895634)
(2,0,452412)
(2,1,534981)
(3,0,639723)
(3,1,905344)
(4,0,321329)
(4,1,978823)
. . .
```

and so on.

If this data is transmitted in a serial fashion over a circuit with well established timing properties (framing, etc.), the actual sequence numbers and data values can be omitted since we know that the "packet" for serial number 1, data 0 (1,0) is followed by the packet for serial 1, data 1, (1,1), etc. Thus, we could transmit only the sequence of MAC and Non-MAC values or

```
(351216)
(895634)
(452412)
(534981)
(639723)
(905344)
(321329)
(978823)
. . .
```

This is an example of lossless data compression and, like the original chaffing, should not be subject to encryption controls. Now, let us suppose that the original message to be sent (with sequence numbers and authentication) was

```
(1,0,351216)
(2,1,534981)
(3,1,905344)
(4,0,321329)
...
```

We note that the serial nature of the connection eliminates the need for the serial numbers. Complementary chaffing also eliminates the need to transmit the data. However, the data can easily be inferred from the authentication. For example, if all that is transmitted is

```
(351216)
(534981)
(905344)
(321329)
...
```

the recipient can easily recover the data by assuming, for example, that the message (with sequence numbers) was

```
(1,0)
(2,0)
(3,0)
(4,0)
...
```

Computing the MACs for this message will give

```
(351216)
(XXXXXX)
(YYYYYY)
(321329)
...
```

where XXXXXX is not 534981 and YYYYYY is not 905344. Thus, the recipient knows that the message was

```
(1,0)
(2,1)
(3,1)
(4,0)
...
```

and can confirm this, if desired, by computing the MACs for sequence numbers 2 and 3 with data bits of 1 and noting that they agree with the received MACs 534981 and 905344 respectively. This is an example of an error correction code, albeit an unconventional one, and again does not represent encryption.

At this point, we have reduced the overhead somewhat, say from 200 to 1 down to about 64 to 1. Can we do better?

3   Lossy Chaffing

With chaffing as described by Rivest, we depend on fact that the probability of
the the random number that replaces the MAC in chaff packets being the actual
MAC for the chaff sequence number and data is very low. In the scheme that
was outlined above, not even this assumption is necessary, although the usual
MAC assumption that $MAC(seq\#, 0)$ is not the same as $MAC(seq\#, 1)$ is. Could
we then transmit less than the entire MAC, say, $f(MAC((seq\#, data))$, whose
size is substantially less than that of MAC and still have a reasonable chance
of determining the data portion of the message? For certain kinds of messages,
notably voice and video among others, a fairly high error rate may be acceptable.
Suppose, for the sake of argument that a bit error rate of 0.1% is acceptable for
voice and that $f(MAC(\ldots))$ is $(MAC(\ldots) mod 2^N)$ for some suitably small N.
What we want is the smallest N for which the probability of a collision between
$f(MAC(Key, Seq\#, 1))$ and $f(MAC(Key, Seq\#, 0))$ is less than the acceptable
rate. Note that this can be viewed as either lossy compression or imperfect error
correction and again is not encryption, *per se*.

HMAC MD5 as defined in [1] has the desired properties that

- a 1 bit change in input results in a change in about 50% of the output bits,
- output bits are divided equally between 0s and 1s, and
- these properties are essentially independent of the position of the bit in the
  output string.

Based on these properties, we can determine how many of the rightmost bits
of the digest would be needed to distinguish between the MAC generated from
a key, a sequence number, and a data bit of 0 and the MAC generated from
the same key and sequence number and a data bit of 1 for a given target bit
error rate. Using a 1 bit MAC would result in a 50% bit error rate. A 16 bit
MAC would result in a bit error rate of about 1 in 65,000, a 10 bit MAC would
result in a bit error rate of about 1 in 1000 (0.1%), and an 8 bit MAC would
result in a bit error rate of about 1 in 250. For many applications these error
rates are unacceptable and MACs of 32 bits or more might be needed to ensure
acceptable bit error rates. However, it is possible to make tradeoffs between chaff
space overhead and error rates over a wide range.

3.1   Using Error Correction Codes

We have investigated whether conventional error correction techniques applied
prior to chaffing with short MACs could reduce the error rate without contribut-
ing significant additional space overhead. To see how this might work, consider
block error correcting codes of the kinds that are applied to semiconductor memory. A code used in the early days of ECC memory used 23 bits to correct all
single bit errors in a 16 bit word.

Let P_{be} be the probability of a bit error. From our earlier analysis, we know
that this is $1/2^M$, where M is the length of the MAC.

The probability of no bit errors in a word of size W is $(1-P_{be})^W$ and the probability of exactly one error in a word is $WP_{be}(1-P_{be})^{W-1}$ thus the probability of one or more bit errors in a word is $1-(1-P_{be})^W$ and the probability of two or more bit errors in a word of length W' is $1-((1-P_{be})^{W'}+W'P_{be}(1-P_{be})^{W'-1})$. Using a 23 for 16 error correcting code, we can compare the number of bits required to transmit a given 16 bit data word using MACs alone ($W = 16$) or MACs plus ECC ($W' = 23$) for a given probability of an uncorrected error under the conservative assumption that the ECC can only correct single bit errors.

For a given MAC size M, we plot the probability of an uncorrected error in a 16 bit word as a function of the total number of bits required to transmit the word. For a scheme using a MAC alone, this is $16M$ while for a scheme using a MAC plus a 23 for 16 error correcting code, this is $23M$. For the MAC alone case, the word error probability is the probability that one or more bit errors occur in the 16 bits sent while for the MAC plus ECC case, it is the probability that two or more bit errors occur in the 23 bits sent. The results are shown in Fig. 1. In this figure, the error rate is plotted on a log scale. The results from the MAC alone case are indicated by a + symbol while those from the combined case are indicated with a ×. The numbers to the right of some of the symbols represent M, the size of the MAC. This can be inferred for the others since M increases as the plot moves down or to the right.

Note that for high bit error rates, (out to about 1 in 16 or 6%, the probability of receiving an error free word is nearly zero, but the MAC alone mechanism provides more efficient transmission. MACs alone are superior out to 17 bits where they are slightly more space efficient than a 12 bit MAC plus ECC for nearly the same error probability (272 bits per word with an error probability of 0.00207 versus 276 bits per word with an error probability of 0.00216). Beyond this point, the situation reverses so that a 23 bit MAC alone has the same space efficiency (368 bits per word) as a 16 bit MAC plus ECC but has a higher error probability (0.0000439 versus 0.0000157). Two additional MAC bits would be required to achieve a comparable error probability with MAC alone.

The difference grows as the MAC size increases. A 20 bit MAC plus ECC slightly outperforms a 32 bit MAC alone with a word error probability of about 1 in 10^7 while using 460 bits as compared to 512. A 38 bit MAC plus ECC outperforms a 64 bit MAC 874 bits to 1024 bits with a word error probability on the order of 1 in 10^{17}.

For cases where a large block of information is to be transmitted as a single unit, the combination of chaffing and the Package Transform [5] as described in [3] is clearly much more space efficient than even the use of fairly short MACs and provides much better error properties as well.

3.2   Multibit Hashes

Another mechanism for reducing the space overhead associated with the MAC is suggested by Pfitzmann[2, Solution to Problem 9-33]. As with the alternative described above, this scheme transmits only the MAC, however, in this case, the MAC is computed over a number of bits, say l bits at a time. The recipient then

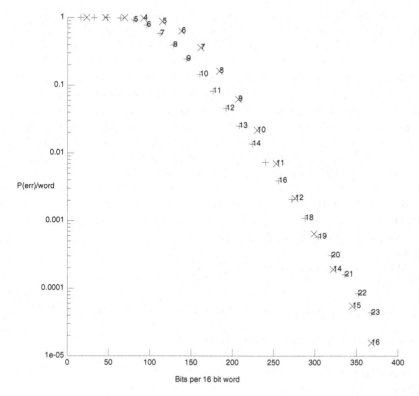

Fig. 1. Space requirements for MAC (+) *vs.* MAC and ECC (×)

computes up to $2^l - 1$ MAC values over the possible l-bit fragments and the sequence number. If the fragments are distributed randomly, an average of 2^{l-1} trial MACs will be required to confirm each fragment ($2^{l-1}/l$ MACs per bit). For $l = 1$ and $l = 2$ the average effort is one MAC per bit transmitted, but the space required for $l = 2$ is half that for $l = 1$. For $l = 8$ the space requirement is reduced by a factor of 8, but the receiver must do about 16 times as much work per bit to obtain the fragment. If the distribution of the fragment values is not uniform, as might be the case if 8 bit fragments represent ASCII codes and the message is in a natural language, ordering the trials should reduce the average effort substantially. Finally, it is possible to combine multibit fragments with reduced MAC lengths (and possibly error correcting codes) for additional space savings. We are in the process of analyzing some of these schemes.

4   Real Time Chaffing

For two way, time constrained, communications such as voice communications, the need to package the transmitted material into large blocks precludes the use of techniques such as the package transform. In the following section, we show a method based on the error correcting notion developed above that appears to allow a 1 bit MAC to be sent as a surrogate for a single bit of data, providing a technique for transmitting digitized voice signals with no space overhead and modest computational overhead.

Going back to the original exposition of the error correcting approach, we note that the recipient decodes the message by assuming that it consists of all 0 bits and correcting the bits for which the computed and transmitted MACs differ. If we could find a 1 bit MAC, say MAC_1, with the property that $MAC\_1(key, seq\#, 1)$ is the complement of $MAC\_1(key, seq\#, 0)$ that also had the statistical property that its output is evenly divided between 1s and 0s for $MAC\_1(key, seq\#, 0)$, we could use the following scheme[1].

```
If (data bit is 0)
   then
      transmit MAC_1(key, seq#, 0)
   else
      transmit not MAC_1(key, seq#, 0)
   . . .
```

The recipient would assume the transmitted bit was 0 and correct as follows:

```
If (received bit = MAC_1(key, seq#, 0)
   then
      data bit = 0
   else
      data bit = 1
   . . .
```

Note that neither the sender nor the receiver needs to compute the MAC_1 of a 1 bit, so any MAC algorithm that has the desired statistical properties will suffice. Again, a simple investigation of hmac_md5 shows that its individual bits have the desired properties as do simple aggregations of them (by byte, for example). Up to this point, we have represented the transmission as a choice between the one bit MAC of the data bit and one bit MAC of its complement (defined as the complement of the Mac of the data bit). When we examined the truth table for transmission function as seen in Fig. 2, we discover that the transmission and receive functions are the equivalent of the logical operation "Exclusive OR" (XOR). Thus the encodings and decodings can be represented as

---

[1] Defining MAC_1 as a one bit reduction (take the low order bit or XOR all the bits) of a suitable multi bit function such as hmac_md5 (the sample implementation from [1]) does not work as there is a 50% probability that this will produce identical MAC values for data bits of 1 and 0. We cheat and define

$$MAC\_1(key, seq\#, 1) = \neg MAC\_1(key, seq\#, 0)$$

to ensure that the complement property holds. The implementation shows this explicitly.

```
Transmitted Bit = Data XOR MAC_1(key, seq#, 0)
```

and

```
Data = Received Bit XOR MAC_1(key, seq#, 0)
```

This means that the same program can be used for both encoding and decoding. Unfortunately, (or perhaps fortunately) this means that the MAC is actually being used to generate the key bits for something that is equivalent to a stream cipher. Whether hmac_md5 or any other authentication code generation mechanism is really suitable for this purpose requires further investigation and is beyond the scope of this paper. Schneier's second edition [6] contains a cautionary note on a related usage in section 14.11. The political implications of this usage are likewise unclear, but when reduced to the limiting case of a one bit MAC for one bit data, chaffing and stream encryption are equivalent.

Transmit			XOR			Receive		
Data	MAC(0)	Xmit	Data	MAC(0)	XOR	Rcv	MAC(0)	Data
0	0	0	0	0	0	0	0	0
0	1	1	0	1	1	0	1	1
1	0	1	1	0	1	1	0	1
1	1	0	1	1	0	1	1	0

Fig. 2. Transmission, Reception, and Exclusive OR

Using hmac_md5 for this purpose seems quite practical and we have constructed a simple demonstration system. In its simplest form, the demonstration system computes a keyed MAC over the key and data formed by concatenating 3 bytes of pad, (0x555555), 1 data byte (0x00) and 4 bytes of sequence number. The sequence number is incremented for each bit of data to be transmitted but the MAC is always computed with the data field set to 0. In the initial system, a distinct MAC is computed for each bit of the input file. The low order bit of the 128 bit digest is XORed with the data bit and the result placed in the output file. A variation of this program computes one MAC per byte of input, XORing the data byte with a one byte MAC produced by XORing the 16 bytes of the digest produced by hmac_md5.

To "...lend an air of verisimilitude to an otherwise bald and unconvincing narrative[2]," we built a simple audio system using the error correction approach outlined above and based on one bit per bit MACs produced by hmac_md5. The data files used for experimentation are audio streams produced by the SPARC Solaris "audiotool." These consist of a 32 byte header (copied unchanged from input to output) followed by a sequence of data bytes representing 8 bit audio samples collected at a rate of 8000 samples per second. The μ-law weighting used is that used for digital telephony in the US.

---

[2] With no apologies to W.S. Gilbert and A. Sullivan

The MAC per bit implementation runs at about 10 times real time; the MAC per byte at about real time, both on an old, fairly slow, SPARC 10. The MD5 implementation used with **hmac_md5** is the reference implementation from [4]. With a more efficient implementation on a faster platform, the application should easily be capable of adequate performance to permit bidirectional telephony.

While detailed statistical analysis of the output has not been performed, the coded files appear random at first glance and certainly sound like white noise when played with the Solaris "audioplay" application.

5 Conclusions

We have shown that more efficient forms of chaffing than those proposed in [3] are possible for data streams in which ordered delivery of data and/or chaff can be assumed. We show that for systems in which each bit has a sequence number and the MAC is computed over the bit and its sequence number, transmitting just this MAC is sufficient to allow the data bit to be recovered through a one step error correction process

For data where modest error rates can be tolerated, the overhead can be further reduced by reducing the length of the MAC. By using a MAC with a length of one bit to authenticate a one bit datum, the space overhead can be effectively reduced to zero. At this limit, however, the sequence of MACs is just a random stream of bits and the transmitted material is exactly that which would be produced by XORing this stream with the data bits, a classic stream cipher.

Thus, it would appear that an information hiding mechanism based on the unregulated technology of strong authentication can be refined to be equivalent to a possibly regulated strong encryption. Although this equivalence only appears in the limiting case its implications for policy makers are unclear.

Acknowledgements

The author wishes to thank Sarah Mocas of Portland State University for encouraging the work presented here. Dick Kemmerer and Ross Anderson also provided useful feedback early in the effort. The not so anonymous reviewer is gratefully acknowledged for pointing out similar work in [2].

References

1. H. Krawczyk, M. Bellare, and R. Canetti. Hmac: Keyed-hashing for message authentication. RFC 2104 (Available at ftp://ds.internic.net/rfc/rfc2104.txt), February 1997. 398, 401
2. Andreas Pfitzmann. Lecture notes for Datensicherheit und Kryptographie, TU Dresden. http://ikt.inf.tu-dresden.de/~pfitza/DSuKrypt.html, March 1998. 399, 403
3. Ronald L. Rivest. Chaffing and winnowing: Confidentiality without encryption. Available from http://theory.lcs.mit.edu/~rivest/chaffing-980701.txt. 395, 399, 403

4. Ronald L. Rivest. The md5 message-digest algorithm. RFC 1321 (Available at ftp://ds.internic.net/rfc/rfc1321.txt), April 1992. 403
5. Ronald L. Rivest. All-or-nothing encryption and the package transform. In *Proceedings of the 1997 Fast Software Encryption Conference.* Springer, 1997. Also on http://theory.lcs.mit.edu/~rivest/fusion.ps. 399
6. Bruce Schneier. *Applied Cryptography.* John Wiley & Sons, 2nd edition, 1996. 402

An Entropy-Based Framework for Database Inference

Ira S. Moskowitz   and   LiWu Chang

Center for High Assurance Computer Systems,
Mail Code 5540, Naval Research Laboratory
Washington, DC 20375, USA
knoweng@itd.nrl.navy.mil

Abstract. In this paper, we discuss the database inference problem. We look at both query-based and partial view-based cases of the problem, concentrating our efforts on classification rules related to the partial view-based case. Based on this analysis, we develop a theoretical formulation to quantify the amount of private information that may be inferred from a public database and we discuss ways to mitigate that inference. Finally, we apply this formulation to actual downgrading issues. Our results are dependent upon the knowledge engine used to derive classification rules. We use C4.5 since it is a well-known and popular robust software tool.

1   Introduction

1.1   Background

Database inference occurs when a user with legitimate access to public information within a database is able to utilize statistical, probabilistic, or logical techniques to infer hidden information. If unauthorized users can infer hidden information, then the privacy of the data may be jeopardized. For example, unauthorized users may be able to infer private patient information from "sanitized" medical records, or private salary information from public company reports. Instances of unsanctioned inference of private information have been well documented in the literature [1,2,3,4,5,6,7]. We focus on the categorical nature of the data and the probabilistic relations between the data. We attempt to keep microdata as unmolested as possible, while allowing changes in aggregate (marginal distributions) values. Previous research noted has taken the opposite approach. We discuss downgrading and query-based situations that differ from those described in the references. We are not concerned with the issues of microdata disclosure that arise in the use of aggregate statistical information, nor with solely logical inferences.

Because existing techniques are inadequate to analyze the probabilistic situations, we present new techniques that we have developed in order to study these probabilistic inferences. Specifically, we review background material from some of our earlier papers [8], [9], [10], and then present a new entropy-based analysis of the database inference problem. Then we demonstrate how these techniques can be integrated into a software tool that we are developing called the Rational Downgrader [11].

A. Pfitzmann (Ed.): IH´99, LNCS 1768, pp. 405-418, 2000.
© Springer-Verlag Berlin Heidelberg 2000

There are two classes of users and, correspondingly, two classes of information, both consisting of *high* and *low*. High information is considered private/restricted information. The user of high information is called High. Low information is public/unrestricted information. A user allowed access to only low information is called Low. High is allowed to use both high and low information. The high information is hidden from Low.

We focus on a database made up of both low and high data. In principle, High should have access to all information (low and high) within the database; whereas Low should only have access to a portion of the information---the low information. Unfortunately, in practice, the supposedly strict boundaries on Low's access to high information are often porous. If Low can obtain "knowledge" about high information, a database inference problem exists. Database inference is a variant of Knowledge Discovery and Data Mining (KDD) [12]. In KDD, the focus is on how to extract as much useful information as possible from a large amount of data. In database inference, we wish to determine how much private information may be inferred (discovered) and how to minimize this leakage. We have expressed [10], for certain situations, the ability or inability of an unauthorized user to infer restricted information by a property called *perfect noninference*. Perfect noninference alone, however is not sufficient for analyzing the database inference problem. We must also consider the condition of *malevolent inference* and the *degree* of the inference. In order to facilitate the analysis of the database inference problem, we break it down into two cases---the query-based case and the partial view case.

1.2 Query-Based

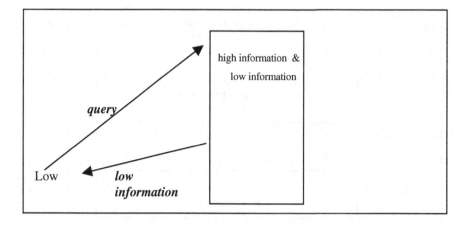

In the query-based case, there exists a database composed of both low and high information. Low is allowed to pose certain queries to the database. These queries should return only low information but, as discussed, Low might be able to deduce the prohibited high information--- the data base inference problem.

Example 1: The database consists of the tuples (Name,Age,Salary). The subtuple (Name,Salary) is considered high information, whereas the subtuples (Name,Age) and (Age,Salary) are considered low information. If Low is allowed the queries Q_1 (Name,Age) and Q_2 (Age,Salary), it may be possible for Low to learn "something" about the high information (Name,Salary). It is this "something" that we wish to quantify.

1.3 Partial View

In this situation, both High and Low each have their own respective databases. By definition, Low's database (L_{db}) is made up only of rows (cases) of low information, whereas High's database (H_{db}) is made up of both the low information and the additional high information. In other words, every row in L_{db} is actually a row or an incomplete row (some values might be missing in order to block the release of high information) from the High database. This is a special case of missing data [13]. L_{db} is the *downgraded* version of H_{db} [14] (We note that downgrading, in such a scenario, is an integral part of some high-assurance system designs. Therefore, the ramifications of downgrading must be well understood). If Low can learn information about the high information from L_{db}, then a database inference problem exists. We wish to quantify what Low may learn. An important distinction is that, in the partial view case, no queries are issued and all of the data is present and ready to be "mined."

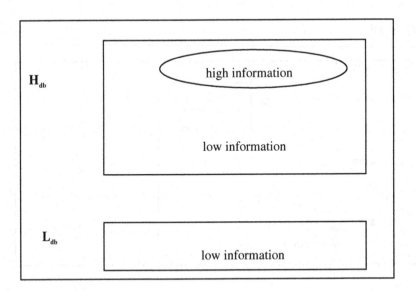

1.4 Partial View-Class Labels

In this paper, we concentrate on a specific type of partial view case. In brief, this is (downgrading) where only certain *class labels* are hidden from Low. We use decision trees to generate the classification rules that describe the relationship between the attribute values and the class labels. We use C4.5 to generate our rules. C4.5 is a well-known and readily available decision tree algorithm that has been widely accepted by the KDD community as useful software for producing classification rules [15]. From the classification rules, we derive a probabilistic model based on outcomes being the instantiations of the different rows comprising the database. (This is how we will derive the distribution B in the this section.) We emphasize that this is in the realm of modeling and engineering. It is not an act of pure mathematics. We assume that the probabilistic relations are representative of the database. Decision trees do not emphasize weak correlations between attribute values (including class labels). Rather, decision trees look for strong statistical correlations between values. These strong correlations are the power behind KDD techniques and are often derived from a subset of the data in question. We are concerned with stopping hidden information from being learned. No one decision tree algorithm or model can faithfully capture all dependencies. However, decision trees in conjunction with a well-reasoned theoretical framework, can capture powerful dependencies that Low might exploit in order to learn high information. We feel that how probability distributions are derived must be discussed in conjunction with any theoretical framework. This point was discussed with the workshop participants and we contrasted our work with how distributions were derived in models of stego systems [16, 17] and certain KDD models [18].

Specifically, there is a relational database DB and all rows of DB are considered sensitive. High is the user or managing authority of all the information in DB. Every case in DB is described by its row. A row is specified by its key k. Row k, r_k, is a (n+1)-tuple and the tuple entries are the attribute values for r_k. The last attribute value is special and is referred to as the *class label*. To avoid confusion, we will reserve the term "attribute" and "attribute value" for the first n entries of any row. It is possible for an attribute value to be missing, which is denoted by placing a ? in that entry. Class labels are never missing in DB. High determines which rows are truly sensitive--the private rows--and which rows need no longer be considered sensitive--the public rows. This is referred to as *downgrading*. Two new databases, H_{db} and L_{db}, are formed. H_{db} is the same as DB except for the designation of rows as either private or public. The row keys of L_{db} are the same as the row keys of H_{db}. If r_k is public in H_{db}, then r_k in L_{db} is identical to r_k in H_{db}. If r_k is private in H_{db}, then the n attribute values of r_k in L_{db} are the same as in H_{db}. However, the class label of r_k in L_{db} is a missing value. Therefore, we see that the low information consists of the private rows with missing class labels along with the public rows (intact). The high information consists of the private rows (intact).

The database L_{db} can be decomposed into two databases: L^-_{db} and L^+_{db}. From these subdatabases we derive two probability distributions A and B. We will model database inference by using the difference between these distributions. The database L^-_{db} consists of the private rows with the class labels missing and L^+_{db} consists of the public rows. In this scenario, A represents the distribution of the class labels given the various attribute values from L^-_{db}. However, since the class labels in L^-_{db} are missing, we are in a quandary. There is nothing we can meaningfully say about the probabilities of the various outcomes (we make a *closure assumption* that the possible instantiations of the missing values are known). We can either say that the distribution A is not well defined, or take a noninformative approach and assume that A is uniform. This is a philosophical debate see [sec 3.3.1, 19]. We choose the latter approach and assume that A is uniform. What is important is that either approach says that Low has no way of choosing one outcome over another! Letting A be an actual distribution facilitates our theoretical framework but in no way changes the concept of inference. What validates this noninformative approach is that our experiment is only run once. By this, we mean that Low only guesses at the missing class labels once. If an experiment is run multiple times, then one could get erroneous estimates of long term behavior (e.g., expectation) by using a uniform distribution when the underlying distribution might not be uniform. In this situation, it would be better to say that no distribution can be derived. However, we are not faced with multiple experimentation and, in our case, saying "I don't know" is equivalent to "uniform."

B represents the distribution of the class labels given the various attribute values from L^+_{db}. Recall our discussion from the beginning of this section that B is derived from decision trees and not from a strict frequency count. Therefore keep in mind that B, and definitions using B, are dependent upon the knowledge engine used to produce the distribution. This is why we use a "good" knowledge engine, the decision tree generator C4.5. Recall also that for both A and B we are implicitly making a realistic *closure assumption* that the set of possible outcomes is known, are the same, and are exhausted by the class labels of L_{db}. Thus, A and B describe the same outcomes but A is based only on the data in the private rows without their class labels---which is not meaningful information---whereas B is based on information from L^+_{db}. We note that in future work we will look at more general partial view cases where attribute values, and not just class labels, may be missing. In this situation A might not be uniform. Thus, we want to have a framework that we can extend to the more general cases. Also, note that in this more general situation we would have to use association rules [20] instead of just classification rules.

Example 2: The first six rows in $H_{db}2$ are public and r_7 is private.

Key	Attribute 1	Attribute 2	Attribute 3	Class Label
r_1	green	soft	cheap	*buy*
r_2	red	soft	expensive	*steal*
r_3	red	hard	expensive	*steal*
r_4	blue	soft	expensive	*steal*
r_5	blue	soft	cheap	*buy*
r_6	blue	hard	cheap	*buy*
r_7	blue	hard	expensive	*steal*

Example2a: $H_{db}2$

Thus, we see that the low database is as follows.

Key	Attribute 1	Attribute 2	Attribute 3	Class Label
r_1	green	soft	cheap	*buy*
r_2	red	soft	expensive	*steal*
r_3	red	hard	expensive	*steal*
r_4	blue	soft	expensive	*steal*
r_5	blue	soft	cheap	*buy*
r_6	blue	hard	cheap	*buy*
r_7	blue	hard	expensive	*?*

Example 2b: $L_{db}2$

L^-_{db} consists of the last row r_7. Inspection of the first six rows in $L_{db}2$ leads one to infer that the missing class label is *steal*. This is the situation against which we wish to guard. We make the closure assumption that the possible outcomes of A and B are *buy* or *steal*. By using our noninformative assumption A is a Bernoulli random variable with ½ being the probability of *buy* and ½ the probability of *steal*.

$$p_A(buy \mid \text{attributes of } r_7) = p_A(steal \mid \text{attributes of } r_7) = ½.$$

Inspection of L^+_{db} (rows r_1 through r_6) gives us two rules:

$$\text{RULE-1: “cheap} \rightarrow buy\text{”}, \quad \text{RULE-2: “expensive} \rightarrow steal\text{”}.$$

These rules are errorless. This means that any row in L^+_{db} that has Attribute 3 = cheap, always has the class label *buy*, and any row in L^+_{db} that has Attribute 3 = expensive, always has the class label *steal*. Note that in this trivial case all decision trees should produce the same rules with the same error rate. C4.5 certainly produces the same errorless rules; thus, we derive 0/1 probabilities for B. Row r_7 has Attribute 3 = expensive; thus, by using B, Low may correctly infer the class label *steal*. Since, in terms of probability, $p_B(steal \mid \text{attributes of } r_7) = 1$, we see that we do have database inference, since Low can obtain the hidden high information. Note that the distributions A and B are different.

To end this section we will give a brief description of C4.5, an invention of J. Ross Quinlan. C4.5 produces decision trees based upon data from a database. C4.5 attempts to derive the strongest rules influencing a special attribute value called the class label. C4.5 does this by using a method involving a weighted mutual information between attribute values and the class labels. Once C4.5 has produced a set of rules it prunes this rule set down to eliminate possibly insignificant effects though a series of sophisticated techniques. C4.5 has been shown to produce good decision trees that accurately reflect real-world situations. C4.5 is a benchmark of the KDD community.

2 Perfect Noninference

Shannon mathematically formalized the idea of secrecy [21] in cryptography. He accomplished this by expressing, in terms of probabilities, the concept of *perfect secrecy*. Let $P(M)$ represent the a priori probability of a message M, and let the conditional probability $P(M|E)$ represent the a posteriori probability of message M after the cryptogram E is received.

Definition 1 (Shannon) Given finite messages M that are enciphered into possible cryptograms E we say that perfect secrecy is achieved iff $.E, .M, P(M \mid E) = P(M)$.

   We develop a similar property for database inference when dealing with the partial view-class label case. We discuss how this theory will also work for certain query-based cases. In future work we hope to develop it for general query-based and partial view cases.

Note: What follow *applies to the partial view-class label case only*. However, certain definitions, such as perfect noninference hold for the query-based case as well [10].

   A and *B* are as before, and share the same sample space *S*. Thus, we have the following definitions (mimicking Shannon's definition, *A* (*B*) takes the place of P(*M*) (P(*M* | *E*)):

Definition 2 ([10]) If the probability distributions *A* and *B* are identical, then we have *perfect noninference*. If *A* and *B* are different, then we have *database inference*.

   Measuring the deviation between the a priori and posterior distributions gives us insight into the amount of database inference that has occurred. Any measurement of database inference should include two factors. One factor is the difference between *A* and *B*. However, a second factor in determining database inference is how close *B* is to being a constant distribution (i.e., the outcome is known with certainty). For this, an entropy-based measure would work. The closer the entropy is to zero, the less uncertainty we have in the distribution. However, entropy alone does not suffice. For example, if the probabilities making up *A* and *B* are simply permuted, there is no difference in entropy but the distributions are certainly quite different. (These discussions are included for future extensions of our work when *A* may not be uniform, e.g., noninformative Bayesian priors.) Also, note that in practice, *perfect* noninference may be impossible to obtain and some more pragmatic approach may be needed. However, as a theoretical tool, perfect noninference gives us a precise way to determine when Low may not learn high information.

   A standard way to measure the difference between discrete probability distributions *X* and *Y*, that share the same sample space *S*, is with the discrimination [22], written as D(*X*‖*Y*). This is also referred to as the Kullback-Liebler distance or relative entropy.

$$D(X\|Y) = \sum_{s_i \in S} p_X(s_i) \log_2 [p_X(s_i) / p_Y(s_i)]$$

(If any probabilities *p* or *q* are zero, the relevant term $p \log(p/q)$ is taken to be its limiting value. Both probabilities are never simultaneously 0 because that occurrence is not considered part of the sample space.) Note that [23] D(*X*‖*Y*) = 0 iff *X* = *Y*, and D(*X*‖*Y*) ≥ 0. However, D(*X*‖*Y*) is not a true distance because D(*X*‖*Y*) • D(*Y*‖*X*), and D(*X*‖*Y*) does not satisfy the triangle inequality. However, it can be "symmetrized" [24] by, for example, letting D'(*X*‖*Y*) = ½ [D(*X*‖*Y*) + D(*Y*‖*X*)]. Discrimination measures the inefficiency [22] of assuming the distribution is *Y* when the distribution is actually *X*.

   Our motivation for using D(*X*‖*Y*) came from [18] where various concepts of measuring the differences between distributions are discussed and Cachin's modeling work [16] in the context of information hiding. However, Cachin is concerned with whether one can determine if there is a hidden stego message inside a cover message. He uses discrimination as an acceptance threshold for existence of the stego message. We, on the other hand, use discrimination to determine the amount of database inference that exists. Of course, since the origins of discrimination are from hypothesis testing it is not surprising that discrimination is useful in both contexts.   We measure the discrimination between the prior probability distribution A and the posterior distribution B.

Definition 3 The **inference** between the prior distribution A and the posterior distribution B is defined to be $D(B\|A)$.

Of course this definition is dependent upon the fact that we have used C4.5.

Note 1: We have perfect noninference iff $D(B\|A) = 0$ and we have database inference iff $D(B\|A) > 0$.

Proof: Obvious.

When we have database inference we measure it by the non-zero inference $D(B\|A)$.

Theorem 1: (well-known): If Y is uniform, and N is the number of non-trivial outcomes of Y (and X) then $D(X\|Y) = \log_2 N - H(X)$, where $H(X)$ is the (base-2) entropy of X.

Proof: The proof is standard and trivial but we include it for completeness. (Note this also appears as Eq. 3 in [16] without proof.)

$$D(X\|Y) = \sum p_X(s_i) \log_2 [p_X(s_i) / p_Y(s_i)]$$
$$= \sum p_X(s_i) \log_2 [p_X(s_i)] - \sum p_X(s_i) \log_2 [p_Y(s_i)]$$
$$= \sum p_X(s_i) \log_2 [p_X(s_i)] - \sum p_X(s_i) \log_2 [1/N]$$
$$= -H(X) + \log_2 [N] \sum p_X(s_i) = -H(X) + \log_2 N \qquad \bullet$$

Corollary: Since A is uniform, the inference is $\log_2 N - H(B)$ and ranges between 0 and $\log_2 N$.

Note 2: For the special case that we have (A uniform), that $D(B\|A) = H(A) - H(B)$, since $H(A) = \log_2 N$. It is interesting to contrast this fact with the difference of entropies as discussed by Anderson [§ 4.1, 25].

Cachin [Def. 1, 16] defined the concept of ε–security for stegosystems. The same ideas can be applied to database inference.

Definition 5 We say that we have ε–inference if $D(B\|A) \dagger \varepsilon$.

Theorem 2: We have ε–inference iff $H(B) \geq \log_2 N - \varepsilon$, where N is the size of the sample space.

Proof: Trivial.

Of course, 0-inference is the same as perfect noninference. In practice, perfect noninference may be impossible to achieve. Therefore, we put forward the idea of ε–inference as a more pragmatic approach.   Therefore, a database that has ε–inference allows ε database inference. Having database inference is not necessarily a bad thing. If using B, instead of A, leads Low away from the correct private information, then allowing Low to know B is actually good. This situation can only occur when L^{-}_{db} is inconsistent with L^{+}_{db}.

Definition 6 If $D(B\|A) > 0$, then we have *malevolent inference* if the odds of Low correctly guessing the private information are increased by using B instead of A.

As discussed above, this can only occur when the low information is consistent with the high information. Thus, the fact that database inference exists does not necessarily mean that privacy has been compromised.

If $D(B\|A)$ is "large" this means that $H(B)$ is small. This smallness, in turn, tells us that B is very specific in designating the outcomes. In fact, if B specifies one outcome with probability 1, then $H(B)$ is 0. However, this must be moderated with a discussion of the malevolence of B. If B is pointing Low away from the correct outcome, then there is no harm in allowing the database inference. On the other hand, if B is pointing Low toward the correct outcome, then the database inference is malevolent. If a system has malevolent inference, we can still live with the system if it has ε-inference, but ε is less than a certain bound.

In KDD, knowledge discovery is considered to be a good thing. In our case, however, it is a bad thing because we are concerned with protecting information privacy. Thus, we wish to protect against Low's ability to learn restricted high information. By using ad hoc notions of database inference, we started investigating this problem in [10]. Since a good defense involves understanding the offense, we must fully understand how KDD techniques apply to databases with both low and high information and then take a data anti-mining (data damming) approach.

Let us apply our theoretical model to Ex. 2. The size of the sample space is 2, A is Bernoulli with $p = \frac{1}{2}$, p is probability of steal, and B is the constant distribution with $p = 1$. Therefore, $D(B\|A) = 1$, which is the maximum possible inference with the given prior distribution A. This is extremely malevolent inference and must be averted. Downgrading as shown in Ex. 1 is harmful and detrimental to High's privacy interests. (Of course, keep in mind that High knows the actual missing class labels.)

Our entropy-based model of inference can also be applied to certain query-based cases. We sketch the method in this paper. Before any queries are issued, Low knows only what the outcomes might be. Therefore, as in the partial view-class label case, A is uniform. We can derive B for the query-based case (in a manner similar to partial view-class label case) if the private information is all from the data in one particular column. In this situation, without loss of generality, we can assume that it is the last column and consider that column to be the class labels. We must also assume that the row keys all come from one column. However, due to the formation of the queries, instantiations of L^{+}_{db} might be different from that of H_{db}. In Ex. 1, the name is the row key and the salary is the class label. However, Q_{2} might return more than one salary for a given age. The Low database might have a different structure. For example, in the next example it would be multiply instantiated attributes. In this case, the probabilities of the different outcomes (multiple instantiations) would be uniformly split in a given row. With this in mind, let us show how the theory can be applied to Ex. 1.

Name	Age	Salary
Bruce	41	$100,000
Paul	41	$200,000
Tim	25	$35,000

Example 3: Consider the following instantiated version of Ex. 1. The private information is the name/salary relationship. Low wishes to know how much Bruce is paid. We assume that Low knows that the salaries are chosen from ($35K, $100K, $200K). Let A represent the a priori distribution of salaries for Bruce. With no other knowledge, Low assigns a probability of 1/3 to each outcome of A. Low is allowed the following two queries: Q_1 returns (name, age) and Q_2 returns (age, salary). From this, Low has the following information: from Q_1 --- (Bruce, 41), (Paul, 41), (Tim, 25), and from Q_2 --- (41, $100K), (41, $200K), (25, $35K). Therefore, Low knows that Bruce makes $100K or $200K. Therefore, the posterior distribution B representing Bruce's salary is P($35K) = 0, P($100K) = .5, P($200K) = .5. Since $A \bullet B$ and we see that database inference exists. The amount of inference is $\log_2 3 - 1$. Note that Q_1 or Q_2 alone give perfect noninference.

3   The Rational Downgrader

We have begun prototyping a software device called the Rational Downgrader [11]. In this section, we briefly review the design of the Rational downgrader and discuss how $D(B\|A)$ is used in conjunction with the Rational Downgrader. We have designed the Rational Downgrader to deal with database inference arising from downgrading that can be modeled as the partial view-class label case (we are investigating extensions to more general downgrading). The Rational Downgrader calls a downgrading decision into question if it allows "excessive" private hidden information to leak via database inference. We plan to use $D(B\|A)$ as the measure of inference, as discussed in the previous section. Again, keep in mind that our results are dependent upon the fact that we are using C4.5. Therefore, what we are considering are inferences with respect to C4.5. If there is too much inference, and it is understood to be malevolent, the Rational Downgrader will modify the initial downgrading decision by changing certain attribute values to missing values. The amount of inference is then analyzed under these new conditions. This is why we have defined a measure for the inference. By using the inference, we are able to decide what is an acceptable level of inference. If the inference is lessened, then we have increased our privacy. However, the instantia-

tion of attribute values as missing values must be performed judiciously so as not to
weaken functionality and performance of the

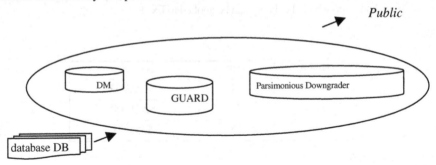

low database excessively. We use a "penalty" function approach to model the performance. We note though that the degradation of performance must be measured
against the increase in privacy due to the lessening of the inference.

The Rational Downgrader is comprised of three related components. The components
are the knowledge-based decision maker (*DM*), the *GUARD*, and the *Parsimonious Downgrader*. After it has performed its initial downgrading, High itself, (or some authority super-
vising High), is the "operator" of the Rational Downgrader.

L^+_{db} is fed into DM. DM produces classification rules since our concern, in the prototype
Rational Downgrader, is the missing associated class labels.

$$DB \rightarrow downgrade \rightarrow L^+_{db} \rightarrow \boxed{DM} \rightarrow Rule\ Set$$

As a research prototype, we use C4.5 [15] for DM. C4.5 uses L^+_{db} as training data and views
L^-_{db} as the test data. Of course, this can be replaced by other sound knowledge-based inference
systems and frameworks or combinations thereof.   Therefore $D(B\|A)$ is understood to be
based upon C4.5 in the Rational Downgrader.

Rules, and the associated probability distribution B learned from DM, are applied to L^-_{db}.
The information learned from L^-_{db} via the DM rules must now be measured. This is the function of the GUARD. Prior to writing this paper, we did not have a way to measure the database
inference! Now, though, we will be using $D(B\|A)$.

$$Rule\ Set \bullet\ L^-_{db} \rightarrow \boxed{GUARD} = pass\ or\ fail$$

The GUARD must determine if excessive inference has occurred and, if so, if the inference is malevolent. If High has assurance that private information will not be leaked, our

analysis is complete (pass). However, if Low is able to glean high information from the public rows—the database inference problem exists (fail). High must reconsider the decisions that it made when it initially downgraded the information. High now redoes its initial downgrading in a parsimonious fashion.

If GUARD = fail, then DB $\rightarrow$ | Parsimonious Downgrader | $\rightarrow L_{db} = L^{+}_{db} \bullet L^{-}_{db}$

Parsimonious downgrading calls the initial downgrading decisions into question and views these decisions as being too liberal if possible database inference, within certain bounds determined by the GUARD, are not taken into account. Parsimonious downgrading is the process of adjusting the downgrading process by making less information publicly available, which it does by inserting missing values for some of the attribute values in the public rows. The idea of parsimonious downgrading was first introduced in [9]. Note that deleting certain aggregate statistics to suppress statistical disclosure is discussed in [26]. This lessening of the amount of public information causes the DM to produce weaker inference rules. We call this *rule confusion*. The net effect of rule confusion is to lessen Low's ability to infer the private class labels (lessen $D(B\|A)$). Of course, hiding additional public information negatively affects the functionality provided by the public rows to Low since data is missing, so it must be done in an intelligent manner (the penalty function). Data cannot be hidden without deleterious effect on system performance. For now, we use a simplistic counting formula for the penalty function and we assign a value of -1 for each missing value. We call the database of adjusted (via the missing values) public rows L_{db}. It is decomposed (as before) into L^{+}_{db} and L^{-}_{db}; of course, L^{-}_{db} is just L^{-}_{db}.

$L^{+}_{db} \rightarrow$ | DM | $\rightarrow$ Rule Set   Rule Set $\bullet$ $L^{-}_{db} \rightarrow$ | GUARD | = pass or fail

After High has performed parsimonious downgrading within the bounds set by an agreed-upon penalty function, the process must start again with the Low database being sent into DM. After DM extracts the rules and applies them to L^{-}_{db} and the inferences have been determined, the GUARD determines the pass/fail decision. If "pass," then High is done. High can now have an assurance that Low will not learn things it is not intended to learn. However, if the GUARD determines "fail," then the process must be restarted.

For future work, one must keep in mind that Low, by seeing missing data, might attempt to insert attribute values to see if non-trivial inferences can be obtained. We refer to this as *restoration*. This becomes a variant of steganography [25]---High attempts to hide data (by changing it to missing values) so that Low does not even know that it has been hidden. We must also study the idea of malevolent inference on only certain pieces of the private information counteracting non-malevolence on other pieces of private information. In other words, we want to look at both global and local effects of database inference and how probabilistic discrimination can filter such inferences.

4   Conclusion

In this paper, we have reviewed different versions of the database inference problem, with particular emphasis on the partial view-class label case. With respect to the partial view-class label case, we have developed a theoretical measure for an entropy-based definition of database inference and have provided illustrative examples. We have discussed extensions of this theory to more general database inference problems. Finally, we have shown how to integrate our theoretical measure into our software tool (the Rational Downgrader).   We feel that C4.5 is a robust way of generating the various probabilities. we are presently running experiments to determine just how robust it is and to compare it with our decision tools..

5   Acknowledgement

We wish to thank R. Heilizer, C. Cachin, the anonymous reviewers, and the workshop participants for their helpful comments.

References

1. G. Duncan and D. Lambert, *The Risk of Disclosure for Microdata*, Jour. of Business & Economic Statistics, Vol. 7, No. 2, April 1989, pp. 207-217.
2. G. Duncan and S. Mukherjee, *Microdata Disclosure Limitation in Statistical Databases: Query Size and Random Sample Query Control*, Proc. IEEE Symp. on Security and Privacy, Oakland, CA, 1991, pp. 278-287.
3. G. Duncan and R. Pearson, *Enhancing Access to Microdata while Protecting Confidentiality: Prospects for the Future*, Statistical Science, Vol. 6, No. 3, 1991, pp. 219-239.
4. L. Willenborg and T. deWall, *Statistical Disclosure Control in Practice,* Lecture Notes in Statistics #111, Springer, 1996.
5. D. Marks, *Inference in MLS Database Systems*, IEEE Trans. Knowledge and Data Engineering, Vol. 8, No. 1, (1996) pp. 46-55.
6. T. Hinke, H. Delugach, & R. Wolf, *A Framework for Inference-Directed Data Mining*, Database Security Vol. X: Status and Prospects, (eds., Samarati & Sandhu) IFIP, (1997) pp. 229-239.
7. J. Schafer, *Analysis of Incomplete Multivariate Data*, Monographs on Statistics and Applied Probability #72, Chapman & Hall, 1997.
8. L. Chang and I.S. Moskowitz, *Bayesian Methods Applied to the Database Inference Problem*, Proc. IFIP WG11.3 Working Conf. on Database Security, Greece, 1998.

9. L. Chang and I.S. Moskowitz, *Parsimonious Downgrading and Decision Trees Applied to the Inference Problem*, Proc. New Security Paradigms 1998, Charlottesville, Virginia.

10. I.S. Moskowitz and L. Chang, *A Formal View of the Database Inference Problem*, Proc. CIMCA'99, Vienna, Computational Intelligence for Modelling, Control & Automation, M. Mohammadian (Ed.), IOS Press, February, 1999, pp. 254-259.

11. I.S. Moskowitz and L. Chang, *The Rational Downgrader*, Proc. PADD'99, London, UK, Apr. 1999, pp. 159- 165.

12. T.Y. Lin, T. Hinke, D. Marks, & B. Thuraisingham, *Security and Data Mining*, Database Security Vol. 9: Status and Prospects, IFIP, (1996) pp. 391-399.

13. A. Kong, J. Liu, J. & W. Wong, *Sequential Imputation and Bayesian Missing Data Problems*, Journal of ASA, Vol. 89, No. 425, (1994) pp. 278-288.

14. M. Kang, J. Froscher, & I.S. Moskowitz, *A Framework for MLS Interoperability*, Proc. HASE'96, (1996) pp. 198-205.

15. J. Ross Quinlan, *C4.5 Programs for Machine Learning*, Morgan Kaufman Publishers, 1993.

16. C. Cachin, *An Information–Theoretic Model for Steganography*, Proc. 2nd International Workshop, Information Hiding'98, pp. 306-318, Portland Oregon, April 14-17, 1998.

17. J. Zöllner, H. Federrath, H. Klimant, A. Pfitzmann, R. Piotraschke, A. Westfeld, G. Wicke, & G. Wolf, *Modeling the Security of Steganographic Systems*, Proc. 2nd International Workshop, Information Hiding'98, pp. 344-354, Portland Oregon, April 14-17, 1998.

18. R. Subramonian, *Defining diff as a data mining primitive*, Proc. KDD-98, pp. 334-338, NY, NY, 1998.

19. J.O. Berger, *Statistical Decision Theory and Bayesian Analysis*, 2nd ed, Springer, 1980.

20. R. Agrawal, T. Imielinski, & A. Swami, *Mining Association Rules between Sets of Items in Large Databases*, , Proc. ACM SIGMOD Conference, Washington DC, May 1993.

21. C. Shannon, *Communication Theory of Secrecy Systems*, Bell System Technical Journal, v. 28, n. 4, (1949) pp. 656-715.

22. S. Kullback and R.A. Leibler, *On Information and Sufficiency*, Ann. Math. Stat., 22:79-86, 1951.

23. *T.M. Cover and J.A. Thomas*, Elements of Information Theory, Wiley, 1991.

24. J.T. Foote and H.F. Silverman, *A Model Distance Measure for Talker Clustering and Identification*, Proc. ICASSP-94, pp. 317-320, 1994.

25. R. Anderson, *Stretching the Limits of Steganography*, Proc. 1st International Workshop, Information Hiding, pp. 39-48, Cambridge, UK, May 30-June 1, 1996.

26. S. Hansen and E. Unger, *An Extended Memoryless Inference Control Model: Partial-Table Level Suppression*, Proc. 1991 Symp. Applied Comp., pp. 142-149.

Covert Information Transmission through the Use of Standard Collision Resolution Algorithms

Talat Mert Doğu and Anthony Ephremides

Institute for Systems Research and Department of Electrical Engineering
University of Maryland, College Park, MD, 20742, USA

Abstract. The objective of this paper is to demonstrate the potential of the wireless medium to host covert channels. We do so by considering a simple covert channel and evaluating its performance. The channel is based on the First Come First Serve (FCFS) spliting algorithm, which is a standard collision resolution algorithm [1,2] that operates in a distributed fashion and coordinates access to a standard collision channel (possibly wireless medium or multi access cable) shared by a large number of users.

1   Introduction

Wireless communication is inherently less private than wire-line communication because wireless (radio) communication can be intercepted without direct physical "tap". Wireless networks are also more easily subject to usage fraud than are their wire-line counterparts for the same reason. Thus unless an initial investment is made in security technology, information providers, carriers, and users will face new threats.

In recent years research on security for wireless networks has mostly concentrated on user authentication, privacy and data integrity problems. More protocol specific issues such as disclosure of location information in mobile IP has also attracted interest. [5] However the threat of covert channels remains to be investigated.

A covert channel exists when a process transmits information by employing an aspect of the system in use, which was not implemented for carrying this type of information. The motivation for the covert information transmission generally lies in security restrictions that prohibit communicating parties to carry out their information exchange using a conventional system. Therefore they manipulate the operation of the system in a way that can be detected by the intended receiver. [4] Wireless communication networks involve numerous variables that can be manipulated in order to convey covert information. Feedback patterns, power levels, coding rates are examples of such variables. Because of the nature of the wireless medium these variables are easy to access and manipulate. Moreover once manipulated the changes can be detected by all users that are in the transmission range.

This paper investigates a covert channel implementation in a multiple access (possibly wireless) channel which uses the First Come First Serve (FCFS)

A. Pfitzmann (Ed.): IH'99, LNCS 1768, pp. 419–433, 2000.
© Springer-Verlag Berlin Heidelberg 2000

splitting algorithm to provide access to individual users. In the next chapter we define our multi-access channel and the operation of the FCFS splitting algorithm. Section 3 introduces the idea for the covert operation and describes two procedures that implement the covert transmission.Section 4 describes the covert reception procedure. In Section 5 the performance of the covert channel is investigated. Section 6 studies the impact of the covert operation on the collision channel performance. Section 8 concludes our paper with a summary of results and insights obtained from this research and indicates areas for future research.

2   Multi-access Channel Model and FCFS Algorithm

We consider the following model of a multiple access channel. A large number of users generate messages in a Poisson manner, at a total rate of λ messages per unit of time. Once a message has been generated its source can transmit it on a common channel. Transmissions start at integer multiples of unit of time and last one unit of time, also called a "slot". If the transmission from two or more sources overlap, a collision is said to occur, and all messages are lost and must be retransmitted at a later time. If only one source transmits the transmission is successful. All sources can observe the channel and learn at the end of a slot whether it was idle or if a success or a collision has occurred. This common feedback is the only information that sources share.

Several methods have been proposed to device an efficient means to share the common channel. Among these methods, the FCFS splitting algorithm is the one known to yield the highest stable throughput of 0.487760 [3]. The rooted binary tree structures in Figure 1 depict the evolution of the FCFS algorithm for a particular pattern of idles, successes, and collisions. Each tree represents a *collision resolution period*, CRP, where the FCFS algorithm initializes at the root vertex. S represents the set of packets in the start of the CRP, and L (left) and R (right) represents the two subsets that S splits into if a collision is observed. Each vertex in the tree corresponds to a subset of backlogged packets. Vertices whose subsets contain two or more packets have two upward branches corresponding to the splitting of the subset into two new subsets. An idle or success observed at S or two consecutive successes observed at subsets of S cause the algorithm to choose a new S and generate a new tree.

As the name implies FCFS splitting algorithm requires splitting of the set of sources with a packet to transmit. For presentation purposes the simplest choice is splitting by arrival time. At each integer time k, the algorithm specifies the packets to be transmitted in slot k (i.e., from k to $k+1$) to be the set of all packets that arrived in some earlier interval, say from $T(k)$ to $T(k) + \alpha(k)$. This interval is called the *allocation interval* for slot k, and is classified by the algorithm as either a left, L, or a right, R, interval. The FCFS splitting algorithm is the set of rules by which the nodes calculate the allocation interval starting point, $T(k)$, the allocation interval length, $\alpha(k)$, and the interval status , L or R, for slot k in terms of the feedback, allocation interval and status from slot $k-1$.

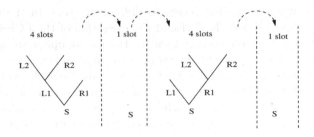

Feedback pattern: c c s s - i -c i s s - s ....

Fig. 1. Evolution of the FCFS algorithm. *c:collision, s:success, i:idle*

3   The Covert Operation

The FCFS splitting algorithm itself is transparent to the users of the shared channel and does not contain any user information. The user information is confined to the packets that are being transmitted according to the rules of the FCFS splitting algorithm discussed in the previous section. However we show that it is possible to convey user information in the number of collisions observed in each CRP. For example, a CRP in which 2 collisions are observed may indicate a "0", while a CRP in which 4 collisions are observed may indicate a "1". Let us denote the covert processes which send and receive information by manipulating the FCFS algorithm by CT and CR, for Covert-Transmitter and Covert-Receiver, respectively. The following assumptions hold for the rest of this paper;

Assumptions:

1. CT and CR share a codebook consisting of integers; $C = \{m_1, m_2, ..., m_i, ...\}$.
2. CT can choose to send or not to send a dummy packet at any slot. This requires a process which can override the rules set by the FCFS splitting algorithm in order to be able to send packets at desired slots.
3. CR is a passive monitor. It does not interfere with the operation of the multi access medium but receives the same feedback as the users of the medium.
4. Apart from CT all other users of the shared channel generate Poisson traffic with a total arrival rate λ and use the FCFS splitting algorithm for accessing the channel.

   Figure 2 (a) and (b) depict the flow charts for procedures 1 and 2, respectively, which create collisions for covert information transfer. Both procedures can be considered as consisting of two operational phases, which are separated by a dashed line in Figure 2. In Phase 1 for both Procedures 1 and 2 CT induces collisions by sending dummy packets at each slot of a starting CRP until the desired number of collisions, m, is observed. m, a positive integer number, is the channel symbol that CT sends to CR. It is assumed that the dummy packets sent by CT contain legitimate information. Hence in the case of the channel being monitored for security the dummy packets will be no different than legitimate packets. Note from Figure 2 that the actions Procedure 1 and 2 implement in the first phase of the covert operation are exactly the same. Thus, both procedures use the same idea of covert information transmission, namely conveying information in the number of collisions observed in a CRP. Even though CT does not obey the FCFS algorithm rules as implied in assumption 2, it must appear as if it is, in order to avoid easy detection of the covert operation. This means that the feedback pattern observed in a CRP where CT creates collisions should be no different than a feedback pattern that might be observed in the normal operation of the system without CT interfering. Phase 2 ensures that the operation of the collision channel under the influence of CT mimics the normal operation of the system. Note from Figure 2 that the actions Procedure 1 and 2 implement in Phase 2 of the covert operation are different.

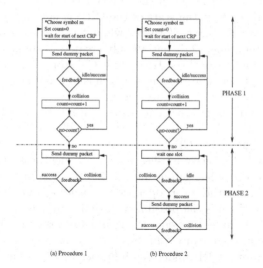

Fig. 2. Flow chart of covert transmission procedures implemented by CT

Consider the first phase. Assume the set S, which contains all packets to be send at the start of a CRP, is empty. Since CT will be sending a dummy packet at each slot, the feedback of the transmission corresponding to S will be a success. This will terminate the CRP and a new CRP will start. The duration of such a CRP is one slot and CT is not able to sent any covert information since no collisions are generated. Now assume set S contains at least 1 legitimate user packet. The transmission of the dummy packet and the packets in S will cause a collision. The root vertex representing the start of the CRP will be split into left ($L1$) and right ($R1$) branches. The FCFS algorithm mandates that the left subset be visited first. This subset may be empty if the splitting procedure put all packets in S into the subset of vertex $R1$. In this case the only packet transmitted in the next slot will be the dummy packet of CT. The feedback will be success and according to the FCFS rules the next enabled vertex will be $R1$. Note that since we observed a collision at the root we know that S contains at least 1 packet. Moreover the success at vertex $L1$ indicates that subset $L1$ is empty. Hence subset $R1$ must contain at least 1 legitimate packet. Knowing that CT will send a dummy packet, the probability of observing a collision at the slot when subset $R1$ is enabled is 1. This collision will split subset $R1$ into subsets $R2$ and $L2$. If subset $L1$ is not empty then the packets in this subset and the dummy packet of CT will generate the second collision and subset $L1$ will be split into subsets $L2$ and $R2$. Observe that given S contains at least one packet and that CT operates in the first phase, we will observe another collision with probability 1. The same reasoning can be applied to the subsequent sets in the binary tree that observe a collision and are split into two subsets since the collision supplies the same information about the parent set regardless of the exact position of the parent set in the binary tree. As a result we observe that given the original set S at the start of the CRP is not empty, CT will be able to create as many collisions as it wishes while it is operating in the first phase.

When CT enters phase 2, it has already created m collisions and would like to stop sending dummy packets. However if CT stops sending dummy packets subsequent right subsets may be empty, which is a situation that can never occur in the normal operation of the FCFS algorithm, and may lead to the detection of the covert operation. Therefore CT needs to continue to monitor and to interfere with the system in order to guarantee that no idles will be observed at right subsets until the end of the CRP.

In procedure 1, CT accomplishes the above mentioned task by sending a dummy packet at every left subset until it observes the first success. Procedure 2 prevents detection of the covert operation by sending a dummy packet in every right subset when there is the possibility of that right subset being empty. This possibility exists in phase 2, whenever a right subset is entered and the previous left subsets did not observe any collisions entirely due to legitimate user packets.

The evolution of a CRP under the influence of Procedure 1 and Procedure 2 can be modeled with Markov Chains. These models are depicted in Figures 3 and 4. Given the FCFS splitting rules, the actions that CT implements, and the Poisson characteristic of the legitimate user traffic, the one step transition probabilities for these Markov chains can be calculated by examining the events that would cause success, collision or idle at each state of the Markov Chain.

4   The Covert Channel

The procedures that CT and CR implement create a discrete memoryless channel(DMC) which we denote as Covert-DMC. The input symbols of this channel are determined by CT and CR by agreeing on the integers that will be used to sent covert information. Based on the number of collisions observed in a particular CRP, the covert receiver CR decides which symbol was sent. At this point it

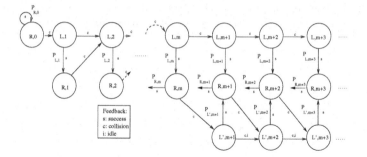

Fig. 3. Markov Chain Model for Procedure 1

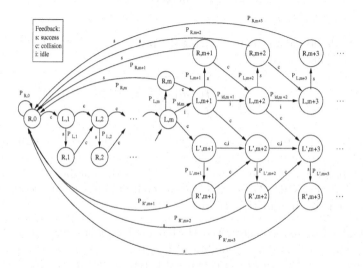

Fig. 4. Markov Chain Model for Procedure 2

is important to note that the observed number of collisions "c" in a CRP may be greater than the number of collisions "m" that CT intended to generate. There are two reasons for these extra collisions:

1. The legitimate user packets that are in the active allocation interval at the start of Phase 2(at state (L, m)) may cause additional collisions.
2. As CT sends dummy packets in Phase 2 to eliminate unusual feedback patterns, these dummy packets may collide with legitimate packets and cause additional collisions.

With this point of view we have a detection problem. Since any M-ary hypothesis testing problem can be decomposed into a series of binary hypothesis testing problems it is of particular interest to investigate the case where CT transmits one of two possible positive integer values m_1 or m_2. Without loss of generality assume $m_1 \leq m_2$. Our observation space consists of all positive integers greater or equal to m_1. Figure 5 visualizes the problem.

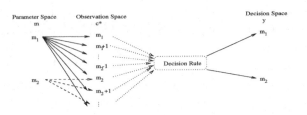

Fig. 5. The detection model.

A suitable decision rule minimazing the probability of error can be expressed in terms of a likelihood ratio test:

$$L(c) = \frac{f(c|m_1)}{f(c|m_2)} \underset{m_1}{\overset{m_2}{\lessgtr}} \frac{w(m_2)}{w(m_1)} \ . \tag{1}$$

where $f(c|m_i)$ denotes the probability that CR counts c collisions given that CT intended to generate m_i collisions in a CRP. Also $w(m_i), i = 1, 2$ denotes the a priori probability of CT to choose $m_i, i = 1, 2$ as the number of collisions to be generated at that CRP. Given the Markov chain models for procedures 1 and 2 we can calculate the function $f(c|m)$.

Consider Figure 3 depicting the Markov model for procedure 1. Let $P_m(R, i)$ and $P_m(L', i)$ denote the probabilities that given the system is at state (L, m), respective state (R, i) or (L', i) is entered before returning to $(R, 0)$ and during the transitions from state (L, m) to state (R, i) or (L', i) no idles are observed. Both $P_m(R, i)$ and $P_m(L', i)$ can be computed iteratively in i. Our analysis reveals that CR will count c collisions if the CRP observes its first idle at state (L', c) or if the CRP terminates from state (R, c) and the transitions leading to that state are not triggered by any idles. Using these observations for procedure 1 we have:

$$f(c|m) = P_{R,c}(s)P_m(R, c) + P_{L',c}(i)P_m(L', c) \ . \tag{2}$$

where $P_{R,c}(s)$ denotes the probability of observing a success at state (R, c) and $P_{L',c}(i)$ denotes the probability of observing an idle at state (L', c).

The Markov model for procedure 2 is shown in Figure 4. Let $P_m(L, i)$, $P_m(L', i)$, $P_m(R, i)$, $P_m(R', i)$ denote the probability that given the system is at state (L, m), respective state (L, i), (L', i), (R, i), (R', i) is entered before returning to $(R, 0)$ and during these transitions no idles are observed. These probabilities again can be computed iteratively in i. Using the FCFS rules and the covert procedures we establish that CR will count c collisions if the CRP observes its first idle either at state (L, c) or (L', c). CR counts c collisions also if the CRP terminates from states (R, c) or (R', c) and the transitions leading to these states are not triggered by any idles. Hence we have:

$$f(c|m) = P_{R,c}(s)P_m(R, c) + P_{L,c}(i)P_m(L, c) + P_{R',c}(s)P_m(R', c) + \\ + P_{L',c}(i)P_m(L', c) \; . \tag{3}$$

where the probability of observing an idle or success at a certain state is expressed by $P_{state}(i)$ and the probability of observing a success at a certain state is expressed by $P_{state}(s)$.

Note that for both procedures, 1 and 2 the probabilities $p_m\{., i\}$ are decreasing as the number of iterations increases. This is because in each iteration the value of the previous step is multiplied by a probability, which must have a value between 1 and 0. The number of iterations to compute $p_m\{., i\}$ depends on both m and i. Thus we can state that $p_m\{., i\}$ is decreasing with increasing i and $p_m\{., i\}$ is decreasing with decreasing m. This observation leads us to the conclusion that for light load conditions ($\lambda \leq 0.2$) the likelihood function $f(c|m)$ is monotonically increasing with increasing m when c is kept constant and $c \geq m$. Thus if the input symbols of the C-DMC are equally probable the decision rule simplifies greatly and does not require the computation of $L(c)$. If the input symbols are equal probable and CR counted c collisions, the decision rule will always choose the maximum of all input symbols which are smaller than or equal to c. For other probability distributions on the input symbols the likelihood ratio $L(c)$ needs to be calculated.

5   Covert Channel Performance

Since we have no a priori knowledge regarding the input distribution we assume that all input symbols are equally probable. Even though this is a special case of the general problem, it simplifies the computation of the decision rule greatly and still remains a good example for demonstrating the tradeoffs and interrelations between the variables of the system. With this assumption the decision rule for the C-DMC chooses the largest of all alphabet symbols (integers) which are smaller than or equal to the number of collisions counted by CR.

Since we know that CT can choose any input alphabet, at first glance it looks logical to make the size of this alphabet as large as possible so that the covert bits send per slot are maximized. But a closer investigation reveals that this approach is not correct. Let $M = (m_1, m_2, m_3, ..., m_n)$ be the n symbol input alphabet of the C-DMC, where each symbol of the alphabet is an integer and the symbols are indexed starting from the smallest value to the largest(i.e. $m_1 < m_2 < m_3 < ... < m_n$). Note that for each symbol in alphabet M, we have a corresponding Markov Chain Model depicting the evolution of the CRP when CT wants to send that covert symbol. Therefore we can associate an expected CRP length in terms of observed slots in a CRP with each symbol in M. Let us denote the set of these expected lengths as $\kappa = (K_1, K_2, ..., K_n)$. κ is also an ordered set where the values of the individual elements increase with increasing index number(i.e. $K_1 < K_2 < ... < K_n$). This increase is due to the increasing number of collisions that need to be created in order to send a symbol in M with a higher index number. Since a CRP cannot terminate while collisions are being observed the expected length of CRPs in which covert symbols of higher indexes are sent, will be larger as compared to CRPs in which covert symbols of lower indexes are sent.

In order to evaluate the performance of the C-DMC we define the raw transmission rate, R as the average covert bits per slot transmitted for a given alphabet M.

$$R = \frac{log(n)}{T} \ . \tag{4}$$

where n is the alphabet size for M that CT and CR share. T is the average transmission time per symbol in the C-DMC for alphabet M. We also define the average decision error probability as:

$$P_e = \frac{1}{n} \sum_{i=1}^{n-1} P_e(i) \ . \tag{5}$$

where n is as defined in the previous expression. $P_e(i)$ is the probability of decision error given that CT intended to send symbol m_i. Finally the average throughput, Tr, for the C-DMC is defined as the average number of correctly received covert bits per slot.

$$Tr = R(1 - P_e) \ . \tag{6}$$

Table (7.1) shows the transmission rate, the average detection error probability and the throughput for both procedures 1 and 2 with a binary input alphabet m_1, m_2. Both symbols, m_1 and m_2, are considered to be equally probable.

Table 1. Performance of C-DMC for a binary alphabet

λ	m_1	m_2	Procedure 1 R(bits/slot)	P_e	Tr(bits/slot)	Procedure 2 R(bits/slot)	P_e	Tr(bits/slot)
0.1	1	2	0.1210	0.2811	0.0870	0.1206	0.0473	0.1149
0.1	1	3	0.1130	0.1556	0.0954	0.1127	0.0061	0.1120
0.15	1	2	0.1416	0.2956	0.0997	0.1407	0.0699	0.1309
0.15	1	3	0.1311	0.1696	0.1089	0.1304	0.0107	0.1290
0.2	1	2	0.1538	0.3094	0.1062	0.1524	0.0917	0.1384
0.2	1	3	0.1418	0.1829	0.1159	0.1408	0.0160	0.1385

Note that both procedures have comparable raw bit rates. However the probability of error for procedure 1 is much higher than procedure 2. This is due to the different actions CT implements during phase 2 of both procedures. If CT implements procedure 1, it will send dummy packets at each slot in phase 2 until it observes the first success. On the other hand if CT implements procedure 2, starting from the first slot of phase 2 CT will monitor the feedback for allocation intervals of left status and choose to sent or not to sent a dummy packet according to the observed feedback. This adaptive behavior of CT in procedure 2 decreases the probability of observing a collision in phase 2. Therefore throughput values for procedure 2 are higher than throughput values for procedure 1.

A second observation from Table (7.1) is that increasing the distance between symbols decreases the detection error probability. However the same action also causes the raw bit rate to decrease since the average number of collisions needed to send a symbol increases when the distance between symbols is increased. Observe that for procedure 1 the effect of the decrease in P_e outweighs the effect of the decrease in the transmission rate such that the throughput is improved by increasing the distance between the symbols by one for all practical values of λ. For procedure 2, on the other hand, increasing the distance between the symbols by one either degrades throughput (for $\lambda = 0.1, 0.15$) or the gain is negligible (for $\lambda = 0.2$).

Finally as the traffic rate, λ, of legitimate packets increases the transmission rate of the C-DMC also increases. This is because with increasing traffic rate the probability of the original allocation interval to contain at least one legitimate user increases. Remember that having at least one legitimate user in the original allocation interval of a CRP is the necessary condition in order to sent covert information in that CRP. An increase in this probability decreases the average symbol transmission time in the C-DMC which in turn increases raw transmission rate. As λ increases, decision error probability, P_e also increases, because a higher λ value implies a higher probability of observing collisions in phase 2 of the covert operations which could lead to decision errors. However, from the table we observe that the increase in R outweighs the increase in P_e for both procedure 1 and procedure 2 since the throughput, Tr, increases with increasing λ for practical values of λ.

Figure 6 investigates the effect of the alphabet size on the throughput of the C-DMC. The figure depicts the throughput values for 13 different alphabets. The first alphabet with only 2 symbols is $M_1 = \{1; 2\}$. The second alphabet is constructed by adding the integer "3" to M_1, i.e. $M_2 = \{1; 2; 3\}$. This procedure is repeated until the last alphabet, $M_{13} = \{1; 2; 3; 4; 5; 6; 7; 8; 9; 10; 11; 12; 13; 14\}$, is obtained. Note that this construction results in the smallest possible average C-DMC transmission duration among all possible alphabets of a given alphabet size. The throughput values for these alphabets are computed using equations for R, P_e, Tr, respectively.

From Figure 6 we observe that there exists an alphabet size for which the throughput of the C-DMC is maximized. This size for the maximum throughput depends on the user traffic rate, λ, and the covert procedure that is being used. This implies that given the covert procedure an adaptive scheme can be used to maximize the throughput. Even though we do not explicitly investigate such a scheme in our thesis, it is clear that such a scheme would need to estimate the legitimate user traffic rate, λ, calculate the stability curve for this λ value

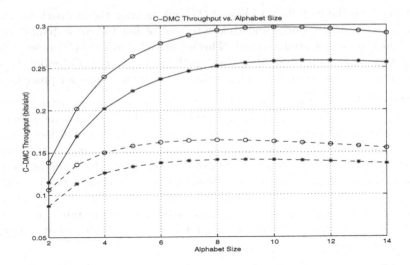

Fig. 6. C-DMC Performance: Throughput vs. Alphabet Size.

and choose an appropriate alphabet size which would maximize the C-DMC throughput without causing instability for the legitimate users.

Figure 7 is a comparison of throughput values for different alphabet constructions. The construction of the alphabets in Figure 7 requires the determination of two variables by the user. The starting integer, SI and the inter symbol distance, ID. Keeping the starting integer and the inter symbol distance small will result in a higher raw bit rate, R, but will increase the decision error probability, P_e. Note that the smallest value for both the starting integer and the inter symbol distance is 1.

The throughput values denoted by "*" belong to alphabets constructed with $SI = 1$ and $ID = 1$. Thus these family of alphabets are the ones used in Figure 6. The throughput values denoted by "o" are obtained for alphabets with $SI = 1$ and $ID = 2$, i.e. $M_1 = \{1; 3\}$, $M_2 = \{1; 3; 5\}$ etc.. Finally, the throughput values denoted by a triangle are obtained for alphabets with $SI = 2$ and $ID = 1$, i.e. $M_1 = \{2; 3\}$, $M_2 = \{2; 3; 4\}$ etc..

We observe that for procedure 2, the construction associated with "*" gives the highest throughput values. This is because the gain obtained by increasing the raw bit rate exceeds the gain obtained by decreasing the already small decision error probability. Therefore the construction with the highest possible raw bit rate is the one which maximizes the C-DMC throughput for a given alphabet size.

In contrast to procedure 2, for procedure 1 the construction with $ID = 2$ results in a better throughput performance. This is because the decision error probability is a more dominant aspect of the operation in procedure 1. Therefore using an alphabet construction which decreases the probability of error increases

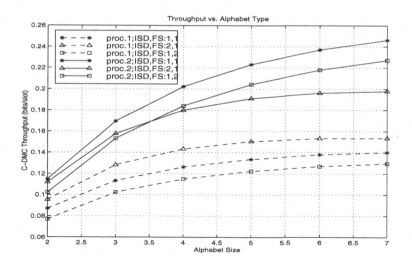

Fig. 7. C-DMC Performance: Throughput vs. Alphabet Construction.

the throughput even though such a construction decreases the raw bit rate as well.

From our investigation of the C-DMC performance in this chapter we conclude that procedure 2 outperforms procedure 1 in terms of achieved throughput in the C-DMC. When using procedure 2 the covert users should employ the alphabet construction with $SI = 1$ and $ID = 1$. Depending on the user traffic rate, λ the alphabet size should be chosen as large as possible without causing instability. If such an adaptive scheme is not available then $M = \{1; 2; 3\}$ is a good choice for the alphabet.

6   Stability Analysis of the Multi-access Channel

The Markov chain models for procedures 1 and 2 enable us to calculate the stable throughput of legitimate user packets under the influence of the respective covert operation. Our calculations use the methods used in [1] for calculating the throughput of the normal operation, and apply them to the new Markov Chain Models that result due to the covert operation. Figure 8 depicts the results of our numerical calculation. Procedure 1 uses the Markov Chain model in Figure 3 for the calculations, whereas procedure 2 uses the model in Figure 4. In both procedures the number of collisions, 'm', that are artificially generated by CT are varied from 1 to 10.

Figure 8 shows that as compared with the normal operation of the FCFS splitting algorithm, the operation under the influence of CT decreases the legitimate user throughput for all values of the covert symbol, 'm', by more than

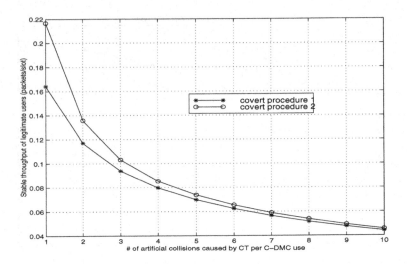

Fig. 8. Legitimate user throughput as a function of artificial collisions created by CT.

50%. This decrease can be explained by understanding how the covert operation alters the normal flow of a CRP.

Without going into the details of the underlying analysis, an intuitive interpretation of the decrease can be given by observing that during the time CT operates in phase 1 no legitimate user packets can be transmitted successfully. In other words CT denies all other users service of the channel during its operation in phase 1. Effectively legitimate users are given the opportunity to use the channel only while CT is in phase 2 of its covert procedure. Even in phase 2, since CT must occasionally sent dummy packets in order to avoid unusual feedback patterns, legitimate users have a greater probability of observing a collision as compared with the normal operation, which also increases the average time a legitimate packet needs to be transmitted successfully.

Figure 8 also shows that in terms of stable throughput of legitimate users Procedure 2 outperforms Procedure 1. The reasons for this lie in the actions that these procedures implement in the phase 2. In procedure 1, CT places its dummy packet always in a left interval. Therefore this dummy packet needs to be transmitted successfully before the CRP can terminate. However in procedure 2, CT places its dummy packet always in a right interval. Therefore there is the probability that due to a collision observed in the corresponding left interval the right interval is returned to waiting and hence the dummy packet need not be sent before the CRP terminates. Furthermore our analysis show that even if a dummy packet is send in procedure 2, the probability of its success is higher than the probability of success of a dummy packet send in procedure 1. Because of the above mentioned reasons the overall interference of CT to the operation of the system is less in procedure 2 as compared to procedure 1, resulting in a higher legitimate user throughput.

7   Conclusion

In this paper we have presented two methods which convey covert information into the feedback pattern of the FCFS splitting algorithm. Our analysis showed that the covert channel created with these methods is a noisy discrete memoryless channel, whose symbols can be determined by the covert users. The symbol set, that the covert users can choose from to form their alphabet, is the set of all positive integers.

We demonstrated that the operation of the FCFS splitting algorithm under the influence of the covert procedures can be modeled with infinite state Markov chains. Using these Markov chains we have analyzed the effect of the covert operation on legitimate user throughput in the multi access channel. Our analysis indicated that the system could support a persistent interference by the covert transmitter, CT, without causing user packet backlog to drift to infinity only if the multi access channel is lightly loaded, i.e. $\lambda \approx 0.1$. Using the Markov models we numerically calculated user traffic rates at which CT could implement the covert operation without causing instability.

We also investigated the performance of the implemented covert channel, C-DMC. However we did not choose the channel capacity as a performance measure. The reason for this was the fact that results obtained by the classical channel capacity analysis provide values in bits per channel use. If the duration of each channel use is not fixed, as in our covert channel model, then these capacity calculations do not provide values that can be expressed in bits/sec. Therefore we felt that a classical channel capacity analysis would not have adequately illustrated the thread of the covert channel. We chose our performance measure to be average correctly received covert bits per slot, which we defined as the C-DMC throughput, Tr. Our results showed that covert procedure 2, which implements a more intelligent interference with the underlying FCFS splitting operation as compared to covert procedure 1, outperformed covert procedure 1 in all practical operating conditions of the collision channel.

By understanding the dynamics of the interference between the FCFS splitting algorithm and the covert procedures we established guidelines for choosing an appropriate alphabet for the covert channel in order to achieve maximum troughput for given channel conditions. Since the channel conditions are dynamic this investigation suggested an adaptive scheme for alphabet selection. We pointed out the neccesary steps for this adaptive scheme. We showed that the alphabet selection constitutes a trade off between the input alphabet size, the average symbol transmission duration and the average decision error probability.

Further research can be conducted on how to modify the covert procedures in order to increase the throughput of the C-DMC. Methods for detecting such covert operation is also of particular interest. Countermeasures for combating covert operation, once it has been detected, needs to be investigated. More over the collision channel model and the FCFS splitting algorithm are rather idealistic abstractions of practical situations. We hope to concentrate our future research on more practical and realistic models and algorithms.

References

1. D. Bertsekas and R. Gallager. *Data Networks*, Prentice Hall, Inc., 1992. 419, 430
2. J. Mosely and P. A. Humblet. *A Class of Efficient Contention Resolution Algorithms for Multiple Access Channels*, IEEE Transactions on Communications, Vol. COM-33, NO.2, February 1985. 419
3. S. Verdu. *Computation of the Efficiency of the Mosely-Humblet Contention Resolution Algorithm: A Simple Method*, Proceedings of IEEE, Vol 74, NO.4, April 1986. 420
4. Ira. S. Moskowitz and A. R. Miller. *Simple Timing Channels*, Proc. of the IEEE Symposium on Research in Security and Privacy, Oakland, CA, 1994. 419
5. C. Kaufman, R. Perlman and M. Spencer. *Network Security*, Prentice Hall, Inc., 1995. 419

The Cocaine Auction Protocol:
On the Power of Anonymous Broadcast

Frank Stajano[1,2] and Ross Anderson[1]

[1] University of Cambridge Computer Laboratory,
New Museums Site, Cambridge CB2 3QG, UK
http://www.cl.cam.ac.uk/~fms27/
http://www.cl.cam.ac.uk/~rja14/
[2] AT&T Laboratories Cambridge,
24a Trumpington Street, Cambridge CB2 1QA, UK
http://www.uk.research.att.com/~fms/

Abstract. Traditionally, cryptographic protocols are described as a sequence of steps, in each of which one principal sends a message to another. It is assumed that the fundamental communication primitive is necessarily one-to-one, so protocols addressing anonymity tend to resort to the composition of multiple elementary transmissions in order to frustrate traffic analysis.

This paper builds on a case study, of an anonymous auction between mistrustful principals with no trusted arbitrator, to introduce "anonymous broadcast" as a new protocol building block. This primitive is, in many interesting cases, a more accurate model of what actually happens during transmission. With certain restrictions it can give a particularly efficient implementation technique for many anonymity-related protocols.

1 Introduction

1.1 Why a Cocaine Auction?

Several extremely rich and ruthless men[1] are gathered around a table. An auction is about to be held in which one of them will offer his next shipment of cocaine to the highest bidder. The seller describes the merchandise and proposes a starting price. The others then bid increasing amounts until there are no bids for 30 consecutive seconds. At that point the seller declares the auction closed and arranges a secret appointment with the winner to deliver the goods.

Why are we interested in this scenario? One reason is that although electronic auctions are a very hot topic (witness the pioneering online auction house

---

[1] To prevent grammatical rules from becoming sexist statements, one would normally split the roles of the principals between male and female personæ; but the drug dealers of our dramatisation look so much more plausible as ugly, cruel cigar-smoking men that it was felt more offensive than flattering to include any ladies. Of course some may now perversely call this an even more sexist statement...

A. Pfitzmann (Ed.): IH'99, LNCS 1768, pp. 434–447, 2000.

eBay [9], whose stock grew 1300% in only seven months after their IPO [19]), their privacy and trust implications have yet to be adequately discussed.

In the eBay model, for example, the auction house's profit is a fixed percentage of the final sale, but at the same time bidders are asked to reveal to the auction house in confidence the maximum amount they are prepared to bid, so that the house can run the bidding process on their behalf without their having to be online for several days. This is putting the fox in charge of the hen house. The auction house could easily and undetectably exploit its knowledge of the bidders' limits to drive up the sale price—possibly introducing a fake bidder—in order to pocket the maximum commission. Users simply have to hope that the auction house will behave properly. EBay addresses some of the other trust concerns, such as whether users should trust other users: there is an interesting "peer review" system in which everyone gets a reliability rating from the principals with whom they interact. But while this mechanism may be valuable, it still cannot be used to justify the trustworthiness of the auction house itself.

We introduce the cocaine auction scenario as an exaggerated case that makes the trust issues unambiguous. We may assume that, in a game with such high stakes and shady players, nobody is going to trust anybody else any more than strictly necessary. We may also assume that the people who take part in the auction all know each other (otherwise one of them might be a police agent), but that no-one who places a bid wants to be identified to the other bidders or to the seller. Nobody except buyer and seller should know who won the auction; and even the seller should not be able to find out the identity of the highest bidder before committing to the sale. But none of the participants should have to trust any other: the protocol cannot rely on a judge or policeman to act as arbitrator and must instead be self-enforcing.

Data protection issues are a further reason for wanting an anonymous auction protocol. In the eBay model, each user has all her transactions logged, together with her personal data, and is at the mercy of abuses by the auction house and other participants, such as the resale of personal information to marketers, insurers or even thieves with a plausible tale ("May I please buy the list of all those who recently bought gold jewellery? I sell a really good polish."). Serious political difficulties may arise from the US practice of storing and reselling such information as this violates the data protection laws of several other jurisdictions, including the European Union. If an auction site were to adopt protocols that prevented it from finding out the identity of bidders (or at least of unsuccessful bidders), then it would be in a much better position to claim that it had taken all reasonable steps to comply with data protection principles.

Finally, there was an amusing case of life imitating art when, the week before this paper was presented at the Information Hiding Workshop 1999, some Internet-savvy scoundrels *did actually offer a shipment of drugs on eBay*, with bids reaching 10 M$ before the auction was noticed and shut down [18].

1.2 Anonymous Broadcast

The second part of this paper examines the anonymity layer on which the auction protocol is built and proposes for it a provocative implementation technique that does not use any cryptography. This novel approach offers substantial performance gains. Interestingly its security, while using mechanisms that were once considered dubious, turns out to be essentially equivalent to that of a cryptographically strong alternative, so long as we use realistic threat models.

Furthermore the anonymous broadcast primitive is also interesting from the protocol modelling point of view in that, for many cases, it gives a more faithful representation of what actually happens.

2 The Cocaine Auction Protocol

2.1 Protocol

We shall now build our anonymous auction protocol assuming the availability of a mechanism for broadcasting messages to all the participants without revealing the identity of the sender ("anonymous broadcast"). The implementation of the anonymity layer will be discussed in section 3.

The other communication primitive we shall use is plain non-anonymous broadcast, where an identifiable principal delivers a message to all the others. Since in our scheme the identity of the seller is known to the buyers, the buyers' messages are anonymous, but the seller's are not.

The basic protocol is fairly simple and is organised as a succession of "rounds" of bidding. Round i starts with the seller announcing the bid price b_i for that round. Buyers have up to Δt seconds to make an offer (i.e. to say "yes", meaning "I'm willing to buy at the current bid price b_i"). As soon as one buyer anonymously says "yes", he becomes the winner w_i of that round and a new round begins. If nobody says anything for Δt seconds, round i is concluded by timeout and the auction is won by the winner w_{i-1} of the previous round, if one exists. If the timeout occurs during round 0, this means that nobody made any offers at the initial price b_0, so there is no sale.

A couple of details need fixing before this protocol will work satisfactorily. Firstly, the seller needs a mechanism to identify the winner: if all the buyers ever say is just "yes", then anybody can go to the seller, offer him the final sale price and obtain the goods in stead of the real winner—which is highly undesirable. This problem can be solved by ensuring that each "yes" message also contain a one-way function of a nonce: before completing the sale, the seller will then ask the winner to exhibit the original nonce, which nobody else could produce.

Secondly, once the auction is over, the seller might prefer to give a *secret* appointment to the winner ("see you on Tuesday at 06:30 in the car park of Heathrow terminal 2") rather than exchanging suitcases of cocaine for cash under the noses of all the losing bidders. On the other hand, the identity of the winner should not be revealed to the seller until the latter commits to the sale. This is to protect the winner from the situation in which the seller says "So who won the auction? Oh, it was you? Well, anyone else would have been fine, but you're from the wrong family, so I won't sell to you after all, even if you've won". To enable the seller to send an appointment to the winner only, but before knowing the winner's identity, we make the previously mentioned one-way function g^x (mod n), where x is the nonce chosen by the bidder and g and n are public system-wide parameters. So each anonymous "yes" message will be of the form g^{x_i}, with x_i chosen arbitrarily by the winner w_i of round i. When the auction finishes, say at round f, with principal w_f committing to buy at price b_f with a "yes" message of g^{x_f}, the seller chooses a nonce y and performs a Diffie-Hellman key exchange [8] with the winner w_f (who is still anonymous) by broadcasting the appointment encrypted under the session key $g^{x_f y}$. The winner is the only buyer who can compute this key.

A number of minor variants to the protocol are possible. For example, before the first round the seller could specify, either algorithmically or by enumeration, the succession of bid prices $\{b_i\}$; then he would no longer have to broadcast b_i at the beginning of each round, because each winner w_i would implicitly refer to the corresponding b_i in the "well known" succession.

A variant at the opposite end of the conciseness v. robustness trade-off [1] is to have the seller broadcast, at the beginning of round i, not only b_i but also the "yes" message ($g^{x_{i-1}}$) of the winner of the previous round. This may help arbitrate races between bidders who both said "yes" to the same b_i. The bidders themselves could include in the "yes" message the value b_i to which they are responding.

We shall not, however, discuss this type of implementation detail any further; let us instead examine some of the ways in which the principals could misbehave, and whether the protocol is (or can be made) robust against them.

2.2   Attacks

There are limits to what can be achieved at the protocol level. It is always possible, for example, to subvert an auction when an appropriate combination of participants colludes against the others. For example, if all the bidders conspire against the seller, one of them can buy the shipment cheaply and divide it with the others later (a practice known as "ringing"), either in equal parts or perhaps even running a separate private auction and splitting the money that didn't go to the seller. Similarly, if the seller plants an ally among the bidders, he can push the final selling price as high as the other bidders will bear (though at the risk of not being able to actually complete the sale). We do not believe that all such attacks can be detected, let alone stopped, by any particular auction protocol: the culprits can plausibly deny their involvement, since the "trace" of externally observable messages of an auction involving a collusion could always have been generated by a "honest" auction as well. Some specific conspiracies may be detectable by protocol level mechanisms, as we shall see; but we will not attempt to guard against the others.

Seller not Selling to Highest Bidder. Does the protocol force the seller to sell to the highest bidder? No, since the seller can always generate the session key starting with the g^x produced by whichever bidder he prefers, and nobody will be able to tell that this happened just by looking at the commitment message. One might object that, so long as the price is strictly increasing from one bid to the next, the seller is guaranteed to lose money if he does not sell to the highest bidder—but the real world is more complicated than that, with all sorts of possible scams and double-crosses. We will differentiate two cases.

In the first, the seller sends an encrypted appointment message to the winning bidder but attempts some treachery in it. For example, he might have a sweetheart deal with one of the participants allowing him to match the best openly bid price, and might send the winner an appointment he has no intention to keep. In such a case, the winner's recourse is to blacken the seller's "good name" by complaining about the disappointment afterwards around the cocaine dealing community. We will consider this case no further.

In the second, the seller encrypts the appointment message using the g^x supplied by someone other than the winner. In this case, the cheated winner can broadcast an accusation and prove that the seller is dishonest, simply by publishing his last x. Anybody can then verify firstly that that x really corresponds to the g^x from the highest bidder and secondly that the message from the seller does not decrypt to anything meaningful using that x. At that point all the bidders take out their machine guns and the seller greatly regrets his dishonesty. Note that the cheated highest bidder manages to accuse the dishonest seller without exposing his identity, since he still sends out x anonymously. So this protocol ensures that most misbehaviour of this sort can be publicly exposed without loss of anonymity for the cheated accuser.

Seller Bidding at His Own Auction. The exception is of course where the seller bids at his own auction in order to raise the price, overshoots, and finds himself the winner. He is unlikely to accuse himself by broadcasting x; but might he offer the shipment to anyone else?

Let us assume that he selects a g^x sent by one of the next-highest bidders, whom we will call Mr. N, and broadcasts an appointment message encrypted under g^{xy}, in the hope that Mr. N (whose identity is unknown to him) will keep quiet in exchange for a chance to buy the goods. When Mr. N sees that he can decrypt the secret appointment using his own g^x, he knows that the seller is cheating, since that message should have been sent to the highest bidder instead. So he can either expose the scam by exhibiting his own x as before and cause the barrels of all the Uzis in the room to converge on the seller; or he can accept the appointment and buy the shipment he would otherwise lose. (He might perhaps haggle over the price when he meets the seller there, but by then he will have lost his ability to cause immediate bodily harm to the seller from the comfort of anonymity).

So, when the seller tries to deal with someone other than the apparent winner, there seems always to be one principal who could expose him as a cheater, although in some sub-cases it is possible that the potential accuser might prefer to stay silent. A seller "with wife and kids", noticing that this situation carries a life risk greater than ε, might never attempt such a scam; but the more adventurous Scarface type on the fast track to the top might occasionally be prepared to run the risk.

Thus in practice the other principals still have no way of knowing for sure that an auction they lost was run "legitimately". So they might want a way for all the participants to verify that the seller did encrypt the secret appointment to the highest bidder, although they should not be able to decrypt the message themselves. They might also want some reassurance that the appointment message decrypts to something meaningful. Both these assurances can be given by a cut-and-choose protocol. The seller broadcasts not one g^y but twenty (perhaps at the beginning of the auction) and once the auction concludes, he then offers a choice of twenty different encrypted appointment messages, such as "06:30 Tuesday in the car park of Heathrow terminal 2", "23:20 Monday behind the George and Dragon", ..., and will reveal up to nineteen of the y values in response to challenges. The same result might probably also be achieved using zero-knowledge proof techniques rather than cut and choose.

It may well be that our drug dealers do not care to pay for the extra complexity of such a protocol. If the main risk is felt to be the seller bidding at his own auction, then even if he overbids and is forced to sell to himself under penalty of being discovered, there is nothing to stop him from running a new auction some time later, pretending to have received a new shipment from his suppliers. (This applies to commodities like cocaine or memory chips, but not to unique and recognisable items such as stolen Rembrandts, where a cut-and-choose protocol might be preferred.)

Deadbeat Bidders. A general consequence of anonymity is that it is hard to hold anonymous principals responsible for anything. In particular, it is hard to guard against "deadbeat bidders", i.e. participants who win an auction and then do not turn up with the cash to buy the goods. With the protocol described so far, they would get the encrypted appointment but not show up, and the seller would not know who to blame. While deadbeat bidders would not gain much (and would certainly not get any free cocaine), their behaviour will certainly annoy the other participants. If repeated undetectably over a series of auctions, deadbeat bidding could amount to a denial of service. One might argue that nonpayment lies outside the scope of the auction protocol, which should only designate a winner and a sale price; but it is still reasonable to seek ways in we might at least identify persistent deadbeats.

The approach used by "respectable" online auctioneers such as eBay is to enable clients to build up a reputation for honest dealing. One might try to transplant this to the cocaine auction by giving each principal a pseudonym; but as soon as the winner turns up to collect his cocaine, the link between his name and pseudonym becomes obvious, unless the actual delivery of goods is also conducted anonymously. In fact, even in the "respectable" case, service denial attacks can be mounted by any principals who can repeatedly acquire new identities.

This problem raises complex issues related to identity certification, which in itself might be a concept that our mistrustful drug dealers unconditionally reject *a priori*. Here we will merely point out a major practical pitfall. Suppose that some acceptable technical mechanism has been devised to create a certification authority. For example, one might set up a k-out-of-n identity escrow scheme with a very high k, say $3n/4$: after a certain level of missed appointments, or deadbeat bids, were detected by the audience, everybody could cooperate to unmask the disruptor, in a way reminiscent of Blaze's "angry mob cryptanalysis" [4]. Mechanisms for setting up the underlying threshold signature schemes without a trusted party are known [7]. But the real problems are likely to come from the application detail, such as the plausibility of the excuse that the subject might put forward to justify his absence (was he arrested "honestly", or did he pay the police to arrest him?).

Do Auction Houses Have a Future? One of the questions asked by many businesses is whether the convergence of computers and communications could destroy their niche. Even banks worry about "disintermediation" as their corporate customers raise loan capital on the markets directly. What does the future hold for auctioneers?

A traditional auction house adds value in a number of ways. Some of these, such as marketing, may be easier to do on the net; others, such as providing assurance that the goods on offer are as described and are the lawful property of the seller, may be harder. But comparing the cocaine auction with existing ones does tell us something about transaction costs. In conventional auctions, bidders must identify themselves to the auctioneer, who can exclude any known deadbeats; and although there is no formal mechanism to detect when a friend of the seller is bidding secretly for him, there is a deterrent in that a seller who buys his own merchandise ends up out of pocket by the auctioneer's commission.

In many sectors of the economy, from securities trading to the provision of airport taxi services, it has been found that regulated markets build confidence and attract custom. The question for regulators is precisely how much to regulate. We hope that comparing conventional auctioneers (and the new online firms such as eBay) with the fully disintermediated environment of the cocaine auction protocol may provide some useful insight.

3   The Anonymity Layer

To make the cocaine protocol usable, we must also supply a mechanism that allows the bidders to anonymously broadcast their "yes" message.

3.1   The Dining Cryptographers

The "dining cryptographers" construction introduced by Chaum [6] addresses precisely this problem. In his now classic story, several cryptographers are gathered around a table for dinner, and the waiter informs them that the meal has already been paid for by an anonymous benefactor, who could be one of the participants or the NSA. The cryptographers would like to know whether they are indebted to one of their own number or to the agency. So Chaum incrementally constructs a protocol through which, after the sharing of what are effectively one time pads between selected pairs of principals, each principal outputs a function of her "I paid/I didn't pay" bit and everyone can later work out the total parity of all such bits. As long as not more than one of the cryptographers says "I paid", even parity means that the NSA paid, while odd parity means that one of the diners paid, even if nobody can figure out who.

Various extensions are then proposed, including one in which the principals are arranged in a token ring and transmit integrity-checked blocks rather than single bits, so that collisions[2] can be detected.

For the system to work, collisions must be controlled by ensuring that the round trip period of the token is much smaller than the typical time between the seller announcing a new price and a bidder responding "I'll buy". Furthermore, the procedure for dealing with collisions must take into account the nature and aims of the principals: it might be inappropriate for us to simply invite colliders to retransmit after random intervals, as Chaum does, since two principals might both retransmit as soon and as often as possible in an attempt to secure the bid, thereby causing collisions ad infinitum.

Pfitzmann proposes an ingenious optimisation [16] that guarantees to resolve a collision between n participants in at most n rounds—while the probabilistic approach suggested by Chaum cannot guarantee an upper bound.

Despite this, the cocaine auction protocol implemented using "token ring dining cryptographers" is fairly expensive in terms of communications. Even ignoring the initial cost of setting up the pairwise one time pads and of any retransmissions caused by collisions, each participant must send at least one message to his neighbour for each round in which one untraceable bid may be sent by one of the parties, plus another one for the second trip round the loop which is needed to communicate the result to all participants. Calling n the number of participants, r the number of rounds of bidding needed before the auction results in a sale and K the "dilution factor" introduced to spread out transmissions over several rounds so as to minimise collisions, the protocol so far described requires $2 \cdot n \cdot r \cdot K$ such messages to be sent. (Pfitzmann's cited construction allows K to be much smaller than in Chaum's case by lowering the retransmission costs on collisions.)

---

[2] Only one cryptographer at a time can say "1" and be heard. Since the resulting anonymous bit is the XOR of those transmitted by the individual principals, if at most one principal transmits a "1" and all others transmit a "0", we can infer as appropriate that nobody said "1" or that one anonymous principal said "1". But if more than one principal sends a "1", the protocol no longer works—it can only tell whether an even or an odd number of principals transmitted a "1".

We shall now show how a simple assumption about the nature and properties of the physical transport layer, directly inspired by a specific implementation technology, dramatically reduces these costly transmission requirements.

3.2 Anonymous Broadcast Based on Physics

The original idea for the cocaine auction protocol arose in the context of the discussion about possible future applications for a short-range radio networking facility such as that provided by Piconet [3]. We envisage that the drug dealers of our story might hold in their pockets little radio transmitters similar in shape and size to car key fobs, and that unobtrusively pressing the button on the device would cause the transmission of the relevant "yes" message (a transmitter with a slow processor, unable to do modular arithmetic quickly, might rely on a precomputed list of g^x for various x).

By using radio, each message sent is automatically broadcast to all principals; and it can be anonymous, as long as we simply omit to mention the sender in the link-layer header. Only one such message is needed per auction round, so in terms of transmissions the entire auction only costs r messages, as opposed to $2 \cdot n \cdot r \cdot K$ (plus the extras we hinted at) for the dining cryptographers implementation.

The savings are dramatic and worth investigating in greater detail. As it turns out, they come from having questioned a basic assumption in protocol modelling, namely that communication is point-to-point. This trick can be exploited in a variety of interesting cases that have nothing to do with auctions.

3.3 A Fundamental Protocol Building Block

Traditionally, cryptographic protocols are described as a sequence of steps of the form

$A \rightarrow B : M$

indicating that principal A sends message M to principal B. In the general case it is proper to assume a primitive that sends a message from a specific sender to a specific recipient; indeed in most cases this is what the communications API offers. Other constructions are typically be derived from this one: for example, broadcasting the same message M to all the members of a domain $\mathcal{D}$ can be represented by a trivial, if inefficient, iteration. Anonymous sending can be achieved by more elaborate constructions which rely on building an untraceable tortuous path across a multiply connected network, in which intermediate relay nodes hide the route that the message is going to take next [5,10], or on diluting the payload in a cloud of messages sent by a community of principals, each of which might have been the actual sender [6], or on broadcasting a message which only some subset can decipher [4].

Let us now reverse the perspective and take "anonymous broadcast" as the fundamental primitive. The following notation

$A ? \overset{\nearrow}{\underset{\searrow}{\longleftrightarrow}} \mathcal{D} : M$

shall signify that principal A broadcasts message M anonymously into the domain $\mathcal{D}$. This means that all principals in $\mathcal{D}$ receive M, and given any two messages M_1 and M_2 that have been anonymously broadcast at different times into $\mathcal{D}$, no principal in $\mathcal{D}$ (except the originators) is able to tell whether they came from the same principal or not.

From here we can derive non-anonymous broadcast by naming the sender in the message, as in

$$A \overset{\nearrow}{\hookleftarrow} \mathcal{D} : M \quad \equiv \quad A\,?\overset{\nearrow}{\hookleftarrow}\mathcal{D} : (A, M)$$

and point-to-point send by naming both the sender and the recipient, as in

$$A \to B : M \quad \equiv \quad A\,?\overset{\nearrow}{\hookleftarrow}\mathcal{D} : (A, B, M)$$

Many security papers are concerned with the strength of the mechanisms used to bind names such as A and B to M: but we are not concerned with non-repudiation, only with its dual, namely plausible deniability. We simply note that a basically anonymous broadcast primitive, coupled with weak mechanisms to name the claimed sender and the supposedly intended receiver, is what *really* happens in practice in many common cases, including radio and ethernet. (Human speech is also a form of local broadcast, anonymous only in crowds, and yet there are many places—not just Japanese paper houses—where it's conventional to ignore messages addressed to others.)

At the physical level, whether in the one-bit bus of ethernet or in the "ether" of radio waves, it is actually the point-to-point messaging facility that is obtained as a composite construction built on top of anonymous broadcast. The practice of prefixing each outgoing message with the globally unique ID that ethernet adapters receive during manufacture is a convention which a malicious node can easily ignore.

Physical anonymous broadcast as a genuine networking primitive requires a shared communication medium and thus is only practical in local networks. In the wide area, its usefulness is limited by issues of transmission power, propagation delay and bandwidth: if only one principal can transmit at a time without collision, larger domains mean that more principals are forced to stay silent while one of them is transmitting. Above a certain domain size, routing becomes the preferred option in order to reduce the transmission power and increase the aggregate bandwidth. So basing a cryptographic protocol on the anonymity properties of the physical broadcast primitive limits it to the local area. The drug barons can hold the efficient version of the auction around a table, with key fobs in their pockets or with an ethernet connecting their laptops, but to hold an auction over the Internet from their swimming pools it appears that they would have to implement the anonymity layer using the more tedious classical techniques. This problem is also faced by Jackson [11], who finds he cannot use the otherwise desirable physical broadcast technique in an active badge application because of power and scalability limitations.

In summary, the anonymous broadcast primitive has two main advantages. The first is efficiency: even before taking anonymity into consideration, in a shared transmission medium sending one message from A to B or sending one message from A to anyone else in the domain has exactly the same cost. It is foolish to use a formalism that hides this, and end up being forced to send $\#\mathcal{D} - 1$ messages rather than one when broadcast is really intended. Moreover, under some assumptions that we shall examine in greater detail next, a shared medium can give anonymity practically for free, thus saving the many redundant messages otherwise needed to hide the real traffic. It is thus convenient to be able to leverage off these valuable properties when designing a higher-level protocol.

The second reason is clarity: by more closely modelling what goes on during the transmission of a message, we are in a better position to evaluate the actual security properties of our system.

3.4　The Strength (or Weakness) of Broadcast Anonymity

Although the network addresses sent out by most nodes in conventional computer and communications systems can be forged easily, it would be naïve to conclude that every transmission on a shared physical medium provides strong anonymity. Pfitzmann, who extensively analysed techniques to reduce user observability in communication networks [13,14,15,16,17], mentioned broadcast over a shared medium as a possible low-level anonymity layer, but then dismissed it in favour of more elaborate solutions based on cryptography as it could not provide unconditional security. This is a valid objection: an opponent who can observe the transmissions at a low enough level will generally be able to distinguish the participants.

For example, in cable and radio transmissions, at the physical level the distance between transmitter and receiver affects both the received power and the transmission delay. Several conspiring nodes who could observe these parameters might well be able to identify the senders of most of the messages. We are not interested in the trivial case in which all nodes but one conspire against the last, but in more serious cases where three or four nodes can, between them, tell whether the last message came from here or from there.

A transmitter might randomly vary its power output to prevent direction finding using signal strength measurements; but the relative amplitude will still be visible, and precise timing information will anyway be what tells most to a well equipped attacker. The game could include directional receiving and transmitting antennas; a "defensive" environment such as a naked Faraday cage that maximises reflections and echoes; or a "hostile" environment with unseen receivers in every ceiling tile and surveillance cameras in every pot plant. Bidders might even use extreme electronic warfare techniques to try to frame each other by causing certain messages to be received by only some subset of participants. Radio-frequency ID systems can identify individual transmitters by their analogue characteristics; to block this, the principals might have several buttons in their pockets which they use once each as they wander around.

However, many of the attacks open to a resourceful opponent are independent of the strength of cryptography in use. Equipment can be abused; keyboard sniffers can be installed in laptops and signal using soft tempest transmitters [12]. If this is impossible, cameras and microphones can be used to observe user input.

There may be infrared lasers to measure bidders' blood oxygen levels and special toilets to collect biological samples to measure stress. One should bear all this in mind when dismissing anonymous broadcast as insecure compared with the "mathematically provable" untraceability of the dining drug dealers' scheme. An opponent who forces us to think about unconditionally secure cryptography may also fly below the mathematics and steal the plaintext at the level of electronics, physics or biology. In such cases, the strength of cryptographic mechanisms is only one factor of many. It is probably fair to say that the attacker equipped to break the anonymity of our physical broadcast will have little trouble in bypassing strong cryptography (wherever it is employed) by simply observing the keys or plaintext directly.

At less exalted levels, we have to consider the economics of the attacker and the defender. It is highly significant that defence (enabling anonymous broadcast) may require only a small change in the firmware of a standard node, and might even be performed in software depending on how "shallow" the network adapter is; but attack (sensing the signal strength, timing, phase, polarisation and/or analogue transmitter characteristics of received messages) is a lower level and thus more expensive operation.

4   Conclusions

We have presented a protocol for anonymous auctions among mutually mistrustful participants and examined its vulnerability to various attacks. Drug dealers made convincing actors for our dramatisation, but our analysis is more general. Online auction houses, commercial companies seeking tenders and even governments calling for bids might all benefit from a scheme in which bidders do not have to reveal their strategies to each other, and in which unsuccessful bidders remain anonymous. As online auctions gain importance and even governments try to move their business online, so will the issues of anonymity, privacy and trust become more critical.

Our analysis showed that introducing a realistic non-cryptographic assumption about the physical nature of the communications medium gave us a dramatic efficiency gain. This "anonymous broadcast" assumption maps directly to the implementation of local area networking environments based on a shared transmission medium such as ethernet or radio. While the strength of its anonymity depends on the threat model, the kind of attacks that might defeat it are uneconomic in many applications and are also likely to defeat "provably secure" cryptography. So, where appropriate, anonymous broadcast may offer significantly better performance, as well as a more accurate model of what is actually going on.

The anonymous broadcast technique is not applicable to the wide area case, so the more efficient version of our auction protocol can only be run locally. But the issues we raised about attacks and deceptions are orthogonal to how the anonymity is implemented: our discussion may provide a useful yardstick even for online auction implementations that use a different anonymity primitive or a different auction protocol.

We conclude by observing that new ideas come from challenging fossilised axioms: it is needlessly limiting to design all cryptographic protocols under the unexamined assumption that communications must perforce be point-to-point.

5 Acknowledgements

We thank the audiences that gave us their valuable feedback during presentations of this research: in particular we appreciated the comments of Bruce Christianson, Markus Kuhn, Stewart Lee, Roger Needham, Larry Paulson and Mike Roe from the security group at the University of Cambridge; of John McHugh and Nicko van Someren at the Information Hiding Workshop in Dresden; and of Raymond Liao at Columbia University. Further useful remarks were offered offline by Andreas Pfitzmann and George Danezis.

References

1. Martín Abadi and Roger Needham. Prudent engineering practice for cryptographic protocols. Technical Report 125, Digital Equipment Corporation Systems Research Center, June 1994. ftp://ftp.digital.com/pub/DEC/SRC/research-reports/SRC-125.pdf. 437

2. Ross Anderson, editor. *Information Hiding: First International Workshop proceedings*, volume 1174 of *Lecture Notes in Computer Science*. Springer-Verlag, 1996. 446, 447

3. Frazer Bennett, David Clarke, Joseph B. Evans, Andy Hopper, Alan Jones, and David Leask. Piconet: Embedded mobile networking. *IEEE Personal Communications*, 4(5):8–15, October 1997. ftp://ftp.uk.research.att.com/pub/docs/att/tr.97.9.pdf. 442

4. Matt Blaze. Oblivious key escrow. In Anderson [2], pages 335–343. http://www.crypto.com/papers/netescrow.ps. 440, 442

5. David Chaum. Untraceable electronic mail, return addresses, and digital pseudonyms. *Communications of the ACM*, 24(2):84–88, February 1981. Unofficial copy at http://www.wiwi.uni-frankfurt.de/~kcotoaga/offline/chaum-acm-1981.html. 442

6. David Chaum. The dining cryptographers problem: Unconditional sender and recipient untraceability. *Journal of Cryptology*, 1:65–75, 1988. Unofficial copy at http://www.scu.edu/SCU/Programs/HighTechLaw/courses/ccp/diningcr.html. 440, 442

7. Clifford Cocks. Split knowledge generation of RSA parameters. In Mike Darnell, editor, *Cryptography and coding: 6th IMA conference, Cirencester, UK, December 17–19, 1997: proceedings*, volume 1355 of *Lecture Notes in Computer Science*, pages 89–95. Springer-Verlag, 1997. http://www.cesg.gov.uk/downlds/math/rsa.pdf. 440

8. Whitfield Diffie and Martin E. Hellman. New directions in cryptography. *IEEE Trans. Inform. Theory*, IT-22(6):644–654, November 1976. 437

9. eBay. http://www.ebay.com/. 435

10. David M. Goldschlag, Michael G. Reed, and Paul F. Syverson. Hiding routing information. In Anderson [2], pages 137–150. http://www.onion-router.net/Publications/IH-1996.ps. 442

11. Ian W. Jackson. *Who goes here? Confidentiality of location through anonymity.* PhD thesis, University of Cambridge, February 1998. http://www.chiark.greenend.org.uk/~ijackson/thesis/. 443

12. Markus G. Kuhn and Ross J. Anderson. Soft tempest: Hidden data transmission using electromagnetic emanations. In David Aucsmith, editor, *Information Hiding: Second International Workshop*, volume 1525 of *Lecture Notes in Computer Science*, pages 124–142. Springer-Verlag, 1998. http://www.cl.cam.ac.uk/~mgk25/ih98-tempest.pdf. 444

13. Andreas Pfitzmann. Ein dienstintegriertes digitales Vermittlungs-/Verteilnetz zur Erhöhung des Datenschutzes *(An IntegratedDigital Services Switching/Distribution Network for Increased Privacy)*. Technical Report 18/83, Institut für Informatik IV, University of Karlsruhe, 1983. 444

14. Andreas Pfitzmann. A switched/broadcast ISDN to decrease user observability. 1984 International Zurich Seminar on Digital Communications, Applications of Source Coding, Channel Coding and Secrecy Coding, March 6-8, 1984, Zurich, Switzerland, Swiss Federal Institute of Technology, Proceedings IEEE Catalog no. 84CH1998-4, 6–8 March 1984. 444

15. Andreas Pfitzmann. How to implement ISDNs without user observability—some remarks. Technical report, Institut für Informatik, University of Karlsruhe, 1985. 444

16. Andreas Pfitzmann. *Diensteintegrierende Kommunikationsnetze mit teilnehmerüberprüfbarem Datenschutz (Integrated services communication networks with end-user verifiable privacy).* Number 234 in Informatik-Fachberichte. Springer-Verlag, Heidelberg, 1990. 441, 444

17. Andreas Pfitzmann and Michael Waidner. Networks without user observability. *Computers and Security*, 6(2):158–166, April 1987. http://www.semper.org/sirene/publ/PfWa_86anonyNetze.html. 444

18. Greg Sandoval. eBay auction goes up in smoke. *CNET*, September 1999. http://news.cnet.com/news/0-1007-202-123002.html. 435

19. StockMaster. http://www.stockmaster.com/exe/sm/chart?Symbol=EBAY. 435

Protecting Secret Keys in a Compromised Computational System

W. P. R. Mitchell

Department of Computer Science, University of Manchester
Manchester M13 9PL
bill@cs.man.ac.uk

Abstract. Software applications which run in a compromised environment and perform sensitive operations, such as providing a secure communication channel between two individuals, require protection in order to prevent them being run by an unauthorised adversary.

This paper looks at how to build in some protection against an adversary who wishes to modify an application so that it no longer authenticates the user before running. This protection works against a casual observer, that is someone who has access only to standard debugging tools, visualisation tools, and decompilers. The tricks given in the paper do not work against an all powerful adversary.

The paper treats the problem of protecting the code fragments dealing with authentication as equivalent to encrypting plaintext without revealing the secret key.

1 Introduction

Consider a software application which is only intended to be used by a specific individual, or within a specified location, or allows privileged access to data by users depending on their role. For example the application may allow one person to secretly communicate with another person over a secure channel. Or the software is a commercial product which is licensed to only run for one person located at any machine in a particular network. Another example is a database which allows some users to have certain privileged access to the data and other users only normal access to the data. It may be perfectly allowable for an individual to check that their own company records are correct, but not to access the personal records of any other individual.

The most obvious way to prevent an adversary from using a piece of software without permission from the rightful user is for the owner to keep it encrypted and only decrypt it when it is being used. However this will not work in a situation where the software is decrypted by a supervisor, but used by a subordinate who may decide to supply a copy of the code to an adversary, or the software is used in an open network where potentially anyone could copy the unencrypted code whilst it is in use. There is then a real need to ensure that the application contains mechanisms which ensure it can not work without proper permission to do so.

A. Pfitzmann (Ed.): IH'99, LNCS 1768, pp. 448–462, 2000.

The application will typically be protected from use by anyone but the rightful owner by means of some kind of key, perhaps a hardware key such as a dongle, perhaps by a smart card, perhaps by communication with a network license manager, or by some password which only the user knows. However the application must contain some secret information which it uses during the authentication stage to validate the key. This is a possible point of attack if a copy of the software falls into the wrong hands.

If an attacker can reverse engineer the authentication process they may then be able to bypass this authentication process altogether. In the case of the communication software the attacker will then be able to impersonate the rightful user, in the case of the software pirate they can then make hacked copies of the application and give them away. Reverse engineering of binary code is a real danger for secure applications, [3] [4], [5], [6] give details of sophisticated decompilation tools and decompilers currently available or under development.

We will regard the problem of preventing the authentication process from being subverted as equivalent to computing the encryption of a piece of plaintext without revealing the encryption key. This paper considers the problem of how to compute the encryption in such a way that the key remains hidden from a casual observer. By this we mean an observer who can only analyse the system through use of standard debugging tools, visualisation tools, and decompilers. It does not include the case of an all powerful observer who can apply any arbitrary technique in analysing the system.

There are secondary problems in protecting an authentication process which we also consider. An adversary may decide that rather than spend time and energy reverse engineering the authentication process they will simply rip it out from the code altogether. This is sometimes possible if the authentication is implemented in a naive way. The protection mechanisms have to be incorporated so they can not be removed by blind attacks which require no understanding of how the code works.

A challenge response authentication often involves the use of a dongle. Checksums of various code fragments are commonly used to decide if the code has been tampered with. There are standard blind attacks against both of these methods which we look at in sections 2 and 3. Finally in section 4 we look at how to hide a secret key whilst encrypting some plaintext with the key.

The protection tricks discussed here are designed to be immune to blind attacks. They are designed to force an attacker to understand how the code works, rather than simply identify vulnerable areas of code which can be bypassed, using standard observation tools. The tricks are also designed so that it is hard to break them down into smaller parts which can be individually attacked through dynamic slicing techniques [7], [10]. This forces the attacker to understand the dynamics of the whole protection mechanism during run time in order to attack any part of it. The tricks are designed to be randomly varying throughout their structure, in essence this makes them appear as self modifying code which operates in an arbitrary fashion. This prevents any standard decompiler from reconstructing any meaningful high level source code.

The tricks involve representing the keys as abstract data types, whose structure is dynamically varied during run time. The same is true for the encryption algorithm. Both the keys and the encryption algorithm are represented through the use of automaton with certain additional features. All of the important encryption operations are translated into operators on automaton which makes it difficult to distinguish operations during run time. The structure of all the operations also dynamically varies during run time.

In order to uncover the computation an attacker will be forced to uncover the semantics of the tricks which is beyond a casual observer. Using that semantic knowledge the attacker then has to identify which parts of the code implement the different semantic operations and data types. Even if the attacker is given this document to work from, assuming that the application is written in some declarative language which is optimised by the compiler, simply using standard observational tools will not enable them to uncover the keys. This is true since recovering the secret key is equivalent to using a decompiler to reconstruct a universal abstract data type interpreter from the static machine code.

1.1   Related Work

One of the most interesting ideas for protecting an application is to build self encrypting code [1]. The idea is that each block of machine code is a decryption cipher, which decrypts the next block of code to run, plus some small part of the application which is encrypted. After running the block re-encrypts itself. This method is a good way to bolt on security after the application is built. It has implications for maintenance since bugs may subtly interact with the modified machine code. It also has portability costs. Finally should an adversary suspect that the code is decrypting itself one block at a time it will then be easy to recapture a fully working version of the unprotected code.

An approach taken in such products as [2] is to build a compiler which uses novel optimising techniques which are not easily reversible, so effectively hiding the authentication process. This has portability issues and is more difficult to maintain than an abstract protection mechanism built into the code itself. The other drawback is that the final code has static protection mechanisms built into it, which by definition are simpler to crack than dynamically varying ones.

Using the idea of hiding values in a higher order abstract data type is not new, in [8], [9], [12] they show how to protect against reverse engineering by such tricks. Their work is concerned with allowing an algorithm to run in such a way that the adversary can not reconstruct the original algorithm, thus protecting the intellectual property contained in the algorithm. This is different from our problem, where we are not concerned with the algorithm being discovered, but with the more difficult problem of hiding some of the values which pass through the algorithm.

In [11] they look at the related problem of how to use a personal key to designate authority to temporary subkeys in a compromised system without revealing too much about the personal key. That paper is not concerned with the actual mechanics of preventing reverse engineering of the authentication process, rather it looks at ways of sharing out some of the attributes attached to the main key without allowing an unacceptable amount of information to leak.

2   Bat Attacks

This section deals with the problem of protecting the application with a hardware key which is only used as part of a simple challenge response mechanism. The response to the challenge is incorporated into a boolean valued test which determines whether the application should proceed or take evasive action.

The most common form of hardware key is a dongle so we will use this term to refer to a generic hardware key from now on. A simple challenge response test using a dongle may look like:

```
if (QuerryDongle(Challenge Value) == Right Response) {
    Continue as normal;
  } else {
    Take evasive action;
  }
```

One weakness with this kind of test is that `QuerryDongle` typically uses a fixed port to communicate whose address is hardwired into the dongle. Current debugging tools can insert break points which occur when that port is used. This effectively locates the point in the code where the boolean test occurs. An attacker can now replace

(QuerryDongle(Challenge Value) == Right Response)

with `True`. Dongle manufacturers commonly warn about this type of attack in their literature.

We call an attack where certain boolean tests are replaced by a constant value (true or false) a boolean adaptation of tests attack (bat attack for short, or sometimes boolean attack).

2.1   Bat Defense

Replace the above simple test with a finite graph G where each node is labeled by a boolean test of the form

(QuerryDongle(v) == r)

and each node has two edges leading from it, one labeled 0 the other labeled 1. The r values are constant and vary from state to state, v is a variable. Choose G in an arbitrary manner. Fix one of the nodes s as the start node.

A sequence of values v_i generates a bit string b as follows. Define states $s_i \in G$ and $b_i \in \mathbb{B}$ inductively, where node s_i is labeled by (QuerryDongle(v) == r_i):

- $s_0 = s$
- $b_i = (\texttt{QuerryDongle}(v_i) \; \texttt{==} \; r_i)$

s_{i+1} is the state for which there is an edge $s_i \xrightarrow{b_i} s_{i+1}$.

Assuming that there are no terminating nodes in G, any sequence of values v_i generates a bit string $b_0 b_1 b_2 \cdots$. Let this bit string be denoted $\mu(G, v_0 v_1 \cdots)$

The application incorporates the graph G and a predetermined set of values v_i together with the precalculated value $\alpha = \mu(G, v_0 v_1 \cdots)$. Before the application runs (or periodically whilst running) it runs through G with values v_i recalculating dynamically $\alpha' = \mu(G, v_0 v_1 \cdots)$. At various places in the code, dislocated from the immediate calculation of α', the application checks $\alpha \; \texttt{==} \; \alpha'$ and only now chooses to continue or take evasive action.

The boolean tests in G can be located in the application code by inserting relevant break points which monitor port traffic. If an attacker wishes to replace any of the boolean tests in G with a constant value then they have a $1/2$ probability of choosing the correct value so that α' will still be α. If there are n values v_i the attacker has only a $1/2^n$ probability of correctly replacing each boolean test without affecting α'. In fact the probability is less than this since there can be many more states in G than n.

This defense has a weakness in that the attacker may discover where the new boolean tests $\alpha \; \texttt{==} \; \alpha'$ are and simply replace them with $\texttt{True}$. This attack is much harder since there is no longer any port communication to give the game away. It is possible to disguise this comparison by hiding α and α' in higher order data types, and then comparing them in a deceitful manner. This is a special case of the next section.

3 Lute Attacks

It is quite fashionable to try to protect applications by calculating checksums on those parts of the code which authenticate the user to ensure that the code has not been tampered with. Some hash function or message authentication checksum (MAC) is used on a part of the code dealing with the authentication process. The resultant value is built into another part of the code. When the application runs it recalculates the relevant hash value whenever necessary to check it is still the same.

If the hash values are used in a simple boolean test they are vulnerable to bat attacks. In order to calculate a hash value of a code fragment the application will need to access some storage device (e.g the disk drive). Such access can be monitored and so break points can be used in the same way as in the dongle case above to locate the boolean tests.

Rather than use a hash value in a boolean test it is sometimes incorporated into a calculation in the application itself. Here is a trivial example which is not particularly secure. If file f has hash value a which is stored as a constant somewhere and h is the hash function, then an assignment $x = b$ can be replaced with $x = b - a + h(f)$. Tampering with f will cause this to give the wrong value to x.

The most obvious attack here is to insert breakpoints on h (assuming this can be achieved by tracking when IO occurs on binary files). From these we can determine what the constants a are and place them in a look up table. Then change the code for h so that it uses the look up table of the values a and simply returns the right value. This is much more work than a bat attack, but still doable. We call such an attack a look up table evaluation attack, or a lute attack for short.

For the rest of this section we will look at one way of representing a constant in terms of a randomly varying abstract data type, and how to defend against a lute attack when performing a checksum on a code fragment.

3.1   Hiding a Constant Value in an Automaton

Let A be a nondeterministic finite state automata with states S and labeled edges E, with labels taken from the set L. Let s_0 be the start state. Choose a function $\delta : \mathbb{N} \longrightarrow S$.

A sequence $l = l_0 l_1 \cdots l_n \in L^*$ determines a value in $\mathbb{B}^N$ as follows. Let $A(l)$ be the set of states which are reached on input l to A. Choose $\beta \in \mathbb{B}^N$ by

$$\beta_i = 1 \Leftrightarrow \delta(i) \in A(l)$$

This provides a mapping from L^*, A and a mapping $\delta : \mathbb{N} \longrightarrow S$, to $\mathbb{B}^N$. Let $\omega(A, l, \delta)$ denote this mapping.

Next consider how to construct an A with string $l \in L^*$ and subset $U = A(l)$, which represents a given value $\beta \in \mathbb{B}^N$. Let $l = l_0 l_1 \cdots l_n \in L^*$. Construct at random a directed acyclic graph (dag) with a single root, using U as the set of leaf nodes, where each branch has length n, and label each edge in the branch with the relevant l_i so that each branch is annotated with l.

Now add edges and states at random (the result is no longer required to be a dag), but in such a way that no new paths are created which have prefix l at the root. The set U now consists of those states which are reached on input l to A, i.e. $U = A(l)$. Choose functions $\delta_1 \{i \in \mathbb{N} \mid \beta_i = 1\} \longrightarrow A(l)$ and $\delta_2 \{i \in \mathbb{N} \mid \beta_i = 0\} \longrightarrow S - A(l)$, putting these together gives a function δ where

$$\delta(i) \in A(l) \Leftrightarrow \beta_i = 1$$

For the given A and l and map δ, $\omega(A, l, \delta) = \beta$. Notice that to a large extent the construction of l, A and δ is completely random. This allows the value β to be dynamically stored in a randomly varying way. The size of A and l can be made arbitrarily large, depending on how much computation is acceptable for the recovery of a constant value.

Any one attempting to recover β would have to locate the map δ, and recover the semantics behind the construction of A. This will be impossible for a casual observer. Notice that it is possible to recover any single bit of β without revealing any of the other bits. To find β_i, recover the set U from the automata and check if $\delta(i) \in U$.

3.2   Varying the Automaton Representation of a Bit String

This section briefly outlines ways to construct new automaton representations of a bit string β from old ones without revealing β and in an efficient manner. One of the goals of using an abstract data type to represent a constant value is to be able to vary the representation dynamically in a random fashion and without revealing the constant. The automaton representation is quite effective at doing this.

A bit string can be hidden by a triple (A, l, δ) as described above. There are simple ways which can be used to change each item in this triple while keeping $\omega(A, l, \delta)$ invariant.

Let $U = A(l)$. Using new states not in A construct a new dag D whose leaves are given by U and where every branch from the root s_0' to a leaf $u \in U$ is annotated by the same word $l' \in L$. Add new nodes and edges at will to D so long as no new paths are constructed which are prefixed by l'. Let A' be the automaton consisting of the union of D with any random subautomaton chosen from A. Take s_0' as the start node for A'. Modify the map δ so that any values $\delta(i)$ which are no longer defined are reassigned to states not in U, let δ' be the resultant map. Notice that

$$\omega(A, l, \delta) = \omega(A', l', \delta')$$

The only unchanged quantity between (A, l, δ) and (A', l', δ') is the set $A(l) = A'(l)$.

The triple (A, l, δ) can also be changed by applying the following graph rewriting rule. For any node u we can add a new node u' so long as we also add the following edges.

- If there is an edge $w \xrightarrow{a} u$ add an edge $w \xrightarrow{a} u'$
- If there is an edge $u \xrightarrow{a} w$ add an edge $u' \xrightarrow{a} w$

Note that if $u \in A(l)$ then we will also now have $u' \in A(l)$. We may also delete any subgraphs which are not path connected to any node of $A(l)$. One may even delete some, but not all, of the nodes in $A(l)$ providing that suitable modification is made to δ so that every undefined value is mapped to some other value in $A(l)$.

The map δ can be modified to a large extent without affecting $\omega(A, l, \delta)$. The only attribute that matters for the map δ is that it maps the correct values into $A(l)$. Thus we may compose δ with any function $\nu : S \longrightarrow S$ so long as $\nu(A(l)) \subseteq A(l)$ and $\nu(S - A(l)) \subseteq S - A(l)$.

Possibly the easiest and most useful modification of (A, l, δ) is to apply a random permutation of the node set. Let $A = (S, E, s_0)$ be an automaton with states S, edges E and where s_0 is the start state. For a permutation $\rho : S \longrightarrow S$ we can define $\rho(A) = (S, \rho(E), \rho(s_0))$, where

$$\rho(u \xrightarrow{l} v) = \rho(u) \xrightarrow{l} \rho(v)$$

Define $\rho(A, l, \delta) = (\rho(A), l, \rho \circ \delta)$. For any $l \in L^*$,

$$\omega(A, l, \delta) = \omega \circ \rho(A, l, \delta)$$

This works since $(\rho \circ \delta)^{-1}\rho(A)(l) = \delta^{-1}A(l)$. Also notice that given $(A', l, \delta') = \rho(A, l, \delta)$ and no knowledge of ρ, it is an NP complete problem to show that (A', l, δ') is isomorphic to (A, l, δ).

Using various combinations of the above modifications can alter the original triple (A, l, δ) into a radically different structure. The modifications are elementary and therefore efficient (in terms of the size of A). This makes it a straightforward matter to dynamically alter the structure representing β in a virtually arbitrary way without revealing β during the modification.

3.3   Lute Defense

Let $T(\beta, r)$ be a function which returns a triple (A_r, l_r, δ_r) where $\omega(A_r, l_r, \delta_r) = \beta$. Function T uses some pseudo-random number generator with seed r to pseudo-randomly construct (A_r, l_r, δ_r) in some way.

The hash function $h(f) \in \mathbb{N}$ is replaced by a function $H(f, r)$. This returns the triple $T(h(f), r) = (A_r, l_r, \delta_r)$ where $\omega(A_r, l_r, \delta_r) = h(f)$. It should be noted that if $H(f, r)$ is merely a call to $T(h(f), r)$ then this will not be secure, since the secondary call to $h(f)$ is still susceptible to a lute attack. The function $H(f, r)$ must build a suitable triple by incorporating the value of $h(f)$ directly into the construction. The checksum constants a are replaced by $T(a, r)$.

The assignment $x = b$ could now be replaced by the following trick pseudo-code. In the code we assume that triples (A, l, δ) are defined as some suitable structure in C++ so that if p is a pointer to a triple (A, l, δ), then $p\text{->}A = A$ etc.

```
\* if the code is unmodified then h(f) == a *\
r = random number;
\\ * is the dereference operator
*p = T(a,r);
ρ = random permutation of states of p->A;
*q = ρH(f, r);
n = random number;
ρ = random permutation of [1,2,..., n];
u = [p, q];
\* supposedly *p is equivalent to *q *\
int y[];
int z[] = random partition of b into n integers;
int e[];
x = 0;
for (i=1; i <= n; i++) {
      e[i] = random choice of -1 or 1;
      y[i] = random element of L*;
};
for (i=1; i <= n; i++) {
      v = random choice of 1 or 0;
      \\ note here * is multiplication
      x += e[i] * ω(u[v]->A, y[i], u[v]->δ) + z[i];
};
```

```
for (i=1; i <= n; i++) {
    v = random choice of 1 or 0;
    x -= e[ρ(i)] * ω(u[v]->A, y[ρ(i)], u[v]->δ);
};
\* now x == b *\
```

A casual observer will not be able to replace H(f,r) by a constant value without destroying the final value of x. The values *p and *q are equivalent in the sense that for all values $x \in L^*$,

$$\omega(\text{p->A}, \ x, \ \text{p->}\delta) = \omega(\text{q->A}, \ x, \ \text{q->}\delta)$$

For the adversary to realise that p is just a permutation of q they would need to recalculate the first value of ρ which is an NP complete problem. Of course if the adversary realises that ρ is computed in the code they could just store it somewhere for later use. However a casual observer will not be able to understand the purpose of ρ or even that it is a permutation of states in an automaton.

The next section turns to the major problem of how to compute the encryption of some plaintext without revealing the key.

4   Hidden Key Computation

If an adversary can not bypass the authentication code contained in the application an alternative is to uncover any secret keys used in the authentication process so that they can use them in a man in the middle attack to fool the software into running. For this section we will restrict our attention to the problem of how to encrypt some plaintext without revealing the secret key used by the encryption cipher. Before we go into this problem in detail we first have to solve the problem of choosing elements of a list in such a manner that the indices of those elements remain hidden. This will be a useful tool which we use when solving the main problem.

4.1   Choosing Elements from a List

This section considers how to choose a subsequence from a list of bits in a manner which hides the locations of the chosen bits. Let $[b_0, \ldots, b_n]$ be a list of bits. The problem is how to construct a subsequence $[b_{i_0}, \ldots, b_{i_m}]$ without revealing the values i_j to a casual observer. In order to simplify the situation only the case of choosing a single bit b_j is considered.

Let $\mathcal{P}_n = \{p_1, \ldots, p_n\}$ be a set of n propositions. Let $\mathbb{B}\mathcal{P}_n$ be the set of propositional formulae constructed from $\mathcal{P}_n$. Let $\beta = [b_0, \ldots, b_n]$, let $\theta : \mathcal{P}_n \longrightarrow \mathbb{B}$ be the valuation given by $\theta(p_i) = b_i$. This extends to a valuation on propositional formulae as usual.

For a set X let $\text{rand}\,X$ denote an element of X chosen at random. Each occurrence of $\text{rand}\,X$ in an expression denotes a separate instance of such a random choice, implying that the value of $\text{rand}\,X$ varies at each occurrence.

For a propositional formula f let $[f]$ denote the set of formulae which can be derived from f by a standard predetermined set of equivalences. For example the set of equivalences might be

$$x \wedge (y \vee z) \;\cong\; x \wedge y \vee x \wedge z \qquad x \vee (y \wedge z) \cong (x \vee y) \wedge (x \vee z)$$
$$\neg(x \wedge y) \;\cong\; \neg x \vee \neg y \qquad \neg(x \vee y) \cong \neg x \wedge \neg y$$
$$x \to (y \to z) \;\cong\; (x \wedge y) \to z \qquad x \to y \cong \neg x \vee y$$
$$x \vee (y \vee z) \;\cong\; (x \vee y) \vee z \qquad x \wedge (y \wedge z) \cong (x \wedge y) \wedge z$$
$$x \wedge y \;\cong\; y \wedge x \qquad x \vee y \cong y \vee x$$

Then, for example, $p \to (\neg q \to r) \in [p \to (q \vee r)]$.

We can construct random tautologies over $\mathbb{BP}_n$ as follows. Pick $f = \mathrm{rand}\,\mathbb{BP}_n$, define the tautology τ as

$$\tau = \mathrm{rand}\,[(\mathrm{rand}\,[\neg f]) \vee (\mathrm{rand}\,[f])]$$

Similarly we can define a random falsehood ∂ (a formula which always evaluates to false) as

$$\partial = \mathrm{rand}\,[\neg((\mathrm{rand}\,[\neg f]) \vee (\mathrm{rand}\,[f]))]$$

Choosing $\beta[i]$ deceitfully

Let P be the set of permutations of $[1, 2, \ldots, n]$. Such a permutation extends to $\mathbb{BP}_n$ in the usual way. That is for $\rho \in P$, $\rho(f)$ is the result of replacing each occurrence of p_i by $p_{\rho(i)}$. Choose a random permutation p of $[b_0, \ldots, b_n]$ such that, if $[a_0, \ldots, a_n] = p([b_0, \ldots, b_n])$, then $a_n = b_j$.

The following code fragment, written in C++ pseudo-code results in the variable x having the value b_j at the termination of the second for loop. A casual observer will not be able to recover the value j even though they can observe the value x.

```
τ[0] = τ;
∂[0] = ∂;
for (int i = 1; i <= n; i++) {
    ρ = rand P ;
    τ[i] = rand [ρ(τ[i-])];
    ∂[i] = rand [ρ(∂[i-])];
}
 x = 0;
for (int i = 0; i <= n; i++) {
    d = disjunctive normal form of   aᵢ ∧ τ[n-i]∨∂[n-i]∧x;
    x = θ(d);
    Phony = Phony ∧x;
};
```

Note that after this code fragment has executed

$$x = b_j \wedge 1 \vee 0 = b_j$$

The sequence $\tau[\mathtt{i}]$, and $\partial[\mathtt{i}]$ are designed to hide the fact that τ and ∂ are only intended to be used for extracting b_j. It would seem that τ and ∂ construct some meaningful sequence which is in fact arbitrary. Making the sequence random ensures that the construction dynamically changes for every instance of finding b_j. Introducing the random permutation ρ means that $\tau[\mathtt{i}]$ and $\partial[\mathtt{i}]$ may well no longer be either a tautology or a falsehood. This implies that any correlation between x and the values a_i is broken.

All the bits b_i are used in the loop, nothing distinguishes one from the other. Only the permutation p distinguishes i. The place where p is used is dislocated from the use of the values a_i which hides the special nature of i.

If the value of x is traced it will take a random sequence of values, which is different on each run, with the exception of the final value which will always be b_j. This could also be hidden by using a two element array $X = [x_0, x_1]$. Replace the second for loop above with this one

```
int r;
int X[2];
for (int i = 0; i <= n; i++) {
    r = rand {0, 1} ;
    d = disjunctive normal form of  aᵢ ∧ τ[n-i] ∨ ∂[n-i] ∧ X[r];
    X[r] = θ(d);
    Phony = Phony ∧X[r];
};
```

Now the value b_j is given by the value $X[r]$ at the end of the for loop. Thus for any particular run b_j might be the value of x_0 or of x_1. Both these values will vary at random over a series of program runs. An observer will have to know which of x_0 or x_1 holds b_j. To make this even more confusing any size array could be used for X. Using a two element array would seem a reasonable choice since that is the minimum number required to ensure there is no statistical relationship between the values in the array and $b_j = a_n$.

4.2 Deceitful Automata

This section discusses how to perform the encryption $\psi_s(k_s, a)$ of text a with cipher ψ_s and key k_s while keeping the key hidden from a casual observer. The proposed method is based on the idea of constructing a graph which represents several parallel encryptions whose intermediate values are all permuted together in seemingly random fashion into a single bit string. This creates the impression that only a single complex encryption is being computed and effectively hides which bits belong to the real encryption cipher.

One of the computations represents $\psi_s(k_s, a)$. The graph has the property that any path of the right length can be used to construct $\psi_s(k_s, a)$ while keeping k_s hidden. The graph is dynamically constructed during run time and will change at random from one execution of the program to the next.

Assume the encryption cipher is an r-round cipher [13] where each round is given by the function $\chi(k^{(i)}, a_i)$, where $k^{(i)}$ is the key material used at the i-th round from the key k, and a_i is the ciphertext of the i-th round. That is the encryption $\psi_s(k,a)$ of plaintext a with key k is given by the iteration

$$\chi(k_r, \chi(k_{r-1}, \ldots, \chi(k_0, a) \cdots)$$

Suppose that the cipher encrypts blocks of size n.

Not all encryption ciphers fit this description, for example the Twofish cipher [14] doesn't. However block ciphers usually include many rounds using essentially the same function, and this part of the cipher can be protected using the ideas in this section.

An extraction function $\varepsilon : \mathbb{B}^{ln} \longrightarrow \mathbb{B}^n$ is any function which returns a permuted subsequence of its argument. An extraction function can be completely specified by a sequence $(i_1, \ldots i_n)$, where

$$\varepsilon(b_1 \cdots b_{ln}) = b_{i_1} \cdots b_{i_n}$$

A block permutation function $\sigma : (\mathbb{B}^n)^l \longrightarrow \mathbb{B}^{ln}$ is any function which can be written as

$$\sigma(x_1, \ldots, x_l) = \rho(x_1 @ \cdots @ x_n)$$

where $\rho : \mathbb{B}^{ln} \longrightarrow \mathbb{B}^{ln}$ is a permutation and @ is append. That is σ appends its arguments together and then permutes the resultant bit string.

A muddled encryption graph is a finite state graph with nodes labeled by l-tuples $(\langle \varepsilon_1, \chi_1 \rangle, \ldots, \langle \varepsilon_l, \chi_l \rangle)$, and edges labeled by block permutations. Each ε_i is an extraction function and χ_i is a round-function of an encryption cipher.

Suppose that

$$(\langle \varepsilon_1, \chi_1 \rangle, \ldots, \langle \varepsilon_l, \chi_l \rangle) \xrightarrow{\sigma} (\langle \varepsilon_1', \chi_1' \rangle, \ldots, \langle \varepsilon_l', \chi_l' \rangle)$$

is an edge A of a muddled graph. The edge A is dovetailed if there is a permutation $p : \mathbb{B}^n \longrightarrow \mathbb{B}^n$ such that for every $(e_1, \ldots, e_l) \in (\mathbb{B}^n)^l$

$$\varepsilon_i'(\sigma(e_1, \ldots, e_l)) = e_{p(i)} \text{ and } \chi_i' = \chi_{p(i)}.$$

A node $(\langle \varepsilon_1, \chi_1 \rangle, \ldots, \langle \varepsilon_l, \chi_l \rangle)$ is interleaving if for all $\alpha \in \mathbb{B}^{ln}$, $\varepsilon_1(\alpha) @ \cdots @ \varepsilon_l((\alpha)$ is a permutation of α. Define a muddled graph where all the edges are dovetailed and all the nodes are interleaving to be a deceitful cipher automaton.

For a node $\eta = (\langle \varepsilon_1, \chi_1 \rangle, \ldots, \langle \varepsilon_l, \chi_l \rangle)$, $\alpha \in \mathbb{B}^{ln}$, and a sequence of keys $k = (k_1, \ldots k_n)$ write $\eta(k, \alpha)^{(u)}$ to denote the tuple

$$(\chi_1(k_1^{(u)}, \varepsilon_1(\alpha)), \ldots, \chi_l(k_l^{(u)}, \varepsilon_l(\alpha)))$$

Where $k_i^{(u)}$ is the key material used by the cipher χ_i in the u-th round of encryption.

Proposition 1.

Let $k = (k_1, \ldots k_n)$ be a sequence of keys and let

$$\eta_1 \xrightarrow{\sigma_1} \cdots \xrightarrow{\sigma_r} \eta_{r+1}$$

be a path in the deceitful automaton D. Let $\eta_i = (\langle \varepsilon_1^i, \chi_1^i \rangle, \ldots, \langle \varepsilon_l^i, \chi_l^i \rangle)$. Let each χ_j^r be part of an r-round encryption cipher ψ_j as described above.

For $a \in \mathbb{B}^n$ define $\alpha_i \in \mathbb{B}^{ln}$ recursively for $0 \leq i \leq r$ as

$$\alpha_{i+1} = \sigma_i(\eta_i(k, \alpha_i)^{(i)})$$

and $\alpha_0 = a@ \cdots @a$, then

$$\varepsilon_i^{r+1}(\alpha_r) = \psi_i(k_i, a)$$

This is a result for any path of length r in the deceitful automaton. Thus every path of length r can be used to calculate the various ψ. The result is true since the edges are all dovetailed so the χ_j^i of each node are all matched together in the α_i sequence.

The deceitful automaton D is used to deceive an attacker as follows. There are various ciphers ψ_i corresponding to the round-functions χ_i which decorate the nodes. Only one of the ψ is the real cipher, say ψ_s, the others are irrelevant. Let χ be the round-function of cipher ψ_s. It would be acceptable to choose all the ψ to be the same as ψ_s, so that every $\chi_i = \chi$. We do not do this here for reasons of generality.

Generate a random path

$$\eta_1 \xrightarrow{\sigma_1} \cdots \xrightarrow{\sigma_r} \eta_{r+1}$$

in D of length r. To perform the encryption $\psi_s(k_s, a)$ calculate the α_r as above using the key-list $k = (k_1, \ldots, k_l)$. The only key in k of interest is k_s the others are all dummies. What matters is that k_s is not discovered by the attacker. For each node η_{i+1} there is a $v \in \mathbb{N}$ such that $\varepsilon_v^{i+1}(\alpha_{i+1})$ corresponds to the value of a after i rounds of encryption with the cipher ψ_s and key k_s. That is

$$\varepsilon_v^{i+1}(\alpha_{i+1}) = \chi(k_s^{(i)}, \chi(k_s^{(i-1)}, \ldots, \chi(k_s^{(1)}, a) \cdots)$$

Since we are placing key k_s as the s-th element of k this implies that for η_1, $v_1 = s$. The value v can be calculated afresh each time the key material is constructed for a particular path.

The key material is stored in a deceitful way in another automaton, as described earlier in section 3.1, and does not appear as a constant anywhere. The other dummy keys are derived from the same storage automaton as k_s but in a random fashion. This means none of the key material is compromised during the encryption. The final encrypted value $\psi_s(k_s, a)$ is given by $\varepsilon_{v_{r+1}}^{r+1}(\alpha_r)$.

An attacker who is only able to naively analyse the computation will not be able to learn how the deceitful automaton is used or which k_i is relevant. The deceitful automaton can be constructed dynamically and changed at random which will confuse any decompiler.

To construct a deceitful automaton generate any number of nodes as seems appropriate with randomly generated ε extraction functions in the labels, but so that each specific node is interleaving. The same set of encipher round-functions is used to construct each node. For any pair of nodes it is possible to construct a dovetailed edge between them, so assign edges between nodes totally at random. This construction allows for the deceitful automaton to be constructed in an almost completely arbitrary manner, and the total number of such automaton is huge. That makes analysing the generated automaton for patterns futile.

For an attack to succeed the attacker must realise that they need to capture the automaton and discover which ψ_i are relevant. Given that (which means capturing ε_s) they can now attempt to backtrack the calculation in the automaton. That requires capturing the relevant nodes and edges and calculating suitable inverses to the various ε and σ in order to recover all the parts of the key material used to reconstruct k_s.

Recall that an extraction function is specified as a sequence of integers. This can also be deceitfully hidden in the guise of an automaton which further complicates any attack. The techniques described in section 4.1 can be used to evaluate the final extraction function, further still hiding any starting point from which to backtrack the calculation of $\psi_s(k_s, a)$.

5   Conclusion

We have shown how to construct various abstract data types which hide secret keys used during encryption, and how to construct an apparently random dynamically varying computation which executes that encryption. The datatypes are essentially automata with some additional features. They are designed so they can be dynamically changed in an apparently random fashion without revealing the original secrets. The true nature of the data is hidden within the semantics underlying the representations which can not be recovered from the code by a casual observer.

The constructions must by their nature make the encryption cipher run less efficiently. However the cost of the extra protection is in some part made up for in their effectiveness. Even if the adversary understands the semantics of the deceitful mechanisms given here, they will still have to perform exponential searches to recover any useful material, since no standard decompiling tool will be able to reconstruct any meaningful source code. Without some sort of high level source code to work with an attacker can not make any use of their semantic knowledge. Also, the authentication process is usually performed sparingly and often is not as time critical as the rest of the application so that the extra cost may not have a great impact on performance.

Looking again at the idea of self encrypting machine code in [1] we can see how to effectively combine that work with the tricks given here. Instead of code which contains its own encryption key, take the key as hidden in some kind of smart card say. Parts of the application stay encrypted until decrypted using the key in the smart card, afterwards they are re-encrypted. Using the tricks here we can disguise the encryption process and hide the key during run time so that a casual observer will not be able to recover a working copy of the application. The encryption process now occurs at a higher abstract level which does not have the weakness of static machine code.

References

1. David Aucsmith, Tamper Resistant Software: An Implementation. Proceedings of Workshop on Information Hiding, Cambridge 1996, Springer-Verlag, Lecture Notes in Computer Science, Volume 1174, pp 317–333. 450, 461
2. DashO-Pro Obfuscator optimising compiler for Java.
   http://www.preemptive.com/DashO/obfuscate.html 450
3. Cifuentes, Cristina and K. John Gough, Decompilation of binary programs. Software — Practice and Experience, vol. 25, no. 7, pp. 811-829, July, 1995.
   http://www.csee.uq.edu.au/~cristina/pubs.html 449
4. C Cifuentes, Partial Automation of an Integrated Reverse Engineering Environment of Binary Code. Proceedings Third Working Conference on Reverse Engineering. Monterey, CA, Nov 8-10 1996. IEEE-CS Press. pp 50-56.
   http://www.csee.uq.edu.au/~cristina/pubs.html 449
5. C Cifuentes, D Simon and A Fraboulet, Assembly to High-Level Language Translation. Proceedings of the International Conference on Software Maintenance, Washington DC, USA, Nov 1998, IEEE-CS Press, pp 228-237.
   http://www.csee.uq.edu.au/~cristina/pubs.html 449
6. C Cifuentes and A Fraboulet, Interprocedural Data Flow Recovery of High-level Language Code from Assembly. Technical Report 421, Department of Computer Science and Electrical Engineering, The University of Queensland, Dec 1997.
   http://www.csee.uq.edu.au/~cristina/pubs.html 449
7. Cimitile A., De Lucia A., Munro M., A Specification Driven Slicing Process for Identifying Reusable Functions, Journal of Software Maintenance : Research and Practice, 8(3), pp145–178, 1996. 449
8. Collberg, Christian, Clark Thomborson and Douglas Low. A taxonomy of obfuscating transformations. Technical Report 148, Department of Computer Science, University of Auckland, New Zealand, July, 1997.
   http://www.cs.auckland.ac.nz/
   ~collberg/Research/Publications/CollbergThomborsonLow97a/index.html
   450
9. Collberg, Christian, Clark Thomborson and Douglas Low. Manufacturing cheap, resilient, and stealthy opaque constructs. Department of Computer Science, University of Auckland, New Zealand, July, 1997. 450
   Also in ACM SIGPLAN-SIGACT Symposium on Principles of Programming Languages (POPL'98), San Diego CA, January 1998.
   http://www.cs.auckland.ac.nz/
   ~collberg/Research/Publications/CollbergThomborsonLow98a/index.html
10. De Lucia A., Fasolino A.R., Munro M., Understanding Function Behaviors through Program Slicing, Workshop on Program Comprehension, IEEE Press, 1996.
    http://www.dur.ac.uk/~dcs1elb/delucia-wpc96.html 449
11. Oded Goldreich, Birgit Pfitzmann and Ronald L. Rivest, Self-Delegation with Controlled Propagation — or — What If You Loose Your Laptop, CRYPTO' 98, LNCS 1462, pp. 153-168. 450
12. Java Code Engineering & Reverse Engineering.
    http://meurrens.ml.org/ip-Links/Java/CodeEngineering/mm_scale.html 450
13. Bruce Schneier. Applied Cryptography, Second Edition, John Wiley & Sons, 1996
    458
14. B. Schneier, J. Kelsey, D. Whiting, D. Wagner, C. Hall, N. Ferguson. Twofish: A 128-Bit Block Cipher, June 1998,
    http://www.counterpane.com/twofish-paper.html 459

StegFS: A Steganographic File System for Linux

Andrew D. McDonald and Markus G. Kuhn*

University of Cambridge, Computer Laboratory, New Museums Site
Pembroke Street, Cambridge CB2 3QG, United Kingdom
a.d.mcdonald@bcs.org.uk
mgk25@cl.cam.ac.uk

Abstract. Cryptographic file systems provide little protection against legal or illegal instruments that force the owner of data to release decryption keys for stored data once the presence of encrypted data on an inspected computer has been established. We are interested in how cryptographic file systems can be extended to provide additional protection for such a scenario and we have extended the standard Linux file system (Ext2fs) with a plausible-deniability encryption function. Even though it is obvious that our computer has harddisk encryption software installed and might contain some encrypted data, an inspector will not be able to determine whether we have revealed the access keys to all security levels or only those to a few selected ones. We describe the design of our freely available implementation of this steganographic file system and discuss its security and performance characteristics.

1 Introduction

Various implementations of cryptographic file systems have been made widely available. Examples include CFS [1] for Unix, TCFS [2] for Linux, and EFS [3] for Windows, which transparently encrypt individual files, as well as the Linux loopback device [4] and SFS [5] for Microsoft platforms, which encrypt entire disk partitions. Cryptographic file systems store files and associated metadata only in encrypted form on non-volatile media. They can provide the user some protection against the unwanted disclosure of information to anyone who gets physical control over the storage unit.

Assuming correctly implemented encryption software is used as designed, and cryptanalysis remains infeasible, an attacker can still chose among various tactics to enforce access to encrypted file systems. Brief physical access to a computer is, for instance, sufficient to install additional software or hardware that allow an attacker to reconstruct encryption keys at a distance. (UHF burst transmitters that can be installed by non-experts inside any PC keyboard within 10–12 minutes are now commercially available, as are eavesdropping drivers that will covertly transmit keystrokes and secret keys via network links.) An entirely different class of tactics focuses on the key holders, who can be threatened with sanctions as long as there remains undecryptable ciphertext on their storage

---

* Supported by a European Commission Marie Curie training grant

A. Pfitzmann (Ed.): IH'99, LNCS 1768, pp. 463–477, 2000.

devices. We are interested in data protection technologies for this latter case, especially considering that attackers can often be more persuasive when the data owner cannot plausibly deny that not all access keys have already been revealed.

Plausible deniability [7] shall refer here to a security property of a mechanism that allows parties to claim to others (e.g., a judge) that some information is not in their possession or that some transaction has not taken place. The one-time pad is a well-known encryption technique with plausible deniability, because for every given ciphertext, a decryption key can be found that leads to a harmless message. However such schemes are only practical for short messages and are not generally suited for data storage.

Anderson, Needham and Shamir [6] outlined first designs for encrypted file stores with a plausible-deniability mechanism, which they called *steganographic file systems*. They aim to provide a secure file system where the risk of users being forced to reveal their keys or other private data is diminished by allowing the users to deny believably that any further encrypted data is located on the disk. Steganographic file systems are designed to give a high degree of protection against compulsion to disclose their contents. A user who knows the password for a set of files can access it. Attackers without this knowledge cannot gain any information as to whether the file exists or not, even if they have full access to the hardware and software.

The authors of [6] outline two different ways of constructing such a system. The first makes the assumption that the attacker has no knowledge of the stored plaintexts and instead of strong cipher algorithms, only linear algebra operations are required. The scheme operates on a set of cover files with initially random content. Then data files are stored by modifying the initially random cover files such that the plaintext can be retrieved as a linear combination of them. The password to access a file corresponds to the subset of cover files that has to be XOR-ed together to reconstruct the hidden file. The number of cover files must be sufficiently large to guarantee that trying all subsets of cover files remains computationally infeasible. We decided not to use this approach in our implementation, because a lot of cover files would have to be read and XOR-ed to ensure computational security. In addition to this prospect of low performance for both read and write access, we felt uncomfortable with the requirement that the attacker must not know any part of the plaintext.

In the second approach outlined in [6], the file system is initially filled completely with blocks of random data. The file blocks are hidden amongst this random data by writing the encrypted blocks to pseudo-random locations using a key derived from the file name and directory password. The file blocks are then indistinguishable from the random data. As blocks are written to the file system, collisions will occur and blocks will be overwritten. This starts to occur frequently after about $\sqrt{n}$ blocks have been used, where n is the number of blocks in the file system, as the birthday paradox suggests. Only a small proportion of the disk space could safely be utilised this way, therefore multiple copies of each block have to be written and a method is needed to identify when they have been overwritten.

Van Schaik and Smeddle [8] have implemented a file system, which they describe as being inspired by [6], however it falls some way short of meeting the security and plausible deniability aims originally described. They neither hide information by linearly combining password-selected subsets of blocks as suggested in the first method, nor do they replicate blocks as in the second method. Instead they mark blocks as 'might be used by the higher security levels'. Hence, from one security level it can be seen that others exist, although the exact quantity of data stored in this way is obscured. In this way, they avoid open files accidentally overwriting hidden data, but at the same time, they also provide inspectors with a low upper bound on the amount of hidden data.

Other steganographic file storage systems in the past have used the idea of storing files in large amounts of non-random but slightly noisy covertexts such as a graphics or audio file. For example, ScramDisk [13] for MS-Windows allows the ciphertext blocks of its cryptographic file system to be stored in the least-significant bits of an audio file. The Linux encrypting loopback block device can also work in this way.

2   Basic Concept

The design of our hidden file system was inspired by the second construction in [6], but it differs substantially from it and is, in our view, more practical and efficient. We do not require the use of a separate partition of a harddisk, but instead place hidden files into unused blocks of a partition that also contains normal files, managed under a standard file system.

While the second construction in [6] allocates blocks purely based on a hash function of the file name, we use instead a separate block allocation table. It fulfills a similar function as the block allocation bitmap in traditional file systems, but instead of a single bit for each block, it contains an entire 128-bit encrypted entry, which is indistinguishable from random bits unless the key for accessing a security level is available. The additional block allocation table has a length that depends only on the partition size. We ensure that it is always present if the steganographic file system driver has been installed on this system, no matter whether it is being actively used or not. The encryption ensures that inspectors can gain no further information from this table beyond the fact that StegFS has been installed. Therefore, we see no need to especially hide its presence, because we do not properly hide the steganographic file system driver itself anyway.

A plausible explanation might have to be given for the installation of the StegFS driver in any case, usually by providing inspectors access to some of the lower security levels that could be filled with mildly compromising material. The privacy protection of our file system is not provided by giving no indication of whether any hidden files are present or not. It is only impossible to find out how many different security levels of files are actually used. Inspectors could of course force the user to fill the entire remaining disk space with new data, which is guaranteed to overwrite most hidden data. Our file system provides no protection against this active attack and we envisage that a user typically has backups hidden elsewhere and would rather have his files destroyed than hand them over.

Our construction has over the ones discussed in [6] the advantage of providing a hidden file system that follows very closely all the standard Unix file system semantics. We have subdirectories, inodes, symbolic and hard links, etc. Error conditions such as lost hidden files in our system are identified and signalled via error codes that correspond to closely related conditions in normal file systems, such that standard software will automatically act appropriately. We can use arbitrary positions for blocks, which allows us to coordinate block allocation with the non-hidden file system that shares the same partition and which also allows us to utilize the entire disk.

3   Implementation

File system support in the Linux kernel [9] is structured into a system call inter-face, a virtual file system (VFS) interface, several file-system specific drivers, a buffer cache and a series of hardware-specific device drivers (Fig. 1). The stan-dard Linux harddisk file system is the Second Extended File System (Ext2fs) [11], but other alternatives such as Minix, DOS, and ISO 9660 can be selected at mount time. Our steganographic file system implementation (StegFS) is installed alongside the normal Ext2fs, Minix, etc. drivers between the VFS interface and the blockbuffer cache.

StegFS partitions are compatible with Ext2fs partitions. The StegFS driver can work on Ext2fs partitions and vice versa. This allows the StegFS driver to be removed entirely from the system and the non-hidden files in the StegFS partition can still be accessed using the standard Ext2fs driver. In such a situation, the StegFS partition will just look like a partition in which unused blocks have recently been overwritten with random bytes using some disk wiping tool.

StegFS contains the full functionality of the Ext2fs driver for compatible access to non-hidden files. In addition, it can store hidden files in the blocks that are currently unused by Ext2fs. As long as no hidden security levels are opened, StegFS behaves almost exactly like Ext2fs. One exception is that when files are deleted, their blocks will immediately be overwritten with random bytes. Another modification is that a small fraction of newly created files is placed at a somewhat more random location on the disk than normal, which will help to plausibly explain to inspectors why sometimes a few unused blocks in the middle of a large range of unmodified free blocks have changed between two inspections. They could either belong to a new hidden file or to one of the non-hidden Ext2fs files that was allocated randomly and later deleted. As soon as hidden security levels are opened, the behaviour of the Ext2fs block allocation routine changes further, such that blocks used by the now visible hidden files will not be overwritten by the Ext2fs section.

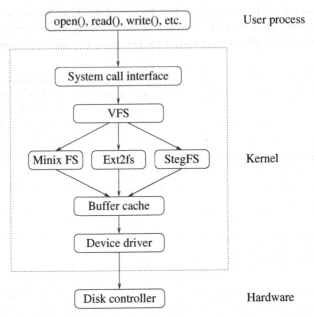

Fig. 1. The StegFS driver in the Linux kernel offers an alternative to the normal Ext2fs driver and includes its full functionality.

We selected Ext2fs, because its widespread use allows us to continue using the non-hidden files in a plausible way even when the StegFS driver has to be removed. Its design is fairly simple and similar to the traditional Unix file system [10]. The use of bitmaps to mark used blocks simplifies block allocation for the steganographic part.

StegFS was built starting with the freely available Ext2fs code. It contains essentially two parallel instances of the Ext2fs functions, an only slightly modified one for access to normal files, and a substantially modified one for access to hidden files. We have effectively two file systems supported in parallel in one driver on one partition. The StegFS implementation adds about 5000 lines of code to the 5400 lines of the Ext2fs driver.

We briefly considered an alternative design in which we would have mounted the same block device multiple times at different security levels. However the VFS interface did not allow this, and the blockbuffer cache was not designed for concurrent access by several drivers to the same block device. We would have had to implement additional synchronization mechanisms between the various drivers and this would have made the design more complex.

When a StegFS partition is mounted as a StegFS file system, it behaves initially almost exactly like a normal Ext2 file system, except for the random overwriting of deleted file blocks and the occasionally more random placement of new files. The user can then use the stegfsopen tool in order to open additional security levels in which hidden files become visible and can be stored. Once the first StegFS level is opened, a directory called 'stegfs' appears in the root directory of the file system. Under this directory additional directories called '1', '2', etc. appear, one for each open security level.

Hidden files are stored in a very similar way to normal Ext2fs files. We also distinguish regular files and directory files. Directories contain file names and inode numbers. Inodes contain file attributes and a list of the blocks assigned to this file. To access a hidden file, we first have to access the root directory of a hidden security level, then traverse the directory path to the inode of the file and finally access the data blocks referenced by the inode. The main difference between normal files and hidden files is that the allocation of new blocks by the Ext2fs driver could overwrite blocks of hidden files when the corresponding security level is not open. In addition, since we cannot plausibly justify sparing any block from being used by the normal file system, we cannot use a fixed location even for the root directory inode of any hidden level.

It is, therefore, necessary that both inodes and data blocks of hidden files are replicated throughout the partition, such that the data can still be recovered after some blocks have been overwritten. The following data structures help the StegFS driver to locate these replicated files.

3.1   Block Table

The block table is the StegFS equivalent of the block allocation bitmap. It contains one entry per block on disk. The main purpose of this table is to store encrypted checksums for each block such that overwritten blocks can be detected. It also stores the inode numbers for blocks containing inodes, such that inodes can be located by searching for their number in the table. The block table is stored in a separate normal non-hidden file.

Each entry in the block table is 128 bits long. It is encrypted under the same key as the data in the corresponding disk block. Each entry consists of the following three 32-bit and two 16-bit variables:

```
struct stegfs_btable {
    uint32_t magic1;
    uint16_t magic2;
    uint16_t iv;
    uint32_t bchecksum;
    uint32_t ino;
}
```

Variable magic1 should always be 0. Variable magic2 is 1 if the corresponding block contains an inode and for a data block it is 0. Variable bchecksum contains the last 32 bits of a block's encrypted contents, which is for our purposes equivalent to a checksum of the block since the blocks are CBC encrypted using the zero-padded value iv as the initial vector. Variable ino contains the inode number of this file. Table entries corresponding to unused blocks contain random data. Note that if we do not know the key for the security level of a block, we cannot distinguish whether is is used or not. Variables `magic1` and `magic2` together contain 47 bits of redundancy that allow us to determine quickly whether a block is used under a security level for which we know the key. The checksum allows us to test whether a block has been overwritten when files were written under Ext2fs while StegFS was not installed. It also allows a StegFS repair tool to eliminate table entries that are unused but look after decryption accidentally like used ones, which might happen with a probability of 2^{-47} per block.

3.2   Inode Structures

The hidden StegFS inodes resemble those of Ext2fs, but contain in addition the number of replicas that were made of the file's inode and data blocks. The list of data blocks has 12 direct blocks, one indirect, one double indirect, and one triple indirect block, just like in an Ext2fs inode. However, instead of just a reference to a single data block, each hidden StegFS inode contains references to all copies of this block (Figure 2).

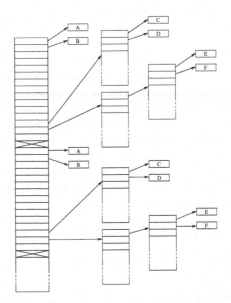

Fig. 2. A StegFS inode contains a sequence of several lists of inodes, each of which points to a different copy of all data blocks for a file. Boxes with the same letter represent blocks containing identical replicated data.

The hidden inodes are 1024 bytes in size, which is the most common size for the blocks in an Ext2 file system. Hence, each inode takes up one disk block. Several copies of each inode are stored to provide redundancy.

In the current version, we can have up to 28 copies of each hidden inode and 14 copies of each hidden file block. The number of copies of the inode and data blocks is inherited from the directory in which the inode is created. The security levels that are used most often can have fewer copies since they are less likely to be overwritten.

The numbers of copies of inodes and data blocks can be altered by a pair of new `ioctl` request types, which provide access to the replication factors that are stored as new attributes in the inodes.

3.3   Virtual File System

The Linux VFS uses generic inode and superblock structures in memory. Both contain a file-system specific section. The StegFS versions of these extend those used by Ext2fs. We augmented the superblock structure by a number of additional fields for managing security levels (e.g., the keys for the currently opened levels), a pointer to the cipher functions structure and the block-table file. We also extended the VFS inode structure, which has to hold the same information as the hidden on-disk StegFS inodes, namely the replication factors and the locations of all replicated data blocks.

The VFS structures are, in the current StegFS version, larger than those for the standard file systems in Linux. Therefore, the kernel must be recompiled at the moment to install StegFS and it is not yet possible to install it just as a loadable kernel module without any other kernel modification.

3.4   Inode Numbers

An inode number is a 32-bit integer that uniquely identifies a file within a file system. In Ext2fs, the location of a file's inode on the disk can be computed directly from its inode number. For hidden files on a StegFS partition, we have to search for the inode in the decrypted block table and hope to find one that has not been overwritten. We decided to distinguish normal and hidden files by their inode number, such that operations on files can easily be directed to either the Ext2fs or the StegFS part of the StegFS driver. Inode numbers of hidden files also indicate the security level in the range 1 to 15

0	1	level	rest of inode number

such that the right decryption key can be selected easily, while non-hidden files have inode numbers of the form

0	0	rest of inode number

In order to avoid that we have to search the entire blocktable for inodes of hidden files, their block locations are selected by hashing the security level key and the inode number together with a hash sequence number. When we create a new file, the hash sequence number is increased until enough free blocks have been found for all copies of the new inode. We go through the same sequence to locate inodes when they are loaded. The decrypted inodes are cached within the VFS, so this search does not have to be repeated often while a file is in use.

3.5 Block Allocation

Data and inode-indirection blocks in the hidden file system are allocated at random locations on the disk. The Linux kernel provides a random number source in form of the /dev/urandom driver, which maintains an entropy pool by hashing timestamps of interrupts [12]. We use this random number generator to select the first free block that we allocate for a file. The first copy of each following block is allocated in the next free block. The additional copies of every block are written starting from completely independent random locations, in order to ensure that the overwrite probability of the various copies remains independent.

Before a block is allocated, we first test whether it is marked as used in the Ext2fs bitmap. If not, we attempt to decrypt the corresponding entry in the block table using each of the known level keys. If for none of the keys the first 47 bits of the decrypted entry are all zero, the block is allocated, otherwise we start the same test on the next free block in the Ext2fs bitmap.

We also tried an alternative method in which each hidden block is assigned completely independently from previous blocks to a random free location. This approach turned out to have both a performance and a security problem. The non-locality of block allocations caused very slow read performance because the harddisk spent most of the time accelerating the read head. In addition, an inspector of the block assignment pattern of the non-hidden Ext2fs files could become suspicious. Ext2fs files would frequently have gaps of single blocks in their assignment pattern, because they had to jump over each single block of the randomly distributed cloud of blocks used by hidden files. Even though the blocks of hidden files cannot be distinguished from deleted files, the large number of supposedly recently deleted single-block files would look rather suspicious and might allow an inspector to estimate the number of blocks occupied by hidden files. It is, therefore, important that the allocation patterns for hidden files are sufficiently similar to the allocation patterns of Ext2fs files with occasionally random placement.

For both normal and hidden files, a block and the corresponding block-table entry are overwritten completely with random bytes when the block is deallocated. This not only ensures that information is really purged when a file is deleted, it also makes deleted normal files indistinguishable from hidden files, as long as the right security level key for a hidden file is not available.

3.6 Block Replication

Multiple copies of both inodes and data blocks are stored on disk, so that if one or more copies are destroyed then hopefully others will remain intact. When reading files, usually only the first copy of any given block will be required. If the checksum for this copy is correct then the block will be decrypted, otherwise further copies will be tried. When writing into a file and only a part of the block is changed, it is first necessary to read and decrypt the corresponding block. After the changes have been made, the corresponding initial vector is modified, the block is encrypted again and written back to disk. The block allocation table entry has to be updated with the new initial vector and checksum. We then have to go through the list of replicated copies of this block and read each of these in order to check whether it has been overwritten in the meantime or is still valid. If the block is still valid, then we just encrypt the new data block for these locations and write it to disk. If the checksum test indicates that the block has already been overwritten, then we allocate a new block if the overwritten one is still in use by a non-hidden or lower level file. We then encrypt and write the data into this block, and update the inode and block table accordingly.

For hidden files, we can never assume that the content of a block is still correct, and so the checksum has to be verified on any access. Most significantly, the fact that we even have to read every copy of a block for the checksum test before we can overwrite it decreases the write performance. A future revision might, therefore, cache the overwrite status of blocks in memory.

Blocks are replicated when data is written out to disk. A simple method to ensure that the full number of copies exists is, hence, to read and rewrite the file. A new tool `rerpl` does this and should be used each time after the disk has been used in a lower security level. Only a small amount of each block in the file needs to be read and rewritten from a user process to regenerate the full number of copies. Inodes are re-replicated automatically by accessing the file, which updates the `atime` in the inode and causes it to be rewritten.

3.7   Key Management

Each hidden file belongs to one of 15 *security levels*. In order to allow groups of security levels to be opened with just a single passphrase, StegFS manages in addition 15 *security contexts*. Each such context gives access to a subset of all security levels and is protected by its own passphrase. In a typical default configuration, security context C provides access to security levels $1, \ldots, C$. This way, for every security level, there exists a passphrase that gives access to this and also all lower security levels. The user can add and remove any security level in any security context to build more complex hierarchies of security levels.

When a user opens a security context C and enters the corresponding passphrase PP_C, then it is hashed immediately using a secure hash function h to produce

$$HP_C = h(PP_C)$$

At the end of the block-table file, a 15×15-element security matrix M is appended, in which each entry is a 128-bit word. If security context C is to provide access to security level L, then

$$M_{C,L} = \{SK_L\}_{HP_C}$$

contains the level key SK_L encrypted with HP_C. All other matrix elements $M_{C,L}$ contain only a random value. The size of matrix M is hardwired like the block table and is independent of the number of security levels and contexts actually used, therefore the open presence of this data does not reveal to an inspector any more information than the presence of the StegFS driver itself.

If disk block i belongs to a hidden file under security level L, then it and the related block table entry are encrypted under the security level key XOR-ed with the block number. So the encryption key for block i will be

$$BK_{L,i} = SK_L \oplus i.$$

Each block is then separately encrypted in Cipher Block Chaining (CBC) mode, using an initialisation vector (IV) that is stored in the corresponding block allocation table entry. We use only a 16-bit counter for this IV, because most files modified by applications are usually recreated entirely and therefore end up with a completely different location for every block, which anyway changes the keys used to encrypt the file and reduces the need to add further variability from a full-sized IV. In addition, as long as fewer than 2^8 inspections take place, inspectors will rarely see two modifications of a hidden block with the same 16-bit IV.

The current implementation offers the two Advanced Encryption Standard candidates Serpent and RC6 as block ciphers (using Gladman's implementations [14] with minor modifications) and the architecture allows other ciphers with the AES block size of 128 bits to be added easily later. An interesting alternative would be to use instead of AES-CBC a variable-length block cipher such as Block TEA [15,16], which would eliminate the need to store an initial vector.

The SK_L for all open levels L are stored in the superblock structure in RAM and these cleartext keys are never written to the disk. The PP_C or HP_C values are overwritten in RAM as soon as the SK_L keys have been decrypted.

4   File System Usage

A StegFS file system has to be prepared as follows. After a partition has been created, we first place a normal Ext2 file system onto it with

```
mke2fs /dev/blockdevice
```

Any existing Ext2 file system can be used as well. We then use the command

```
mkstegfs /dev/blockdevice /path/to/btab
```

to fill all the empty blocks in the Ext2 file system with random data and create the block table file, whose size only depends on the size of the partition.

The block table also contains the space to store enough encrypted keys for 15 different security contexts and levels. The number 15 is hardwired and is deliberately not made user configurable, so as to give users plausible deniability for the number of security levels for which memory was allocated. They can then claim that the software forced them to allocate 15 levels even though they needed only 1 or 2. The program prompts for a passphrase for each context. The StegFS file system is now ready and can be mounted with:

```
mount /dev/blockdevice /mnt/mntpoint -t stegfs \
  -o btab=/path/to/btab
```

In order to open one of the StegFS security levels to access or deposit hidden files and directories, we use the command

```
stegfsopen /mnt/mntpoint contextnum
```

where contextnum is either the number of the security context that is to be opened, which by default gives access to security levels 1 to contextnum, or zero if all evidence of hidden files shall be removed. When this command is completed, the hidden files of each opened level become accessible in the subdirectories /mnt/mntpoint/stegfs/1/, /mnt/mntpoint/stegfs/2/, etc. If write operations have taken place while fewer or no security levels were open, the tool rerpl should be used to refresh all hidden files and ensure that the required number of replicated blocks is restored. The number of copies of each inode and copies of the blocks of a file can be controlled using the tunestegfs utility. The stegfsctrl tool allows the user to add and remove security levels from contexts, such that the linear default hierarchy of security levels can be broken up.

StegFS is available under the GNU General Public License from the authors in the form of a patch against Linux kernel 2.2.12 [9] plus user tools and can be downloaded via the Internet from

- ftp://ftp.kerneli.org/pub/kerneli/net-source/StegFS/
- http://ban.joh.cam.ac.uk/~adm36/StegFS/
- http://www.cl.cam.ac.uk/~mgk25/stegfs/

5   Other Design Issues

In our current implementation, the buffer cache keeps hidden blocks only in their encrypted form. This ensures that other file systems never can see plaintext block contents and do things with them that are beyond our control (such as writing parts of them to disk). It also means that decrypted buffers are not retained in memory since the buffer into which a block is decrypted will be overwritten immediately when the next block is re-encrypted. In addition, this helps to retain consistency between functions so that we do not get confused over whether a buffer cache entry is encrypted or not, however we will experience some performance degradation.

The hidden file system implements hard links, but these are only allowed within the same security level. An attempt to create a hard link across security levels will result in an EXDEV error code, the same error that occurs when hard links across devices are requested. This way, we prevent users from accidentally moving a file from a higher to a lower level instead of copying and deleting it, or create a link from a lower to a higher security level. Since inode numbers indicate security levels, a higher security level inode number that found its way into a lower level directory would indicate to an inspector that there are higher security levels in use. Users are responsible for not leaving traces of higher security levels (e.g., symbolic links, paths, log files, shell histories) in lower levels.

6   Performance

We have evaluated the performance of StegFS using the Bonnie [17] benchmark tool. The tests ran on an AMD K5 PR150 100 MHz processor, using a 1 GB partition of a Fujitsu 1.2 GB IDE disk. Bonnie attempts to measure real I/O speed by operating on files that are much bigger than the cache to render it ineffective. In real applications, access locality will lead to more cache hits and therefore better performance.

The table below compares the performance of the Ext2fs driver with the performance for normal and hidden files under StegFS, using a replication factor of 5 for both inodes and data blocks of hidden files.

| | Sequential Output | | | Sequential Input | | Random |
	Per Char [kB/s]	Block [kB/s]	Rewrite [kB/s]	Per Char [kB/s]	Block [kB/s]	Seeks [1/s]
Ext2fs	1835	3839	1964	2216	5476	31.4
StegFS normal	1628	2663	1761	2075	4872	31.3
StegFS hidden	44	45	10	374	420	2.6

Access speed to non-hidden files is roughly comparable to that for the standard Ext2 file system. A clear performance penalty is paid however for the high level of security provided for the hidden files.

We also performed a simple transaction write test, which wrote 256 bytes to a file, rewound the file position back to the start and called fsync() to commit all inode and data blocks to disk. Ext2fs managed to perform 45.10 of these transactions per second, while StegFS achieved 45.05 for non-hidden and 5.26 for hidden files.

The major reasons for the significantly lower performance of hidden files are the need to write replicated blocks, the encryption and decryption overhead, as well as the need to first check whether a block has been overwritten. Performance has greatly improved compared to earlier versions of the file system that spread block locations across the disk randomly.

We also performed some basic tests to verify the survivability of files while they are hidden. We first created with StegFS 250 hidden files, each 100 kB in size. We then unmounted the StegFS partition, mounted it again under Ext2fs and created another 250 files, each 100 kB long, this time openly visible. We finally remounted the file system under the StegFS driver and checked the integrity of the hidden files. Each test was repeated 100 times. With only a single copy of each hidden inode and data block, an average of 2.43% of the files were lost. With a replication factor of two, this fell to 0.08%. A replication factor of three, meant that only 0.005% of the files were lost. When four or more copies of the inode and data blocks were created, all of the files remained fully intact in this test. A larger number of copies will increase the survival chance of hidden files, but it will also reduce the disk capacity and the write performance.

7 Conclusions

We have created a practical implementation of a steganographic file system. It offers the following functionality:

- Users can plausibly deny the number of files stored on the disk.
- The confidentiality of all hidden file content is guaranteed.
- Deleting hidden or non-hidden files leads automatically to their secure destruction.
- Several layers of plausibly deniable access can be used such that lower layers can be voluntarily compromised without revealing higher ones.
- The existence of higher layers is plausibly deniable.
- The installation of the driver can be plausibly justified by revealing one lower layer and by referring to the additional security advantages provided by the product.
- A moderate amount of write accesses performed while not all hidden layers are opened is unlikely to damage data in hidden files.
- Write access to hidden files between inspections cannot be distinguished from non-hidden files that have been created and deleted.
- Non-hidden files continue to be accessible when the StegFS driver and its block allocation table are temporarily removed.
- The full Unix file system semantics are implemented.

Our project was inspired by [6], however the technique that we eventually chose, namely the use of an openly visible encrypted block-allocation table, differs from the two originally suggested constructions. Our system allows us instead to completely fill the disk safely when all hidden levels are open, and the only storage overhead comes from the adjustable replication of blocks. In addition, our scheme allows us to share a partition with a normal widely used file system, which simplifies installation and provides an additional degree of plausible deniability by making hidden files indistinguishable from unused blocks.

Like [6], we did not attempt to cover in this implementation the following functionality of a steganographic file system:

- Hidden presence of the steganographic file system driver
- High-performance write access to hidden layers
- Integrity protection of files
- Protection against the filtering of the entire disk content

Hiding the presence of the driver would require it to be attached, like a Trojan Horse, to another large and obfuscated application. The performance of write accesses might be somewhat increased by better caching of accesses to the block allocation table, but it will ultimately remain limited by the replication requirement that provides the survivability of hidden data during write accesses to lower layers.

References

1. Matt Blaze: A Cryptographic File System for Unix. In Proceedings of 1st ACM Conference on Computer and Communications Security, Fairfax, Virginia, November 1993, pp. 9–16. ftp://ftp.research.att.com/dist/mab/cfs.ps 463

2. Giuseppe Persiano et. al: TCFS – Transparent Cryptographic File System. DIA, Universita' Degli Studi Di Salerno, Italy, http://tcfs.dia.unisa.it/. 463

3. Encrypting File System for Windows 2000, Microsoft Windows 2000 White Paper, Microsoft Corp., 1998, http://www.microsoft.com/windows/server/Technical/security/encrypt.asp 463

4. Linux Kernel International Patches, http://www.kerneli.org/. 463

5. Peter Gutmann: Secure FileSystem (SFS) for DOS/Windows. Internet Web page http://www.cs.auckland.ac.nz/~pgut001/sfs/. 463

6. Ross Anderson, Roger Needham, Adi Shamir: The Steganographic File System. In David Aucsmith (Ed.): Information Hiding, Second International Workshop, IH'98, Portland, Oregon, USA, April 15–17, 1998, Proceedings, LNCS 1525, Springer-Verlag, ISBN 3-540-65386-4, pp. 73–82. http://www.cl.cam.ac.uk/ftp/users/rja14/sfs3.ps.gz 464, 465, 466, 476

7. Michael Roe: Cryptography and Evidence. PhD thesis, University of Cambridge, Computer Laboratory, 1997. http://www.ccsr.cam.ac.uk/techreports/tr1/ 464

8. Carl van Schaik, Paul Smeddle: A Steganographic File System Implementation for Linux, University of Cape Town, South Africa, October 1998. Software available on http://www-users.rwth-aachen.de/Peter.Schneider-Kamp/sources/sfs/. 465

9. Linus Torvalds, et al.: Linux 2.2 – Kernel. C source code, http://www.kernel.org/, 1991–. 466, 474

10. Maurice Bach: The Design of the UNIX Operating System. Prentice Hall, 1986. 467

11. Rémy Card, Theodore Ts'o, Stephen Tweedie: Design and Implementation of the Second Extended Filesystem. In Frank B. Brokken et al. (eds.): Proceedings of the First Dutch International Symposium on Linux. State University of Groningen, 1995, ISBN 90-367-0385-9. http://www.mit.edu/~tytso/linux/ext2intro.html 466

12. Peter Gutmann: Software Generation of Practically Strong Random Numbers. In Seventh USENIX Security Symposium Proceedings, San Antonio, Texas, January 1998, pp. 243–257. http://www.cs.auckland.ac.nz/~pgut001/pubs/random.pdf 471

13. "AMAN" <scramdisk@hotmail.com>. ScramDisk – disk encryption software. http://www.scramdisk.clara.net/. 465

14. Brian Gladman. AES algorithm efficiency. http://www.seven77.demon.co.uk/cryptography_technology/Aes/. 473

15. Roger M. Needham, David J. Wheeler: Tea extensions. Draft technical report, Computer Laboratory, University of Cambridge, October 1997, http://www.ftp.cl.cam.ac.uk/ftp/users/djw3/xtea.ps. 473

16. David J. Wheeler, Roger M. Needham: Correction to xtea. Draft technical report, Computer Laboratory, University of Cambridge, October 1998, http://www.ftp.cl.cam.ac.uk/ftp/users/djw3/xxtea.ps. 473

17. Tim Bray: Bonnie file system benchmark, 1990, USENET newsgroup comp.arch, http://www.textuality.com/bonnie/ 475

Nonbinary Audio Cryptography[*]

Yvo Desmedt[1,2], Tri V. Le[1], and Jean-Jacques Quisquater[3]

[1] Department of Computer Science, Florida State University
Tallahassee, Florida FL 32306-4530, USA
desmedt@cs.fsu.edu
lvtri@uwm.edu
http://www.cs.fsu.edu/~desmedt
http://www.uwm.edu/~lvtri/
[2] Department of Mathematics,
Royal Holloway – University of London, UK
[3] Dept of Electrical Eng., Microelectronic laboratory, Université Catholique de
Louvain
Place du Levant, 3, 1348 Louvain-la-Neuve, Belgium
Quisquater@dice.ucl.ac.be
http://www.dice.ucl.ac.be/crypto/jjq.html

Abstract. Visual cryptography, introduced by Naor-Shamir at Eurocrypt '94, only requires primitive technology to decrypt the ciphertext. However, a disadvantage of it is that the "ciphertext", as a random looking transparency, is suspicious to a censor. The solutions recently proposed by Desmedt-Hou-Quisquater to avoid these problems are neither user friendly, having a low bandwidth, nor are tested. In this paper we present three schemes that overcome these problems. As in one of the Desmedt-Hou-Quisquater's schemes, a share (or a ciphertext) corresponds to an audio signal, such as music. While in the Desmedt-Hou-Quisquater scheme the plaintext was binary, in our schemes the plaintext can also be speech, or any other audio signal. By introducing variations of the one-time pad we guarantee perfect secrecy. The ciphertext is non-suspicious, when tested with human ears, is indistinguishable from normal music.

Keywords: audio cryptography, information hiding, perfect secrecy, visual cryptography, speech encryption.

1 Introduction

The hacker community and the research on computer security has demonstrated that a practical computer cannot be made completely secure. Operating systems must be trusted. If the running software can write, Trojan horses can be introduced (such as computer viruses, etc.). To make matters worse, today's Trojan

---

[*] This research was done while Yvo Desmedt and Tri V. Le were at the University of Wisconsin – Milwaukee. Their research is now funded by NSF CCR-9903216.

A. Pfitzmann (Ed.): IH'99, LNCS 1768, pp. 478–489, 2000.

horses are not only common in software but a Pentium chip having more than 5 million transistors also allows for these.

Several methods have been suggested to reduce the impact of potential attacks. Some have, for example, suggested to detect intruders, e.g. using artificial intelligence, [16,10,9]. An old idea is to check the correctness of the programs, e.g. [18,22]. A more theoretical idea is to have the program check itself [4]. However, this still requires a trusted subroutine.

Naor and Shamir [15] have opened the door for computer programs that can be verified without the use of a computer. In this way, a human can check the correctness of a computation even if one cannot trust that the computation will be done correctly (one assumes that the computer has a single user and is not connected to a network). Their research has mainly focussed on guaranteeing privacy. So, the decryption requires only primitive technology. Although a computer is needed to generate the ciphertext and the key, having no need for a computer to decrypt, one can verify the correctness of a visual encryption without relying on an untrusted computer. We demonstrate that this idea can be extended towards computation in which one has more conditions that just the requirement for privacy (see end of this section).

The way visual cryptography achieves its goal is by having the key and the ciphertext (in other words, the secret shares [2,19] of the plaintext), correspond to dots printed on respective transparencies. By stacking one on top of the other, the plaintext is revealed.

A major disadvantage of visual cryptography, as pointed out by for example, Desmedt-Hou-Quisquater [8], is that random transparencies stick out from those written in the clear. Also Biham [1] recently addressed this issue, but the obtained ciphertext (and key) transparency is different enough from normal ones to allow a censor to block the delivery. Steganography, which may be older than cryptography [14], solves this problem. However, in many schemes the privacy is not perfect and many such schemes have recently been broken [13].

Desmedt-Hou-Quisquater combined the concept of visual cryptography with steganography to obtain the following schemes:

Cerebral cryptography [8] in which the ciphertext and the key (the secret shares) look like normal pictures. Combining the key and the ciphertext by looking through a 3-D viewer (similar to an old Viewmaster) a stereogram is obtained, which is the plaintext, that was encrypted.

Audio cryptography [7] in which the ciphertext and the key correspond to music in which the phase has been changed. Playing the ciphertext and the key together one can obtain music which is either loud or quiet depending whether the plaintext is 0 or 1.

Noise-cancelingcryptography [7] in which the first share is obtained by having some low significant bit of each pixel in a picture being replaced by a random value. The one-time pad is used to create the second share in a similar way. Using a Mach-Zehnder interferometer Desmedt-Hou-Quisquater claim that one can decrypt.

We already mentioned the problems with Biham's approach. We will now discuss the problems of the Desmedt-Hou-Quisquater schemes:

1. Many humans are unable to see the stereogram in cerebral cryptography. Moreover, the steganography used only fools a human sensor. Indeed, although a computer cannot obtain the cleartext from a single picture, it can easily detect that one of those pictures is suspicious and censor it.
2. The obtained bandwidth of audio cryptography is very low, i.e. in the order of 1bit/sec.
3. Although noise-canceling cryptography seems to have a high bandwidth, nobody has tested the feasibility of the decryption of this method, so far we know.

So, these problems motivate the research on a crypto-system satisfying the following conditions:

- the scheme guarantees perfect secrecy, i.e., intercepting one share does not reveal any information about the plaintext.
- a human censor (and preferable a computer) cannot distinguish a share from a daily life media, such as recorded music.
- no general purpose computer or sophisticated hardware is required to decrypt.
- the obtained bandwidth is sufficiently high.
- the method can easily be tested.

To achieve the last condition, we preferred choosing audio technology above visual, even though visual media allows for a much higher bandwidth.

In this paper, we: 1) refresh the reader's knowledge on radio and Fourier transform as well as notations needed to understand the paper (Section 2), 2) discuss the general techniques and the particular schemes used (Section 3), 3) prove that our schemes guarantee perfect secrecy (Section 4), and 4) report on the testing of the schemes (Section 5).

2   Background

2.1   Fourier Transform and Discrete Fourier Transform

We will use capital letters, e.g. $F(\omega)$, for the result of the Fourier transformation of a signal written in lower case, e.g. $f(t)$, where ω is in the frequency domain and t is in the time domain. The readers familiar with Fourier transforms, etc., may skip the rest of this subsection.

In the paper, a signal is modeled as a continuous function $f : \mathcal{R} \mapsto \mathcal{R}$, where $f(t)$ means the value of the signal measured at time point t in some chosen scale. When it is more convenient to use complex numbers, we will take $f(t)$ as a complex-valued function. Function $f(t)$ is called time domain model of the signal f.

The signal f also has its frequency domain model as a complex-valued function $F(\omega)$, obtained from its time domain function $f(t)$ through a Fourier transform:

$$F(\omega) = \frac{1}{\sqrt{2\pi}} \int_{-\infty}^{\infty} f(t) e^{-i\omega t} dt$$

One can get back the time domain function $f(t)$ from $F(\omega)$ through the inverse Fourier transform:

$$f(t) = \frac{1}{\sqrt{2\pi}} \int_{-\infty}^{\infty} F(\omega) e^{i\omega t} dt$$

For periodic signals (of period 2π) with finite energy, we have the trigonometric form, known as the Fourier series:

$$f(t) = \frac{a_0}{2} + \sum_{n=1}^{\infty} a_n \cos(nt) + b_n \sin(nt)$$

where constants a_n, b_n are determined by the integrals:

$$a_n = \frac{1}{\pi} \int_0^{2\pi} f(t) \cos(nt) dt$$

$$b_n = \frac{1}{\pi} \int_0^{2\pi} f(t) \sin(nt) dt$$

Rewriting each individual frequency as:

$$a_n \cos(nt) + b_n \sin(nt) = c_n \cos(nt + \phi_n)$$

where $c_n = \sqrt{a_n^2 + b_n^2}$, and $\phi_n = \arctan(b_n/a_n)$, we have c_n and ϕ_n are the amplitude and phase of the nth frequency, respectively. Sometimes, it is also convenient to write the signal $f(t)$ as:

$$f(t) = \mathbf{Re} \sum_{n=0}^{\infty} F_n e^{int}$$

where $F_n = c_n e^{i\phi_n}$, is the complex number, whose absolute value c_n, denoted as $|F_n|$ is the amplitude, and whose argument ϕ_n, denoted as $\arg F_n$, is the phase of the nth frequency e^{int}. In other words, F_n is the coefficient of nth frequency in the signal $f(t)$.

Assuming that the period of the signal $f(t)$ is 2π, then by *Nyquist* theorem, we have: if $\{f_n := f(nd) | n = 0, 1, 2, ...\}$ is sampled at sampling frequency $N = 1/d$, then $f(t)$ can only be restored correctly up to frequency $N/2$:

$$f(t) = \sum_{n=0}^{N} F_n e^{int}$$

Correspondingly, we have discreet Fourier transform (DFT) to compute the coefficients F_n from the sequence $\{f_n\}$:

$$F_k = \frac{1}{\sqrt{N}} \sum_{n=0}^{N} f_n e^{-(2\pi i/N)kn}$$

and inverse discreet Fourier transform (iDFT):

$$f_n = \frac{1}{\sqrt{N}} \sum_{k=0}^{N} F_k e^{(2\pi i/N)nk}$$

By *Cooley and Tukey*'s theorem [6], we have efficient algorithms to evaluate these transform in $O(N \log(N))$ time.

2.2 Human Auditory System

The human auditory system is a complex system consists of the ears, the communication links to the brain, and the brain itself [21]. The ears act as microphones, receive air waves from the environment, convert them into electrical pulses and then send them through the communication links to the brain for further cognitive processing.

Modern research [21] has shown that the human ears work in real-time as a frequency analyzer. They have a set of nerves, each one contains a hair of different lengths and, thus, resonates to different frequencies. Usually, the outer nerves have longer hair and, therefore, resonate to lower frequency. Because each hair can only resonate to a specific frequency, the set of auditory nerves and their hairs make up a real-time frequency analyzer which sends the power level of each frequency to the brain in the form of impulsive signals.

This is the reason why the ears are sensitive to the power level of each individual frequency but not the phases individually. Only the relative phases among frequencies would be important to the ears and the brain. Hence, when we shift each frequency by the same phase, then the new audio signal is indistinguishable to the human auditory system. In our tests, when we choose a small number of samples (i.e. 512) for doing DFT, the phases of the signal can be shifted by an arbitrary angle with little distortion in the quality of the resulting signal. This phenomenon will be used later in some of our techniques.

3 Techniques

3.1 Main Idea

Our goal is to seek for some hiding place in the human auditory system in order to hide a signal. One of the good candidates for such a place is the masking effect happening in the human brain. This effect appears when both very high and very low power level signals are presented. The high power signal tends to mask the low power one. This can be demonstrated in the case where we have a phone conversation in the street and a sudden big truck comes by. While the truck is passing we cannot hear anything on the phone. Although the masking effect is greater at higher and lower frequencies, it does appear at every frequency in the audible range [11]. We will use this fact later to choose the best power spectra for the carrying signal.

Physics brings us a noise-canceling effect, also used in [7]. When signals of the same power, but of opposite phases, are played together, they cancel each other out. This makes us hear nothing.

3.2   Hiding Aspect

In the first two methods (the phase shifting and frequency flipping methods), we applied DFT to 512 samples at a time only. To avoid frequency leakage problem when doing DFT, we did not apply it directly on the cover (the music), but only on the message (the speech). This way we avoided bad impacts on the audio quality of the shares.

First we let $m''(t)$ be the original message signal, but slightly modified to $m'(t)$, depending on the method, as we will explain later. To guarantee that the shares are audible, we created temporary signals, called *preshares*, from the (modified) message signal $m'(t)$. We call their sum $m(t)$, i.e., $m(t) = s_1(t) + s_2(t)$. To recover the message we evidently need $m(t)$ sounds very similar to the original message signal. The actual shares were then made by mixing the preshares with the covering signal $c(t)$, e.g. a music signal, as follows:

$$share_1(t) = ks_1(t) + (1 - k)c(t)$$
$$share_2(t) = ks_2(t) + (k - 1)c(t)$$

where k is some small positive constant chosen between 0 and 1. It was chosen small enough so that the masking effect occurred.

We note that this addition is done in the time domain.

3.3   Perfect Secrecy

To guarantee perfect secrecy we obviously need $s_1(t)$ and $s_2(t)$ to be independent of the message, as in [20].

Definition 1. *Given signals* $m'(t), s_1(t), s_2(t)$. *We call the following statements*

$$\forall t_0, m_0' \in R : \mathrm{P}(m'(t_0) = m_0', s_1) = \mathrm{P}(m'(t_0) = m_0')\mathrm{P}(s_1)$$

$$\forall t_0, m_0' \in R : \mathrm{P}(m'(t_0) = m_0', s_2) = \mathrm{P}(m'(t_0) = m_0')\mathrm{P}(s_2)$$

independence condition.

It was not simple to achieve this condition for our setting, as will be evident later. Some of the schemes we developed had to be rejected, since they did not satisfy perfect secrecy. Moreover we need to be careful, since $s_1(t)$ and $s_2(t)$ are analog signals [3]. By working with discrete values and choosing discrete random values we avoided the last problem.

3.4   Decryption

The decryption method used in [7]'s audio cryptography consisted of playing the first share on speaker one and the second share on speaker two. Theoretically this should work for our non-binary audio crypto-systems, too. Indeed, $share_1(t) + share_2(t) = k(s_1(t) + s_2(t)) = km(t)$. However, tests have demonstrated that this does not work. There are two problems. First the mixing obtained is not good enough, and so one only hears the cover (the music). In order to solve this problem an inexpensive audio mixer suffices. Secondly, even using an audio mixer, one is still unable to hear the message. The reason is that k is so small, we cannot hear the message clearly. This is solved using an (old fashioned) amplifier. In Section 5 we will report in more details about the tests.

Note that the result of the decryption method is $m(t)$ the modified message. As long as $m(t)$ sounds similar to the original message, we have achieved the decryption goal.

3.5   Common Techniques

In the following sections, we choose a fixed signal, $g(t)$, with non-flat power spectra, where the lower and higher frequencies get more power than the middle ones. In the first two methods (the phase shifting and frequency flipping methods), we modify the original message $m''(t)$ as follows. First $m'(t) := m''(t)$. Secondly, for all ω: if $|M''(\omega)| > |G(\omega)|$ we make $|M'(\omega)| = |G(\omega)|$. In the modular amplitude method $m'(t) = m''(t)$. How $m(t)$ depends on $m'(t)$ will be explained later.

4   Particular Schemes

4.1   Phase Shifting Method

The chosen phase of the first preshare is uniformly random modulo 2π. The amplitude of the preshares corresponds to the one of $g(t)$. Using elementary properties of trigonometry we guarantee that the amplitude of the sum of the preshares is the same as the one of the message. Using the properties of the auditory system (see Section 2.2) the resulting decryption will sound like the original message.

Theorem 1. *Assuming that $m'(t)$ is the message modified as explained in Section 3.5 and $c(t)$ is the covering signal, and that the signals $s_1(t)$ and $s_2(t)$ are determined by the following formula:*

$$S_1(\omega) = e^{ir_1}|G(\omega)|, \qquad \text{where } r_1 \in_R [0, 2\pi)$$
$$S_2(\omega) = e^{ir_2}|G(\omega)|, \qquad \text{where } r_2 = r_1 + 2\arccos(|M'_\omega|/|G_\omega|) \text{ modulo } 2\pi.$$

then we have the independence condition. Moreover, the amplitude of $m(t)$, the sum of the shares, is twice the amplitude of $m'(t)$.

Proof. Clearly $r_1 \in_R [0, 2\pi)$, hence is uniformly random[1] and independent of $m'(t)$. Also

$$r_2 - r_1 = 2\arccos(|M'(\omega)/G(\omega)|) \bmod 2\pi$$

is independent of r_1, therefore:

$$r_2 = r_1 + 2\arccos(|M'(\omega)/G(\omega)|) \bmod 2\pi$$

is also uniformly random and independent of $m(t)$.

Consequently, $S_1(\omega)$ and $S_2(\omega)$ are independent of $m(t)$, and so are their inverse Fourier transform $s_1(t)$ and $s_2(t)$.

Now using elementary trigonometry, we obtain $M(\omega) = S_1(\omega) + S_(\omega) = 2e^{i(r_1+r_2)/2} * \cos((r_2 - r_1)/2) * |G(\omega)| = 2 * e^{i(r_1+r_2)/2} * |M'(\omega)/G(\omega)| * |G(\omega)| = e^{i(r_1+r_2)/2} * 2 * |M'(\omega)|$.

4.2   Frequency Flipping Method

Since analog signals do not add up modulo 2π, as one can do in the one time pad, we anticipate that such a modulo approach can create a hard to understand decryption (see Sections 4.3 and 5 for a discussion on this topic). Our idea is to work modulo $G(\omega)$, where $G(\omega)$ is an upper bound on the signal, but when a reduction would be needed we replaced the output by zero. This scheme turned out not to guarantee perfect secrecy. The following modification of this idea, explained in the next theorem, however, maintains the security.

Theorem 2. *Assuming that $m'(t)$ and $g(t)$ is the message and carrier signal respectively. Let r_1 and r_2 be chosen from the following ranges:*

$$r_1 \in_R [0, 2\pi),$$
$$r_2 \in_R [-|G(\omega)|, |G(\omega)|]$$

Then the signals $\mathbf{S}_1(\omega)$ and $\mathbf{S}_2(\omega)$, determined by the following formulas:

$$\mathbf{M}^\star(\omega) \in_R \{\pm|\mathbf{M}'(\omega)|\}$$
$$\mathbf{S}_1'(\omega) = r_2$$
$$\mathbf{S}_2''(\omega) = \mathbf{M}^\star - r_2$$
$$\mathbf{S}_2'(\omega) = \text{if } (|\mathbf{S}_2''(\omega)| \le G) \text{ then } \mathbf{S}_2''(\omega) \text{ else } -\mathbf{S}_1'(\omega)$$
$$\mathbf{S}_1(\omega) = e^{ir_1}\mathbf{S}_1'(\omega)$$
$$\mathbf{S}_2(\omega) = e^{ir_1}\mathbf{S}_2'(\omega)$$

satisfy the independence condition, where $\delta(x)$ is a real function over the complexes, which equals 1 when $|x| \le G$, and be 0 otherwise. Moreover, the amplitude of $\mathbf{M}(\omega)$, the sum of the shares, is the amplitude of $\mathbf{M}'(\omega)$ or zero.

---

[1] One can choose an element with uniform probability in the interval $[0, 2\pi)$. Note that we actually choose r_1 as a uniform random (modulo l) multiple of $2\pi/l$, where l is an integer.

Proof. For short notations, we dropped the variable ω and use the capital letters $C, G, S_i, S_i', M, M', S_2''$ only. We need to prove that each of $\mathbf{S}_1$ and $\mathbf{S}_2$ is independent of M. We do this by first showing that $\mathbf{S}_1'$ and $\mathbf{S}_2'$ are independent of M. Then, because r_1 is independent of anything else, it is straightforward to obtain that $\mathbf{S}_1$ and $\mathbf{S}_2$ are independent of M.

Now $\mathbf{S}_1' := r_2$ is chosen randomly, independent of anything else, so it is independent of M. For each real value $v \in [-G, G]$ and each complex value $\alpha \in \mathcal{C}$, $|\alpha| \leq G$, we then compute:

$$
\begin{aligned}
P(\mathbf{S}_2' = v \mid \mathbf{M} = \alpha) &= P(\mathbf{S}_2' = v \mid \mathbf{M}^\star \in_R \{\pm|\alpha|\}, \mathbf{M} = \alpha) \\
&= P(\mathbf{S}_2' = v, |s_2''| \leq G \mid \mathbf{M}^\star \in_R \{\pm|\alpha|\}, \mathbf{M} = \alpha) \; + \\
&\quad P(\mathbf{S}_2' = v, |s_2''| > G \mid \mathbf{M}^\star \in_R \{\pm|\alpha|\}, \mathbf{M} = \alpha) \\
&= P(\mathbf{S}_2'' = +v, |\mathbf{S}_2''| \leq G \mid \mathbf{M}^\star \in_R \{\pm|\alpha|\}, \mathbf{M} = \alpha) \; + \\
&\quad P(\mathbf{S}_1' = -v, |\mathbf{S}_2''| > G \mid \mathbf{M}^\star \in_R \{\pm|\alpha|\}, \mathbf{M} = \alpha) \\
&= P(\mathbf{S}_2'' = +v \mid \mathbf{M}^\star \in_R \{\pm|\alpha|\}, \mathbf{M} = \alpha) \; + \\
&\quad P(\mathbf{S}_1' = -v, |\mathbf{S}_2''| > G \mid \mathbf{M}^\star \in_R \{\pm|\alpha|\}, \mathbf{M} = \alpha) \\
&= P(\mathbf{M}^\star - r_2 = +v \mid \mathbf{M}^\star \in_R \{\pm|\alpha|\}, \mathbf{M} = \alpha) \; + \\
&\quad P(r_2 = -v, |\mathbf{M}^\star - r_2| > G \mid \mathbf{M}^\star \in_R \{\pm|\alpha|\}, \mathbf{M} = \alpha) \\
&= P(\pm|\alpha| - r_2 = +v) + P(r_2 = -v, |\pm|\alpha| - r_2| > G).
\end{aligned}
$$

But we have:

$$
\begin{aligned}
P(\pm|\alpha| - r_2 = +v) &= P(r_2 = \pm|\alpha| - v) \\
&= (\delta(|\alpha| - v) + \delta(-|\alpha| - v))/2G,
\end{aligned}
$$

and also

$$
\begin{aligned}
P(r_2 = -v, |\pm|\alpha| - r_2| > G) &= P(|\pm|\alpha| - r_2| > G \mid r_2 = -v)P(r_2 = -v) \\
&= P(|\pm|\alpha| + v| > G \mid r_2 = -v)/2G \\
&= (P(||\alpha| + v| > G) + P(|-|\alpha| + v| > G))/2G \\
&= (2 - \delta(|\alpha| + v) - \delta(-|\alpha| + v))/2G,
\end{aligned}
$$

so

$$
\begin{aligned}
P(\mathbf{S}_2' = v \mid \mathbf{M} = \alpha) &= P(\pm|\alpha| - r_2 = +v) + P(r_2 = -v, |\pm|\alpha| - r_2| > G) \\
&= (\delta(|\alpha| - v) + \delta(-|\alpha| - v))/2G \; + \\
&\quad (2 - \delta(|\alpha| + v) - \delta(-|\alpha| + v))/2G \\
&= 1/G,
\end{aligned}
$$

which is independent of α. Hence $\mathbf{S}_2'$ is independent of M. And so is $\mathbf{S}_1$ and $\mathbf{S}_2$.

4.3   Modular Amplitude Method

In this method we pretend that the signals belong to the reals modulo a number. We compute the preshares this way, which will create errors when decrypting.

Theorem 3. *Assuming that $m'(t)$ is the original message and $f > 1$ and $|m| < max$, then the signals $s_1(t)$ and $s_2(t)$ determined by the following formula:*

$$
\begin{aligned}
s_1(t) &\in_R [-max, 0] \\
s_2(t) &= m(t)/f - s_1(t) \bmod max
\end{aligned}
$$

satisfy the independence condition. The probability that $m(t) = s_1(t) + s_2(t) \neq m'(t)$ is less or equal to $2/f$.

Proof. This is one-time pad over the reals modulo max, so independence condition is automatically satisfied.

Now, $P(m/f - s_1 \geq max) = P(s_1 \leq m/f - max) \leq P(s_1 \leq max/f - max) = 1/f$ and $P(m/f - s_1 < 0) = P(m/f < s_1) \leq P(-max/f < s_1) = 1/f$. These are the only cases where a reduction modulo max is done.

5   Testing

We did several tests using a pair of an audio mixer and an amplifier (model Apollo and TEAC 2), which are both analog devices. The mixer has four input lines but we used only two of them. The dynamic range of the amplifier is about 40dB. The cover signal is a piece of music from Beethoven's *For Elise*, and input signal is a speech by President Clinton. Both were sampled at approximately 11 kHz.

All three methods were very well at playing back each of the shares. They are clean of noises and we could not distinguish them from the original music. In other words, the quality of the cover was completely maintained in the shares.

The following results were obtained when decrypting the ciphertext by playing each pair of the shares together, using the mixer and the amplifier. For the phase shifting and frequency flipping methods, the speech was clearly understandable. We were not only able to understand the text but also to recognize the voice of the speaker. For the modulo amplifier method, we clearly heard some clicks. These clicks made it hard to recognize the speech. We had a trade-off between the number of clicks and their amplitudes proportionally, but with a linear mixer and linear amplifier we failed to achieve the goals when using the modulo amplifier method. We predicted that with a very nonlinear amplifier or very nonlinear speaker, the quality of the reconstructed plaintext would be improved in the modular amplitude method. We expect to have such a demo within a few weeks.

Another problem we faced when playing both the shares at the same time was synchronizing them so that they would start at the same time. Available analog techniques [12] allows one to play two streams at almost identical starting times, with timing errors less than $0.5\mu s$, much better than what we need, i.e., $10\mu s$. The notable point is that these analog techniques require the use of neither a complex computer nor an integrated chip in their functioning.

These tests can be found at http://www.cs.fsu.edu/~desmedt/nonbinary/

6   Conclusions

We presented three methods which achieve a better bandwidth than the binary audio cryptography introduced by Desmedt-Hou-Quisquater. Our methods guarantee perfect secrecy, do not need a computer to decrypt and the shares are non-suspicious to a censor, improving on the visual cryptography properties of Naor-Shamir. Our method can be generalized to allow decryption from 2-out-of-l shares in a similar way as proposed by [8].

As we pointed out in the introduction, visual media allows for higher bandwidth. It is an interesting question whether our techniques can be adapted to a visual media such that decryption is possible without relying on expensive studio-type equipment.

References

1. E. Biham, September 21–26, 1997. Lecture given at Daghstuhl, Germany. 479
2. G. R. Blakley. Safeguarding cryptographic keys. In *Proc. Nat. Computer Conf. AFIPS Conf. Proc.*, pp. 313–317, 1979. vol.48. 479
3. G. R. Blakley and L. Swanson. Infinite structures in information theory. In D. Chaum, R.L. Rivest, and A. T. Sherman, editors, *Advances in Cryptology. Proc. of Crypto'82*, pp. 39–50. Plenum Press N. Y., 1983. Crypto '82, Santa Barbara, CA, August 1982. 483
4. M. Blum and S. Kannan. Designing programs that check their work. *21st ACM STOC*, pages 86–97, 1989. 479
5. G. E. Carlson. *Signal and Linear System Analysis*. John Wiley & Sons, New York, second edition, 1998.
6. J. M. Cooley and J. W. Tukey. An algorithm for the machine calculation of complex Fourier series. *Mathematics of Computation*, 19, pp. 297–301, 1965. 482
7. Y. Desmedt, S. Hou, and J.-J. Quisquater. Audio and noise-canceling cryptography, 1998. Rump session of the second Information Hiding Workshop, April 15–17, 1998, Portland, Oregon. 479, 483, 484
8. Y. Desmedt, S. Hou, and J.-J. Quisquater. Cerebral cryptography. In *Preproceedings of the second Information Hiding Workshop*, 1998. April 15–17, 1998, Portland, Oregon. To appear in the proceedings, Lecture Notes in Computer Science, Springer-Verlag. 479, 488
9. D. Endler. Intrusion detection applying machine learning to solaris audit data. In *Proc. of 14th ACSAC*, Phoenix, Arizona, 1998. 479
10. A. Gosh, J. Wanke, and F. Charron. Detecting anomalous and unknown intrusions against programs. In *Proc. of 14th Annual Computer Security Applications Conference*, Phoenix, December 7-11 1998. 479
11. D. M. Howard and J. Angus. *Acoustics and psychoacoustics*. Focal Press, Oxford, 1996. 483
12. Eric D. Daniel and C. Denis Mee and Mark H. Clark. *Magnetic Recording* [Timing errors between tracks, page 327]. IEEE Press, New York, 1999. 487
13. Information hiding workshop, 1998. April 15–17, 1998, Portland, Oregon, proceedings to appear in the Lecture Notes in Computer Science, Springer. 479
14. D. Kahn. *The Codebreakers*. MacMillan Publishing Co., New York, 1967. 479
15. M. Naor and A. Shamir. Visual cryptography. In A. De Santis, editor, *Advances in Cryptology — Eurocrypt '94, Proceedings (Lecture Notes in Computer Science 950)*, pp. 1–12. Springer-Verlag, May 9–12, 1995. Perugia, Italy, May 9–12. 479
16. M. Newberry. *Active intruder Detection: Some Aspects of Computer Security and User Authentification*. PhD thesis, University of New South Wales, ADFA, Department of Computer Science, Canberra, Australia, 1991. Active intruder Detection: Some Aspects of Computer Security and User Authentification. 479

17. A. V. Oppenheim and A. S. Willsky. *Signal & Systems*. Prentice-Hall, Englewood Cliffs, New Jersey, second edition, 1997.
18. R. Sandhu. The RRA97 model for role-based administration of role hierarchies. In *Proceedings of 14th ACSAC*, Phoenix, Arizona, December 7-11, 1998. 479
19. A. Shamir. How to share a secret. *Commun. ACM*, 22, pp. 612–613, November 1979. 479
20. C. E. Shannon. Communication theory of secrecy systems. *Bell System Techn. Jour.*, 28, pp. 656–715, October 1949. 483
21. S. W. Smith. *The Scientist and Engineer's Guide to Digital Signal Processing*. California Technical Publishing, San Diego, CA 92150-2407, 1997. 482
22. D. Thomsen, D. O'Brien, and J. Bogle. Role based access control framework for network enterprises. In *Proc. of 14th ACSAC*, Phoenix, Arizona, 1998. 479

Author Index